AMERICA IN 1857

AMERICA IN 1857

A Nation on the Brink

KENNETH M. STAMPP

New York   Oxford
OXFORD UNIVERSITY PRESS
1990

Oxford University Press

Oxford   New York   Toronto
Delhi   Bombay   Calcutta   Madras   Karachi
Petaling Jaya   Singapore   Hong Kong   Tokyo
Nairobi   Dar es Salaam   Cape Town
Melbourne   Auckland

and associated companies in
Berlin   Ibadan

Published by Oxford University Press, Inc.,
200 Madison Avenue, New York, New York 10016

Oxford is a registered trademark of Oxford University Press

Library of Congress Cataloging-in-Publication Data
Stampp, Kenneth M. (Kenneth Milton)
America in 1857: A nation on the brink
/ Kenneth M. Stampp.
p.   cm.   Includes bibliographical references.
ISBN 0-19-503902-5
1. United States—Politics and government—1857–1861.
I. Title.   E436.S78   1990   973.6'8—dc20
90-31374

9 8 7 6 5 4 3 2 1

Printed in the United States of America
on acid-free paper

To the memory of Selma Stampp

Preface

This book is about a crucial year in the antebellum American sectional conflict. History, of course, does not usually divide itself neatly into twelve-month segments, but, as a time frame, a year is no more artificial than a decade, or an "age" (of Jefferson or of Jackson), or a century. In a way, it is perhaps less artificial, for it is a span of time imposed not by some human decimal contrivance but by the inexorable mechanics of the solar system. The rhythm of the seasons, to some degree, regulates the lives of nations as well as individuals. Each new year marks a new beginning with its fresh hopes and brave resolutions. At year's end each winter solstice brings its coda, recapitulating gains and losses, successes and failures.

In 1856 three events had worsened the already strained relations between the North and South: first, a violent struggle between proslavery and free-state parties for control of Kansas Territory; second, a bitter controversy over the question of congressional authority to exclude slavery from the western territories; third, an exciting presidential campaign during which numerous Southerners threatened secession if the young Republican party, with its antislavery platform, should elect its first presidential candidate. In the autumn, the political crisis dissipated when peace was restored in Kansas and when the national Democratic party won the presidential election and control of both houses of Congress.

The year 1857 dawned with widespread expectations of a diminution of sectional tensions. On March 4, James Buchanan began his administration with a commitment to resolve the Kansas question and restore harmony between the sections. Most Northerners and Southerners were relieved that a secession crisis had been averted and hoped once more for a durable political settlement. All that was required, many believed, was to permit the qualified voters of Kansas Territory to elect delegates to a constitutional convention, to authorize that body to frame a state constitution acceptable to the majority, and to provide for its submission to popular ratification. With Kansas admitted to statehood, peace between the sections would be restored. All remaining sectional issues, the optimists claimed, were manageable, for a conflict over slavery in any of the other territories seemed unlikely.

These were the fair promises that produced a general mood of optimism in the early months of 1857. By December the mood had changed, and the year ended with a political disaster that brought the nation a long step closer to disunion and civil war. Kansas had become the source of a new and far more disruptive sectional conflict; Buchanan had lost the confidence of most of the Northerners who had voted for him; and the national Democratic party had suffered a wound so deep that, in spite of all healing efforts, it did not recover until after the Civil War. As a result, 1857 was probably the year when the North and South reached the political point of no return—when it became well nigh impossible to head off a violent resolution of the differences between them. At least a few observers, even without the historian's hindsight, understood at that time the significance of what had occurred. How that point was reached is the central theme of this book.

To devote a book solely to the year 1857 can be justified only because it encompassed a political crisis which proved to be decisive in the coming of the Civil War. Yet, in that crowded year many nonpolitical events and problems, great and small, also aroused the interest of editors, reporters, diarists, letter writers, and others who left records of one kind or another. Because they formed the matrix in which the crisis developed, some required attention: crime, corruption, nativism, land speculation, railroad building, a business panic and economic recession, a religious revival, filibustering in Nicaragua, affairs of the Mormons in Utah, among others. Many were directly or indirectly relevant to the crisis. Others, although irrelevant to it, were significant simply because they occupied the public mind at a time when the nation was moving ever closer to a political catastrophe.

The subject of this book required frequent assessments of popular attitudes and of the responses to events among Republicans, Democrats, and other political groups, North and South. For this period, long before well-structured public opinion polls were available, political assessments such as these must be based upon cautious use of newspapers, manuscripts, and government documents. They can never be made with precision. Contemporary newspapers, although highly partisan, were useful as both reflectors and molders of local attitudes. Political editors, while advocating or defending party policies, revealed a great deal about the feelings and prejudices of their readers. Because the speeches of Congressmen during Senate and House debates were often intended for home consumption, they provided clues to the sentiments of their constituents. A large proportion of the letters received by politicians were self-serving and therefore unreliable barometers of general attitudes. Some, however, written by political lieutenants in their states or districts, were intended to provide accurate information about local public opinion however distasteful it may have been. Occasionally an issue aroused voters sufficiently to produce a spontaneous flood of letters to Congressmen, and reactions were revealed with unusual clarity.

I have taken a few liberties with my sources. Spelling, punctuation, and the use of capital letters in many manuscripts are eccentric, and I have changed or corrected them when necessary to clarify meaning without enclosing the changes in brackets. I have also corrected typographical errors in my quotations from newspapers. Finally, I have not used ellipses at the start and finish of quotations.

Politics in the decade of the 1850s is not one of the neglected subjects or periods of American history. A full bibliography of relevant books and articles would run to many pages. In addition to my footnote citations, I want to acknowledge my special debt to the writings of Don E. Fehrenbacher, Eric Foner, William E. Gienapp, Michael F. Holt, Robert W. Johannsen, Allan Nevins, Roy F. Nichols, David M. Potter, Richard H. Sewell, and Joel H. Silbey. From their various perspectives they provided a rich background for my study, as well as many shrewd observations about the events of 1857. If my perspective or interpretations sometimes differed from theirs, that in no way diminished my respect for their scholarship.

The help of many others was more direct. Richard F. Hill, Henry F. May, and Robert L. Middlekauff read the entire manuscript, and I accepted with gratitude most of their suggested revisions. Richard N. Current read only a small portion of it, but my debt to him is impossible to measure. Over the many years since graduate school days, through correspondence, conversations, and his own publications, he has influenced markedly my understanding of the years of the American sectional conflict. Mark W. Summers, while a graduate student at Berkeley, served for a year as an unusually resourceful research assistant. William E. Gienapp hastened the completion of my research by lending me microfilms from his personal collection. Dorothy Shannon spent many hours transcribing hundreds of notes taken with a tape recorder.

The staffs at all the research libraries I visited were, without exception, helpful and generous with their time. I am especially grateful to the Henry E. Huntington Library for liberal research grants and for the ideal working conditions it provides. Martin Ridge, Senior Research Associate at the Huntington, was responsible in many ways for making my sojourns there both productive and pleasant. The University of California at Berkeley, where I taught for thirty-seven years, provided both time and financial assistance for my research, and the support has continued since my promotion to the rank of professor emeritus. Sheldon Meyer, of Oxford University Press, waited patiently for the completion of the manuscript, meanwhile offering both encouragement and understanding. Leona Capeless edited the manuscript with her customary skill and tact.

The contribution of my wife Isabel to the research and writing of this book was so substantial as to approach collaboration. She accompanied me on research trips, assisted in note taking, and was a thoughtful critic in all the stages of the manuscript's preparation. The book would never have been written without her support, and I am grateful for her remarkable patience.

Berkeley   Kenneth M. Stampp
December 1989

Contents

AMERICA IN 1857

CHAPTER **1**

A New Year
and a Fresh Start

New Year's Day, 1857. "Another year. God prosper the same and make it more abundant in good works!" This was the prayer of the urbane New Yorker George Templeton Strong, who, like most of his countrymen, had been deeply affected by the public calamities of 1856 and, looking ahead, hoped for better times. Strong, a successful Wall Street lawyer, after devoting the morning to "diligent work," amiably observed the custom of the day and spent New Year's afternoon making social calls, and the evening with his family, entertaining at home. Everywhere old friends met to exchange good wishes, announce firm resolutions for self-improvement, and share their thoughts about what the future would bring. Some found the day a good time for resolving old grievances and renewing friendships. "The process is as pleasant as enchantment," observed the Kentucky editor George D. Prentice. "One has merely to call on a ruffled friend in order to blot out the past and make the future blossom like the rose."[1]

The new year dawned in Washington beautifully with a mantle of fresh fallen snow that set off its attractive squares and public buildings, while briefly covering its muddy, unpaved streets and softening the contours of its numerous drab shops and ramshackle residential districts. Here, too, the day brought the customary exchange of social visits. Congressmen and members of the Cabinet were "at home" to receive friends and visiting constituents. At the White House, President Franklin Pierce, nearing the close of his administration, was his naturally gracious, genial self, in the morning receiving members of the diplomatic corps and officers of the army and navy, and in the afternoon opening the doors to the public.[2] Though he appeared as cheerful as the occasion demanded, the President must have found it hard to conceal the bitterness that lay within him.

Pierce was a lame duck, denied nomination for a second term at the Dem-

ocratic national convention the previous June, waiting now for the inauguration
of his Democratic successor, James Buchanan, before retiring to his home in Concord, New Hampshire. His mood this day contrasted sharply with his mood four
years earlier when, savoring a sweeping victory over his Whig opponent Winfield
Scott, he had looked forward to the presidency as the culmination of a long political career. He had won his party's nomination with little personal effort, for a
deadlocked convention had compromised on him, a dark horse, after forty-eight
futile ballots had shown that none of the leading contenders—Lewis Cass, James
Buchanan, and Stephen A. Douglas—could muster the two-thirds majority
required for a nomination. Pierce, a handsome man of engaging charm, modest
talents, and vague, unsteady principles had been acceptable to party leaders in all
sections. Given his undistinguished political record, they could hardly have
expected him to provide strong executive leadership, but few had anticipated the
need for it in the period of domestic peace and economic prosperity that followed
the political crisis of 1850. According to the national Democratic platform, the
great compromise of that year was to have been the "final settlement" of all issues
dividing North and South, and Pierce had been inaugurated at a time when more
than a few optimists had foreseen a new era of good feelings.

The initial enthusiasm for Pierce soon died. As President, he was weak and
vacillating, showing little capacity for growth in meeting his responsibilities.
Almost from the start he fell under the influence of the southern wing of his
party, especially the state-rights extremists such as Jefferson Davis of Mississippi,
whom he appointed Secretary of War. Howell Cobb of Georgia and other southern Democratic Unionists complained that they were ignored in most matters of
policy and patronage. Pierce, an ardent believer in "manifest destiny," encouraged, with remarkable ineptitude, the desire of proslavery expansionists to
"detach" Cuba from Spain; and he looked benevolently on their active support
of the Tennessee-born filibuster, William Walker, who, with a small army of
American freebooters, seized and briefly held control of the government of
Nicaragua.

Most devastating in its consequences was his decision in 1854 to commit his
administration to support the Kansas-Nebraska Act sponsored by Senator Stephen A. Douglas of Illinois. That measure provided that in the newly formed
territories of Kansas and Nebraska the slavery restriction incorporated in the
Missouri Compromise of 1820 was to be "inoperative and void." Applying
instead the principle of "popular sovereignty," it gave the people who migrated
to Kansas or Nebraska the right "to form and regulate their domestic institutions
in their own way," thus potentially opening to slavery a part of the public
domain in which it had previously been prohibited. The ultimate passage of that
act, by recklessly unsettling existing sectional adjustments, brought down on the
heads of both Douglas and Pierce the wrath of the northern majority, including
more than a few Democrats. In the resulting revived and intensified sectional

conflict, the Pierce administration had pursued a distinctly prosouthern policy and consequently bore much of the responsibility for its culmination in a northern political revolution.

A thoroughly distraught President then found himself embroiled in a violent partisan struggle for control of Kansas Territory. In 1855 proslavery Kansans, illegally aided by proslavery voters crossing over from Missouri, captured the first territorial legislature and legalized slavery. Soon after this fraudulent election, free-state settlers met at Topeka, drew up an antislavery constitution, elected a governor and legislature, and put their own government in motion. Since neither government had a clear claim to legitimacy, another, better supervised, election would seem to have been in order; but Pierce chose instead to ignore the frauds and recognize the territorial legislature, giving it support with proslavery judicial appointees and federal troops. In the summer of 1856 the sporadic bloodshed that had become a part of life in Kansas escalated into something approaching full-scale civil war. Missouri "border ruffians" and volunteers from other slave states came to the aid of the proslavery cause, but they were greatly outnumbered by free-state settlers pouring in from the North. Meanwhile, in the midst of an unusually exciting presidential election, reporters on assignment and other Kansas correspondents supplied the partisan eastern press with vivid, often distorted or exaggerated accounts of Kansas in flames. Finally, in September 1856, Pierce's third Kansas governor, John W. Geary of Pennsylvania, arrived and, combining firmness and tact, brought the rash of murders and pillaging and clashes of armed bands to an end.

Peace was restored in time to help the Democrats narrowly win the presidency and gain control of Congress, but not before a momentous political change had occurred in the North. During the turmoil of Pierce's administration the Republican party had gradually taken shape, first achieving a national organization at Pittsburgh in February 1856, then nominating a presidential candidate, John C. Frémont, at Philadelphia the following June. The new party was put together from the fragments of other parties—northern Whigs whose national organization had disintegrated; "anti-Nebraska" Democrats angry about the repeal of the Missouri Compromise; Free-Soil partisans who demanded federal legislation to exclude slavery from the territories; a few political abolitionists from the Liberty party; and a large segment of the currently powerful northern anti-Catholic nativists—the so-called North Americans—who either joined the Republicans or formed coalitions with them in state and local elections.[3]

In 1856 the Democratic platform, framed at the party's nominating convention in Cincinnati, was written to appeal to a national constituency. It endorsed the principle of popular sovereignty but deliberately left its exact meaning unclear, claiming only that fairness to both sections demanded that the slavery question be decided by a majority of those who settled each territory. The Republicans at Philadelphia wrote a forthright free-soil platform which incorporated the bold affirmations of the Declaration of Independence, demanded the immediate admission of Kansas as a free state, and contended that it was "both the right and the imperative duty of Congress to prohibit in the Territories those twin relics of barbarism—Polygamy and Slavery."[4] Their campaign stressed the need to protect the rights of free labor by checking the aggressions of the southern "Slave Power." Democrats, exploiting northern race prejudice, attacked the "Black" Republicans as "amalgamationists" and reckless abolitionists whose triumph would destroy the Union.

In the election the nativist American party candidate, Millard Fillmore, endorsed by a remnant of the old Whigs, carried only Maryland. Frémont, supported by many North Americans who deserted Fillmore, carried all but five of the free states. James Buchanan's electoral majority came largely from the South. Though the Democrats elected another President and won substantial majorities in both houses of the Thirty-fifth Congress, the campaign of 1856 also positioned the Republicans as their strongest opposition in a radically altered national party system.

A brief period of political quietude normally follows a presidential election, but on this occasion the heated rhetoric of the campaign and the tension between North and South abated only slowly and never completely. On December 1 the lame-duck session of the Thirty-fourth Congress assembled, and on the following day President Pierce sent that body his fourth annual message. The occasion might well have inspired a retiring chief executive to assume an air of magnanimity, to attempt pacification and avoid provocation, perhaps to review recent events with some measure of detachment, to express gratitude that Kansas was at peace, above all, to appeal to the better natures and national loyalities of Northerners and Southerners alike. Pierce, unfortunately, was not in that mood. Unable to express publicly his feelings toward those within his own party who had turned against him, he made an unseemly and highly partisan attack on his critics without.

Pierce placed full responsibility for the troubles in Kansas, first, on northern "propagandist colonization" designed to promote its "peculiar views of policy" and, second, on the attempt of free-state settlers "to erect a revolutionary government" with the sedulous aid of outside "agents of disorder." In a pointless attack on the Missouri Compromise, he came close to claiming the right of slaveholders to carry their property into *all* of the territories. Lashing out at the Republicans, he accused them of seeking not only to prevent the expansion of slavery but to achieve its abolition in the southern states as well. They sought to prepare the country for civil war "by appeals to passion and sectional prejudice, by indoctrinating its people with reciprocal hatred, and by educating them to stand face to face as enemies rather than shoulder to shoulder as friends." The recent election, Pierce gloated, was an emphatic rebuke to those who would organize the voters into "mere geographical parties."

A few months earlier the message would have served the Democrats well as a stirring campaign pamphlet; in December it served no purpose other than to infuriate Republicans and titillate Pierce's southern friends. A simple motion to print the message brought Senator John P. Hale of New Hampshire to his feet to protest the circulation of that "very extraordinary and unprecedented" document which accused "a vast majority of the people of eleven States . . . of want of fidelity to their constitutional obligations, and of hostility to the Union." Senator Benjamin F. Wade of Ohio, holding Pierce responsible for the proslavery outrages in Kansas, asked how he could then accuse Republicans of courting a civil war. Others hurled the charge of sectionalism back at Pierce and his pro-southern administration. In the House, Representative Lewis D. Campbell reminded the President of his inaugural pledge that the "repose which the country then enjoyed . . . should receive no shock" during his term. Yet the country had experienced "a fearful array of section against section produced by his official action, and the Union of the States [had been] shaken to its very center." Representative John J. Perry of Maine heaped ridicule on the President, "abandoned by his friends and smarting under the lash of popular indignation," turning on his political opponents "with characteristic malignity" and boasting that they were "crushed out."[5]

Southern Congressmen rose to Pierce's defense. His indictment of the Republicans, they insisted, was borne out by their Philadelphia platform and the words of their editors and political leaders. Their antislavery party was indeed a threat to the Union's peaceful survival. Northern Democrats doubtless wished for a less provocative presidential message, one that would not have forced them to defend a failed administration and thus expose themselves to its taint. Senator William Bigler of Pennsylvania, a ponderous speaker and ineffective debater, while defending the President's right to alert the country to the perils of anti-slavery agitation, soon found himself on the defensive when Wade pressed him for a definition of popular sovereignty. Senator George E. Pugh of Ohio argued lamely that Pierce was not the first President to write a politically controversial annual message. Lewis Cass, the venerable but decrepit Senator from Michigan, thanked Pierce for his warning that congressional action to exclude slavery from the territories would culminate in the secession of the South.[6] Others said what little they could in his behalf.

For several weeks sectional partisans continued to range over the issues of the last campaign: "Bleeding Kansas," whether the Constitution empowered Congress or a territorial legislature to prohibit slavery prior to statehood, the justice or injustice of the federal fugitive-slave law, the morality or immorality of the southern system of slave labor, the alleged sinister designs of the Slave Power and the "Black" Republicans. Even the possible revival of the African slave trade, prohibited for half a century and once believed dead as a political issue, did not seem too farfetched for serious debate. Only in late December, when Congress recessed for the Christmas holidays, did the country begin to experience the normal post-election political lull and a reprieve from the fierce rhetoric evoked by the summer violence in Kansas and the presidential campaign.

At the dawn of the new year, because of better tidings from Kansas, the cooling of tempers, and, no doubt, the magic of the season, the mood of the unhappy President was not the prevailing mood of the country at large—or at least not of the majority of those whose thoughts are a matter of record. A new year is always, in some measure, a fresh beginning, and many, like the conservative editor of the Washington *National Intelligencer,* seemed confident that 1857 would be "a new point of departure." Another President would soon be inaugurated; Kansas, like other western territories, was again open to peaceful settlement; commerce, manufacturing, and agriculture were flourishing; and, after the secession threats of the autumn, the Union once more seemed secure— secure, said an optimistic Pennsylvanian, "until the people of the United States become vastly more foolish and insane than they ever have yet proved themselves." Even a disappointed Illinois Republican conceded that the feeling, "generally speaking throughout our Republic is buoyant. The prospect before the nation is well calculated . . . to induce gratitude to Divine Providence."[7]

Looking back on the recent election, *Harper's Weekly* waxed lyrical about its ultimate vindication of the American political system: "Four millions of active, intelligent, free citizens have united in this judgment . . . . Frauds are committed here, numbers of uneducated citizens vote there; but, as a whole, the suffrage of the American Republic is free, honest, intelligent, and it is *universal.*" The canvass had been unusually irritating and inflammatory; "and yet, how complete is the calm that succeeds the gale! We claim it . . . a credit to our national system of government." The outcome, according to this conservative journal, brought the triumph of no party but of "the principles of Compromise and Union." There remained no room for doubt that, "with an immense majority of the American people, North, South, East, or West, attachment to the Union is the paramount idea. The Union is only another name for freedom, progress, and civilization, and as such it is regarded."[8]

Euphoric outbursts such as these in the early weeks of 1857 came largely from political conservatives—a decided majority of the national electorate—who felt immensely relieved that, by the defeat of the Republican party the previous November, a major sectional crisis had been avoided. During the campaign Republicans had ridiculed southern talk of secession as a game of bluff, an attempt to frighten northern voters. Nevertheless, there is good reason to believe that the states which seceded in 1860-61 would have seceded quite as readily in 1856-57 if Frémont had been elected. In the states of the Deep South, not only the southern-rights radicals—the "fire-eaters"—but political leaders of more moderate temperament had sounded warnings as clear as those they would sound four years later. Hints of disunion had been heard even in North Carolina, and Virginia's Governor Henry A. Wise had appeared ready to lead his state's secessionists in the event of Republican success.[9] Alexander H. Stephens of Georgia, one of the more conservative politicians of the Deep South, speaking with considerable emotion, congratulated the country upon its "safe deliverance." A conservative northern editor was grateful that "the word disunion, late so frequent of utterance with fanatics, has almost ceased to be spoken." In his forecast for the new year, an independent Philadelphia editor (a rare breed in the 1850s) predicted fair political weather with "peace and prosperity." The new administration, he thought, would open "with the noblest opportunities, and under the happiest auspices."[10]

The 1856 presidential election returns could be manipulated to gratify almost anyone's wishes, and northern and southern conservatives chose to find in them evidence of a Republican political disaster. Frémont, they noted, had carried only eleven of thirty-one states; he had polled less than one-third of the popular vote. Even in the free states, in spite of the repeal of the Missouri Compromise and the violence in Kansas, with all its attendant violence elsewhere, Buchanan and Fillmore together had defeated Frémont by a majority of nearly 300,000 votes.[11]

Now it appeared that Republicans would soon be deprived of the Kansas issue, for Governor Geary confidently expressed his determination to prevent another outbreak of violence in that troubled territory. "Times never before looked so encouraging as now," wrote an exuberant correspondent from the antislavery town of Lawrence.[12] Moreover, in addition to the restoration of peace, all the signs seemed to point to the territory's early admission as a free state. The New York *Herald* proclaimed the November election "substantially a popular verdict" in favor of that result. It was convinced that Buchanan regarded the outcome as such—"and from the backtrack which poor Pierce has taken with his border ruffians," it thought that he, too, had been made "to feel the public warning and to obey it." The Washington *Union*, Pierce's administration organ, seemed to concur. If soil and climate and the will of the majority resulted in making Kansas a free state, "in harmony with the great democratic principle of popular self-government . . . not a word of complaint will be uttered by democrats." Southerners, according to a Tennessee Democratic editor, only demanded that "no outside influence shall be brought to bear upon this question; but that it shall be left solely to those whom it concerns, viz: *the people of the Territory themselves.*"[13]

With Kansas admitted to statehood, many conservatives dared to hope for improved relations between North and South, for no other territory seemed to possess a potential for the shattering conflict over slavery that it had experienced. In Nebraska Territory, political controversy centered on the purely local issue of where to situate the territorial capital.[14] Both Oregon and Minnesota territories

were preparing for statehood, and their imminent admission as free states was a
matter beyond dispute. In Washington Territory, Congress had already acknowledged that slavery was prohibited by territorial law. Utah Territory, controlled
by the Mormons, was on the eve of a bitter conflict with federal authorities, but
the issues were only vaguely relevant to the politics of sectionalism. New Mexico
Territory, sparsely settled, was then of national interest primarily as an area
through which a transcontinental railroad might be built. What a triumph, then,
lay within Buchanan's grasp if, by a fair application of the principle of popular
sovereignty, he could bring Kansas in as a free state and persuade the South to
acquiesce! That, the historian George Bancroft assured him, would be "the great
healing measure ... which will call down on your administration the loud
applause of the civilized world and of succeeding generations."[15]

Once the Kansas crisis had been resolved, conservatives looked forward
expectantly to a rapid decline of the Republican party. Since the Republicans did
not propose to interfere with slavery in the southern states, the Democratic Cincinnati *Enquirer* demanded that they explain "what particular question connected with slavery is now before the people." That subject, it believed, was giving way to others "which more engross the public mind." The Chicago *Times,*
Douglas's political organ, happily announced that the slavery debate was "about
ended for the present. All parties are tired of it, and none more so ... than the
Black Republicans themselves." Benjamin F. Perry, a South Carolina Unionist,
rejoiced that this northern sectional party was "crushed, and the broad, bright
banner of Democracy waves victoriously over the North and the South, the East
and the West." Small wonder that an Indiana Democrat celebrated his party's
"bright future," for it had "out lived the fanaticism of all the conglomerated isms
of the day."[16]

In the light of all these death notices, however dubious their sources, Republican Senator Lyman Trumbull of Illinois may have been a little disturbed by a
letter from one of his constituents. The writer, a former Democrat who had voted
for Frémont to protest the repeal of the Missouri Compromise, confessed that he
nevertheless had "some degree of faith in Mr. Buchanan." He would not condemn Buchanan in advance but would judge him by his works. "If his course
shall commend itself to my sense of fairness and justice I will applaud him."[17]
Here was a potential danger. Having existed as a national organization for less
than a year, the Republican party, as Trumbull's correspondent indicated, had
not yet had time to develop enduring loyalties among its supporters; and, as a
minority party, its future hinged upon events beyond its control. If it should
falter, if significant numbers of Frémont voters should show signs of uncertainty
about their future political course, not only the Democrats but the nearly defunct
Whigs and declining American party were prepared to welcome them. Henry
Winter Davis, an American party Congressman from Maryland, told the Republicans that after Kansas achieved statehood their party would have "nothing to

do" and therefore had "no future." Henceforth, wrote a southern Whig-American editor, voters would have to choose between the American or Democratic party. "There is no middle ground."[18]

Oddly enough, the Republicans, who read the election returns rather differently, recovered quickly from their disappointment at Frémont's defeat, and most of them began to sound almost as euphoric as their critics. Given the youth of their organization and its limited resources, they proclaimed it a triumph to have carried all but five of the free states. In those states Frémont's majority over Buchanan was more than 100,000 votes; nationally Buchanan would be a minority President with only 45 percent of the popular vote. In 1860 Republicans, by holding the states they had carried in 1856, would need only Pennsylvania and either New Jersey or Indiana or Illinois to gain an electoral majority.[19] In the five northern states that they had lost the combined Frémont-Fillmore vote had nearly equalled or actually exceeded Buchanan's; in Pennsylvania the Democratic majority was barely a thousand. With the nativist anti-Catholic, anti-foreign movement waning, Republicans had good reason to anticipate substantial accretions of support from the American party. Soon after the election Senator Trumbull received reports that in Illinois the trend was already evident. One lifelong "firm and ardent Whig" who had voted for Fillmore informed him that henceforth he would be found "battling with the Republicans." Another predicted that at least three-fourths of the Fillmore voters would join the Republicans.[20]

More immediately, the party benefited from its control of most northern state legislatures, which sent a half-dozen new Republican Senators to the Thirty-fifth Congress. The strongly antislavery wing rejoiced when, in January, the Massachusetts legislature almost unanimously re-elected Senator Charles Sumner, the party's authentic martyr. On May 22, 1856, Representative Preston S. Brooks of South Carolina had entered the Senate chamber and, finding Sumner at his desk, had severely beaten him with a gutta-percha cane. Brooks had resented some personal references Sumner had made to his relative, Senator Andrew P. Butler, in the course of a long and unusually bitter speech which Sumner had titled "The Crime Against Kansas." However great the provocation, the assault had created a northern sensation and brought countless wavering voters into the Republican fold. "Nothing ever was so unlucky," wailed an old Whig. "Providence itself seems to be on the side of the republican party." Edward Everett, a conservative Whig-American, recalled that when the news of the attack reached Boston, "it produced an excitement in the public mind deeper and more dangerous than I have ever witnessed." To the conservative George Templeton Strong, Brooks's violent act was nearly the last straw. Much as he disliked "antislavery agitators," he feared that "the reckless, insolent brutality of our Southern aristocrats may drive me into abolitionism yet."[21] For more than three years, during Sumner's slow recovery, his Senate seat remained empty, thus serving the Republican cause more effectively, perhaps, than it otherwise could have done.

Elated Republicans were less certain than their opponents that the Kansas issue was settled—though one of them suspected that the recent election might have "frightened the rascals" into making it a free state. In any case, a free Kansas would not end the crusade against the Slave Power, for, in their view, it remained strong and aggressive. The task ahead was to consolidate Republican forces, to spread "sound antislavery principles," and thus to assure victory four years hence.[22] "Frémont is not elected," wrote one of the faithful, "but the election has been as successful as a defeat can be." Republicans were happy, observed another, "because the Democracy had such a bad scare." Gideon Welles, a Connecticut Republican editor, had never known a defeated party "so full of vigor and enthusiasm." When Ohio's Republican presidential electors met, the feeling among them "was by no means that of a disappointed or defeated party." In fact, wrote Carl Schurz, the leader of Wisconsin's German-American Republicans, "there has never been a more victorious defeat . . . and never has a beaten army gained so many advantages after a lost battle." Looking to 1860, one of the more euphoric exulted: "We all think there is 'a good time a-coming.' Because we think our cause a holy one."[23]

Few Republicans took seriously southern warnings that secession would be the inevitable consequence of their political success. Senator John P. Hale, the Free Soil party's presidential candidate in 1852, challenged Southerners with a prediction that in 1860 the Republican party would "wind up this dynasty." If the exclusion of slavery from the territories were to provide grounds for disunion, he taunted, "now is the time to begin." Slavery was already prohibited in Oregon by federal law, and when Republicans had the power they would surely prohibit it in Kansas and Nebraska as well. Pointing to Frémont's impressive vote, Hale asked, "do you not read the handwriting on the wall?" The Chicago *Tribune* ridiculed the secessionists as "pretenders simply" who lacked the power to accomplish their goal. They claimed to speak for the South, but their own people would "resist to the death any *overt* action against the union." Southerners, like Northerners, would cling to it in order to "enjoy the liberty it was intended to establish."[24] Republicans had to believe that to be true, or, given the strong Unionist sentiment of northern nationalists, there would have been little basis for their euphoric mood.

Soon after the election, disunionism did seem to fade into a rather vague and distant threat. The Boston abolitionist William Lloyd Garrison and his small sectarian following, believing that the Constitution and Union were bulwarks of slavery, had been preaching disunion for years, but they managed thereby merely to compromise the antislavery cause. In the South the extreme state-rights, pro-secession Democrats were potentially more dangerous. They interpreted the election in still another way, deriving from it, surely no cause for euphoria, but reason to hope for ultimate success. Journals such as the New Orleans *Delta,* Charleston *Mercury,* and Natchez *Mississippi Free Trader* made much of the fact that Buchanan would be a minority President and that Republicans needed only thirty-five more electoral votes to win the presidency. Moreover, observed Edmund Ruffin, a Virginian and a prince among fire-eaters, the victory, "such as it was," was possible only because Buchanan, aided by large sums of money sent from New England and New York City to buy votes, managed to eke out a tiny majority in his home state of Pennsylvania. Buchanan's election, "if thus gained by bribery," Ruffin thought "worth even less than I had before estimated it." The *Mercury* argued that Southerners should regard the election as a warning rather than a triumph. The South had entered the contest "as a question of life and death. We have come out of it barely with life." The *Mississippi Free Trader* claimed to read in the "volcanic upheavings of the Southern heart . . . the prophesy of a sectional convulsion, wider, deeper, and more decisive than we have yet seen."[25] These southern ultras had no faith in Buchanan or the northern Democrats, whom they considered virtual free soilers pledged to make Kansas a free state and ready to betray the South in order to save the party in the North.

In Congress and on the stump the fire-eaters persisted in their agitation, admonishing the South to prepare for the eventual free-soil assault on slavery not only in the territories but in the states as well. Lawrence M. Keitt, a radical Congressman from South Carolina, reproached the "pious conservatives" whose "lachrymose appeals" for the Union lured Southerners into a false belief that with Buchanan's election their interests were secure. The trend, he said, was toward the formation of geographical parties based on "the rivalry of local interests [and] the conflict of different social systems." The inevitable crisis could not be resolved by "treacherous compromises, or quieted by sentimental invocations." Southern slavery, Keitt asserted, must be accepted as a "primordial fact, rooted in the origin of things." If the South submitted to the "vulgar tyranny" of "Black" Republican rule, "her soil will be filled with scathed and blackened ruins, and the Government will be established upon the usurpation of her rights."[26]

With the presidency, both houses of Congress, and the Supreme Court securely in the hands of the national Democracy, the secessionists' gloomy message made few converts. The Charleston *Courier* was certain that even South Carolina, where secession agitation had been especially strong, would now go "harmoniously for the Union." On a visit to Charleston Edmund Ruffin conferred with the rabid fire-eater Robert Barnwell Rhett and found him disheartened, "mainly because there are no proper leaders—men who have the will and ability and also the necessary influence with the people." Ruffin was appalled to find that some of the South's strongest men were "seekers of high federal office . . . and therefore are self-bribed to a course of inactivity, or submission." Others, once ardent secessionists, had "abandoned the struggle in sullen despondency or despair." In Mississippi a friend warned Jefferson Davis that the "visionary" secessionist editor of the New Orleans *Delta* assumed to speak for him and was thereby alienating his old political friends. In New Orleans, *DeBow's Review,*

which published Ruffin's pro-secession essays, complained about its small subscription list; nothing seemed "capable of arousing the South to a moderate support of its literature." Similarly, in Charleston the *Southern Quarterly Review*
made "pathetic appeals for the merest crumbs of subsistence."[27] Clearly, the winter of 1856-57 was a discouraging time for the secessionist radicals.

One can only speculate about the turn national politics might have taken if
the new President, backed by the northern Democracy and a strong southern
administration party, had exhibited both determination and political skill in
directing the affairs of Kansas. Had he arranged an honest election for a constitutional convention, persuaded the delegates to submit their constitution to the
voters for ratification, and thus speedily secured the admission of a free Kansas,
he would have redeemed a virtual pledge that northern party leaders had made
during the campaign of 1856. They had frequently assured voters that the Democratic party's great principle of popular sovereignty would achieve that result,
and much of the optimism among conservatives early in 1857 was premised on
its success. Though other issues would have remained for Republicans to exploit,
and others soon would emerge, few illustrated more graphically their charge that
an aggressive Slave Power threatened the rights of free labor than the current
attempt to plant slavery on the prairies of eastern Kansas.

Accordingly, northern Democrats repeatedly accused the Republicans of
attempting to keep the Kansas controversy alive—of directing the action of the
territory's free-state party with the sole aim of creating an issue for the next
presidential campaign. But as the months of 1857 passed it appeared increasingly
evident that the Republican cause required no tactics as cynical as that. The performances of the "border ruffian" territorial legislature and, ultimately, of the
Buchanan administration served them well enough. In fact, the Republicans
could not have been better served if they had themselves written the script.

CHAPTER **2**

Politics and
the Social Milieu

Early in 1857, amid the optimistic forecasts of northern conservatives, Dr. Gamaliel Bailey, the militant antislavery editor of the Republican Washington *National Era,* voiced a sharp dissent. After the recent exciting campaign he thought it natural that people should long for a respite from political agitation. But he cautioned them not to expect the present calm to be more than a lull in a political storm whose end was not in sight. "The well-organized Slave Interest has elected its President," he warned, and Buchanan, a veteran politician, could not be expected to "falsify the record of his life." Why, then, "yield to vain hopes ... instead of reasoning from his antecedents, his well-known character, and the circumstances by which he is surrounded?" Should it become Buchanan's policy to support the free-state cause in Kansas and to wrest from the Slave Power its control of the national government, Bailey would admit "that the Ethiopian can change his skin and the leopard his spots."[1]

Another dissenter, Lawrence M. Keitt, the South Carolina fire-eater, strove to arouse southern conservatives with his own apocalyptic vision of impending events. Soon after Congress reassembled in January he renewed his attack on those who shouted "around the chariot wheels of the Union," foretelling "the advent of a political millennium at the election of Mr. Buchanan." They could not alter the fact that the South was "driving down the darkling tide of events to the moment when she will have to take her own safety into her own hands." Were not her resources sufficient to support a government of her own? "With the great nerve of commerce [cotton] in her hands, has she anything to fear from the Powers of the world?" The loss of southern cotton "would cover England with blood and anarchy, and shake down the strongest thrones of Europe."[2]

Persistent appeals such as these to antislavery and proslavery warriors annoyed conservatives who hoped to prolong the post-election political lull and create a climate for enduring sectional peace. Congress eventually wearied of the debate over Pierce's annual message and turned its attention to a heavy legislative agenda, much of which divided members along lines other than political or sectional. Only occasionally did an item of business touch some legislator's sensitive nerve and evoke a passionate defense of state, section, or party. From time to time Republicans amused themselves by inviting northern and southern Democrats to reconcile their different interpretations of the party's great principle, popular sovereignty. Could a territorial legislature prohibit slavery if it chose, they asked, or must the decision be postponed until the territory was ready for statehood? Most northern Democrats took the former position; most Southerners took the latter; but many party leaders tended to equivocate, suggesting that it was a constitutional question perhaps best left to the United States Supreme Court. However, with Kansas awaiting the policy of a new President, with slavery a matter of little concern in the remaining organized territories, the issue lacked focus and was, at least temporarily, in abeyance.

Late in January an unexpected event briefly but poignantly recalled the previous year's political sensation: the caning of Charles Sumner in the Senate chamber. Sumner, a descendent of New England Puritans, was a graduate of Harvard College and Harvard Law School. He was a scholar of the law and briefly taught at Harvard. Impressive in both voice and appearance, he was a classic, elegant nineteenth-century orator who, while sometimes insensitive to the impact of his words, composed his Senate speeches with meticulous care. His dedication to the antislavery cause was complete, and political abolitionists thought of him as their chief congressional spokesman.

In the months after the assault, Sumner, though elevated to sainthood by his antislavery admirers,[3] had been stung by Democratic charges that either he was too cowardly to return to Washington or he was feigning incapacity in order to bask in his martyrdom. After his re-election, he considered an immediate resumption of his senatorial duties, but his physician and associates urged him to remain at home until he had fully recovered. One day a friend found Sumner seated in the Athenaeum Library in Boston, looking well and speaking easily with a firm voice. But the change in him was evident when, bracing his back with his hands, he rose to his feet and walked with a cane "quite feebly, instead of his peculiarly vigorous stride." Unable to sit upright through a whole day, he still found it physically impossible to deliver his intended speech, which he promised would be, compared to his last one, "what first proof brandy is to molasses-and-water." He thought of resigning, but after some inquiry he was persuaded, probably quite easily, that the Massachusetts legislature could not be trusted to elect a suitable successor. On March 7, after returning to Washington to cast one crucial vote and to be sworn in for a second term, Sumner boarded a ship for Europe. Until late in the year he traveled in Great Britain and on the Continent, seeking to recover his health and enjoying the hospitality of statesmen and the London and Paris literati.[4] Meanwhile, through a voluminous correspondence, he kept in touch with events at home and was generous with both commentary and advice.

Sumner's assailant, Preston S. Brooks, was a handsome young man of thirty-seven, the son of an Edgefield, South Carolina, planter, a graduate of South Carolina College, and a veteran of the Mexican War. He was extremely popular among his southern congressional colleagues, and they and most of the southern press had defended his caning of Sumner as an appropriate response to an intolerable affront to both his family and his state. Brooks's penalty for his offense had been light. The Senate had taken no action on the ground that it lacked jurisdiction; the House, unable to win the two-thirds majority required to expel him, had merely adopted a resolution of censure. Brooks had then resigned and returned to South Carolina, where he received a hero's welcome. He had been toasted and banqueted and presented with several symbolic silver canes—and had been quickly re-elected to his congressional seat.[5] In January he was in Washington finishing his term in the Thirty-fourth Congress.

On the evening of January 27, while the national capital was nearly paralyzed by a heavy snowfall and a severe freeze, the startling news slowly spread that Preston Brooks was dead. Though he had been ill with a fever and sore throat for several days, neither his friends nor his two physicians had thought his condition serious enough to cause alarm. But he was suddenly stricken with a "spasmodic paroxysm" that impaired his breathing, and within a few minutes, after "violent heaving of the chest and lungs," his breathing stopped. His death was attributed to suffocation caused by croup, or "acute inflammatory sore throat." Brooks's physicians had treated him with warm poultices and at the last minute had called for warm water and salt, presumably to be used as an emetic, but they were too late. One witness was distressed that they had not resorted to "leeching and blistering" Brooks's throat; he was convinced that this ancient and still widely used treatment would have saved him.[6] Some physicians of that day probably would have agreed.

In Congress none would publicly speak ill of the deceased. In the Senate, Republicans listened quietly to the eulogies pronounced by Josiah J. Evans of South Carolina, Robert M. T. Hunter of Virginia, and Robert Toombs of Georgia. Only Toombs, his eyes filled with tears, alluded to the assault on Sumner, observing that Brooks had "come among us in evil times," when the revered principles and leaders of one section "were objects of the bitterest vituperation and invective by the representatives of another." The House, too, was silent during the eulogies—silent even when John H. Savage of Tennessee compared the caning of Sumner with Brutus's stabbing of Caesar and observed that posterity had applauded. "Brooks and Brutus—Caesar and Sumner," wrote one indignant New York Congressman, "what an alliterative allusion—nobody was foolish enough to make a fuss about it." Both houses resolved, "in token of respect for the memory of the deceased . . . [to] wear the usual badge of mourning for thirty days." The funeral service on the floor of the House was attended by the President, President-elect, heads of departments, members of the Supreme Court, and members of Congress. As soon as the weather permitted, Brooks's body was returned to his Edgefield home for another huge funeral ceremony and final burial.[7]

Southern editors filled their columns with eulogies. The *Southern Quarterly Review* published a biographical sketch of Brooks and a long defense of his "castigation" of Sumner. The writer, describing Brooks as "a man of high honor and talent, whose graces and accomplishments would have commended him to the most polished society of Europe," deplored his "execration" in the northern and British press. Brooks had confronted Sumner in the Senate only when he was unable to find him elsewhere. He had waited patiently for the Senate to adjourn, and for the ladies to leave the chamber. His only weapon had been his gutta-percha cane—"he had no revolver, no bowie-knife, no instrument of death." For this act, the South claimed him "as the gallant defender of her rights and her institutions."[8]

Republicans and abolitionists could hardly have failed to discern in Brooks's sudden and untimely death the hand of the Almighty. Charles Francis Adams, in one of the less judgmental comments, wrote privately that although to many the event would seem "like a providential visitation," Brooks at heart had been "a simple, good natured creature" whose associations with slaveholders had "tended to brutalize him." While appalled by the attempt to "canonise an assassin," Adams wished "peace to his ashes." Sumner's correspondents were less charitable. "He has gone to his maker to render an account for his deeds," wrote one. "God has 'caused judgment to be heard from heaven,'" wrote another. "Everybody (north) was quoting scripture. . . . 'Vengeance is mine saith the Lord: I will repay.'" In the epitaph of an unforgiving abolitionist editor, Brooks was "in character a coward of the basest sort, in conduct a brutal ruffian." He and his victim epitomized the societies to which they belonged. "Sumner, in the power of a cultivated intellect, in the graces of refinement, in the nobility of a pure patriotism . . . stood for what the North, in some measure, is and should be altogether." Brooks "was the South, treacherous, insolent, imbruted and tyrannical."[9]

After all had been said that could be said of Preston S. Brooks, good and bad, the last word was *Requiescat in Pace!* As for Sumner, three years later he did deliver his promised speech, "The Barbarism of Slavery," and, until his death in 1874, many more in behalf of racial justice for American blacks.

The principal accomplishment of the lame-duck Congress was the adoption, late in the session, of a new tariff which reduced significantly the import duties imposed by the relatively low Walker Tariff of 1846. The passage of this bill was remarkable, because the two branches of the Thirty-fourth Congress, elected in

1854, were divided politically, the House being controlled by Republicans and North Americans, the Senate overwhelmingly by Democrats, most of them from the South. At its first session the House had wrangled for two months over a matter of no greater substance than the choice of a Speaker. At length a coalition of Republicans and Americans elected the North American, Nathaniel P. Banks of Massachusetts, whose fairness and parliamentary skill soon won the respect of nearly everyone. Prior to this last session, the political and sectional battles generated by affairs in Kansas had given Congress little time for other business.

Passage of the Tariff of 1857 was possible because it did not represent a victory of one section over the other; nor did it produce a clear division between parties. Its supporters included Democrats, Republicans, and Americans; representatives of northern merchants, manufacturers, and railroad interests; and spokesmen for southern farmers and planters. Opposition came largely from two economic groups: the iron manufacturers of Pennsylvania and the wool growers of New England and the West. Conservatives may have found it encouraging to witness this Congress at last engaged in a comparatively low-key debate over a major piece of legislation with far less of the bitter animosity between parties and sections than had been common during the preceding three years. During the debates some members, as some always will, ignored the subject before them and delivered set speeches on the slavery question, largely for home consumption, but most of their colleagues were determined to pass the tariff bill and would not be distracted.

The impulse for a reduction of tariff schedules came in part from a problem confronting the United States Treasury Department. Its revenues, derived largely from duties on imports, exceeded government expenditures, and federal law required the surplus to be taken out of circulation and locked in government subtreasury vaults. Fearing that Congress would be tempted to indulge in wasteful expenditures or finance the projects of political favorites, a commercial editor argued that sound policy required the government to collect no more revenue than it needed to defray legitimate expenses. Moses H. Grinnell, a New York shipping merchant, warned Congress that unless it acted to stop large sums from flowing into the Treasury, the economy would experience a "general crash" before the end of the year.[10]

As soon as it appeared that the tariff was to be revised, all the free-trade and protectionist ideologues reaffirmed their traditional positions, all the local interest groups rose up and demanded to be heard, and a brigade of lobbyists descended upon Washington. William Cullen Bryant's free-soil, free-trade New York *Evening Post* made the classic case for laissez-faire. American ingenuity was the basis of national prosperity, it claimed, and needed no "fostering," no "officious interference of the federal legislature." Fostering stifled enterprise, made it "barren and uninventive." Excessive tariff revenues, a Democratic editor charged, were the source of the federal waste and corruption that were "eating to the vitals of our Republican system." The interests of the industrial and commercial classes were best served by permitting them to be governed "by their own natural laws."[11]

For thirty years southern cotton, tobacco, and rice planters had been protesting that a protective tariff, by increasing the cost of the goods they consumed, was discriminatory legislation designed to enrich the manufacturers of the North. The Tariff of 1846 had been a step in the right direction, but even it "betrayed too great an inclination to offer incense to the idol of New England capital." Representative John Letcher of Virginia argued that any tariff "arranged for the purpose of *protecting domestic manufacturers* . . . robs the majority for the purpose of placing money in the pockets of the minority; therefore it is . . . utterly subversive of every principle of justice and fairness in legislation." A South Carolina editor described the present tariff debate in Congress as a "great struggle between Right and Wrong, between Wisdom and Folly, between the producers and consumers of the whole country and a few pampered, bloated monopolists." The tariff was a favorite theme of the fire-eaters, who considered it a prime example of how Northerners turned the federal government into "an instrument for promoting their own peculiar interests." The South's staple crops, said the Charleston *Mercury,* were the country's principal exports and, since they paid for its imports, were "the great source of public revenue." Yet they received no protection but lived "by their own vitality."[12]

The protectionist argument was as old as Alexander Hamilton's Report on Manufactures and Henry Clay's American System. Now its most effective protagonist was the Philadelphia economist Henry C. Carey, whose influence was evident in the appeals of many protectionist editors and politicians. Carey and his followers stressed the advantages of national self-sufficiency, the need to enable American industry and labor to compete successfully with European manufacturers, the benefits of a large domestic market for the products of American agriculture, and the importance of producing at home the military equipment required for national defense. "I prefer a Pennsylvania forge to a Birmingham one," said Representative Justin S. Morrill of Vermont. The result of a low tariff, Representative Amos Granger of New York predicted, would be "another financial *crash.* Come it will, and it is only a question of time."[13] Both protectionists and free-traders claimed to hold the keys to prosperity and continued economic growth.

Behind the ideologues stood the myriad economic interests whose welfare depended, often quite critically, on the schedules of duties, and whose conflicting demands made the writing of a tariff bill that satisfied all producers and consumers well-nigh impossible. The Tariff of 1857 was no exception. In January a Washington correspondent described the economic warfare then in progress: "The woolen manufacturers ask for the repeal of the duty on wool. . . . The owners of iron mills are pitching into the owners of works for making fire-bricks. . . .

The railroad companies . . . are making war on the small class of iron-masters who make railroad iron." A Washington lobbyist urged the "rail road men" to organize against the "Iron Men" and "go from room to room" to gather votes. The Louisiana legislature demanded a tariff on foreign sugar; the Ohio legislature instructed its Congressmen to vote for the admission of sugar duty free. But Horace Greeley, an ardent protectionist, feared that if the duty on sugar were removed, "Iron, Cotton, Woolens, etc., must share its fate."[14]

The pleas of several small New York entrepreneurs to Senator William H. Seward illustrate the serious effect that seemingly minor changes in duties might have on the fortunes of individuals. A manufacturer of carbonate of soda complained that the duty on his product was to be removed, while the duty on his raw material, soda ash, was to be retained, a change that threatened his "hard earnings for twelve years past." Another small capitalist had recently invested in an enterprise to produce zinc, all of which was then imported from Europe. He begged for the retention of the duty on zinc for a few years, promising that it would soon result in a supply sufficient to meet domestic needs. A third entrepreneur protested against the proposed repeal of duties on "whiting" and "American Paris White," for the manufacturers found it "exceedingly difficult" to compete with English imports.[15]

The most serious conflict of interests was between the New England manufacturers of woolen goods and the producers of raw wool. Because the Tariff of 1846 had reduced the duties on the former and increased them on the latter, the manufacturers were desperate for relief. One of them petitioned Seward for his support, claiming that unless Congress came to their aid, "we shall have to stop what little machinery are now running." Surely Seward understood that it was "to the interest of the whole country to . . . have our cloth made at home." When it became evident that a majority would not approve a tariff increase, the manufacturers sought protection in another way: by a reduction in the duty on raw wool, which they knew could win the support of Congress, the Secretary of the Treasury, and the President. John W. Wolcott, their chief lobbyist, assured Speaker Banks that by admitting raw wool duty free the manufacturers would be able to compete successfully with the British in the Canadian market, and Banks would receive the gratitude of his native state. "You have no idea of the feeling here upon this subject," Wolcott wrote.[16] From this strategy grew a strange alliance between protectionist New England manufacturers and free-trade New York merchants, southern planters, and western Democrats.

Lewis D. Campbell of Ohio, chairman of the House Committee on Ways and Means, had introduced a tariff bill in the previous session of the Thirty-fourth Congress, but debate did not begin until January 1857. Campbell's bill, whose principal provision was an increase in the list of non-manufactured goods admitted duty free, did not satisfy many Southerners, and several of them proposed either a 20 percent reduction of all duties, or a uniform 20 percent duty on all imports. Nevertheless, on February 20, Campbell's bill, with minor amendments, won House approval by a vote of 110-84. The bill had the united support of neither protectionists nor free-traders, nor of any party or section. As in all tariff legislation, the only keys to most Congressmen's votes were the economic interests of their states or districts.

The House bill, which placed raw wool valued at less than twenty cents a pound on the free list, elicited a flood of protests from the wool growers. Representative Benjamin Stanton of Ohio angrily denounced it as "essentially a manufacturers' bill" whose sponsors assumed "that the interests of agriculture are altogether subordinate and secondary." Another agricultural interest, the Kentucky and Missouri hemp growers, complained that the new tariff would not give them adequate protection from Manila hemp. A Missouri Congressman cautioned eastern manufacturers that they were "putting the knife to their own throats," for they would drive traditional western protectionists "into the ranks of the free-traders of the South."[17]

The Senate referred the House bill to its Committee on Finance, whose chairman, Robert M. T. Hunter of Virginia, on February 24, offered a substitute. In addition to expanding the free list, he proposed to reduce all tariff schedules by 20 to 25 percent. His purpose, he said, was gradually to approach "revenue duties upon all articles consumed by the masses, and at the same time . . . to give the manufacturer those articles free of duty which are used only by himself." His bill, which reduced the duty on iron from 30 to 24 percent, caused Pennsylvania's iron manufacturers to join the wool growers in the ranks of the disgruntled. The Senate debated Hunter's substitute for a single day and, early in the morning of February 26, adopted it by a vote of 32-12. The opposition included the Senators from Vermont and Pennsylvania, Seward of New York, and several Senators from the West. Sumner obliged his constituents by taking his seat to cast his vote with the majority, which included nearly a united South. After a conference committee had accepted the slightly revised Hunter substitute, both houses passed it overwhelmingly. On March 3, President Pierce signed the bill as one of his last official acts.[18]

The new tariff's expanded free list and reduced schedules of duties did achieve the desired reduction of federal revenues, but it was hardly a measure designed to win widespread praise from protectionists. Though a Boston manufacturer thanked Hunter for his service to the country, he observed that the tariff was "not entirely satisfactory to any of the leading interests of New Eng." The Boston *Advertiser* found it good only "as it is better than nothing." Greeley's protectionist New York *Tribune* was grateful that it had not done greater injury to "our imperiled industrial interests." Yet the free-trade New York *Evening Post* also gave it only partial approval, because it still accepted "the old doctrine of discrimination for the sake of protection." The Charleston *Mercury,* ignoring the fact that the tariff had been written by a southern-rights Virginian and adopted with southern votes, found little in it to praise.[19]

At the time of its passage, the Tariff of 1857 caused serious dissatisfaction only in Pennsylvania and among the wool growers in other states. A Pittsburgh Congressman claimed that it would "strike down the great industrial interests" not only in Pennsylvania but throughout the North. Vermont's senator Jacob Collamer remembered bitterly that the manufacturers of woolens had "struck hands with a new set of friends ... not their old friends, the wool growers and farmers of the country." Early in January the Philadelphia *North American* had found it hard to believe that Congress, whose "sacred duty" was to protect every national interest, would legislate against the iron industry, which was the "central column" of Pennsylvania's prosperity.[20] Before the end of the year Republicans would discover in this discontent an issue with which, in 1860, they might hope to enlist Pennsylvania in their cause.

"You see how things are going on after the old fashion in Congress," wrote a Washington observer. "Nobody seems disposed to introduce new or decided measures so near the outgoing of this luckless administration." Nevertheless, Congress, as usual, was burdened with a mountain of routine matters—the reading and referral of petitions and memorials, private bills concerning claims of various kinds, pension proposals for war veterans and their descendants, affairs of the District of Columbia, and appropriation bills—each item finding at least a few Congressmen prepared to speak at great length on one side or the other to mostly inattentive colleagues. On one occasion Senator Sam Houston of Texas paused in his speech to complain of the noise and disorder. He recalled the "august and solemn appearance" of the Senate when the Fathers sat there, when it was a "majestic body" and "no one was permitted to put his foot on his desk."[21]

Though little was accomplished, some long-standing issues of more than routine significance received a vigorous airing. One of these was a proposal to build a transcontinental railroad subsidized by a federal land grant from the public domain. In 1850, Congress had made huge land grants to Alabama, Mississippi, and Illinois for railroad construction, two and a half million acres of which went to the Illinois Central Railroad, and since then every western state had been clamoring for similar support. By 1857, eight states, four northern and four southern, had received federal grants totaling nearly twenty-one million acres for the benefit of scores of railroad projects. In 1856 the Republican platform had favored "immediate and efficient" federal aid for a transcontinental railroad; and late in the campaign, Buchanan, in a bid for California's vote, gave it his support as a measure essential to national defense.[22] A federal subsidy would doubtless receive a great deal of southern support, provided that Congress agreed to a line along a southern route with its eastern terminus at Memphis or New Orleans. Opposition came largely from doctrinaire southeastern state-rights Democrats who denied the constitutionality of any form of federal aid for internal improvements, and from those who thought, with good reason, that too many of the land-grant measures smelled of corruption.

Once again Congress was unable to frame an acceptable transcontinental railroad bill and provided instead for the construction of two wagon roads to California, one starting from Fort Kearney, Nebraska, the other from El Paso. It also authorized the establishment of overland mail service, and soon thereafter the Postmaster General awarded John Butterfield and associates a contract to carry the mail on semiweekly stagecoaches. Late in the session the Senate approved a bill, introduced by Senator John E. Weller of California, to build a telegraph line to the Pacific coast, but the House failed to act. To Californians the railroad and telegraph were matters of far greater importance than most of those to which Congress devoted its time. "If our people prosper," wrote one impatient San Francisco editor, "it is in spite of a retrograde government. Washington, in fact, is a perfect incubus on the nation." Sectional politicians had wasted years debating which route the railroad should follow. The editor suggested that they cease "caning each other in the Capital, or shooting each other in Kansas" and apply their competitive energy to the construction of both a northern and a southern line. Then Californians "would be in a position to enjoy the sport amazingly."[23]

The promotors of a transatlantic cable, supported by Senator Seward, had greater success. After a long debate Congress voted to authorize the President to negotiate an agreement with Great Britain for cooperation in laying a cable between Newfoundland and Ireland and for its use on equal terms. The Newfoundland, London, and New York Telegraph Company was granted an annual subsidy of $70,000 to construct and operate a telegraphic connection between Newfoundland and New York. Those who denied the constitutionality of federal appropriations for internal improvements were doubly incensed because the cable project lay outside the boundaries of the United States and the termini would be controlled by the British. Kentucky's American party Senator John B. Thompson suspected that the enterprise was controlled by some of Seward's "un-Americanized New Yorkers." Moreover, he doubted the project's feasibility, suggesting that the cable would be broken by an iceberg or a whale or a shark. Speaking for the majority, Representative Lewis D. Campbell of Ohio praised the project as "one of the greatest of the age" and declared his readiness to meet "our ancient enemy . . . midway on the ocean, and shake her cordially by the hand."[24]

Before adjournment Congress rejected a bill, introduced by Senator Clement C. Clay, Jr., of Alabama to discontinue the bounty that for many years had been granted to vessels, mostly from New England, engaged in cod fishing. In defense of the bounty, Seward explained that its purpose was to promote commerce, increase the merchant marine, and provide "a nursery for seamen required by the United States Navy." His argument did not impress Southerners, and Clay voiced their customary objections. Twenty-five states of the Union, he complained, were forced to pay tribute to this "pet nursling of the Government," the "codfish aristocracy" of New England. To take money from one class of the community and pay it to another class, "not in consideration of public service, but in consideration of their doing their own business," was a form of government tyranny.[25]

The southern interest in government economy diminished considerably when Congress discussed a proposal to establish a naval station on the south Atlantic coast. When the question of its location arose, the unity of the southern state-rights Democracy quickly vanished. Senator Alfred Iverson of Georgia, in typical promotional hyperbole, described the great commercial future of Brunswick. "The State of Georgia asks this at the hands of Congress," he said, for Florida and South Carolina had already received their "hundreds of thousands of dollars" from the federal treasury. But North Carolina congressmen wanted the naval station at Beaufort, North Carolina, and South Carolina congressmen wanted it at Beaufort, South Carolina. All claimed to have the best port with the deepest channel, the most accessible timber supply, the most salubrious climate, and the most defensible position. Eventually Iverson won the prize for Brunswick.[26]

Because of the intensity of sectional and partisan feelings generated by the Kansas conflict of the previous year, the published proceedings of the Thirty-fourth Congress contain as many acrimonious debates as can be found in the records of its most tumultuous predecessors. Yet the House managed to conclude its business on a remarkably tranquil note. On March 3, just before its adjournment, Representative William Aiken of South Carolina introduced a resolution of thanks to Speaker Nathaniel P. Banks, who would soon join the Republicans, for the "able, impartial, and dignified manner" in which he had discharged his duties. When several northern and southern Democratic partisans objected, Representative James L. Seward of Georgia spoke for the resolution, asserting that he took "great pleasure" in "doing justice to a political adversary." The resolution won overwhelming approval, a token of the somewhat better feeling that had prevailed during the lame-duck session. The following day the country's political fate passed into the hands of a new Democratic administration and a strongly Democratic Congress.[27]

A surprising entry appears in the 1857 journal of Ralph Waldo Emerson, that transcendental optimist who usually spoke so glowingly about American individualism and democracy. On this occasion he wrote indignantly about the "class of privileged thieves who infest our politics," those "well dressed well-bred fellows ... who get into government and rob without stint and without disgrace." Emerson's complaint was by no means rare. Soon after the adjournment of Congress, *Harper's Weekly* denounced "the pecuniary corruption omnipresent in our Legislative Halls, which controls land grants and steamer contracts, and is incarnated in that gigantic corruption-fund, the public printing." Political dishonesty, it claimed, existed everywhere, and its form was no more offensive at Washington than at Harrisburg or Albany. The Cincinnati *Enquirer,* noting the numerous charges of widespread corruption among those holding offices of trust, deplored "the class of inferior men who have come out of public stations far richer than they went into them." According to the New York *Herald,* the lobby had become the "third estate in the government . . . the overshadowing evil at Washington . . . a rapacious monster." Lobbyists were the source of the schemes "for fleecing the public through the exclusive privileges of land grants, exemptions, bounties, contracts, patent monopolies, and other devices."[28] Though the political scandals of the post-Civil War Grant administrations are better known, those of the prewar decade were sensational enough, and 1857 was a vintage year.

John W. Wolcott, one of the shadowy figures who composed the *Herald's* "third estate," illustrated the ways of the lobbyists while Congress was considering the tariff bill. Lawrence, Stone & Company, a Massachusetts manufacturer of woolen goods, had employed Wolcott to win support for the reduction of duties on raw wool. In a variety of ways he helped the company spend $87,000 to promote the cause. Thurlow Weed, a powerful Albany Republican and Seward's close political ally, received $5000, the editor of the New York *Journal of Commerce* $3500, and a congressional clerk $1000 for their assistance. Wolcott spent the balance on his lobbying activities in Washington, much of it for payments and loans to Congressmen. Later, when Lawrence, Stone & Company went bankrupt, a congressional investigating committee summoned Wolcott to testify, but he refused to reveal names or give details of his operations.[29]

On January 6, the New York *Times* published a letter from James W. Simonton, its Washington correspondent, accusing several Congressmen, unnamed, of corruption in attempting to secure a land grant for a railroad in Minnesota Territory. Three days later, Representative William H. Kelsey of New York had the letter read in the House and moved that the Speaker be instructed to appoint a committee to investigate. Several members objected to wasting the time of Congress on accusations made by "penny-a-line" newspaper writers, "those demented fragments of humanity" who hung about the chamber eavesdropping on private conversations. However, the House approved the investigation when Representative Robert T. Paine of North Carolina assured his colleagues that there was substance to the charge. He himself had been approached by a member of the House who informed him that a favorable vote on the Minnesota land bill would guarantee a payment of $1500. Paine received the offer "with feelings of indignation" and promised to give evidence before the committee.

As the five-man committee, chaired by Kelsey, began its work, the New York *Tribune* reported that "the master spirits of the lobby were hastily packing up and departing." Henry J. Raymond, editor of the New York *Times,* was summoned to testify, but he was distressingly weak on facts to support the charges of his paper. Simonton refused to name the guilty Congressmen or reveal his sources on grounds of confidentiality, and he was briefly held for contempt of the House and placed in the custody of the Sergeant-at-Arms. Other witnesses provided enough evidence to enable the committee to bring charges against four members and to recommend their expulsion.

Francis S. Edwards, a New York Fillmore American, was the unfortunate Congressman who offered a bribe to the honorable gentleman from North Carolina. William A. Gilbert, a New York Republican, had voted for an Iowa land grant "for a corrupt consideration." He had also agreed to procure the passage of a bill for government purchase of copies of a book on pension and bounty land laws and to divide the proceeds with the author. William W. Welch, a Connecticut Republican, was accused of involvement in Gilbert's book-purchase scheme and of demanding payment for supporting a private pension claim. Orsamus B. Matteson, another New York Republican and a thorough scoundrel, had procured "a large sum of money and other valuable considerations" for the passage of the Iowa land bill. In addition, because Matteson claimed that other Congressmen had banded together to demand payment for their support of federal land grants, the committee accused him of "falsely and wilfully" defaming the character of the House, thus proving himself "unworthy to be a member thereof."

When the House took up the committee report, Edwards and Gilbert resigned, after which it tabled resolutions to expel them. The majority voted to drop the charges against Welch on the ground of insufficient evidence. Matteson also resigned, but in his case an overwhelming majority voted to reject his resignation and then expelled him. Having disposed of the culprits, the House voted to expel the reporter Simonton from the floor, presumably because of his refusal to name his sources.[30] Surprisingly, one of the fish caught in the committee's net was the Republican editor Horace Greeley, not for bribery but for transferring a $1000 draft from an Iowa railroad company to a Washington lobbyist. The revelation damaged Greeley's reputation as a reformer and amused his many conservative critics.[31]

To southern partisans the striking fact of the scandal was that three of the investigated Congressmen were Republicans and none was a Southerner. "As a body," wrote Edmund Ruffin, "the majority of the northern members of congress are ... corrupt, and destitute of private integrity." The Charleston *Mercury* branded the free-soil Republicans a "party of hucksters and swindlers ... ready to sell all its advantages and influence to the highest bidder." The defense of public morals and republican institutions depended upon the South, claimed a Nashville editor. If the South were to lose its controlling influence, "that moment the government will commence its decline." Embarrassed Republicans could only respond that a party was not responsible for the misdeeds of individual members. "What section, what State, what party, is immaculate?" asked the Washington *National Era*. The New York *Herald*'s sardonic comment was that the investigating committee had merely scratched the surface, that "nine-tenths of the spoils and plunder jobs of Congress, and the briberies and corruptions of the lobby . . . are yet untold."[32]

Scandals at the state and local level included election frauds. Since state election laws were often poorly drawn, polling places were inadequately supervised, and ballots were printed by the parties themselves, the opportunities for fraud were abundant enough. After an election the defeated party almost habitually accused the victors of fraud, usually exaggerating its extent and seldom providing adequate supporting evidence. Nevertheless, the charges sometimes were valid, especially in urban centers with well-organized political machines. Urban immigrants were the source of much of the illegal voting, for party leaders found judges who would naturalize compliant followers in large numbers on the eve of elections, often in violation of naturalization laws. In Philadelphia, for example, several thousand illegal votes helped the Democrats carry Pennsylvania for Buchanan by a small plurality. Voting irregularities were by no means exclusively a phenomenon of the large cities. In May 1857 a Virginia Whig-American described scenes of "bullying, intemperance and fraud" during an election in Albemarle County. "Lots of foreigners were naturalized for the occasion . . . [and] Irish bullies were brought from the R. Road to coerce and drive the reluctant, and overawe the timid."[33]

Most of the financial corruption resulted from the temptations dangled before politicians by land speculators, railroad promoters, government contractors, and seekers after bank charters or street railway franchises. Often the politicians were themselves investors in western lands, town properties, railroad projects, or banking enterprises, and the distinction between the public good and private interests could easily become blurred in their minds. Thurlow Weed, for example, while editing the influential Republican Albany *Evening Journal* and carefully managing Seward's political career, also exerted great influence over the action of the state legislature, played lobbyist for various business enterprises (including the New York Central Railroad, whose president, Erastus Corning, was a power in the state Democratic party), and seized his opportunities to make a fortune for himself. Men like Weed made a mockery of the New York state railroad commission's attempts at regulation, for the railroads, through their lobbyists and lawyers, had more influence in the courts and legislature than the commission.[34] Each party had its share of worldly men, some of them far less scrupulous than Weed, all of them, like their patrons, caring more about practical affairs than about abstract political ideologies.

In New Jersey, during the legislature's winter session, wine seemed to be the lubricant used effectively by the banking and railroad lobbyists to expedite passage of bills beneficial to their clients. According to one reporter, the flow "increased in proportion to the importance of the interests at stake." During a dinner for legislators at the Trenton House, agents of the Camden and Amboy

Railroad saw that wine was served copiously. Later, when the legislature reassembled, "there were not a few dizzy-headed members among them, and . . . bills were carelessly rushed through on their final passage." In Ohio a committee of the General Assembly accused the Democratic Board of Public Works of fraud in the awarding of contracts for repairs on the state canal system. In the Hoosier state, Democratic Governor Joseph A. Wright, in his January message to the General Assembly, charged that fraud and bribery explained the recent chartering of the Bank of the State of Indiana, a charge substantiated by a subsequent legislative investigation. In Wisconsin, two Milwaukee Democrats, Byron Kilbourn and Moses Strong, obtained from the legislature a two-million-acre share of a federal land grant for their La Crosse and Milwaukee Railroad. After the line went bankrupt, a joint committee reported wholesale bribery of legislators, other influential politicians, and newspaper editors. Republican Governor Coles Bashford had accepted a bribe of $50,000 for signing the bill and soon thereafter moved to Arizona.[35]

Some officeholders were quite capable of finding ways to line their pockets without help from the outside. In June, when an interest payment on Ohio's bonded debt was about to fall due, the Republican state treasurer, William H. Gibson, revealed that his Democratic predecessor and brother-in-law, John G. Breslin, had embezzled $550,000 in state funds. Because Gibson had kept the theft secret for six months, Governor Salmon P. Chase forced him to resign. Breslin, after being indicted by a grand jury, fled to Canada.[36]

In frontier California, where the influx of gold-rush adventurers and the resort to vigilante justice were vivid episodes in its recent past, public corruption remained a persistent problem in state and local politics. By 1857, San Fransisco had acquired a relatively responsible city government, and some of the more notorious political scoundrels had been driven from the state; but an Oakland resident could still complain that legislators were guilty of "more bribery and corruption than they will ever be able to repent for." The malfeasances of officeholders, observed a Sacramento editor, had given California "a name and a reputation . . . which carries no claim to respect among honorable men." The immediate cause of public indignation was the exposure of fiscal irregularities by the state treasurer and controller, both of whom were impeached and forced out of office. Then came the discovery of defalcations and speculations with government funds at the United States Mint in San Francisco. "One after another the disclosures of official corruption are given to the people," wrote one despairing observer, "each astounding and sickening, and each scarcely appreciated till it is succeeded, equalling and exceeding it in infamy."[37]

In New York City, Mayor Fernando Wood of Tammany Hall first campaigned as a political reformer, a friend of the poor and downtrodden, but soon became, above all others, the sordid symbol of antebellum urban corruption. By 1857 the behavior of Wood and his political minions had become so outrageous

that even some of the sachems of Tammany, now determined to break his control, welcomed Republican and American party support of a movement to drive
him from office. Under Wood, raged the New York *Times,* "rowdies become
Aldermen, Common Councilmen, and Policemen, lead parties, sit in caucuses,
vote away our money, and divide our taxes between them." City Hall was a
"sink of corruption," cried David Dudley Field in a speech to Ninth Ward
Republicans. All the laws against vice were now unenforced and might as well
be repealed, Henry Ward Beecher told his congregation at Plymouth Church in
Brooklyn. *Harper's Weekly* described the councilmen as "a mere mob," the heads
of departments "as lawless as eastern pashas," but it placed responsibility on the
citizens themselves and especially on the "best men," the "men of property and
intelligence," who had withdrawn from public life. Looking upon politics as "too
vulgar," they had surrendered power "to men inferior in every proper recommendation . . . who follow politics just as any other money-making business."[38]
Too often, as in this complaint, the critics overlooked the fact that the "best
men," though seldom on the receiving end, were sometimes on the other end of
the bribery.

The Fernando Woods, the lobbyists in Washington and the state capitals,
the corrupt Congressmen, the defalcating officeholders, the bribe-givers, and the
bribe-takers, all were affiliated with one or another of the national parties, some
of them prominent leaders in their states. All had fought under the banners of
Buchanan or Frémont or Fillmore the previous year. All, posing as men of principle, had taken stands on some of the great national issues—slavery expansion,
popular sovereignty, Kansas, the relative merits of free and slave labor, federal
land and fiscal policies, among others. None, fortunately, was a typical man of
his party, but collectively they were an integral part of the nation's political
matrix, and no party organization was entirely free of their taint. Corruption
was not a new phenomenon in American politics—Daniel Webster, for example,
had been paid an annual retainer by the second Bank of the United States while
defending it on the floor of the Senate—but corruption had become distressingly
common in this period of accelerating commercialization and industrial growth.

In 1857 the regulatory machinery, taxing powers, and disbursements of
national, state, and local governments touched the lives of the American people
far less than they do today. Yet, given the nature and omnipresence of antebellum
American politics, the political lull following the presidential election of 1856
was necessarily of short duration. Nothing quite matched the excitement of a
presidential campaign, but important state or city elections always seemed to be
pending somewhere. Several contests early in the year tested the capacity of the
Republican party to survive the defeat of Frémont and the restoration of peace
in Kansas. New Hampshire Republicans elected a governor, won overwhelming
control of the state legislature, and re-elected all three of their Congressmen. In
Rhode Island they elected a governor and won a plurality in the legislature. In

Connecticut, Republicans and Americans, in an uneasy coalition, elected their state ticket by a considerably reduced majority and lost two congressional seats. These reverses resulted in part from a damaging internal struggle between quondam Whigs, Americans, and Democrats for control of the party. Gideon Welles, a free-soil Democrat, complaining that the Whigs were trying to rebuild their party under a new name, refused to participate in the campaign.[39] Connecticut Republicans clearly had not yet achieved an identity of their own.

Two city elections were more encouraging. In Cincinnati a Republican-American fusion ticket, supported by many German Protestants, defeated the Democratic candidates for mayor and other city offices. To a Democratic editor the behavior of the Germans was "inexplicable and unreasonable." Having received the protection of the Democrats when the nativists were on a rampage, they now had rushed, "with unmanly and cowardly haste, to kiss the sandals of those who so lately had carried the uplifted rod of chastisement over them." In Chicago, "Long John" Wentworth, editor of the *Democrat* and a very recent convert to Republicanism, was the first candidate of his party to be elected mayor, a heartening result in a state that Buchanan had won. In this case, according to a disgusted Senator Douglas, feuding Democratic factions were responsible for their party's defeat. "Never," he wrote, "did a party throw away its favour and waste its strength so foolishly and uselessly by personal quarrels, resentments and desire for revenge."[40]

The political press, the principal reading matter of the American public, was another reason for the ubiquity of politics. A few of the metropolitan newspapers, such as the New York *Times, Herald,* and *Tribune* and Chicago *Tribune,* though deeply involved in politics, had sufficient circulation to make a profit from subscriptions and advertising and could assert their independence when they chose. However, the vast majority of dailies and weeklies were intensely partisan publications whose editors depended for survival on government printing contracts, or postmasterships, or some other form of party subsidy. Political news and editorial commentary filled their columns, some of it thoughtful and edifying, but much of it intended simply to advance the interests of the party, with a singular indifference to fairness or accuracy. "As a general thing," wrote the editor of a small nonpolitical weekly, "political papers hold truth in sovereign contempt . . . and any effort to get an honest sentiment out of one of them, would result about as favorably as the effort to pass a tin sixpence for a gold dollar."[41]

Contemporary journalism was not only partisan, it was extraordinarily personal, often bordering on the libelous, and bitter editorial feuds, some of them culminating in physical violence, were a source of lively public entertainment. There was nothing unusual about a Democratic editor's attack on Horace Greeley as "Old Drab . . . the most conscienceless and shameless libeler in these United States," whose paper was "charged to the muzzle with the coarsest and most reckless slanders of the purest and most exalted characters in the nation." Politicians were the targets of similar volleys from their editorial critics. The Democratic Detroit *Free Press,* for example, described Michigan's newly elected Republican Senator, Zachariah Chandler, as "a preposterous ignoramus ... a loafer and an ass, and, comparatively speaking, an idiot."[42] Whatever their defects, the party editors were seldom dull, and few households lacked at least a weekly newspaper of their preferred political stripe.

Finally, antebellum politics was almost inseparable from other aspects of American culture. A political campaign, like a religious revival, was in part a social event, an entertainment, and in part a crusade waged on high moral grounds with a strong emotional charge. In a scale of values, loyalty to one's party and belief in its principles often ranked only slightly below devotion to one's church and faith in its creed. In rural and small-town America, where social diversions were few, party and church were the principal institutional competitors for their members' leisure time; and, Sundays excepted, the party seemed to win a large share of it. Printed political speeches and newspapers were doubtless read more widely than printed sermons and religious tracts. Moreover, the church was not always a refuge from politics, for the "political parsons," especially those of the Republican persuasion, often laced their sermons with political homilies. Both the deep interest in politics and its social role as popular entertainment explained the astonishing turnout at the parades, barbecues, and party rallies and the willingness of audiences to sit or stand long hours listening to political speeches and debates.[43]

When out of office, distinguished politicians were much in demand as lecturers, enlightening or entertaining the public through lyceums, literary societies, and lecture associations. Soon after retiring from office, Caleb Cushing of Massachusetts, Pierce's conservative, prosouthern Attorney General, was deluged with lecture invitations. The venerable Thomas Hart Benton of Missouri, a Jacksonian Democrat and Senator for thirty years, now out of favor with the proslavery wing of his party, devoted much of the last year of his active life to a lecture tour, pleading for the Union and striving to "pacify the public mind." Edward Everett, the conservative Massachusetts Whig and one of the most celebrated orators of his day, was the unchallenged man of the year on the lecture circuit. On scores of occasions, to help raise money for the construction of the Washington Monument, he delivered a filiopietistic oration on the first President to packed houses in every part of the country. In Cincinnati, according to a reporter, an "immense audience" listened quietly for two hours to his "clear, vigorous narrative, his vivid and graphic pictures, his pure and elevated reflections ... all pervaded by a glowing earnestness ... and warmth of patriotism which awoke a sympathetic response in every heart."[44] But Everett was still an active politician, and his patriotic message was Whiggish to the core.

The year 1857, of course, brought its myriad private concerns and public events that were a vital part of its history, though only remotely, if at all, related to politics. As the months passed a new political and sectional crisis slowly developed, but much of the time the attention of the public at large was focused on other matters. Even the correspondence of national politicians was full of digressions concerning personal business and financial operations, the private affairs of friends and relatives, constituents' requests for seeds or useful government publications, and pension applications and claims. The diary of the New York lawyer George Templeton Strong indicated that—after being caught up in the political excitement of 1856—his profession, the affairs of Trinity Church and Columbia College, of which he was a trustee, and the opera, concerts, and sumptuous dinners once again monopolized his time. Weeks passed without a reference to politics. In the voluminous correspondence of two North Carolina planting families, the Pettigrews and Lenoirs, the outside world seldom intruded. Gossip and family problems, the weather, sickness, births and deaths, horses and crops filled the pages of their letters.[45] The workaday world of merchants and manufacturers, artisans and shopkeepers, farmers and day laborers was abundantly filled with occupational worries and family cares.

Matters of local interest from time to time were sufficiently newsworthy to merit at least a few lines in the political press. In New York one learned that the chief engineer for the construction of Central Park, then "a pestilential spot, where rank vegetation and miasmatic odors attaint every breath of air," recommended a thorough drainage of its marshes. On the evening of January 26, reporters covered the grand opening of Philadelphia's splendid Academy of Music, whose architects were influenced by Milan's La Scala. The first evening's entertainment included a ball for the city's elite and a performance of Verdi's *Il Trovatore*. The following month the New Orleans press described a "brilliant ball" at the St. Charles Hotel, where the ladies, "dazzling in the extreme," were dressed "in the most recherché fashion, set off by the sparkle of diamonds and other jewels." One reporter doubted that any other city in the Union could produce such an elegant display. A Chicago editor discussed the current interest in spiritualism, the belief that, through the agency of a gifted medium, the living could communicate with the spirits of the dead. Though skeptical, he conceded that the "testimony upon the reality of the manifestations" had become too strong to be wholly disbelieved. Perhaps a commission of the "most unexceptionable men" should be created to examine the claims of the spiritualists, "with a view to wrest that subject from the control of the half crazy montebanks or the thoroughly corrupt knaves who now use it to delude the public and replenish their own pockets."[46]

Among the vicissitudes of life that often found their way into the news were the dramatic turns of the weather, a major concern of farmers and planters, and sometimes of the rest of the population as well. In late January, along the Atlantic coast from New England to the Carolinas, a record snowstorm and bitter cold brought transportation and communication to a virtual halt. In Virginia, freight and passenger trains were unable to move for almost a week. A farmer reported that his sheep were buried "four or five feet by a drift." In the North Carolina piedmont the temperature fell to two degrees below zero, and snow drifts were as deep as six feet. "The old folks about here," wrote one observer, "say that this is 'the master snow ever they seen,' with the exception perhaps of a similar one that came 'about fifty years ago.'"[47]

With the bad weather came an increase in colds, pneumonia, and other respiratory ailments for which physicians still frequently prescribed the traditional heroic remedies of bleeding, blistering, and violent purging. Descriptions of amazing new patent-medicine panaceas filled the advertising pages of every newspaper, claiming cures for these and all other human afflictions. One issue of the Detroit *Free Press* offered Holloways's Pills and Ointment to "disinfect the blood and the secretions, and cure external and internal complaints, by destroying their seeds in the vital fluids." A dose every two days of Dr. Shallenberger's Fever and Ague Antidote would bring an immediate cure, "and in no case will the second chill occur after commencing the medicine." More remarkably, Helmbold's Highly Concentrated Compound Fluid Extract of Buchu cured "all diseases of the bladder, kidneys, urinary and sexual organs . . . female complaints, chronic gonorrhea . . . and all diseases arising from excesses and imprudencies in life." Women, whose menses were a matter of much tender concern, could choose between Dr. Duponco's French Golden Periodical Pills, or The Great English Remedy, "prepared from a prescription of Sir James Clarke, M.D., Physician Extraordinary to the Queen." One of the advertisers warned readers to "Beware of quack nostrums and quack doctors"![48]

A New York editor made an alliterative leap from health to hoop skirts, which had just come into fashion. After women overcame their initial prejudice, the new style vied "with many of the more noted methods for improving the exterior contour of the female form . . . as well as conducing to health." Any competent physician would agree that its lightness would be an improvement over the former "ponderous bundle of individual skirts numbering twenty or more." When the price of whalebone hoops had doubled because of a diminishing supply, steel hoops were suggested as a substitute. Some, however, feared that they might attract lightning.[49]

Every locality seemed to have its own special anxieties. A San Francisco editor deplored the "frightful" divorce rate in that young state, indicating "a terrible amount of family difficulties and domestic quarrels," leading in turn to a "pernicious system of references . . . to private lawyers, unscrupulous and perhaps often licentious themselves." The columns of California newspapers were filled with accounts of legal disputes over land titles between recent settlers and those who demanded recognition of older Spanish or Mexican grants. The press in the port cities of the old Northwest fretted about losses from marine disasters on the Great Lakes, which had exceeded three million dollars the previous year. Affluent New Yorkers complained about the high wages paid domestic servants. "Ten, twelve and fifteen dollars are freely asked," rather than the wages "once thought liberal, of six, seven and eight dollars a month." In upstate New York a clergyman cautioned the Teachers' Association of Southern Oneida County against the evils that resulted from "mere secular knowledge without religion . . . when employed as the instrument of unprincipled selfishness, in the general scramble . . . to be rich." And in Concord, Massachusetts, a small group of reformers was more broadly concerned about human destiny. Proposing to organize a Universalist Society, it invited everyone "in favor of the Universal Salvation of all mankind" to a meeting at the Middlesex Hotel to elect officers. An amused Richard Henry Dana, Jr., asked, "Could this have happened out of New England?"[50]

Three serious social problems, more general in scope, did spill over into the arena of sectional politics. The first involved the fifteen southern states and their four million black slaves, who constituted a third of the southern population. Proslavery propagandists depicted the slaves, both domestics and field hands, as living comfortably and contentedly on the plantations of their white masters, with whom they shared strong feelings of respect and affection. On the surface an air of tranquility often did seem to prevail, but underneath, as in all slave societies, there was an element of coercion, for the master's authority was rooted in the threat, if not always the exercise, of physical force. The behavior of slaves was unpredictable; various forms of resistance by individuals, usually passive but sometimes violent, were common. Large-scale conspiracies or insurrections occurred infrequently, but those that had occurred, especially the Nat Turner rebellion in Southhampton County, Virginia, in 1831, were vividly remembered. Hence the slave codes of all southern states severely restricted the movements of slaves, required whites to be present at their gatherings even for religious services, provided for slave patrols to police rural districts, and, short of deliberate murder or maiming, gave masters almost a free hand in enforcing discipline. The psychology and political behavior of antebellum white Southerners is comprehensible only if the persistent dread of slave insurrections is taken into account. The fear expressed by a group of Charlestonians in 1822 still persisted three decades later: "We should always act as if we had an enemy in the very bosom of the State, prepared to rise upon and surprise the whites, whenever an opportunity afforded."[51]

Usually the forebodings of a possible slave rebellion were local and vague, but there were times when they suddenly became widespread and acute—for example, in the autumn of 1856 and the early weeks of 1857. As a rule the southern press considered the subject too delicate for public discussion, and the evidence of "Negro troubles" appeared only in private letters and diaries. On this occasion the Richmond *Enquirer* candidly reported that "recent rumors of impending insurrection" had "excited a sensation of uneasiness and apprehension throughout the community." White Virginians could count themselves fortunate that they had experienced only a "passing panic," for there was evidence of a "very prevalent spirit of mutiny, if not a general purpose of revolt, among the slave population." The *Enquirer* feared that the state was not sufficiently protected "against the danger to which we find ourselves perpetually exposed" and called for more effective measures of defense.[52]

A New Orleans editor, after a long delay, reluctantly published news of "slave disturbances" in Kentucky, Tennessee, and Mississippi. Other intelligence indicated that slaves were in a "much unsettled state of mind," with "symptoms of agitation" numerous and widespread. An Austin editor reported "discoveries of insurrectionary movements" in Texas, Louisiana, Mississippi, and Tennessee. Georgia citizens had just recovered from the "fright into which some of them were thrown" by rumors that a slave insurrection was to occur during the Christmas holidays. Yet, there was no insurrection anywhere—nothing but panic inspired by rumors, most of them apparently unfounded, revealing more, perhaps, about the state of the southern white mind than that of the black. "The whole South has been shaken as with an earthquake of terror," exulted a northern abolitionist editor. "It seemed as if some avenging angel had swept over the whole Slaveland pouring out the vial of his wrath."[53]

In retrospect, when the panic had passed, the southern proslavery press claimed to know that the source of unrest, however extensive it may have been, was not to be found in the character of the slaves or in the treatment they received. For the African race was "peculiarly adapted, as if by Providence intended, for their present relation in society." No other race was "so submissive, so domestic, so contented with their condition, and so easily governed as the negro." Southern slaves were complacent and happy "beyond the laboring classes of any other nation." Both blacks and whites understood that the existing relationship was best "for the interest of both races." So ran the traditional proslavery argument.

If, then, there had been unrest, its source must have been located outside the South. Many believed that the recent presidential campaign, "with an abolitionist [Republican] in the field as a formal candidate," had excited some of the slaves and "led to expressions unusual from such sources." Republicans, one southern editor charged, had sent "secret missionaries" to tell the slaves "that Frémont's election would be the signal of their liberation." It would be the "greatest mercy" to the slave "to preserve him from contact with those . . . who would mislead him to his inevitable doom." Northern conservatives must put down this war upon slavery, or the South would "at once make the issue of disunion."[54] In short, the very existence of the Republican party threatened the security of the South.

The second politically sensitive social problem grew out of the huge influx of immigrants to the United States—two and a half million during the 1850s, reaching a peak just prior to 1857—most of whom settled in the North. Immigrants constituted half the population of New York City and were a majority in western cities such as St. Louis, Chicago, and Milwaukee. Only about 12 percent of the immigrants came from the traditional sources in Great Britain and northern Ireland; more than two million came from Germany and southern Ireland. Though the country was still sparsely settled and labor was in short supply, large numbers of native-born citizens reacted with hostility to the recent immigrants in their midst. Many seemed to feel threatened by the sheer number of newcomers. Some xenophobes accused the immigrants of clannishness and undue fondness for Old World customs and habits of dress and, unfamiliar with the concept of cultural pluralism, believed that they could not be assimilated. Because so many of the Irish were poor, unskilled laborers and lived in urban slums, the nativists associated them with crime and pauperism. Native-born workers resented them as economic competitors who undercut their wages. Others, notably the old Whigs, feared the immigrants' political power, their support of urban Democratic machines, and viewed them as a source of political corruption and therefore a threat to democratic institutions.

All of these fears had contributed to the upsurge of antiforeign sentiment, but to the nativists by far the most distressing fact about the newcomers was that most of them—about half of the Germans and nearly all of the Irish—were Roman Catholics. Before the 1850s the United States, in its religious life, had been overwhelmingly a nation of Protestant sects, and the principle of religious freedom generally had been understood in that context. Now the presence of a substantial Catholic minority required a more liberal view of that principle than a great number of Protestants were ready to accept. The resulting anti-Catholic nativism was a form of bigotry rooted in disagreements over Christian doctrine dating back to the Reformation, and in fear of the temporal power of the Vatican and its American hierarchy. To some of the more hysterical nativists, every Catholic immigrant was an agent of the Pope.

A Protestant crusade that began with published exposures of alleged papal plots soon had inspired the formation of a variety of secret societies, the largest of which was the Order of the Star Spangled Banner. Members, who were sworn to secrecy, refused to reveal their activities and were soon popularly labeled the "Know Nothings." By 1854 the nativists had turned to politics, capturing the legislatures of several northern states, electing most of the anti-administration Congressmen, and briefly threatening to supersede the Whigs as a major party. Organizing nationally as the American party, their 1856 presidential candidate, Millard Fillmore, had polled 22 percent of the popular vote.

Even then, however, Know-Nothingism had begun to disintegrate as an independent political movement. Nativists failed to persuade Congress to change the immigration or naturalization laws, and they had only limited success in changing state suffrage requirements. Far from purifying American politics, Know-Nothing rowdies were responsible for election day riots in Baltimore, Louisville, and other cities. Finally, when the American party refused to incorporate a plank opposing slavery expansion in its national platform, the North Americans broke away and supported Frémont. By 1857 the northern wing of the American party, though still exerting considerable power in several states, was rapidly losing its membership to the Republicans. "Its leaders have scattered, its best men have deserted, its rank and file are disheartened," reported *Harper's Weekly*.[55] The violence in Kansas had given the Republican crusade against the Slave Power and its program of slavery expansion greater urgency to northern voters than the nativist crusade against Catholic immigrants.

Even so, a reservoir of nativist anti-Catholic sentiment still existed in 1857 and continued to be a force in state and national politics. A Philadelphia American clung to his hope that his countrymen would "liberate themselves from the fetters of foreign bondage, insolence and ignorance." The Boston capitalist Amos A. Lawrence publicly lauded the American party's effort to "cherish a pure nationality" and to deny to foreigners the political power "which should belong to those alone who are educated to exercise it." Massachusetts still had a Know-Nothing governor, Henry J. Gardner, who warned the legislature against the voting of "aliens born, aliens unnaturalized, and aliens entirely ignorant of our institutions." In Congress the Americans continued to deplore the influence of the "Irish brigade" and other "foreign recruits" on the outcome of presidential elections, as well as "the intrusion of religious influence on the political arena." On April 4, Louisville Americans swept the city election, and George D. Prentice, the brilliant but venomous Know-Nothing editor of the Louisville *Journal*, rejoiced in the defeat of the "illiterate hordes of Irish papists and German infidels which infest our country." Prentice was obsessed with the belief that "crafty and ambitious" European monarchs were systematically exporting "a vast army of paupers and criminals" and "a sufficiency of the Roman Catholic element to . . . give into the hands . . . of the papal hierarchy the control of our State and Federal governments." In June, the last of the major Know-Nothing riots occurred in Washington, when a contingent of Baltimore "Plug Uglies" arrived to prevent the Irish from voting in a District election.[56]

The persistence of the social phenomenon of nativism in 1857, as manifested in the hostility toward Irish Catholics, can be understood more easily when placed in the broader context of virulent prejudice against other ethnic or racial groups considered unassimilable. The Milwaukee *Sentinel* expressed the common desire of most native-born white Protestants "to see the different elements, which make up our population, blend together more and more perfectly . . . and gradually forgetting their different origins, their national or religious prejudices, their old habits and customs, form one homogeneous and happy AMERICAN brotherhood." If the Irish were not considered a likely ingredient in that blend, others were even less so. The same feeling was evident in an upstate New Yorker's description of the Jews of New York's Chatham Street. These petty merchants, he wrote, dealt "mostly in cheap jewelry and old clothes; but in the various forms of buying and selling there is no filth, filthy enough to soil [their] hands." Whether you bought their wares or borrowed their money, "you may gratuitously set yourself down as cheated." In California the majority opinion was that the presence of the Chinese, who could never "mingle or amalgamate," was "an evil which should be abated, even at the risk of using objectionable means." New England philanthropists sometimes showed concern for the plight of the American Indian, but, more typically, a Chicago editor disliked him "any way he could be served up. In his own forests he is a cross between the tiger and the hog. . . . He is a cruel, revengeful, faithless, bloody animal."[57] As for the country's black population, nearly four million lived in bondage, the remaining half million existing as a despised and proscribed minority. Only a small group of abolitionists had the courage to advocate their integration into American society, an idea that the Democratic friends of the Irish seemed to regard as a sign of insanity.

The third social problem with sectional ramifications was an increase in crime and lawlessness that seemed to advance hand-in-hand with industrial growth and urbanization. "We are constantly hearing of some new and startling act of enormous wickedness," wrote a Nashville editor. "We can rarely take up a newspaper that does not contain an account of a 'Bloody Tragedy,' 'A Horrid Murder,' 'A Gigantic Swindle,' or some other nefarious crime. . . . Moral depravity of every character, is rampant in the land." Not only individuals but urban mobs had become "riotous and seditious, having no respect for the laws or the officers of the law." A Chicago editor remembered a time when a murder or other serious crime would shock the whole community. "Not so now. . . . The present condition of things . . . exhibits a degeneracy truly deplorable and alarming." Never before, claimed a San Francisco editor, had the American press been so filled with reports of crime. "A bloody epidemic seems to be sweeping over the country."[58]

Discounting editorial hyperbole, remembering also that crime and lawlessness were familiar enough in the rural society of earlier years, the alarm of these editors had a solid basis in fact. The annals of crime in 1857 provide a rich variety of illustrations. Beaver County in western Pennsylvania was the center of an "extensive business" in counterfeiting the coin of the United States. In Louisville, after a jury acquitted four free blacks of a murder charge, a mob broke into the jail and lynched three of them, while the fourth cut his own throat. "It was another damning outrage upon law and order," wrote a local editor. "We have said a thousand times that there was no law in Louisville." On a visit to Chicago, Mrs. Stephen A. Douglas reported that a series of robberies had "set the world nearly crazy here and alarm me terribly." According to the Chicago *Tribune*, homicide, "in all its bloody variety of forms," had become so common in the western states "that we have been obliged to let them pass without notice in our columns." California, observed a San Francisco editor, did not escape the national epidemic of crime. "In the mines, on the mountains, in the plains . . . the bowie-knife and the revolver have been unusually busy. Every day the intelligence is borne to us of some bloody encounter."[59]

New York City, with its cosmopolitan population of 600,000, had become the cultural capital of the country; but its Bowery Boys and other street gangs, its immigrant slums and grog shops at the notorious Five Points, and its corrupt and politicized police had helped to make it the crime capital as well. Because of the recent numerous unsolved homicides, observed the *Evening Post,* everyone asks "whose turn it will be next to be strangled, or knocked on the head, or stabbed in the heart by some of these prowling assassins who strike so surely and make their escape with such dexterity." No one dared go abroad at night "without some provision against assault." The frequency of garroting on busy streets had "created a panic," wrote George Templeton Strong. "Most of my friends are investing in revolvers and carry them about at night." One frightened woman, when her husband went out in the evening, locked the doors, lit the gas burners and candles, went to bed, and waited, "momentarily expecting to be Garotted or murdered in some way."[60]

By far the most notorious crime of 1857 was a murder that occurred on the night of January 30 in a New York boarding house on Bond Street. The case was a sordid one involving persons hitherto unknown, with little to distinguish it from numerous other homicides except that it contained a spicy bit of sex and the chief suspect was an audacious woman with a questionable past. The woman was Mrs. Emma Augusta Cunningham, a widow and mother of two grown daughters and two young sons. The previous May, Mrs. Cunningham had leased the house on Bond Street from its owner, Dr. Harvey Burdell, a dentist, who continued to live there along with several other boarders, among them John J. Eckel and George V. Snodgrass. Relationships among the inhabitants of the house were in some manner complex, but conflicting testimony makes it impossible to determine the facts. Mrs. Cunningham, a woman "not destitute of artful charms," may have been the mistress of Dr. Burdell, or of Eckel, or perhaps of both. Dr. Burdell, a man of "irascible temper, few, if any friendships, and unsocial habits," owned property worth $100,000 and had no direct heirs. Mrs. Cunningham claimed to have married him, but Burdell denied it, and the clergyman who performed the ceremony was not sure whether the bridegroom was Burdell or Eckel using Burdell's name. By January, relations between Burdell and Mrs. Cunningham had become stormy, and Burdell apparently tried to evict her and rent the house to another woman.

On the morning of January 31, Burdell was found dead in his blood-spattered room, the victim of strangling and fifteen stab wounds. At an incompetently conducted coroner's inquest all the inmates of the house testified that they knew nothing of the murder and had heard nothing on the night it occurred. No witness was found who could give direct testimony of any kind. Nevertheless, a grand jury indicted Mrs. Cunningham and Eckel for murder, and Snodgrass as an accessory before the fact. By then the case had become a sensation. "No murder during the present century has created greater excitement," reported *Harper's Weekly*. Permeating every grade of society, it was, according to the *Herald,* "the sole topic of conversation in the street, the omnibus, the saloon, [and] at the theater." Day after day hundreds of people stood in front of the house on Bond Street, seeming, one New Yorker thought, "to derive relief from protracted contemplation of its front door." People bought newspapers "for nothing but news of the murder." Until the termination of the trial the case so absorbed the public that even the political press was distracted from politics, not only in New York but throughout the country. An occasional editor expressed sympathy for Mrs. Cunningham as the victim of Dr. Burdell's unfaithfulness. Some, while covering the case, scolded the public for its morbid interest. The New York *Tribune* thought it similar to the fascination with the story of Macbeth, "which informs the traditions and legends over which silly minds are wont to quiver."[61]

James Gorden Bennett, whose widely read New York *Herald* featured the story almost daily, tried and convicted Mrs. Cunningham in his columns before she could be tried in a court of law. Early in February the *Herald,* finding the evidence "frightfully against" her, suggested that she might have poisoned her first husband, that her life had served "to harden her heart and steel her nerves," that her associates were such "as no honest woman would willingly keep," and that she and Eckel had speculated "on the happy coincidence of a 'handy blow' on the doctor's head." Convinced that the murder was instigated by jealousy, revenge, and a desire to obtain the victim's estate, the *Herald* concluded that the guilty party must be a woman, for these passions were "stronger with women than with men." Moreover, no man would stab his victim fifteen times, but a "slighted woman might do so." Mrs. Cunningham was "the woman scorned, like whom, the poet tells us, hell has no fury." Perhaps she was innocent, and perhaps she could prove it; but this was "a fair view of the present aspect of the case."[62]

The jury decided otherwise. On May 9, after her trial before a Court of Oyer and Terminer, the jury took just a half hour to find Mrs. Cunningham "not guilty." The prosecution then dropped its cases against Eckel and Snodgrass. Few disputed the jury's decision, but some joined the *Herald* in complaining that the prosecution furnished "a melancholy commentary on the manner in which justice is administered in New York." The unsolved Bond Street murder would be remembered "either as one of the most successful crimes or as one of the most lamentable failures of justice on record." The *Herald's* last comment was a cynical prediction that Mrs. Cunningham would now resume her place among the fashionable of Saratoga Springs, with her social standing enhanced by her trial. "New York society is so singularly constituted that we must be prepared for all such startling inconsistencies."[63]

Many speculated about the causes of the "melancholy phenomenon" of crime in America, and most of those advanced in 1857 would be echoed by subsequent generations of troubled citizens. Some blamed the breakdown of the patriarchal family and the failure to discipline children. Others thought that cases like the Bond Street murder were the products of a "luxurious, licentious, money-worshipping . . . diseased society." Still others repeated the nativist charge that most of the crime was perpetrated on a peaceful population "by criminals from abroad." The clergy, too, was accused of neglecting its responsibilities while the country's youths were "learning to cheat and to lie, to rob and to kill."[64]

Those responsible for enforcing the laws and administering justice were the targets of much of the criticism. The police in New York and other cities, said the critics, were political appointees, uneducated, inexperienced, caring only for their salaries while they lasted, lacking the esprit of officers of the law in London. Governors were accused of abusing their pardoning power, thus letting "criminals of the worst character loose upon the community." The Chicago *Tribune* complained that twenty years had elapsed between a recent hanging and the one that preceded it in that city. In the interim many scoundrels had escaped the noose because of the "squeamishness of jurors, the ingenuity of attorneys, and the carelessness of courts." Calling for an end to the "sentimentality that poisons our criminal jurisprudence," the *Tribune* hoped that hangings would thereafter occur more frequently. However, "in the name of humanity," it objected to public executions.[65]

In 1853, Wisconsin had abolished capital punishment, and, in 1857, Republican legislators defeated an attempt to restore it. The debate over the issue raged on in the press. Nothing but the death penalty would deter murderers, argued the Milwaukee *Sentinel*. A correspondent, deploring the "mawkish sympathy" of sentimentalists for the "incarnate devils" who commit murders, defended "the right of society to protect itself." The chief object of punishment was not the reformation of the criminal but *"the prevention of crime."* God, who knows the human heart, had given Noah His law for the punishment of the murderer: "Whoso sheddeth man's blood, by man shall his blood be shed." But history, replied another, taught that the death penalty had proven a total failure in preventing murders. Wisconsin had a large immigrant population, which the Know-Nothings blamed for crime; yet Wisconsin compared favorably with other states in that respect.[66]

Southern partisans made much of the crime rampant in northern cities and had their own explanation for it. Crime, proclaimed the Richmond *Enquirer* in a typical analysis, was the result of universal freedom and equality, which ultimately produced "universal demoralization and anarchy." The North's so-called free society produced its "noxious efflorescence in personal prostitution and social corruption, in private vice and public disorder . . . adulteries, forgeries, wholesale swindling, garrotting, murders, mobs, conspiracies and treason." After describing these unpleasant scenes, the *Enquirer* found it comforting to contemplate "the peaceful homes and pure hearths, the personal security and public tranquility of Southern life." There the institution of the family was the center of social life, and domestic slavery gave it strength. Slavery, in fact, was the "great conservative element of our society, which builds up and sustains . . . the noblest social system in the world."[67]

Thus, replied a New York editor, Southerners, having recovered from their slave-insurrection panic, had resumed their "vituperation" of the North. They were "stung and irritated by the general condemnation which the voice of civilization had pronounced upon slavery, and relieve themselves in this way."[68] Even crime, it seemed, could not be discussed without becoming an issue in sectional politics and without generating a debate over the relative merits of free and slave societies.

If fame were to be measured by the attention a person received in the national press, Mrs. Emma Augusta Cunningham would surely have been 1857's woman of the year, for she probably was the subject of more editorial columns than all other American women combined. In one sense, that was odd, for women, in addition to their traditional roles in the family, by then had become an important, if exploited and low-paid, part of the urban labor force. They were attending normal schools, women's colleges, and a small but growing number of coeducational institutions. They dominated the teaching profession at the elementary level and were slowly forcing their way into other professions. Some northern middle-class women, while waging their own battle for women's rights, were playing a major role in the reform movements of the day, especially in the temperance and antislavery crusades. These concerns led them, with their male cohorts, to seek remedies through political action and, increasingly, to take an interest in state and national politics. During the Frémont campaign, one thoroughly politicized woman, Lydia Maria Child, declared that she would almost lay down her life to have him elected. A Philadelphia woman, a Democrat, professed a deep political interest "in all that relates to the welfare of the country."[69]

Since women were not voters, for the most part the heavily political press ignored them as politically irrelevant. On one unusual occasion *Harper's Weekly* featured a front-page article about "Two Noble Women," Florence Nightingale and Annie M. Andrews, the latter a native of New York who had served as a nurse in a Norfolk hospital during a yellow fever epidemic. The serious tone of the article contrasted sharply with the typical burlesquing of women reformers and advocates of political rights. For example, when a Wisconsin Republican legislator moved to amend a proposed referendum on black suffrage to include suffrage for women, the Democratic minority supported him "to get a political advantage by making the bill odious." The legislator, reported the Milwaukee *Sentinel,* presented his argument "to the great amusement of the members," including the Republicans, for it was "funny, very."[70]

A Philadelphia editor took as advanced a stand on the woman's-rights movement as his male readers would tolerate without dismissing him as a fanatic. Declaring that women suffered more than was commonly realized, he approved the repeal of laws under which they were made the slaves of their husbands, and he favored opening more occupations to them and paying them higher wages. At present there were thousands of "ill paid, overworked women, in our large cities, struggling in weariness and sorrow to earn a scanty pittance." But their cause was weakened by "much of the nonsense" spoken by those who would not accept the fact that "women will still be women" and that they would be ill served if taken out of their "proper sphere." Women had a distinct sphere of their own and were "fitted for a different class of employments." It was "absurd" to claim that their intellects fitted them "for the forum, for the bar, for the pursuit of abstract science, or recondite philosophy. As women as a class, never have excelled in any of these, so we may be sure they never will." Yet, if women were "deficient in the logical faculty," they were "superior to the other sex in many respects."[71]

If, by the standards of the day, this liberal response to the woman's-rights movement was tolerable within the mainstream of masculine thought, so was the ridicule heaped upon it by conservatives. A New York editor would not object to women speaking in public but hoped never to see his mother or sister "in that conspicuous position." He would not object to "strong-minded" women voting, since "in these days of corrupt politics, it is considered no very great sacrifice to resign." But women had been too much indulged, and he thought it was time for the organization of a "men's rights society, and the calling of a convention." Fortunately, wrote a Richmond editor, southern women were "perfectly content that their husbands, fathers, brothers and sons shall do the voting at the hustings, while they remain in the quiet, comfort and elegance of their happy homes." Current editorial standards seemed to permit references to married women as merchandise. *Harper's Weekly,* complaining of their extravagance, confessed "that the toast of 'dear woman' suggests to our calculating instincts a question of dollars and cents. What does a *dear* woman cost?" A wife, wrote a New York editor, was getting to be a luxury "beyond the reach of men of moderate means." The price would have to come down, "or the stock of old maids for the next generation will be frightful to contemplate. We want a cheaper article of dry goods for the market; something in the calico line, warranted to wash."[72]

A teacher who recommended a young lady from a middle-class family for admission to Antioch College revealed a great deal about current attitudes toward women's education. The applicant, she wrote, had read Ovid, but an expurgated edition which contained "only the beauties of the author, clear of all his obscenities and indelicacies." The applicant wrote "*well* for a girl." She was spirited but "very *governable.*" Before entering Antioch her parents were sending her to a Philadelphia lady "*to learn politeness and good manners.*" Every girl, wrote a Philadelphia editor, should be educated to be a wife and mother, whatever occupation she may temporarily pursue. Women who lack this training would drive husbands into "evil courses" and to "seek amusement elsewhere." A girl should be taught to be "womanly"; to educate her "to depend on herself entirely . . . is to render her . . . less feminine." Though she should learn to think independently, "she should not become mannish, or, as the world calls it, 'strong-minded!'"[73]

There were rebels outside the ranks of the organized woman's-rights movement—a San Francisco woman, for example, who signed her letter to a local editor "Muggins' Wife," and who will have the last word. She did not claim to be one of the "strong minded," but she resented women being assigned "the lowest rank in the human species." It was impossible, she wrote, for wives "to cherish a profound respect for their husbands" unless they deserved it. She did not approve of divorce, but she was "indignant that men should be considered wholly blameless in all domestic difficulties. Innumerable homilies are written on the duties of wives—have *husbands* no duties? Or are they models whose actions must pass unquestioned?"[74]

After the cold winter of 1856-57, the signs of spring's arrival were especially welcome. In New York City, early April found the first shad of the season in the fish markets. The organ-grinders reappeared, playing their "musical jargon" at busy corners and before the hotels and saloons. The lazzaroni also returned, begging passers-by for pennies. The military paraded the streets, "strutting after the glorious music of . . . fine brass bands." And the milliners opened their bandboxes of spring fashions to show their "delicate treasures straight from beautiful Paris."[75]

The arrival of spring also brought an end to the post-election political lull. A new President had been inaugurated, and soon thereafter a controversial court decision and new troubles in Kansas embroiled friends and foes of the administration in a political conflict whose climax, coming near the end of the year, would prove more disastrous to both the Union and the national party system than any that had occurred before.

James Buchanan:
President-elect

Rarely has an American President entered the White House as superbly trained for his responsibilities as James Buchanan. Born in 1791 near Mercersburg, Pennsylvania, the son of a Scotch-Irish farmer and small merchant, Buchanan graduated from Dickinson College, read law, and in 1812 opened an office in Lancaster, launching what proved to be a highly successful and lucrative legal practice. Two years later he entered politics as a Federalist and served two terms in the state legislature. In 1820 he was elected to the first of five successive terms in the House of Representatives, and during the political realignments of those years he became a Jacksonian Democrat. In 1831, President Jackson appointed him American minister to Russia, a post he resigned in 1833 to enter the United States Senate, where he remained for more than a decade. After his career as a legislator Buchanan gained valuable administrative experience as President Polk's Secretary of State, and additional diplomatic experience under Pierce as American minister to Great Britain. He was sixty-five at the time of his election to the presidency, a shrewd veteran of four decades in state and national politics and a respected elder statesman.

Throughout his public life Buchanan had been a loyal party man, and on most policy issues he had become a firm believer in the principles of Jacksonian Democracy. Unlike Jackson, he was not a dynamic and charismatic leader, nor was he one of the truly gifted politicians of his own day, the peer of Benton, Douglas, or Seward. Always cautious and conservative, short on imagination and wit, he had been a diligent, knowledgeable, and competent legislator, but he had not won distinction as an orator or skilled debater, or as the author of important legislation. In his diplomatic career he was remembered for his complicity in 1854 in framing the so-called Ostend Manifesto which, to the delight of southern expansionists, had urged the Secretary of State to acquire Cuba from Spain by purchase if possible, by force if necessary. Living in London during the fierce controversy over the Kansas-Nebraska Act, he avoided involvement on either side, keeping his doubts about the wisdom of the measure strictly to himself. Thus he improved his prospects for the Democratic presidential nomination in 1856, a prize he had sought four years earlier and lost to Pierce.

Six feet tall and heavy set, his white hair crowning an impressive head, Buchanan was an imposing figure, neatly but not stylishly dressed, always wearing a large white collar and neckcloth. Defective vision in one eye caused him to squint and tilt his head to the side when engaged in conversation. Henry S. Foote, a Mississippi politician who knew him well in the years before his presidency, remembered Buchanan as a man of "solid and vigorous intellect," though less than a man of genius, and not well read in the classics or literature. He doubted that Buchanan had ever uttered a genuine witticism, but on social occasions he sometimes abandoned his customary circumspection and became charmingly facetious. Foote believed him to be a man of "inflexible integrity . . . exceedingly truthful and confiding," delighting more than most public men "in what is sometimes called 'cronyship.'"[1]

Buchanan needed cronies, for he was a bachelor. Early in his career he had been engaged to a young woman of Lancaster, but the engagement was broken and she died soon after. Cherishing this romantic memory, he never again seriously considered marriage and, if one can judge by the lack of public gossip about his private life, apparently abstained from intimate relationships outside of marriage as well. He found innocent pleasure in the company of the attractive women to whom some of his friends were married. At the same time he lavished paternal affection and financial support on numerous nieces and nephews who had become orphans at an early age.

Reserved and lacking personal warmth, Buchanan was nevertheless gregarious, enjoying the capital's social life and informal gatherings of his favorite political associates, most of them Southerners or men with southern connections. While living in Washington he had roomed for many years with Senator William R. King of Alabama, a fellow bachelor, who was elected Vice President in 1852 and died the following year. When he was President-elect his most trusted advisers included Senator John Slidell of Louisiana, a transplanted New Yorker turned ardent Southerner; Senator Jesse D. Bright of Indiana, owner of lands and slaves in Kentucky; Representative J. Glancy Jones of Pennsylvania, formerly a southern clergyman; Governor Henry A. Wise of Virginia; and Robert Tyler, son of former President John Tyler of Virginia. Young Tyler, now living in Philadelphia but still a loyal Virginian, had worked hard in the presidential campaign and sought thereafter to influence Buchanan in behalf of Governor Wise and the South.

Not only in his personal relations but in his ideological beliefs, Buchanan felt most comfortable with the southern wing of his party. He was a strict constitutionalist and, except for the proposed transcontinental railroad, opposed federal appropriations for most internal improvement projects. He sympathized with the expansionists who coveted Cuba and other regions in Latin America suitable for slavery. He shared the southern view of popular sovereignty, which held that the people of a territory could not prohibit slavery until they were ready for statehood. He despised both abolitionists and free-soil Republicans, and the rather considerable difference between them seemed too subtle for him to grasp. Perceiving no inherent injustice in the southern slave system, he could never understand the passion of its critics. In his third annual message to Congress Buchanan claimed that the slaves were "treated with kindness and humanity.... Both the philanthropy and the self-interest of the master have combined to produce this humane result." Shortly after his election he assured a southern Senator that the "great object" of his administration would be "to arrest, if possible, the agitation of the Slavery question at the North and to destroy sectional parties. Should a kind Providence enable me to succeed in my efforts to restore harmony to the Union, I shall feel that I have not lived in vain." In short, in the northern antislavery idiom of his day, Buchanan was the consummate "doughface," a northern man with southern principles.[2]

Apart from political friendships and ideology, there were compelling practical reasons for Buchanan's solicitude for the South. Nearly two-thirds of the electoral votes that had made him President had come from the slave states. The Democratic majority in both houses of the new Thirty-fifth Congress was dominated by Southerners. The South was nevertheless the sensitive, disaffected minority section that felt threatened by a northern, free-soil, mostly Republican majority and expected much from a President so deeply in its debt. Buchanan's party had by no means become a southern sectional party, but its center of gravity had shifted there, and to alienate the South would have been a disaster for him and for the Democrats.

Clearly, if Buchanan's goal was to restore the harmony of the Union, part of his task was to conciliate the South and thereby to isolate the small secessionist faction. If, in addition, he would destroy sectional parties, he would first have to take care that his own party did not become one. He needed to increase its appeal to northern voters. To that end he would have to construct his Cabinet with care, win the loyalty of leading northern Democrats, including Senator Douglas, and use his patronage in a manner best calculated to strengthen the party as a national organization. Buchanan's desire to arrest the antislavery agitation of northern abolitionists was an impossible goal as long as slavery showed its present vitality. How far he succeeded in his more limited object of weakening the Republicans would depend on how well he handled the fortunes of the Democratic party and, most important for the immediate future, how skillfully he managed affairs in Kansas. He would forget at his peril the assurance that party leaders had given northern voters that their great principle of popular sovereignty would bring Kansas into the Union as a free state. At the very least Buchanan needed to avoid giving the slightest cause for doubt that the majority in Kansas, in a fair election, had made the decision for or against slavery. Achieving his goals, then, would require the best use of his political experience and acumen; moreover, he would need to show a considerable capacity for growth, rare in a man of his age, for the challenge he faced was unlike any he had known before.

The first task was to form a Cabinet. Soon after the election, while Buchanan pondered this problem at Wheatland, his country estate near Lancaster, he felt the tug of the sections as their spokesmen maneuvered for advantage. "We have elected a President, as the defender . . . of State Sovereignty," wrote a Memphis editor. "He must surround himself with no doubtful politicans, who . . . have been distinguished by their readiness to barter away Southern interests." A Georgian was wholeheartedly in favor of a "Union Cabinet," as long as it contained "zealous defenders of the Constitutional rights of the South." Buchanan would commit a grave error to ignore the militant southern-rights Democrats "by whose support, mainly, he carried the Southern States." To lose their confidence would "paralyze his administration and render it impotent for good." An Alabama Democrat, believing that Buchanan had some "dark spots" in his record on the slavery question, demanded a Cabinet "of the *Jeff. Davis* order of state rights men," but feared that the South was "about to be fooled."[3]

John Appleton of Maine, an old friend who had been Buchanan's secretary in London and his chief clerk in the State Department, now serving him as a confidential observer, offered shrewd advice on the southern problem. With Minnesota and Kansas likely to be admitted as free states, he urged the President-elect to "yield pretty generously to the weaker part of the Union" in order to "keep things quiet." Moreover, if his Cabinet included men whom the South could trust, he could "do more for Northern opinion" than would otherwise be possible. The southern-rights men, Appleton reported, were "a little nervous," because many of them had favored the nomination of Pierce over Buchanan, and they were "very anxious" to communicate with him. They would have much strength in the new Congress and could be "mischievous" if not dealt with fairly. Buchanan heeded the advice and wrote a friendly note to Jefferson Davis, who responded cordially to his wish to renew their "old relations of friendship and confidence."[4]

A few weeks later Appleton reviewed Buchanan's problem from the perspective of northern Democrats. Both his inaugural address and his Cabinet would doubtless show that his principles were southern, and with that the South ought to be satisfied. If too much were yielded to that section, "might not this furnish a pretext to the North for further agitation?" This was the concern of the party's northern wing, and Appleton thought it best that Buchanan should know it. George Bancroft warned him that the opposition of the "rabid Pro-Slavery Nullifiers" was less dangerous than their love. "Their friendship was the death of the reputation of Pierce. . . . You have only to disregard them . . . and the country will bear you up." He feared that Buchanan, too, would be ruined by truckling to the "ultra Southern party," a danger that he did not fully understand.[5]

Bancroft's fear was justified, for Buchanan's whole outlook made him decidedly more sensitive to admonitions from the South than from the North. He did succeed in enlisting the support of James Gordon Bennett, the maverick editor of the New York *Herald,* the city's most popular daily newspaper. Bennett, for personal more than policy reasons, had broken with Pierce and in the last presidential campaign had thrown his support to Frémont. But he cheerfully accepted Buchanan's election, describing it as a victory not of the Democratic party but of the conservative, Union-loving people of the country. Buchanan responded with gratitude and offered the flattery that Bennett demanded, predicting that they would "get along well together and all the better because each will pursue an independent course." Bennett promised his full support "in governing this difficult, troublesome, tumultuous, agitating republic of ours," and his often unpredictable paper at once became Buchanan's strong and almost unquestioning ally.[6] It was a major coup for the President-elect.

Buchanan heard other cries of anguish from western Democrats who felt that their section was being neglected. The Cincinnati *Enquirer* was appalled at the ignorance of the "greatness and resources of the West, which prevails among the representatives of the ancient and declining States of the Seaboard." It contrasted the generous federal expenditures for coastal surveys, lighthouses, breakwaters, and navy yards in the East with the "miserable parsimony" with which the urgent needs of the West were served. Buchanan, it complained, was not getting enough advice from western Democrats, and it feared that the West would continue to be "left to rough its own way in the world, without countenance or sympathy from the parent government."[7] Senator Douglas was the obvious politician for Buchanan to consult about western discontents.

Sectional jealousies were only part of Buchanan's problem. He also felt the pressure of all the state Democratic organizations, some of them weak, some powerful, many split into warring factions almost as eager to defeat each other as their Republican enemies. The National Democratic party, like the National Republican party, was a congeries of state parties which coalesced every four years to nominate a presidential ticket, construct a national platform, raise and distribute campaign funds, and coordinate other campaign activities. The national committee was an important party agency in presidential election years, but at other times the state organizations were quite autonomous, interpreting party principles in the manner best suited to appeal to their local constituencies.[8]

In his political role a President could hope to win the support of the state organizations only by pursuing policies generally acceptable to them and by discreet use of his patronage. Buchanan's Cabinet appointments were his most highly prized patronage plums and, therefore, were crucial to both his roles—as President and as party leader.

In one case after another Buchanan discovered that a proposed Cabinet appointment, desirable from a national perspective, would please one faction of a state organization but incur the hostility of another. In New York, for example, Democrats had for years been divided between the Hard Shells and Soft Shells, a division having more to do with patronage than ideology, except that the latter faction included most of the free-soilers of the 1840s. Since President Pierce had favored the Softs, the Hards threw their support to Buchanan at the national convention in 1856. Only an uneasy truce enabled the two factions to meet in a state convention and agree on a gubernatorial candidate and a slate of presidential electors.[9] After the election Buchanan eventually decided against appointing any New Yorker to his Cabinet.

The loyalties of Virginia Democrats were divided between Buchanan's friend, Governor Henry A. Wise, and the ardent southern-rights Senator, Robert M. T. Hunter. Wise, a rough-hewn, hot-tempered, garrulous, ambitious politician, eyed Hunter's Senate seat in 1857, and, perhaps in 1860, a presidential nomination. His strength was centered in the western counties, and he enjoyed the editorial support of the Richmond *Enquirer.* Hunter, a more cultivated man with support among the eastern slaveholding gentry, also had presidential ambitions, and his cause was advanced by a new paper, the Richmond *South,* edited by the fire-eater Roger A. Pryor.[10] Similar personal rivalries were evident and troublesome to Buchanan in Georgia and Mississippi.

Indiana's Democratic politics was enlivened by the rivalry between Senator Jesse D. Bright, the prosouthern party boss, and retiring Governor Joseph A. Wright, who now seemed determined to contest Bright's re-election for a third term. Actually the Indiana legislature had to elect two Senators, because the Democrats in 1855 had broken a quorum and prevented a Republican-Know-Nothing majority from electing their candidate. Buchanan bought off Wright with the promise of a high federal appointment, but Bright's friends made it clear that they did not want him in the Cabinet. The Democratic caucus then nominated Bright for the full term and Dr. Graham N. Fitch for the short term. This time the Republicans and Know-Nothings, now in a minority on a joint ballot, bolted in order to prevent the election of Bright and Fitch. Democratic legislators, in a bold move, then met without the Republicans and elected their candidates. Eventually the Democratic Senate, after refusing to seat James Harlan of Iowa, whom the Republicans had elected under identical circumstances, seated both Bright and Fitch, and Buchanan thus gained two loyal senatorial friends.[11]

Democratic party rivalry in California centered on a similar senatorial contest. One of the aspirants, Dr. William N. Gwin, a native of Tennessee and leader of the "Chivalry," the prosouthern wing of the state Democracy, had been elected to the Senate in 1849. His rival, David C. Broderick, an Irish Catholic working-class veteran of New York's Tammany Hall, was the leader of a faction determined to destroy the power of the "Chivs." In 1855, Broderick had prevented Gwin's re-election, and in 1857 the term of California's second Senator, John B. Weller, also expired. As a result, when the Democratic-controlled legislature met in January, it had to elect two Senators, one for a four-year term and one for a full term. Broderick won the Democratic nomination for the full term, and after his election he had the power to determine who the other Senator would be. To the astonishment of everyone, he gave his support to Gwin, who accepted it on the most humiliating terms. Gwin had to sign a written agreement to relinquish all California patronage to Broderick, and in a public letter he thanked Broderick and his friends for their "timely assistance" in securing his election.[12] It was a crushing defeat for the Chivalry—provided, of course, that Buchanan would respect the bargain and abandon Gwin for the brash and abrasive Broderick.

Pennsylvania Democrats were proud that they had secured the nomination of James Buchanan, their state's first presidential candidate, but after his election the local party factions proved to be among the most troublesome of all. A host of state and county politicians, who in various ways had supported him during his long career in public life, made pilgrimages to Wheatland in search of their rewards. Given a free hand the President-elect would have liked to place several of his most trusted Pennsylvania friends in strategic positions where they could be of special value to his administration. The term of one Pennsylvania Senator, Richard Brodhead, was about to expire, and Buchanan hoped he could be replaced by Judge Jeremiah S. Black, head of the state supreme court and the ablest and most learned of his local friends. Senator William Bigler was not close to Buchanan, but he would be reliable, and if his skills as a debater and parliamentarian were not impressive, his votes at least would be at the President's disposal. The Pennsylvanian whom Buchanan wanted above all others for his Cabinet was Congressman J. Glancy Jones, a friend with whom he felt comfortable and who would share his attitudes on questions of policy. Finally, he would have been pleased to give the editorship of the Washington *Union,* the national party organ, to his most devoted political friend, John W. Forney.

Forney was a special case and needed to be dealt with first. Ardent, impetuous, voluble, and talented, he had linked his career with Buchanan's many years ago, first as an editor in Lancaster, then as editor of the Philadelphia *Pennsylvanian.* By 1847 he seemed to have dedicated his life to making Buchanan President, but the enterprise failed in 1848 and again in 1852. Four years later, after helping him gain the coveted nomination, Forney lodged his wife and children at Wheatland for much of the summer while serving as chairman of the state

Democratic committee and directing the drive to win Pennsylvania's crucial electoral vote. "I saw him many times during the contest," a friend recalled, "and he always seemed to be wholly absorbed in what he evidently regarded as the great battle of his life." In addition to campaigning personally, he mobilized speakers, badgered editors, raised funds, assessed Democratic office-holders, spent money of his own—and, later, became the target of most of the Republican charges of illegal voting in Philadelphia and several doubtful districts. After the election, Buchanan was sincerely grateful to his faithful friend, declaring that of all those who had helped the cause in Pennsylvania, Forney had done "the most to secure the Triumph of our ticket." The Washington *Union* and its lucrative Congressional printing contract seemed to be a well-earned and appropriate reward for this energetic and experienced editor. Forney himself asked for nothing more.[13]

Unfortunately, after giving Forney reason to hope that the *Union* would be his, Buchanan learned that Southerners, including Virginia's Governor Wise, disliked and distrusted Forney and were adamantly opposed to his selection as principal editorial spokesman for the administration. Why it should have taken Buchanan so long to discover this fact is not clear, but eventually he concluded that the *Union* would have to be edited by someone more generally acceptable to Democrats in both sections. Finding another place equally suitable for the mercurial Forney would not be easy, and in his effort Buchanan suffered a major political disaster.[14]

Forney was shocked by the loss of his anticipated prize and the substantial income that it entailed. In his view, nothing less than an office of the first rank would be an adequate substitute and a sufficient expression of Buchanan's gratitude for his long years of service. A Cabinet appointment would have been acceptable to him, but hardly to the Southerners who had opposed his editorship of the *Union,* or to J. Glancy Jones, a political rival who had been promised Pennsylvania's place in the new administration. Forney's talents and temperament were quite unsuited to the responsibilities of an executive department, and at no time did the President-elect consider him for a place of that kind. Buchanan's predicament eased a little when Forney asked instead for his support when the Democratic legislative caucus met to nominate a candidate for the United States Senate. Forney's nomination and election would have solved a major problem and, at the same time, removed the chief obstacle to a Cabinet appointment for Jones. However, every solution seemed to create another problem, for Buchanan had already promised to support Judge Black for the Senate and now had to ask him to give way to Forney. Fortunately, Black and Forney were political friends, and Black, suppressing his disappointment, agreed.[15]

Buchanan had never before intervened in his party's legislative caucus, but he threw his support to Forney because of his determination to provide an office for him "first and above all others." Writing to one Democratic legislator, he expressed his regard for the other candidates but desired to make clear his preference. "When asked I have always said that I preferred Col. Forney. I should esteem it a friendly act toward me for any person in or out of the Legislature to support him." In early January, once again full of hope and brimming with gratitude for Buchanan's "warm and generous heart," Forney assured him that he would not be ashamed of his "poor printer boy."[16]

On a joint ballot of the two houses the Democrats in the Pennsylvania legislature had only a small majority of five, but Buchanan gambled that his prestige as President-elect would enable him to hold virtually every member of his party in line. Yet he knew that in his state, as elsewhere, Democrats were divided into factions and that Forney had made enemies there as well as in the South. Senator Broadhead, still hoping for re-election, would surely use what influence he had against Forney. Before Buchanan's intervention most Democratic legislators had expected their colleague Henry D. Foster, a former Congressman, to be nominated by the party caucus, and many of them resented the effort of an outsider, no matter how distinguished, to dictate their choice. Governor Wise and other Southerners were unhappy about the prospect of Forney entering the Senate; and in Philadelphia, Wise's friend, Robert Tyler, acquiesced with extreme reluctance, warning that his nomination "cannot fail to produce a bitter feud." Bigler, responding to Buchanan's wish, used his influence for Forney, but a political friend advised him "to keep out of it as there will be a fierce contest," with the outcome far from certain.[17]

When the Democratic caucus met on January 9, eight supporters of Foster refused to attend, and of those who did attend, thirty-five cast votes for Forney and twenty-six for other candidates. What the dissidents would do when the legislature met in joint session was uncertain. "Though my friends are sanguine of my election *I am not,*" a discouraged Forney informed Buchanan. "I feel that you have discharged your whole duty to me, and, whatever my necessity, I can make no demands."[18]

Forney's pessimism resulted not only from the divided vote of the Democratic caucus but from the united action of the Republican and American party legislators. The opposition appeared ready to support almost anyone given a chance to defeat him because of his role in the last presidential campaign. "It would be a great victory if we could send a Republican . . . to the U.S. Senate," wrote Buchanan's famous Lancaster neighbor, Thaddeus Stevens. "If you tender the nomination to S. Cameron I have reason to believe that he can get enough of his old friends to elect him." Stevens's candidate, Simon Cameron of Harrisburg, was a self-made capitalist with investments in banking, railroads, and mining, a former Democratic Senator, a former Know Nothing, now a Republican. Cameron understood the opportunity presented him by the opposition to Forney and by his continued friendly relations with a number of Pennsylvania Democrats. At the caucus of Republicans and Americans, Charles B. Penrose of Philadelphia reported that several Democrats would vote for Cameron and permitted a committee to interview the defectors at his hotel. The caucus then unanimously endorsed him, though some agreed reluctantly and only for the first ballot. What Buchanan thought of Cameron, who had helped defeat his bid for a presidential nomination in 1852, was stated clearly in a party organ, the Philadelphia *Pennsylvanian:* "His triumph would only serve to demonstrate that corruption, duplicity, intrigue, and chicanery were the true passports to honorable distinction."[19]

On January 13, the day of the joint legislative session, as one observer recalled, the opposition sat in "quiet anxiety," the Democrats in "sullen apprehension," feeling that "there was some subtle miasma in the political atmosphere." As the roll was called the legislators voted as expected, until the clerk reached the name of William B. Lebo, a Democrat from Schuylkill, who cast his vote for Cameron. The stunned Democrats then heard two more of their members, Samuel B. Manear of York and G. A. Wagenseller of Schuylkill, give Cameron their votes, the first "in a feeble voice," the other in a "distinct and defiant tone." Cameron, with the unanimous support of the opposition, received 67 votes, Forney, 58, and Foster, 7.

Buchanan's inability to control the Democratic factions in his own state was a severe blow to his prestige. Moreover, Cameron's election placed his bitter enemy in the Senate and left the increasingly troublesome problem of John W. Forney still unsolved. Forney himself vowed, briefly at least, to bear his defeat with "becoming fortitude." Within a few weeks his interest in a Cabinet appointment had revived.[20]

Among the congratulatory letters sent to Cameron, one from a Democrat expressed pleasure at the rebuke to Buchanan "for his insolent dictation to the members of the legislature." Others interpreted his election variously as a "repudiation of Forney," a vindication of "sound Americanism," a demand for "the protection of home industry," or a victory for free soil.[21] Democratic editors poured their scorn on the three apostates who, after attending and approving the action of the Democratic caucus, "earned an immortality of infamy by basely betraying their constituents and their party." However much southern Democrats may have disliked Forney, they could hardly rejoice at the increase of Republican strength in the Senate. The Richmond *Enquirer* thought the loss of a Democratic Senator from a northern state, "in this, our hour of peril . . . a matter of more than ordinary concern."[22]

Few Democrats believed that the three renegades had given their votes to Cameron for honorable reasons. Their action, charged the Washington *Union,* bore "upon its face the strongest presumptive evidence of bargain and corruption." Most of the Democratic members of the Pennsylvania legislature signed a petition to the United States Senate Committee on the Judiciary charging that Cameron's election "was procured, as they are informed and believe, by corrupt and unlawful means," and requesting an investigation. Three members of the state senate informed Senator Bigler that they had witnesses ready to testify that all three of the defecting Democrats had sold their votes for cash, and they asked for time to present their evidence. Instead, on March 11, during a special session of the Democratic-controlled United States Senate, the Judiciary Committee reported the allegations "too vague and indefinite" to justify an investigation. It urged the Pennsylvania legislature to investigate the matter itself and make a case before asking the Senate to act. During the debate, Senator Cameron, who had already been seated, asserted that he was too proud of his state "to believe that any man in her legislature could be bought to do any unworthy act." At that point, but hardly for that reason, both the Senate and the Pennsylvania legislature dropped the case.[23]

Cameron's political reputation doubtless contributed to the suspicion that old friendships did not explain the three votes that elected him, or, for that matter, his nomination by the party caucus. The surviving evidence is far from conclusive but sufficient to keep the suspicion alive. One Uniontown friend apparently did not think that Cameron would be offended if he were told of a legislator whose vote might be for sale, or of a local Democrat who was "not very scrupulous in either opposing old friends or in serving new ones." Part of the uncertainty grew out of Cameron's generous policy of making loans to political friends or contributions to their campaigns, thus placing them under obligation to him. One recipient of a loan assumed, mistakenly, that he would not be pressed for payment, for he had agreed, "if elected to do a certain thing, which I supposed a 'quid pro quo.'" Another correspondent referred to a $500 payment promised him if Cameron were elected, vowing that he would reveal nothing before any investigating committee. Precisely what he had done to earn the payment was not clear, but he acknowledged receipt of half the amount and asked for the rest. In any case, whatever the facts may have been, Cameron survived the accusations and in his own state managed before long to build and control a powerful Republican political machine.[24]

"There is such a number and such a cross firing of the Cabinet making cliques," the New York *Herald* observed in early January, "as to render this Cabinet game for the plunder very fierce, funny and interesting." Among others, there were the two Virginia cliques of Wise and Hunter; the two Pennsylvania cliques of Forney and Jones; two or three New York cliques; two or three cliques of southern fire-eaters "of different degrees of temperature"; and two or three northwestern cliques loyal to Senators Cass, Douglas, or Bright. Since the election the *Herald* estimated that "from thirty to fifty positive members of the new Cabinet [had been] telegraphed from Washington, and combinations from these men amounting to at least fifty different Cabinets."[25]

As the weeks of January passed, with the Washington air full of rumors, Buchanan was bombarded with advice, pleas, and warnings from all directions and by every party faction. He listened to friends and tolerated the blandishments of others, but he made no public announcements while searching for the seven Cabinet officers whom he thought best able to serve both national and party interests. He was determined to appoint men who could work harmoniously with him and with each other, rather than representing a variety of political perspectives. During these trying days John Appleton continued to send him perceptive reports about areas of discontent and suggested ways to deal with them. To help with his heavy correspondence Buchanan persuaded his nephew, James Buchanan Henry, a young lawyer, to come to Wheatland and serve as his secretary.

Buchanan tried first to build his Cabinet around the friends he knew best and trusted most—Wise, Slidell, Bright, and Glancy Jones—but Wise preferred to continue in his present post as governor of Virginia, and Slidell and Bright preferred to remain in the Senate. Since only Jones agreed to accept an appointment, the President-elect was obliged to consider other political friends and some candidates with whom he was less familiar. He knew that New England, the old Northwest, and both southern Unionists and southern-rights Democrats would have to be represented, and that none of them had a candidate behind whom all factions would unite. He would have liked to accommodate those who urged him to broaden his base by appointing a conservative old-line Whig, but Democratic partisans were reluctant to surrender even one place to their recent foes.[26] While wrestling with these exasperating problems, Buchanan for the first time might well have begun to wonder why he had struggled so long for the office whose cares were already upon him.

For the office of Secretary of State, the premier position in rank and prestige, he considered two old friends, Howell Cobb and Robert J. Walker, whom he had known while in Congress and in the Polk administration, and who had backed his presidential nomination the previous year. Cobb, a Georgia Unionist, had supported the Compromise of 1850 from his position as Speaker of the House, had then served as governor of his state, and in 1855 had returned to Congress. He had campaigned effectively for Buchanan in New York, Pennsylvania, and Indiana, and he was now eager to take the State Department (but nothing less) in part as a means of advancing his own ambition for a presidential nomination in 1860. Walker, a native of Pennsylvania, had moved to Mississippi to practice law, engage in land speculations, and pursue a political career. Twice elected to the United States Senate, he had resigned to become Polk's Secretary of the Treasury. While holding that office he had successfully sponsored the Tariff of 1846, managed the financing of the Mexican War, and strongly supported southern expansionist ambitions in both Cuba and Central America.

Either Cobb or Walker would have been quite acceptable to Buchanan. Unfortunately, both were controversial, receiving enthusiastic support and vigorous opposition in about equal measures. Cobb was the favorite of the southern moderates and had the approval of Slidell and a group of Pennsylvanians, including Forney, who appreciated Cobb's sympathy after his defeat for the Senate. The opposition came mostly from Jefferson Davis and other southern-rights Democrats in the Deep South, but he was also opposed by Wise and Douglas, the latter remembering Cobb's refusal to support him at the last Democratic national convention. Walker, the expansionist, anti-protectionist, and sometimes reckless speculator, was the candidate of the southern-rights faction, of Douglas and the aggressive northern "Young America" Democrats, and of some New York business interests. His opponents were the conservatives who regarded him as unsteady, too flamboyant, too sympathetic to filibustering enterprises, and too close to New York speculators. Cobb made it clear that he would not accept a place in the Cabinet if Walker were given the state department.[27]

During the stalemate some suggested that Secretary of State William L. Marcy, a talented New Yorker and one of the ablest men in the Pierce administration, be continued in office, but Buchanan wanted no holdovers, especially one who had opposed his presidential aspirations in the past. As a last resort others proposed Lewis Cass of Michigan, who was about to retire from the Senate and would welcome an opportunity to remain in Washington. The old general, now in his seventy-fifth year, was a veteran of the War of 1812, and of the Jacksonian political wars as well. In his decrepitude he could hardly be a source of strength to the administration, hardly more than a figurehead whose age and infirmities would conveniently make him a rival of no one. This was a poor reason for appointing Cass Secretary of State, but if all else failed Buchanan might be persuaded to consider him as a compromise candidate.[28]

As Buchanan weighed these alternatives, he also conferred with advisers at Wheatland and in Philadelphia about other possible Cabinet appointments. He knew that Douglas hoped to secure a place for one of his friends, either William A. Richardson of Illinois, who had lost his seat in the House, or Judge Samuel Treat of St. Louis. Neither was likely to contribute to the harmony of the Cabinet, and Slidell warned him against offending Bright by appointing "any decided partisan of Douglas." Governor Wise wanted an appointment for his fellow Virginian, ex-Governor John B. Floyd, but objected to Cobb, Bright, Forney, Walker, or Slidell. South Carolina's southern-rights Democrats wanted a place for one of their own, Francis W. Pickens. Judge Black had his Pennsylvania champions after he agreed to give up the Senate. Retiring Governor Herschel V. Johnson of Georgia informed Buchanan that he would be a candidate if Cobb declined to serve. Mrs. Cobb, another woman deeply interested in politics, was exasperated by the behavior of her husband's opponents, the "abominable, conceited" southern-rights men, and wished that they would "hold their tongues and pens still through all time." She hoped that Buchanan would soon "relieve the suspense which reigns in every heart." Late in January, John B. Lamar, Cobb's brother-in-law, expressing the growing impatience, complained that the long delay in announcing a Cabinet was opening "all the old sores" in the South.[29]

Slidell had urged Buchanan to visit Washington before selecting his Cabinet, because his friends wanted to see him. "You will of course be immensely annoyed," Slidell warned, "but . . . you cannot correctly feel the public pulse any where else." Marcy thought that if the President-elect were puzzled about the Cabinet problem before, "he will not be less so after his arrival. I do not know two prominent men who will present to him concurrent views." Nevertheless, Buchanan finally agreed to come, arriving on January 27 and taking rooms at the National Hotel. He called on President Pierce at the White House and met the members of Congress and other dignitaries. After a long interview, Cobb concluded that he had not yet made any firm decisions about the Cabinet, including the State Department. Bright, Wise, Slidell, and Douglas also conferred with him. After his departure on February 3, Cobb was even more puzzled, concluding now that his chief rival for Secretary of State was not Walker but Senator Hunter of Virginia. "You have left the cabinet makers more confounded than ever," Bigler wrote Buchanan. "They say that before your visit they had some things settled, now all is mystery to them."[30]

The Washington visit did help Buchanan make his final Cabinet choices, but it was also the occasion of two more pre-inauguration disasters. The first involved Senator Douglas, his chief rival for the 1856 presidential nomination, the most powerful Democrat in the old Northwest, the champion of popular sovereignty, and the embodiment of the nationalistic, expansionist, go-ahead spirit of his Young America followers. Short, stocky, pugnacious, a brilliant debater and fiercely ambitious, the "Little Giant," then in his forty-sixth year, believed that Buchanan would be the last President to represent the Democracy's Old Guard and that his party's future belonged to him. Douglas was a masterful politician. According to an editor who traveled with him from St. Louis to Chicago, "He knows everybody; can tell the question that affects each locality; call the name of every farm owner on the way; tell all travelers something of the homes they left . . . and suggest what they are adapted for in this life, and what place they deserve in heaven." Such a man, he concluded, "wrapped up with the one idea of preferment, power, and dominion among men, is not easily to be put down; and his opponents might as well believe at once, that when they fight him they fight a strong man—a little giant indeed."[31]

After the death of his wife three years earlier, Douglas had gone through a distressing period of heavy drinking and indifference about his personal appearance. Then, shortly before Buchanan's visit, Douglas had married Adele Cutts, the daughter of a government clerk, a beautiful, charming, and gifted young woman in her early twenties. His second marriage proved to be both a healing and transforming experience, bringing a notable change in his disposition, manners, and dress. His Washington house became one of the centers of the capital's social life, in which, according to one observer, Adele was soon "quite as prominent . . . as her husband [was] in the political arena." When Douglas called on the President-elect at the National Hotel, Buchanan congratulated him on his improved appearance since his marriage, to which Douglas responded with the suggestion that he try the same remedy himself.[32]

Buchanan was the guest of honor at one of the Douglases' elegant dinners, but his conversations with the Illinois Senator on political matters were not pleasant. Even though Douglas had withdrawn in his favor at the Democratic national convention and campaigned vigorously in his behalf, he had never liked Douglas personally and showed little interest in his Cabinet recommendations. Nor would he assist Douglas in his effort to freeze out Bright in their rivalry for control of the patronage in the Northwest. Concluding that all the patronage would be given to Bright, Douglas prepared for battle, vowing that if he were the object of attack, he would fight all his enemies "and neither ask nor give quarter." He wanted nothing for himself, he said, "only a fair share for my friends." Convinced that he was being treated as an outsider and that his advice was being ignored, he saw no alternative but to "return every blow they may give."

Back at Wheatland, Buchanan heard from Slidell that Douglas was "in a very morbid state of mind, believing or affecting to believe that there is a general conspiracy to put him down." He was especially disposed "to run amuck" against anyone who had a good word for Bright.[33] As a result, Buchanan would begin his administration with this powerful Illinois Senator more suspicious and disgruntled than it was necessary for him to be. No doubt the natures and goals of the two men would have made it impossible for them to think well of each other personally, but the President-elect had made matters worse by dealing with Douglas insensitively and by giving more time and attention to the desires and opinions of lesser men. Douglas was not a man to trifle with, as Buchanan would learn at considerable cost.

In addition to incurring the ill will of Douglas, Buchanan returned home a sick man, one of the victims of the so-called National Hotel disease which afflicted guests and employees at the time of his stay. There were various explanations for it. Some traced it to the water taken from the hotel cistern, into which rats poisoned with arsenic had fallen. Others attributed it to a poisonous miasma rising from the hotel's sewers, cesspools, and sinks. The most likely cause was the contamination of both food and water by a sewage back up resulting from frozen plumbing during the bitter cold of late January. The disease itself was probably paratyphoid fever. The symptoms were severe and persistent diarrhea and inflammation of the colon, effective treatment for which was then unknown to the medical profession. On February 25, after Buchanan had endured several weeks of misery, the public was informed that visitors would no longer be received at Wheatland before the inauguration.[34]

Meanwhile, the friends and foes of Cobb and Walker continued their pressure on the enfeebled President-elect through the mail. Douglas refused to write directly, but Bigler reported that he had expressed "a most decided preference" for Walker, manifesting "much feeling on the subject" and declaring the appointment "eminently wise for the country." Slidell told Buchanan that he did not trust Walker's associates and thought Cobb would be a safer Secretary of State. Among the many letters on the subject, one from Glancy Jones may well have been the most important in helping Buchanan to make his final decision. The fact that Cobb and Walker were "neck and neck," he wrote, had "produced a wonderful unanimity, in a project: to take Cass for [the] State Dept. representing solely the whole West, and in this the whole South together with Douglas and Bright are ready to acquiesce." Moreover, Cass wanted the appointment so much that he would take it on almost any terms, suppressing his chronic anglophobia, permitting Buchanan to name an Assistant Secretary of State, and even allowing him to keep foreign policy decisions mostly in his own hands.[35]

Buchanan had never cared much for Cass, but the compromise, suggested many times before, seemed by mid-February to be the only way to avoid a potentially serious party division. On February 19, Slidell and Bright conferred with Cass and verified his acceptance of the rather humiliating terms. Two days later Buchanan wrote him a flattering invitation to accept the office of Secretary of State. "This it was my desire to do from the beginning," he said, "and I have only doubted in consideration of your age. I am happy, however, to learn ... that you are now as capable of mental labor and physical exertion as you were ten years ago." Cass accepted without delay. Some believed that the appointment was only a temporary one, until someone better fitted for the office could be found, but that proved not to be the case.[36]

On the day that Buchanan sent his offer to Cass he also invited Cobb to join his administration as Secretary of the Treasury. The Georgia Unionist had determined earlier to accept no office other than the State Department, and in late January he told his wife that he felt "more and more reluctant to go into the cabinet." Some of his friends urged him to refuse "second place" lest it weaken his position in 1860, but John B. Lamar warned him that another Georgian might be appointed instead and "foist himself on the people four years hence as *the* man of Georgia." Cobb had a most agreeable interview with Cass and decided that, because of Cass's seniority, he could without humiliation accept the Treasury Department after all.[37]

Before Buchanan could complete his Cabinet, he was forced to make a painful decision concerning his own state. When Forney learned that there would be no place for him, he mobilized his party friends to urge the appointment of Judge Black rather than Glancy Jones. The pressure was so great that, on February 17, Buchanan informed Jones that because of the party situation in Pennsylvania he would not be able to give him a Cabinet post. He added that he might appoint Black to be Attorney General and suggested that Jones accept an appointment as minister to Berlin. In his reply Jones withdrew his name to save Buchanan embarrassment, adding bitterly that everyone would know that the influence against him was "the Forney clique, Judge Black being only Forney's second self." He begged Buchanan at least not to appoint Black, "so that my enemies may not have a double triumph." Though declining the Berlin appointment, he promised to "remain your *true* and *steadfast* friend," and he did. John Appleton, acting as peacemaker, urged Buchanan "to have Jones at Wheatland for a few days, and come with you to Washington."[38]

Late in February, Buchanan made three more appointments. His Secretary of War would be Governor Wise's candidate, John B. Floyd of Virginia, a state-rights Democrat and former governor, an amiable, unenergetic man of no great talent. The patronage-rich Postmaster Generalship went to Aaron V. Brown of Tennessee, a lawyer, former governor, and proslavery expansionist, a man in his sixties in physical decline. Jacob Thompson, appointed Secretary of the Interior, was a hard-nosed, wealthy, self-made Mississippi planter, a southern-rights Democrat who had opposed the Compromise of 1850, and a former chairman of the House Committee on Public Lands. These three joined Cobb to give the Cabinet a southern majority.[39]

Buchanan delayed his last two appointments until after his arrival in Washington for the inauguration. Yielding to advice from Pierce's friends and from the South, he abandoned his first choice for a New England representative, Nathan Clifford of Maine, for Isaac Toucey of Connecticut, a loyal party man, whom he made Secretary of the Navy. Before appointing Black the Attorney General, Buchanan had to write another awkward letter to Glancy Jones asking to be released from a promise not to appoint any Pennsylvanian other than him. Again Jones agreed, and Black gratefully promised to forget their past differences "for the sake of the harmony which is required by the public service." He assured Buchanan that no act of his would ever threaten the unity of his administration.[40]

Buchanan thus succeeded in forming a harmonious Cabinet that would loyally support his plans to suppress slavery agitation and undermine the sectional Republican party. It was a Cabinet of Democratic moderates, containing no true representative of the northern free-soil wing or of the southern fire-eaters. But it was far from a distinguished body. In temperament, ability, and political skill Cobb was probably the best of the President's men. Black and Thompson were vigorous and able but narrow and saturnine. Brown and Toucey handled their departments with reasonable efficiency, but neither made a significant impact on executive policy. Nor did Floyd, whose administrative slackness eventually bred corruption and embarrassed the President. Cass, as expected, was a cipher.

The most serious defect in the Buchanan Cabinet was its lack of a young, articulate representative of the northern Democracy—someone who could express its views on Kansas policy and the meaning of popular sovereignty, and prevent the administration from appearing to be wholly a body of Southerners and doughfaces. None of the northern members was capable of playing that role. The President and his advisers were eager to weaken the sectional antislavery agitators, but they were poorly equipped to check the sectionalization of their own party. None of them appeared to give much thought to the matter, or to be aware of its urgency. For outside advice from the North they were more inclined to listen to friends such as Bright, Bigler, and Glancy Jones than to those they viewed as malcontents, such as Douglas.

Even Buchanan's trusted northern adviser, John Appleton, could not alert him to the needs of the northern Democracy. Reading a draft of his inaugural address, Appleton found a statement supporting the southern proslavery position that the people of a territory could not exclude slave property until they were ready for statehood. He urged Buchanan to delete it to avoid taking issue with Northerners whose interpretation of popular sovereignty upheld the prior right of a territorial legislature to prohibit slavery if it chose. Appleton questioned the wisdom "of presenting without necessity a merely abstract question where opinions are known to be divided." He pointed to the need for a revival of the northern Democratic party, without which the next presidential election would be a purely sectional contest, probably ending in disunion. He reminded Buchanan that "the northern democracy cannot make bricks without straw." Appleton's advice went unheeded.[41]

The long intraparty struggle over Buchanan's Cabinet appointments, though less than edifying, clearly illustrated both the disruptive factionalism that plagued both parties and the intensity of political feelings at the time of Buchanan's incumbency. It also illustrated the remarkably complex blend of desires that motivated the politicians engaged in the party battles—part patronage, part profit, part power, and underneath it all, part principle. Four years later a Republican President-elect would find himself in a similar predicament.

After his victory in November 1856, Buchanan must have looked forward to inauguration day, March 4, 1857, as the triumphant end of a ten-year quest and the joyful culmination of a long and unusually successful political career. Unfortunately, because of his persistent illness, the occasion turned out to be a wretched ordeal requiring all his fortitude to see it through. Two days before the event, on a cold and blustery morning, he rode in his carriage from Wheatland to Lancaster, accompanied by his niece, Harriet Lane, his nephew, James Buchanan Henry, and his housekeeper, Hetty Parker. Church bells rang as a procession of townspeople and a marching band escorted him to the railroad station, where a special train waited to carry his party to Baltimore. There, at Barnum's Hotel, he was scheduled to attend a reception and dinner in his honor, but he was forced to excuse himself and take a private room for several hours of rest. Arriving in Washington that evening, he rejected the advice of his physician and returned to the National Hotel, where the proprietor, an old Lancaster friend, welcomed him. He spent the next day meeting with political friends and considering his last-minute Cabinet appointments.[42]

Inauguration day in Washington was mild and clear, bringing an early taste of spring and lifting the spirits of the tens of thousands who had come on special trains, in stagecoaches and carriages, and on horseback to witness the ceremony. They filled the rooms and lobbies of every hotel and boardinghouse, or found lodgings in private homes, or, as a last resort, paid fifty cents to camp on cots in a circus tent. In the morning they were awakened by a salute from the Washington Navy Yard and Arsenal, and soon the streets were filled with visitors and the members of military companies, fire companies, brass bands, Democratic clubs, and others who were to participate in the grand inaugural parade.

General John A. Quitman, a wealthy Mississippi planter, Congressman, and fire-eater, commanded the parade as it marched down Pennsylvania Avenue to meet Buchanan at the National Hotel. After a delay caused by the late arrival of President Pierce, who almost had been forgotten, he and the President-elect climbed into an open barouche and the parade continued to the Capitol. Before them marched the military units and the bands, as well as a float featuring the Goddess of Liberty. Following them were the political clubs with their bands and banners, another float with a liberty pole and a large American flag, and a fully rigged miniature ship-of-war built at the Navy Yard. Arriving at the Capitol, Vice President John C. Breckinridge of Kentucky first took the oath of office in the Senate chamber, after which he led the procession to the platform built over the steps of the east portico. Buchanan, dressed in black, medicated, and fortified with brandy, was loudly cheered as he stepped forward to deliver his inaugural address.[43]

Speaking in a loud, clear voice, he began with the inevitable platitudes about the Constitution, the Union, and the need to preserve the nation's free institutions. Passions had been aroused during the last campaign, but when the decision had been made, "the tempest at once subsided and all was calm." The voice of the majority had been heard, he claimed, though he had in fact been elected by a minority of the popular vote. In order to show that his administration would be motivated only by a desire to serve the country, Buchanan then made a serious political error by announcing that he would not be a candidate for re-election.

Turning to the question of slavery in the territories, he endorsed the principle of popular sovereignty, commending Congress for applying the "simple rule, that the will of the majority shall govern." In the words of the Kansas-Nebraska Act, the people would be left "perfectly free to form and regulate their domestic institutions in their own way, subject only to the Constitution of the United States." Buchanan noted that a difference of opinion existed concerning the proper time for the people of a territory to make their choice. Fortunately, he said, passing lightly over a question of serious concern to both North and South, this was "a matter of but little practical importance." Moreover, it was a judicial question which belonged to the Supreme Court of the United States, before whom it was then pending. He understood (better, in fact, than his audience knew) that the Court would "speedily and finally" settle the issue, and, "in common with all good citizens," he would cheerfully submit to its decision. Buchanan then offered gratuitously his private opinion that, under the Kansas-Nebraska Act, the appropriate time for the people to decide would be "when the number of actual residents in the Territory shall justify the formation of a constitution with a view to its admission as a State into the Union."

In another statement, obviously made with the problem of Kansas in mind, he seemed to commit his administration to a policy about which there could be no subsequent dispute. The "imperative and indispensable duty of the Government of the United States," he said, was "to secure to every resident inhabitant the free and independent expression of his opinion by his vote. This sacred right of each individual must be preserved." It would have been difficult for anyone not to understand that this statement was a pledge that delegates to the Kansas constitutional convention would be chosen in a fair election and that the constitution would be submitted for ratification by popular vote.

Buchanan next described the supreme goal of his administration: the restoration of peace between the sections. With the question of slavery left to the people of each territory under the terms of the pending court decision, "everything of a practical nature" concerning slavery would have been decided. All agreed that slavery in the southern states was beyond the jurisdiction of the federal government. "May we not, then, hope that the long agitation on this subject is approaching an end, and that geographical parties to which it has given birth . . . will speedily become extinct?" Then the public mind would be diverted from slavery to other matters "of more pressing and practical importance." The anti-slavery agitation of the past twenty years, Buchanan claimed, had accomplished no good for the master, the slave, or the country, and it could ultimately "endanger the personal safety of a large portion of our countrymen where the institution exists." He called on everyone who loved the Union "to suppress this agitation," which, since the passage of the Kansas-Nebraska Act, was "without any legitimate object." Then the Union would survive, as Providence intended, to be "peacefully instrumental by its example in the extension of civil and religious liberty throughout the world."

In the remainder of his address, Buchanan considered the matters which to him, presumably, were of "more pressing and practical importance" than slavery. One was an embarrassing surplus in the federal treasury, which might produce "extravagant legislation" and "wild schemes of expenditure." He suggested that the surplus be applied to paying off the public debt, to enlarging the navy, and to any "great national objects for which a clear warrant can be found in the Constitution." The particular national project he had in mind was the construction of a transcontinental railroad, which he described as a "military road" sanctioned by the Constitution because it was necessary for the defense of the Pacific Coast. In favoring federal aid for this project he took issue with Governor Wise and other southern state-rights Democrats who had denied its constitutionality.

Closing on an expansionist note, and probably thinking of Cuba, Buchanan suggested that "in the progress of events" the United States might "still further extend [its] possessions."

All in all, the program he announced was extremely ambitious and, in some respects, remarkably unrealistic. A fair settlement of the Kansas problem was certainly within reach, and he would have thereby deprived the Republicans of one of their most effective issues. His posture as defender of the Constitution and the Union did rally much conservative support for him in both the North and South. On the other hand, in his desire to destroy the Republicans he underestimated the extent of northern sympathy for their program of federal action to exclude slavery from the territories and to check the alleged aggressions of the Slave Power. He apparently missed the irony of his suggestion that Providence had destined his country, with its four million slaves, to serve as a model of civil liberty before the world. Finally, Buchanan's belief that there were national issues of more substantive importance than slavery was a monumental misconception shared by many of his contemporaries, but rejected by many others. After taking the oath of office, administered by the Chief Justice of the United States, Roger B. Taney, it was his misfortune to begin his presidential term trammeled by a web of faulty calculations and lacking advisers prepared to question them.

On inauguration day Buchanan was doubtless relieved that he had managed to complete his address without an embarrassing interruption. His last duty that day was to make an appearance at the inauguration ball. It was a grand affair held in a large temporary building adjacent to City Hall, richly decorated and lighted with gas chandeliers. Of the ladies present, one of the guests thought that Mrs. Douglas, "dressed in bridal white, with a cluster of orange blossoms on her classically formed head," was the most beautiful. Buchanan and Miss Lane appeared only briefly. After their departure the festivities continued until dawn, with dancing, food in abundance, and plenty to drink.[44] It was a night to remember, for the Democrats would wait a very long time—twenty-eight years, in fact—before they would have another inauguration to celebrate.

A change in administrations was always an occasion for the victorious party to indulge in a certain amount of self-congratulation. One Democratic editor perceived the inauguration not only as a party triumph but as a "happy illustration of the genius and spirit of republican institutions and a prouder spectacle than . . . all the rounds of regal splendor or of royal coronations." The retiring President gave up his office "not as an expelled monarch, driven by the tide of revolution and the curses of an outraged people, but with the approving conscience of an honest patriot." Another party editor was certain that "a submission to the decrees of the ballot box" had become a "fixed and settled" American tradition, which from the force of habit was "almost second nature with our population."[45]

Democrats were sanguine about the prospects of the new administration. Considering the likely consequences of Frémont's election, the Detroit *Free Press* thought that "the heart of every patriot cannot but be filled with joy at the fact that democracy has possession of the reins of power—that James Buchanan is President of the United States." The new President, said the New York *Herald,* would begin with "indications of a peaceful, dignified, satisfactory and successful administration, both in regard to our internal and external relations." The Washington *Union,* with John Appleton the temporary editor, believed that the "wild dreams of the fanatic" were giving way to "the great question of sustaining the Union and crushing out its enemies." Conservative old Whigs, "for the sake of the country," also wished Buchanan success, one of them suggesting that the time was auspicious for a nonpartisan "experiment in political pacification."[46]

Before leaving Georgia, Howell Cobb reported optimistically that the administration had the "unbounded confidence" of the southern people. "Even the Know Nothings admit that it promises to be the fairest and ablest *democratic* administration we have ever had." A Texas fire-eater was gratified that Buchanan had accepted the southern version of popular sovereignty, would assure the South "fair play in Kansas," and would support the acquisition of Cuba. A Virginia Democrat, looking anxiously beyond the present to an uncertain future, viewed the Buchanan administration "as the last hope of our Republic." Unless it was able to bring about a revolution in the sentiments of the northern people, "a Black Republican must inevitably be chosen President at our next election, our Union in all probability [will] be dissolved and the institutions of the South placed in the most fearful peril."[47]

Few Republicans greeted Buchanan's inauguration with more than a grudging bow to the will of the people. The Chicago *Tribune* assured him that it would not permit "political differences, or passion, or prejudice" to influence its judgment; but "knowing all the details of his career—how servile and pliant he has been ... to Southern dictation ... we cannot look forward with confidence to such an Administration as the times demand." In his inaugural address, the Milwaukee *Sentinel* asserted, the President had recognized "his obligations to the pro-slavery party who elected him" and renewed "his promises of fidelity to their views and interests." He denounced slavery agitation, observed the New York *Evening Post,* yet he put forth "the most monstrous doctrines," claiming the right of slaveholders to invade every territory. "While he is stirring the subject freely ... he exhorts those who differ with him not to meddle with it. We cannot take Mr. Buchanan's advice. If he agitates the subject so must we." Charles Francis Adams saved his gloomy forecast for his diary: "The next four years are to be more industriously employed than ever to uphold a tyranny which the progress of the age is doing its best to undermine and destroy."[48]

CHAPTER 4

The President,
the Chief Justice,
and a Slave Named Scott

Unfortunately, Buchanan's White House entourage and official advisers included no diarists to record, day by day, his domestic life, personal relationships, and shifting moods, or to discuss and interpret the formal business transacted at Cabinet meetings, his conferences with individual department heads, and the complex manner in which policies evolved during his presidential years. The voluminous correspondence of the President and some of those close to him, notably Black and Cobb, the facts and rumors served up by friendly and unfriendly reporters, and the recollections, more or less reliable, of his associates tell us much about life behind the White House doors. But there are gaps at crucial times— occasions when an instinctively reticent President seemed determined to deny his countrymen, then and forever, access to the inner workings of his administration. Secrecy soon begot suspicion that there were things Buchanan feared to have known about its purposes and about who was in control. With this advantage, Republicans found it politically useful to accuse him of weakly abdicating his authority to a prosouthern Cabinet clique and of becoming a willing tool of the Slave Power. Eventually their highly partisan accusation hardened into a durable tradition that has affected Buchanan's historical reputation ever since. Considering its durability, the tradition was based on a remarkably insubstantial foundation.

During the difficult weeks immediately following the inauguration, while heavily burdened with both domestic and administrative problems, Buchanan continued to endure the misery of the National Hotel disease. Recovery finally came in mid-April, but his nephew, Elliott Eskridge Lane, Harriet's elder brother, who had come to the White House to manage his uncle's business affairs, died of the disease that same month. Though James Buchanan Henry continued to serve as his private secretary, he felt Elliott's loss deeply. Meanwhile the President had to deal with a teapot tempest stirred up by Harriet Lane and his housekeeper, Hetty Parker, both of whom were determined to take command of the White House staff. Miss Lane, after threatening to leave, won the battle; Miss Parker returned to Wheatland and was replaced by a steward in a clearly subordinate position. With his efficient niece now in undisputed charge, Buchanan found comfort in a regime of domestic peace.[1]

Harriet Lane's role in the White House went far beyond the management of the President's household. She also supervised a substantial and much needed refurbishing of its rooms and furnishings. Above all, this young woman, still in her twenties, assumed responsibility for the President's social affairs, making good use of her experience as a hostess during her uncle's diplomatic sojourn in London. Miss Lane, together with the southern members of the Cabinet, and Lord and Lady Napier, who had just taken over the British embassy, helped to make Buchanan's presidential years memorable ones for Washington society. "Of the Napiers," one socially prominent woman recalled, "it may be said that no ministerial representative . . . ever more completely won the hearts of Washingtonians." During their tenure the embassy "was conspicuous for its complete absence of ostentation and its generous hospitality." She described Miss Lane as "not beautiful so much as handsome and healthful and good to look upon," possessing "great tact, and a perfect knowledge of Mr. Buchanan's wishes." Entering the life of the capital at a trying time, she helped "to keep the surface of society in Washington serene and smiling." To the President, who thoroughly enjoyed the dinners and entertainments she planned, Miss Lane was indispensable. She remained with him throughout his presidential years, postponing marriage until well after his retirement.[2]

As chief executive, Buchanan was fully engaged, working at his desk, answering letters, meeting with his Cabinet, or receiving callers from early morning until late afternoon. After several meetings Cobb reported that the members of the Cabinet got on harmoniously and that "everything promises well." If there was a complaint it was that the President tried to handle too much executive business, did not delegate enough to his subordinates, and involved himself in too much detail. As expected, he managed foreign affairs with the aid of his friend John Appleton, whom he appointed Assistant Secretary of State. He developed a personal interest in his Cabinet officers and did not hesitate to question them about their private affairs. Cobb related one such occasion to his wife: "Says he, 'you are rich, I suppose?' 'No,' says I, 'I am not.' 'But,' he replied, 'Mrs. Cobb is, I understand and that is the same thing.' 'How much,' says he, 'is her estate.' I replied about two hundred and fifty thousand dollars. 'Well,' says he, 'why don't you pay that debt of fifteen thousand, that you say you owe?' Don't you think the old Gentleman is quite curious about such matters?" Buchanan, in good humor, apparently told the Cabinet one day that he knew they all were anxious to be his successor, especially Cobb.[3]

As the months passed, the harmony in the Cabinet proved durable, but the initial formality gave way to an easy informality, with the President given the new title of "the old squire." Without exception his department heads respected him, supported his policies, and, while expecting him to consider their advice, knew that he was not easily deterred from his course once it had been set. Late in April, Black wrote to Cobb, who was in Georgia, about a Treasury Department appointment which they both favored. Black had discussed the matter with Buchanan, who "listened with attention" but postponed a final decision. "He is a very stubborn old gentleman," Black observed, "very fond of having his own way and I don't know what his way is about this matter." According to Secretary of War Floyd, "Mr. Buchanan was different from Gen. Jackson; . . . Gen. Jackson could be *coaxed* from his purpose, but . . . Mr. B. could neither be coaxed nor driven." In the summer, when Kansas affairs worried the administration, Black wrote that the "great old captain" of the ship "looks calmly up into the sky and gives his orders quietly—orders which will keep her head steady on true course." In July, Floyd described the hiatus in Washington when the President was away on a holiday: "We meet in Cabinet, and 'discuss' very much; but I believe we all feel it to be a sort of game of solitaire,—the play of Hamlet with the part of Hamlet left out." Before the end of the year Cabinet members were aware that Buchanan had already upbraided Floyd for his careless handling of some War Department business. None of them found evidence of weakness in him during his administration's first critical months.[4]

No serious Cabinet crisis developed until the threatened disruption of the Union following the election of Abraham Lincoln. Before that there were no resignations, forced or voluntary, the only replacement resulting from the death of Postmaster General Aaron V. Brown in 1859. Cass was loyal and cooperative, signing without protest dispatches that were written in his name. Buchanan was fond of Floyd in spite of his shortcomings, all of which were attributable to carelessness rather than venality. He found no fault with the performances of Toucey and Brown in their respective departments. Thompson was ambitious, humorless, and personally unattractive, but Buchanan respected him, appreciated his efficiency, and was charmed by his beautiful young wife. Black was an old friend who shared the President's feelings about Republicans and abolitionists; he was learned, witty, sharp of tongue and pen, honest and straightforward, and a formidable antagonist. Buchanan found in him a reliable and powerful administration advocate, and a source of strength at critical times.

Cobb soon became Buchanan's personal favorite. The youngest member of the Cabinet at forty-one, he was cheerful, easy of manner, gregarious, a fine talker, fond of good food and wine, and always ready with a jest, in short, a convivial, rotund, "jolly Falstaff." Buchanan found his company so agreeable that he was often a guest at the White House during his wife's frequent visits to Georgia. The Cobbs once introduced the President to a pretty young widow from Athens, Mrs. Elizabeth C. Craig, whose charms won for her, too, an invitation to live at the White House. Contemplating matrimony, she accepted, but after several months of futile flirtation she gave up and went off to marry someone else.

In his political role, Cobb soon became the Cabinet's premier, presiding at meetings when Buchanan was away. Though lacking experience in fiscal matters, he managed the Treasury Department remarkably well. He was a shrewd, ambitious politician and clearly hoped for a presidential nomination in 1860. Meanwhile, he served the administration faithfully, proving to be a most valuable aide in its relations with southern Democrats. Cobb, the Unionist, was anathema to the fire-eaters, but his contacts with moderates, such as Alexander H. Stephens, assured the administration of an opportunity to make its case when it was threatened with southern disaffection. He contributed to the shaping of administration policy, but always as the President's loyal adviser, never as a usurper of his authority.[5]

The Vice President, John C. Breckinridge, though an experienced Kentucky politician, was given no role to play other than his constitutional duty to preside over the Senate. He was consulted about Kentucky appointments but never about questions of policy, in part, perhaps, because he had favored the renomination of Pierce, but mostly because there was no tradition of vice-presidential involvement in executive affairs. Soon after the inauguration Buchanan deeply offended Breckinridge by responding to a request for a private interview with a suggestion that he call on Miss Lane instead. Friends of the President tried to conciliate the indignant Vice President with the disingenuous explanation that this was his usual way of arranging private interviews. The established rule, Floyd assured Breckinridge, was that "when a gentleman who has been invited to visit Miss Lane is announced to the President, he breaks off all other interviews and engagements to attend promptly that summons." Thus the President's suggestion "was intended as the highest mark of respect, instead of a slight." The Vice President was not persuaded, and he had no private interview with Buchanan for more than three years.[6]

Even before the inauguration the New York *Herald* warned Buchanan that his first trouble would be the "hungry office beggars." They would "come upon him from all quarters, hopping and croaking, like the frogs of Egypt, . . . for the ravenous democratic stumpers, collectors and distributors of cash, speeches and documents . . . will be at the elbow of their anointed chief, clamorous for their expected reward." The *Herald* predicted that there would be at least ten applicants for every available office. "Truly this is a noble country," mocked a Mobile editor. "There can be no danger to republican institutions surely, as long as there are so many found ready to bear its burthens," all of them "constrained by a sense of duty to meet any responsibility which the public interest may impose." Congressmen as well as the President were set upon by the office seekers. Senator Bright, after his recent bitter fight for re-election, had the gall to complain about them: "Office, office, office, office seekers, office seekers, office seekers, how these words ring in my ears."[7]

In the years before civil service reform and the introduction of a merit system the patronage, more than the financial contributions of corporations and private citizens, was the oil that lubricated political machines, federal, state, and local. A conscientious executive gave some thought to the qualifications of an aspirant for public office, but the system required that first consideration be given to party service. Senator Bigler's objection to a proposed appointment to a postmastership in his state was motivated, he said, "by a sense of duty to our party and to myself." The candidate had "never left the impress of his will on the politics of the ward in which he lives, much less on that of the County and State. He has had no part in our struggles for ascendancy." A Wisconsin postmaster angrily claimed that a group seeking his removal were "violent, red mouthed, crazy, mischievous, sore headed negro worshippers, and black amalgamationists—men who would ... tramp in the dust an honest democrat." Though salaries were low and government bureaucracies were still relatively small—in Buchanan's day approximately 20,000 were in federal employment—a political place was the goal of most diligent party workers.[8]

If the party in power lost an election, the victors, having promised reform, would soon undertake a thorough housecleaning in the civil service. When, in 1857, Pennsylvania Democrats elected a governor, a local party leader greeted the "glorious triumph" with the observation that "once more the *faithful* will be in motion for the little patronage in the gift of our State Administration." In Massachusetts, after Republicans defeated the Know Nothings, a call went up for "a vigorous application of the gubernatorial foot to the backsides of nearly every office-holder in the Commonwealth."[9]

"To the victors belong the spoils" was a slogan coined by a Democrat, but Whigs and Republicans applied the principle with equal conviction whenever given the opportunity. By 1857 the spoils system was not only universally practiced but, according to its theoretical defenders, it had become an essential ingredient of effective governance in a democracy. A Democratic editor claimed that the questions of competence and honesty were not the only ones to be considered by a President in making appointments, for some competent and honest men were "wholly unfit for offices which carry with them a share of political power." A Democratic President had "a duty to fulfill to those who elected him." He must always ask whether an appointee would use his influence "to promote the interests and increase the power of [the] Democracy."[10]

Hardly an appointment, high or low, was made on merit alone. Federal clerkships, post offices, customhouses, navy yards, land offices, and Indian agencies were filled with persons of varying degrees of ability and integrity but of unswerving party loyalty. So were federal judgeships and district attorneys' offices. Even an applicant for a captain's commission in the United States Army, when soliciting Senator Bigler's support, knew that it was less essential to list his qualifications than to assure him that he was a Democrat and had "always labored for the success of the Democratic party." The American diplomatic service was equally politicized; adequate training and language proficiency seemed to count for little. "The low tone of our European ambassadors is so common that it is taken as a natural thing in the Old World," observed the New York *Tribune*. "Diplomacy is the sewer through which flows the scum and refuse of the political puddle. A man not fit to stay at home is just the man to send abroad." Buchanan illustrated the uses to which the service was put when he sent ex-Governor Wright of Indiana to Berlin in order to clear the way for Bright's re-election to the Senate. Wright himself provided another illustration when he recommended a friend for a diplomatic appointment merely because he was "very desirous to visit Europe" and needed "something that will pay expenses." He was, of course, known for his "devotion to Democratic principles."[11]

Some applicants for federal appointments resorted to professional office-brokers to work in their behalf; but the most common tactic was a letter of solicitation, with supporting letters from friends, to the President, or a member of the Cabinet, or a Congressman. The letters took a variety of forms. There was the flattering approach: "The announcement . . . of your appointment and confirmation as Attorney General . . . has given me . . . intense satisfaction. . . . I tender you my heartiest congratulations. Meanwhile—alas that I am constrained to mention *business* at such a time—let me ask you to keep in remembrance my application for director of the U.S. Mint." The reluctant approach: "My democratic friends have urged me to *consent* . . . that my name shall be presented to the President for the office of Post Master of Harrisburg." The weary party veteran's approach: "I am heartily tired of the perplexity of an Editor's life. . . . If, therefore, in the distribution of the *good* offices, Mr. Buchanan should see proper to select me to fill one, I would feel truly grateful." The heavy-handed approach: "Within the last seven years, I have done you several good deeds. . . . I intend to be faithful to your interests hereafter. Am I not entitled to a *quid pro quo?*" And, occasionally, the candid approach: "I am well aware that you have scores of applications of a similar nature. . . . Yet like other hungry aspirants desiring to suck at the 'public pap' I look to you for aid."[12]

The spoils system was not without its critics, but they were always most plentiful among the members of a defeated party. George D. Prentice, the Whig-American editor of the Louisville *Journal,* denounced the system as "the expedient of a demagogue, not the policy of a statesman." It was based on the assumption "that government is an affair of personal ambition and emolument instead of the common good." The only appropriate test to apply to an incumbent, Prentice claimed, was the test of fitness; to remove him merely to reward another was "trifling with the public interest" and "a gross public outrage." President Buchanan had no right "to make the organs of the national body subservient to the appetites of his clamorous partisans."[13] Perhaps Prentice's high-mindedness would have carried more weight had he judged earlier Whig administrations by the same standard.

Buchanan, following the practice of his day, used the patronage to benefit his party and to reward his political friends; however, he was somewhat inhibited by the fact that the federal offices at his disposal were already filled with Democrats appointed by Pierce, many of whom had been assessed a percentage of their pay to support his presidential campaign. "The pressure for office," he had predicted, "will be nearly as great as though I had succeeded a Whig administration."[14] Fortunately for him, Jacksonian Democrats had favored not only the spoils system but the principle of rotation in office. Rejecting the idea of a professionally trained civil service as elitist, they believed that officeholders should serve a single four-year term and then return to private life. With rare exceptions Buchanan's policy was to permit the Pierce incumbents to complete their terms, after which he replaced them with his own appointees.

The announcement of this policy brought down on the administration and Democratic Congressmen a flurry of protests from unhappy incumbents and a deluge of candidates to replace them. Hundreds of "greedy, impatient and insatiable spoilsmen," reported the New York *Herald,* had gathered in Washington "like wolves and vultures upon the heels and flanks of a wasting army." For months after his inauguration, patronage letters formed the bulk of Buchanan's correspondence, and daily Cabinet meetings were devoted principally to considering appointments. A critic suggested that the minor offices, at least, might be filled "without a solemn conclave of the eight highest dignitaries in the land." The President, he charged, was employing his Cabinet as if it were "little more than a nominating board and appointing council for the distribution and dispensation of Executive patronage."[15]

Nevertheless, the patronage was a serious business that could cripple the new administration if ineptly handled. Party editors, for example, had to be rewarded with jobs to sustain the party press, preferably postmasterships which gave them both an income and free use of the mails. Postmasters played the role of agents for the administration, reporting on local political affairs to the Assistant Postmaster General, Horatio King. Meanwhile, an ambitious Cabinet member, such as Cobb, had his own purposes, using the Treasury Department patronage to advance his personal political career. Even when the patronage was skillfully managed, disappointments were inevitable, and neglected political friends could easily become dangerous political enemies. As Cobb noted, some of the place seekers whose hopes were blighted left Washington in anger, "swearing vengeance."[16]

In dispensing his patronage Buchanan confronted not only the problem of a superfluity of applicants but, as in the selection of his Cabinet, state and regional intraparty rivalries. One of his most important appointments—and one of the most profitable—was the editorship of the national party organ, the Washington *Union,* which had usually received the House and Senate printing contracts when Democrats were in control, as they would be in the Thirty-fifth Congress. The editor in turn subcontracted the printing to a remarkable entrepreneur, Cornelius Wendell, a Republican from Albany who had built a printing plant in Washington and purchased a half interest in the *Union.* Wendell paid the editor a percentage of his huge profits derived from outrageous charges for congressional printing. Representative William Smith of Virginia, demanding reform of the system, asserted that every man who had obtained the printing contract had "grown suddenly rich," realizing in a year a fortune seldom acquired through the labors of a lifetime.[17]

That such a prize should be permanently granted to a single party newspaper, especially one of the character of the *Union,* was bound to cause resentment among other Democratic journals. "It is not a newspaper in any sense of the word," sniffed the New York *Herald.* "It is a mere political flysheet . . . the 'trade circular,' so to speak, of the President." The Cincinnati *Enquirer,* resenting the neglect of the western Democratic press, denounced the connection of the *Union* "with a company of jobbers and speculators, composed of men of all parties . . . a body of enormously rich monopolists, who do not care a fig for the Democracy." The character of the paper was so well known, wrote Douglas's Chicago *Times,* that it was "of no possible account to the party or to the public." Clearly, the *Herald* observed, the printing contract had become so tempting "as to aggravate the jealousy and the cupidity of some of the brethren itching for a share."[18]

Buchanan ignored the critics and, having decided against Forney, turned first to his friend John Appleton to edit the *Union.* Appleton began at once to negotiate with Wendell and the paper's co-owner, Alfred O. P. Nicholson of Tennessee, who agreed to accept him as editor and proprietor with an unusually generous salary of $6000 a year in addition to a share of the profits from any printing contracts the *Union* might obtain. When Appleton subsequently accepted the position of Assistant Secretary of State, Buchanan selected William A. Harris of Missouri to replace him, and Wendell agreed to the change. Harris was a former Virginia Congressman with some editorial experience, but above all he was a devoted and reliable party hack. Assuming control of the *Union* on April 15, he announced that the President would receive "all the support which party ties and personal friendship can inspire." He confessed "a faith and devotion to the great principles of the democratic party as strong and abiding as . . . [to] the principles of the Christian religion itself."[19] Under Harris the *Union* was less a party organ than an administration organ, following wherever it led, willingly accepting occasional editorial assistance from Attorney General Black.

By appointing no New Yorker to his Cabinet, Buchanan had avoided early involvement in that state's Democratic jungle warfare, but he could not escape it when the time came to fill federal offices. The Hards, led in New York City by Augustus Schell, a wealthy businessman and member of the national committee, and upstate by Daniel S. Dickinson, a former Senator, could claim much for their support of Buchanan's presidential nomination. The Softs, no longer a united group, were the Pierce men and the incumbent officeholders, but their leaders—August Belmont and other powerful banking and mercantile interests in New York City, and Dean Richmond and Erastus Corning in Albany—were determined to have their share of the new administration's patronage. Hards and Softs were united temporarily in an effort to defeat a third political force: Mayor Fernando Wood and his disreputable band of ward heelers, thugs, and corruptionists, who controlled city patronage and aspired to control state and federal patronage as well.

One of the most coveted federal offices was that of Collector of the Port of New York, an office that, one way or another, seemed to pay well and provided the incumbent with his own considerable customhouse patronage. To no one's surprise, the collectorship went to Buchanan's friend, Augustus Schell. Other desirable positions at the Brooklyn Navy Yard, as well as judicial appointments and postmasterships, favored the Hards but also recognized other party factions. Unfortunately—and perhaps inevitably—no faction was altogether satisfied with its share, and the internecine strife within the New York Democracy raged on, causing the administration no end of annoyance. Few of the officeholders served the public well—James Gordon Bennett, though saying nothing in the *Herald,* privately described Buchanan's appointments as "horrible."[20]

Neither the New England nor the Southern states provided a party battlefield comparable to New York. The rivalry between Governor Wise and Senator Hunter in Virginia and between Jefferson Davis and Senator Albert G. Brown in Mississippi, as well as the tension between southern moderates and fire-eaters, created only minor disputes over appointments. Fewer Pierce incumbents were removed in the South, and Buchanan had four southern Cabinet officers to advise him when replacements were to be made. In Louisiana the administration deferred to the wishes of Senator Slidell.

Patronage matters were not as easy in the West, where many Democrats felt that their section seldom received its fair share of the spoils. The Cincinnati *Enquirer,* still seething over the *Union* and the printing contracts, insisted that western claims were "paramount in importance to those of any other section."

Yet the older states, both North and South, treated the West "as a mere serf or ally, to be used and courted . . . and to be discarded after being used." At odds on all other subjects, they agreed "in their view of the manner in which the West shall be treated."[21]

Buchanan's western appointments did little to lessen these discontents. Indiana's Senator Bright, after informing Black that he would be "damaged for all time" unless he had the administration's "decided sympathy," was given control of his state's patronage. His rival, Ex-Governor Wright, did receive the Berlin mission after threatening a "severe division" in the state organization if he were not compensated for withdrawing from the senatorial contest. Subsequently, because Wright's resentful political friends carried on the feud, the pro-Bright party organ piously denounced them as "the disappointed and the selfish" who regarded the patronage as "the sole end and purpose of party organization." These "indiscreet and short-sighted men," it charged, were distracting and dividing the Indiana Democracy in their "scramble . . . for the miserable flesh-pots of office." As in New York, the administration was unable to repair a dangerous party split.[22]

In Illinois, in spite of the coolness between them, Buchanan did not question Douglas's right to control the state patronage. Anti-Douglas Democrats could be found, but none seriously challenged his command of the party organization. "I could not oppose him successfully if I would, nor would I if I could," wrote one of his local opponents. "I might hold him down, but . . . so great is his intellectual strength that the whole Democratic house in Illinois would fold with him." When Buchanan applied his policy of rotation in office, one friend of Douglas usually succeeded another. In the case of the Chicago postmastership, Douglas was pleased to have rotation applied in order to remove Isaac Cook, who was both corrupt and incompetent, and to replace him with William Price, who agreed to subsidize the pro-Douglas editor of the Chicago *Times,* James W. Sheahan. On one occasion, when Buchanan, without consulting Douglas, appointed Col. R. B. Carpenter disbursing officer for a new post office and customhouse in Chicago, Douglas bluntly demanded his "instant removal." He was compelled, he said, to make an issue of it "to ascertain whether the administration recognize him or me as the organ of the Party. . . . To delay is to create mischief. Things cannot remain as they are." Carpenter was removed.[23]

Douglas's discontent grew out of the administration's rejection of numerous appointments he desired outside Illinois, especially out of his failure to place a friend in the Cabinet and others in the foreign service. Several of his recommendations for Kansas appointments were honored; and his close friend and political ally, William A. Richardson, after failing to obtain a foreign embassy, accepted the governorship of Nebraska Territory. Other political friends, notably former Illinois Congressman John A. McClernand, received nothing. "Our recommendations have been totally disregarded," one Douglasite complained. Illinois Democrats were being "proscribed," he believed, "because we happen to have a prominent candidate for the Presidency." Douglas impatiently informed Buchanan that in the past, while other states had received Cabinet appointments and foreign missions, Illinois had been treated "with a neglect which could not fail to wound the pride of all her working Democrats." Noting the same "apparent neglect" of his state's claims by the new administration, he hoped that it "would do justice in the future appointments."

Most irritating was Buchanan's decision to appoint J. Madison Cutts, Douglas's father-in-law, to the office of Second Comptroller of the Treasury in place of one of the Senator's old Illinois friends. Douglas was annoyed because he had not been consulted, and because it enabled the Republican press to accuse him of nepotism. In a letter of protest he asked to be assured that the appointment was the President's "voluntary act," that it was not motivated by the family relationship, and that it would not be counted as part of his state's share of the patronage. In a curt reply, Buchanan informed Douglas that the appointment would be his own, "proceeding entirely from my regard for Mr. Cutts and his family, and not because Senator Douglas has had the good fortune to become his son-in-law." Douglas then published the correspondence in order to refute the charge of nepotism, but the whole affair did nothing to improve relations between the President and the disgruntled Senator.[24]

In his California appointments Buchanan pleased an old political friend while making a dangerous new political enemy. Late in January, Senators Gwin and Broderick together took the long journey to Washington by way of Panama, the latter, in accordance with their agreement, anticipating a free hand in dispensing the California patronage. Gwin, who was entitled to take his Senate seat at once, enjoyed the sympathy of southern friends when he explained the indignity he had suffered at the hands of his young colleague. Broderick, whose term would not begin until March 4, remained with friends in New York until the eve of Buchanan's inauguration. Soon after taking the oath of office he called on the President with his recommendations for federal appointments, but, to his chagrin, he was told to submit them in writing. Buchanan's sympathies were entirely with Gwin and California's prosouthern Democratic Chivalry, not with this presumptuous northern free soiler, and he refused to respect the patronage bargain that Broderick had obtained. Gwin honored the bargain to the extent of making no recommendations of his own, but the administration consulted him, rather than Broderick, before appointments were made. Early in April, Gwin gleefully informed a California friend that Broderick was departing for home "in a great rage. . . . His denunciations of the President and Cabinet are gross in the extreme." Meanwhile, he wrote, "I spent yesterday in visiting the Cabinet and the President with whom I had [patronage] talks."[25]

The New York *Tribune* speculated that Broderick soon "may discover that he is a true Republican and will cross the political lines." Broderick tried instead to capture the California state Democratic convention and secure the nomination of an anti-administration candidate for governor. He failed, and the Chivalry nominated and elected their own candidate, John B. Weller, in spite of the refusal of the Senator's friends to campaign in his behalf. Defeated in California as well as in Washington, bereft of patronage, Broderick's political future was uncertain at best. "Please mark my words," wrote one of the California Chivalry, "Broderick will be found acting with the Black Republicans before his Senatorial term expires."[26]

Buchanan, knowing the Pennsylvania Democracy well, probably anticipated the problems that the patronage would cause him there. Even his rotation policy would not open enough federal offices to accommodate all the political friends he had cultivated over the years, as well as, among others, the friends of Forney, Senator Bigler, Glancy Jones, Robert Tyler, Mayor Richard Vaux of Philadelphia, and the rival editors of Pittsburgh's two Democratic newspapers, the *Post* and *Union*. The most lucrative appointment, Collector of the Port of Philadelphia, went to one of Buchanan's and Forney's Lancaster friends, Joseph B. Baker. Other offices were divided among the factions, with none of them altogether satisfied, none wholly disappointed. After the appointments had been made, the cries went up from those whom the President had neglected, including several local party leaders who had been loyal to him for many years. One of them, an unsuccessful candidate for naval officer at Philadelphia, poured out his bitterness in a letter to Bigler: "I feel that I have been most unjustly and outrageously treated. Like an old horse, after being worked almost to death . . . I am turned out to starve and die."

Another protest, which revealed the petty vindictiveness of which Buchanan was sometimes capable, came from James Campbell of Philadelphia, who had been Postmaster General in the Pierce administration. Although he had been Buchanan's political friend for many years, he had naturally favored Pierce's renomination but claimed to have worked hard for Buchanan during the campaign. Nevertheless, he wrote, "Not a single friend of mine has received office at your hands, but on the contrary my friendship for any man has been good cause for his proscription." Campbell suffered the fate of many who had once supported Pierce.[27]

Foremost among those who felt abandoned was John W. Forney, whose sorrows were many and whose capacity for mischief Buchanan did not sufficiently heed. In later years Forney claimed that at the time of Buchanan's inauguration "I was 'dead broke,' having contributed all my personal means to the cause of my favorite." As he recalled, his "whole heart" had been in the campaign, and Buchanan's election was his "all-sufficient reward."[28] Forney apparently did spend a considerable amount of his own money for the cause, but his subsequent correspondence with the administration suggests that he considered it an investment, perhaps a speculation, but certainly not a gift requiring in return nothing more substantial than the pleasure of witnessing Buchanan's inauguration. His desire to be editor of the Washington *Union* and his battle for a Senate seat had made that clear enough.

After his defeat in the senatorial election, Forney was quiet for a time, except to assure Buchanan that he disapproved of those who interfered in his behalf and tried "to press my name upon your attention." In short, he expected Buchanan to treat him fairly without the intervention of others. In a typical reluctant-applicant letter to Cobb, Forney noted how eager his friends were for him to be given a Cabinet appointment. "I can go into no secondary place," he added, "I can become no mere office-holder." At length, Mrs. Forney, mother of five children and expecting a sixth, having discovered that John Appleton had become editor of the *Union,* took up her husband's cause. "Do tell me what is to become of us," she asked in an appeal to Buchanan, "there is nothing now but the Post Master General. . . . I am sure he would not disgrace the position." They had no money for a fresh start, for Forney had spent not only his own in the campaign but hers as well. "My dear sir, " she wrote, "he has grown old, he neither eats or sleeps, I sometimes fear for his mind"; yet he had "the same confidence in you he ever had, he knows you will do what you think best."[29]

By February, Forney was in a deep depression, drinking too much and growing resentful as his disappointments mounted. John Appleton wrote Buchanan in alarm: "There is a good deal of soreness here which requires emollients. . . . If you would write a kind letter to Forney, invite him to Wheatland and talk freely and frankly with him, it would have an excellent result." Appleton reported that Forney was considering, apparently for the first time, establishing a paper of his own in Philadelphia, but it was then "only a floating plan which may not last." He suggested, as an alternative, helping Forney to acquire the Philadelphia *Pennsylvanian,* which was not prospering under its present ineffective Democratic editor, William Rice. Buchanan responded by offering Forney instead either the naval office at Philadelphia or the consulate at Liverpool in gratitude "for the signal services which you have rendered the Democratic party," and as a token of his own "warm feelings of friendship." Forney, disappointed at being offered far less than he felt he deserved, declined them both, claiming to be "no applicant for position" at his hands. Though he had "suffered deep and bitter humiliation" since the election, he assured the President that he would remain loyal to the man "whose cause I have given the best years of my life, and upon whose election . . . I have expended every effort . . . and nearly every dollar I had in the world."[30]

Forney's transparent resentment did not move Buchanan to suggest something better. For several months after the inauguration, not wishing to be "regarded as an encumbrance" to the President, he directed his increasingly desperate appeals to his friend, the Attorney General. With Black's support he made

an attempt to purchase the *Pennsylvanian,* promising to make it a faithful administration organ, but Rice refused to sell at a reasonable price. By May, Forney
was ready to accept the Quebec consulate, or "any other respectable paying
office" Buchanan would give him. Again he was offered nothing but the Liverpool consulate, and an exchange of letters with the President in June culminated
in an angry expression of his "just indignation" at the manner in which he had
been treated. Finally, on June 28, having abandoned hope of an acceptable
appointment, he informed Black that he had decided to return to Philadelphia
and start a paper of his own. "I am full of the scheme," he wrote, "and feel
certain of a triumph."[31]

Forney's subsequent public announcement that he would begin publication
of the Philadelphia *Press* on August 1 angered the proprietor of the *Pennsylvanian* and startled the administration. In his prospectus the editor promised to
"sustain the policy of the present national administration," and in the first issue
he gave it his "heartiest approbation." However, two letters from Forney to
Buchanan, though again professing his support, were far from reassuring, for he
no longer wrote as a suppliant but with an air of confident independence. "I do
not think you have ever truly appreciated me," he chided, "but I predict that
you will do so." Friends had advanced the needed capital, he reported, and he
already had an impressive subscription list. He denied responsibility for those
predicting that he would join the opposition: "You who know me better . . . can
be safe in trusting to me as you have in the past. Have faith." In his reply the
uneasy President "heartily and cordially" reciprocated Forney's "friendly spirit"
and wished him success.[32]

Editorials in the *Press,* which quickly became Pennsylvania's leading Democratic newspaper, were consistently favorable to the administration, but Forney's private sentiments were less so and quite disturbing. "The worm will turn
when trampled on," he warned Black, "and I will not submit to being *persecuted
by Mr. Buchanan!*" He desired "to be understood as the supporter of the men
and measures" of the administration, he told the President, but he would be "no
sycophant to power." The *Press,* he explained to Vice President Breckinridge,
was his "last struggle for independence," enabling him to tell "the great men at
Washington that I can do without patronage or office."[33] Friends of the administration feared that Forney's paper would deepen party divisions in Pennsylvania. Robert Tyler informed Buchanan that the *Press* seemed to have attracted "a
strange mixture of your bitterest enemies and many of the office-holders, who
should be your devoted friends." William Rice confessed that the *Pennsylvanian*
was losing subscribers to its young rival and that he was "utterly sick of the
fight."[34]

Soon after Forney launched the *Press,* Buchanan began to suspect that his
purpose was to advocate "the claims of a particular individual [Douglas] to the

Presidency," and he warned Joseph B. Baker, head of the Philadelphia custom-house, to "have nothing to do with it." Baker assured him that Forney had no such purpose, but he was not convinced.

Meanwhile, a remarkable change was occurring in Buchanan's recollection of how the Democrats had carried Pennsylvania in the campaign the previous year. His memory of Forney's role rapidly faded, and the importance of Robert Tyler's influence with foreign voters, especially with the Irish of eastern Penn-sylvania, grew ever larger until, in his mind, it had become decisive. Few men had done more than Tyler, Buchanan now contended, "to elevate me to my present position and . . . I am personally attached to him very warmly."[35]

By late summer both Buchanan and Black were ignoring Forney's advice concerning Pennsylvania appointments. "Elevation to power is apt to increase the distance between former friends," a disillusioned Forney observed. "But I am not too old to profit by the lesson."[36]

Although Buchanan devoted an appalling amount of time, before and after his inauguration, to patronage disputes, he somehow managed to attend to other political problems as well. Because one of his major goals was to end the contro-versy over slavery in the territories, he had noticed with considerable interest a case involving that question which had recently been argued before the Supreme Court, and he had referred to it in his inaugural address. The case, originating in suits for freedom by four Missouri slaves, Dred Scott, his wife Harriet, and their two young daughters, had been making its way through the state and fed-eral courts for more than a decade. By the time it reached the Supreme Court hardly anyone in public life—politicians, lawyers, or judges—seemed to remem-ber that the future of Scott and his family was at stake, or to consider what effect the endless delays, postponements, and rehearings might have on their lives. The Scotts had lost their identity as living persons; they had dissolved into a case, an abstract constitutional issue which, regardless of what the judges might decide, many believed would have no practical effect upon the question of slavery in the existing territories. Moreover, contrary to Buchanan's stated wish, the Court's decision, when finally rendered, intensified, rather than arrested, slavery agita-tion, and for a time in 1857 Republicans found it a more effective weapon than Kansas in their attacks upon the Slave Power. For the new President the decision proved to be another political disaster.[37]

Dred Scott, like most slaves, was illiterate, and the sketchy accounts of his life are derived mostly from the testimony of the whites who owned him and his family or knew them during their legal battle for freedom. He was born in Vir-ginia around 1800 and became the property of a small slaveholder named Peter Blow. Early in the nineteenth century, like thousands of Virginians, Blow migrated westward, taking his large family and six slaves first to an Alabama cotton plantation, then, in 1830, to St. Louis, where he rented a boarding house and operated it as the Jefferson Hotel. His wife Elizabeth died the following year, and Peter Blow died soon after, on June 23, 1832. Around the time of Blow's death Scott was sold to Dr. John Emerson of St. Louis, but in subsequent years several members of the Blow family continued to show considerable interest in his welfare.

In 1834, Dr. Emerson, having obtained a commission in the United States Army as assistant surgeon, was assigned to Fort Armstrong, Illinois, and Dred Scott accompanied him as his personal servant. Two years later Emerson was transferred to Fort Snelling on the west bank of the Mississippi River near the future site of St. Paul, then part of Wisconsin Territory. The place in which Scott now lived was located in a part of the Louisiana Purchase where slavery had been prohibited by the Missouri Compromise of 1820. At Fort Snelling, Scott met a young woman, Harriet Robinson, who was the slave of a federal agent at a nearby Indian agency, and they were married. After the marrige, Dr. Emerson acquired title to Mrs. Scott and, eventually, to the Scotts' two daughters.

Late in 1837, Emerson was transferred to Fort Jesup, Louisiana, where he remained long enough to court and marry Eliza Irene Sanford of St. Louis, who was there on a visit to her sister and brother-in-law, Captain Henry Bainbridge. The following year the peripatetic doctor, returned to Fort Snelling with his wife and the Scotts, and in 1840, after depositing them in St. Louis, he traveled to Florida on his last military assignment. Finally, in 1842, after endless complaints about his health and requests for transfer from whatever post he happened to occupy, he received an honorable discharge and returned to his family and civilian life in St. Louis. Emerson died on December 29, 1843, leaving his estate, including the Scott family, to his wife. He named his wife's brother, John F. A. Sanford, one of the executors, but the court appointed her father, Alexander Sanford, instead.

During the next few years, while in the employment of Mrs. Emerson's brother-in-law, Captain Bainbridge, the movements of the Scott family are uncertain, but early in 1846 they were back in St. Louis and hired out to a local man named Samuel Russell. According to Dred Scott's later account, he then tried to persuade Mrs. Emerson to permit him to "hire his own time"—that is, to find work for wages, as some owners of urban slaves permitted a favored few to do—to enable him to buy freedom for himself and his family. If his unsubstantiated account is accurate, Mrs. Emerson refused.

In any case, on April 6, 1846, Dred and Harriet Scott commenced their decade-long ordeal in the state and federal courts: they petitioned the judge of the Missouri circuit court at St. Louis for permission to bring suits for freedom because of their long residence in a state or territory where slavery was prohibited. When their petition was granted, the Scotts, claiming to be "free persons," filed separate charges against Mrs. Emerson for holding them as slaves, and for assault, claiming that she had "beat, bruised and ill-treated" Dred and temporarily imprisoned him. The Scotts' attorney was a white man, but it is not clear whether he, or the Scotts, or a member of the Blow family had first suggested the action. Whoever was responsible, the suit at the outset was nothing more than an action to gain freedom for the Scotts; it was not initiated as a test case and had no political significance.

The cases seemed simple enough, because the Missouri courts on a number of occasions had granted freedom to slaves whose owners had taken them for long periods of residence in free states or territories. Yet, delays and complications developed from the start. Mrs. Emerson did not file her plea of not guilty until November, and the suits were not tried until June 30, 1847. Because of an absurd defect in the testimony—failure to prove that the Scotts belonged to Mrs. Emerson—the jury brought in a verdict in favor of the defendant. On December 2 the court granted the Scotts' motion for a retrial; Mrs. Emerson's attorney promptly filed a bill of exceptions; and the case automatically went to the Missouri supreme court on a writ of error. Another delay followed until June 1848, when the supreme court dismissed the writ of error and permitted the retrial in the circuit court to proceed. After a longer delay caused by two postponements, the retrial began on January 12, 1850. By then Mrs. Emerson had moved to Springfield, Massachusetts, to live with a sister, and her brother John Sanford supervised the case in her behalf. This time the jury brought in a decision in favor of Dred Scott, and the defense prepared an appeal to the state supreme court. Both sides agreed that Dred Scott's case was identical to that of his wife's and that the decision in his case would be sufficient to settle both.

The attorneys had filed their briefs by March 1850, but the court's repeated postponements put off a decision for two years. By then much had changed. The lower court had placed the Scotts in the custody of the sheriff, who hired them out for the benefit of Mrs. Emerson, provided she established her right to hold them as slaves. Sectional tensions had mounted prior to the adoption of the Compromise of 1850, and the slaveholding interest in Missouri, as elsewhere, had become increasingly resentful of antislavery attacks from the North. In addition, the United States Supreme Court, in the case of *Strader v. Graham* (1851), refused to review a decision of the Kentucky court of appeals that the brief sojourn in Ohio of a group of Kentucky slaves did not make them free men. Chief Justice Taney declared that the laws of Kentucky, not of Ohio, determined their status once they had returned to Kentucky. The *Strader* case was significantly different from Dred Scott's case, but one of Mrs. Emerson's attorneys made use of it in a supplementary brief, arguing that the law of Missouri must prevail regardless of whether Scott might have been given freedom in Illinois or Wisconsin Territory. His brief also exploited the fears of slaveholders and referred darkly to the designs of abolitionists and the dangers of a large free black population.

On March 22, 1852, Judge William Scott, a strongly proslavery Democrat, delivered the court's decision in the case of *Dred Scott v. Emerson,* in which

Judge John F. Ryland concurred. Reversing the decision of the lower court, he ruled that Dred Scott was by Missouri law still a slave. Missouri was not bound to respect or enforce the laws of other states, especially when they were "conceived in a spirit hostile to that which pervades her own laws." Conditions, Judge Scott asserted, were not as they had been when Missouri slaves were freed in cases such as this. Now both individuals and states were "possessed with a dark and fell spirit in relation to slavery," and they advocated measures "whose inevitable consequences must be the overthrow and destruction of our government." Concluding with a fanciful *obiter dictum,* Judge Scott suggested that the introduction of slavery had been, "in the providence of God, who makes the evil passions of men subservient to His own glory, a means of placing that unhappy race within the pale of civilized nations."

Judge Hamilton R. Gamble, a conservative Whig, dissented. He did not deny the right of Missouri to refuse to enforce the laws of other states, but he argued that Missouri's judicial precedents were all in favor of freedom for Dred Scott, and he deplored the introduction of politics into the case. Concurring with Gamble's dissent, the historian Don Fehrenbacher concluded that Judge Scott's decision, "rendered nominally against Dred Scott, was primarily an expression of mounting southern anger and an act of retaliation against antislavery words and deeds." In short, the Scott family's six-year quest for freedom in the courts of Missouri was lost in a volley of sectional, proslavery rhetoric.[38]

That was the end of *Dred Scott v. Emerson,* but not of Dred Scott's case. In the following months one of Scott's attorneys died, another moved to Louisiana; Mrs. Emerson married Dr. Calvin C. Chaffee, a Massachusetts Republican; and Mrs. Chaffee's brother, John F. A. Sanford, now living in New York City, either purchased the Scott family or assumed responsibility for them as her agent. Another St. Louis attorney, Roswell M. Field, a native of Vermont with strong antislavery sentiments, perceived in the new situation an opportunity to initiate a suit for Scott's freedom in the federal courts. Article Three, Section Two, of the Constitution gave them jurisdiction over controversies between citizens of different states, and, on November 2, 1853, Field initiated an action of trespass in the United States Circuit Court for the District of Missouri.

The suit claimed that Scott was a citizen of Missouri and that he and his family were being illegally held as slaves. The defense responded with a plea in abatement, claiming simply that the court had no jurisdiction because Scott was a Negro and therefore not a citizen of Missouri. Judge Robert W. Wells, without giving an opinion on the controversial subject of Negro citizenship, ruled that it was sufficient for this case that Scott was a resident of Missouri. The brief trial began on May 15, 1854. After the arguments of counsel were completed, Judge Wells, apparently with regret, explained the law governing the case to the jury in such a way as to make its verdict in Sanford's favor almost inevitable. Scott, as the state supreme court had previously ruled, was still a slave by Missouri law.

Counsel for Scott promptly filed a bill of exceptions in order to initiate the anticipated appeal to the United States Supreme Court.

Field's next task was to find a Washington attorney to argue Scott's case,
as well as the money to pay his fee and other expenses. He wrote to the free-soil
Republican Montgomery Blair, son of the old Jacksonian Francis Preston Blair
and a former attorney in St. Louis, now practicing before the Supreme Court,
and asked him to take the case. Field suggested that "the cause of humanity may
perhaps be subserved," while, at the same time, "a much disputed question would
be settled by the highest court in the nation." Blair, after conferring with his
father and with Dr. Gamaliel Bailey, editor of the Republican Washington
National Era, agreed to act as counsel for Scott without fee. Bailey in turn promised to raise money for court costs and incidental expenses, which ultimately
amounted to the nominal sum of $154.68.

Blair was a good choice, for he was an able and experienced lawyer who,
though a conservative Republican, was strongly committed, as a free soiler, to
the cause embodied in Dred Scott's case. Sanford retained a formidable pair of
proslavery attorneys to represent him: Senator Henry S. Geyer of Missouri, an
anti-Benton Democrat, and Reverdy Johnson of Maryland, a former Whig Senator and Attorney General, and a constitutional lawyer of great distinction. Blair
needed assistance, but he found none until late in the litigation, when George
Ticknor Curtis of Massachusetts, brother of Associate Justice Benjamin R. Curtis,
agreed to join him in arguing certain constitutional issues before the court.

On December 30, 1854, in the ninth year of Dred Scott's pursuit of freedom,
the Supreme Court, late in its term, received the record of *Dred Scott v. Sandford,*
with Sanford's name misspelled and never corrected. Given the history of the
case, no one should have been surprised that it was carried over to the next term,
and that argument before the Court did not begin until February 11, 1856. By
then even Montgomery Blair apparently thought that weightier matters were at
stake than the fate of an obscure black family named Scott.[39]

As he prepared his brief, Montgomery Blair could hardly have been sanguine
of success, not only because of the talent of opposing counsel but because of the
current composition of the Supreme Court. Of the nine justices, five were southern proslavery Democrats, two were northern Democrats, one was a northern
Whig, and one was a northern Republican. The Chief Justice, Roger B. Taney of
Maryland, then in his eightieth year, had been appointed by Andrew Jackson in
1835 to succeed John Marshall. He had been an intensely partisan Jacksonian
before his appointment, but in subsequent years he had won high praise for his
lucid opinions and effective leadership of the Court. Nevertheless, his judicial
robes had only partially concealed his persistent partisanship, especially on matters relating to slavery and the sectional conflict. Taney's proslavery proclivities
had been evident in several previous decisions, notably *Strader v. Graham* in

which he pronounced a *dictum* which, if accepted by the Court, would deny freedom to a slave in a case such as Dred Scott's. His age and chronic physical afflictions had taken their toll, giving his face, according to one reporter, a "sinister expression" suited to the role of malevolent villain that his antislavery critics would assign him.

Three of the southern associate justices—James M. Wayne of Georgia, John Catron of Tennessee, and John A. Campbell of Alabama—were firm defenders of southern rights. The fourth, Peter V. Daniel of Virginia, was a proslavery zealot, a judicial fire-eater, who refused to tread on northern soil and hoped that every southern man would be "prepared for any extremity" to resist a northern attempt to exclude slavery from the territories. Of the two northern Democrats, Samuel Nelson of New York was reluctant to have the Court involve itself in the politics of slavery expansion; but Robert C. Grier of Pennsylvania was as closely tied to the southern wing of the Democratic party as his friend James Buchanan. Benjamin R. Curtis of Massachusetts, the conservative Whig justice, was in bad repute among Republicans of his state for his readiness to enforce the Fugitive Slave Act of 1850, but he shared their belief in the power of Congress to prohibit slavery in the territories. Justice John McLean of Ohio, a former Jacksonian Democrat, now a Republican, was deeply involved in party politics. He had sought a presidential nomination in 1856 and still hoped for one in 1860, when he would be seventy-five years old.[40]

The Dred Scott case was reviewed not only by a highly political Court but in an atmosphere of great political excitement following the passage of the Kansas-Nebraska Act and the emergence of the sectional Republican party. The Court had the case before it during the presidential campaign of 1856, during the months of violent conflict between proslavery and free-state factions in Kansas, and during an angry congressional debate over constitutional issues relating to slavery in the territories. Both southern and northern Democrats, including Douglas, were now denying that Congress had the power to prohibit slavery in the territories, even though it had previously exercised the power in a half-dozen territorial acts, as well as in the Missouri Compromise. But Democrats still disagreed among themselves about the right of a territorial legislature to exclude slavery prior to statehood. From time to time exasperated partisans affirmed that these were constitutional questions that could be resolved only in the federal courts; and Congress itself had worded the Compromise of 1850 and the Kansas-Nebraska Act in such a way as to invite a judicial settlement.[41]

However, *Dred Scott v. Sandford,* as it first came before the Supreme Court, still focused on Scott's suit for freedom and not on any facet of the territorial question. Blair, when he filed his brief, showed no desire to introduce it, for he claimed freedom for his client only because of his extended residence in the state of Illinois. Beyond that he merely reaffirmed the ruling of the lower court that Scott had at least limited citizenship, qualifying him to bring suit in a federal court. During the four days of oral arguments counsel for the defense revived the contention that Scott, a Negro, was not a citizen and denied the Court's jurisdiction. At this point the defense made its fateful decision to introduce the territorial issue and argued that the Missouri Compromise was unconstitutional. But even then it seemed doubtful that the Court would get involved in that knotty problem. Early in April, after several conferences on the case, Justice Curtis wrote privately that the Missouri Compromise would not be considered, "a majority of the judges being of opinion that it is not necessary to do so." The Court was divided on the question of jurisdiction, and, on May 12, it decided on still another delay, ordering Dred Scott's case to be reargued at its next term. Both sides were to consider the validity of the lower court's ruling on limited Negro citizenship. The case would thus be decided after the presidential election, sometime early in the year 1857, approximately eleven years after the Scott family's suits for freedom had begun.[42]

When reargument before the Court began on December 15, the potentially broad political significance of the case had become evident, and public interest in it had increased considerably. On the question of Scott's citizenship and right to bring suit raised by the defense's plea in abatement, Blair claimed that this already had been settled by the circuit court, whose decision should be left standing. Even though Negroes were segregated socially and denied political rights, he argued, they were no less than "*quasi* citizens" who possessed other rights of citizenship, including the right to bring suits in the courts. Counsel for the defense argued that the jurisdictional issue raised by the plea in abatement should be reviewed to determine whether the circuit court's decision was erroneous. Geyer argued further that Dred Scott was a slave and not a citizen of Missouri or of the United States, and that even a deed of manumission would not make him a citizen. In short, he asked that the lower court's decision on the plea in abatement be reversed and the case dismissed for lack of jurisdiction.

Turning from the question of jurisdiction to the grounds for Dred Scott's suit for freedom, Geyer and Blair debated the effect that living in a free state for two years had on his status as Emerson's slave. Geyer argued that Emerson had not been a resident of Illinois but merely a "sojourner" while on military duty, thus providing no grounds for Scott's emancipation. His most telling argument was that when Scott returned to Missouri his status was determined by its laws, not by those of Illinois, whose laws Missouri was not bound to enforce. Blair, in turn, argued that Emerson had been a *resident,* not a sojourner, in Illinois, for he had claimed residency nowhere else. He also cited the precedents in Missouri's own courts for granting freedom to slaves in cases such as Scott's, and he accused the Missouri supreme court of a political motive for rejecting them. Interstate comity, he concluded, obligated Missouri to respect the Illinois law against slavery.

The defense counsel's argument against Scott's freedom after his return to Missouri from Illinois was equally applicable to his condition after his return to Missouri from Fort Snelling. However, in this case they elected to argue instead that the slavery restriction imposed by Congress in the Missouri Compromise was unconstitutional, thereby, as Don Fehrenbacher observed, converting "Dred Scott's private case ... into a public issue" and turning the courtroom into a "political arena." Both counsel for Scott and for Sanford debated this question at length.

Article Four of the Constitution, briefly and somewhat ambiguously, grants Congress the power "to dispose of and make all needful Rules and Regulations respecting the Territory or other Property belonging to the United States." Since the precedents and seventy years of constitutional interpretation, based on this provision, supported the right of Congress to prohibit slavery in the territories, counsel for the defense were obliged to defy the precedents and defend a position recently taken by extreme proslavery partisans. They argued that the constitutional reference to territory was merely intended to authorize Congress to dispose of public lands, not to give it unlimited control over the property of those who inhabited those lands. Congress had power to establish temporary territorial governments, but this power did not include the right to legislate against slavery. Such legislation, including the restriction in the Missouri Compromise, was an affront to the people of the southern states. Moreover, defense counsel maintained, it was unconstitutional, because it deprived them of the right, enjoyed by settlers from the northern states, to carry their property into the territories.

Blair, now ably supported by George Ticknor Curtis, argued that Article Four not only empowered Congress to establish territorial governments but granted legislative authority to "make all needful rules" for them, subject only to the limitations explicitly stated in the Constitution. Whether the prohibition of slavery in any territory was "needful" was a political question requiring a political remedy, not the intervention of the courts. Counsel for Scott noted that Southerners, including John C. Calhoun, had supported the Missouri Compromise line, while others more recently had been willing to extend it through the territory acquired in the war with Mexico. Finally, they denied that Southerners were excluded from territories where slavery was prohibited and noted how many had settled in them. Nor was the equality of the states thereby impaired, for the territories were in no respect subject to their legislative authority.[43]

The reargument of the case lasted four days, until December 19, after which the long wait for the Court's decision began. Considering its composition, few believed that Dred Scott would emerge from his ordeal a free man. "It seems to be the impression," wrote Montgomery Blair, "that the Court will be adverse to my client and to the power of Congress over the Territories."[44] Yet, when the judges began their deliberations, it was by no means certain that a decision against Scott's freedom would require an opinion on the constitutionality of the slavery restriction embodied in the Missouri Compromise. They might easily have decided his case on narrower grounds. For example, the Court might have sustained the lower court's ruling on the plea in abatement concerning Dred Scott's citizenship, proceeded directly to the question of Scott's status as a result of his residence in Illinois or at Fort Snelling, and simply upheld the lower court's decision that his return to Missouri subjected him to the laws of that state. Or the Court might have reversed the lower court's ruling on the plea in abatement, concluded that Dred Scott was not even a quasi-citizen of Missouri, and ordered it to dismiss the case for lack of jurisdiction.[45]

No doubt the Supreme Court, if it so desired, had sufficient grounds for exploring the broader question of congressional power after it had been thoroughly debated by counsel for Scott and Sanford. Moreover, the Court had been exposed to considerable political pressure to render a decision on that issue. Alexander H. Stephens, for one, had been "urging all the influences [he] could bring to bear" on that body to rule on the constitutionality of the slavery restriction in the Missouri Compromise. Anticipating an adverse decision, Stephens believed that the Court would thereby also deny the power of a territorial legislature to prohibit slavery.[46] In previous cases the Taney Court had rarely dodged an opportunity to decide a question involving slavery when presented to it. Even so, on this occasion, rather than yielding to outside pressure or giving vent to their own strong feelings, the justices might have considered what precisely was to be gained from a broad decision on congressional power at a time when the Democrats controlled the executive department and both houses of Congress. Posterity judges Supreme Court justices not only by their judicial erudition but, like Presidents and Congressmen, by the quality of their statesmanship as well.

Nearly two months passed before the Court began its second round of conferences on the fate of Dred Scott. This time the delay resulted from the tragic death, on January 3, of Justice Daniel's young wife, who had been fatally burned when a candle ignited her clothing. The Court recessed to attend her funeral, then put off the Scott case until Daniel had sufficiently recovered from his bereavement to resume his judicial duties.[47]

On February 14, when deliberations finally began, one southern and the four northern justices favored accepting the lower court's ruling on the plea in abatement, thus refusing to take up the question of Negro citizenship; the five southern justices wanted to deny the constitutionality of the slavery restriction in the Missouri Compromise; Curtis and McLean would have upheld it; and the two northern Democrats, Nelson and Grier, urged the Court merely to accept the decision of the lower court that Dred Scott was still a slave under Missouri law. With the Court thus divided, Nelson and Grier prevailed, and Nelson agreed to write a brief opinion that would have elicited dissent only from Curtis and

McLean. Declaring it unnecessary to review the plea in abatement, he passed directly to the question of Scott's claim to freedom and concluded, as the lower court had done, that his status was determined by the law of Missouri, not by that of another state or territory. If Nelson's opinion did less than justice to Dred Scott, it would at least have done so without provoking a national explosion, and to that extent there was an element of judicial statesmanship in it.

The opinion that Nelson thought he had written for the Court ultimately proved to be his opinion alone. A few days later the southern majority, in an abrupt shift, decided that judicial statesmanship dictated another course: it approved Justice Wayne's motion to take up the broader issues involved in the case, including the constitutionality of the congressional restriction on slavery in the Missouri Compromise. Chief Justice Taney willingly assumed the task of writing the Court's opinion. Why this sudden about-face? The traditional explanation has been that Curtis and McLean, for their own selfish reasons, had forced the majority's hand by their evident intention to prepare comprehensive dissenting opinions not only favorable to Dred Scott's claim to freedom but covering the territorial question as well. More recently, Don Fehrenbacher, in his study of the case, suggested instead that the change of plan merely spelled "victory for those justices who had wanted all along to issue an emphatically pro-southern decision." His explanation seems to fit the historical facts a good deal more comfortably, for the Court's southern majority apparently hoped that a firm judicial decision would terminate the divisive political controversy over slavery in the territories.[48]

Obviously the authority of the decision would be weakened if it had the approval of only a bare majority of the Court, especially one consisting entirely of Southerners. Could one of the northern Democrats be persuaded to join them? Nelson, who had already written his opinion, was a less likely prospect than Grier, whose commitment to a narrow opinion was less firmly fixed. Since Grier was a Pennsylvanian, it occurred to Justice Catron of Tennessee that Buchanan might be of assistance, and he seemed to discern no ethical problem in soliciting a politician to intervene for the purpose of influencing the action of one of the justices in a case before the Court. Buchanan, eager to have a judicial decision on the territorial issue, seemed equally indifferent to the ethics of the matter and readily complied.

This extraordinary correspondence began innocently enough on February 3, when Buchanan wrote Catron asking whether the Court was likely to give its opinion in the Dred Scott case before the day of his inauguration. Catron replied that the timing depended upon the Chief Justice, but he would "ascertain and inform" the President-elect within a few days. On February 10 he wrote less discreetly that some judges might write opinions touching the territorial question, but he thought that the court's decision would "*settle* nothing." His own opinion, he added, was that Congress clearly had the power to govern the territories.

A contrary decision "after a practice of 68 years would . . . subject the Sup. Court to . . . ridicule." However, Catron believed that the Missouri Compromise violated the terms of the Louisiana Purchase treaty of 1803, which protected the property, including slaves, of all inhabitants prior to statehood. Thus, in his view, "the Treaty settles the controversy."

Nine days later Catron sent Buchanan the welcome news that the majority had decided to give an opinion on the constitutionality of the Missouri Compromise. He might "safely say" in his inaugural address that the Supreme Court would thus "decide and settle a controversy" which had "so long and seriously affected the country." Catron then asked Buchanan to "drop Grier a line, saying how necessary it is . . . to settle the agitation by an affirmative decision of the Supreme Court, the one way or the other." Grier, he reported, believed the Missouri Compromise to be unconstitutional, but he was inclined, like Nelson, to avoid the issue—"to take the smoothe handle for the sake of repose." On February 23, in response to an urgent note from Buchanan, Catron reported that the two dissenters were ready and the five Southerners were nearly ready; but, he added, "I want Grier *speeded.*"

On the same day, Grier, unaware of Catron's involvement, wrote a long reply to the letter he had received from Buchanan urging a broad decision. He had shown the letter "to our mutual friends Judge Wayne and the Chief Justice," both of whom agreed that it was desirable to have "an expression of the opinion of the Court on this troublesome [territorial] question." Claiming that Curtis and McLean had forced the issue on the majority, Grier revealed that he was now "anxious that it should not appear that the line of latitude should mark the line of division in the court." Nor did he think it wise for the majority opinion to be founded on "clashing and inconsistent arguments." Hence, "On conversation with the chief justice I have *agreed to concur with him.* . . . There will therefore be six if not *seven* (perhaps Nelson will remain neutral) who will decide the compromise law of 1820 to be of *non-effect.*" Grier assured Buchanan that none of the other justices would be told "about *the cause of our anxiety* to produce this result." This, he admitted, was "contrary to our usual practice," but he, as well as Wayne and the Chief Justice, thought it proper to apprise the President-elect "in candor and confidence [of] the real state of the matter." Thus, three southern justices, one compliant northern justice, and the President-elect secretly made a pawn of Dred Scott in a game of judicial politics.[49]

In this manner Buchanan, at the time of his inauguration, knew that the Court was about to declare the congressional restriction on slavery incorporated in the Missouri Compromise invalid. Yet, in his inaugural address, when he referred to the pending decision, Buchanan predicted that it would settle a different question—that is, whether a territorial legislature, prior to statehood, could prohibit slavery. This issue had not been raised in the Dred Scott case, and neither Catron nor Grier had alluded to it in their letters to him. There is no clear explanation for Buchanan's seemingly unwarranted prediction except that, like proslavery Southerners, he believed that if Congress could not prohibit slavery in the territories it could not delegate that power to a territorial legislature. It had always been his private opinion, he said, that the proper time for the decision about slavery was when a territory was ready for statehood. In mid-February, Glancy Jones, apparently sharing the same view, had informed Buchanan, without revealing his source, that the "reasoning of the [Court's] opinion" would cover the question of territorial authority to exclude slavery.

Another possibility, suggested by Don Fehrenbacher, is that Buchanan may have seen a copy of Taney's opinion or have been told of its contents, for Taney was the only justice who gave an opinion on the issue that divided northern and southern Democrats—the right of the people of a territory, prior to statehood, to decide for or against slavery.[50] The President's contemporary critics had an easier explanation, for he was seen at the inaugural ceremony on March 4 engaged in a brief whispered conversation with the Chief Justice shortly before delivering his address. Whatever the truth of the matter, there was hypocrisy, surely, in Buchanan's inaugural pledge that, "in common with all good citizens," he would "cheerfully submit" to the Court's decision, "whatever this may be."

At eleven o'clock on the morning of March 6, reporters and spectators crowded the cramped quarters of the United States Supreme Court on the ground floor of the Capitol. They were there to hear Chief Justice Taney read the opinion of the Court in the case of *Dred Scott v. John F. A. Sandford,* and thus, after eleven years, to decide the fate of Scott and his family. More important to most of the audience, it was widely understood that the opinion would also address the constitutional controversy over the rights of slaveholders in the western territories. In a few days Taney would turn eighty, "growing more feeble in body," as Justice Curtis observed, but retaining "his alacrity and force of mind." Having managed in two weeks to write an opinion which, after subsequent revisions, would run to fifty-five pages, the exhausted Chief Justice, his hands trembling and his feeble voice growing ever fainter, now read from his manuscript for more than two hours. Taney's voice may have been weak, but his words were not, for they bristled with uncompromising defiance of abolitionists, free soilers, and Republicans. In essence, Don Fehrenbacher concluded, his opinion was "a work of unmitigated partisanship . . . more like an ultimatum than a formula for sectional accommodation." In its scope—its bold rulings on matters for which constitutional authority is vague or nonexistent—Taney's opinion was a breathtaking example of judicial activism.[51]

Affirming at the outset that the plea in abatement was before the Court, Taney devoted nearly half of his opinion to the issue of Scott's right "to sue as a citizen in a court of the United States." The question, he said, was whether Negroes descended from slaves could become members of the political community formed by the federal Constitution, "and as such become entitled to all the rights, and privileges, and immunities, guarantied by that instrument to the citizen." In Taney's opinion, they could not, for, whether slaves or free, "they were not included, and were not intended to be included, under the word 'citizens' in the Constitution." Rather, at the time of the framing of the Constitution, they were regarded "as a subordinate and inferior class of beings, who . . . had no rights or privileges but such as those who held the power and the Government might choose to grant them."

Taney conceded that a state may confer on a person "the rights of citizenship . . . within its own limits," but it did not follow that such a person thereby became a citizen of the United States. Nor was he necessarily "entitled to the rights and privileges of a citizen in any other State"—presumably in spite of an explicit statement to the contrary in Article Four, Section Two, of the Constitution. A state could not by its own laws grant United States citizenship to persons whom the framers of the Constitution intended to exclude. The Constitution in fact names no such persons, but Taney held that members of the "negro African race" had been excluded, and their emancipation by state law did not raise them to the rank of citizens.

Taney argued further that the "unalienable rights" of "all men" affirmed in the Declaration of Independence did not apply to the descendants of those who had been imported as slaves. They were not, at the time it was written, "acknowledged as a part of the people, nor intended to be included in the general words used in that memorable instrument." In the "civilized and enlightened portions of the world" they were then considered "altogether unfit to associate with the white race . . . and so far inferior, that they had no rights which the white man was bound to respect; and . . . might justly and lawfully be reduced to slavery for his benefit." Hence, it was "too clear for dispute, that the enslaved African race . . . formed no part of the people who framed and adopted this declaration." Nor had the state of public opinion changed when the Constitution was adopted, for in that document, too, "they were not regarded as a portion of the people or citizens of the Government then formed." Since then racial attitudes may have changed, but the Constitution remained unchanged and, until amended, it must be interpreted as it was intended to be at the time of its adoption.

After "a full and careful consideration of the . . . facts stated in the plea in abatement," the Court's opinion, Taney concluded, was that "Dred Scott was not a citizen of Missouri within the meaning of the Constitution of the United States, and not entitled as such to sue in its courts; and consequently that the Circuit Court had no jurisdiction of the case, and that the judgment on the plea in abatement is erroneous." The path to this startling opinion was littered with misrepresentations of the status of both slaves and free blacks in the late eighteenth century, with other historical inaccuracies, and with confusing statements about the nature and origin of state and federal citizenship. To bolster his opinion Taney rewrote the Declaration of Independence to read "all *white* men are created equal," and he amended the Constitution to transform it into a racist document.

Two justices—Wayne and Daniel—explicitly concurred in Taney's denial of Negro citizenship; and four others—Campbell, Catron, Grier, and Nelson—acquiesced, Curtis and McLean being the only dissenters. Taney's ruling on this point, therefore, was accepted 7-2 as the opinion of the Court.

Having ruled that Dred Scott was not a citizen and hence was not entitled to sue in a federal court, Taney proceeded to examine the merits of his case on the grounds that a second jurisdictional question was embodied in his claim to freedom. Whatever opinions some may have entertained in favor of the citizenship of a free Negro, he reasoned, "no one supposes that a slave is a citizen of the State or of the United States." Hence, if the Circuit Court was correct in ruling that Scott was still a slave, Taney argued that it should have dismissed the case for lack of jurisdiction without rendering a judgment in favor of either party. The Circuit Court's judgment in favor of the defendant was then as erroneous as its ruling on the plea in abatement. Taney therefore proceeded to inquire "whether the facts relied on by the plaintiff entitled him to his freedom."

Were Scott and his family free because of their stay in territory where slavery was prohibited by the Missouri Compromise? That, said Taney, depended on whether Congress had the constitutional power to impose such a restriction. What was the intent of Article Four, Section Three, of the Constitution, which authorized Congress to "make all needful rules and regulations" respecting the territory of the United States? According to Taney's own imaginative reading, this power was meant to apply only to the territory belonging to the United States in 1787, not to territory subsequently acquired. "It was a special provision for a known and particular territory, and to meet a present emergency, and nothing more." The principal object was to authorize the sale of public lands and to make the necessary rules and regulations for that purpose, not to give "supreme power of legislation."

The territories acquired since 1787, Taney claimed, were not intended to be held as colonies "and governed by Congress with absolute authority." Nor could citizens who migrated to a territory "be ruled as mere colonists, dependent upon the will of the General Government, and to be governed by any laws it may think proper to impose." Territories were acquired for the benefit of the people of the several states, and the federal government served as their "trustee acting for them, and charged with the duty of promoting the interests of the whole people of the Union." Federal power over the citizens of a territory was "strictly defined, and limited by the Constitution," especially by the due-process clause of the Fifth Amendment which protected both the rights of person and the rights of private property.

According to Taney, to deprive a citizen of his (slave) property merely because he brought it into a territory of the United States, "could hardly be dignified with the name of due process of law." Moreover, he asserted, "if Congress itself cannot do this—if it is beyond the powers conferred on the Federal Government—it will be admitted, we presume, that it could not authorize a Territorial Government to exercise them." Since the power of a territorial government over slavery was not an issue in the Dred Scott case, Taney's opinion on this point was *obiter dictum*—extrajudicial—and none of the justices who wrote concurring opinions discussed it. Nevertheless, his view of territorial power was part of the accepted opinion of the Court, an opinion with which at least four other justices (Wayne, Daniel, Campbell, Catron, and probably Grier) would have concurred had they seen fit to address the issue.

Some seemed to think, Taney observed, that there was a difference between slave property and other property, "and that different rules may be applied to it in expounding the Constitution of the United States." Yet nothing in the Constitution gave Congress greater power over slave property or entitled it to less protection than other property. Rather, it imposed on Congress "the duty of guarding and protecting the owner in his rights." Accordingly, it was the opinion of the Court that the prohibition of slavery in territory north of the Missouri Compromise line was unconstitutional and therefore void, "and that neither Dred Scott himself, nor any of his family, were made free by being carried into this territory." The Court's opinion meant, of course, that not only the slavery provision of the Missouri Compromise but all other acts of Congress excluding slavery from various territories had been equally unconstitutional. A restriction thus imposed on congressional power to govern the territories, unmentioned in the Constitution, unknown to its framers, undiscovered for many years thereafter, but recently devised by John C. Calhoun and other proslavery partisans, was now, according to the opinion of the Court, the law of the land.

Taney then considered whether Dred Scott was free because he had lived with his owner for two years in the state of Illinois. This question, he said, had been decided in the case of *Strader v. Graham* involving slaves briefly taken from Kentucky to Ohio and then returned to Kentucky. In spite of Scott's much longer stay in Illinois, Taney ruled that when he returned to Missouri "his *status,* as free or slave, depended on the laws of Missouri and not of Illinois." The opinion of the Court, therefore, was that the judgment of the circuit court in favor of the defendant must be reversed, "and a mandate issued, directing the suit to be dismissed for want of jurisdiction."[52]

Among the concurring justices, Wayne required only a few pages to approve the opinion of the Court in every respect. Nelson's longer opinion concurred to the extent of holding that Dred Scott's status was determined by Missouri law, but he made no reference to the question of Negro citizenship and only a brief and indecisive allusion to the Missouri Compromise. Grier, in less than a page, accepted Nelson's opinion on the status of Scott and Taney's opinion on the Missouri Compromise. Daniel's long concurring opinion supported Taney on almost every point, but his argument was more extreme, claiming that slave property deserved *greater* protection than other forms of property and denying the constitutionality of the Ordinance of 1787. Catron and Campbell avoided the issue of Negro citizenship; and, except for denying the power of Congress to prohibit slavery, Catron did not share Taney's limited conception of its authority to govern the territories. Because some concurring justices did not explicitly concur with every part of Taney's decision—for example, on whether the plea in abatement was before the Court and on Negro citizenship—there has been much confusion about what the Court actually had decided. The most plausible assumption is, as Don Fehrenbacher concluded, that since Taney's decision was acknowledged to be the decision of the Court, silence indicated concurrence, not dissent.[53]

The lengthy opinions of the two dissenting justices, read on March 7, agreed on nearly all substantive issues, except that Curtis accepted Taney's opinion that the plea in abatement was before the Court and McLean did not. Because Curtis's opinion was better constructed and more lucid, because he was a conservative Whig and lacked political ambition, his dissent carried more weight than McLean's and attracted more attention.

On the issue of jurisdiction Curtis maintained that if Dred Scott resided in Missouri and was a citizen of the United States, he could not be deprived of his right to sue a citizen of another state in the federal courts. The question, then, was "whether any person of African descent, whose ancestors were sold as slaves" could be a citizen of the United States. If such a person could be, Scott was entitled to be recognized as a citizen by the Court, because the defense had presented no other reason for denying his citizenship.

The Constitution, Curtis noted, acknowledged that United States citizenship existed under the Articles of Confederation, a status which then was derived only from state citizenship. Accordingly, it was necessary to determine whether free persons of African descent were citizens in any of the states at the time the Constitution was adopted, for that document did not deny citizenship to any group which then possessed it. Curtis showed that in five states Negroes were not only recognized as citizens but "possessed the franchise . . . on equal terms with other citizens." Moreover, Curtis found in the Articles of Confederation a provision conferring upon the citizens of the several states, not excluding free Negroes who were citizens, "the privileges and immunities of general citizenship." He concluded that under the federal Constitution, "every free person born on the soil of a state, who is a citizen of that state by force of its Constitution or laws, is also a citizen of the United States." Hence the claim in the plea in abatement that Dred Scott was of African descent was not sufficient to prove that he was not a citizen of the United States, "and the judgment of the Circuit Court overruling it was correct." Curtis, one should note, did not claim that Scott was in fact a citizen, only that the defense had failed to establish that he was *not* a citizen.

Curtis next presented his reasons for dissenting, first, from the majority's assumption of authority to examine the constitutionality of the Missouri Compromise, and, second, from the conclusions it had reached. After the majority had decided that the Court lacked jurisdiction, he denied that it had the right to consider the merits of the case and held that its opinion was not binding "when expressed on a question not legitimately before it." This was all the more true when the case involved a "great question of constitutional law, deeply affecting the peace and welfare of the country." Having almost, but not quite, called the opinion of the Court on the Missouri Compromise *obiter dictum,* Curtis claimed his own right to judge the merits of the case because of his opinion that the Court did have jurisdiction.

He offered strong historical evidence that the framers of the Constitution were fully aware of the need to grant Congress sufficient power to govern not only the existing territory but "all territory belonging to the United States throughout all time." To meet this need the Constitution explicitly declared that Congress shall have power to make "*all* needful rules and regulations," without qualification; and those who argued that slavery was excepted, would have to show that these words were "not to be understood according to their clear, plain, and natural signification." Curtis noted "eight distinct instances" between 1789 and 1848 in which Congress had prohibited slavery in western territories in legislation signed by seven Presidents, beginning with Washington.

What positive prohibition, he asked, could be found in the Constitution restraining Congress from excluding slavery from territory north of the Missouri Compromise line? The only one suggested was the due-process clause in the Fifth Amendment. But slavery existed only by the municipal laws of individual states, and slaves ceased to be property when taken to places where such laws did not exist. Territories were outside the jurisdiction of states, and it was reasonable to assume that the framers of the Constitution intended "to leave to the discretion of Congress what regulations, if any, should be made concerning slavery" in each of them. Congress, McLean claimed, could legislate the exclusion of slavery from a territory if it thought the institution "injurious to the population . . . or on any other ground connected with the public interest." Such legislation, Curtis concluded, was no more a violation of due process than similar prohibitions passed from time to time by various slave states.

These arguments, with much elaboration, led both Curtis and McLean to conclude that the slavery restriction in the Missouri Compromise was "constitutional and valid." In slightly different ways they also concluded that Dred Scott had resided in Illinois and at Fort Snelling sufficiently long to "terminate the rights of the master" and, regardless of the laws of Missouri, to make him a free man. Accordingly, both their opinions affirmed that "the judgment of the Circuit Court should be reversed, and the cause remanded for a new trial."[54]

It would be difficult to dispute Don Fehrenbacher's conclusion that, apart from questions of morality and justice, the opinions of Curtis and McLean seem more persuasive than the opinion of the Court, and that they, rather than the majority, were the "sound constitutional conservatives." The opinion of the Court included several radical innovations, among them, the first judicial invalidation of congressional legislation of major importance, and "denying to Congress a power that it had exercised for two-thirds of a century." McLean, in his own way, may have been as much a partisan as Taney; yet his private expression of dismay was genuine enough: "I did not suppose it was possible for some of my southern brethren to evince that entire indifference to historical facts, and the rulings of the court, as is shown in the opinion of the chief justice."[55]

Curtis and McLean gave copies of their dissenting opinions to the press without delay; but for many weeks the public had only sketchy accounts of the opinion of the Court, for the Chief Justice would not release it until he had found time to make revisions. Both dissenters heard rumors that Taney was making material alterations, and Curtis, on April 2, sent a request to the Clerk of the Supreme Court for a copy of the opinion as soon as it had been printed. The clerk, William T. Carroll, replied that the Chief Justice had instructed him not to give a copy to anyone until it was published in the official Court reports. When Curtis wrote directly to Taney expressing disbelief that the order applied to a member of the Court, Taney replied that it did, explaining that he did not want his opinion "hurried before the public ... by irresponsible reporters, through political and partisan newspapers." He added testily that he saw no reason why Curtis should need a copy, for "you announced from the bench that you regarded the opinion as extrajudicial, and not binding upon you or any one else."

On May 13, Curtis replied indignantly that he did not think it necessary for a member of the Court to give a reason for requesting a copy of the Court's opinion. He now explained that he wished to determine whether there was truth in reports that the opinion from which he had dissented "had been revised and materially altered," and whether it might be necessary for him to make corresponding alterations in his dissent. Although the Court's opinion, along with the concurring and dissenting opinions, were finally published late in May, the increasingly unpleasant exchanges between Taney and Curtis did not cease. On June 11, after delaying for almost a month, Taney wrote a long reply asserting that reports of material changes in his opinion "had no foundation in truth." He had merely added "proofs and authorities" to support the "historical facts and principles of law" advanced by the Court but denied in the dissenting opinions.

He berated Curtis for rushing his opinion into print, thereby encouraging partisan attacks on the Court and seeking to "impair its authority." After a final bitter
exchange their correspondence came to an end.

Curtis, however, inserted a memorandum in his records concerning the
"many material additions" that Taney had made to the decision he had read
from the bench. Having heard the original opinion read on two occasions, he
concluded that subsequent additions amounted to "upwards of *eighteen* pages,"
all of them "*in reply* to my opinion." In short, Curtis charged that Taney had
"withheld his opinion . . . for the purpose of concealing the fact that the original
was retained to be altered." Other evidence indicates that Curtis's charge was
essentially true.[56]

During his correspondence with Taney, Curtis seriously considered resigning from the Court, and on September 1, after some hesitation, he sent his resignation to President Buchanan. His usual explanation was that the salary of a
judge was not sufficient to support his family in Washington, but in private he
once wrote that he had lost confidence in the Court and did not "expect its
condition to improve." Buchanan accepted his resignation with a curt, almost
rude, note written by Attorney General Black. Some friends expressed sympathy
for Curtis's decision; others deplored it as "unmanly." "I esteem and respect
him," wrote one Boston friend. "But I have never known a resignation which
seemed so much to be like a desertion." Charles Francis Adams, a Republican
critic, thought it ironic that Curtis, with his past record of hostility to the antislavery movement, would appear to posterity "as a champion of principles, for
his *opposition* to which he obtained his seat on the bench."[57]

In May 1857, Taylor Blow of St. Louis, a member of the family that had
once owned Dred Scott, acquired title to him and his family and emancipated
them. Scott, after a brief life in freedom, died in obscurity on September 17, 1858,
but his case before the Supreme Court had by then written his name indelibly in
the political and constitutional history of his country. The numerous arcane passages in the Court's opinion, as well as the uncertainty about what had actually
been decided, would intrigue future generations of historians and jurists.
Whether the majority of justices thought that their decision would help to resolve
their own generation's political crisis, whether they expected it to give effective
protection to slave property in the territories, or whether they understood it to
be merely a bold assertion of slaveholders' rights that even the judiciary could
not sustain, are interesting questions. If they anticipated some material benefit to
the South—if they believed that their decision would encourage a triumphant
march of slaveholders to Kansas or to other western territories—many Southerners were a good deal wiser than they.

Whatever its practical value, most Southerners seemed to find in the Dred
Scott decision at least welcome relief from the moral stigma they believed inherent in congressional restrictions on the expansion of slavery into the western

territories. They found in it, too, confirmation of their racial justification for holding the southern black population in slavery, though Senator James M. Mason of Virginia suspected that Taney's opinion might be "too strong for stomachs debilitated by the sickly sensibilities of a depraved morality." Abolitionism, exulted the Richmond *Enquirer,* had been "staggered and stunned" and the "diabolical doctrines" of northern fanatics repudiated.[58]

Southerners also celebrated the vindication of their constitutional doctrines. The Supreme Court—"that great tribunal . . . before whose decisions all parties and all factions must give way"—had determined that the territories belonged "no less to the people of the Southern than to those of the Northern States." The decision, predicted the Richmond *Whig,* would "set at final rest all those vexed Constitutional questions" associated with the controversy over slavery. The Charleston *Mercury* gloated that proslavery radicals had been "simply a step in advance" of the Supreme Court "in declaring what was the law of the land, and seeking honestly and faithfully to enforce it." Best of all, wrote another editor, the decision "puts the whole basis of the Black Republican organization under the ban of the law, . . . and forms a basis upon which all conservative men of the Union can unite." To defy the Court would be treason, a subversion of law and order.[59]

Moral and constitutional vindication, however, was not easily translated into a tangible southern advantage. In the months after the Court's decision slaveholders rarely moved their slaves into the territories that were legally open to them, and the slave population of Kansas actually declined. While the Court was still deliberating the case several southern Congressmen, among them James L. Orr of South Carolina, had observed that merely prohibiting congressional or territorial exclusion laws would have little effect. Anticipating Douglas's famous Freeport Doctrine of 1858, Orr noted that every slaveholding community protected the rights of the master with a code of laws and police regulations, "without which the institution would not only be valueless, but a curse to the community." But if a slaveholder were denied that protection, he would be "as well excluded as if the power was vested in the Territorial legislature, and exercised by them to prohibit it." A Kentucky editor knew of no power "to compel a Legislature to act when they are determined not to act." The secessionist Charleston *Mercury* was perhaps not altogether disappointed when it confessed that, for the "practical attainment" of southern rights, the Dred Scott decision was "just so many idle words."[60]

Nevertheless, by firmly upholding the Supreme Court as the final arbiter of all constitutional issues (rather than the sovereign states, as Calhoun had done), Southerners had raised the stakes in the next presidential election. Suppose a new President had the opportunity to change the composition of the Court; suppose the new Court, no more partisan than the old, found the ruling in the Dred Scott case on the authority of Congress over slavery in the territories extrajudicial and rejected it; suppose Congress, with the blessing of the Court, then prohibited slavery in all the territories. By their own repeated declarations, the choice open to Southerners would be acquiescence or revolution. Thus, even their victory over what many of them perceived as mere constitutional abstractions was far from secure.

Among northern Democrats, a few editors were openly critical of the Dred Scott decision, or denied that their party was responsible for it, or elected to ignore it. George Bancroft was certain that the Chief Justice, "so far as history is concerned," was "altogether in the wrong," especially in saying that white men "ever regarded the black race as having no rights." The South, he thought, had gained nothing from the "extreme notions" put forth by the Court, while north-ern Democrats had been "dreadfully routed in consequence."[61] A few others, such as the New York *Herald* and the administration organ, the Washington *Union,* joined Southerners in giving the opinion of the Court unqualified support. Caleb Cushing, Pierce's Attorney General, defending the decision in a speech at New-buryport, declared that the Court deserved the country's "profound respect," praised the justices for their "exalted character," and described the Chief Justice as "the very incarnation of judicial purity, integrity, science and wisdom."[62]

Most northern Democratic editors and politicians, while praising the Court and claiming vindication of their party's principles, read the opinion not quite as Taney had written it. They wholeheartedly embraced his ruling on Negro citi-zenship, claiming it to be a doctrine "entertained and promulgated by the dem-ocratic party" and celebrating it with an outburst of racial demagoguery. "The Black Republican party favor the full *citizenship* of the negro—the Democracy oppose it," asserted the Indianapolis *Indiana State Sentinal;* that was the funda-mental issue between them. The decision, according to the Detroit *Free Press,* destroyed "the underpinnings of negro worship" and prostrated "that detestable ism in the dirt." Douglas described the settlement of the Negro-citizenship ques-tion as the "main proposition" of the decision. "No one," he said "can vindicate the character, motives and conduct of the signers of the Declaration of Indepen-dence, except upon the hypothesis that they referred to the white race alone."[63]

Northern Democrats were equally enthusiastic about the Court's invalida-tion of the Missouri Compromise and other congressional restrictions on slavery in the territories. The decision, claimed the Cincinnati *Enquirer,* was a "complete vindication" of the Kansas-Nebraska Act, which had "only swept an illegal and unconstitutional measure from the statute book." How could the Republican party survive, asked the Sacramento *Union,* "without materially modifying their articles of political faith?" Never before, exulted Douglas's Chicago *Times,* had the "creed of an entire political party [been] swept away from the consideration of all honest people, by the solemn and profound adjudication of the supreme tribunal." Only "wild and reckless agitators," Republicans were warned, would defy the Supreme Court, "one of the most important branches of their government."[64] These editors wrote with the conviction of recent converts, for it was not until the passage of the Kansas-Nebraska Act in 1854 that most northern Democrats, including Senator Douglas, had begun to question the constitutionality of the Missouri Compromise. A few years earlier Douglas had called it "sacred."

After praising the opinion of the Court on Negro citizenship and the limits of congressional power in the territories, the Detroit *Free Press* noted in passing that it had also covered some other matters which were merely "incidental or subsidiary" to these. In this manner most northern Democratic spokesmen chose to disregard Taney's (and Buchanan's) embarrassing assertion that territorial legislatures had no more power than Congress to prohibit slavery prior to statehood—a clear invalidation of popular sovereignty as they understood its meaning. Ignoring the taunts of Republicans, the Chicago *Times* asserted that the Court had ruled that the platform of the Democratic party, which left "the final determination of the existence or non-existence of slavery . . . with the people of a territory," was constitutionally "true and legitimate." The *Indiana State Sentinel* boldly insisted that the "great doctrine" of popular sovereignty had been "approved, affirmed, sanctioned and established" as the "salutary rule" for all the territories.[65]

One resourceful Democratic editor revised Taney's opinion on territorial jurisdiction over slavery to make it more palatable to his readers. Taney, he claimed, simply meant "that whilst a territory remains a territory—*if there are local laws to protect it*—slaves may be holden there. That is all." Douglas, however, in a major speech at Springfield, Illinois, on June 12, chose neither to disregard nor distort Taney's *dictum*. Rather, echoing the words of various Southerners, such as James L. Orr, he gave the substance of what became his Freeport Doctrine during his debates with Abraham Lincoln the following year. Yielding to the opinion of the Court, Douglas agreed that the slaveholder's right to carry his property into the territories continued "in full force under the guarantees of the Constitution." But this right, he said, remained "barren and worthless . . . unless sustained, protected and enforced by appropriate police regulations and local legislation," and these "must necessarily depend upon the will and wishes of the people of the Territory." Accordingly, Douglas concluded, "the great principle of popular sovereignty and self-government" was "sustained and firmly established by the authority of this decision."[66]

Eventually proslavery Southerners would respond with a demand for congressional *protection* of slavery in the territories to implement the opinion of the Court, but at the time of its delivery Douglas's speech won more praise than criticism from them. Meanwhile, without denying the constitutional rights claimed by southern slaveholders, he had managed to assure northern Democrats that popular sovereignty, as they defined it, was compatible with the Dred Scott decision, and that slavery would not be forced upon an unwilling majority in any territory. As a result, although most northern and southern Democrats continued to interpret popular sovereignty in different ways, Taney's opinion, by itself, did not disrupt their national organization.

To understand the impact of the Dred Scott decision on the Republicans, one needs only recall that their chief unifying principle, as stated in their Philadelphia platform the previous year, was that Congress had "both the right and the imperative duty" to exclude slavery, that "relic of barbarism," from the territories. Accordingly, for all practical purposes, the opinion of the Court, as Democrats freely advised, was an order to their party to disband.

Republicans responded with angry defiance. Congressman John F. Potter of Wisconsin called the decision "sheer blasphemy . . . an infamous libel on our government . . . a lasting disgrace to the court from which it issued, and deeply humiliating to every American citizen." It was, according to the New York *Tribune,* "entitled to just so much moral weight as would be the judgment of a majority of those congregated in any Washington barroom." A Boston Republican asserted that the opinions of this proslavery Court deserved no more respect "than those of any other sectional caucus of partisans." The Chicago *Tribune* branded Taney's opinion "shocking to the sensibilities and aspirations of lovers of freedom and humanity," for it set back "the current of progressive ideas and christian humanity" and threatened a renewal "of the iniquitous despotism . . . of barbarian ages."[67]

The dissenting opinions of Curtis and McLean were soon available in pamphlet form, and Republicans gave them wide circulation. Other lengthy dissents soon appeared, among them a sharp attack on the Court by Timothy Farrar, a Boston lawyer, published in the *North American Review*. Farrar doubted that the decision would have any practical significance, except that the public would no longer believe in "the sound judicial integrity and strictly legal character of their tribunals." Thomas Hart Benton, though dying of cancer, turned on his former Jacksonian colleague, the Chief Justice, and wrote a short, heavily documented book strongly defending the constitutionality of the Missouri Compromise and claiming broad powers for Congress over the territories. Among the numerous assaults on the Court from northern pulpits, the most sensational was a series of four sermons by the Rev. Dr. George B. Cheever, pastor of the Church of the Puritans in New York City. Cheever justified violent resistance to the Court's decision if necessary, for the laws of God must be upheld against those of a wicked government.[68]

Most of the northern legislatures controlled by Republicans registered additional formal protests. In Maine, both the legislature and the state supreme court dissented. The New York legislature adopted resolutions declaring Taney's opinion "erroneous" and claiming that the Court had "lost the confidence and respect of the people of this State." In Ohio the legislature not only denounced the decision but adopted measures against slaveholding or the kidnapping of free blacks, and the supreme court ruled that any slave brought into Ohio would automatically be emancipated. State Republican conventions in Ohio and Wisconsin, after hearing party orators deliver scathing attacks on the Court's decision, adopted platforms containing sweeping dissents.[69]

The burden of most Republican protests was that the Dred Scott decision had wrought a profound change in the status of slavery in the American republic. The Revolutionary Fathers and the framers of the Constitution, they recalled, had viewed slavery as a temporary evil and anticipated its rapid decline. Their feelings of moral repugnance to the institution were evident in their candid acknowledgment of the equality of all men in the Declaration of Independence, and in their refusal to use the word *slave* in the Constitution. As long as slavery survived, they intended it to be a local institution subject to the laws of individual states—laws that had no validity beyond their borders. In short, in their political order, freedom was national and slavery was local. The Supreme Court, however, by extending the laws of the slave states over the territories, had reversed that order and made freedom local and slavery national. Its decision, said the New York *Evening Post*, had transformed what had once been the South's "peculiar institution" into "a federal institution, the common patrimony and shame of all the states." According to the Milwaukee *Sentinel*, the government of the United States now stood "before the world as a government whose flag carries slavery wherever it waves!"[70]

Two logical corollaries to the recognition of slavery as a national institution, many Republicans warned, would be the reopening of the African slave trade, and, in due course, the introduction of slavery into every state of the Union. The opinion of the Court would furnish sufficient grounds for the owners of slaves to claim the right to hold them in the free states not only as temporary sojourners but as permanent residents. If the Constitution recognized slaves as property, in no respect different from other property, reasoned the Chicago *Tribune*, "then no State Court, Legislature, or State Constitution can deprive the owner of such slave property . . . in any State into which he may see proper to emigrate." In the light of the Court's opinion, no state law could prevent someone from "opening a slave pen and an auction block for the sale of black men, women and children right here in Chicago." Carl Schurz foresaw the day when slaves would be seen "working side by side with the freeman on the beautiful fields of Pennsylvania, and on the broad prairies of Illinois." Then Georgia's Senator Robert Toombs would prove his boast that one day he would "call the roll of his slaves under the shadow of the Bunker Hill monument."[71]

To Republicans the Dred Scott decision was the last in a chain of sinister events beginning with the annexation of Texas and including the War with Mexico, the passage of the Fugitive Slave Act of 1850, and the adoption of the Kansas-

Nebraska Act. Each event, they claimed, was part of a conspiracy promoted by the southern Slave Power and assisted by its northern doughface allies. The ultimate goal of the conspirators was the conversion of the American republic into a slave empire ruled by "a pampered and powerful oligarchy of some 350,000 Slaveholders." The fact that Taney's decision had been rendered soon after Buchanan's inauguration was not fortuitous, for there had been an understanding between them—in Seward's words, "a coalition . . . to undermine the National Legislature and the liberties of the people." On inauguration day, spectators were "unaware of the import of the whisperings carried on between the President and the Chief Justice." Two days later, Seward noted, the Court ruled that the Missouri Compromise violated the rights of slaveholders in the territories, thus making their rights "paramount to the authority of Congress." Here was evidence, charged the New York *Evening Post,* that the Supreme Court had joined the administration in a conspiracy "of the most treasonable character." Thus far had the conspiracy progressed, wrote another editor. "To what lengths it may yet go, we cannot tell, for the democratic party in the past has always yielded to every demand of the Slave Power."[72]

Republican leaders were more cautious in their attacks on Taney for his opinion on Negro citizenship than they were for his invalidation of the Missouri Compromise. In a society sorely afflicted with Negrophobia, their party was already vulnerable to Democratic racial demagoguery—to charges that its freesoil platform was a mask to conceal their ultimate goal of racial equality, both political and social. Actually, Republicans were themselves guilty of more than a little racism, for many of them opposed either the enfranchisement of free blacks or their full social integration. Even so, they rarely showed sympathy for Taney's rash assertion that at the time of the Revolution persons of African descent, free or slave, had possessed no rights which white men were bound to respect. The New York state legislature voiced an almost unanimous Republican protest when it denounced this proposition as *"inhuman, unchristian, atrocious*—disgraceful to the Judge who uttered it, and to the tribunal which sanctioned it."[73] Republicans usually accused Taney of describing a present rather than a past condition, but since he denied United States citizenship and the "unalienable rights" affirmed in the Declaration of Independence to blacks of his own day, their error was hardly significant.

Some Republican protests went a good deal further. They rejected Taney's denial to a person of African descent "the possible right of citizenship of the United States," thereby "closing the door of national justice to him as an outlaw." Lincoln, in a speech at Springfield on June 26, insisted that, contrary to Douglas, the authors of the Declaration of Independence "intended to include *all* men." They did not declare men "equal *in all respects,"* but claimed them to be "equal in 'certain inalienable rights, among which are life, liberty, and the pursuit of happiness.' This they said and this they meant." One reason for the Chicago

Tribune's objection to Taney's opinion was its legalization "of the 'prejudice of color,' which is not only without the shadow of support from the Constitution of the United States, but is condemned by the increasing light of civilization." Free blacks were "left to the mercy of every ruffian," complained a New England editor, "to suffer without redress, every indignity and wrong that can be heaped upon them." No nation, he warned, could "contain within itself an abased caste, without being itself tainted with their abasement."[74] From sentiments such as these Democrats built their indictment of "Black" Republicans as racial "amalgamationists."

Republicans met the challenge of the Dred Scott decision to their existence as a party in two different and somewhat conflicting ways. First, they attacked the Court for infringing upon the legislative authority of Congress. "From being expounders, they have become makers of the law," complained one editor. "It requires but a moderate degree of ingenuity on the part of any judge to make a plausible argument in justification of any decision required by personal or party interest." Another editor found "something prophetic in Jefferson's frequent warnings against the encroaching tendencies of the Supreme Court," its disposition "to enlarge its jurisdiction." Some party leaders suggested specific reforms, such as requiring the appointment of justices in proportion to the population of the North and South, or providing for the election of judges for a fixed term. Senator Trumbull of Illinois appealed to a power higher than the Court, "The People," who would in due time "reform this sectional court by increasing the number of Judges, or otherwise placing upon the bench a fair proportion of Northern members." One way or another, the Chicago *Tribune* promised, the people would recover their lawmaking prerogatives—"and if the ousting of a Bench full of Pro-Slavery judges is necessary to a resumption of this right, let it be done with as little delay as possible."[75]

However, reforming the federal courts would be a slow and difficult process, and Republicans meanwhile would expose themselves to charges of recklessly assaulting the judicial branch of the government. Consequently they resorted more frequently to an immediate remedy which Justices Curtis and McLean had presented to them in their dissenting opinions: they argued that once the Court had disclaimed jurisdiction over the Dred Scott case, its opinion on the constitutionality of the Missouri Compromise was *obiter dictum* and therefore not binding. Timothy Farrar's essay in the *North American Review* reasoned that if Negroes were not citizens and could not sue, that necessarily would be the end of the case. "There is nothing afterwards before the court to be judicially adjudicated or considered. The parties are out of court. . . . Anything else done afterwards is extrajudicial. It cannot affect parties or their rights, and is of no consequence to anyone, unless it be to the newspapers and debating clubs." In a typical editorial a Republican journal professed respect for the Supreme Court and agreed that its decisions, when "lawful and binding," must be accepted as the law of the land. But its opinion on the Missouri Compromise, "being founded on no case actually before the court . . . is nothing more than the opinion of so many private men." Accordingly, as another editor boldly affirmed, the Republican party would "continue to assert, with unabated confidence . . . that it is the right and duty of Congress to provide Governments for Territories and to secure justice and extend liberty, by prohibiting Slavery therein."[76]

In addition, Republicans took full advantage of their opportunity to ridicule Senator Douglas for his "contemptible quibble" in trying to reconcile his "great principle" of popular sovereignty with the Dred Scott decision. He "wriggles in and wriggles out in a manner which is most pitiful," observed the *Illinois State Journal;* but if he agreed that slaves could be held as property in the territories, how could territorial governments refuse to protect the slaveholders? Every territorial officer took an oath to support the Constitution of the United States. Hence, if the Constitution authorized slavery in the territories, how could they, "in consistency with their oaths, defeat its intention? . . . How absurd it is, then, to talk of popular sovereignty!"[77]

Convinced that the Supreme Court's Dred Scott decision, together with recent events in the territory of Kansas, had clearly revealed the aggressive intentions of the southern Slave Power, northern antislavery forces anticipated substantial accretions of public support. "[The] fiercer the insult, the bitterer the blow, the better," exulted one abolitionist journal. "If anything can galvanize [the country] into vitality again, it will be a succession of shocks like that." Speaking before the American Anti-Slavery Society in New York, Frederick Douglass noted that the history of the movement proved that "all measures devised and executed with a view to . . . diminish the anti-slavery agitation, have only served to increase, intensify, and embolden that agitation." Even a conservative Boston Whig wondered how abolitionists could be denied the right to campaign against slavery in the southern states if slavery were a national rather than a local institution.[78]

The more moderately antislavery Republicans also expected the Dred Scott case to win new converts to their party. That "outrageous" decision, one of them claimed, was "the best thing that could have happened." In their journals and on the stump party leaders sent out their message: "The remedy is—UNION, ACTION, AND THE BALLOT BOX!" Let the North elect a Congress united for freedom, let the next President be a Republican, "and 1860 will mark an era kindred with that of 1776." If the Slave Power's hold on the federal government were to be broken, northern voters "must lay aside all differences of opinion on other questions, and rally as one man . . . for the overthrow of the Oligarchy and its allies in the free States." Southerners insisted that slavery agitation must cease; yet, Republicans charged, they had themselves provoked it for their own purposes through their proslavery Court. They demanded that the North "give way without protest, and without resistance," but that was no longer possible. "The agitation and excitement can never cease till Freedom is made national and Slavery completely sectionalized."[79]

The Dred Scott decision brought the post-election political lull, which had prevailed in the early weeks of 1857, to an abrupt end. Taney's invalidation of the Missouri Compromise was unquestionably a major milestone in the developing sectional crisis of the 1850s. As much as any previous event, it lent credence to the charge of abolitionists and Republicans that the southern Slave Power conspired to make slavery a national institution. Yet, in spite of the fact that the decision evoked widespread apprehension and much anger in the North, Republican attacks on the Court majority seemed to bring the party little additional support. In fact, in several northern state elections later that year, Republicans either won by a reduced majority or suffered a clear defeat.

That the decision of the Court made less of an impact on the northern electorate than events in Kansas the previous year was doubtless due to its failure to ignite a struggle over the status of slavery in any existing territory. Since it did not affect the right of territories to prohibit slavery when they were ready for statehood, it had no bearing on affairs in Minnesota or Oregon, and it brought no significant influx of slaves to territories elsewhere. Thus Taney's opinion, however provocative, produced no concrete results. Moreover, though long exploited by Republicans, it was soon overshadowed by another bitter controversy over affairs in Kansas—a controversy that produced a far more decisive national crisis. In retrospect, the Dred Scott case, though the sensation of the spring, did not prove to be the crucial political event of 1857.

CHAPTER 5

The Heart of the Matter: Slavery and Sectionalism

The debate between the sections and political parties over the Dred Scott case, though often shrill and hyperbolic, nevertheless clearly illustrated both the substantive issues that divided North and South and the manner in which the parties tried to deal with them. Whether or not the Court's decision would have any practical significance for the existing territories, the various reactions to the case did make clear—as the Kansas controversy had done the year before—the centrality of the slavery issue in the sectional conflict. The issue assumed many forms. Northern abolitionists aimed their attacks directly at slavery in the southern states, denouncing it as immoral and its survival as a national disgrace. Most Republicans, who did not consider themselves to be abolitionists, hoped to promote its ultimate extinction indirectly by preventing its expansion, or by resisting enforcement of the Fugitive Slave Act. Others avoided frontal assaults by stressing only the need to check the aggressions of the southern Slave Power. Proslavery Southerners, not without reason, claimed to see no significant difference between these several forms of attack, regarding each as a dangerous threat, varying only in its degree of subtlety.

Southern editors, politicians, and literary champions, in turn, frequently elected not to speak directly of the need to defend slavery but stressed instead the more abstract and elevated concepts of southern honor or constitutional rights. In most cases the terms were interchangeable, for as they were generally used the concepts of rights and honor were almost invariably linked to slavery. The Richmond *Enquirer* made the linkage explicit when it argued that secession would be justified "only when the honor of the slave states" was "outraged by a Black Republican control of the country.... Let Congress enact another boundary line, beyond which slavery shall not go, and we would say repeal it, or the

South should go out of the Union." Similarly, Alexander H. Stephens insisted that the territorial issue was important not so much because he expected slavery to expand westward, but because it involved the important principle of "constitutional right and equality. . . . A people who would maintain their rights must look to principles much more than to practical results." But Stephens also linked his principles to slavery. "If the slightest encroachments of power are permitted or submitted to in the Territories," he warned, "they may reach the states ultimately."[1]

Republicans often anticipated Seward's assertion the following year that an "irrepressible conflict" divided the advocates of free and slave labor, as well as Lincoln's declaration, in his "House Divided" speech, that the Union could not survive half slave and half free but would become "*all* one thing, or *all* the other." The Chicago *Tribune* claimed that the sectional conflict was "no accident" but sprang "from the contest between nonslaveholders and . . . the Oligarchs who rule upon *Slave Labor*." Sectionalism, wrote another Republican editor, had destroyed the old political parties and rendered their platforms obsolete, "and now nothing remains but an issue upon the great principles of humanity and liberty as opposed to wrong and slavery." A substantial segment of the Republican electorate seemed to believe that slavery, or slavery expansion, or the Slave Power, or some combination of these, was not only the central issue in national politics but the sole issue. One of Seward's correspondents described a single Republican goal: to "contest every inch of ground, expose every scheme of the slave power, and keep the public mind agitated on the great question of freedom." Looking to 1860, another expected a Republican victory to be the dawn of the day when "that blighting curse of slavery shall be swept from our fair and fertile land."[2]

Proslavery Southerners could, on occasion, speak with equal bluntness about what was at the heart of the sectional conflict. It involved "but one subject," wrote an Alabama editor, and that was slavery. "Other questions may for a time occasion agitation . . . but they can never result in a disruption of the Union." The tariff, federal appropriations for internal improvements, and national banks, said the editor of *De Bow's Review*, were "but means of ordinary oppression," which the minority South might have to endure. "Slavery restriction and slavery extinction, on the other hand, . . . [would drive] the South back, at a single step, into worse than barbarism." No nation could survive, a Texas Congressman believed, "unless a preponderant majority of its members be one in fundamental opinion."[3]

In a series of editorials the Richmond *Enquirer* developed its own version of the irrepressible conflict. "The slavery question," it claimed, was "the single source of all the intestine trouble" which endangered the Union. For the past fifty years slavery agitation had been "growing greater and fiercer and wilder, widening its circle with each succeeding year." As a result the North and South were "divided into two antagonistic sections," between whom there existed "an intensity of animosity" seldom found "even among separate and distinct nations in times of peace." The *Enquirer* saw a national crisis rapidly approaching and believed that the presidential election of 1860 would, "in all probability, determine the result." In that contest "the dangerous doctrines of abolitionism" must be defeated, or the South would "secede at once" and form a southern republic.[4]

Abolitionists, Republicans, and proslavery Southerners, of course, did not speak for the entire body politic. Conservative old Whigs and northern Democrats emphatically rejected the concept of an irrepressible conflict. They denied that the slavery controversy in its various guises had been spontaneously generated by an aroused electorate, thereby forcing reluctant politicians to take up the proslavery or antislavery cause. Rather, they charged, certain opportunistic northern and southern politicians had themselves politicized slavery. Then, for their own partisan purposes, they had exploited the resulting sectional conflict and turned the attention of voters away from more important issues. Northern conservatives accused Republican leaders of recklessly resorting to slavery agitation in order to form a new sectional party through which they hoped to win political power. Their platform needlessly called for the exclusion of slavery from territories that were geographically and climatically unsuited for it. Abolitionist agitation, they claimed, merely intensified the southern defense of slavery, thus postponing the time when natural forces would bring about its demise.

Edward Everett viewed the sectional conflict from this perspective. "In all this wretched struggle," he wrote, "it is mournful to reflect that the real difficulties spring more from the selfish passions of men than the necessities of the case." In the border states, slavery was already declining from "natural causes." If only "intemperate and too often unprincipled agitation of the subject for electioneering purposes at the North could be stopped, Slavery would disappear in 5 years in several of them." Thomas P. Akers, a Democratic Congressman from Missouri, complained of the Republicans' pointless "lectures on the ethics of slavery." He had hoped that they would cease "at least until capital is needed for another presidential campaign." Serious national problems demanded the attention of Congress, he said, yet that body ignored them and engaged in a "driveling discussion" of slavery, which all knew could have no other effect than to "deepen the animosity and embitter the strife" between the sections. From the conservative perspective, then, slavery was not the fundamental cause of the sectional conflict. Rather, the politicians and other antislavery agitators were themselves the cause, for they brought it on deliberately, needlessly, and irresponsibly.[5]

Implicit in this conservative explanation was the assumption that there were national problems of greater importance than slavery on which Republicans should have focused, that other available issues would have resonated with voters quite as effectively, that politicians were free to create and politicize whatever issues they pleased, and that they probably would have fared as well with one issue as another. Yet, the inability of the remnants of the Whig party, after the decline of nativism, to find and effectively politicize alternative issues, discredited their indictment of antislavery Republicans. Among Democrats no politician tried more desperately than Stephen A. Douglas to keep slavery out of national politics; yet he was obliged repeatedly to grapple with it. Before the end of the year 1857, his own Illinois constituents *forced* him to take a stand on one slavery issue or risk the loss of his Senate seat. Politicians, in fact, can successfully politicize only those issues that have real or at least symbolic significance, and then only when external conditions make them relevant to the concerns of their constituents. Those who joined the slavery debate in one or another of its forms understood not only their constituents but the social climate of the mid-nineteenth-century Western world far better than their critics.

By the year 1857 southern slavery had existed for more than two centuries and was then an entrenched and flourishing institution, providing most of the labor for the production of the South's staple crops. Nearly 400,000 masters had a capital investment of $2 billion in nearly 4,000,000 slaves distributed over fifteen southern states. Their "peculiar institution," as they called it, had survived the American Revolution, the abolition of slavery everywhere in the New World except Brazil, Cuba, Puerto Rico, and Dutch Guiana, early manumission movements in the southern states themselves, and many years of organized northern abolitionist agitation. The constitutional right of each state to regulate its own domestic institutions protected slaveholders from federal interference—except that they demanded, and received, federal assistance, through the Fugitive Slave Act of 1850, in recovering runaways. Over the years southern politicians, publicists, clergymen, and men of letters had developed a systematic defense of slavery as a benign and socially beneficial institution for which the South need make no apology. Arguing from the Scriptures, historical experience, economic necessity, scientific evidence, and social theory, they had produced a vast body of writing—probably more extensive than in any other slaveholding country—to prove that slavery was not merely a necessary and temporary evil but a positive good.

"There was a time," recalled the Richmond *Enquirer,* "when not a few of the wisest and best men of Virginia concurred in the opinion that negro slavery was an evil." After further investigation, however, opinion changed, and slavery was accepted "not as a 'mildew, a blight and scourge,' but a social, political and moral blessing, a special boon of Providence both to the African and Anglo Saxon races." A Virginia clergyman confessed that after having been all his life a "quasi-abolitionist," he had recently been influenced by the Scriptural defense and concluded that he had been "in error." He was greatly relieved, for in the past his conscience had been "more or less offended by slavery."[6]

Yet, the defense could never rest its case, for the proslavery argument always seemed to require additional props or further embellishment to disarm potential opposition from within the South or to refute the ceaseless attacks from without. If critics marshaled statistics to show that the slave states lagged behind the North in education, railroad building, manufacturing, and commerce, the defense preferred a standard "less gross" than material development by which to judge a people. Virginians prized their "personal virtues and individual dignity," the "traditional glory" of their state, "the valor of her sons . . . the moral ascendancy which she maintains in the confederacy." If critics described the South as undemocratic, the defense replied that the conservative, stabilizing influence of slavery was "essential to the existence of a legitimate republic," for it served as a "counterpoise" to the "dangerous tendencies" of white manhood suffrage and the potential "evils of Red Republicanism." If critics attacked slavery as cruel and unjust, the defense portrayed the institution as a "Patriarchal form of Society" which fostered "affection and confidence" between masters and slaves and provided the latter with "all the comforts, and even luxuries known not to their wants only, but to their desires." If critics appealed to southern nonslaveholders for support, the defense confidently asserted that they were as "prompt and resolute . . . in resisting the Abolitionists and sustaining Southern rights" as their slaveholding neighbors.[7]

White Southerners, an intensely religious people, most of them affiliated with the Baptist, Methodist, and Presbyterian churches, were particularly sensitive to abolitionist attacks on slavery as unchristian. The issue had already divided northern and southern Baptists and Methodists, and in 1857 the New School Presbyterians also split along sectional lines after their General Assembly, at a meeting in Cleveland, resolved that the holding of slaves was contrary to church doctrines. Southern members then organized their own General Assembly, because, as one editor explained, they did not wish "to contaminate the pulpit with politics." Alabama Methodists were reassured when their Conference voted to expunge from their discipline the rule forbidding "the buying and selling of men, women, and children, with an intention to enslave them." These matters were not the proper concern of Christian churches, wrote a Virginian, for Christ, while on earth, had not "troubled himself with the political or social condition of men." Since slavery existed in His day, it was "inconceivable that he should not have said that the system was wrong, if it was so in fact."[8]

Proslavery partisans almost invariably stressed the racial basis of their institution—the need for white masters to control an inferior race for the benefit of both. Slavery alone, they said, would preserve the South's Anglo-Saxon culture and prevent the disaster of racial assimilation. Hence, the lot of blacks in America was "one of inevitable subordination to the whites." All who understood them, claimed a Texas Congressman, knew that they would not work "unless under the pressure of physical compulsion." Since to blacks freedom would simply mean freedom from toil, they would attempt to survive by "theft, rapine, or beggary," thus exposing the country to "terrific outrages of crime and disorder," and eventually to "exterminating strife." Africans were *"a race in childhood,"* exhibiting "all the simplicity, credulity, and unreflecting instincts of the child, with a nature as little complicated and as easily analyzed." Why, then, asked a Kentucky editor, would any "wise and humane man take the responsibility of abolishing slavery in the South?"[9]

And how did free blacks fare in the northern states? asked the defenders of slavery. Which of them treated blacks as social or political equals? "What Northern State desires them as inhabitants, or does more than tolerate them, as a nuisance they would gladly be rid of?" "Ye hypocrites," scoffed a Kentucky editor, "reform yourselves, before you preach to us." On the other hand, the fact that many northern abolitionists did advocate political and social equality for blacks led one proslavery writer to deplore them as "a sad commentary upon [northern] civilization. When white men can come down to a brotherhood and companionship with negroes . . . it would almost seem that society itself is as yet an experiment, threatened with failure."[10]

Abolitionism, said slavery's defenders, was only one of many signs of the North's social degradation. "Python," in an essay titled "The Relative Moral and Social Status of the North and South," described the North as far more "socialistic, and communistic, or if you please, purely democratic" than the South. One could detect in northern society a "standard of licentiousness . . . which characterized that of Rome just prior to the commencement of anarchy and civil war." In contrast, wrote Elwood Fisher of Virginia, the "elevated rural society of the South," produced a people notable for "a warm heart and open hand, for sympathy of feeling, fidelity of friendship, and high sense of honor . . . and when the North comes into action with the South, man to man, in council or in the field, the genius of the South has prevailed." Slavery was the foundation upon which the South's social edifice was built, and it could only be removed "by tearing and rending asunder the elements of Southern society—destroying its civilization and progress, its safety and happiness, its very existence."[11]

In this manner proslavery partisans waged their endless battle against critics whom they could neither convert nor conquer. By 1857 the *Southern Literary Messenger,* a monthly published in Richmond and once dedicated exclusively to literature, science, and art, was devoting much of its space to essays defending the South and black bondage. *De Bow's Review,* another monthly, had begun publication in New Orleans in 1846 to promote southern industry, commerce, and agriculture, vowing to ignore sectional politics. Within a few years it, too, had opened its columns to both secessionists and the most zealous defenders of slavery.

The year 1857 marked the publication of two additional book-length defenses of slavery. Dr. Josiah C. Nott and George R. Gliddon, ethnologists and prominent members of the so-called American school of anthropology, had already written articles and an earlier book, *Types of Mankind* (1854), claiming that Negroes belonged to a separate species of man, a species innately inferior to that of the Caucasian. To the dismay of some orthodox proslavery Christians, they advanced, in these and in a second book, *Indigenous Races of the Earth* (1857), a theory of polygenesis, which denied the Old Testament account of creation.

One of slavery's more extreme partisans, George Fitzhugh of Virginia, while contributing numerous essays to the Richmond *Enquirer* and *De Bow's Review*, had published *Sociology for the South; or, the Failure of Free Society* (1854), and three years later he published a second book, *Cannibals All! or, Slaves Without Masters*. Fitzhugh argued that the northern and British working classes would have been better off under a paternalistic system of slavery than they were under ruthless capitalist masters in a so-called free society. But he took pains to assure white Southerners that in their biracial society he advocated only the continued enslavement of the inferior black laboring class. The South, Fitzhugh confidently predicted, would "lead the thought and direct the practices of christendom," which would eventually see that it had "acted a silly and suicidal part in abolishing African slavery—the South a wise and prudent one in retaining it." To accomplish their goal he acknowledged that Southerners would have to "disprove and refute the whole social, ethical, political, and economic philosophy of the day."[12]

Fitzhugh boldly asked the question that arose logically from the southern proslavery argument: Could one defend black slavery and at the same time denounce as immoral the African slave trade that had made it possible? Was it piracy deserving capital punishment, as federal law provided, "to buy idle, savage cannibals in Africa, bring them to America, subject them to a milder slavery, colonize, christianize, and make them useful and industrious beings[?]" Was the importation of slaves from Africa, others asked, in any way less moral than the legal interstate slave trade between the Upper South and the Deep South? Edmund Ruffin thought that the suffering and cruelty associated with the African slave trade could be prevented and the "middle passage" made "comfortable" if it were made legal and properly regulated.[13]

The great majority of proslavery Southerners were appalled that anyone would even suggest the reopening of a trade that had been prohibited for half a century. Yet, by 1857 some of the more ardent spirits, most of them from the Deep South, were advocating the repeal of the federal restriction and the importation of additional black laborers. A committee of the South Carolina legislature reported that the interests of the South required the trade to be reopened, but after a sharp debate the report was tabled. The legislatures of Alabama and Texas considered resolutions of a similar nature but took no action. Leonidas W. Spratt of South Carolina raised the question at a southern commercial convention that met in Knoxville, but the delegates only agreed to appoint him chairman of a committee to consider the matter.[14]

The movement to reopen the African slave trade, whatever its proslavery logic, was a flight from political reality, an embarrassment to the South, and served no purpose other than fortifying the abolitionist and Republican charge that free labor was threatened by an aggressive Slave Power. A South Carolina Congressman, William W. Boyce, tried to repair the damage with a resolution, approved by a vote of 125 to 8, asserting that public opinion in both the North and South was "utterly opposed to the reopening of the slave trade." Governor Herschel V. Johnson of Georgia asked his legislature to consider the harm that could result from agitating this question. The trade, he said, was "adverse to the sentiments of the civilized world," and to support it would divide the South, alienate northern Democrats, and "rouse to a still higher pitch the prejudices of other nations against us."[15]

Although northern antislavery leaders made a plausible case for the presence in the South of an aggressive Slave Power, proslavery partisans were in fact on the defensive, at least ideologically, most of the time. They complained that both northern literary journals and the school books marketed by northern publishers were tainted with an antisouthern bias. These books, charged the Richmond *Enquirer,* were "brimful . . . of a sickly sentimental philanthropy" and indoctrinated southern children with "antislavery sentiments, and a false social philosophy from their earliest years." Moreover, the South had been too dependent on northern-trained teachers. It needed teachers "born upon Southern soil, educated at Southern schools, [and] familiar with Southern society." The duty of both parents and teachers, wrote an Alabama editor, was to instruct southern youth that slavery was "both wise and humane . . . the foundation and fortress of the South in all her interests and relations." Every book "which in words or by implication" taught otherwise "should be burned or banished instantly."[16]

Except in a few border states, the time had long since passed when southern editors, politicians, teachers, clergymen, or private citizens could publicly advocate even the gradual abolition of slavery. Southern postmasters repeatedly refused to distribute antislavery literature. During the presidential election of 1856, Benjamin S. Hedrick, professor of chemistry at the University of North Carolina, was condemned by his colleagues and dismissed by the administration for supporting the candidacy of John C. Frémont. In the summer of 1857 the editor of the Quitman *Texas Free Press* was driven from the state, as he claimed, "for daring to allow . . . the free discussion of Slavery . . . and for declaring Editorially that such free discussion was the inalienable right of free men." An indignant North Carolina slaveholder canceled his subscription to the *Missionary Herald,* because its criticism of slavery was "hastening the arrival of one of the bloodiest revolutions ever known in the history of man."[17]

One of the striking features of the proslavery South was the inability of its white citizens, through their press, politicians, and literature, clearly and consistently to define themselves—to determine what it was that gave them their distinct identity. Some celebrated the American Revolutionary tradition, others rejected it. Some spoke as patriotic nationalists, others as extreme sectionalists. Some boasted of the South's economic fluidity, social mobility, and countless self-made men; others proudly described their society as stable, conservative, and aristocratic. Some promoted factories, railroads, and shipping lines and believed in economic "progress" as ardently as Yankees; others romanticized a static, traditional, agrarian civilization. Entrepreneurial slaveholders produced staple crops for world markets through the most commercialized large-scale agricultural system in the country; yet their propagandists described them as a class of hedonistic, open-handed patriarchs living by some precapitalist code of values.

The identity problem diminished considerably when a white Southerner, forgetting his section's slave population, simply defined himself as a citizen of the American republic and professed his faith in its providential mission to mankind. In that mood a Tennessee editor could write: "We are on the right side of all the great questions that agitate the world. . . . Kings and oppressors are in dread of our power. Humanity, groaning under tyranny and wrong, look to us for succor and support. . . . Our system not only justifies, but encourages the loftiest ambition on the part of the humblest citizen." A North Carolinian, however, remembering the slave population, seemed to hope one day for a changed southern identity. In a letter to Senator Seward he blamed "no man for being a Freesoiler— were I north I should be one. . . . I am here where I was born and raised and will support to the death the institutions which are a part of us, but do hope and feel that the time will come when all things will become new."[18]

The Democratic party still managed in 1857 to maintain a national organization, strengthened in the South by accretions from the Whigs, but weakened in the North by defections to the Republicans. A party whose constituents included southern administration Democrats, southern fire-eaters suspicious of Buchanan and northern Democrats generally, German and Irish Catholic immigrants, northern urban merchants and workingmen, and northwestern farmers, was necessarily a fragile body requiring the art of skillful politicians to prevent its fragmentation. Many Democrats, north and south, clung to a traditional Jacksonian platform on issues relating to money, banking, the tariff, internal improvements, and federal land policy, and these issues still had considerable importance in both state and national politics. But in 1857 these were not the political topics that, day after day, filled the columns of the party press, monopolized Congressional debates, or, if surviving records are an accurate barometer, occupied the minds of rank-and-file party members when they wrote to their Congressmen. In fact, some party spokesmen claimed that, given the urgency of other national problems, the Democracy could no longer use these traditional issues to define itself.

Hostility to the anti-Catholic nativists and their demands for state prohibition laws, changes in voting regulations, and a longer residency requirement for naturalization, motivated the Democratic party's ethnic voters far more than its opposition to a national bank or federal appropriations for internal improvements. Although some Democrats had joined the nativist movement, the party had been far more forthright than Republicans in denouncing religious bigotry and the Know-Nothing platform. "We believe that there is liberty in plenty for all," ran a typical defense of the immigrants, "and that we shall have none the less of it, because others enjoy it with us." After describing the immigrant contribution to the country's economic growth, one editor charged that the "real secret of this war upon foreigners" was that they voted "with the Democratic party—that is their sin and no other."[19] Anti-nativism was a source of strength to the national Democracy, arousing no significant dissent from any of its constituencies.

In contrast, Democrats shamelessly—almost proudly—flaunted their own form of ethnic bigotry. Anti-black racism, which they exploited with savage invective during every political campaign, was another unifying force and source of party strength. As their response to the Dred Scott decision indicated, race was an issue on which northern and southern Democrats found common ground, and they succeeded in establishing themselves as preeminently the "white man's party," while branding the "Black" Republicans as the "nigger party," the "wool heads," or the "amalgamationists." The Democratic party, boasted the Philadelphia *Press,* "ignores all Quixotic efforts to raise an inferior race to a position of equality for which it is physically and mentally unqualified. The condition of the negro . . . is a mere secondary consideration." When New York Republican legislators favored repealing a property restriction on black suffrage, a Democratic editor denounced them as "the sable part of the legislature, who rank themselves with negroes, and wish to reduce their wives and daughters to the same level." An Ohio Republican's proposal to enfranchise blacks exposed him to the wrath of the Cincinnati *Enquirer:* "When such a base conspiracy against civilization— such an impious defiance of Providence—so gross an outrage on reason, decency and humanity shall be consummated, our political and social system will be shaken . . . and the people pushed to the verge of a great civil convulsion and revolution."[20]

Racial equality was only one of the heresies of which Democrats accused the Republicans. According to the Washington *Union,* "The black-republican party comprises within its ranks all the *isms* of the North. . . . Mormonism, abolitionism, free-soilism, spiritual rappings, women's rights, socialism, free-loveism, and know-nothingism, have sprung up from this corrupt state of political profligacy and religious infidelity, and are now . . . madly bent on ruling or ruining the country." Calling for a coalition of all conservatives, the *Union* described the

Democracy as the party that defended "law, order, government, the constitution, private property, marriage, religion . . . against the virulent assaults of the black republicans." The Republican party, charged Caleb Cushing, was "a jumble of freaks and follies" dedicated to "all the humbugs of the day." It was, said the *Democratic Review,* a party of "quacks" disseminating ideas "imported from Europe, or generated in fanaticism." If any new sect arose subversive of the "common moralities of life . . . we know always that they will become, and naturally are, members of the Republican party."[21]

Both northern and southern Democrats recognized slavery as a local institution wholly within the jurisdiction of the individual states, and they shared a hostility to abolitionists as irresponsible fanatics who threatened the Union and domestic tranquility. They agreed, too, that there was no significant difference between abolitionists and Republicans, the former being the vanguard, providing the leadership, and keeping the party up to the mark in its war against the South. Moreover, some northern Democratic editors showed considerable sympathy for the southern proslavery argument. The Cincinnati *Enquirer,* rejecting the "absurd falsehoods" about the mistreatment of slaves, claimed that "humanity and interest" had improved their condition. According to the New York *Herald,* "when Sambo is his own master he will work neither for love nor money," but in slavery he is a productive laborer, "rollicking and happy over his corn cake and bacon." An Illinois editor asserted that if his state were to legalize slavery, the prairies "would be made to smile as a lovely garden." The New York *Day Book,* a Democratic weekly published by Dr. John H. Van Evrie, was so outspoken in its proslavery sentiments that it won much admiration in the South. A Mississippi slaveholder praised it for exerting "a wider and healthier influence on the public mind than any other paper now published in the Union."[22]

Even so, the northern wing of the Democracy never seemed to be proslavery quite enough to allay the suspicions of the southern fire-eaters. These southern-rights Democrats, claimed the Charleston *Mercury,* were the purest defenders of the party's original principles, but they were also "citizens of the South, determined to protect and defend her institutions." Free-state Democrats usually held abolitionists responsible for the angry posturing of the fire-eaters, but occasionally they lost patience with them. "There are dangerous agitators in the South as well as the North," complained the normally prosouthern Cincinnati *Enquirer.* "We allude to the mad-caps, who are always overflowing with wrath against the whole North . . . and who would establish slavery in the new States . . . whether it is acceptable to them or not."[23] By 1857 the agitation of this minority of extreme southern partisans had made the slavery issue a potential threat to the unity of the Democratic party.

The immediate danger arose from the determination of the fire-eaters to make the admission of Kansas as the sixteenth slave state a test of the Democratic party's readiness, as well as ability, to protect southern interests within the

Union. Yet, during the presidential campaign of 1856, northern Democrats had assured voters, especially in the pivotal state of Pennsylvania, that popular sovereignty would produce a free Kansas. With a substantial free-state majority in Kansas, that territory could have become a slave state only by a refusal to submit the issue to a popular vote—in other words, by a repudiation of a basic party principle as it was understood by Democrats in *both* the North and South. That the result of such a course would be a political disaster for the northern wing of the party was obvious enough to elicit from its spokesmen a virtually unanimous demand that the will of the people of Kansas be determined in a fair election.

"A single difficulty is, at this time, presented to Mr. Buchanan," advised the Detroit *Free Press* soon after his inauguration. "We allude to the situation of affairs in Kansas." The North would accept the *principles* of the Kansas-Nebraska Act, but it would "abide by nothing less than the faithful *enforcement* of those principles." Douglas's Chicago *Times* estimated that five-sixths of the Kansas settlers were opposed to slavery; the New York *Herald* was certain that even the "desperate expedients of a pro-slavery Legislature" would fail to make Kansas a slave state. The Cincinnati *Enquirer* predicted that when the controversy was ended and Kansas had entered the Union as a free state, Senator Douglas would occupy "in the love and confidence of the people as lofty a position as any statesman and Democrat ever attained." Few doubted the New York *Herald*'s warning that the issue of a free Kansas presented to the Democracy as a national political organization "the simple issue of life or death—consolidation or annihilation."[24]

In the South, administration Democrats were constantly harassed by the fire-eaters in their own party and by an opportunistic coalition of rather desperate Whig-Americans. The alienated radical southern-rights Democrats, many of them secessionists, all of them distrustful of Buchanan, had free access to the columns of *De Bow's Review,* as well as the Richmond *South,* Charleston *Mercury,* Natchez *Mississippi Free Trader,* and New Orleans *Delta.* In them secessionists such as Edmund Ruffin, Lawrence M. Keitt, and Robert Barnwell Rhett could sound their warnings that the national Democratic party was an unreliable defender of southern rights. The editor of the *Free Trader* vowed that he would see the party "rent into a thousand atoms and sent hurtling into eternal oblivion" before he would agree to lose Kansas through the "treachery" of a Democratic administration. The *Mercury* accused administration Democrats of disloyalty to the South: "With them, the paramount object of patriotic desire is the preservation of the Union and the success of the National Union Democracy. For this, they are ready to sacrifice the South." Opposing them were the southern-rights Democrats, who were "something more than Democrats"; they were "Southern men, with Southern sympathies in their hearts, and Southern interests in their mind." The *Delta,* viewing the South "from Virginia to Texas," claimed to read the signs of an approaching storm. The southern-rights wing of the Virginia

Democracy was "growing restive"; the heart of South Carolina palpitated "with the suppressed excitement of a coming battle"; Texas was ready "to bare her brawny arm"; and the chivalry of Mississippi was "prepared for the issue," only awaiting "the tocsin's call." Early in the year Keitt predicted that in six months "a powerful opposition organized against Mr. Buchanan" would develop in the southern Democratic party.[25]

The attack on the other flank of the southern administration Democrats came from the American party, which in 1856 had carried Maryland for Fillmore and polled a substantial vote in Virginia, Kentucky, Tennessee, Missouri, and Louisiana. Except in New Orleans and border cities such as Baltimore, Louisville, and St. Louis, few of the immigrants had settled in the slave states, and southern nativists therefore stressed their danger as potential allies of the Republicans in the northern states and western territories. An American party editor reported that the Germans had been "thoroughly abolitionized"; another accused Seward of plotting to "array all this foreign vote in support of Black Republicanism, and in antagonism to the South." If the immigrants' political power were not checked, nativists warned, the ultimate result would be Republican control of Congress and "the inevitable destruction of Southern rights." In 1857, in various southern state and Congressional elections, the American party combined with the remnants of the old Whigs to nominate "opposition" candidates, but their campaigns, though vigorously waged, were seldom successful.[26]

In spite of political defeats, southern Whigs and Americans continued to challenge the Democracy and had visions of a triumphant resurgence as members of a new national conservative party. Representative Henry Winter Davis of Maryland optimistically noted that Buchanan, having failed to win a majority of the popular vote, took office with his party's principles rejected in advance and his administration "paralyzed before its birth." Alexander H. H. Stuart, a prominent Virginia Whig, urged party leaders in his state to take the initiative in forming a powerful national coalition for "the patriotic purpose of wresting the government from the hands of the spoilers." Predicting the admission of Kansas as a free state and the consequent demise of the Republican party, the Richmond *Whig* was ready to welcome even the "rankest and most uncompromising" of its members into a political movement dedicated to "defeating and prostrating the Democratic party." The new opposition party might be called Whig, or American, or take some other name, as long as it attracted a "thoughtful, sedate, constitution-abiding, conservative class of men."[27]

Unfortunately for the Whig-Americans, with the decline of nativism they were bankrupt when it came to ideas and issues with which to build a platform. As a result they oscillated between a course of proslavery demagoguery and conservative Unionism. In the first role they tried to surpass the Democrats as defenders of the South. The American party, proclaimed an Alabama spokesman, pledged "an unfaltering devotion to Southern rights, Southern interests, and Southern honor." In contrast, the Richmond *Whig* described "the duplicity, hypocrisy, and recklessness" of the Democrats in their dealings with the South. Each Democratic administration came to power "with honeyed professions of devotion to Southern rights" but left a record of shameless betrayal. Now Buchanan's aim was "to intrigue Kansas into the Union as a *free* State, as the best and only means of re-uniting and re-organizing the shattered forces of the Northern Democracy." If his "insidious and treacherous" policy succeeded, the *Whig* concluded, the Southern Democracy would have surrendered Kansas, "without protest or remonstrance, into the . . . perpetual control of Northern Free-soilers and Abolitionists." In this manner, feigning sympathy for the fire-eating dissidents, the Whig-American press cynically exploited both the division in Democratic ranks and the fears of the proslavery South.[28]

Simultaneously, and with remarkable unconcern about consistency, southern Whigs and Americans portrayed themselves as responsible Unionists standing against the radical agitators of the North and the reckless southern-rights Democrats of the South. In this role the Richmond *Whig* deplored the "pernicious slavery agitation" that was "fanned and kept alive for the sole purpose of continuing the Democratic party in power!" On the eve of a state election the *Whig* urged voters to "put an extinguisher upon the fire-brands which the demagogues and spoilsmen of the State are perpetually casting among them." Whig Representative Emerson Etheridge of Tennessee charged that only Democratic incendiaries advocated the repeal of the laws and treaties prohibiting the African slave trade. The Montgomery *Mail* insisted that, unlike the Democrats, the Whigs were innocent of fostering "that slavery agitation which has inflicted so much of evil upon our common country." As long as the Democracy could win elections "on the plea of being special champions of Southern institutions, does any man suppose they will let the slavery question die out?" The ultimate aim of the southern "secession Democracy," according to the Nashville *Republican Banner,* was to secure the election of a northern antislavery President, thus preparing the South "to imbibe the poisonous South Carolina malaria." A Virginia Whig hoped that the revival of his party would rescue the South "from the grasp of the *pseudo* democracy" and revive "that national feeling so essential . . . to the integrity of the Union."[29]

Southern administration Democrats, showing concern about both the fire-eaters in their party and the dangerously opportunistic Whig-Americans, searched for ways to maintain their position as reliable defenders of the South's special interests within the structure of a national political organization. Contrary to their critics, party leaders had not invented the slavery issue in order to politicize it. Rather, they had responded aggressively to an increasing barrage of antislavery attacks and to the resulting fears of their proslavery constituents.

"[It] would be more than folly," wrote a Tennessee Democrat, "to shut our eyes to the fact that a majority of the . . . people of the United States regard slavery as an evil. . . . We affirm only what every intelligent man knows to be true."[30]

The desire of the great majority of southern Democrats to protect slavery within the Union caused a few to revive John C. Calhoun's demand that in Congress a balance be restored between the sections. One proposal was to give the South full representation for its slave population rather than for only three-fifths as provided in Article One of the Constitution. The Richmond *Enquirer* proposed instead to maintain sectional equality in the Senate by permitting slavery to expand so that a new slave state could be admitted to the Union along with each new free state. Thus the South would be armed with the power to veto "oppressive legislation against its rights and its institutions." This system, claimed a Florida Congressman, would have been unnecessary had there been no northern attack on southern institutions, "no scheming to interfere with them . . . no hostile prejudice nursed and disseminated against them."[31]

In the North the New York *Herald* stood almost alone in supporting the idea of a sectionally balanced Senate, suggesting the division of Texas into three or more slave states and the annexation of Mexico and Cuba from which others could be created. Republicans, of course, ridiculed the proposal, and northern Democrats rejected it as impracticable. Douglas claimed that it would violate the principles of the Democratic party, especially its commitment to popular sovereignty. Southerners themselves seldom took the proposal seriously. A Whig editor called the *Enquirer*'s suggestion "utterly preposterous," while a Democratic editor tactfully observed that it was not marked "with the usual discretion and statesmanship of that paper."[32]

Finding no way for the South to escape its plight as a political minority, southern administration Democrats claimed that their party was its strongest— indeed, its last—defense within the Union, and throughout 1857 they urged Southerners to rally to their support. The Richmond *Enquirer,* the most influential southern administration journal, launched a sharp assault on the rebellious fire-eaters. It denounced the "idle twaddle" of the secessionists who regarded themselves as the "anointed defenders" of southern rights and were "constantly issuing bulls of excommunication" against those who did not "swear allegiance to their rickety platform." It quoted the "editorial ravings" of the Charleston *Mercury* to illustrate "the hopeless insanity which marks a leading organ of the new 'Southern party.'" A Georgia editor, joining the attack, scolded the *Mercury* for its "excessive sensitiveness on the subject of Southern rights," and a South Carolina neighbor found "something slightly morbid" in its "desponding tone." None of these Democratic journals disputed the right of secession, or its necessity if a Republican were elected President, but to them it would be warranted only if all other southern defenses had failed. In the summer of 1857 the *Enquirer* saw "nothing to justify a disruption of the confederacy" and believed that the Union could be saved by a Democratic administration's "impartial enforcement of the Constitution."[33]

The *Enquirer,* in spite of much evidence to the contrary, argued that the national Democracy had never before been as harmonious as it was at present. It saw no issue relating to slavery over which northern and southern Democrats could differ. Buchanan owed his election to the South, and it was not in his nature "to turn his back upon men who have supported him with such generous confidence." Paying the President the ultimate compliment, the *Enquirer* affirmed that it would "as soon entrust the rights and honor of the South to James Buchanan as to Mr. Calhoun himself, if he were alive." An Alabama editor agreed that if the South were to remain in the Union its security would depend upon "a cordial, united support of the democratic party." The hope of the South, wrote a South Carolinian, was "the pillar of fire which leads on the great Democratic column." In short, the need of the hour was for a politically solid South united in the Democratic party, for an opposition party would merely "divide our vote and give the victory to the Black Republicans."[34]

Conservative leaders of the southern Democracy clearly understood that there were limits beyond which northern Democrats could not be pushed if they were to cooperate in maintaining a national organization. The policies of the Pierce administration and the behavior of the Kansas "border-ruffian" legislature had been heavy loads for them to bear. Accordingly, for the sake of party unity, an impressive number of southern Democrats conceded that there might well be an antislavery majority in Kansas and that its admission as a free state was perhaps inevitable. No Southerner, according to a Georgia editor, expected Buchanan to "make Kansas a slave State against the wishes of her people." The principle of the Democratic party was that "states *may* come into the Union, either with or without slavery as the people shall choose, not that Kansas shall come in as a slave State, whether her people want it or not." The Richmond *Enquirer* poured its scorn on southern ultras who would deny to the people of Kansas "the right of holding a fair, impartial election." Rather than having a "family quarrel" among Democrats, a Mississippi editor preferred to "let Kansas go." Others argued that if Kansas would not be a slave state Buchanan was at least trying to "make it a state safe for the Democracy." A Texas Democrat concluded that the admission of Kansas as a free state was essential if the Buchanan administration were to accomplish "the greatest amount of good."[35]

By 1857 it was clear that a united national Democratic party was the only political organization strong enough to prevent a Republican victory in the presidential election of 1860. Though it was obviously self-serving for southern administration Democrats to make that claim, their appeal to the South on that score was nonetheless valid, especially their warning that it would be disastrous to alienate the party's northern wing. The Louisville *Democrat* reminded Southerners that northern Democrats had "to stand up against the pulpit, most of the press, and all the combined forces of fanatics and factions of every shape and color." Where would the South be now, asked the *Democrat,* without the steady support it had received from its northern allies? "They are the friends of the South; they have given a thousand proofs of it."[36] The price of their continued support, conservatives seemed to understand, was an honest election in Kansas followed, in all probability, by its admission as a free state.

On July 4, 1857, in a speech at Framingham, Massachusetts, Wendell Phillips, scion of an aristocratic Boston family and a brilliant antislavery orator, gave his views of the relationship between abolitionists and Republicans. A political party, he said, was "but a weathercock—it will point which way you make it." The task of abolitionists was to provide it with principles. Phillips willingly served "down in the trenches, making the moral highway," knowing that he would be "thrown aside" when the work was finished. Then, when Republicans rode over it "in triumph," abolitionists would welcome their use of what they had built. Only, Phillips begged them in mock humility, "do not kick us as you do so. Recognize the service we did and do you."[37]

Phillips had a point. Though most Republican leaders denied any connection with or sympathy for abolitionists, they were deeply indebted to them for helping to develop in the North a moral climate in which at least a mildly antislavery political party could flourish—one that dared call slavery a "relic of barbarism." Abolitionists had long ago coined the term "Slave Power" and developed the concept of a Slave Power conspiracy to nationalize slavery, which Republicans now exploited with great success. They had created an image, now widely accepted, of slaveholders as hostile to democracy, enemies of free labor, and violators of civil liberties such as freedom of speech and of the press. On the eve of the twenty-fourth annual meeting of the American Anti-Slavery Society, an abolitionist editor boasted of the movement's achievements during the past quarter-century. "It has made the subject of slavery a household topic at every fireside in the country," he wrote. "It has opened hundreds of newspapers to the discussion of the subject. . . . It is no small triumph to have built up a political movement, far as it fell short of what we discerned to be the only principle of genuine life."[38]

All that may have been true, but abolitionists in 1857 were oppressed by a nagging feeling of failure. William Lloyd Garrison reminded the faithful that their goal was not merely to resist the fugitive-slave law, or to make Kansas a free state, or to exclude slavery from the western territories. Rather, it was "to effect the immediate, total, and eternal overthrow of Slavery, wherever it exists on American soil, and to expose and confront whatever party or sect seeks to purchase peace or success at the expense of human liberty." Yet slavery was undeniably flourishing in the southern states, and the abolitionists' ultimate goal seemed as remote as it had been in the 1830s. "After the agitation of nearly twenty-five years," wrote one disheartened antislavery leader, "the slaves are still in bondage, their numbers have greatly increased, and no effective measures are adopted in a single Slave state ... for their liberation." While less exposed to violence than in earlier years, abolitionists still confronted an unsympathetic northern majority who considered them annoying troublemakers—a threat to the Union and to profitable trade relations with the South, and a disruptive force in the churches. Though by no means free of prejudice, in their racial attitudes they were considerably in advance of their contemporaries, whom they alarmed by opposing legal, political, economic, and, sometimes, social discrimination against free blacks. Northern racism was in fact the principal cause of hostility to the antislavery crusade, for it created deep anxieties about the social consequences of liberating millions of black slaves.[39]

Some of the more politically pragmatic antislavery leaders—Sumner of Massachusetts, Salmon P. Chase and Joshua R. Giddings of Ohio, and George W. Julian of Indiana, among others—had joined the Republican party, but the purists among them spurned it for its refusal to support their campaign to end slavery in the southern states. Oliver Johnson, editor of the *National Anti-Slavery Standard,* recognized that many Republicans viewed their party as a vehicle for attacking and weakening slavery; nevertheless, he found it too "compromising and political" for his taste. The party, he claimed, lacked principles and had been "founded merely on a shifting expediency." To join them would be an "utter betrayal of the cause to which we are devoted." At its annual meeting in New York the American Anti-Slavery Society addressed the Republicans with a resolution asserting that "if it would be a curse and crime to plant [slavery] in Kansas, it is no less criminal and disastrous to perpetuate it in Carolina." Republican leaders, wrote a Boston abolitionist in disgust, were "disclaiming any intention or *desire* to abolish slavery.... They are skulking the charge of having any sympathy with the Abolitionists.... Their behavior is most base—their position is most cowardly and contemptible."[40]

The dispute among antislavery leaders over support of the Republican party illustrated the internal conflicts which long before 1857 had left them organizationally fragmented and their cause consequently damaged. Some had joined earlier antislavery political movements—the Liberty and Free-Soil parties—but the sectarian followers of Garrison in the American Anti-Slavery Society had opposed all political action. Some read the Constitution as an antislavery document; but Garrison read it as a proslavery "covenant with death" and "an agreement with hell." Some were strong defenders of the Union, but the Garrisonians cried "No Union with Slaveholders" and urged the political separation of North and South. Some were pacifists, but by the 1850s a growing number was prepared to resort to violence, especially in resisting the capture of fugitive slaves. Some favored and some opposed uniting abolitionism with the woman's-rights movement. Some worked within the Protestant churches; others repudiated them for temporizing and for admitting slaveholders to their communion and fellowship.[41]

Differences over programs and tactics sometimes degenerated into bitter personal feuds, with Garrison especially prone to speak ill of those who did not agree with him in all respects. For example, he severely rebuked Gerrit Smith, a prominent New York abolitionist, for suggesting that the day of emancipation might be hastened if slaveholders were compensated for the loss of their property. This, growled Garrison, was the latest of "the eccentricities, gyrations and somersets of Mr. Smith, whose powers of reasoning and moral discrimination seem to be getting more and more obfuscated." Smith resented the "unkind and uncandid" treatment he had received, and Samuel J. May, another abolitionist, told Garrison that his attack was "the worst, the most unjust thing" he had ever done. Frederick Douglass, a celebrated black abolitionist orator, who had broken with the Garrisonians, was often the target of their wrath. Douglass, one of them wrote, after "wriggling and turning" to adjust his views to those of other men, found that he had "the confidence of very few, the respect, I venture to say, of none." In a speech at Canandaigua, New York, Douglass, in turn, accused his critics of racism. "Your humble speaker," he said, "has been branded as an ingrate, because he has ventured to . . . plead our common cause as a colored man, rather than as a Garrisonian." Henry Ward Beecher, the antislavery pastor of Plymouth Church in Brooklyn, also had his abolitionist enemies, one of whom thought he lacked "a particle of the sacred fire—all of his fuel having burnt into sentimental ashes." If abolitionists could not treat each other with respect, Gerrit Smith asked, "why should we wonder if the public feel no respect for us?"[42]

The profound differences within the northern antislavery movement were evident in the actions of two conventions that met in 1857. The first, a gathering mostly of Garrisonians, met in Worcester, Massachusetts, in January to consider the wisdom of a dissolution of the Union. A handful of Massachusetts radical Republicans attended, and one of them, Francis W. Bird, presided, but both local and national antislavery Republican leaders repudiated their action. In an address to the convention, Garrison reaffirmed his contempt for the Union, calling it "an insane experiment to reconcile those elements which are eternally hostile." Disunion, he claimed, by removing the support of the federal government, would "paralyze the power of the master, and therefore, render emancipation certain." Other speakers, among them Wendell Phillips, Thomas Wentworth Higginson, and Stephen Foster, argued that as long as the Union existed Northerners shared the guilt of slavery with its southern defenders. The convention did nothing but harm to the abolition movement and to Garrison's leadership role, for it was clear that even the great majority of abolitionists opposed it. A proposed second disunion convention in the autumn was cancelled, ostensibly because of unfavorable economic conditions but actually because it had so little support.[43]

The following August an antislavery convention with a more conservative goal met in Cleveland and formed the National Compensation Emancipation Society. Led by Gerrit Smith, Elihu Burritt of Massachusetts, a self-taught linguist and ardent pacifist, Benjamin Silliman, a distinguished scientist at Yale, and Mark Hopkins, president of Williams College, the new society adopted resolutions declaring that the free states must share responsibility for the existence of slavery and claiming that "immeasurable advantages" would accrue to both sections if it were abolished. Accordingly, it was proper for Northerners, "in a generous and brotherly spirit," to join Southerners in bearing the cost of ridding the country of this "moral and political evil." To this end the society proposed that Congress pay participating southern states the sum of $250 for each slave emancipated, and each of the "wronged and destitute" freedmen the sum of $25 to help them obtain "humble homes upon this continent, or upon another, should they prefer . . . removal from the land of their birth." Speaking in support of this program, Smith denied that it recognized the right of property in man, but he urged abolitionists to have "a loving heart . . . for the slaveholder as well as the slave." Their aim, said Burritt, must be to abolish not only slavery but "the alienation and distrust which grow out of its existence." Proslavery Southerners and Garrisonian abolitionists united in ridiculing both the plan and its authors. What right had Burritt and his society, asked the *National Anti-Slavery Standard,* "to chaffer with the stealers of men for the human beings they have stolen?"[44]

As these two conventions indicated, the divisions within antislavery ranks were wide, but common to all was an essentially moral appeal that had developed over the years. Though some spoke against the slaveholders more harshly than others, all stressed their betrayal of the secular principles of the Declaration of Independence; the hypocrisy of a nation claiming to be a model republic while tolerating slavery; the sinfulness of Christian masters holding as slaves black men and women who were their equals in the sight of God; the corrupting and degrading impact of slavery on the lives of both masters and slaves; and the cruelties inherent in the slave trade, the disruption of slave families, and the physical punishments necessary to maintain slave discipline. All shared a conviction that a sinister Slave Power plotted to transform the republic into a slave empire. Speaking at a July 4 celebration in Boston's Tremont Temple, the Rev. William R. Alger warned his audience: "Day and night they are plotting for new fields, reckless of the means, and devising new entrenchments. . . . Can we endure this, and sit tamely down, and do nothing to stay the advance of the all-grasping despotism?"[45]

By 1857 the obvious failure of the abolitionists' original program of peaceful "moral suasion" to convert the slaveholders had produced a new militancy in their ranks. Some had turned to the Republican party, hoping to make it more vigorously antislavery. Some were ready for violence, not only to protect fugitive slaves but to strike at the Slave Power itself. The Massachusetts abolitionist, Thomas Wentworth Higginson, for one, preached disunion but was also ready to use "any weapon, so that for one instant in our lives we may know the sensation of being freemen!" Another, Theodore Parker, a Boston Unitarian clergyman, had once thought that "this terrible question of Freedom or Slavery in America would be settled without bloodshed; I believe it no longer."[46]

Abolitionists had always feared that failure to abolish slavery peacefully would one day lead, in the words of Frederick Douglass, to a "wildly and deadly struggle for freedom." Now, however, some in despair seemed to anticipate a slave insurrection with less fear than hope. Henry C. Wright, a Massachusetts Congregational clergyman and long a pacifist, boldly asserted: "A Baptism of blood awaits the slaveholder. . . . So be it. The retribution is just . . . unless they willingly and penitently let their slaves go free." A Garrisonian editor hesitated to advocate insurrection, but he argued that a "state of natural warfare" existed between masters and slaves and claimed "the perfect right of every oppressed people to rise on their oppressors." Eventually, he predicted, "the Moses of these modern Hebrews" would emerge and deliver them from their bondage. A successful insurrection would "enoble the whole race," for it was not slavery that degraded the African but *the endurance of slavery.* " Let the slaves "make good their determination, and the world accords to such heroism its place in human esteem."[47]

The abolitionists, though a small and divided minority, nevertheless had at their command an arsenal of eloquent voices and fluent pens. These weapons, together with their single-minded dedication to the antislavery cause, enabled them to broadcast their message more successfully than their numbers and the public hostility to them would seem to have made possible. One of the remarkable features of the northern press in the 1850s was the degree to which editors, though rarely expressing sympathy for abolitionists, had been influenced by them in their descriptions of slaveholders, southern society, the southern economy, and even slavery. Accordingly, the turn of the abolitionists from "moral suasion" to the contemplation of violence was a matter of no small significance in the annals of the American sectional conflict.

Soon after the presidential election of 1856, Republican leaders began to think of 1860 and how to strengthen their coalition of antislavery Whigs, Free-Soilers, Anti-Nebraska Democrats, and antislavery nativists. They were most concerned, of course, about the northern states they had lost—New Jersey, Pennsylvania, Indiana, and Illinois—in each of which the American party had polled a substantial vote. Because of the decline of nativism as a political movement, Republican strategists hoped that American party voters would soon join their ranks. Since the Republican party was by no means their only possible refuge, their support could not be taken for granted. Some Fillmorites who worried about disunion threats favored instead a conservative coalition with the Democracy. Others, like their southern Whig-American counterparts, still hoped for a collapse of Republicanism and a rebirth of the party of Webster and Clay. Edward Everett's belief in the soundness of Whig principles was not shaken by the party's recent decline. "I voted for Mr. Fillmore," he wrote, "in common with the great mass of my political friends . . . as the candidate adopted by the patriotic Whig party." In a letter to Fillmore a New York Whig predicted a mass movement of Republicans to his party within two years; a Wisconsin Whig assured him that 1860 "would witness the Party again spreading its branches from one end of this our beloved country to its utmost limits." Fillmore himself urged the Whigs to stand firm, "organize their forces, rally round the flag of the Union . . . and protect it . . . regardless of all consequences and all sacrifices."[48]

These fantasies about a future Whig revival put some of the conservative northern Fillmore voters beyond the Republican party's reach. A further complication was the existence of a substantial and influential group of antislavery Republicans who opposed pandering to nativist prejudices and insisted that coalitions with them would corrupt the party and compromise its principles. Moreover, as Horace Greeley and others argued, nativism would undermine the Republican effort to convert the territories into free states. "It has been foreign immigration which has peopled the West," observed a critic of nativism, planting it with "a hardy and industrious race of freemen." Senator Seward's record of sympathy for Catholic immigrants earned him an invitation to a St. Patrick's Day supper given by the Hibernian Providential Society of Albany. By his "consistent, able and fearless advocacy" of immigrants' rights, he had "laid them under obligations which cannot soon, or readily, be forgotten." Edward L. Pierce of Massachusetts, a strong antislavery Republican and Sumner's close friend, writing glowingly of his party's bright future, urged its members "to be generous to all ranks, conditions, and nativities . . . and thus in the fullness of time we shall organize victory."[49]

Nationally the Republican party refused to endorse any of the nativist voting or naturalization "reforms"; at the state level, except in Massachusetts and Ohio, it rarely conceded more than vague support for protecting the "purity" of the ballot box. Prior to 1856, in a dozen northern states, many Republicans had joined nativists in supporting state laws prohibiting the sale or possession of intoxicating beverages—laws clearly directed against the beer-drinking Germans and whiskey-drinking Irish. Because the laws lost numerous challenges in the courts and were seldom effectively enforced, most of them were soon repealed. By 1857, though the temperance crusade was still a political force, Republicans had abandoned it as too divisive and a major obstacle to their bid for at least the German Protestant vote in the western states.[50]

Yet, practical Republicans knew that they could not win the next presidential election without a massive movement of Fillmore Americans to their party, and in state elections in 1857 they still felt obliged to place former nativists on their tickets in Massachusetts, Connecticut, New York, Pennsylvania, and Ohio. Republicans faced a delicate problem: they needed to hold the hard-line opponents of nativism, increase their support among German voters, and yet smooth the path to Republicanism for antislavery nativists. Numerous Republican editors, some of them subtly, some coarsely, dealt with the problem in a manner rather less admirable than effective. They avoided indiscriminate nativist attacks on immigrants and, writing off the Catholic vote, focused instead on the Irish as a source of political corruption, and on the Slave Power and Papists as the twin enemies of free labor and Republican institutions.

In Pennsylvania the Harrisburg *Telegraph,* recalling the last election, deplored the votes, "many of them illegal and fraudulent," of the "priest-ridden foreign rabble." The Springfield *Illinois State Journal* boasted that Republicans had "never laid claim to the Irish vote," conceding that it was "entirely 'Dimicratic.'" The Germans, on the other hand, "awakened to the pro-slavery tendencies of the sham Democrats," were "not at all like 'the bog trotters.'" Reporting a local Democratic meeting, the Chicago *Tribune* accused the "Emerald Islanders . . . in pursuance of Irish tactics," of running roughshod over the German delegates. Such were the manners of the "half-civilized horde" who gave the northern Democracy its strength "and the American name its deepest disgrace." These ethnic attacks found a receptive audience within the Republican party. One New York Republican privately expressed a belief that his "celtic fellow citizens" were "almost as remote from us in temperament and constitution as the Chinese."[51]

A Republican editor, denying that he felt any prejudice against the Irish, objected only to "that great mass of them" who, as Democrats, were doing "the dirty work of the proslavery party" and aiding the spread of black servitude in the United States. A belief in the principle of despotism animated both "the propagandists of slavery and the propagandists of Popery," claimed the Chicago *Tribune,* and it was fitting "that they should pull politically in the same traces." The greatest threat to American liberty was that it might be "crushed between the upper and nether mill-stones of . . . Catholicism and Slavery." Republican opposition to the proscription of immigrants, the *Tribune* insisted, did not mean that it would aid "the growth and spread of an odious hierarchy in the very heart of the Republic."[52] Expressions of anti-Catholic nativism such as these were never written into a Republican national platform, but they were easy to detect in speeches at local party meetings and in some state and county platforms, thus giving the party its durable reputation as the haven of native-born Protestants.

The Republican attacks on Irish Catholics no doubt encouraged the movement of northern Fillmore voters to its support. At the same time some Republican leaders, aware of the prevalence of racism in the North—and often themselves partaking of it—tried to portray their party, rather than the Democrats, as the authentic white man's party. Their opposition to the expansion of slavery, they claimed, was to protect the interests of white settlers. The Republican members of the Illinois state legislature adopted resolutions declaring that the basic issue between their party and the Democracy was whether the territories "shall be reserved for free white people, or surrendered to the negroes and their masters." They accused proslavery Democrats of "driving white men at the point of the bayonet from Kansas, to make more room for negro slaves." A Wisconsin editor made the point more crudely: "No slaveholders and no niggers in the territories—white men must own and forever occupy the great west. . . . Nigger slaves shall not be allowed to work among, associate nor amalgamate with white people. . . . These are Republican ideas."[53]

Lincoln, in a speech at Springfield on June 26, addressed the obsessive fear of American racists: "amalgamation." There was, he noted, "a natural disgust in the minds of nearly all white people, to the idea of an indiscriminate amalgamation of the white and black races." He assured his audience that when Republicans claimed that the Declaration of Independence was meant to include *all* men they did not mean that they wanted "to vote, and eat, and sleep, and marry with negroes!" Lincoln ridiculed the "counterfeit logic that, because I do not want a black woman for a *slave* I must necessarily want her for a *wife*. I need not have her for either, I can just leave her alone." Slavery, he charged, was "the greatest source of amalgamation." Hence he favored "separation of the races" by excluding slavery from the territories and by urging free blacks to colonize somewhere outside the United States. Senator Lyman Trumbull, one of the Republican party's most outspoken racists, refused to argue with Chief Justice Taney about the "degradation" of persons of African descent, nor would he discuss their "amalgamation with the whites," or placing them "on a level with the white race." He knew of no party "advocating such repulsive notions."[54]

Republican politicians and editors who, because of their constituents' racial fears (and perhaps their own), tried to portray their party as a safe vehicle for white men to ride, were, if nothing else, realists. Given the racial attitudes of the 1850s, no party—not even one appealing primarily to northern voters—could have adopted a platform advocating equal political and legal rights for blacks without suffering total defeat. As an Indiana Republican warned, if his party permitted the Democrats to define the issue between them as "the equality of the black with the white race we shall be beaten not only in Indiana but in the Union from this time forward." Yet, in spite of Trumbull and other party racists, Republicans never succeeded in establishing themselves as *the* white man's party, in part because even at their most blatant they rarely matched the virulence of the Democrats in racial demagoguery. During the last presidential election, Lincoln recalled, "We were constantly charged with seeking an amalgamation of the white and black races; and thousands turned from us."[55] Since Republicans always found themselves on the defensive when Democrats confronted them with the race issue, their best strategy was to avoid it as much as possible.

The Democrats had another advantage: Their party was almost unanimously opposed to granting civil or political rights to free blacks, and the great majority of the most rabid Negrophobes, regarding it as the anti-Negro party, was in its ranks. Republicans, on the other hand, were less united, some refusing to claim that their party was the white man's party and taking politically dangerous positions on one or another racial issue. Even as conservative a paper as the Springfield *Illinois State Journal* deplored the racial hysteria of its Democratic rival, the *Register,* denounced the state's constitutional exclusion of free blacks, and demanded that they be "treated something like human beings." They were, it said, at least entitled to "the common and natural rights which are guaranteed to the humblest citizen, and the privilege of suing for them in our courts of justice." Lincoln may not have wanted a black woman for a wife and may have denied that she was his equal "in some respects," but, he added, "in her natural right to eat the bread she earns with her own hands without asking leave of anyone else, she is my equal, and the equal of all others."[56]

In general, Republicans, in spite of their racism, seemed to be somewhat less obsessed than Democrats with fantasies about the "black peril," somewhat less hostile to moderate proposals to improve the lot of blacks in America, and a good deal more tolerant of racial "extremists" such as Charlie Sumner. Their party counted among its leaders Ohio Congressman Joshua R. Giddings, who made known his hope that one day "all distinctions . . . of complexion shall cease, and the whole family of man shall constitute one brotherhood." It included a Portland, Maine, editor, who dared assert that the nation's future was bound up with that of the Negro: "We cannot shake him off by trampling him under foot. If he goes down, we go down with him. If he rises to the condition of a *man,* we may go onward . . . sure of preserving our own liberties as long as we respect the rights of all." It also included some Republican philanthropists who helped to support a high school for black girls in Washington, D.C.—an institution, the *National Era* reminded its proslavery critics, that neither shook the foundations of the Union nor brought down the price of stocks.[57]

The racial issue on which many Republicans were most inclined to take a liberal stand was black suffrage. In 1857, black males had the ballot in only a few New England states and in New York, where they were required to meet a $250 property qualification not required of whites. The *National Era* exaggerated when it claimed that the great majority of Republicans favored extending the franchise to blacks, but it was true that nearly all existing support came from members of their party. In the New York legislature, for example, the Republican majority, over the almost unanimous opposition of the Democrats, voted to amend the state constitution by removing the property restriction imposed on black voters. The amendment had the support of Greeley's *Tribune,* but because of a legal technicality it was not submitted to the voters—who would almost certainly have rejected it, as they did three years later. In an Iowa constitutional convention the same year the Republicans voted to submit a black suffrage referendum, but it was overwhelmingly defeated.[58]

The most dramatic battle over black suffrage in 1857 occurred in Wisconsin, where the legislature's Republican majority, after a prolonged debate, submitted the issue to the voters at the state election in the fall. The Republican state convention cautiously endorsed the referendum with a vague resolution opposing "the proscription of any man on account of birthplace, religion, or color," and most of the party press, with varying degrees of enthusiasm, gave it their support. The Milwaukee *Sentinel,* one of the measure's strongest advocates, described the service of blacks during the Revolution and asked whether "some small degree of consideration" was not due to a "proscribed and unjustly treated class of citizens." Democrats lost no time in seizing the issue, insisting that black suffrage was tantamount of "giving negro husbands and negro progeny to our fair daughters and sisters." Their state convention promised to resist "the odious doctrine of Negro equality." If blacks were given the right to vote, one Democratic editor warned, Wisconsin would soon become "a grand asylum for the animalized free Negro hordes who curse our eastern and southern cities." The black suffrage referendum was defeated, but an impressive 41 percent of the voters favored it. Opposition was heavily concentrated in Democratic districts, while most of the support came from Republican strongholds. In fact, one analysis of the election returns estimated that more than 60 percent of the Republicans who voted on the referendum gave it their support.[59]

Most assuredly the Republican party of the 1850s was not committed to a policy of racial justice for the northern free black population. Its national platform was silent on the subject. Yet there were some in the party who, in their day, appeared to the general public as dangerous radicals. Even the more conservative Republicans took positions on racial issues significantly different from those taken by Democratic politicians and the Democratic press. That was why they were vulnerable to the attacks of racist demagogues, and why race was an issue they rarely cared to stress.

In the presidential campaign of 1856 the Republican party's Philadelphia platform was a decidedly antislavery document. Though it did not propose to violate the Constitution by interfering with slavery in the southern states, it described the institution as a "relic of barbarism," asserted the "right and imperative duty" of Congress to exclude it from the territories, and reaffirmed the principles of the Declaration of Independence. Most of those who favored political action against slavery perceived the Republican party to be at least moderately antislavery and gave it their support. During the campaign, Democrats portrayed it not only as a party of "amalgamationists" but, equally inaccurately, as a party of "rabid abolitionists." After losing the election, many Republican moderates and conservatives concluded that their party had assumed too radical an antislavery posture and hoped to change it a little before the next national campaign. In 1857, therefore, party leaders, after assessing their recent gains and losses, debated both publicly and privately their future course. What eventually emerged was a Republican party still divided between radicals such as Giddings, moderates such as Lincoln, and conservatives such as Trumbull, with the moderates generally controlling state and national party organizations but skillfully avoiding serious defections of either radicals or conservatives. The moderates appeased the conservatives by giving the party a somewhat less radical image, and the radicals by preserving much of the substance, if not the rhetoric, of the antislavery Philadelphia platform.

Each wing of the party, of course, gave its own interpretation and emphasis to the Republican party creed. Conservatives continued to stress the need to preserve the territories for free white labor, assured the South that they had no desire to interfere with slavery in the states, and acknowledged an obligation not to interfere with the enforcement of the federal fugitive-slave law. Some proposed the restoration of the Missouri Compromise line and hoped to make their party "acceptable to the freemen of the South at least." One New England conservative wanted to rid the party of "a few demagogues" such as Seward and Greeley and unite "all the Old Line Whigs and Fillmore men into one party." A California Republican claimed that the principal concern of most Frémont voters in his state was not the slavery issue but the transcontinental railroad.[60] Realistic Republicans such as Thurlow Weed and Simon Cameron, in exerting political influence to advance their business ventures and in building their New York and Pennsylvania political machines, provided a foretaste of politics in the post-Civil War "Gilded Age." In their view, political probity sometimes had to give way to political necessity, and the only valid standard for judging a party platform was success.

At the other end of the Republican spectrum were the antislavery radicals, full of the reform spirit of their age, often exuding the enthusiasm characteristic of religious revivals. "Next to my God and my family," wrote one of the crusaders, "Republicanism, with its just and philanthropic aims, has my deepest interest." Republican doctrines, another believed, were "emanations from the 'Throne of Thrones,' written on the hearts of men by the finger of Omnipotence," and eventually men would respond "to God's voice within them." From his perspective in Europe, Sumner observed with regret that slavery prevented his country from fulfilling its divine mission to serve as a model democratic republic. "In fighting our battle at home," he asserted, "we are fighting the battle of Freedom everywhere." Radical Congressmen sometimes matched the rhetoric of the fallen Sumner in their strictures against slavery—for example, John A. Bingham of Ohio: "You may call the State which enslaves and sells its own children, and manacles the hand which feeds and clothes and shelters it, *republican;* but truth, and history, and God's eternal justice, will call it despotism, equally criminal and equally odious, whether sanctioned by one or many, by a single tyrant or by the million." The new Congress would seat another radical, Owen Lovejoy of Illinois, brother of Elijah P. Lovejoy, an abolitionist who twenty years earlier had been murdered in Alton by a proslavery mob.[61]

One political abolitionist, Congressman George W. Julian of Indiana, explained with unusual candor why he had joined the Republican party. Although he disliked its ambition for immediate success, its "deplorable coalitions," and its "bad leadership of ambitious politicians," the party nevertheless stood "fairly committed to the policy of divorcing the Federal Government from slavery, and to the prosecution of this policy as an unmistakable protest against its existence." Excluding slavery from the territories was like "the first dose of medicine" for the national malady, "an essential part of the whole process of cure." The authors of the Philadelphia platform had taken positions and proposed practical measures "sufficiently broad and catholic for all anti-slavery men" who believed in the use of the ballot. "They expressed their reverence for our fathers, and announced principles that in their working must put an end to slavery." Indeed, they had "virtually proclaimed war against the institution, and the determination to rescue the nation from its power." Julian hoped that with better leadership his party would correct its errors and shortcomings. "To this end," he concluded, "as a Republican, I shall steadfastly labor hereafter, as I have done heretofore."[62]

Where did the moderates—the mainstream Republicans—stand? Almost all of them subscribed to the general principles of the Philadelphia platform, acknowledged that Congress had no constitutional authority to interfere with slavery in the southern states, denied any connection between their party and the abolitionists, and shared Lincoln's views on race relations. In their criticisms of slavery and opposition to its expansion moderate party spokesmen often emphasized its adverse impact on white labor more than on its injustice to blacks. They sometimes appeared to be less engaged in a moral crusade against slavery than in an assault on the South and on the slaveholders who, according to them, controlled it. The expression of these attitudes has led some historians to question the validity of the Republican party's traditional antislavery image, suggesting instead that it was motivated chiefly by hostility to blacks and to the southern Slave Power.[63]

That is a fair description of conservative Republicans and of statements made at various times by many moderates. It does not of course describe the radicals, who were the keepers of the party's conscience and whose support the party could not afford to lose. Nor is it an accurate *general* description of the moderates, some of whom never used racist arguments against slavery expansion but stressed slavery's damaging effect on *both* whites and blacks. The Philadelphia platform did not oppose slavery expansion on racial grounds, and that platform was repeatedly endorsed by moderate Republican governors, legislatures, and state and local party conventions. It seems quite likely that some genuinely antislavery Republican leaders used racist arguments against slavery expansion as a political expedient designed to increase popular support. They had found, observed the Chicago *Tribune,* "that it is far easier to convince the multitude that Slavery is a baleful evil to them, than to possess them with the idea that it is a cruel wrong to the enslaved."[64]

Both Republicans and abolitionists made it clear that racial prejudice did not prevent them from taking strong moral positions against the institution of slavery. Lincoln was typical of the moderate Republicans in his repeated declarations that opposition to slavery did not require him to believe in the social equality of the races, or even in the enfranchisment of blacks or granting them citizenship. Moreover, it would have been difficult for a Republican to have negative feelings about the South, or to perceive a threat to free white labor from an aggressive Slave Power, without developing antislavery sentiments as well. How could one hope to "reform" the South or to undermine the Slave Power without anticipating a change in the southern labor system? To lessen anxieties about the consequences of emancipating four million black slaves, some Republicans suggested that they could be colonized abroad; others comforted northern racists with the prediction that they would remain in the South.

In defining their goals, party spokesmen rarely managed to isolate the Slave Power from slavery. Rather, their hostility to one almost inevitably produced hostility to the other. For example, in 1857 the Massachusetts state Republican platform opened with a description of "the alarming encroachments of the Slave Power," then explained its aggressions as "the natural results of the inherent wickedness of slavery." The Wisconsin state Republican platform included an identical description of the Slave Power, followed by an attack on slavery as "a crime against humanity of the deepest dye," which could "no more be constitutionalized or legalized, than theft, robbery or murder." A resolution adopted by Michigan's Republican legislature also affirmed the need to check the Slave Power's "encroachments," then demanded the repeal of the Fugitive Slave Act, the exclusion of slavery from all the territories, and the abolition of slavery in the District of Columbia. A moderate New York Republican thought it likely that the "designs of the slave-power in acquiring further supremacy" would cause "the welfare of the Republic . . . and the voice of the people [to] warrant . . . the extirpation of slavery itself." In a private letter, Governor Salmon P. Chase of Ohio, whose antislavery credentials were impeccable, expressed a desire for his country to take an honorable place among the nations of the world. "I know this cannot be as long as the Slave Power controls the land. I wish therefore to overthrow the Slave Power." Chase, like most Republicans, believed that the Slave Power could not be overthrown without exerting "the influence of the General Government on the side of Freedom." Then, he believed, his country "would soon be redeemed."[65]

In their public statements, Republicans usually took pains to dissociate themselves from the abolitionists; yet some of them, in spite of ideological and tactical differences, corresponded with abolitionists and sympathized with their goals. Radicals such as Chase, Sumner, and Giddings were on friendly terms with antislavery leaders who would not join their party; even Charles Francis Adams, a moderate Republican, counted a few of them among his friends and correspondents. Prudent Republicans must have been disturbed by the appearance in Milwaukee on June 17 of two abolitionists, Gerrit Smith and the notorious John Brown, fresh from his violent escapades in Kansas, to address the Republican state convention. Equally surprising, the Chicago *Tribune,* a major party organ, after explaining why it disagreed with the abolitionists, confessed its "profound respect" for them. "We award them the credit of perfect sincerity and of benevolence without alloy of selfishness. Many of them have sacrificed ease and position, and others have laid down wealth and social standing . . . in obedience to the demands of conviction. . . . Such men are never to be despised."⁶⁶

The harsh provisions of the Fugitive Slave Act of 1850, denying alleged fugitives trial by jury and forcing Northerners to assist in their capture, stretched to the limit the obligation Republicans felt to obey the laws of their government. "The surrender of a human being," the New York *Evening Post* commented bitterly, "who has exhibited his fitness for freedom by encountering the dangers of escaping from slavery, is a most repulsive task." Charles Francis Adams heard a Boston clergyman, one Sunday morning, declare his refusal to respect the law. The audience listened quietly, "and no one afterwards raised his voice much to disapprove." In 1857, New Hampshire and Wisconsin followed the example of several other northern states by passing "personal liberty laws," which, in defiance of federal law, gave alleged fugitives the protection of habeas corpus and trial by jury and prohibited any state officer from assisting in their capture or detention. Thus, commented a Milwaukee editor, Wisconsin had applied "the shield of State Sovereignty to protect citizens . . . from the aggressions of the Slave Power."⁶⁷

On various occasions Republicans represented alleged fugitives before federal commissioners appointed under the Fugitive Slave Act, or in the state courts. In Indianapolis, George W. Julian defended a black named West, who was claimed by a Kentucky slaveholder. When Julian lost the case, he joined other antislavery men in an unsuccessful attempt to help West escape. A similar case in Cincinnati led first to a violent clash between a deputy United States marshal and citizens attempting to rescue two fugitives, then to a legal clash between state and federal courts. Republican editors again found merit in traditional southern defenses of state rights; one of them warned the federal "minions of the slave power" that the states were "sovereign within their own territorial limits." In Wisconsin the arrest in 1854 of a Republican editor, Sherman Booth, for assisting a fugitive slave to escape had subsequently led the state supreme court, in a remarkable assertion of state sovereignty, to declare the federal Fugitive Slave Act unconstitutional. In 1857 the Republican legislative majority agreed to elect James R. Doolittle to the United States Senate only after he defended the court's decision and the constitutionality of Wisconsin's personal-liberty law. In the fall election, the Republican state platform denied the power of Congress to pass a Fugitive Slave Act and asserted that, since such a law did not exist in Wisconsin, anyone attempting to return a fugitive to slavery would be guilty of kidnapping.[68]

Democratic politicians and editors, using evidence such as this to identify the "Black" Republicans as abolitionists and advocates of racial equality, repeatedly denied the party's legitimacy as a traditional American political organization. It was, they charged, a reckless, sectional, "one-idea" party whose very existence threatened the survival of the Union. Republican leaders felt their vulnerability to this charge and took pains to refute it. Their program, they claimed, was national in scope and would have the support of a mass of southern nonslaveholders if the Slave Power had not destroyed freedom of speech and of the press. Proslavery partisans were free to speak in the northern states, but a Republican exposed himself to grave risk merely to travel in the South. The Republican press made much of southern antislavery martyrs such as John C. Underwood, driven from his Virginia home for attending the Republican national convention; Benjamin S. Hedrick, discharged from his post at the University of North Carolina for supporting Frémont; and Cassius M. Clay, whose antislavery newspaper in Lexington, Kentucky, had been destroyed by a proslavery mob.

A sensational book entitled *The Impending Crisis of the South*, written by Hinton R. Helper, a Southerner, and published by a northern press in June 1857, gave the Republican defense precisely the support it needed. Helper, the son of a North Carolina yeoman farmer and small slaveholder, had concluded that slavery was retarding both the economic and the cultural progress of the South. Dedicating his book to southern nonslaveholding whites, he used the 1850 census to compile statistical tables showing that the North had far surpassed the South in commerce, manufacturing, and even in agriculture, and that the average value of an acre of northern land was more than five times higher than an acre of southern land. Helper concluded that slavery was the sole cause of the discrepancy and that the immediate rise in land values resulting from its abolition would more than compensate the slaveholders for the value of their slaves. Meanwhile, he charged, "the lords of the lash are not only absolute masters of the blacks . . . but they are also the oracles and arbiters of all non-slaveholding whites, whose freedom is merely nominal, and whose unparalleled illiteracy and degradation is purposely and fiendishly perpetuated." Having no desire to live among free blacks, Helper proposed to levy a tax on slaveholders to pay the cost of colonizing them in Liberia or Latin America.[69]

Helper's book found few southern readers, but it won enthusiastic praise from the Republicans. The Washington *National Era* hoped that it would be "scattered broadcast throughout the country," for it would "open the eyes of the blind upon this subject." An optimistic Pennsylvania Republican believed that

Helper expressed "a widely spreading sentiment at the South," and that half the slaveholders of Virginia were "emancipationists at heart, and free-soilers secretly." The Republican National Committee immediately considered publishing a cheap edition of *The Impending Crisis,* and during the congressional campaigns the following year the party distributed an abridged version, prepared by Helper and endorsed by many Republican leaders.[70]

The border city of St. Louis bolstered the Republican effort to refute the charge of sectionalism by giving the party its first substantial foothold in a slave state. In 1856, Frank Blair, son of Francis Preston Blair and a resident of St. Louis, was elected to Congress as a free-soil Democrat. A friend of Thomas Hart Benton, an advocate of the free-state party in Kansas, and a champion of Frémont, Blair had the support of the St. Louis *Missouri Democrat,* edited by B. Gratz Brown, of the Bentonites (but not of Benton himself), and of much of the city's German population. In March Blair's supporters nominated John M. Wimer for mayor on a platform declaring that the gradual emancipation of Missouri slaves, with compensation to their owners, would be "neither impracticable, unwise, or unjust" if it appeared to be "for the best interests of the people." On April 8, Wimer was elected by a substantial majority, a victory, according to the *Missouri Democrat,* "for the free white working men of St. Louis." In his inaugural address Wimer asserted that the "skilled and intelligent labor of free white men is more productive than the compelled labor of slaves." The racist appeal of this border-state emancipation movement was clear enough. "It will be asked—what will be done with the niggers?" remarked the *Missouri Democrat.* "We answer that charity begins at home, that we are only interested for the whites. . . . We will, nevertheless, suggest that our colored folks might be shipped to Liberia."[71]

Proslavery Southerners, already concerned about the loyalty of the border slave states, were shocked by the emancipationist victory in St. Louis and the election of Blair, a "Black" Republican, to Congress. They found what consolation they could in the belief that cities everywhere were "controlled by corrupt influences." Republicans warmly embraced the St. Louis antislavery party, racism and all. It was enough that it had determined "to throw off the deadening and blighting influence of slavery" and come to terms with "the progressive spirit of the age." The Washington *National Era,* usually a voice of the Radical Republicans, in its enthusiasm, praised the "able and enlightened course of that large and influential Press, the *Missouri Democrat.*" Even Frederick Douglass, though recognizing that the St. Louis election was "purely a white man's victory," was happy that white men, "bad as they generally are, should gain a victory over slavery."[72]

To many Republicans it was significant that the St. Louis victory was made possible by the votes of German settlers and emigrants from the free states. To a few the victory suggested that at least the Upper South might be "redeemed" if it were systematically planted with communities of northern free farmers and artisans. John C. Underwood, a New Yorker by birth, after selling his property and leaving his Virginia home, returned to the North and urged various Republicans to unite in a colonization project. Early in 1857 he aroused the interest of Eli Thayer, a Massachusetts Congressman and founder of the New England Emigrant Aid Company which had assisted free-state emigrants moving to Kansas. In April, Underwood and Thayer, with the support of Greeley and numerous northern merchants, bankers, and manufacturers, obtained a charter for the North American Emigrant Aid and Homestead Company from the New York legislature. The purpose of the company was to purchase uncultivated lands in Virginia, distribute part of it to settlers in small plots, and sell the rest to make a profit. Industry as well as agriculture was to be encouraged; railroads were to be constructed; and villages of free artisans were to be planted. As the project grew, the promoters expected the slaveholders to sell their lands and migrate to the Deep South, thus transforming Virginia into a free-labor state.

Thayer bought land for the company in western Viriginia on the south bank of the Ohio River and founded a colony which he named Ceredo. However, the company was inadequately financed; the colony attracted few settlers; and by the end of the year the enterprise had collapsed. Some Southerners had viewed the project with amusement, some with anxiety, and a few with anger. Republicans had welcomed colonization as an antislavery program both peaceful and practical, and at least a few continued to hope that the South's redemption might come in this gradual, painless way.[73]

By 1857 Republicans were thinking of broadening their appeal by adding some economic planks to their national platform—and three years later they did. But the national Republican party continued to be, as it had been in 1856, an antislavery party stressing the need to protect free labor from the aggressions of the Slave Power. The conservative wing called their party the white man's party and used racist arguments in opposing the expansion of slavery. The radicals— the political abolitionists—were more aggressively antislavery in both their rhetoric and their goals, and more concerned about the plight of northern free blacks, most of them favoring black citizenship and black suffrage. The moderate, mainstream Republicans could on occasion speak of the need to exclude slavery from the territories in order to protect white labor, but just as often they justified exclusion either as an antislavery measure or as a way to undermine the Slave Power. They attacked slavery in the southern states only indirectly, for they acknowledged the constitutional limits of federal power. They emphatically denied any desire to secure the equality of the white and black races; yet they often spoke with feeling about rights which, according to the Declaration of Independence, *all* men were entitled to enjoy.

Mainstream Republicans did oppose slavery on moral grounds and hoped for its ultimate extinction, but apart from opposing its expansion they were seldom clear about how or when this might occur. Charles Francis Adams, for example, believed that great reforms "must in the nature of things move slowly." He favored going on, as in the past, "reforming opinion in the Free States," educating the "rising generation in a determined hostility to the spread of slavery," infusing "the genuine spirit of liberty into the still torpid regions of the Middle and Western States," and then trusting "to time and the providence of God for a favorable result." Adams was not sure that he would live to see the end of slavery. "But it will come, and in a peaceful form of settlement. All that we want, to accelerate it, is honest and competent leaders."[74] That was hardly a program, but abolitionists were equally vague in explaining theirs.

In 1857, however, all Republicans agreed that their immediate goal was to secure the admission of Kansas to the Union as a free state. Ironically, the Republican platform's demand for the prohibition of slavery by congressional action was neither attainable to them as a congressional minority nor relevant to the existing situation in Kansas. The voters in that territory were about to elect a constitutional convention in preparation for statehood, and the surest way to the Republican goal was to make certain that the antislavery majority would prevail in a fair election. In other words, Republicans found themselves obliged, temporarily at least, to support the popular sovereignty platform of Senator Douglas and the national Democrats.

CHAPTER **6**

Popular Sovereignty, Kansas Style

The early emigrants to all western territories found life hard and rough, and often violent. Among their shared experiences were Indian wars resulting from white encroachments on lands that were part of Indian reserves; lawlessness and the eccentricities of frontier justice; corruption at the government land offices; bitter conflicts over land claims and the planting of town sites; and political battles over the location of territorial capitals, transportation lines, and banking facilities. Those who settled Kansas Territory after its creation in 1854 experienced all of these trials, but much that they suffered was unique. No other territory became the object of such intense sectional rivalry, or endured the ordeal of civil war, or forced its people to choose between two rival governments, neither of which could establish its legitimacy beyond dispute. Except for the Mormon migration to Utah, no territory received as many settlers who were in some degree motivated by commitment to a cause as well as by the usual anticipation of economic opportunities. Kansas, observed the Richmond *Enquirer,* was "the battleground on which the South and the enemies of the South have met and struggled for the mastery."

Radical proslavery partisans viewed the Kansas conflict almost in apocalyptic terms. *"Kansas must come in as a slave state or the cause of southern rights is dead,"* wrote a Georgian. If the administration supported the free-state cause, he believed that Buchanan would "richly deserve death," and he hoped "some patriotic hand" would inflict it. The loss of Kansas, warned the Charleston *Mercury,* would soon mean the loss of Missouri as well, for it would then be nearly surrounded by free states. "Kentucky stands next, then Virginia." Antislavery Northerners agreed. "Momentous consequences for weal or for woe, hang upon the result," one of them asserted. If Kansas were won for freedom, "the honor of more than a 'Roman Triumph' will be due to the Spartan band, by whom that decision shall have been achieved." Another was convinced that if the South lost Kansas it "could never get on an equal footing again." Then the day could not be far off when Southerners "would see the beauty, profit and thrift of Free Labor" and abandon slavery.[1]

Neither side was willing to leave the outcome altogether to chance. Eli Thayer's New England Emigrant Aid Company, with the Boston conservative Whig philanthropist Amos A. Lawrence serving as treasurer, sold stock and solicited contributions to encourage and assist northern emigration to Kansas. The company speculated in territorial lands, helped to found and finance the free-state town of Lawrence, and subsidized the free-state journal, the *Herald of Freedom*. The editor, G. W. Brown, a Pennsylvania free soiler, moved to Kansas with his family and an emigrant party of nearly three hundred that he had organized with Thayer's support. Kansas-aid societies in New York, Chicago, and other communities also assisted northern emigrants, but most of them came independently from the middle Atlantic states and Ohio valley.[2]

Proslavery Southerners heard exaggerated stories of the efforts of northern Kansas-aid societies to "seize" a territory that they believed was rightfully theirs, and the most ardent of them tried countermeasures to "rescue" it for the South. However, slaveholders were not easily persuaded to risk their property in a disputed territory where the future of slavery was at best uncertain. The great majority of southern emigrants were nonslaveholders from the states of the Upper South, some of whom gave no support to the proslavery cause. By 1857, with only a few hundred slaves in Kansas, with a substantial free-state majority already there, and with a host of northern emigrants expected to arrive that spring and summer, the outcome of the Kansas controversy should have been clear enough.

Yet, Kansas Territory was still governed by a proslavery legislature. It had been elected with the aid of thousands of illegal votes cast by Missourians who had invaded the territory from the adjoining slaveholding hemp and tobacco growing counties lying along the Missouri River. These "border ruffians" were led by ex-Senator David R. Atchison and his lieutenant, B. F. Stringfellow, both of whom publicly announced their determination to win Kansas for slavery at any cost and boasted of their roles in the election frauds. "We had at least 7,000 [Missouri] men in the territory on the day of the election," Atchison informed Senator Hunter of Virginia. "We are playing for a mighty stake . . . [and] the game must be played boldly." At its first session the territorial legislature enacted the Missouri slave code and provided harsh penalties for any person who denied the legality of slavery in Kansas. "This body of men," declared the *Herald of Freedom* early in 1857, "forced upon the Territory against the wishes of four-fifths of its inhabitants . . . we hold in utter contempt."[3]

Leadership of the free-state party was in the hands of three strong-willed men: Dr. Charles Robinson and Samuel C. Pomeroy of Massachusetts, both agents of the New England Emigrant Aid Company who came to Kansas with Thayer's first emigrant group; and James H. Lane, a former Democratic politician from Indiana—a bold, ambitious, magnetic leader gifted with a rough eloquence—and the most militant of the three. They were the guiding spirits of the convention that met at Topeka in October 1855 to frame a free-state constitution and nominate candidates for state offices. The free-state party approved the constitution in December by a vote of 1,731 to 46 and early in 1856 elected a legislature and chose Robinson for governor.

Meanwhile, the proslavery supporters of the territorial legislature, now confronted with an organized and formidable opposition, had met in convention at Leavenworth and formed the Law and Order party. In the spring of 1856, backed by their legislature and judicial officers, by the Pierce administration, by federal troops, and by Atchison's Missouri irregulars, they organized a territorial militia and mobilized against the free-state "revolutionaries." Warrants were issued for the arrest of free-state leaders, and both sides called on their eastern friends for arms and reinforcements. Civil war began in May when proslavery forces entered Lawrence, destroyed the office and presses of the *Herald of Freedom*, burned the Free State Hotel and "Governor" Robinson's residence, and looted several shops. A few days after the "sack" of Lawrence, the militant abolitionist John Brown led a small party, including four of his sons, to Pottawatomie Creek and retaliated by dragging five proslavery settlers from their cabins and brutally murdering them.

For nearly four months thereafter the press was filled with accounts of battles, skirmishes, and raids, of victories and defeats for one side or the other. Peace was not restored until September, when a vigorous new territorial governor, John W. Geary, arrived. Supported by federal troops, he dissolved the proslavery militia and persuaded Atchison and his "border ruffians" to abandon plans for another attack on Lawrence and to go home. Some free-state guerrillas were arrested, and the proslavery hotspurs were soon persuaded that further violence would have serious consequences. By the end of the year, proslavery Missourians had abandoned their efforts to obstruct the passage of free-state emigrants, who thereafter were able to travel freely through Missouri by wagon, by railroad, or by boat up the Missouri River.[4]

The war was over, but the surviving bitterness and mutual suspicion was a legacy not soon forgotten. The devastation of the conflict, Governor Geary reported, "had impoverished many good citizens." Partisans on both sides, he charged, had "committed acts which no law can justify; and the people of Kansas have been the victims." No traveler, wrote the Lawrence *Herald of Freedom,* could visit the territory "without having forced upon him painful evidence of poverty and misfortune." Editor G. W. Brown recalled his own tribulations: "Our press type, office and fixtures were destroyed because we advocated Free

State Principles. For four months we were imprisoned. . . . Our family was broken up and scattered, and our property was gone." Only the contributions of northern friends "and the devotedness of Mrs. Brown to the cause" enabled the *Herald of Freedom,* on November 1, 1856, to resume publication.[5]

Democratic politicians were as aware as their opponents of the manner in which the Kansas territorial legislature had been elected, and they had tried to avoid facing the northern electorate as its defender during the presidential campaign of 1856. In June of that year Senator Robert Toombs of Georgia introduced a bill which, in effect, would have rejected both the "border ruffian" legislature and the Topeka free-state government and initiated a procedure that would have secured the early admission of Kansas to statehood. The Toombs bill provided for the taking of a new territorial census supervised by federal commissioners appointed by President Pierce. All adult white male residents were to be registered as voters, including free-state settlers driven from the territory but who had returned by October 1. In November they would elect delegates to a constitutional convention which would meet the following month. Congress would be pledged to accept the convention's constitution whether or not it recognized slavery, and Kansas would be admitted to statehood at once even though its population was less than the normally required minimum. With this measure—by all appearances a fair compromise—Democrats hoped to eliminate Kansas as a political issue or, if defeated, at least to place themselves in a better strategic position for the national campaign.

Republican Congressmen opposed the Toombs bill. Although they were accused of cynically trying to keep the Kansas issue alive to gain a political advantage, there were other plausible reasons for their opposition. Pierce's previous Kansas appointments hardly encouraged them to trust his judgment in selecting the crucial federal commissioners. Even if he chose impartial commissioners, could they cope with the territory's proslavery judges and sheriffs, or prevent another invasion of Missourians on election day? Was the Toombs bill a mere campaign ploy? Was it a trick designed to make Kansas a slave state once the election was over? Republicans may have been unduly suspicious, but they responded to the proposal at a most unfavorable time: after Democrats, including Senator Douglas, had defended the "bogus" Kansas legislature for more than a year, shortly after Brooks's assault on Sumner, and in the midst of the Kansas civil war. The bill easily passed the Democratic Senate, but the Republicans defeated it in the House, proposing instead to admit Kansas as a free state under the Topeka constitution. Douglas, angry and frustrated, damned the Republicans for their partisanship. "An angel from heaven," he cried, "could not write a bill to restore peace in Kansas that would be acceptable to the Abolition Republican party previous to the presidential election." To Republicans, however, the Toombs bill smelled of the earth rather than heaven.[6]

The lame-duck session of the Thirty-fourth Congress, which met from

December 1856 to March 1857, had no greater success in resolving the Kansas stalemate. The Toombs bill was dead, and there was no possibility of the Democratic Senate accepting the free-state Topeka constitution. The "bogus" territorial legislature, therefore, continued to be the de facto government, recognized by the administration in Washington, by Governor Geary, and by Samuel D. Lecompte, the proslavery chief justice of the federal court in Kansas. All the county probate judges, sheriffs, and justices of the peace were loyal to the legislature, which had appointed them. In addition, the House of Representatives, by a close vote, had seated the intensely proslavery John Whitfield as territorial delegate. Under those circumstances members of the free-state party, whatever their feelings, could not avoid, in some degree, giving tacit recognition to the authority of the territorial government. Even the Lawrence *Herald of Freedom* eventually recognized it as "the government *de facto* though we all deny its being such *de jure*."[7]

The Kansas government was nonetheless a travesty of Douglas's "great principle" of popular sovereignty, and by 1857 even many of its friends were deserting it. When Geary became governor the days of the "border ruffians" were over, and Atchison, their principal leader, returned to Clinton County, Missouri, to manage his estate. In a mass meeting at Westport, Jackson County, on the Kansas border, local Missourians announced their determination to preserve the peace and extended to emigrants from both sections "a hospitable welcome and all the protection of persons and property." Early in the year the proprietor of the Atchison *Squatter Sovereign,* the leading proslavery newspaper, sold out for lack of support, and its new owners turned it into a free-state organ. It was a sign that control of Atchison and other proslavery towns along the Missouri River in northeast Kansas was rapidly being lost to free-state settlers. In March, after spending several months in the East, "General" James H. Lane, who had commanded the free-state militia, returned to Kansas and settled in Doniphan, another former proslavery town. On a visit to Atchison he was cordially entertained by none other than Dr. J. H. Stringfellow, the former proslavery editor of the *Squatter Sovereign.*[8]

Proslavery Southerners were discouraged about Kansas prospects, and many abandoned hope of planting slavery there. Late in the spring, Atchison advised a South Carolina friend that it was futile to raise any more money for the cause. "At one time we had high hopes," the Richmond *Enquirer* recalled sadly, "that in Kansas we should soon have another outpost protecting the institutions of the South. But we are no longer laboring under any such flattering illusion." Why had the South failed? The reason, according to the *Enquirer,* was that Northerners were "more migratory and more fanatical" than Southerners. "Prompted by the cupidity which characterizes the roving Yankee in his search for gain . . . they rush to Kansas in hordes; while the Southern people, having stronger local attachments, less avidity for the 'almighty dollar' and more congenial comforts at home, were not so active in the enterprise."[9]

Only a few months earlier the *Enquirer* had itself been urging the South not to surrender but to "arrest the advance of abolitionism, and to defeat the policy which would restrict the extension of slavery." Remembering the promises and predictions southern Democratic politicans had made during the presidential campaign that the South would have Kansas, some, especially in the Deep South, would not give up the fight. In April a proslavery emissary from Kansas arrived in South Carolina to address public meetings held to raise money. "Pro-slavery still survives and has the mastery in Kansas," claimed the Charleston *Mercury.* "The North will be defeated, and Kansas will be gained to the South." All that was needed was "but one effort more" to secure Kansas and to protect the slave-holding region of western Missouri. "While we have a prospect of getting Kansas," admonished a Texas editor, "upon this question are we called to unite all our energies." In Kansas the proslavery Leavenworth *Journal* bravely assured its friends, who were "a little faint-hearted," that their cause was "bright and promising."[10]

With the territorial government still in proslavery hands, free-state partisans were far from confident that the battle for Kansas had been won. In January the *Herald of Freedom* urged northern emigrants to come early, not only to find the best locations for settlement but to "checkmate" proslavery emigrants who would try to win Kansas by their votes as others had tried by violence. "Those who think that the freedom of Kansas is already secured, are laboring under a great mistake," warned the Chicago *Tribune.* The soil and climate of eastern Kansas were as suitable for slavery as those of the border slave states, and if rooted there it would "cast its deadly shadow over that land" and degrade free labor. "On then with the emigration," the *Tribune* urged. "Let the good and true men of the North, who are seeking new homes in the West, hasten their preparations."[11]

"Governor" Robinson visited Boston, New York, and Washington in January soliciting financial aid for his free-state government. The Vermont and Michigan legislatures appropriated money for the relief of northern settlers in Kansas, to be used if conditions required it. The Massachusetts legislature appropriated $100,000, only to have the bill vetoed by the conservative Know-Nothing governor, Henry J. Gardner. The Kansas State Committee of Massachusetts, formed the previous year by a remarkable coalition of abolitionists, Republicans, and conservative businessmen, issued an appeal for funds to aid free-state settlers. "They look especially to Massachusetts and New England for such aid," it claimed. "The sons of the Pilgrims in the West appeal to their brethren in the East. . . . The efforts to defend freedom must be equal to the efforts to crush it."[12]

Among the Kansas free-state emissaries who visited the East in the winter and spring of 1857 was John Brown, whom one reporter described as "a hale and vigorous old man of fifty-seven, of a spare figure, with piercing dark-blue eyes, and a face expressive of indomitable will." In spite of his involvement in the Pottawatomie massacre, Brown won the admiration of many prominent men and women of Boston and Concord and thrilled them with his bold assertion that freedom in Kansas could only be won by the sword. Henry David Thoreau introduced him to Ralph Waldo Emerson, who heard him speak in Concord's town hall. Brown "gave a good account of himself," Emerson wrote. "One of his good points was the folly of the peace party in Kansas." On April 8 a group of thirty Bostonians, including Charles Francis Adams, Samuel Gridley Howe, and Amos A. Lawrence, met at the home of W. R. Lawrence on Beacon Street to hear Brown explain his plan to organize a company of one hundred "minute men" to fight for the free-state party if violence broke out again. The Kansas Committee and various individuals, vicariously joining Brown's military enterprise, gave him money to finance it and to support his family. How Brown actually spent the money is unclear.[13]

The astonishing power of John Brown's personality affected not only the abolitionists but philanthropic businessmen such as John Carter Brown of Providence and Amos A. Lawrence. The former contributed $100 to the cause of "that sturdy friend of liberty for Kansas and his brood of little Browns." His motive, he said, was to help "a *poor* but *worthy* family," for he rejoiced that there yet remained "*some northern* men true to the great cause of freedom." Lawrence, although too conservative to join the Republicans, was Brown's most generous patron. He thought that if there was a renewal of violence in Kansas, Brown would be the "best man" to lead the defense of the free-state party, provided there was "some controlling power near him." Lawrence believed Brown to be "a pious man and loyal to his government," and asserted that he had "done and suffered more to keep slavery out of Kansas than any other man, except perhaps Robinson."[14]

Fortunately for the people of Kansas, the civil war did not resume in 1857, and John Brown soon decided to wage his private war against the Slave Power elsewhere. With large-scale violence apparently a thing of the past, Lawrence turned his attention to the Emigrant Aid Company's Kansas properties and encouraged with generous gifts the development of a system of public education and the founding of a college. "It was fortunate for Kansas," wrote a Republican admirer of Lawrence, "that she early enlisted the services of so noble and munificent a patron."[15]

In the spring of 1857, the Rev. George B. Cheever, speaking to a Boston audience at the invitation of the New England Emigrant Aid Company, described the ingredients of "a perfect Christian colonization" of Kansas: "the church, the ministry, the word of God, the meeting-house, the Sabbath school, the plough, the sawmill, free schools, and free labor." Some of that year's northern emigrants still moved to Kansas in companies dedicated to the free-state cause. For example, one of the promoters of a company from upstate New York expressed its desire to take with it "such means of culture," including a free press,

as would "give tone and character" to the territory and help to plant free institutions. The Emigrant Aid Company assisted several small parties by securing
reductions in train fares, but its role was now a small one compared with the
unassisted movement of individual emigrant families from the states of the Old
Northwest.[16]

In March the St. Louis *Missouri Democrat* reported that the city was filled
with strangers, "all destined for the fruitful plains of Kansas." They came to St.
Louis by rail from Cleveland, Indianapolis, and Chicago; and they traveled from
St. Louis to Kansas either by rail to Jefferson City and then by steamer up the
Missouri River, or by steamer all the way. When they arrived they settled somewhere temporarily and began their search for land. "Persons hunting claims are
to be found going in all directions over the Territory," wrote a Kansas correspondent. "New towns are being laid off ... [and] there will be considerable
speculation in town property." Missouri speculators had already invaded the
Shawnee Reserve in eastern Kansas, which was Indian land, and they organized
to defend their illegal claims against newcomers who, according to reports, proposed to make their own equally illegal claims and become actual settlers.[17]

Land claims, the promotion of town sites, and the procuring of town charters were as prolific sources of trouble in Kansas as in other western territories,
but the conflicts were intensified by the fact that they frequently pitted proslavery
and free-state partisans against each other. To make matters worse, Congress had
opened Kansas to settlement before portions of Indian land reserves had been
acquired by treaty and before public lands had been surveyed and opened for sale.
Settlers were permitted by law to be "squatters" on unsurveyed land in the public
domain, and they were given preemption rights—that is, the right eventually to
buy their land at the minimum price of $1.25 an acre at the government land
offices. Squatting on Indian lands under the jurisdiction of the federal Office of
Indian Affairs was always illegal. Because of the slowness of the surveyors, no
settler in Kansas was able to acquire title to his land until the first public sale in
November 1856. Additional sales occurred in 1857, each of them attracting large
crowds which included, as one observer noted, "honest squatters, speculators,
sharpers, traders, etc., who were there on legitimate business," as well as "a large
number of horse thieves [and] not a few gamblers ... with their ... chuck-a-
luck, and other games spread out to view."

Both Pierce and Buchanan managed to exacerbate the Kansas land controversies by filling the federal land offices and Indian agencies with incompetent or
corrupt appointees, most of them proslavery partisans. As in other territories,
they, along with governors, judges, and lesser territorial officials were themselves
frequently involved in land speculations, joining the Missourians and emigrants
from both North and South in often violent disputes over claims. The settlement
of Kansas had begun at the height of the land speculation mania of the 1850s,
which had been stimulated by national prosperity, a growing foreign market for

American wheat, high commodity prices, and a great influx of European immigrants. *"All the world and the rest of mankind are here,"* a proslavery politician wrote from Leavenworth. "Speculations run high. Politics seldom named, *money* now seems to be the question." Investors in Kansas lands included eastern politicians, bankers, and capitalists, some of whom also set up loan offices where settlers could borrow money for land purchases at rates averaging close to 40 percent.[18]

Free-state politicians were as heavily involved in land speculations as their proslavery counterparts. One of "Governor" Robinson's private enterprises was the development of a new town on the Missouri River, which he named Quindaro, and which he hoped would become as prosperous as Lawrence. "I am strongly tempted," he wrote to his wife, "to spend my time in cultivating a part of my claim and have no other business except to buy and sell property and loan money if I have any to loan. . . . Just think of 5 per cent a month or 60 per cent a year for money." Robinson claimed to have come to Kansas with about $2000, and in 1857 he valued his Kansas property at $195,300. He did not think it was "a sin politically to be industrious and make a little money if possible," for money was "essential to success in politics."[19]

To Thayer the New England Emigrant Aid Company had always had a dual purpose: to encourage and assist free-state emigrants to Kansas, and to make money for its investors through land speculation and the development of town sites such as Lawrence. However, Amos A. Lawrence never expected the company to make a profit. To him its sole purpose was "to explore and plant capital in Kansas and thus make settlements; to make arrangements by which emigrants can go there (at their own expense) and as cheaply as possible." In May 1857, Lawrence resigned as treasurer of the company, explaining that in his opinion its main object, "the incitement of free emigration to Kansas," had been accomplished. Thereafter, with its role in the Kansas crusade rapidly diminishing, it was essentially a land company trying, without success, to make a profit.[20]

Lawrence was practical enough to realize that the current interest in land speculation would "form a great element" in encouraging free-state emigrants to come to Kansas. "That will be rife," he predicted. "Fortunes will be made and lost in rapid succession." Mocking the moral pretensions of Robinson, Lane, and other free-state politicians, a proslavery editor charged that they had "made a good thing" of the Kansas troubles. "All of them have grown fat on the blood of suffering Kansas. The reason of their course is apparent to everyone." But who in territorial Kansas, whether proslavery, antislavery, or neutral, was not trying, like Robinson, to "make a little money"?[21]

Although the restoration of peace enabled Kansans to repair whatever property damage they may have suffered and to endure only the normal hardships of frontier life, the political problem of two governments, both with dubious credentials, remained unresolved. Governor John W. Geary, having demonstrated both courage and skill in implementing his program of pacification, seemed to be ideally suited as well for the task of establishing a single legitimate source of political authority. An energetic young Pennsylvania Democrat in his mid-thirties, Geary had seen military service in the Mexican War and subsequently gained political experience in California, where he served as San Francisco's first mayor. He came to Kansas sharing the administration's negative feelings about the free-state party, but he quickly developed a more balanced view and a determination to see justice done to both sides. The problems of the territorial government were daunting enough to tax to the limit even his considerable talents. Among other problems, he found a moribund judicial system and the treasury virtually without funds. Most counties had failed to pay assessments, and the sheriffs had been unwilling to risk life and limb attempting to make collections.[22]

After an extensive tour of the territory and numerous interviews, Geary gradually began to turn against the proslavery party and to appreciate the folly of its continued support by the national administration. In January he sent President-elect Buchanan a candid report concerning the state of affairs in Kansas. Proslavery leaders and most of the territorial officers, he claimed, had "entered into a secret league, called the 'Blue Lodge,' with the deliberate purpose of making this 'a slave state in or out of the Union.'" He urged Buchanan not to support this "specious and transparent movement," for he was convinced that at least three-fourths of the actual citizens were in favor of making Kansas a free state. Geary warned that the territory's proslavery leaders, whose actions had made them "deservedly odious," were not capable of organizing a successful Kansas Democratic party.[23]

Nevertheless, on January 12 the proslavery party, by then thoroughly hostile to Geary, met in convention at Lecompton. Small in number but determined to fight on, the party remained in the hands of reckless men: John Calhoun of Illinois, the surveyor-general appointed on the recommendation of Senator Douglas, and intent on being the territory's Democratic political boss; L. A. Maclean, his chief clerk, a crude, blunt man and a fierce partisan; John W. Whitfield of Tennessee, the territorial delegate and formerly a federal Indian agent; A. J. Isaacs, a land speculator and former district attorney; Chief Justice Samuel D. Lecompte of Maryland; and Judge Sterling G. Cato of Alabama, neither of whom made any pretense of judicial impartiality. Under their guidance the convention, having made it clear that none but proslavery men would be welcome, brazenly changed the organization's name from the Law and Order party to the National Democratic party. Resolutions called for a constitutional convention to prepare for statehood, endorsed the principle of popular sovereignty, and urged the people of Kansas to "rally to the defense of law and order." On a motion from the floor the delegates also resolved unanimously that the territories were "the common property of all the states," and that all persons were free to emigrate to Kansas and were "entitled to protection by law, of their property, of every species and character."

Asserting that henceforth "we fight under the banner of the National Democracy," the proslavery Lecompton *Union* invited men of all parties to join in "putting down the foul Black Republican conspiracy designed to overthrow the Constitution of our beloved country." The Lawrence *Herald of Freedom* denounced the convention as a "noisy, swearing, smoking and excited crowd" gathered from the river towns of Kansas and Missouri, bent on violence against Governor Geary and other "abolitionists." Geary seemed unconcerned, reporting that the convention was sparsely attended and produced "no serious harm." Its purpose, he believed, was merely to adopt the name "National Democracy" and to oppose some of his official acts.[24]

By January the free-state leaders were divided in their reactions to Geary, some finding the proslavery party's hostility to him encouraging, others refusing to trust any appointee of the Pierce administration. "Governor" Robinson had resigned the previous month to support a hopelessly unrealistic proposal by his mentor, Amos A. Lawrence, that Kansas be admitted to statehood under the Topeka constitution with Geary as governor. The *Herald of Freedom* shared Robinson's confidence in Geary, urging Republican editors not to "throw obstacles in his way." But the suspicious citizens of Osawatomie, at a public meeting, resolved that any member of the free-state party who collaborated with the territorial government would be regarded as a spy and socially and politically ostracized.[25]

When the free-state legislature met at Topeka early in January, Robinson was not in attendance and the body lacked a quorum. Governor Geary, though receiving assurance that nothing unlawful would be done, nevertheless had his "confidential agent" there and reported to Washington that he was "prepared to act as circumstances might require." Action was unnecessary, for the legislators only adopted a memorial asking for admission as a free state, after which they adjourned until June. Before their adjournment a deputy United States marshal appeared with a writ for their arrest, issued by Judge Cato, on the grounds that they had illegally attempted to assume public offices. They offered no resistance to being taken as prisoners, and on appearance before Judge Cato they were released on bail. (The following May the court made the whole affair a pointless farce by declaring the cases *nolle prosequi*.) "Certain parties," Geary charged, had attempted to thwart his peaceful policy and "to excite renewed bitterness between the opposing political parties of the Territory." The response from Washington was a rebuke not to Cato but to Geary for failing to act more firmly against the Topeka pretenders. "You will, I have no doubt," wrote Secretary of State Marcy, "take care that restless and evil minded men are not permitted again to stir up civil strife in the Territory." Apparently Geary, by incurring the hostility of the proslavery party, had also lost the confidence of the Pierce administration.[26]

On January 12, the day of the proslavery party's convention, the territorial legislature also met at Lecompton, a busy town on the south bank of the Kansas River which served as the territory's capital. The fact that Governor Geary acknowledged the legality of that body did not pacify its members; nor did his message, though its tone was conciliatory and his advice to them eminently wise. He urged them to follow a course of "moderation and justice," of respect for the ballot box, and of "unqualified submission to the will of the majority." He recommended the repeal of the test oath required of voters as "wrong, unfair, and unequal upon the citizens of different sections of the Union"; a transfer of the power to appoint probate judges and other public officers from the legislature to the electorate; adoption of strict residential requirements for voting and severe penalties for "false voting"; and repeal of the section in the slave code that destroyed "freedom of speech and the privilege of public discussion" concerning slavery in Kansas. Geary also advised the legislature, when Kansas was ready for statehood, to require the convention to submit its proposed constitution to a "direct popular vote . . . to give it sanction and effect." Finally, he announced with pleasure that Kansas was at peace and had "entered upon a career of unparalleled prosperity."[27]

The legislature ignored nearly all of Geary's recommendations. It did repeal the oath required of voters to support the federal Fugitive Slave Act, and a law making it a felony to deny the legality of slavery in Kansas. This was done not to accommodate the governor but to ward off a proposal then before Congress to repeal all acts of the legislature. Most of its objectionable proslavery legislation still remained in force, and it now added another provocation by making it a capital crime to engage in "rebellion" against the territorial government. "Every man in the Territory of ordinary penetration," protested an antislavery editor, understood that this act had been passed "for the express purpose of preventing Free State conventions." As a final challenge to the free-state party the legislature passed a banking act which located the principal bank at Leavenworth, with branches in various towns, the notable exceptions being Lawrence and Topeka.[28]

During its month-long session relations between the legislature and Governor Geary worsened as they went through a series of hostile confrontations. One of the controversies involved Chief Justice Lecompte, considered by Geary negligent, incompetent, and blatantly partisan. The last straw was a case involving one Charles Hays, indicted for murder, released by Lecompte on token bail, rearrested on Geary's order, and released again on a writ of habeas corpus. Geary then asked for Lecompte's removal, and Pierce reluctantly sent the Senate his nomination for a replacement. The legislature denounced the governor for interfering with an "honest, high-minded, and capable" judge while engaged in the discharge of his duties, and Senator Toombs of Georgia praised Lecompte for refusing to be "intimidated or seduced." The Senate eventually rejected Pierce's nominee, and Lecompte, to Geary's dismay, continued to serve as chief justice.[29]

A second bitter conflict arose when the Board of Commissioners of Douglas

County appointed William T. Sherrard, a violent proslavery man, to the vacant office of sheriff. Geary, knowing Sherrard's reputation, refused to issue the necessary commission. When the legislature demanded an explanation, he replied that "many good citizens" of the county had complained that Sherrard's "habits and passions rendered him entirely unfit" for the office. He had been involved in "several drunken broils—fighting and shooting at persons with pistols." Sherrard, after threatening the governor's life, accosted him one day as he was leaving the legislative chamber, cursed him, and spat on him. The legislature had passed resolutions defending Sherrard; but on February 19, after the spitting incident, friends of Geary in Douglas County met at Lecompton to pledge their support. When Sherrard and his cronies tried to break up the meeting, shooting began, and before the bloody encounter came to an end Sherrard had wounded John W. Jones, Geary's clerk and brother-in-law, and Jones had shot and killed Sherrard. Subsequently a company was formed to protect both Jones and Geary, but Jones, who was arrested and released on bail, absconded.[30]

While Geary was embroiled with the legislature the proslavery editor of the Lecompton *Union* subjected him to a drumfire of abuse. "He came here with a smiling countenance . . . [but] bearing to us inward hatred," it charged. "The thin veil falls, and we see him, *as he is,* our enemy." Defying all evidence to the contrary, the *Union* insisted that the majority in Kansas was "emphatically Pro-Slavery." All that was necessary to make Kansas a slave state was to uphold the existing laws. "Does any one doubt our power to do so? . . . We can get along without the Governor's assistance, if he witholds it." All the constables, magistrates, sheriffs, marshals, and judges, the *Union* boasted, were on the proslavery side—"it is *our* duty to sustain and uphold them."[31]

The legislature easily matched the audacity of the *Union*'s editor when, on February 14, without waiting for Congress to pass an enabling act, it adopted a bill providing for a constitutional convention with the clear intention of making Kansas a slave state in spite of the territory's antislavery majority. The bill specified that during the month of March the county sheriffs and their appointed deputies, or the probate judges in counties having no sheriff, were to take a census of all free male citizens of the United States over twenty-one years of age, and of all other white persons residing in their counties. By April 10, lists of qualified voters were to be filed with the probate judges, who could hear challenges until May 1, after which the lists were to be submitted to be the governor and to each county. On the basis of these lists the governor was to apportion convention delegates among the counties. The boards of county commissioners were to determine the polling places, and to appoint "three suitable persons" for each place to be judges of the election. The election of delegates was to be held on the third Monday in June. Voting was restricted to "every bona fide inhabitant of the territory" over the age of twenty-one who was a citizen of the United States, who had resided in his county for at least three months, and whose name was on the voting list. Delegates to the convention were to meet at Lecompton on the first Monday in September with authority to "form a constitution and state government."

The cynical partisanship of the convention bill was clear to everyone. By its provisions emigrants arriving during the three months prior to the election, who would be overwhelmingly from the northern states, were ineligible to vote. Moreover, as the *Herald of Freedom* correctly observed, "every avenue to the polls" was in proslavery hands. The census takers, judges, and clerks of election all would be creatures of the legislature. No provision was made for the submission of the constitution to the electorate for ratification, and the legislature did not intend that it should be submitted. "Every contingency has been provided for in this compact and complicated scheme," observed the St. Louis *Missouri Democrat*. "The convention will be packed from the foundation-stone to its eve-stone, and every honest man in Kansas will therefore see the propriety of shunning it as he would Pandemonium itself."[32]

Governor Geary's last act for the Pierce administration, which he had served better than it deserved, was to veto the territorial legislature's convention bill. In his veto message he criticized the flaws in the method of taking the census, the exclusion of recent emigrants from the election, and the lack of sufficient guarantees of an honest count. Most of all he stressed the bill's "material omission"— its failure to require that voters be given a chance to approve or reject the convention's work. Geary questioned whether Kansas, with her meager resources and small population of perhaps thirty thousand, was ready for statehood, and he suggested that the majority might be inclined to vote against any constitution at that time. In any case, the position "that a convention can do no wrong . . . and that its constituents have no right to judge of its acts," was "extraordinary and untenable."[33]

Ignoring Geary's objections, the legislature easily passed the convention bill over his veto. At that point the thoroughly exhausted governor, confronted by hostile territorial legislators and judges, receiving no encouragement from the Pierce administration, and threatened with physical violence, wondered, in a letter to Amos A. Lawrence, how much longer he could "sacrifice pecuniary interests, comfort, and health" to continue his "almost thankless work." On March 4 he sent in his resignation. Stopping in St. Louis on his way east, he poured out his bitter feelings to the editor of the *Missouri Democrat*. He accused the Pierce administration of failing to honor its pledge to support him. In spite of threats of assassination, the commander of the federal troops in Kansas, General Persifor F. Smith, had refused to give him military protection, and he was forced to spend his own funds for that purpose. His mail had been tampered with. Thus, according to his interviewer, Geary "more than confirmed" the reports of outrages by proslavery ruffians and asserted that "the half [had] not yet been told."[34]

On March 23, Geary met with Buchanan and the Cabinet and gave his final report on conditions in Kansas, apparently with little effect. He had aroused too much hostility in the South for the administration to embrace him; moreover, it had been deluged with denunciations of the ex-governor from the territory's proslavery politicians. Some northern Democrats, too, considered him "dangerous," and suggested that he be treated "with decided denunciations . . . based on his cowardice and treason to the party." More often they shared the New York *Herald*'s sympathy for Geary's effort to check "the outrageous doings of the border ruffians." Republicans praised him moderately, giving him credit for stopping the intrusion of armed bands from Missouri and for "such measure of peace as the territory has enjoyed since his appointment."[35]

Geary's term as governor of Kansas had lasted a scant six months. He was the third governor appointed by Pierce and decidedly the most successful, for he had ended the civil war and sent the Missouri "border ruffians" home. Yet, when he departed, the tainted Lecompton territorial government and the shadow Topeka state government were still competing for recognition, and the constitutional convention that was to meet at Lecompton in the fall appeared less likely to resolve the political impasse than to introduce a further complication. This was the shape of the two-year-old Kansas problem as it was dropped in Buchanan's lap immediately after his inauguration.

The governorship of Kansas was one of the less lucrative and least attractive appointments the President could offer an ambitious politician. It was also one of the most important, for the continued success—perhaps the survival—of the Democratic party as a national organization required a prompt settlement of that territory's political future—one arrived at in a manner whose fairness no reasonable person could dispute. Northern Democratic leaders had promised no less than that during the presidential campaign, and they knew that fairness was not to be expected from the Lecompton constitutional convention without forceful executive leadership. "It is manifest," a Pennsylvania Democrat warned Attorney General Black, "that . . . unless the public are convinced that there is a fair field and no favor between the pro-slavery faction and its opponents—we may soon add Pennsylvania to the domains of Northern fanaticism. . . . We must have no failure from any cause this season." Buchanan needed to be "firm and determined," wrote a Michigan Democrat. If he wavered over Kansas the party would be in "imminent danger" of losing the entire North. How the President dealt with that problem, a Philadelphia editor believed, would "go far to determine the complexion of parties for the next four years."[36]

Buchanan decided to offer the Kansas governorship to Robert J. Walker of Mississippi, whom he had earlier considered for his Cabinet and who seemed to have the ideal combination of talent, energy, political experience, ambition, and daring for the job. Since the end of his service as Secretary of the Treasury in 1849, Walker had been engaged in a variety of speculative schemes involving western lands, railroad promotions, California mining, and the construction of a canal through Central America. Though a Pennsylvanian by birth, he had lived in Mississippi long enough to build a law practice, acquire slaves and a plantation, and become a force in state politics. More recently Walker's speculations had brought him to New York, where he had established other valuable business and political connections. His appearance belied his aggressive character. In his mid-fifties, he was a frail, wizened little man, no more than five feet two inches tall, weighing not much over one hundred pounds. But he was fearless and still politically ambitious. For a man of his imagination a Democratic presidential nomination would not have seemed an unrealistic ultimate goal.[37]

In the fall of 1856, Walker, a strong supporter of Buchanan, had published a campaign pamphlet entitled "An Appeal for the Union." In it he stated bluntly his belief that Kansas, because of the nature of its soil, climate, and population, would not become a slave state. Buchanan had read the pamphlet and in a letter to Walker called it "excellent" and "stamped with all the ability of its author." He thought it "well calculated to do good to the cause" and hoped to have a German translation for circulation in Pennsylvania's German counties. The President was thus quite aware of Walker's position before offering him the Kansas appointment, and he gave no sign of disagreeing with it.[38]

Buchanan did not merely offer Walker the appointment—he begged him to take it. "It was a long time before I would agree to go to Kansas," Walker later testified before a congressional committee. "But the request was renewed from time to time with great earnestness by the President, and by many friends through whom he communicated with me." Douglas put heavy pressure on him, declaring that the success of the Kansas-Nebraska Act depended upon his consenting to go. When Mrs. Walker objected to her husband's acceptance, the President called on her, told her that he might "save the country," and persuaded her to give her consent. Walker's final acceptance entailed great financial sacrifice and considerable risk to his health and political future. "It is a most hazardous experiment," one political friend warned him. "I tremble for your reputation." Quite possibly he agreed to go to Kansas in part out of a patriotic sense of duty. But he also seemed confident that he could succeed where others had failed, and the political rewards of success were worth the risk. "After that of President," wrote one northern editor, "there is not a more responsible officer in the whole country than the Governor of this territory. The eyes of the whole Union are fixed on him."[39]

Walker laid down certain terms before accepting the Kansas appointment, to all of which the President readily agreed. Frederick P. Stanton, a former Tennessee Congressman then practicing law in Washington, was to be appointed secretary of the territory, and General William S. Harney was to be given command of 1500 federal troops, whose support would be available to the governor if needed. Most important, in a letter to Buchanan, dated March 26, Walker made clear the policy he intended to pursue and the support he expected from the administration: "I understand that you and all your cabinet, cordially concur in the opinion expressed by me, that the actual, *bona fide* residents of the Territory of Kansas, by a fair and regular vote, unaffected by fraud or violence, must be permitted, in adopting their State constitution, to decide for themselves what shall be their social institutions." This was the "great fundamental principle" of the Kansas-Nebraska Act, and he expected the whole people of Kansas to "participate, freely and fully, in this decision."

Buchanan, in his reply through Secretary of State Cass, dated March 30, fully concurred and made his own policy equally clear: The territorial legislature having authorized a convention, "the people of Kansas have the right to be protected in the peaceful election of delegates for such a purpose. . . . When [the] constitution shall be submitted to the people of the territory, they must be protected in the exercise of their right of voting for or against that instrument, and the fair expression of the popular will must not be interrupted by fraud or violence." In short, although the territorial legislature had made no provision for submission of the constitution for ratification or rejection, the President and Governor Walker both agreed that its submission in an honest election was the only way to determine the popular will. Both seemed determined that the popular will should prevail, and for the next several months there was no outward sign of disagreement between them.[40]

The northern Democratic press almost unanimously approved Walker's appointment. It was, asserted the New York *Herald*, "immeasurably the most important act, thus far, of the new administration," one that would "in all probability . . . settle the Kansas imbroglio." Walker, predicted the Detroit *Free Press*, would not govern that territory as a northern or southern partisan, for he was "a Union man—a sectionalist upon no subject and in no respect." Such a man, of course, was not to the taste of the southern fire-eaters who, like the Charleston *Mercury*, still insisted that Kansas belonged to the South and demanded a governor who would save it from the abolitionists. Walker, growled Edmund Ruffin, was an "unprincipled adventurer . . . authorized and instructed by the President to use his official influence to make Kansas a non-slavery state." However, the Richmond *Enquirer*, in its enthusiastic approval of Walker, was decidedly more representative of southern Democratic opinion. He was, it claimed, a man of integrity and "unclouded judgment," with a clear understanding of the rights and interests of both sections. Even the Lecompton *Union* greeted the appointment with "exquisite satisfaction," for Buchanan had given the territory "a first class statesman . . . who hails from the South."[41]

As for the Republicans, some professed to believe that Buchanan, perceiving the need to admit Kansas as a free state in order to save the northern Democracy, had slyly sent Walker, a southern man, to accomplish that result. The New York *Tribune*, considering his background, was not hopeful but generously declined to prejudge him. Most Republicans judged Walker at once and harshly. This "broken down financier and worn out political hack," sneered the Milwaukee *Sentinel,* was "just the sort of man to continue to the bitter end the unfortunate troubles of Kansas." The Chicago *Tribune* suspected a nefarious plot. Walker's purpose, "with his honeyed words," it charged, was to persuade the free-state party to recognize the validity of the laws of the "bogus" legislature and thus to trap them into admitting the legality of slavery in Kansas. He was a "vagabond fortune hunter, a political black-leg," and his promise of a fair vote was a "cheat and a snare." In Kansas the editor of the *Herald of Freedom* promised to "try and throw a healthy influence around him" but feared that Walker would join the border ruffians, who stood "ready to embrace him." Unfortunately for the new governor, he would begin his tenure with suspicious partisans, North and South, ready to destroy him if he would not serve their cause.[42]

In April, as Walker settled his affairs in the East and prepared to depart for Kansas, he reviewed the present condition of the territory and weighed the policy choices that he could realistically consider open to him. The territorial legislature, whatever the manner of its election, he felt obliged to recognize as the legitimate legislative body whose laws must be enforced. Accordingly, he would be obligated to deny the legality of the Topeka free-state government, but he could leave it undisturbed as long as it made no effort to govern. The election of the Lecompton constitutional convention could no longer be prevented, but he could encourage the free-state majority to vote for delegates and insist that the constitution be submitted to the electorate for approval or rejection. Walker knew that in a fair election the majority would almost certainly reject slavery, but he could try at least to create a solidly Democratic state, for the free-state party included a substantial number of northern and southern Democrats. Finally, he was as eager as Buchanan to have Kansas ready for statehood when the Thirty-fifth Congress began its first session the following December. He may well have read the New York *Herald*'s euphoric prediction that with the Kansas issue satisfactorily settled, "the democracy and the administration . . . are upon their feet again, and Mr. Walker may command an unparalled popularity for the succession."[43]

From mid-April to late May, pending Walker's arrival, Frederick P. Stanton, the territorial secretary, served as acting governor of Kansas. Although he had been a proslavery Tennessee politician, he made it clear, in an address to the people of the territory, that he shared Walker's determination to have "a full and fair expression" of the popular will on the subject of slavery. To avoid any pretext for resistance to the action of the constitutional convention the election of delegates must be free of fraud and violence, and the convention must "provide for submitting the great distracting question" of slavery to a vote of all the "actual *bona fide* residents of the territory."[44]

On April 24, having accepted an invitation to visit Lawrence, Stanton was received cordially by free-state leaders and had tea at the home of Charles Robinson. After this ceremony of reconciliation he addressed with candor and firmness a gathering of citizens in front of the Cincinnati House. After speaking glowingly of the future of Kansas and expressing his hope for continued peace, he evoked cries of protest when he insisted that the laws of the territorial legislature, recognized by Congress as valid, must be obeyed and taxes paid. Far more agreeable to Stanton's audience was his declaration that, although he was a proslavery Southerner, he had no desire to force slavery on people opposed to it. He reiterated his determination to have the issue submitted to the electorate and confessed that he had always believed that Kansas would become a free state. Rapport with his audience restored, he closed amid good feelings all around, dined at the Cincinnati House with local notables, and spent the rest of the evening in pleasant conversation. The next day he toured the town and mingled with the people whom he found most agreeable.[45]

The convivial atmosphere of Lawrence during Stanton's visit did not change the free-state party's decision not to participate in the election of delegates to the Lecompton convention. On March 10 a party convention at Topeka had adopted resolutions denouncing the method prescribed by the territorial legislature for taking the census and compiling the voting lists, asserting that there was no adequate protection against fraud, and noting the legislature's failure to require the submission of the constitution to the voters. Another resolution claimed that the Topeka constitution had the support of the majority of Kansas citizens and urged Congress to approve it and grant the territory immediate statehood. During this convention Robinson agreed to withdraw his resignation as governor and resumed his role as head of the inactive Topeka state government.[46]

Eastern friends of the free-state party deluged it with well-meaning but conflicting advice concerning its response to the approaching delegate election. Some, including the New York *Times* and the more radical Washington *National Era,* urged party members to vote, arguing that the consequences of not voting would be more damaging to their cause than voting and losing the election. "If they do not contest it," advised the *National Era,* "their strength will be unfelt and unascertained, and the evidence of fraud cannot be demonstrated. If they go into it heartily . . . they may be outvoted; but if this is done by illegal votes, they can demonstrate the fact." Those who advised antislavery Kansans to vote were reacting to Democratic warnings that, if the election of convention delegates went to the proslavery party by default, the responsibility for the constitution they would write would rest on those who refused to vote. They were also sensitive to the charge in the Democratic press that Republicans were prepared to permit Kansas to become a slave state in order to keep up the slavery agitation until after the presidential election of 1860.[47]

Others shared the opinion of the Chicago *Tribune* that the best course was "to pay no heed to the enactments of the Felon Legislature and to stand by the Topeka constitution." The New York *Evening Post* advised "unyielding resistance to usurping authority at every hazard." Amos A. Lawrence encouraged Robinson to follow a course of "passive opposition to the bogus laws" and predicted that "if persisted in by the people, it must prevail." Seward, on the other hand, thought that the Kansas free-state party had always done best when left "to act according to the necessities of the hour" and advised outsiders to refrain from interfering. Charles Francis Adams was distressed by the division of opinion and concerned about the dilemma free-state Kansans confronted: "If they go in and vote for the new convention, they do so at every disadvantage. . . . If they do not, their silence will be construed as consent, and congress will be called upon to ratify the Constitution as the result of a fair expression of the popular will."[48]

Free-state Kansans were themselves divided over the issue of voting, and their leadership was weakened by a dispiriting feud between "Governor" Robinson and G. W. Brown, whose *Herald of Freedom* grew increasingly critical of Robinson and openly doubtful that the Topeka government would ever be accepted by Congress. What were they to do? Along the Kansas border, one antislavery partisan claimed, "all Missourians are enrolled to vote," while in many interior free-state counties "whole neighborhoods are passed unnoticed." At this juncture an Indiana Republican Congressman, Schuyler Colfax, wrote to Robinson and suggested a strategy. Go to the governor, he advised, with "a frank, direct, comprehensive proposition, so framed that its justice and fairness would be apparent to all men." Ask him to appoint election officers representing both parties with instructions to compile new voting lists, and to station federal troops along the Kansas border to prevent another Missouri invasion. If the governor rejected this proposal, free-state leaders could suggest submitting both the proslavery constitution and the Topeka constitution to a vote, with the understanding that he would recommend the one favored by a majority to Congress. If both proposals were rejected, Colfax assured Robinson that it would "absolutely annihilate any party at the North that would dare to continue opposition to your rights."[49]

On April 25, the day after Stanton's address to the people of Lawrence, Robinson and several other citizens presented him with a letter containing a proposal similar to the one suggested by Colfax. At present, they claimed, there was no assurance that the vote for convention delegates would be fair. Many names had been omitted from the registry lists, while well-known citizens of Missouri were registered. However, if a fair election were intended, they would "overlook the past and go into the election" on the following conditions: First, two persons should be elected in each district, one by the proslavery and one by the free-state party, to take a new census and register all legal voters. Second, the apportionment of delegates should be based on the returns thus made. Third, each precinct should have four judges of election, two proslavery and two free state. Finally, the names of three of the judges should be required to validate a certificate of election.

Stanton replied the following day. He could not consent to new proceedings in opposition to those sanctioned by the territorial legislature. Rejecting the charge that the laws of Kansas had been enacted by an illegal body elected by voters from Missouri, he asserted that it was his duty to enforce them. Although he could not control the probate judges, he hoped that they would correct their voting lists. He reminded Robinson and his friends that they had "very generally, indeed almost universally, refused to participate in the pending proceedings for registering the names of the legal voters."

In spite of his friendly overtures to the citizens of Lawrence, Acting Governor Stanton had concluded his visit with a virtual concession that legally he could not prevent the election of convention delegates from being conducted precisely as the territorial legislature had intended—that is, with nearly all of the free-state voters refusing to participate. The election, predicted the New York *Herald,* would be carried unanimously by the proslavery party. The convention would have "unlimited power in favor of slavery" and would "doubtless exercise it in the adoption, unanimously, of a pro-slavery State constitution."[50] If that were the outcome, how could northern Democrats ever again make a persuasive case for Senator Douglas's "great principle" of popular sovereignty? How could President Buchanan hope to settle the controversy over Kansas by the end of the year? Indeed, how could the Democratic party survive as a national organization if, during his administration, still another crisis developed in that troubled territory?

In the early weeks of May, as the delegate election approached, it appeared that the party's fate was in the hands of Robert J. Walker, the kinetic little governor, who would soon be on his way to Kansas brimming with confidence that an inaugural address he carried in his baggage would soon put everything right.

Before leaving Washington, Walker asked President Buchanan to read certain crucial passages in his inaugural address. Having secured his approval, he went to New York and had dinner with some business and political friends, whom he assured that the people of Kansas, before a constitution was adopted, would be given an opportunity for a "full, free, and solemn" expression of their will. On his way west he stopped in Chicago to confer with Douglas and to let him read his inaugural address, thus making certain that there was no difference between them. At St. Louis he boarded a steamer for the journey up the Missouri River, finding among his fellow passengers a Republican Senator, Henry Wilson, a notorious abolitionist, Samuel Gridley Howe, and the Rev. John Pierpont, all from Massachusetts. Disembarking at Leavenworth on May 25, he attended a rather alcoholic reception where he had his first encounter with a free-state leader, "General" Lane, and found him quite cordial.[51]

The following day he visited Lawrence. At the Unitarian church he found a capacity crowd turned out to hear rousing antislavery speeches by Wilson, Pierpont, and Howe. After praising the beauties of Kansas, Wilson promised to go home "more than ever condemning the policy which would expose these fertile fields to the footsteps of the slave." "Governor" Robinson spoke of the tribulations of free-state citizens, warning the new governor that they would make a "big rumpus" if he did not protect their rights, but assuring him that they would be his "best friends" if he did. Walker was invited to speak, and in his brief remarks he promised both to enforce the territorial laws and to insist that the constitution framed by the Lecompton convention be submitted to a fair vote of the people.[52]

On May 27, Walker was in Lecompton to deliver his inaugural address. Parts of his address bordered on the flamboyant and the whole was considerably longer than it needed to be; but he clearly stated the policy to which the administration was committed, and he gave free-state citizens the promise of fairness that he hoped would persuade them to participate in territorial elections. The convention about to be chosen, he said, was properly authorized by the territorial legislature, and it was his duty to see that the election was free from fraud or violence. He urged all qualifed voters to go to the polls, warning those who refused that their acquiescence in the result must be assumed. With equal force he sounded a warning to those who would serve as delegates: It was his "clear conviction, that unless the Convention submit the constitution to a vote of all the actual resident settlers of Kansas, and the election be fairly and justly conducted, the constitution will be and ought to be rejected by Congress."

Walker stressed the importance of keeping slavery agitation out of Congress and presidential elections, predicting that if the question of slavery in Kansas could be fairly resolved, "the safety of the Union [would] be placed beyond all peril." There was, he claimed, a law of nature that would determine the future of slavery in Kansas. It was evident in "the isothermal line . . . regulating climate, labor and productions, and, as a consequence profit and loss," which could "no more be controlled by the legislation of man than any other moral or physical law of the Almighty." Walker assured the proslavery party that even though nature excluded slavery from Kansas the state need not be controlled by the "fanaticism of Abolitionism," nor should it become an asylum for Missouri's fugitive slaves. South of Kansas, he said, was a great region "admirably adapted by soil and climate for the products of the South," and there a new slave state might soon be created. He closed with a burst of passionate oratory in praise of the brave men and women who were building the West: "The march of our country's destiny, like that of his first chosen people, is marked by the foot-prints of the steps of God."[53]

Walker's immediate concern was the impact of his address on the proslavery and free-state parties in the territory. His aim, he later explained, had been "to unite the free State democrats with the pro-slavery party and all those whom I regarded as conservative men" in order to make Kansas a Democratic state. He was encouraged by the fact that the eight Democratic candidates for delegates to the constitutional convention from Douglas County (Lecompton), including John Calhoun, were already committed to favor submitting the constitution to the voters. Unfortunately, his assertion that Kansas was not suited for slavery turned the most aggressive proslavery leaders against him. At a dinner given by the territorial legislature after his inaugural address, Maclean hurled insults at him and threatened him with the fate of his predecessors. Subsequently a proslavery delegation went to his office and demanded that he say no more about submitting the constitution for ratification. Nevertheless, the governor had widened a division in proslavery ranks. For example, the Lecompton *Union,* after helping to drive Governor Geary out of the territory, responded to Walker with remarkable warmth. Although dissenting from his opinion concerning slavery in Kansas, it praised his address as "able and statesman-like ... a masterly production," and approved his stand in favor of referring the constitution to the electorate.[54]

Walker's inaugural was most successful in building trust between him and the free-state party. "We hail his advent among us with pleasure," responded the *Herald of Freedom.* "Governor Walker is a Southern man, but he is ... too much of a man to be led by the pot-house politicians who will surround him at Lecompton." On a second visit to Lawrence shortly after his inaugural he listened to numerous citizens relate their past difficulties, and he was reported to have said privately that although the past could not be changed, "the future is in our keeping, and every wrong can be redressed." In an interview with one prominent citizen the governor asserted that the idea of admitting Kansas to the Union without submitting its constitution to the people was "too monstrous to be tolerated either here or at Washington." Reporting to Cass, he was emphatic in his warning that without a popular vote a peaceful settlement of Kansas affairs was unlikely and "a most disastrous civil war" a distinct possibility.[55]

On June 6, Walker was in Topeka to address a large mass meeting of the free-state party. Having abandoned hope that its members would participate in the election of delegates to the constitutional convention, he stressed the importance of their voting in the fall when a new territorial legislature was to be elected, and when it was his intent to have the Lecompton constitution submitted for ratification or rejection. He urged them to abandon the illegal Topeka government and warned that he would suppress any attempt to put it into operation. Walker confessed that he could do nothing about the registration procedures for the election of convention delegates, but that election, he argued, was less important than the subsequent vote on the finished constitution. On that occasion, he promised them, the constitution would be submitted to the *whole* people—not only to those registered under the territorial law, or to those now in residence, but to all who would be actual residents in the fall. If the majority voted against the constitution, that would be the end of it. If the Lecompton convention refused to submit the constitution to a vote, Walker would join them in opposition to it, adding that he was confident that the President and Congress would oppose it as well. Both the President and the Cabinet, he assured his audience, knew his views and had approved them before he accepted his appointment as governor.[56]

In spite of Walker's assurances, a free-state convention met in Topeka on June 9 and, with "General" Lane presiding, reaffirmed their desire for admission to statehood under the Topeka constitution and urged the free-state legislature to remain in readiness to assume political control if necessary. The Topeka legislature met on the same day, but it was careful to avoid collision with federal authorities. Governor Walker was there and spoke to the members, making it clear that if they took no action he would not disturb them. Actually, the legislature lacked both unity and a quorum, and in its weakened condition, with "Governor" Robinson again ready to abandon the cause, it was unable to do more than maintain a shadowy existence and await developments in the fall. On June 13 it adjourned.[57]

Two days later the election of delegates to the constitutional convention took place, with the result a foregone conclusion. Senator Douglas, either from inexplicable ignorance or from unwillingness to admit that popular sovereignty could be turned into a farce, had asserted publicly that the territorial election law was "just and fair," and that he believed it would be "fairly interpreted and impartially executed." Those who refused to vote, he said, would have to bear the responsibility if the result were not to their liking. Yet, abundant evidence that the election had been rigged was available to all who would see. Partly because of free-state recalcitrance and partly because of the indifference of proslavery officials, the census had not been fairly taken; less than half of the adult males were on the voting lists; and the apportionment of the sixty delegates was weighted heavily in favor of a few counties along the Missouri border where proslavery sentiment was strongest. If anything more were needed to control the result, proslavery officers alone would canvass the election returns.

By election day members of the free-state party had patched up their differences and decided overwhelmingly, even if registered, not to vote. As a result, with only token opposition from a few hundred free-state Democrats, approximately 1800 proslavery voters elected 60 delegates who were unanimously, though in varying degrees of intensity, proslavery. Seven thousand registered voters stayed away from the polls, and another 10,000 adult males were unregistered. As one northern Democrat reported, "There are about 20 to 25,000 votes in Kansas. About 9000 were registered—about *2000 voted!* Comment is unnecessary." In short, the delegates had been chosen by less than 10 percent of the potential voters, and by the summer of 1857 that probably represented nearly the full strength of the Kansas proslavery electorate.[58]

Democrats accused the free-state voters of being the "obedient servants" of the Republican party, less interested in the exclusion of slavery from Kansas than in keeping up "anarchy and strife" until the next presidental election. Actually, after the arrival of Governor Walker the free-state party gradually evolved a strategy of its own. As one prominent Kansan, Henry J. Adams, explained it to Governor Chase of Ohio, the strategy was based on Walker's statement "in the most positive terms" that the constitution framed at Lecompton must be submitted to the voters. Adams believed that free-state partisans would turn out in force and vote it down. They would also participate in the election of a new territorial legislature in October. Then, with that body in free-state hands, "we can call a new convention and readopt the Topeka Constitution and submit it again to the people for ratification." Eighty to 90 percent of the population, Adams predicted, would approve. All this could be accomplished without making any concessions to the proslavery party other than "voting under their bogus laws," and without "coming in collision with the general government."[59]

Shortly after the delegate election, showing no concern about the result, Walker exuded confidence in a letter to Buchanan. "I have been in a constant whirl of business and excitement since my arrival here including seven public addresses," he reported. Although he found "restless men" among both proslavery and free-state partisans, he was certain that the "vast majority" of the people were with him. He credited his inaugural address and other speeches for preventing the free-state legislature from adopting and enforcing a code of laws, but he warned that it would do so in the fall if the constitution were not put to a vote. In fact, the principal cause of tension in the territory was the fear that a proslavery constitution would be "forced by a minority upon the majority." Hardly anyone, Walker claimed, denied that the majority wanted Kansas to become a free state. Still, he was convinced that all would be settled satisfactorily if the convention did its work properly. The governor's confidence, of course, rested principally in his faith that in all of his public addresses he spoke the President's mind as well as his own.[60]

Early in July, President Buchanan read Governor Walker's cheerful letter in a mood decidedly less buoyant. Patronage problems still bedeviled him, and he had just received the alarming news that a disappointed and now independent John W. Forney, without administration approval or support, was about to publish his own newspaper in Philadelphia. He was also aware of the fear among northern Democratic leaders that the recent Kansas election might lead to another political disaster: an attempt by the proslavery convention to attain statehood with a proslavery constitution not ratified by a popular vote. At the moment, however, Buchanan was most distressed by the cacophonous roars of protest emanating from southern Democratic presses and politicians over Walker's inaugural address and other speeches delivered in Kansas. To the "blood and thunder organs" of the ultra state-rights Democracy, observed the New York *Herald,* the governor was "guilty of the most heinous of political crimes": he had expressed the opinion that Kansas was not suitable for slavery, and he had predicted that Congress would not accept the Lecompton constitution if it were not submitted to the people for ratification.[61]

The fire-eaters led the attack on Walker, not only because of his demand that the constitution be approved by the electorate but also because he had rejected the legislature's restrictive suffrage requirements. He was, the Charleston *Mercury* raged, the "greatest Abolitionist in Kansas," and it urged the convention to "despise his counsels and defy his threats." The Jackson *Mississippian* joined the radicals who demanded that Buchanan uphold the principle of federal nonintervention by the prompt removal of his "cunning and treacherous appointee." If Kansas were lost, South Carolina's Lawrence Keitt asserted, it would be lost by a federal official, a "political mountebank," who had traveled through the territory "corrupting and debauching, tricking and bullying, wherever free-soil objects could be accomplished by these base means." Walker was not the only villain, Keitt believed, for Buchanan also had "a finger in the pie." His aim was to bring Kansas in as a free state in order to save the northern Democracy. If Walker were not removed, wrote Judge Thomas W. Thomas of Georgia, "we are ruined, and ought to be if we sustain Buchanan. . . . Our victory is turned to ashes on our lips, and before God I will never say well done to the traitor or to his master who lives in the White House."[62]

Southern protests were not limited to the fire-eaters. Moderate administration Democrats avoided attacks on the President, but many expressed their hostility to Walker. In Georgia the Democratic state convention, meeting June 24, adopted resolutions praising Buchanan and the party's Cincinnati platform but demanding Walker's removal for violating the nonintervention provision of the Kansas-Nebraska Act. Two weeks later the Mississippi Democratic convention resolved that Walker's inaugural address was "a dictatorial intermeddling with the performance of a high public duty already entrusted by law to a convention selected from the people of Kansas with which Governor Walker had no right to interfere." In Montgomery a public rally declared Walker's demand for submission of the constitution improper and a gross violation of the principle of popular sovereignty.[63]

Buchanan realized the gravity of the southern rebellion when it extended to some whose loyalty he took for granted and could scarcely do without. Slidell of Louisiana turned against Walker and began to talk like a fire-eater. Toombs angrily denounced Walker's "folly" in demanding a vote on the constitution and hoped that the convention would refuse to comply. Lucius Q. C. Lamar, writing from Mississippi, denied that he was an enemy of the administration, but he warned that if it supported Walker's policy, "the enthusiasm of the party will vanish, [and] the energy and momentum of an approving public sentiment will be irretrievably lost." Alexander H. Stephens's disaffection, expressed in a public letter to his Georgia constituents, was especially painful. It was the convention's right, he claimed, to submit the constitution for ratification or not as it chose. Governor Walker, however, had declared that the people could not form their constitution in their own way, but only "in his way or in that in which Congress shall see fit to dictate." This issue, Stephens argued, involved "everything recognized as State Rights and State Sovereignty," and he could not believe that Buchanan would support Walker's "outrageous and monstrous" doctrine.[64]

Stephens's letter was doubtless motivated in part by the attempt of Georgia Whig-Americans to exploit the Walker controversy during a particularly bitter gubernatorial campaign then in progress. In every southern state the opposition party, in a typical display of opportunism, flayed the Democrats for betraying the proslavery cause in Kansas and professed great sympathy for the courageous protests of southern-rights radicals against administration policy. "It is well known that Walker's programme was prepared before he left Washington, and approved by Buchanan and his Cabinet," wrote a Tennessee Whig editor. "We submit to the people of the South if this is the feast to which they were invited in the support of Mr. Buchanan." The Richmond *Whig* accused the administration and "that hermaphrodite locofoco, the Hon. Robert J. Walker, now free soil Governor of Kansas," of a "deliberately concocted plot" to drive slavery out of that territory. The Louisville *Journal* described Buchanan's dilemma: If he appeased his southern critics by removing Walker, he would simply "drive the Northern Democracy to the farthest limits of mortal fury."[65]

His dilemma was in fact more apparent than real. To have removed Walker a few months after his appointment for announcing and defending what, in most respects, was the President's own Kansas policy, would have been a personal humiliation and a political catastrophe, and he never considered it. Every major northern Democratic newspaper strongly supported Walker and the administration. The New York *Herald* was convinced that Walker was "the faithful representative in Kansas of the President and his Cabinet, and must be sustained. . . . The fate of the administration and the destiny of the Union depend upon the nerve and pluck of our honest President. If he shrinks, like poor Pierce, he is lost." Forney, defending Walker in the Philadelphia *Press,* observed that the submission of state constitutions for ratification was the prevailing practice in both North and South; to deprive Kansans of that right "would be a disgraceful comment upon the boasted theory of popular sovereignty." The Cincinnati *Enquirer* noted that Congress had explicitly required the Minnesota convention to submit its constitution to the voters for approval. It doubted that "any party or faction had ever assumed so weak and untenable a position" as the southern politicians who opposed submission of the Kansas constitution. The Albany *Atlas and Argus* insisted that Congress had a duty, when a territory applied for statehood, to determine whether its constitution had the approval of a majority of its citizens.[66]

Letters supporting Walker from northern Democrats matched those opposing him from southern Democrats in both numbers and urgency. "For heaven's sake," a Pennsylvanian wrote Attorney General Black, "don't let Mr. Buchanan give way to the secessionists." Another warned him to beware of the men in the South who would do anything "to destroy a Penna. President, or a republican form of Govt." Buchanan received a most welcome letter from Glancy Jones, a friend with strong southern connections, praising his instructions to Walker and pledging his unqualified support. Senator Douglas wrote directly to Walker. "I have never hesitated," he assured him, "to express the opinion that the constitution ought to be referred to the people for ratification." He was confident that the convention would permit the bona fide inhabitants to vote on the constitution and exclude those who entered the territory "for the mere purpose of participating in the contest." It was "all important," Douglas concluded "that the convention shall make such a constitution as the people will ratify, and thus terminate the controversy."[67]

Early in July the administration's most impressive support came from the Democrats of Kansas. A convention called by the territory's Democratic Central Committee met at Lecompton to nominate a candidate for delegate to Congress. Taking the name of the "National Democracy of Kansas," the convention counted among its members emigrants from both the North and the South, some of whom were reported to be proslavery men. After they had unanimously endorsed Walker's efforts to keep the peace and uphold the law, a proslavery delegate introduced a resolution pledging support of the new constitution even if it were not submitted for ratification. The resolution was defeated by a vote of 42-1. "Does not the controversy end here?" asked the Democratic Detroit *Free Press.* "Is there any appeal from this action? . . . If Governor Walker has the unanimous approval of the democracy of Kansas, need he care what conventions in Georgia and Mississippi may say of him?"[68]

Several southern Democrats tried to persuade Buchanan that the party in their section was as united in demanding Walker's removal as the northern wing was in voicing its support. The Charleston *Mercury* claimed that no issue in the past had "brought the South into more complete Union than the proceedings of Governor Walker in Kansas." Writing from White Sulphur Springs, Virginia, a favorite summer watering place of southern planters and politicians, Slidell informed the President that he had not met anyone who did not strongly oppose Walker's course. All assumed that he viewed the governor's "foolish speeches" as they did and would soon make his opinion known. Francis W. Pickens of South Carolina, also writing from the Springs, claimed to find the same "universal condemnation of Gov. Walker's extra official conduct and speeches." Pickens reminded the President of his debt to the South and of the precarious position in which his administration and the Democratic party would find itself without southern support. In one way or another, he concluded, Walker's speeches must be repudiated, or "the whole South will believe that he was sent there expressly to over awe the Convention and dictate to it."[69]

These claims of southern unanimity in favor of Walker's removal were at best disingenuous. Actually, in spite of the noisy clamor against him, the South was divided, a fact of which the Buchanan administration was well aware. The gentry at White Sulphur Springs had only to read the influential Richmond *Enquirer* to discover their error. Submission of state constitutions for ratification or rejection, it asserted, though not always done in the past, was "highly proper" and "more in accordance with Democratic sentiment and the spirit of our institutions." Virignia's constitutional conventions had twice required ratification, the *Enquirer* recalled, adding that it was far more imperative in Kansas where only a small minority had voted in the delegate election. Moreover, "so many frauds have been committed there that the voters place no confidence in their legislative bodies." The *Enquirer* also recognized the right of Congress to reject a constitution when it clearly did not represent the will "of a majority of the *bona fide* residents . . . fairly ascertained by general suffrage."[70]

Similar editorials appeared in Democratic journals in Louisville, Nashville, Memphis, Milledgeville, and New Orleans. The Memphis *Appeal,* denouncing the war on Walker as "ill advised, unnecessary, and fraught with danger to the unity and harmony of the Democratic party," thought it "entirely proper that the Constitution should be submitted" and doubted that Congress would admit Kansas without ratification. In Milledgeville the *Federal Union* agreed that Walker had exhibited "considerable vanity" and "magnified his official importance," but accused some southern editors of being "entirely too hasty" in condemning him. As long as Democrats in Kansas were satisfied with his conduct, the editor saw "no reason to believe that he [had] done any substantial harm" and refused to endorse the Georgia convention's demand for his removal. The New Orleans *Picayune,* like many Southerners, often wavered and contradicted itself but eventually came out squarely for the principle of popular ratification. A proslavery constitution, it warned, written by convention delegates who exclude "the public voice from the decision, avowedly because they are afraid of being overruled, would be a calamity to Kansas . . . and to the slaveholding cause generally."[71]

Howell Cobb received numerous assurances from Georgia that the administration had general support and that the hotheads were gradually cooling off. After the"hasty and ill conceived action of our State Convention," one friend informed him, there had been time for reflection and a "better feeling" had developed. None fully approved of Walker's speeches, but the action of the Kansas Democratic convention had "opened the eyes of many" to their "imprudent and false position." Another friend sent "many thanks to Mr. Buchanan for daring to think and act for himself." Many now regretted the convention's resolutions, he claimed, and thought the whole matter was "a tempest in a teapot," especially since they had learned, "very much to their surprise," that Walker had the support of Kansas Democrats. After a trip to Kansas, James L. Orr of South Carolina told Cobb that Walker had not affected public opinion in that territory but had merely "conformed to what was public opinion among our friends when he got there."[72]

In Virginia the controversy over Walker became an issue in the rivalry between Governor Wise and Senator Hunter. Wise backed the administration's Kansas policy, and his attacks on Hunter through the Richmond *Enquirer* eventually forced the Senator to deny that his opposition to Walker implied hostility to the President. Beverley Tucker joined the dispute with a letter defending Walker that appeared in the *Enquirer* after Roger Pryor refused to publish it in the Richmond *South*. As a minority, he wrote, the South could not afford to be in the wrong. Walker was bound by the Kansas-Nebraska Act and by his instructions from the administration "to use every honorable means in his power to secure to the people of that disturbed Territory the free exercise of their elective rights." If the result were the admission of Kansas as a free state, "it must be by a *fair vote;* and to make it a slave state by any other process would not only disease the cause of the South, but would inevitably, in the end fail of its purpose."[73]

Walker was hardly the man to leave his defense entirely to others. Writing to Cass on July 15, he did not let modesty weaken the case he could make for himself. He repeated his conviction that only his promise of a vote on the constitution had dissuaded the Topeka legislature from adopting its own code of laws; and he claimed an important role at the territorial Democratic convention in securing its endorsement of administrative policy. He predicted that if a proslavery constitution were adopted against the will of the majority, free-state Democrats would be driven into the arms of the Republicans, Kansas would elect an abolitionist legislature, two abolitionist Senators, and an abolitionist Congressman, and the proslavery constitution would then be quickly abolished. "Indeed," Walker wrote, "the only real question is this: whether Kansas shall be a conservative, constitutional, democratic and ultimately free state, or whether it shall be a republican and abolition state." His policy alone would prevent that last "most calamitous result." As for the attacks from the South, they did not concern him, because he was certain that he could justify his course to reasonable Southerners when he could address them. Walker cared nothing for the hostility of the disunionists, "whose censure is praise," and whose approbation he neither sought nor desired.[74]

Walker's letter, however self-serving, was a reasonably accurate statement of the crucial role he had played in supporting the administration as well as of the likely result of accepting a proslavery constitution without ratification by the electorate. Buchanan had already received corroborating evidence from several Democratic friends with firsthand knowledge of Kansas affairs. George N. Sanders, a Kentucky adventurer and speculator, after two weeks in the territory, reported that the "wide awake and indefatigable little governor" had persuaded all parties that he had "the material interest of the territory much at heart." Simeon M. Johnson, writing from Leavenworth, praised Walker for his skill in winning public confidence without yielding to either side while "pressing his scheme of securing a fair vote." The extreme proslavery men, "now in a futile minority," disliked yielding political power into other hands. Nevertheless, he assured Buchanan that if Walker's policy were sustained, "a great triumph awaits your administration and the democratic party."[75]

The most forceful supporting letter came from Pennsylvania's usually unassertive Senator Bigler, who reported from St. Louis after an extensive land-speculating tour of Kansas. "I regret exceedingly to witness the bad temper of some of our southern friends," he wrote, for they apparently did not understand "the real state of parties" in that territory. "All probability of Kansas becoming a Slave State by the will of the majority, has vanished long since," Bigler asserted. "This is the opinion of the prominent proslavery men as fully expressed to me at all points on my tour." There was, he warned, "great danger of a much worse result—the organization of a Black Republican State," and it would require unity and skill among Democratic leaders to defeat that "dreaded result." In almost the identical words used by Walker, he claimed that the only question was whether Kansas would enter the Union "under the auspices of your Administration as a democratic State or as an abolition State!" Bigler understood the feelings of the southern dissidents, but they could not "change the fates—they wish a Slave State and yet no policy they could suggest at all admissible could produce such a result. . . . Let Gov. Walker be sustained and all will be well."[76]

With convincing evidence that Walker had the solid support of northern Democrats and of most Kansas Democrats, as well as influential defenders in the South, Buchanan was in a strong position to deal with the southern dissidents. He and his Cabinet could have wished that the governor had been less prone to windy speech making, and they clearly felt that his reference to an "isothermal line" pitting nature against the survival of slavery in Kansas, whether true or not, would have been better left unsaid. Even so, the dissidents' defense of the farcical election of convention delegates and opposition to Walker's demand for a popular vote on the Kansas constitution was too weak a cause around which to rally the South against the administration. The danger—indeed, the certainty—of a northern Democratic rebellion if a proslavery constitution were forced upon an unwilling majority was a far more compelling force behind Buchanan's course of action.

On July 12 he wrote a personal letter to Walker assuring him of his continued support. "The point on which your and our success depends," he affirmed, "is the submission of the constitution to the people of Kansas. And by the people I mean, and have no doubt you mean, the actual *bona fide* residents who have been long enough in the Territory to identify themselves with its fate." Three months, he thought would be a reasonable residence requirement, which would have given the vote to all emigrants arriving before early August. In words clear and emphatic, Buchanan repeated: "On the question of submitting the constitution to the *bona fide* resident settlers of Kansas, I am willing to stand or fall." That, he wrote, was the basic principle of popular sovereignty and "the foundation of all popular government." If the convention would adopt that principle all could be settled harmoniously, and Walker would "return triumphantly" from his "arduous, important, and responsible mission." Then the attacks from Georgia and Mississippi would "pass away and be speedily forgotten." Buchanan approved of Walker's principal goal in Kansas—"to build up a great democratic party there ... composed of pro-slavery and free State democrats." In a final word of caution he advised Walker, in the future, not to express his opinion that the Kansas climate was not suitable for slavery, because he exposed himself to the charge of "violating the principle of non-interference."[77]

Buchanan avoided personal confrontations with the southern dissidents, but throughout the summer of 1857 he and his Attorney General spoke indirectly and frequently through the columns of the administration's political organ, the Washington *Union*. Collectively these *Union* editorials contained a sweeping endorsement of both Walker's policies and opinions. When the Kansas convention had completed its work, one of them argued, it would still be necessary to determine whether the constitution reflected the will of the people "on the question, not only of slavery, but upon all others." If it did, Kansas should be admitted whether slave or free. If it did not, no one could pretend "that a constitution condemned by a majority of the people should be forced upon them, no matter under what forms and by what authority adopted." Given the present condition of Kansas, claimed an editorial written by Black, there was no way to determine the will of the people "except by their own direct expression of it at the polls." A constitution not subjected to that test would "never be acknowledged by its opponents to be anything but a fraud," and the controversy over Kansas would be "prolonged for an indefinite time to come." Ratification was all the more essential because the convention had not been authorized by a congressional enabling act, but only by the initiative of the territorial legislature. Black reminded critics that Walker was a southern man sent to Kansas by an administration pledged to defend southern rights, and he was entitled to "sympathy, comfort, and aid from the South."

On several occasions the *Union* boldly defended statements of Walker that were particularly offensive to the dissidents. His opinion that Kansas would become a free state, it claimed, was less an argument than a simple truism. Moreover, if the constitution were not approved by a popular vote, the chances were "a thousand to one" that Congress would reject it. Walker's prediction, therefore, was true, and, his warning was "timely and just." Finally, the *Union* denied the charge that he had abolitionized Kansas, because it "had been brought into its present condition perhaps a year or more before he went there."[78]

Cobb served both Buchanan and his own political ambition well by defending administration policy in the South, especially in his Georgia base where he strove to avoid a party division. He feared that the agitation of the dissidents would encourage the Kansas convention to refuse submission of the constitution to a vote, that Congress would consequently refuse to accept it, and that the country would then find itself in another "fearful crisis." Writing to Alexander H. Stephens he expressed regret that Walker had offered an opinion about the future of slavery in Kansas, but he slyly suggested that the governor, expecting it to become a slave state, had only meant to assure free-state partisans that they would be given a chance to be heard. Cobb argued that without submission of the constitution the administration "could not justify and carry through" the territory's admission to statehood. His own wish, he admitted, was that the Kansas constitution would say nothing about slavery, leaving the legislature to settle the matter when it was no longer a national political issue. In a letter to John B. Lamar he complained of the foolish demand for Walker's removal "when all *the democrats and pro-slavery men in Kansas* are satisfied with him."[79]

Cobb's most effective defense was addressed to Lucius Q. C. Lamar of Mississippi, whose opposition to Walker he regretted. After his usual concession that the governor had made some unwise statements, he agreed that his threat to oppose the admission of Kansas if the constitution were not ratified was wrong. Nevertheless, he argued, it was "the right and duty" of Congress to know that the constitution reflected the will of a majority of her citizens, and a vote for ratification or rejection was the best way to settle the matter. Cobb pointed to his own state where a constitution had once been submitted and rejected, and to the Minnesota enabling act requiring constitutional ratification. If Walker had violated the principle of nonintervention, then so had Congress and the President. In view of the small vote for convention delegates, Cobb confessed that he would "feel at great loss for a good reason" to justify a refusal to require ratification of the Kansas constitution. The question would be asked "again and again . . . why refuse to submit *to qualified voters,* if you believe that it was approved by them, and if you do not so believe, then do you desire to force upon an unwilling people a constitution they condemn?"[80]

Hoping to speed the process of Kansas statehood and to avoid alienating the whole of the northern Democracy, realizing moreover that it had no viable alternative, the administration thus gave its firm support to Governor Walker. Yet, this prosouthern President and Cabinet were distressed to find themselves exposed to so much criticism from southern Democrats. All of them despised Republicans and abolitionists, all believed that organized and subsidized northern emigrants were the original source of the troubles in Kansas, and all would willingly support the admission of Kansas as a slave state if a proslavery constitution were ratified in an honest election. The administration felt all the more uncomfortable when the Republican press began to heap praise on Walker for his courageous inaugural address. The New York *Evening Post* called it an "important concession to the popular sentiment of the North," indicating that Buchanan still had "some of his senses about him" and knew enough at least "to go in when it rains."[81]

In spite of such taunts, the Cabinet stood loyally behind the President— Black with his *Union* editorials, Cobb with his cajoling letters to southern friends. Jacob Thompson, who disliked Walker personally and had been his political rival in Mississippi politics, defended him with considerably less conviction. In one sour note to Black he claimed to have lost himself in Walker's "many givings out" and thought it required a "skillful tactician" to do justice to the President without wounding the governor. Even so, Henry S. Foote, the Mississippi Unionist, heard "from the lips of Mr. Jacob Thompson" the welcome news that Buchanan was determined to stand by Walker whatever the consequences to himself and his administration. Another of the Cabinet's Southerners, Postmaster General Aaron V. Brown, sent Walker a friendly letter of advice. He shared the governor's opinion that submission of the constitution to a vote would be the best policy, as well as his conclusion that Kansas would be admitted as a free state. He urged Walker only "to fix the record" so that the administration could not be accused of permitting the decision to be made by "a horde of imported [northern] voters." The governor was doubtless especially pleased to receive a cordial letter from Cobb, his old political friend, assuring him that no one desired Kansas to enter the Union with a constitution that did not have the approval of its people.[82]

In short, throughout the summer the President and Cabinet had given Walker every reason to feel secure.

In July, Governor Walker found an opportunity to demonstrate to Southerners his impartiality in administering territorial affairs. It grew out of an attempt of some citizens of Lawrence to bypass the territorial legislature in adopting a city charter and in electing a mayor, aldermen, and other officials. The charter empowered the city government to levy taxes and to adopt the usual ordinances to protect the health of citizens and preserve public order. Each city officer was to take an oath to support the constitution of the United States "and of this state"—that is, to support the Topeka government, not the territorial government whose legality Walker recognized. To justify their action the charter committee asserted that since the territorial government had not been elected by the people of Kansas, a charter could not be accepted from it, and the state government had not yet provided for the organization of municipal governments. Hence the only alternative to the community's present unorganized condition was a charter "springing directly from the people."

Walker's intemperate and overbearing response greatly exceeded the requirements of this minor challenge to territorial authority; it can only be explained in political terms as a heavy-handed effort to redeem himself in the eyes of his southern critics. On July 14 he called on General Harney for a regiment of dragoons to act as a posse comitatus to deal with a "dangerous rebellion" in Lawrence. The next day he addressed a long, grandiloquent proclamation to the people of Lawrence accusing them of attempting to "involve the whole territory in insurrection, and to renew the scenes of bloodshed and civil war." In another extravagant passage he charged that a rebellion "so iniquitous, and necessarily involving such awful consequences," had "never before disgraced any age or country." Accordingly, he had ordered a force of federal troops to the vicinity of Lawrence to arrest their "revolutionary proceedings," and he promised to accompany them "to prevent, if possible, any conflict." In a letter to Cass he claimed that Lawrence was the "hotbed of all the abolition movements" in the territory, whose purpose was "to perpetuate and diffuse agitation throughout Kansas."[83]

Walker rode with his dragoons to the outskirts of Lawrence, found its citizens going peacefully about their business, and, although looking rather foolish, had the dragoons camp there for the next two weeks. Like the majority of the citizens of Lawrence, the *Herald of Freedom* did not approve of the charter movement, but it gently rebuked the governor for his hasty and ill-advised action. "We had no idea that the preservation of the Union depended upon our allowing dead horses to remain in our streets," wrote another Lawrence editor. "Is vaccinating our little children an act of insurrection?" Nevertheless, Walker, still claiming that a revolutionary spirit prevailed, informed Cass that it was "indispensably necessary" to have a force of 2000 regular troops stationed at Fort Leavenworth, which he claimed "would probably prevent a conflict." Repeating his request near the end of the month, he feared the "most serious consequences" if the troops were not sent. Yet, he admitted that Lawrence's charter government had not been organized and that "a highly respectable conservative party" had formed to prevent any challenge to the territorial government.

Cass responded with assurance that the President approved of the governor's action against Lawrence, but he cautioned him to use "discretion as well as firmness" and to await an overt act of resistance before resorting to military force. During Buchanan's absence on a holiday at Bedford Springs, Pennsylvania, Cass reported the Cabinet's sober conclusion that Walker, in requesting additional troops, had exaggerated the seriousness of the crisis, and its perhaps justifiable suspicion that he was "endeavoring to make a [political] record for the future." Secretary of War Floyd suggested, less credibly, that the attacks on Walker from the South had caused him to hope, if he failed, to throw the blame upon the administration or the War Department. That thought led Floyd to wonder whether the appointment of Walker was "going to turn out very profitable." Buchanan clearly did not share these suspicions.[84]

By August 3, Walker had cooled off sufficiently to report that the conservative party controlled Lawrence and that, thanks to his vigorous action, no "insurgent government" had been established there or elsewhere. He then withdrew the troops from the vicinity of Lawrence and sent them west to protect frontier settlers during a rash of Indian attacks. Whatever else Walker may have accomplished by his military demonstration, he was temporarily spared the embarrassment of praise in the Republican press. Party editors now called him a "despot" bent on "crushing out the liberties of the people." He had been shaken by the attacks of the Georgia and Mississippi conventions, they charged, and to "appease their wrath" he now sought "to provoke an unnecessary war with the free State party."[85]

Walker's use of the military also elicited a letter of protest to the President, signed by forty-three distinguished citizens of Connecticut, including Professor Benjamin Silliman of Yale, Horace Bushnell, James Brewster, and Timothy Dwight. "The fundamental principle of the constitution," they affirmed, "is, that the people shall make their own laws and elect their own rulers." Hence, they were astonished to learn that the President, through the governor of Kansas, was employing an army to force the people to obey laws which "they never made, and rulers they never elected." The signers accused Buchanan, "to the great derogation of our national character," of violating his solemn oath to support the Constitution, and of "levying war against [a portion of] the United States." Yet, they would pray that with the aid of the Almighty, Buchanan would make his administration "an example of justice and beneficence and . . . protect our people and our constitution."[86]

This protest gave Buchanan the opportunity for which, quite obviously, he had been waiting. As Walker had exploited the Lawrence charter issue, he found in the Silliman letter a chance to balance the sectional and political scales. The style of his long reply, dated August 15, and subsequently published in the Washington *Union,* betrayed his enthusiasm for combat with northern Republicans and abolitionists; but the principal audience toward which it was directed was in the proslavery South. Accusing his critics of not knowing the facts, he related his version of events since the creation of Kansas Territory. Buchanan admitted that there had been controversy over the election of the territorial legislature, but when he became President he found the government of Kansas "as well established as that of any other territory." His duty, therefore, was to protect it "from the violence of lawless men, who were determined either to rule or ruin," and for this reason he had sent a military force to the territory. In his account, responsibility for the presence of the military rested entirely with free-state partisans, whom he accused of spurning the ballot box and attempting to establish a "revolutionary government" of their own.

In the light of the Dred Scott decision Buchanan claimed that slavery had been legal in Kansas from the beginning. How this could ever have been doubted he found a mystery, for when a territory had been acquired by the "common blood and treasure" of all the sovereign states none of the partners could be excluded "by prohibiting them from taking into it whatever is recognized to be property by the common constitution." A convention would soon meet to frame a constitution for the state of Kansas, and that would be the appropriate time for "qualified resident citizen" to express their opinion "at the ballot box on the question of slavery." Once again it would be the President's duty to employ federal troops, if necessary, to defend the convention against violence—and, he added, to protect those eligible to vote when the constitution was "submitted to them for their approbation or rejection." Buchanan concluded by admonishing the gentlemen from Connecticut to use their influence against northern antislavery agitation, which had produced "much evil and no good, and which, if it could succeed in attaining its object, would ruin the slave as well as his master."[87]

Although Buchanan had again made clear his assumption that the Kansas constitution would be submitted to the electorate, he presented it in such an attractive proslavery package that most southern dissidents responded favorably. Writing to Stephens, Cobb called the President's letter "a great document" that would "tell powerfully in our state." Cobb's brother, Thomas R. R. Cobb, reported that Toombs had become a strong administration man, calling "Mr. B's letter to the Forty Fools from Connecticut . . . the *greatest State Paper for the South* that [had] ever emanated from the Executive Chair since the days of Washington." A Louisiana friend assured Buchanan that his letter satisfied "every Southern man not pre-determined to make an issue" with him. He enclosed a letter from Governor Robert C. Wickliffe expressing "much pleasure" with the President's reply and "the most perfect confidence" in him.[88]

Republicans understood Buchanan's purpose. The Washington *National Era* found it impossible "to resist the conviction that the opportunity was chosen to set the Administration right with the discontented South." His response to the Silliman letter was nothing more than "a solemn act of submission to the nullifiers," claimed the St. Louis *Missouri Democrat,* and it should have been addressed not to Mr. Silliman but to Mr. Keitt, the South Carolina fire-eater. Some detected the hand of the Slave Power again at work. Buchanan now claimed that the Constitution protected slavery in all the territories. "What next?" one editor asked. Perhaps he would decide that it protected slavery in all the states as well. "Why not this? The step is not longer than the others—the doctrine no more startling now than the others were at first."[89]

During the long, hot Kansas summer of 1857 territorial politicians busily prepared for the critical events of the fall: the election of a new territorial legislature, the meeting of the constitutional convention at Lecompton, and the popular vote to ratify or reject the constitution, which both Buchanan and Walker had solemnly promised. Although the violence of 1856 had thus far been avoided, the future was still cloudy. In August, "Governor" Robinson was tried in Judge Cato's court for "usurping" the office of state governor, but he won acquittal on the ground that he could not usurp an office which the court claimed did not exist.[90] His shadow Topeka government was inactive, but its course was unpredictable if there were more election irregularities. "General" Lane was again trying to recruit a free-state militia and boldly issuing "general orders" to mostly nonexistent volunteers, but that, too, could change. Free-state partisans knew that in an honest election, if they turned out in force, their numbers would be overwhelming. With the Kansas press now almost solidly behind them, how could they lose?

That was the question on the minds of the territory's minority of proslavery partisans, and of their agents who would control the Lecompton convention. They still had the strength, if they dared, to do considerable mischief, and they knew that there were reckless proslavery radicals in the South who would back them. Circumstances had given this handful of obscure men the power to threaten the unity of the national Democratic party, and thereby to imperil the Union as well.

Dog Days

"Today is the fourth of July!" wrote a patriotic Texas editor, the anniversary of the day, eighty-one years ago, that brought "to each lover of liberty the hope for the world's redemption." Although it was a day of feasting and celebration throughout the land, a Virginia editor urged his readers to spend it soberly "as the Great National Sabbath," consecrated to the memory of the Revolutionary fathers. "Let us, in grateful remembrance," he advised, "cherish the emotions which this day awakens." The spirit of the day seemed to inspire most Northerners and Southerners, momentarily transcending their differences, to acknowledge their common heritage, history, and nationality, and to share feelings of pride in all they had achieved. In a burst of optimism the New York *Times,* while recognizing the danger inherent in sectionalism, denied that the people of the North and South hated each other. Rather, it claimed, they exuded "a glowing American nationality whereof the vitality [had] not yet escaped." Hence, in spite of recent controversies, the *Times* could not believe that disunion—"the final catastrophe, the annihilating deluge"—was near at hand. Its optimism stemmed not only from the day but from a widespread hope, during the summer of 1857, that in Kansas a peaceful political settlement might soon be reached.[1]

Politically, Washington was a quiet place when the oppressive heat and enervating humidity of summer descended upon it, and when the malodorous and miasmatic vapors rising from the Potomac River bottom gave warning that the malarial season was at hand. The federal bureaucracy still manned department offices, transacting their routine business, but legislators fled the city when Congress was not in session, and the higher judicial and executive officers escaped when they could. For several weeks in late July and early August, Buchanan was away at Bedford Springs, his favorite summer resort in the mountains of western Pennsylvania. During his absence the Cabinet met but did little. After his return he wrote his reply to the Silliman letter and then left Kansas affairs in Governor

Walker's hands. Not until September, with the approaching constitutional convention and territorial election, did the administration again actively involve itself in the territory's problems.

Although the capital's political life was in a state of quiescence, August was a busy month in the South, where numerous hard-fought and remarkably vituperative state and congressional elections occurred. Among the Democrats sharp personal rivalries, especially in Virginia, Georgia, and Mississippi, and harsh disputes between the fire-eaters and pro-administration moderates were the chief threats to party success. For the distressed coalitions of Whigs and Americans these elections were nothing less than battles for survival. They soon abandoned their efforts, half-hearted at best, to press nativist issues and tried instead to exploit the divisions among Democrats. Some, posing as the South's most loyal defenders, saddled the administration with responsibility for Governor Walker's alleged surrender to the Kansas abolitionists. In the Louisville *Journal,* George D. Prentice noted the "fearful agitation now raging in the bosom of the Democracy upon the subject of Kansas," because some in the South would unite with the northern Democracy on any terms, "honorable or dishonorable, just or unjust."[2]

On the other hand, the Richmond *Whig,* putting on the party's other face, spoke one day as a responsible conservative looking forward to the end of slavery agitation and the dissolution of sectional parties. Then all the elements of opposition, including former Republicans, could stand "shoulder to shoulder . . . in compact and sold array, against the Democracy." Democrats responded to sentiments such as these with hints that the opposition party, whatever its name, had secret antislavery sympathies and was content to play "merely 'second fiddle' to Black Republicanism." It should be clear to all, warned a Georgia editor, that there were only two great political parties in the United States, one of which was destined to win the presidential election of 1860. Before that time every state election would strengthen one national party or the other. Opposition leaders knew that the defeat of the Democracy in any southern state would merely give aid and comfort to the "Black" Republicans; yet they battled on to achieve that end. The one important issue in these state elections, Democrats claimed, was this: "Shall the Black Republicans, or the Democracy, rule the country, shall Wm. H. Seward, or a sound Democrat be elected in 1860?" In such a contest local issues counted for little.[3]

In their extremity the Whig-Americans reached far back into their past to revive an issue associated with the name of the great Whig leader Henry Clay. They proposed to distribute among the older states, which had received no land grants to aid in the construction of railroads, the proceeds from the sale of public lands in proportion to their populations. Whig Senator John Bell of Tennessee had introduced a bill for that purpose in the last session of Congress. Although it did not pass, the southern opposition press took up the cause with enthusiasm and tried to make it "the great and paramount issue" of the state campaigns.

The Louisville *Journal,* in rehearsing the old arguments for distribution, was pleased to "revive something of the glorious past." Why should not the old states, asked the Richmond *Whig,* share the profits of public land sales along with newer ones such as Illinois and Iowa? With distribution, Virginia could extinguish its public debt, complete all its railroad projects "with the utmost dispatch," and check the drain of its population to the Southwest.[4]

The Democrats disposed of distribution, the Whigs' "great hobby" of the state campaigns, with ridicule. In a speech at Raleigh, Tennessee's Governor Andrew Johnson pronounced it a "fossil remain, dug up and thrown into the canvass" in order to divert attention from the true issues. A Nashville editor dismissed it as an "old and exploded issue . . . thoroughly repudiated by the country." Moreover, he discovered in Bell's proposal a potentially dangerous threat to southern slavery. Concede to the federal government the right to divide its revenues among the states for any purpose, he warned, and "you sanction the exercise of a power by the General Government which would enable a Black Republican Congress to apply the same revenues to the emancipation of our slaves."[5]

Nothing could save the Whig-Americans that summer. Although the Kentucky American party was one of the strongest and best organized in the South, it lost control of the legislature, failed to elect its candidate for state treasurer, and elected only two Congressmen, W. L. Underwood and Humphrey Marshall, for a net loss of four. Louisville, however, where mobs of Plug Ugly nativists had controlled the polls for several years, remained in American party hands. In Maryland, in the fall, thanks to the Plug Uglies, Rip Raps, Blood Tubs, and other gangs of Baltimore thugs, and to the demoralization of the Democrats, the Americans scored their only statewide victory. They retained control of the legislature and elected their gubernatorial candidate, Thomas H. Hicks, and four of the state's six Congressmen. Earlier a mob of Baltimore Plug Uglies had invaded Washington on the day of a municipal election and engaged in riots that left six dead and many wounded before they were suppressed by a company of United States marines. The long and notorious record of violence involving nativist mobs was another reason for the decline of the southern Whig-Americans.[6]

The disasters accumulated rapidly. In Virginia the Democracy was seriously divided between Governor Wise's moderate administration faction and Senator Hunter's disaffected southern-rights ultras, and they aired their differences through the columns of their respective organs, the Richmond *Enquirer* and Richmond *South.* Wise eventually forced Hunter to profess at least qualified loyalty to the administration by threatening to contest his Senate seat before the legislature when he would seek re-election in December. The feud was no help to the Whig-Americans. Somehow the Democrats temporarily patched up their differences, met in a reasonably harmonious convention, and on May 28 carried every congressional district in the state.[7]

In North Carolina, opposition candidates, calling themselves American-Whigs, ran in only four of the eight congressional districts and lost in all but one. Tennessee Whig-Americans had a strong leader in John Bell and ran on a Unionist platform opposing slavery agitation and supporting distribution to pay off the state debt and to finance a system of public education. However, the Democratic charge that they were allies of the abolitionists appeared to be more effective, and the Democrats elected Isham G. Harris governor, won both houses of the legislature, and sent Andrew Johnson, the retiring governor, to the United States Senate. The Alabama opposition called itself the "Whig and American party"; the Democrats called it the "American and Plug Ugly party." In fact, it was hardly a party at all. As a result, it could find no candidate to run for governor against the Democrat, A. B. Moore; it was defeated in every congressional district; and it won only 5 of 33 seats in the upper chamber of the legislature and 15 of 100 in the lower.[8]

Texas Democrats expected an easy time of it when they met in convention on May 5 and nominated Hardin R. Runnels for governor on a strong southern-rights platform. A week later Senator Sam Houston, the venerable old Jacksonian Democrat and hero of Texas independence, having joined the American party two years earlier, announced his candidacy. Although the Whig-Americans endorsed him at their convention in early June, Houston campaigned as the "independent anti-caucus" candidate. The Democrats, he informed Thomas L. Rusk, his Texas friend and senatorial colleague, had made the issue "Houston and anti-Houston. So now the whips crack, and the longest pole will bring down the persimmons. The people want excitement, and I had as well give it as any one."[9]

Houston was an excellent stump speaker, and with his dual message of nativism and Unionism he did make the campaign exciting. Worried Democrats, describing him as an unreliable defender of southern rights, exploited the fact that he had voted against the repeal of the Missouri Compromise and accused him of opposition to the Dred Scott decision. Their alarm increased when Senator Rusk, amid rumors that he might remain neutral or even endorse Houston, ignored numerous requests that he announce his support of the Democratic platform and ticket. "For God's sake," the chairman of the state central committee wrote him, "as you value the great cause of the Democracy in Texas, break the silence at once." Finally, on June 28, Rusk wrote the desired letter for publication, declaring his intention to cast his vote for the Democratic candidate. In the August election Houston polled 41 percent of the vote, but the Democrats elected their entire state ticket and won overwhelming control of the legislature.[10]

In Missouri the result of an August gubernatorial campaign, made necessary by the election of Democratic Governor Trusten Polk to the United State Senate, distressed proslavery Southerners almost as much as the free-soil victory in St. Louis the previous spring. James S. Rollins, a former American, ran as an independent with the support of the Whig-Americans, the St. Louis antislavery party, and many of the Benton Democrats. Rollins, himself a slaveholder, did not favor immediate emancipation, but he affirmed that a day might come when Missouri would find it to her economic advantage to convert to a free-labor system. His opponent, Robert S. Stewart, was a strongly proslavery anti-Benton Democrat. Although the contest did not offer a clear choice between free and slave labor, it was widely perceived as such. The result was very close, Stewart winning by a scant margin of 329 votes in a total of more than 95,000. The St. Louis *Missouri Democrat* insisted that the election was stolen from Rollins by fraud.[11]

Better news for proslavery Democrats came in October when state elections were held in Mississippi and Georgia. Whig-Americans in Mississippi nominated James L. Alcorn, a prominent Delta planter and politician, for governor, but he declined, preferring his chances for a seat in Congress. After their second nominee also declined, their third choice, E. M. Yerger, described as a man "addicted to hopeless undertakings," ran against William McWillie, a southern-rights Democrat, who won in a landslide. Every Whig-American congressional candidate was defeated, including Alcorn, who lost to L.Q.C. Lamar, and in the new legislature the party was reduced to a feeble minority.[12]

The Georiga state election demonstrated that in 1857 southern Democrats, even when troubled with factional divisions, could defeat the best the opposition Whig-Americans could offer. James Jackson, the Democratic candidate for Congress in the Sixth District, informed Cobb that there was "trouble every where in Democratic ranks" because of Governor Walker's speeches. His effort to defend the administration for not recalling Walker had alienated "a good many fire-eating Democrats." At the party's state convention the dissidents defeated Cobb's favorite candidate for the gubernatorial nomination, John H. Lumpkin, by supporting several competing candidates. After a score of futile ballots, with none able to obtain the required two-thirds majority, the convention agreed to appoint a committee representing each of the congressional districts and to accept whichever candidate it chose. Linton Stephens, Alexander's brother and author of the convention's anti-Walker resolution, proposed to that body the nomination of Joseph E. Brown, an obscure southern-rights Democrat from the upcountry, and both the committee and the convention approved. "I knew you would be astonished at the result," Mrs. Cobb wrote to her husband, advising him to "take patiently what the *leaders* of the So[uthern] Rights Democracy choose to serve up to you." Politics, she concluded, was "like a filthy pool—now and then throwing up mud and slime from its bottom."[13]

At their state convention the optimistic Whig-Americans chose an exceptionally promising candidate: the young Unionist Benjamin Hill, a brilliant lawyer, fluent speaker, and able debater. Their platform was a model of opportunism, combining distribution and nativism with attacks on the administration for betraying the South, bold assertions of southern rights, and professions of Unionism. Somehow Hill managed to persuade Brown to join him in a series of joint debates, and the result for Brown was so disastrous that he soon withdrew. Toombs and Stephens then took him in hand and helped him wage a successful campaign. The Whig-American defeat was less decisive than in most other southern states. Although the Democrats won a large majority in the legislature, Hill polled 45 percent of the popular vote, and the opposition elected two of Georgia's eight Congressmen.[14]

Collectively these Democratic victories in the 1857 state elections indicated an accelerating southern trend toward one-party politics. The opposition coalitions of Whigs and Americans under their various names were still a political force in the border slave states, but they were in a condition of rapid decline elsewhere and near death in South Carolina, Alabama, and Mississippi. Many of the ablest Whig leaders, such as Toombs and Stephens, had deserted to the Democrats, and those who remained failed utterly to put together a viable platform. Instead they wavered between a course of conservative Unionism and efforts to surpass the Democrats in southern-rights radicalism. Meanwhile, the Democrats, with the powerful assistance of a prosouthern administration, survived the summer crisis over Governor Walker and had remarkable success in portraying themselves as the most reliable defenders of the South's interests and institutions. Only a united South, they warned, acting through the national Democratic party, could defeat the "Black" Republicans in the next presidential campaign.

August witnessed another familiar southern political event: the meeting in Knoxville of delegates to a convention ostensibly to consider ways to strengthen the South's economy, but primarily to provide a sounding board for the southern-rights radicals who controlled it. Southern commerical conventions had met frequently since the late 1830s, and in earlier years delegates had focused on improving transportation, building factories, and promoting direct trade with Europe in order to reduce their section's dependence on northern merchants and manufacturers. Although many Southerners had long lamented the lack of a local cotton textile industry and of a fleet of home-owned merchant vessels, they continued to invest most of their capital in the profitable commerical production of their great staple crops. Hence, calls for economic diversification were still common. "To allow the North the entire foreign trade of this great country," the Richmond *Enquirer* scolded, "would be to acknowledge that the South is either incapable, from barrenness, to furnish freight and travel enough to sustain a line of ocean steamers, or that our people have not the public spirit to embark in such an enterprise." The Charleston *Mercury* deplored the seeming willingness of Southerners to permit all their business "to pass through the hands of Northern merchants," thus making themselves "hewers of wood and drawers of water" to those who would "dishonor all that we hold dear in our social organization."[15]

By the time of the Knoxville convention these gatherings had become the playthings of the extremists. Its aim, according to the committee which called it together, was the "advancement and security of the South" through the dissemination of "correct, enlarged, and faithful views" of southern rights. When the convention opened on August 9 more than 700 delegates representing eleven of the slave states were in attendance, most of them from Virginia and the Deep South. Each delegation was given as many votes as its state had in the Electoral College. J.B.D. De Bow, editor of *De Bow's Review*, was elected president and delivered an address entitled "The Rights, Duties, and Remedies of the South." The rights he emphasized were the right of Southerners to control their slave property "without external let or hindrance," and the right to carry their slaves, "under due protection of law," into the territories "purchased by the common blood and treasure." De Bow described a bleak future: the admission of many more free states, the repeal of the Constitution's three-fifths compromise, and, eventually, the "proclamation from the National Capital ... of *universal and unconditional emancipation*." He called for a united South to resist the power which "promotes servile insurrections, the laying waste of fields, the paralysis of industry, the recession of civilization." Are we prepared, he asked, to surrender our slave labor "to the theorists, the pseudo philanthropists, the socialists, and agrarians, and their selfish, unscrupulous, or deluded followers?" The clear implication of De Bow's words was that the South must seek its safety not through the national Democratic party but through independence.

After a long debate the convention voted to permit northern reporters to attend its sessions and then turned to the consideration of resolutions and committee recommendations. It adopted the usual appeals for the investment of capital in manufacturing enterprises and in the development of shipping lines between European and southern ports. E. B. Bryan of South Carolina, a radical among radicals, proposed a resolution recommending the repeal of the American agreement with Great Britain, in the Webster-Ashburton Treaty of 1842, to maintain a naval squadron on the west coast of Africa to help suppress the slave trade. The discussion was heated, but a motion to table the Bryan resolution was defeated by a vote of 42 to 62. Subsequently it was adopted by a vote of 66 to 26, the opposition coming from Maryland, North Carolina, and Tennessee. Another resolution directly advocating the reopening of the African slave trade was by far the most divisive, provoking much opposition from states of the upper South. Yet, a motion to table it was defeated, and a motion to refer it to a committee with instructions to report the following year passed by a vote of 52-40.

Other favorite projects of these angry and defiant southern-rights partisans passed with little opposition. In order to prevent a decline in the number of families having a direct interest in the preservation of slavery, they urged each southern state to exempt one or more slaves from seizure for debt. They recommended the founding of a great southern university and the preparation of textbooks suitable for the education of southern students. They demanded the termination of the federal bounties paid to New England fishermen. When a delegate offered a resolution that was pro-Union in spirit, they voted to lay it on the table. Finally, they agreed to meet in Montgomery the following year.[16]

The reluctance of convention delegates to seat northern reporters resulted from the ridicule they customarily received in the northern press. The Knoxville convention, commented a Philadelphia editor, "facetiously calling itself commercial," was in fact "a political club ... of secessionists in disguise." He described its members as "impracticable ideologists" and "reckless demagogues," and its proceedings "of a piece with its constituent elements." These gatherings of southern-rights radicals received a great deal of criticism from moderate Southerners as well. A practical Virginian, writing in the Washington *National Intelligencer,* thought that their calls for industrialization and direct trade with Europe made sense only to those who sought an independent southern nation. There were, he asserted, "natural causes" for the South's specialization in the production of staple crops and the North's development of commerce and manufacturing. Given the nature of their soil and climate, Southerners had "fulfilled their mission" in developing an agricultural economy, and they should no more be reproached for it than Northerners for failing to produce cotton and sugar. Commercial conventions may continue to meet, he concluded, "and resolve and re-resolve" that the South must be independent of the North, but the interest in profit would "carry the trade to the North in spite of all our patriotic resolutions." And so it did.[17]

Before adjourning, the Knoxville convention, after briefly discussing American foreign policy, had adopted a resolution demanding that the federal government assert its exclusive control over Central America. By the Clayton-Bulwer Treaty of 1850 the United States and Great Britain had agreed that neither country would colonize or establish dominion over any part of Central America, and that any canal built through Panama or Nicaragua would be neutral and open to the ships of all nations on equal terms. The treaty had many critics, among them southern proslavery imperialists who looked southward for potential areas of political and economic expansion. The eventual acquisition of the West Indies and Central America, they believed, was a vital part of the nation's Manifest Destiny, a blessing to all who would fall under its benevolent jurisdiction. Edmund Ruffin, like most other American expansionists, was confident that "the conquest of these mongrel and semi-barbarous communities, by any civilized power, would be a benefit to the conquered and to the world."[18]

If the American government was sometimes slow in pursuing its destiny, there were men of action—filibusters—prepared to point the way. Cuba had been the principal target of the filibusters in the recent past. Early in 1857, Henry A. Crabb, imagining that he saw opportunity beckoning in Mexico, led a small band of Americans across the border to support Ignacio Presqueira in a revolution against the governor of Sonora. The revolution succeeded, but, in April, Pres-queira turned on Crabb and his men as enemy invaders, defeated them in battle, and executed them. These filibusters had recklessly ignored opportunities to escape to the United States, where they would only have risked a trial for violat-ing the neutrality laws.[19]

By far the most notorious of the mid-century filibusters was a young Ten-nessean named William Walker. Remembered as the "gray-eyed man of destiny," Walker was in fact a shy, unimpressive but restless little man who sought fame in Nicaragua. He first tried several honorable professions, earning a medical degree from the University of Pennsylvania, studying law and gaining admission to the bar in New Orleans, then turning to journalism. In 1850 he moved to California and soon thereafter discovered his true calling in the life of a filibuster. His career began in 1853 when he raised a small army of adventurers for an invasion of Mexico aimed at the seizure of Lower California. The invasion failed, and on his return to California he was indicted for violating his government's neutrality laws, tried in a federal court in San Francisco, and acquitted by a friendly jury.

Walker's great enterprise began in 1855 when the leader of a revolution against the government of Nicaragua invited him to join his cause. With a small force of volunteers he arrived in time to participate in military engagements that culminated in victory and the formation of a provisional government. Appointed commander in chief of the army, he commanded mostly soldiers of fortune recruited in the United States and loyal to him rather than to civilian authorities. In 1856, Walker repudiated the provisional government, arranged a presidential election which he won with ease, and began to rule as a dictator. He invited American settlers to come by promising them land confiscated from those opposed to his government. One of his decrees repealed the Nicaraguan law against slavery. By this act, Walker later wrote, his government deserved to be judged, for it was "the key to its whole policy." Its wisdom or folly, he claimed, "involved the wisdom or folly of the American movement in Nicaragua; for on the re-establishment of African slavery there depended the permanent presence of the white race in that region." As the culmination of his dream, Walker hoped to lead in the formation of a confederation of Central American states.

Walker's dream turned into a nightmare when the other states—El Salva-dor, Honduras, Costa Rica, and Guatemala—fearing him as a threat to their independence, formed an alliance to overthrow him. Walker lost most of his sup-port among Nicaraguans, and his army was decimated by disease and desertions. He had also made a formidable enemy of Cornelius Vanderbilt by revoking the charter of his American Accessory Transit Company and seizing its property, giving his favor instead to George Law's rival United States Mail Steamship Com-pany. Southern expansionists rallied to Walker's support, but in vain. In the spring of 1857 he was besieged in the town of Rivas by the overwhelming forces of the Central American allies. On April 30, Captain Charles Henry Davis, of the sloop-of-war *U.S.S. St. Mary's,* negotiated the surrender of Walker and some three hundred officers and men to American authorities. Walker departed, abandoning the dead and wounded, showing no concern for the civilian victims of his invasion, still claiming to be the rightful president of Nicaragua, and vowing one day to return.[20]

Walker and his staff were escorted first to Panama, then sailed to New Orleans, arriving on May 27. Ten thousand admirers were at the dock to greet him and escort him to the St. Charles Hotel. Addressing the cheering crowd, he assured them that his recent defeat would not deter him, that he would soon return to Nicaragua with another army, and that his cause would triumph. The local press praised his "heroic qualities" and expressed the "prevailing faith, that the star of his destiny, though dimmed for a season, will yet shine out with renewed luster." Walker received flattering attention throughout the South. A Texas editor, describing the "Nicaragua fever" in his state, wrote that Southerners could not "contemplate without emotion and sympathy, the southern extension of American settlements upon the continent." Jefferson Davis lauded Walker and held the British and northern abolitionists responsible for his defeat. The armies of the allies, he charged, were their cat's-paw in their outrageous attempt to prevent the reintroduction of slavery in these tropical lands. Even the Richmond *Enquirer* joined in the chorus of praise. "Central America, with its rich resources and its dilapidated republics," it asserted, offered "an inviting field to the enterprise and genius of such men as Walker."[21]

Walker also had his friends and admirers within the business community of New York City and among the expansionist Democrats of the Old Northwest. Was not his ambition honorable? asked the Cincinnati *Enquirer.* Would not his success have "conferred a benefit on the world, and especially on the country which was the arena of his ambition?" Walker was the pioneer of a movement that would yet triumph, and one day his critics would "marvel that they could ever have been so short-sighted and narrow minded." The praise of an eastern Democratic editor was considerably more restrained. He judged Walker's enterprise "premature and ill considered" and noted that some of his followers were fugitives from justice, who sought "to wipe out the memory of a tainted life by a career of desperate and honorable adventure." Yet, he could not condemn these "ill guided" men for undertaking "what seemed to them, at first, a glorious, an American cause."[22]

Sharp criticism of Walker came mostly from old Whigs and Republicans. The Washington *National Intelligencer* commented tartly on the reception that New Orleans had given a man whose action was "condemned by the common law of all mankind," and whose success consisted of a safe retreat from a country which he had "ravaged with fire and sword, after strewing it with the bones of his victims." A Chicago Republican, deploring the lives that had been wasted, thought it "almost a pity that Walker had not been caught and hung." No felon more richly deserved the gallows, and none owed a greater debt to justice. The "cotton men," he charged, were responsible for all the filibusters, their object being the acquisition of more slave territory "to balance the rapidly increasing power of the free states."[23]

Walker traveled to Washington to promote his cause, and on June 12 he had an interview with the President. His claim, often repeated, was that he alone could restore order, revive Nicaragua's economy, and provide the conditions for safe transit across its territory. There is no record of Buchanan's response, but his subsequent action made it almost certain that he gave Walker no encouragement to undertake another invasion. Filibusters may have been popular in the South, but he found them a source of great embarrassment in American relations with Great Britain. After his interview Walker wrote an open letter to the President full of outrageous claims. He had gone to Nicaragua, he asserted, to plant a colony and had become a naturalized citizen of the Republic. Political leaders there told him that he was "the only hope for the Democrats, not only of Nicaragua, but of all Central America," and they begged him and his men to remain. When he was elected president he had accepted the office reluctantly after being persuaded that it was his duty. Finally, in a gesture of supreme ingratitude, he held Captain Davis responsible for his defeat and surrender, accusing him of undermining the morale of his troops and insulting their commander.[24]

Walker went on to New York to enjoy another enthusiastic reception and accept the tribute reserved for a national hero. Thereafter, for the remainder of the summer, he was busy preparing for a triumphant return to Nicaragua and the resumption of his presidential office.

In Walker's account of his Nicaraguan adventure he clearly revealed his low opinion of the native Indians and "half-castes" while claiming to be the rightful president of their republic. Under his rule he expected white settlers to direct the labor of Indians and black slaves, and the disorderly "half-castes" soon to become extinct. Those who praised him and his fellow filibusters usually displayed similar ethnic and racial attitudes. For southern imperialists it was a simple matter of applying the ideas underpinning their proslavery argument to the populations of the West Indies and Central America.

Walker's enterprise, argued a Kentucky editor, was "no ordinary scheme of lawless outrage." Rather, it was another step in the relentless spread of Caucasian civilization. Wherever the white race lived it was supreme, and wherever it went it conquered. "Its abounding and invincible vitality subdues and assimilates the inferior races as readily as the individual does the fruit of the field." According to a Tennessee expansionist, men such as Walker merely fulfilled the destiny of the Anglo-Saxon race. It was "only a matter of time" until backward regions, such as Nicaragua, would "give way before that ever onward march." Nearly the whole population of Central America was of "mixed blood," Edmund Ruffin wrote in disgust, "and no distinction made between, or repugnance of any one color to another. . . . Taken together . . . the people are worthless, and afford no hope of their improvement . . . and their extinction will be a benefit to America." In Cuba, a New Orleans editor observed, except for a few Spaniards in Havana, "they but eat, drink, sleep and die. That is the sum of their earthly existence." Yet their land was rich in natural resources and commanded a strategic position on one of the great highways of commerce. Eventually, when this mixed breed "of negro, Indian, and degenerate European races" had shown its incapacity to seize these opportunities, its lands, "by every law human and divine, revert to us and us alone. We have a preemption right in the Gulf."[25]

Senator James S. Green of Missouri bolstered the southern racial rationale with a strategic argument, invoking the inherent national right of self-defense. If that right required the acquisition of Cuba, he was for it "whether with or without the consent of Cuba or the consent of Spain." Others stressed the political advantage. A Texas Democrat, in a letter to Attorney General Black, conceded the need to admit Kansas as a free state in order to appease the northern wing of the party. In addition, to avoid angering the South, he urged the acquisition of Cuba and Santo Domingo and their restoration to the white race. "We want Cuba," wrote another Texan. "It will make two good Southern States." To some, annexation was a conservative national measure, one that would strengthen the Union by restoring the sectional balance. One way or another the South was bound to have Cuba, vowed the Richmond *Enquirer,* for Manifest Destiny pointed to it "with the finger of fate."[26]

Southern expansionists had a most sympathetic friend in President Buchanan. His interest in the acquisition of Cuba from Spain dated back to his term as Secretary of State in Polk's administration, and he had subsequently shown sympathy for the use, if necessary, of means more drastic than peaceful purchase. Yet, in his inaugural address he assured the world that the United States would not acquire additional territory except through means "sanctioned by the laws of justice and honor." Accordingly, no other nation would have a right to interfere if "in the progress of events we shall still further extend our possessions."

In January, Buchanan had received encouraging word from Horatio J. Perry, former secretary of the American legation in Madrid, of a favorable prospect that Cuba could be "peaceably separated" from Spain and annexed to the United States. Two years of "intelligent, constant action," Perry believed, should be sufficient to negotiate a purchase on satisfactory terms. In March, Senator Toombs conferred with the President on annexation prospects. He suggested that American citizens buy up the Spanish bonds held by British citizens, using them as leverage in negotiating a purchase treaty. Late in the year Buchanan authorized Christopher Fallon, financial agent to the queen mother, to suggest that "a transfer of the Island to the United States for a reasonable and fair price would greatly promote the interests of both countries." Fortunately for Buchanan, it was all in vain, and he was spared another angry battle between the Slave Power and its militant antislavery critics.[27]

The racial and ethnic justification of expansionism was by no means an exclusively southern rationale, for Northerners, especially the nationalistic Young America Democrats, echoed the sentiments of their proslavery compatriots. The Detroit *Free Press,* for example, thought that belief in equality of the races was "great nonsense." The Chinese and the Africans were what they had been three thousand years ago and would be three thousand years hence. "Neither is the equal of the Anglo-Saxon and never can be." Caleb Cushing, after retiring from Pierce's Cabinet and returning to Newburyport, Massachusetts, used the occasion of a large public reception to defend Manifest Destiny in particularly brutal terms. In the course of American expansion, he said, "it happens that men, nations, races, may, must, will, perish before us. That is inevitable. There can be no change for the better save at the expense of that which is. Out of decay springs fresh life." Such was the fate of the Indian tribes and of the Latin Americans who were "wasting away by apparent incapacity of self-government." They suffered one province after another to "relapse into pristine desolation, and thus to become prepared to receive the people and the laws of the United States."[28]

While Cushing described a biologically amoral world in which the fittest survived, others viewed Manifest Destiny as a benevolent process directed by the "finger of Divine Providence." To them it was simply God's plan for the weaker to seek the protection of the stronger—for "the ignorant and distracted to take refuge in the arms of the wise and calm." The most intelligent portion of the Latin American population understood this themselves and desired "nothing more ardently than the introduction of Anglo-Saxon institutions into the countries they inhabit." Somewhat less benevolently, *Harper's Weekly* perceived in the political supremacy of Christian countries evidence of their cultural superiority over non-Christian countries. That was a curious argument, for this journal clearly did not rank the Catholic countries of Latin America among the international elite.[29]

Some northern Democrats hoped that geographic expansion might provide a solution to the potentially disruptive problem of Kansas. The Cincinnati *Enquirer* urged Southerners to stop wasting their energies "in a vain and hopeless attempt to extend slavery into Kansas" and turn to the tropics, where slave labor was profitable and where they could enhance both their political and economic power. The New York *Herald* told southern ultras that it was time for them to "throw aside their hobby horses and look things in the face as they exist." Rather than launching a senseless attack on the administration over Kansas they should strive to procure two or three new states elsewhere. "Let them take a stand upon the purchase of Cuba," the *Herald* advised. "Mexico, too, is offering three or four new states to their hands."[30]

Whatever northern Republicans might have thought of Manifest Destiny under different circumstances, in the prosouthern political context of the Pierce and Buchanan administrations it meant nothing more than swaggering Slave Power aggression. They would have none of it. Southern Whig-Americans, in their conservative Unionist posture, also denounced the arrogant doctrine "that we, as a nation, may at any time . . . seize upon the property of any neighbor that happens to be weaker than ourselves." The Democrats, charged a Tennessee Whig editor, were a "manifest-destiny, or rather a manifest-destruction party" bent on spreading American influence "by fire and sword." Alexander H. H. Stuart, a Virginia Whig, deplored "the cormorant appetite" of southern expansionists for a different reason. The consequence of expanding the area of slavery to the south, he feared, was the contraction of its area along the northern border. Virginia "must set her face against the acquisition of new territory," or she would lose her "productive labor" and suffer "a radical change in her domestic institutions."[31]

Meanwhile, southern expansionists such as John A. Quitman, a flamboyant Mississippi Congressman and friend of the filibusters, were abetting Walker in his plans for a new invasion of Nicaragua. Buchanan, however, found their activities an embarrassment during some difficult negotiations with Great Britain over the meaning of the Clayton-Bulwer Treaty. The question at issue was whether that treaty obligated the British government to renounce a protectorate it had previously established over the Mosquito Indians on the coast of Nicaragua, as well as its assertion of jurisdiction over the Bay Islands off the coast of Honduras. These matters, although seemingly trivial, involved important American concerns: the control of an anticipated isthmian canal and the protection of transit rights between the Atlantic and Pacific. Inevitably they aroused the endemic anti-British feelings of the American public and provoked a rash of truculent editorials in the press. The Baltimore *Republican,* denouncing Britain's "grasping ambition" and "treacherous double-dealing policy," thought a war with her might "prove a blessing to the country." Many demanded repudiation of the treaty and assertion of American hegemony over Central America.[32]

Buchanan drew on his considerable diplomatic experience and his friendly London connections in achieving an amicable settlement. He startled the British government with an unwelcome proposal to abrogate the Clayton-Bulwer Treaty and write a new one whose terms both would understand. Preferring the existing treaty with its restrictions on American activity in Central America, the British soon accepted the American interpretation, recognizing Nicaraguan sovereignty over the Mosquito coast and Honduran sovereignty over the Bay Islands.[33] As these negotiations progressed, Buchanan watched the movements of the filibuster

Walker with growing concern. Another attempt to invade Nicaragua, he concluded, would have to be stopped.

In mock sympathy for Buchanan and his problem with filibusters, the New York *Times* suggested that he appoint William Walker governor of Utah Territory. Then let him take his brave followers to Salt Lake City, plant a settlement of "gentiles," and challenge the power of Brigham Young and his dedicated Mormon followers.[34] During the summer of 1857 Young and the members of his Church of Jesus Christ of Latter-day Saints were more often the source of public vexation than public levity. Like the recent Catholic immigrants, they were severely testing the strength of the American commitment to the constitutional guarantee of religious freedom. Moreover, having developed patterns of community organization and family life that were both different and unpopular, they had isolated themselves culturally from other Americans. In Utah they had, in effect, applied the principle of territorial popular sovereignty—the right "to form and regulate their domestic institutions in their own way"—rather differently than Douglas had intended.

After some early hardships the Mormons had enjoyed ten years of peace and prosperous growth in the Great Salt Lake basin, and their missionaries had brought in thousands of converts from the East and from Europe. Yet their past experiences with hostile neighbors, persecutions, and flight were still too recent to be forgotten. The church had been founded in 1830 in upstate New York soon after Joseph Smith had incorporated in the Book of Mormon miraculous revelations he claimed to have received from God. In his search for a new Zion, Smith had taken his followers from New York to Kirtland, Ohio, then to several locations in Missouri, then to a town site in Illinois which he named Nauvoo.

Everywhere they settled the Saints had irritated the "gentiles" who lived nearby, in part because of their close-knit communitarian social organization, in part because they prospered, and in part because of their conviction that Mormonism, being the only true faith, made them a "chosen people" and gave Joseph Smith, their prophet, the power to communicate directly with God. In Hiram, Ohio, Smith was seized by a mob and tarred and feathered. In Missouri, after fleeing from one community to another, some of the more militant Mormons formed the secret Danite Band and engaged in violent conflict with the "gentiles." In 1839, following the massacre of seventeen Mormons at Haun's Mill, the arrest and imprisonment of Smith and other church leaders, and the destruction of their community at Far West, the Saints left Missouri, carrying with them particularly bitter memories.

In Nauvoo they flourished economically and their membership grew to more than thirty thousand. Soon their Illinois neighbors turned as hostile to them as the Missourians. It was there, in the early 1840s, following another alleged revelation, that Joseph Smith and a few dozen other leaders of the church secretly adopted the practice of "plural marriage." The practice briefly caused a crisis within the church itself, and, in spite of Smith's public denials, sensational reports of Mormon polygamy began to circulate among the "gentiles." A few years later the Nauvoo phase of Mormon history came to an end. In 1844, Smith was arrested for destroying the press of a Mormon dissenter who had published an attack on him. On June 27 a mob took him and his brother from the jail at Carthage and murdered them. The following year the Mormon Council of Twelve announced that the Saints would leave Illinois.

In the summer of 1846, under the brilliant leadership of Brigham Young, Smith's successor as head of the church, the epic Mormon migration to the valley of the great Salt Lake began. In 1849, church leaders held a constitutional convention and formed a provisional government for the State of Deseret. However, by a provision of the Compromise of 1850, Congress placed the Mormon settlements within the boundaries of the new territory of Utah, and President Fillmore appointed Young governor and superintendent of Indian affairs. Thus, with the temporal powers of the territorial government and the spiritual powers of the Mormon church united in his hands, Utah became a theocracy ruled by a prophet whose word was law in matters both religious and secular. Secure in their own domain, the leaders of the church, at a general conference in 1852, for the first time publicly acknowledged and defended the Mormon practice of plural marriage.

Only a leader of Young's ability and strong will, backed by the strict discipline of the church, could have made a success of the settlements planted in so unpromising a place. Born in 1801 in rural New England, he spent his young manhood in upstate New York learning several trades as an apprentice. He was much affected by the fervor of the religious revivals then sweeping through the region, winning converts for the Methodists, Baptists, and Presbyterians, and spawning a variety of new sects. In 1832, Young was baptized a Mormon and rose rapidly to a position of leadership. After the death of Joseph Smith most Mormons turned to him as the man best able to head the church in a time of crisis. At his headquarters in Salt Lake City the new prophet used the organization that Smith had created to establish a despotism at once ruthless and benevolent. The Saints revered him as a stern but caring father, one who, knowing the will of God, must be trusted and obeyed.[35]

In civil affairs, Young governed with a compliant territorial legislature. In church affairs, he was assisted by a complex hierarchy of councils, a Presiding Bishopric, and a Patriarch. Locally the church was organized into groups of congregations called "stakes," each of them governed by a three-man presidency, and each congregation, or ward, by a presiding bishop. The church had no official clergy; rather, the men in each ward thought worthy formed a lay priesthood, whose duties, like those of the bishops, were civil as well as religious.[36]

In spite of the success of their church and their remarkable economic achievements—evident in their growing capital city, thriving towns, and productive irrigated farmlands—the Saints in Young's mid-nineteenth-century kingdom still suffered from the frailties of other men and women. Young himself could be harsh, arrogant, and crude, as well as kind and benevolent. In the words of his biographer, he sometimes "shared with most public men the subtleties of policy that gave every appearance of duplicity." In his territorial government he not only made no distinction between church and state but saw no need to grant the legislative and judicial departments independence from his executive authority. He made "gentiles" feel that they were not welcome in his domain, as he did the non-Mormon federal officers who reached the territory in 1851 and, finding it impossible to perform their duties, soon departed. He was equally inhospitable to blacks, for his racial attitudes differed little from those of the "gentiles," except that he gave his racism the Mormon church's own special religious gloss.[37]

The Saints, like other religious communities, finding it difficult to live consistently by the precepts of their church, occasionally required exposure to the emotional exhortations associated with revivals. One such revival, known as the Reformation, began in the fall of 1856 (a year of bad crops) and reached its peak in 1857. Mormon leaders called on their people to confess their sins, repent, and seek a second baptism as a token of renewed commitment to their covenants. Jedediah M. Grant, Young's zealous counselor, led the movement, sending out missionaries to catechize individual church members and sermonize congregations. They were successful, and many of the Saints gained a new enthusiasm for their faith that, in some cases, bordered on religious frenzy. Some sought absolution for their sins by confessing them to Brigham Young. "I fell into transgression," wrote one penitent. "I wish to serve the Lord but this is constantly before me. . . . If you forgive me, I believe the Lord will." Writing to Young from abroad, a missionary reported that the more he saw and felt "the corruptions of the world," the more "pure and holy" he felt the atmosphere of Utah and its "principles of righteousness."[38]

An intimate part of the Reformation of 1856-57 was the Mormons' strong defense of plural marriage and a substantial increase in the number of polygamous families. Although percentage estimates vary widely, the great majority of Mormon households remained monogamous; but many of the Saints, in these years of unusual religious enthusiasm, turned to polygamy as a way to demonstrate their full acceptance of church doctrine. Their conviction that polygamy, as in the days of the Hebrew prophets, was sanctioned by God, was fortified by the practical fact that among Mormon converts women outnumbered men. The system thus addressed a social problem and helped to fulfill the church's teaching that marriage and motherhood were both the duty and proper sphere of women. Brigham Young, serving as a model with his numerous wives and children, warned that those who opposed the "plurality of wives" would be damned.

Polygamy, one husband of many wives advised, would help to keep a man "fresh, young, and sprightly."[39]

Whatever its religious justification, polygamy was a heavy burden to those devout men and women who practiced it and yet could not suppress altogether their doubts about its morality. Many may well have adjusted to it successfully, but the records left by those less fortunate are too numerous to suggest that Joseph Smith and Brigham Young had found a viable alternative to the trials of monogamous marriage. Among Young's many responsibilities was that of marriage counselor for the Saints, who wrote to him for advice concerning family problems, for approval of proposed plural marriages, and for permission to obtain divorces. Men seemed to have accepted polygamy more readily than women, and some could write about it with a kind of casual ease seldom found in the letters of their wives. "As this is a day of Reformation," wrote one, "we feel a desire to reform in all things, and . . . we would like to know if it is our privilege to get more wives." "Not wishing to trouble you with a long communication," wrote another, "I come to the question at once, can I have the privilege to get me another wife[?]" Still another, already married to several women, reported that he was the choice of two more and wanted to know whether it was his privilege and "duty to take them whether I want to or not."[40]

The experiences of two women, though not typical, were not rare. One of them, a widow, agreed to a polygamous marriage when she was without a home during a severe winter. Since then, she wrote, "I have felt entirely miserable in my feelings [for] he is a man I cannot love . . . [and] the thought of having to live with a man that I indeed cannot feel happy with has brought me down nearly to the grave." Another widow, destitute and the mother of a small child, found refuge in the home of a Mormon family and agreed to become a second wife. Unfortunately, she found it "utterly impossible to live there in any degree of quietness or comfort—his wife being so utterly opposed to polygamy . . . making herself so miserable while I remained there, that . . . I have been compelled to leave." Confessing that she knew little of Mormonism, having been baptized only recently, she asked for a divorce as the only available remedy.[41]

Mormonism was a political issue of a kind rarely encountered in 1857, because, with few exceptions, Northerners and Southerners, whether Democrats, Republicans, or Americans, could unite wholeheartedly in condemning it. Long viewed with hostile suspicion, the Reformation heightened the eastern perception of Mormon leaders as lawless tyrants and their followers as crazed fanatics shamelessly justifying their wicked deeds in the name of religious freedom. To outsiders, the practice of plural marriage was by far the Saints' most shocking crime. Numerous travelers returning from Utah fed the eastern press sensational reports of life among the Mormons, especially lurid tales of lecherous old men forcing young girls into polygamous liaisons. "The women are worse off than the slaves in Turkish harems," reported a Philadelphia editor. "Not Paris in the worst days of the first French Revolution witnessed so complete a prostration of all the forms of justice—such a perfect reign of terror as seems to be pervading all ranks alike of the saints and the sinners there." According to the New York *Times,* Mormon women were coerced to enter "the already overstocked harems of the elders," and children were "compelled to submit to a fate worse than death." Another editor refused to "disfigure" his columns with the details of life in Utah, or to ask his readers to imagine them, for no mind "unaccustomed to bestiality and miserable hypocrisy" could conceive of such depravity.[42]

Congressmen were sensitive to demands for federal action to protect the country "from the filthy streams of Utah," and they responded with hot rhetoric and many threats. Douglas, forgetting for the moment his "great principle" of popular sovereignty, denounced the Mormons as "outlaws and alien enemies" and called on Congress "to apply the knife and cut out this loathsome, disgusting ulcer." Repeal the act creating Utah Territory, he suggested, place the Mormons under federal military rule and punish the lawbreakers! Republicans would not let Douglas escape so easily. He was the author of the organic act that had created Utah Territory, they reminded the public, and the Mormons had simply applied "the Douglas doctrine of 'self-government' . . . to practice their horrid obscenities." Republicans had always believed in the supremacy of Congress over the territories, not in "that new-fangled and absurd Squatter Sovereignty" which protected Brigham Young and his "lustful and beastly crew." Lincoln taunted Douglas for his "considerable backing down" from his principle of self-government for the territories, claiming it to be further proof that the principle was only a "deceitful pretense for the benefit of slavery."[43]

Douglas's organ, the Chicago *Times,* had earlier defended the Mormons' right to practice polygamy in the name of religious freedom and popular sovereignty, but it soon joined the hue and cry against them. A few other editors occasionally spoke up in their defense, claiming that polygamy violated no federal law, but they had little support. Even Southerners who had spoken most strongly against federal interference with the domestic institutions of Kansas argued that Utah was a different case. How were these "unchristian outlaws" to be dealt with? asked the Richmond *Enquirer.* Since their social institutions were "revolting alike to civilization and law," it would be a travesty to recognize their right of self-government unless they relinquished their "barbarous code of laws" and conformed to "the usages of civilized society." The *Enquirer* did not advocate federal action beyond the government's constitutional authority, but when "the interests and honor of the people of the States" are in jeopardy, "it should energetically exercise the powers with which it is entrusted."[44]

By the time Buchanan took office, public sentiment favoring both a firm assertion of federal authority in Utah and the curbing of Brigham Young's political power had made some kind of response on his part almost mandatory. The press was full of calls on the administration for "prompt and decisive action" to vindicate the Constitution and laws of the United States, to dethrone "King Brigham, " and to emancipate his subjects from their "abject bondage." One correspondent, on his return from Utah, warned Attorney General Black that Mormon leaders were boldly declaring their intention to "erect an immense polygamous Hierarchy in defiance of the United States and entirely independent of its control." Senator Bigler informed the President that a *"universal sentiment"* demanded action. Robert Tyler urged him to "seize this question with a strong fearless resolute hand," adding the tempting suggestion that the "eyes and hearts of the Nation may be made to find so much interest in Utah as to forget Kansas!"[45]

The crisis in the relations of the federal government and the Mormon-controlled territorial government did not occur suddenly. Rather, a series of events and a cluster of problems had been slowly drawing them toward a potentially violent conflict—one in which each party considered the behavior of the other intolerable. Fillmore's non-Mormon appointees returned from Utah with complaints that their authority was ignored, that Governor Young controlled everything, and that "gentiles" were mistreated. Federal Judge W. W. Drummond, gave the Mormons ample reason to complain about his morals and honesty, but his conflicts with them centered on their rather unorthodox judicial system. Another federal judge, George P. Stiles, an excommunicated Mormon, stubbornly upheld the authority of the federal courts in spite of threats of physical violence. In December 1856 a mob broke into his office, seized and burned his law books, and carried off the records of his court. Early in 1857, having received no protection from Young, Drummond and Stiles returned to Washington to make detailed reports concerning lawlessness in Utah. A third federal judge, John F. Kinney, managed to establish better relations with the Mormons, but his official comments about the quality of justice rendered in the territory's probate courts were highly critical.

Two other federal officers had sharp encounters with the Mormons. David H. Burr, appointed surveyor general by Pierce, alarmed the Saints because their titles to the lands they occupied were far from clear. Fearing that Burr's surveys might lead to federal efforts to evict them, they obstructed his work until, in the spring of 1857, he fled the territory. Garland Hurt, a federal Indian agent, worked effectively among the Indians of Utah, and when his policies clashed with those of the Mormons he refused to join the other federal appointees in flight. His reports, along with those of Burr, had a considerable impact on Buchanan.

The Saints viewed matters in a rather different light. In addition to their memories of past persecutions and suspicions of the intentions of all non-Mormon territorial officers, they resented several recent federal affronts. In 1856, Hiram Kimball had won a government contract for carrying the mails between Utah and the East, and Young took over the contract, hoping to form a profitable business enterprise for the church. On June 10, 1857, Kimball received word from

Washington that his contract had been cancelled. In addition, Congress had repeatedly rejected the Mormons' petitions for statehood. On the last occasion, in 1856, they had held a convention, adopted a constitution, and prepared a petition for presentation to Congress. But their congressional delegate reported that there was no possibility of approval, and the matter was dropped. With every avenue to the political autonomy they undoubtedly sought apparently closed, the frustrated Saints, in the midst of their religious Reformation, gave vent to some hot rhetoric and defiant threats of their own. Hostility to the "gentiles" increased, and church leaders sounded incendiary warnings of an impending battle with the federal forces of evil.[46]

For several months after Buchanan's inauguration the eastern press reported various acts of violence in Utah. Some of the reports, but not all, were based on unsubstantiated rumors. One that was more than a rumor concerned William Parrish, a disenchanted Mormon who had abandoned his faith. When he tried to escape from the territory in order to avoid the wrath of his neighbors, he and one of his sons were ambushed and murdered. The Parrish story was one of many in the newspapers that spring, all of which fortified the decision Buchanan reached in May to remove Brigham Young and appoint a non-Mormon governor. Pierce had tried to replace him in 1854 when his term expired, offering the post to Lt. Colonel Edward J. Steptoe, who was then in Salt Lake City. Steptoe declined, and Young continued to serve as governor, although technically in an interim capacity until a replacement arrived.[47] Young himself clearly did not regard his tenure in those terms.

The governorship of Utah Territory was an even less attractive federal position than that of Kansas, and Buchanan had trouble finding a qualified person willing to risk his career and possibly his life in a confrontation with Brigham Young. His first choice, Ben McCulloch, twice declined, and others were considered until mid-June when Alfred Cumming, a Georgian with both nerve and ability, was persuaded to accept. Buchanan also appointed three new federal judges, a marshal, a territorial secretary, and a new superintendent of Indian affairs. He ordered 2500 troops with large supply trains to accompany them to Utah, there to serve as a *posse comitatus* if they were needed to protect federal officials and enforce the laws. Buchanan first placed General William S. Harney in command of the expedition, but Governor Walker insisted that he was needed in Kansas and persuaded the administration to keep him there. Throughout July and August the army moved westward from Fort Leavenworth without their commanding officer, until, early in September, Harney was replaced by Colonel Albert Sidney Johnston. By then the troops had advanced as far as Fort Laramie; but at the high elevations of that region winter would soon be closing in, and the expedition was still hundreds of miles from Salt Lake City.[48]

In his first annual message to Congress, Buchanan explained the reasons for his decision to appoint a new governor and to send a military force to Utah. As head of the Mormon church, he said, Brigham Young claimed to rule its members "by direct inspiration and authority from the Almighty," and his power therefore had been "absolute over both church and state." Nearly all federal officers had been forced to withdraw from the territory for their own personal safety, with the result that no government remained "but the despotism of Brigham Young." Accordingly, the President felt it his duty to restore "the supremacy of the Constitution and laws." With the religious opinions of the Mormons, although "revolting to the moral and religious sentiments of all Christendom," he claimed no right to interfere. Defiant civil acts against federal authority were another matter. Young, Buchanan charged, had been making military preparations for several years and laying in stores of provisions; he had been "tampering with the Indian tribes and exciting their hostile feelings against the United States." These acts, among others, had necessitated military action of sufficient strength to cope with the "frenzied fanaticism" of the Mormons and to convince "these deluded people" that resistance would be futile.

The War Department did not officially notify Governor Young of the military expedition until the troops were on their way. In a letter, dated July 28, General Harney informed him that the government intended to create a military department in Utah Territory similar to those in other parts of the country, and that an army was en route and would establish its headquarters at "some suitable position." Harney noted that the army would need forage and supplies and promised to pay liberal prices. He stressed the "advantages accruing to any community by the promotion of a proper intercourse between themselves and their government."[49]

Young had learned of the military expedition well before Harney's bland communication reached him. On July 22 he and some 2500 Saints had gathered at the head of Big Cottonwood Canyon, in the mountains southeast of Salt Lake City, to celebrate the tenth anniversary of the Mormon pioneers' arrival at their desert home. It was to be a three-day outing, a joyous occasion with speeches, music, dancing, and feasting. At noon on the 24th, however, four horsemen arrived, one of them from eastern Kansas, with a report that a "gentile" governor was on his way with an army to supersede their prophet and take control of their government. That evening, after the festivities, the Saints were called together and told the ominous news. Mormon leaders had feared and even predicted this action, but the news came as a shock nonetheless, and their celebration ended on a very somber note.[50]

Two days later counselor Heber C. Kimball sounded the call to arms in an angry speech full of threats, vowing that he would fight the invaders to the death. Stop the advancing army, he urged, seize its cattle and supply trains, and use them to feed and clothe the Mormon people! "Who would not rather die than bow down to the yoke of the enemy?" asked a speaker in the Salt Lake City

Tabernacle. "Would you, if necessary, brethren, put the torch to your buildings and lay them in ashes ... rather than submit to their military rule and oppression?" The federal government, Young claimed, had long been seeking a pretext for striking "a fatal blow at the kingdom." After their past exposures to violence, the Saints were determined that "if a mob again attack us, whether led by their own passions, or constitutionally legalized by the General Government ... we will resist their aggressions, by making an appeal to God, and our own right arms."[51]

Mobilization and preparations for all contingencies followed. Daniel H. Wells, commander of the territorial militia, called the Nauvoo Legion, ordered his force of about 2000 men to prepare for battle against an invading army. Brigadier General Franklin D. Richards ordered regimental officers to be ready for marching orders on short notice, to see that grain was not wasted, and to report any person who sold grain "to any Gentile merchant or temporary sojourner." The militia and other men mustered into military service participated in regular military drills. Missionaries were called home, and Saints in distant communities were asked to sell their property and return with arms and ammunition. In August, Young often spoke of severing the Mormon ties with the United States. "The time must come," he said, "when there will be a separation between this kingdom and the kingdoms of this world." He issued a defiant proclamation prohibiting military forces from entering his territory. If they did enter, Mormon leaders vowed that the Saints would burn their fields, destroy their settlements, and retreat to mountain strongholds for a long season of guerrilla warfare. Eventually some considered the alternative of another exodus and a renewed search for a Zion where they could live independently and in peace.[52]

The first encounter between the Mormons and the federal military was peaceful but unproductive. On September 7, Captain Stewart Van Vliet arrived in Salt Lake City to assure Young and other leaders that the army had no hostile intentions and to arrange for the purchase of supplies. His mission failed, but while there he listened to Mormon speakers who related their grievances and denied that they were in rebellion. Van Vliet was moved by what they said, and after carrying his message to the army he went on to Washington to urge an attempt at a peaceful settlement. His efforts were seconded by John Bernhisel, Utah's territorial delegate, and by Thomas L. Kane, a sympathetic "gentile" who had pleaded the cause of the Saints for many years.

Meanwhile, an angry correspondence between Young and Colonel Edmund Alexander, who commanded federal forces until Johnston's arrival, bristled with wild accusations and dire menaces. Young repeated his order to federal troops— that "armed, mercenary mob"—to stay out of Utah, and he placed the territory under martial law. He directed the Nauvoo Legion to fortify and defend Echo Canyon, thus blocking the shortest approach to Salt Lake City through the Wasatch Mountains. In an effort to halt the army's advance, he sent out squads of "Mormon Raiders" to destroy its supply trains and stampede its horses and cattle. On one expedition the raiders seized and burned 74 wagons in three supply trains and captured 1400 head of cattle. That proved to be the major action of the "Mormon War" before Johnston's small army, without having fought a battle, went into winter quarters near burned-out Fort Bridger, some 115 miles northeast of Salt Lake City.[53]

Although it was a war without battles, it was not one without tragedy and death. The army suffered heavy losses from sickness and the bitter cold of a mountain winter. In addition, a group of angry Mormon civilians and militiamen in southern Utah, threatened by the approaching army, caught in the frenzy of their Reformation, and incited by the inflammatory speeches of their leaders, took their revenge for past injuries on a company of "gentile" emigrants passing through their land. Remembered as the Mountain Meadows Massacre, Mormon historians have never confronted this lamentable episode without pain. Local Indians were accomplices in the crime, but not the instigators as some participants claimed in order to diminish their own guilt.

The Mormon alliance with the territory's Indian tribes began soon after the Saints arrived in Utah and wisely worked to win their friendship. They traded with them, established Indian missions, and preached to them from the Book of Mormon. The missionaries also competed with federal Indian agents for their loyalty, often suggesting that the government of the United States was their common enemy. In the summer of 1857, with the approach of the army of "gentiles," Governor Young sent out instructions for a campaign to win Indian support for the Saints in the impending conflict. He advised Elder Jacob Hamblin in southern Utah to seek "by works of righteousness" the Indians' confidence, "for they must learn that they have either got to help us or the United States will kill us both." Writing from northern Utah, one of the Saints reported that he had preached to the Shoshone Indians and described the Book of Mormon "as writings of their fathers." Since some of them had several wives, he told them that the American soldiers were angry "because we would not throw away that good Book and all our wives but one." Late in August, Elder Hamblin escorted a group of Indian chiefs to Salt Lake City for a conference with Young. Shortly after that meeting they were back in southern Utah and participated in the carnage at Mountain Meadows.[54]

The victims were members of an emigrant party, led by Captain Alexander Fancher, passing through Utah on its way to California. Numbering about 140 men, women, and children, most of them were Arkansas farmers and their families. The rest were Missourians, including a few reckless young men called the "Missouri Wildcats." Starting their long journey late in March, they had the misfortune to reach Utah in early August at the height of the Mormon fury over the threatened invasion, when "gentiles" were viewed with particular hostility. In the past emigrants had been able to purchase supplies in Utah, but, following

Young's order, the Saints refused to do business with members of the Fancher party. When they reached Salt Lake City they either were advised or decided on their own that the season was too late to risk taking the northern route across the Sierra. Instead they elected to take the longer southern route along the Old Spanish Trail.

As the emigrants traveled southward through Utah they experienced increasing hostility from the Saints and met the same refusal to sell them supplies. Apparently there were some rude exchanges between them, and some of the Missourians were accused of making provocative boasts about the treatment of Mormons in their state. One town refused to permit the emigrants to pass through, and at Cedar City their effort to purchase supplies again failed. From there they moved on to Mountain Meadows, a lush valley where they paused to rest their livestock before the long journey across the desert. Once more the emigrants found no one willing to replenish their dwindling supplies, and their relations with the Saints worsened. Some resorted to theft.

On September 6, at a meeting of the local Stake High Council in Cedar City, a decision was reached to deal with the emigrants before the United States Army arrived, and some strongly favored doing away with them. They sent for John D. Lee, who lived at Harmony and had considerable influence among the surrounding Indians. The next day James Haslam, an express rider, departed for Salt Lake City with a message to Young, the contents of which are unknown. Arriving on September 10, he delivered the message, and three days later he was back in Cedar City with Young's reply. It was addressed to Elder Isaac C. Haight and told him not to meddle with the Fancher party. Young added that the Indians would "do as they please" and that good relations with them should be preserved. In short, the Indians were to be given a free hand, which may lend added significance to his recent conference with their chiefs—and exposed him to suspicion of being at least an accessory before the fact.

Whatever their message to Young may have been, the Saints did not wait for his reply. The emigrants had already been attacked by the Indians, and they were under siege for several days during the second week of September. Three of them tried to break out and summon relief from Cedar City, but they were caught and killed, one by a white man, the other two by Indians. It was then that the Saints apparently decided that the whole Fancher party, except for the infants who could not talk, would have to be put to death. According to their plan, John D. Lee was to entice the emigrant party into a trap, and the grisly work was to be executed by Indians and Mormon militiamen under the command of Major John M. Higbee.

On September 11, Lee and William Bateman passed through the siege line and told the emigrants that they could be saved if they would surrender their weapons, wagons, and cattle to the Indians and walk with the militia back to Cedar City. The astonishingly gullible emigrants agreed. As they departed the small children and wounded men were transported in two wagons; the women and older children walked behind them; and the men followed single file, each with a militiaman beside him. When they reached a point where Indians, by pre-arrangement, were concealed in a forest of scrub oak, Major Higbee ordered the procession to halt and gave the command, "Do your duty!" Each militiaman promptly shot and killed the man at his side. Lee killed the wounded men in one of the wagons. The Indians fell upon the screaming women and older children, slaughtering them with knives and hatchets—thereby, it was said, enabling the Saints to avoid the shedding of innocent blood. When all was quiet, the Saints and Indians collected their booty and departed, leaving their 120 victims behind. Eighteen infants were taken back to Cedar City and eventually sent to relatives in the East.

In the aftermath of the massacre no one offered to accept responsibility. Brigham Young was innocent. Other church leaders were innocent. In most Mormon accounts the Saints involved, if not quite innocent, had been overwhelmed by their bitter memories of past wrongs and became the tragic victims of the hysteria caused by the threatened military invasion. Members of the Fancher party, however, were not deemed innocent, because some of them had behaved badly during their passage southward from Salt Lake City. Nor were the Indians, who in many accounts bore prime responsibility for the massacre. Eventually the question of guilt was settled judicially by the arrest and trial of a single man. Twenty years after the event, with the charges against all other Mormons dropped, John D. Lee, having already been excommunicated from his church, was convicted of murder in the first degree by an all-Mormon jury. On March 23, 1877, he was taken to Mountain Meadows and shot, thus dying for the sins of many Saints.[55]

One might have hoped that the horror of Mountain Meadows would have a sobering effect on both Mormons and "gentiles," but there was no sign that it did. At least two more emigrants were subsequently killed in the vicinity of Fillmore City by Indians aided and abetted by Mormons. One of the Local Saints protested to Young that this "order of things" illustrated "the spirit of blood thirstiness which was the prevailing topic in the reformation here last winter and spring." The "gentile" press demanded retribution. "Virtue, christianity, and decency," declared one editor, "require that the vile brood of incestuous miscreants who have perpetuated this atrocity shall be broken up and dispersed." In December, Buchanan asked Congress for more troops.[56]

During the winter, Young wisely concluded that continued resistance was futile and that he would have to surrender executive authority to Governor Cumming. In advising this course, a friend in the East asked Young how a man of his ability could have shown such bad judgment. By defying the federal government, he warned, Young "would only be the means of sending to an untimely grave many who are probably worthy of a better fate." Eventually the mediation of

Thomas L. Kane, whom Young trusted as an old friend, and the tact of Governor Cumming brought the conflict to an end. The following summer Cumming took up residence in Salt Lake City, and the army, after marching through the capital, established its base farther south. By all outward appearances the political order in Utah had changed, but in reality the center of power in the kingdom of the Saints remained firmly in the hands of Brigham Young.[57]

In the summer of 1857 skeptical foreign visitors could have found cause for amusement at America's self-image as a model republic, a beacon of hope for all mankind. Consider what they might have observed or read about in the press: southern proslavery extremists discussing the reopening of the African slave trade; deadly election-day Plug Ugly rioting in the national capital; William Walker recruiting a band of filibusters to invade Nicaragua; Governor Walker threatening the "insurrectionary" citizens of Lawrence with a military occupation; an army marching westward to protect the legally appointed governor of Utah Territory; Brigham Young shaking his fist in angry defiance; a body of Saints massacring a party of "gentiles." That was not all. For two weeks in July the streets of New York City were the scene of rioting and bloodshed.

New York's summer violence had its roots in a legislative measure placing the municipal police under state control. The city's police force, first organized in 1845, was by 1857 badly in need of reform. Under the supervision of a board controlled by Democratic Mayor Fernando Wood, it had become deeply involved in Tammany Hall politics. Some of the police were the allies of street gangs and other criminal elements who made certain districts of the city unsafe even in daylight. In April the legislature, controlled by upstate Republicans, passed a Metropolitan Police Bill similar to an act of the British Parliament which had created London's Metropolitan Police. Under its provisions Mayor Wood's police board was abolished and replaced by a five-man state commission appointed by the governor. In passing the bill the Republican majority responded in part to pressure from its upstate temperance constituents, who demanded more vigorous enforcement of the Sunday closing law against grog shops. Unfortunately, Republican Governor John A. King exposed the state commission to charges of partisanship by selecting four of its five members from his own party.[58]

Protests from New York City were not limited to Mayor Wood and his disreputable henchmen. "Our crime is to have held different opinions on political matters from the rural constituencies of the State," Harper's Weekly charged. "It has been our unhappiness to disapprove and nullify a liquor prohibition act which was much esteemed in the rural districts." Governor King's partisanship, complained the New York Times, had "imperiled the practical working of . . . what must have been at best a doubtful experiment." Disgusted with the whole controversy, George Templeton Strong concluded that the sole purpose of the police bill was to take power out of the hands of Mayor Wood, "that King of Scoundrels," and put it in the hands of "the other scoundrels at Albany." The New York *Herald,* raising the banner of self-government, claimed that this usurpation of municipal power stemmed from the desire of a Republican legislature to humiliate a Democratic city.[59]

Some Democrats now viewed Mayor Wood, with all his corruption, as the champion of municipal freedom, and one assigned him a place in history not merely respectable but "august and memorable." He defended the city against "the boldest stroke of usurpation ever planned in this country," wrote a party editor, one that "Federalism in its haughtiest days would not have ventured upon." Wood refused to surrender. He maintained his own police force, made additional appointments to it, and promoted some members, described by one critic as "notorious ruffians and brawlers," to the rank of captain. On May 29, supporters of the mayor held a rally at National Hall, where speakers called on citizen volunteers to defend New York's charter rights with bayonets if necessary. For a time the city faced the prospect of two commissions and two police forces confronting each other in battle array. After some skirmishing between them, a regiment of the New York National Guard arrived to preserve order. New York, *Harper's Weekly* reported sadly, "presents to the eyes of her sister cities the disgraceful spectacle of confirmed anarchy."[60]

Wood averted more serious violence by retreating a little and taking his case to court. Early in July, when the New York Court of Appeals upheld the constitutionality of the legislature's bill, the mayor gave up. He ordered his municipal police to disband and turned the station houses over to the new metropolitan police. As a result, members of the old police force felt betrayed and cursed the mayor for deserting them.[61]

On July 4 the first of the riots broke out and continued through the following day. The participants included discharged members of the municipal police, Irish and German immigrants, and members of street gangs such as the Dead Rabbits, Blackbirds, Bowery Boys, and Roach Guards. Apart from gang rivalry, the anger of the mobs seemed to be directed against the new metropolitan police, and the Sunday closing of grog shops. In the Irish sixth ward the Dead Rabbits and Bowery Boys battled each other from behind barricades with brickbats, rocks and pistols, and the new metropolitan police were not yet well enough organized and sufficiently trained to deal with violence on so large a scale. Before peace was restored on the evening of the second day, six persons had been killed and scores wounded.[62]

A few days later there were new disorders and more casualties. In the eleventh ward, two clubs, the Blues and the Forty Thieves, waged a private war. In the seventeenth ward, German and Irish immigrants, the Dead Rabbits, and some of the disbanded municipal police engaged in guerrilla warfare against the metropolitan police. The Germans were angry because the police, for the first time, were enforcing a law closing the beer halls on Sundays, thus depriving them, as one sympathizer explained, "of the simple pleasure of drinking lager beer, on their only day of recreation." On July 14, before the disturbances had ended, George Templeton Strong visited the police station at the corner of Third Street and the Bowery—"the outpost or advanced guard of law and order." The police rarely ventured east of it. He deplored the fact "that there should be a whole ward . . . which I cannot walk through tonight without serious risk—and that no vigorous effort is made to suppress the disorder."[63]

For nearly two weeks, observed the New York *Herald* in mid-July, the principal business of the newspapers of this city had been to chronicle "riots and disturbances of the peace, all of them serious and menacing in their general aspect, and some of them resulting in a deplorable loss of life." The source of all the trouble, it insisted, was "the unwise, uncalled for and unconstitutional" interference of the state legislature in the affairs of the city. The New York *Times* probed deeper. Some, it noted, thought the solution was to close down the dramshops on Sundays and holidays; but drinking was one of the few pleasures open to the poor of the city. Even members of the street gangs, "ignorant, depraved scoundrels" though they were, deserved "something more at the hands of the State than a scarcity of whiskey, and volleys of musketry." If wealthy citizens hoped for an end to mobs and riots, the *Times* suggested that they contribute to the charitable agencies that tried to assist those living in poverty. Meanwhile, the rioters merely repaid "in bitter measure, the neglect of the Christian and educated classes." They controlled elections; their corrupt leaders plundered the city; they endangered property and defied the law. "This is their answer to the selfishness of churches and the avarice of the rich."[64]

To its very end the summer was filled with an unfortunate sequence of dismal events, great and small. Early in August the intrepid adventuress Mrs. Emma Augusta Cunningham was back in the national news, again providing good copy for editors and titillating reading for the public. This time she was the principal in a bizarre attempt at fraud. During Mrs. Cunningham's trial for the murder of Dr. Harvey Burdell, she had claimed not only to be the victim's widow but to be pregnant with his child. After the jury found her not guilty, although Burdell's estate remained in the hands of a public administrator, she and her children continued to occupy his house on Bond Street. Having failed to persuade the court that she was Burdell's widow, her only chance to establish a claim to his property was to bear a child and prove him to be the father.

In due course Mrs. Cunningham appeared in public looking quite pregnant. She told a Dr. Uhl, who had been her medical adviser before the murder and during her trial, that her child was due in August, but she apparently asked for no prenatal care. Eventually Uhl began to doubt her pregnancy and reported his suspicions to District Attorney A. Oakey Hall. Although refusing to sign an affidavit, he agreed to cooperate with Hall in exposing the fraud if such it proved to be. Late in July, Mrs. Cunningham confessed to Uhl that she was not pregnant and brazenly offered him $1000 if he would procure for her a newborn infant from the almshouse. Uhl, pretending to agree, obtained the infant, and a birth was announced. On August 4, Mrs. Cunningham was arrested on a charge of attempting to procure a fraudulent heir to the Burdell estate.

Once again the house on Bond Street attracted crowds of the morbidly curious. There and elsewhere in the city, the *Times* reported, "shoeless urchins" did a brisk business selling the scurrilous "Cunningham-baby ballads." "Here you are," they shouted, "Mrs. Cunningham's baby, only one cent." "We do not wonder that crowds surround the house," commented the *Evening Post*, for the crimes committed there "served to render the spot accursed." *Harper's Weekly* looked back on the Cunningham case "with a feeling of unmitigated horror." In the annals of crime it could find none "so consistent throughout, so marvelously conceived and wondrously executed, so regular and obedient to the laws of art." Nor could it find "a parallel to Mrs. Cunningham in all the long list of female reprobates from Lucrece Borgia to our own days." A Philadelphia editor, however, found "singular comedy" in the "unblushing impudence" of the fictitious birth she contrived so soon after her trial for murder.[65]

Mrs. Cunningham's attempted fraud shared the news columns that August with accounts of a more propitious public enterprise: the laying of a transatlantic cable to provide telegraphic communication between New York and London. Cyrus W. Field, the project's chief promoter, had conceived the idea as early as 1853 and enlisted the support of other New York entrepreneurs, among them, David Dudley Field, Peter Cooper, and Moses Taylor. By 1857 American and British ships had made the prelminary surveys; a satisfactory agreement with Great Britain had been reached; and the Newfoundland, London, and New York Telegraph Company had built a telegraph line between New York and St. Johns, Newfoundland. Messages between them, which had taken several weeks by mail, now passed through a half-dozen independent telegraphic circuits in less than an hour. With the completion of this western connection, work could begin on th‿ transatlantic cable between Newfoundland and Valentia Island, Ireland, a distance of over 2000 miles. British capitalists joined Field and his associates to form the Atlantic Telegraph Company. The American and British governments assisted the enterprise by providing ships and engineers.

The public followed the exciting venture with deep interest and great expectations of a dramatic change in the history of mankind. It was, wrote the New York *Herald,* "the grandest work which has ever been attempted by the genius and enterprise of man." The resulting rapid exchange of ideas between nations, the New York *Evening Post* predicted, would "make the great heart of humanity beat with a single pulse." Soon, wrote a Tennessee editor in an euphoric flight of fancy, the whole world would be "chained and bound together by this mystic tie." The nations would become one family. They would then be able to "assemble around a common council board and engage together in diplomatic deliberations, or about a common altar and mingle their voices in devout worship to the same great Creator and Ruler." More than that: "Wars are to cease. The kingdom of peace will be set up." The nations of the earth would henceforth "be actuated by good will towards each other," and display "all the affections which should bind together a common brotherhood." Unfortunately, these millennial fantasies vanished abruptly late in August when news arrived that the cable had broken several hundred miles west of Valentia Island. After another failure the following year, Field was unable to fulfill his dream until 1866.[66]

The summer ended with two disasters of a kind all too familiar to the American public. On September 5 there was a collision between an express passenger train and a wood train on the Camden and Atlantic Railroad about twelve miles from Philadelphia. Three passengers were killed and many were injured. A week later the steamer *Central America,* en route from Havana to New York, sank with the loss of 400 lives. The vessel was only a few years old, yet it began to leak soon after leaving port. The fires went out for want of coal, the engines stopped, and when a storm came up it foundered helplessly. The life boats it carried were insufficient for more than 300 passengers, yet it carried 600. "Every day a ship is lost," wrote a New York editor as he reviewed other recent marine disasters. Some were "enveloped in fearful mystery." The details of others were so distressing "that it were better that the same uncertainty should surround them." Each was a victim of the "inevitable perils of the deep to which all are liable who go down to the sea in ships."[67]

All in all, it was not the best of summers—and the autumn proved to be no better.

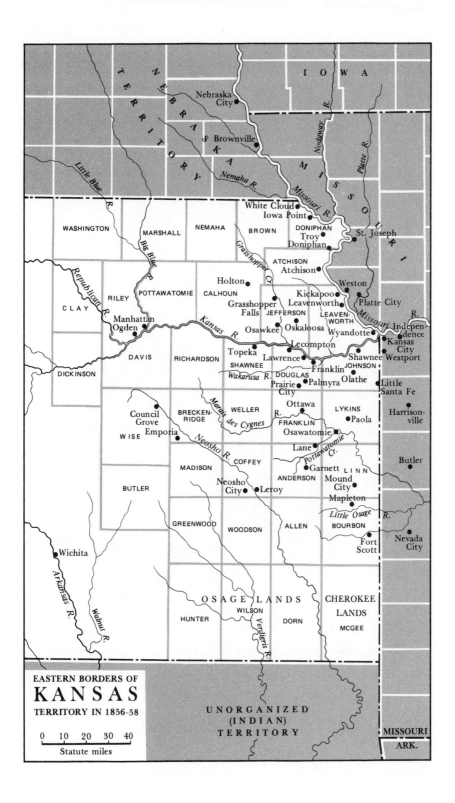

EASTERN BORDERS OF
KANSAS
TERRITORY IN 1856-58

0   10   20   30   40
Statute miles

OUR NEW PRESIDENT.

James Buchanan, *Harper's Weekly*. Bancroft Library, University of California, Berkeley.

Buchanan's Cabinet, *Harper's Weekly*. Bancroft Library, University of California, Berkeley.

John W. Forney. Files of the National Archives.

Chief Justice R. B. Taney. Files of the National Archives.

Charles Robinson. Kansas State Historical Society,
Topeka.

James Lane. Kansas State Historical Society, Topeka.

R. J. Walker. Files of the National Archives.

GEN. WILLIAM WALKER, OF NICARAGUA.—[FROM A PHOTOGRAPH BY MEADE BROTHERS.]

William Walker, *Harper's Weekly*. Bancroft Library,
University of California, Berkeley.

S. A. Douglas. Files of the National Archives.

CHAPTER **8**

Flush Times and
an Autumn Panic

On the first day of autumn Robert C. Winthrop, descendant of John Winthrop, conservative Whig politician, and gentleman scholar, sat at his desk in his comfortable Boston home and considered the state of the Union. For almost a month, no doubt, he had been reading daily accounts in the local press of a series of economic calamities that had startled the country and produced a condition of near business paralysis: a sharp decline of prices on the New York Stock Exchange, merchants in distress, banks in dire peril, railroads facing bankruptcy, land values collapsing, factories reducing their operations or shutting down, the ranks of the unemployed steadily growing. The news was all the more dismaying when it appeared that some of the men who controlled the failing enterprises, once respected for their probity, were guilty of unethical business practices, a few even of outright peculation. In a gloomy letter to a friend, Winthrop reflected the current widespread feelings of disillusionment and despair. "For myself," he wrote, "I am afraid that my moralizings do not do me much good, and may be only the result of disordered nerves or a bad digestion; but the world never seemed to me a less hopeful place than in this month of September, in the Year of our Lord 1857."[1]

How sadly these sentiments contrasted with the economic euphoria evident in the business community and in the editorial columns of the urban press a few months earlier! The buoyant boosterism of the Cincinnati *Enquirer* as recently as June typified the general optimism that had prevailed during the previous decade of prosperous growth. Cincinnati, it proudly claimed, presented to the world "a picture of progress heretofore unknown to the history of cities." Having grown in a half-century from a small village to a thriving city with a population of 115,000, its "solidity and continued prosperity" had become "matters of special wonder." Cincinnati's commercial economy, long based on a flourishing steamboat trade with St. Louis, Memphis, New Orleans, and other river towns, had recently expanded as a result of railroad connections with the Great Lakes and the East. The *Enquirer* predicted that continued growth and prosperity would further augment her "marvelous greatness."[2]

The immediate cause of the *Enquirer's* exuberance was the completion of the final segment of the Ohio and Mississippi Railroad, which connected Cincinnati and East St. Louis. Building this 340-mile road through hilly terrain had been expensive, and Cincinnati had taxed its citizens in order to purchase one million dollars of the company's stock. But the anticipated rewards were to be great, for the city, already linked to the East by the Baltimore and Ohio and the Marietta and Cincinnati railroads, was now situated on a 900-mile trunk route between Baltimore and St. Louis. From this position Cincinnati merchants, like those of St. Louis, hoped that their rail and river transport would enable them to compete successfully with Chicago for the southern and western trade. Both cities held grand celebrations, and excursion trains starting from Baltimore and East St. Louis carried distinguished guests along the entire line. The Chicago *Democrat* generously congratulated the promoters of the Ohio and Mississippi. Nevertheless, in a typical example of intercity rivalry, the *Democrat* boasted that Chicago, with the Illinois Central recently completed and with its own strategic eastern rail connections, would defeat any challenge from Cincinnati or St. Louis in the race to become the West's leading metropolis.[3]

Other western cities—Cleveland, Toledo, Detroit, Indianapolis, and Milwaukee—had their boosters and promoters, all resting their faith on the magic of the iron rails. On April 15, Milwaukee celebrated the completion of the Milwaukee and Mississippi Railroad. After a hundred-gun salute a special train transported officers of the company and guests to its western terminus at Prairie du Chien, where it received a two-hundred-gun salute. Carried away by the occasion, the Milwaukee *Sentinel* rejoiced that the long-awaited day had arrived when, "starting betimes from the shores of Lake Michigan, the iron horse does at evening slake his thirst in the brimming Mississippi." The event was a harbinger of prosperous times for Milwaukee, the *Sentinel* predicted, if its merchants would only reach out for the opportunities within their grasp.[4] The Milwaukee press was also full of news about other railroad projects—the Milwaukee and Horicon, the La Crosse and Milwaukee, the Milwaukee and Beloit, the Milwaukee and Watertown, the Lake Shore, the Air Line to Fond du Lac, and, with the aid of a federal land grant, a line to connect Milwaukee with Minnesota and the Lake Superior region—some under construction, others mere promotions.

Much of the economic boom of the 1850s centered on feverish railroad construction and the consolidation of smaller lines into trunk lines such as the Boston and Albany, the New York Central, the New York and Erie, the Baltimore and Ohio, and the Pennsylvania Railroad. During the decade more than 20,000 miles of tracks were laid, of which nearly 2500 were completed in 1857. Everywhere politicians, merchants, and land speculators regarded the railroads—"those wonder working agencies of modern civilization"—as precursors of an economic millennium. They had opened the immense West, wrote a Boston editor, "made valuable that, which from lack of means of communication was before worthless . . . annihilated distance and made the land a neighborhood." The Detroit *Free Press* predicted that within five years, if certain projected railroads were built, the state's resources would be developed well beyond what would be possible in thirty years without them. A Harrisburg editor praised the Pennsylvania Railroad for its "uninterrupted career of success . . . of which all Pennsylvanians should feel proud." The Southern states, too, were caught up in the railroad mania. Several of them, notably Virginia, subscribed generously to railroad stock, while Georgia built the Western and Atlantic between Atlanta and Chattanooga as a state enterprise. Railroads, observed a New Orleans editor, were changing the city's economy in ways undreamed of only ten years ago.[5]

The railroads were financed in a variety of ways. In addition to the stock subscriptions of various states, cities, and counties, the companies sold their securities to investors and speculators on the New York Stock Exchange and to foreign, especially British, investors. The Milwaukee and Mississippi and other Wisconsin lines, by promising high dividends, persuaded thousands of farmers living along the right-of-way to buy railroad stock with personal notes secured by mortgages on their farms. The railroads then sold the mortgages to eastern bankers to obtain a portion of the funds required for construction and the purchase of rolling stock. Federal aid in the form of land grants from the public domain began in 1850 when the state of Illinois received 2.5 million acres to subsidize the construction of the Illinois Central Railroad. Between 1850 and 1857 the railroad projects of eleven western and southern states were assisted by federal land grants totaling 22 million acres. The grants proved to be a stimulus not only to the railroads but to land speculation and to a considerable amount of corruption growing out of the competition of rival promoters for a share of the land at the states' disposal.[6]

The possibility of a railroad to the Pacific coast had been discussed off and on for more than a decade, and President Buchanan gave it his support in his inaugural address. During the Pierce administration the War Department had conducted preliminary surveys of four possible routes, one northern, one central, and two southern, and estimated the costs and engineering problems involved in each. The southern route through Texas, New Mexico Territory, and California to San Diego was the shortest and appeared to be the least expensive, and the Buchanan administration was decidedly partial to it. Early in 1857 the Southern Pacific Railroad, with land grants from the state of Texas, began building westward from the Louisiana border, thereby arousing in New Orleans exciting visions of the riches to be gained if it were to become the eastern terminus of the first, and perhaps the only, Pacific railroad. A local editor could not contemplate the result without resorting to the romantic imagery of locomotives "rioting over the prairies of Texas . . . rejoicing along the valleys of the Gila," bringing with them "the arts of peace . . . the song of joy, the voice of prayer, the hum of thrift."[7]

Memphis, St. Louis, and Chicago had other visions. An Illinois advocate of the central route was convinced that·a railroad traversing the belt of territory between the thirty-eighth and forty-second parallels would be profitable from the start. A great tide of emigrants would follow the line as it was constructed, "and the beautiful country on the shores of the Pacific, and large portions of the inter-mediate and fertile region would be occupied by an enterprising population."[8] Thus, in 1857, as in earlier years, the sectional controversy over the route of a Pacific railroad prolonged the political stalemate, while Californians fumed at the exasperating failure of eastern politicians to act.

Persistent skepticism about the feasibility and need for the project was a further deterrent. Trade with California and with the Far East was cheaper, some insisted, along existing water routes than it would be by rail to the Pacific coast. Others, mostly southern Democrats, revived Jacksonian arguments against the constitutionality of federal subsidies for internal improvements. "The Federal Government was not instituted to make roads," protested a Louisville editor. "Its framers had no such purpose in view." The people themselves, argued a Tennes-sean, were better able to accomplish "all that is good in human progress, than the heavy machinery of government." Besides, what hope did the minority South have of persuading Congress to approve a route favorable to its interests? That, in fact, was the nub of the matter.[9]

Only rarely, in this time of blind faith in the benevolence of railroad cor-porations, did anyone propose government regulation to improve their safety or to assure their faithful performance as public-service enterprises. In January 1857, Governor Chase, in his message to the Ohio legislature, observed that the rail-roads had become a new power in the state and proposed the creation of a com-mission to regulate their operations. One of Chase's correspondents feared that this "untried and novel element in the State may grow up and rapidly become very pernicious to the interests of many classes of citizens." Hence, he urged that the commission be empowered to control rates and supervise the railroads' rela-tions with shippers, passengers, and landholders along their lines. At present, he wrote, there was nothing to prevent a railroad president or superintendent, "by a single sweep of the pen, from affecting the value of every acre of *producing* land . . . on any of your trunk lines." He could just as easily destroy the profit of a wheat farmer, or an iron manufacturer, or a coal producer.[10]

The legislature ignored Chase's proposal—and well that it did, declared a Democratic editor, for neither the public nor the railroads would submit to such "audacious pretensions." Expressing the extreme laissez-faire philosophy of the mid-nineteenth century, he asserted that private companies could manage their own affairs far better than public officials. "The whole experience of the country is against such a policy. No good patriotic citizen . . . would justify or propose such interference with the rights of individuals. It could only originate in the mind of a selfish partisan, intent on personal aggrandizement." This, of course, was a Democratic editor's attack on a Republican governor, but Chase was also rebuffed by a Republican legislature.[11]

The untrammeled free enterprise of a laissez-faire political economy did seem to be working wonderfully well. Nowhere on earth, boasted the *Illinois State Journal*, could any nation match the progress and prosperity of the United States. "In intelligence, enterprise, adventure, rugged independence, and sterling qualities of the heart," no people excelled the Americans. The thriving young city of Chicago, with its flourishing commerce and burgeoning manufacturing enterprises, was both child and symbol of the dawning industrial age. It made almost everything that was made elsewhere, claimed the Chicago *Tribune*, and competed successfully, "by the excellence of the market, with larger, wealthier, and longer established factories in the East." The textile mills and other industries of New England and Philadelphia expanded and prospered, as did the iron works of western Pennsylvania, the American merchant marine, and the commercial houses of New York City. The foreign and domestic markets had been strong and prices correspondingly high for the wheat of western farmers and the cotton of southern planters. Even Virginia emerged from long years of agricultural depression to share in the general prosperity. Improved agricultural methods, the use of fertilizers, and crop rotation restored the productivity of its depleted soil. Augmenting the prosperity of the 1850s was the great influx of foreign immigrants, who expanded both the domestic market and the labor supply. In addition, the flow of gold from California increased specie reserves and thus enlarged the basis for bank loans to railroads, industry, and agriculture.[12]

The number of banks of various kinds—state-owned banks, private banks chartered by states with free-banking laws, and unchartered private banks operated by individuals or partners—had increased to meet the credit needs of the expanding economy. Between 1850 and 1857 the number of banks nearly doubled, totaling by then more than 1500. Most were located in the East, approximately sixty of them in New York City, which had become the nation's financial center and the place where many country banks deposited their reserve funds. With the federal government wholly withdrawn from banking after the demise of the second Bank of the United States in 1836, regulation of these fiscal institutions rested altogether with the individual states. Some required them to support their issues of bank notes with adequate specie reserves and to report regularly concerning their loans and deposits; others were lax, enabling bank officers to take risks that made the value of their note issues uncertain at best. Occasionally the banks themselves organized a regulatory system. In New England the

Suffolk Bank of Boston initiated a method which virtually forced country banks to back their notes with adequate reserves. In New York a Clearing House, organized in 1853, indirectly performed a similar regulatory function for the banks of that city. Nationally the banking system, though seriously flawed and vulnerable in a crisis, had somehow managed to provide most of the financial support for the economic growth and prosperity of the past decade.[13]

Easy credit, improved transportation, and generally high prices for wheat, corn, and cotton had accelerated westward migration and the sale of public lands. "Your true home is in the West!" Horace Greeley advised poor workingmen and marginal farmers in the eastern states. "Seek it, and rear your children there to larger opportunities than await them on the rugged hillsides or in the crowded streets of the East!" Much of the migration still went to the states of the Old Northwest, such as Wisconsin, whose population grew from 305,000 in 1850 to an estimated 730,000 in 1857. The Illinois Central attracted a host of settlers to its lands with offers of seven years' credit and a small down payment. With the advantage of railroad connections to Chicago and the East, emigrants were willing to pay a relatively high price of $10 to $24 an acre for good land.[14]

But the flow of emigrants moved increasingly to the tier of states across the Mississippi River and to the territories further west. "Long lines of cars on the Chicago and Mississippi road, are constantly filled with emigrants . . . wending their way to Kansas and Nebraska," reported the *Illinois State Journal.* The editor expressed sympathy for the eastern communities that were losing their "most energetic and industrious population," but he reflected contentedly that nothing could deter these restless people from their search for a Golconda in the West. Southern slaveholders as well as small farmers were attracted to the rich lands of Louisiana's Red River valley and the prairies of eastern Texas. A North Carolina planter wrote Senator Rusk that he and a half-dozen of his neighbors had "taken the Texas fever" and hoped to "better their fortunes" planting cotton there.[15]

Land for speculation as well as land to farm attracted many of those who attended the public sales. "Nearly the whole West swarms with speculators," reported the Washington *Union,* "who neither intend to cultivate the soil nor settle there, but who expect to realize fortunes without labor out of the *bona fide* settlers." Land speculation, observed a Wisconsin editor, had become a mania. "Merchants have shut up their shops, lawyers have left the bar, farmers have laid down the shovel and the hoe, manufacturers have abandoned their business to turn land agents and real estate dealers." In Minnesota, complained a territorial politician, people were "so engrossed in speculating" that they had no time for politics. In May, when the Minnesota railroad land grants were put up for sale, "the cormorants [were] gathered there from all quarters . . . all engaged in a general scramble for the spoils." Lots on the best street in Omaha, which had sold for $500 in the spring of 1856, went for $5000 a year later. In a Kansas land sale, reported a correspondent, five-eighths of the land went to eastern speculators.

Like his predecessors, Governor Walker was an active participant in the business.[16]

"These things cannot last," warned the Washington *Union*. "The laws of trade and business produce unerring consequences." There were always Jeremiahs, of course. Soon after Congress reduced the duties on foreign imports Greeley's protectionist *Tribune* began to argue that the current prosperity was "bloated, unsound, and factitious" and to see the skies "gloomy and lowering." Europe would now flood the American market with its manufactures and contrive "to run us yearly deeper and deeper into her debt." One morning, Greeley predicted with remarkable prescience, the country would wake up and find that its economy had been brought to a dead halt, probably because of "some comparatively trivial . . . unlooked for incident." The real cause, in fact, would be "too much extravagance . . . too much buying abroad, and on time, of things which we should make at home."[17]

Others, from time to time, betrayed anxiety about the possible consequences of the current heavy speculation in railroad securities and land. This was an age, fretted a Philadelphia editor, in which men sought to grow rich without labor, and speculation was their favorite means. A prudent man might well be tempted to bury his money in the earth rather than involve himself with Wall Street's "bulls and bears, who seem, between them, to give value to the merest bubble." Western land speculators, another feared, held more land than could be settled in twenty years. Many of them were men of modest means, who had borrowed at high interest rates and would be ruined if declining commodity prices should cause land values to fall. In May, Amos A. Lawrence wrote "Governor" Robinson concerning the lands of the New England Emigrant Aid Company, warning that a general collapse was inevitable. "Now is the time to sell," he advised, "and lend the money to those who think differently."[18]

Still others worried that the country had been "too 'fast'" and that "the day of reckoning and atonement" was at hand. Railroad promoters had accumulated enormous debts, and they were not realizing the anticipated large dividends. By summer some promoters were finding it difficult to secure payments on stock subscriptions; one of them had to spend "two hard and dreary weeks . . . going from house to house raising stock" for the Jacksonville, Alton, and St. Louis Railroad. In May and June the New York papers nervously noted a decline in the shipping business. "Our wharves are crowded with ships," reported the *Herald*, "most of them without employment; and those that have found something to do have accepted it at rates ruinously low." A Boston paper revealed that 6000 New England cotton looms had been stopped during the summer—nothing serious, it thought, merely a temporary adjustment to demand.[19]

Late in June, *Hunt's Merchants' Magazine*, an important commercial publication, suddenly, but briefly, grew alarmed. Business activity in the spring, it confessed, had created "considerable uneasiness in regard to the future," especially about economic conditions in the West. Land speculation in that section seemed to have reached its peak; but now money was scarce and interest rates high, and those who had acquired property might find it difficult "either to pay for it, or to sell it without great loss." Railroads, it believed, were valued so highly that they were "no longer constructed to facilitate the cultivation of the soil, but for mere purposes of local speculation." Continued profitable trade with the West would depend upon the success of the year's crops and the avoidance of a financial crisis. Meanwhile, the country needed to return "to the old spirit of patient productive labor."

A month later *Hunt's* had regained its cheerful outlook. It was now convinced that there were no signs of an imminent commercial crisis, and the world should be able to "breathe more freely during the dog-days." In fact, it complained that some listened to the doomsayers "far too much for the peace of the country," for their "croakings" alarmed the superstitious. Even the following issue, which apparently went to press before the last week of August, reported that the country continued prosperous, and no trouble was in sight. Rather, "the people are industriously engaged in productive pursuits, and there can be no permanent distress while such engagements are continued."[20]

Editor Freeman Hunt had plenty of support from his complacent journalistic colleagues. In mid-August the New York *Independent* ridiculed the talk of a financial crisis indulged in "by the whole tribe of long-faced bears," predicting instead a more favorable money market, rising stock prices, excellent crops, and an improvement in trade. According to the Chicago *Democrat,* the general feeling was that the recent signs of an impending economic crisis had "passed away," and that financial prospects were "growing better daily." Farmers everywhere were "blessed with abundance, and as a natural result their demands on manufacturers for goods must be great." Late in August an editor from upstate New York, during a visit to New York City, found money so plentiful "that accommodations on good paper [could] be easily had on reasonable terms." With crops abundant and expectations of a large fall trade, he concluded: "We shall have better times!"[21]

Such were the confusing economic observations and forecasts that editors, politicians, and businessmen served up to the public during the spring and summer of 1857. Some of them were based on wishful thinking, most of them on available, often unreliable, economic information which contemporary observers, with their necessarily imperfect vision, weighed and interpreted in different ways. In later years economic historians, with better perspective and a clearer perception of the dynamics of business cycles, have measured the events preceding the Panic of 1857 more accurately, but they continue to dispute their relative importance. Some stress international conditions: the dependence of the American economy on British trade and capital investments; the unfavorable American balance of trade and the resulting export of specie; the decline of European markets for American farm staples; and the curtailing and partial liquidation of British investments in American securities. Others stress domestic conditions: the shortcomings of the American banking system, especially the inadequate specie reserves of many banks and their inability to cooperate in times of crisis; the frenzy of speculation in land and railroad securities; the weak and overburdened credit structure; the eventual cyclical decline in railroad and industrial investments; and the enormous increase in agricultural production, which exceeded domestic demand. Yet, in the years immediately preceding the panic these domestic and international conditions interacted with each other in so complex a manner as to make their separation almost impossible.

Both had provided ample cause for apprehension. After a brief but sharp contraction in 1854, the prosperity of the 1850s reached its peak in the middle of the decade. Immigration declined after 1854, and by the end of 1856 government lands sales, bank loans and discounts, and domestic trade were falling off. During the previous two years the Crimean War, which deprived western Europe of Russian wheat, had provided an expanded international market for American cereals at a time when production was rising faster than demand at home. When, early in 1856, peace was restored, American farmers lost a large part of their foreign market, and American shippers soon found themselves in a recession. By the spring of 1857, imports had begun to diminish; earnings of the Erie, New York Central, and other railroads were disappointing; and new England textile mills had substantial inventories but few buyers. In July the Stark Mills of Manchester, New Hampshire, suspended operations; others in Lowell and elsewhere soon followed.

Meanwhile, a significant change had occurred in international financial markets. The Bank of France, weakened by the loss of specie during and after the Crimean war, was obliged repeatedly, in a period of economic expansion, to draw specie from the Bank of England. This, in turn, led to substantially increased interest rates in London, which tempted British investors to sell off American securities and put their money in less speculative and often more remunerative domestic securities. The result was a decline in the price of shares on the New York Stock Exchange. The decline of security values weakened the American banking system by reducing the value of the assets supporting it. In short, an economic recession had already overtaken the economy before Greeley's "unlooked for incident" brought on a crash.[22]

In 1857 the Ohio Life Insurance and Trust Company was one of the most highly respected financial institutions in New York City. Although it was a branch of a Cincinnati corporation, the Wall Street office appeared to enjoy considerable freedom in managing its own affairs. In spite of its name it did not write insurance but served as a bank of deposit capitalized at approximately $2 million.

The bank's managers enhanced its reputation for prudence by refusing to issue bank notes. Instead they used the deposits from brokers and private individuals to make advances to commercial houses, especially in the West, on good security. They frequently borrowed from other New York banks to redeem the company's drafts when western merchants offered them in payment for supplies purchased in the East. The bank also served as agent for the state of Ohio in transferring funds and paying interest on the public debt; and it did considerable business with Ohio corporations and state banks. According to the New York *Herald,* for many years "no bank was favored with more deposits, nor was there any which was abler to loan on adequate security than the New York branch of the Trust Company of Ohio."[23]

On August 24, Charles Stetson, the company's president, made a shocking announcement: "The unpleasant duty has devolved upon me to state that this company has suspended payment." Stetson explained that the suspension had resulted from the failure of certain parties to repay their loans; but he assured the public that, except for losses from these loans, the company's capital was "sound and reliable." The truth was far less comforting. The company had in fact invested much of its capital in speculative railroad bonds; the cashier was involved in a large embezzlement; and total liabilities were reported between $5 and 7 million. The New York branch quickly brought down its Cincinnati head-quarters, and within four days stockholders saw their shares decline more than 85 percent. A Cincinnati editor described a depressing local scene of small depos-itors crowding the street in front of the bank anxiously asking for "the best mode of securing and realizing their claims." All they could be told was "to wait for something to turn up."[24]

Most of the New York banks were creditors of the Ohio Life and Trust, and the panic began among them and on the stock exchange. The banks called in their loans, pressured interior banks to redeem their notes in specie, and sharply increased interest rates, refusing all requests to lend on promissory notes and bills of exchange. For several weeks stock prices declined steadily, with rail-road shares among the most vulnerable. Soon the papers were filled with dismal news about bankrupt brokers and speculators, bank failures, mercantile houses closing their doors, and manufacturers suspending operations. George Templeton Strong's diary recorded the mood on Wall Street as the panic took its toll: "O Posterity, Posterity, you can't think how bothered, bedeviled, careworn, and weary were your enlightened ancestors in their counting-rooms and offices and bank parlors during these bright days of September, A.D. 1857." In a time such as this even a Wall Street lawyer might grow concerned about lost innocence and sentimental about the simple life of earlier days. He wondered why the men of business wasted the sunshine and imperiled their health "in a long, grim battle with endorsements and due-bills and time-contracts, instead of living their lives in freedom and peace and pure air with a competency and a cow."[25]

In the weeks after the failure of the Ohio Life and Trust some put on a bold face and tried to restore confidence by denying that there was cause for serious alarm. "The 'panic'—if there was one—has pretty much subsided," a Boston editor announced in early September, "and the 'crash' which was confidently promised by the croakers has not come." Another insisted that a general collapse like that of 1837 was "an absolute impossibility." A month later the New York *Tribune,* finding some encouraging economic news, claimed that many thought the sky was brightening. Until late September the Chicago *Tribune* maintained that the "bursting of bubbles in New York . . . need not alarm anybody in the West," for its prosperity was built on a better foundation. It saw no cause for despair, or even a "serious growl," if all the gamblers in grain, stocks, paper money, and frontier real estate, as well as the "red-dog and wild-cat" banks, were bankrupted. In the South, too, there was much confidence that the Wall Street panic would be a purely local affair and was "not quite so serious a thing" as some imagined.[26]

Eventually even the optimists lost heart and were obliged to admit that all classes and sections were in some degree suffering from the impact of the panic. On September 29 the Chicago *Tribune* faced reality: "There is little use in attempting to delude ourselves or our readers with the fiction that the money market is easier. . . . Western men must make up their minds to go through a winter of extraordinary pressure." A week later a Nashville editor reported that confidence in the local banks was "utterly destroyed" and that the community was responding "like a terror stricken army." Many would suffer severely, he predicted, for no city was free from the panic's "destructive ravages." In New York, early in October, Strong described the mood of merchants and bankers on three terrible days. October 8: "Bluer and darker every day. . . . Failures many and important." October 9: "This has been the bluest day yet; distrust and despondency universal." October 10: "We seem foundering. Affairs are worse than ever today, and a period of general insolvency seems close upon us. . . . People's faces in Wall Street look fearfully gaunt and desperate."[27]

At the heart of the panic following the suspension of the Ohio Life and Trust was the fear that the fragile American banking system could not withstand the pressures suddenly placed upon it. Could individual banks, given their limited specie reserves and inability to collect on their loans, meet the demands of frightened depositors for the redemption of their notes in coin? Would there be a general suspension of specie payments, with unpredictable results? On August 27 a Boston paper reported the failure of five banks in New England and one in Virginia. Within the next few days other country banks in New England, upstate New York, Missouri, and Nebraska Territory suspended payment on their notes. These suspensions were sufficiently alarming to prompt the Secretary of the Treasury to act. Cobb, "much and anxiously exercised" about the financial crisis, arranged for the redemption of several million dollars worth of Treasury bonds and the minting of $4 million in gold coins in order to increase the specie holdings of savings banks.[28]

Cobb was commended for his action, but it had little appreciable effect. On September 25 the Bank of Pennsylvania in Philadelphia, the state's leading financial institution, closed its doors, producing "the wildest excitement" throughout the city. Long lines of depositors then formed at other Philadelphia banks, demanding coin for their notes and deposits, and the following day those banks also suspended specie payments. Simultaneously the banks suspended in Baltimore, Harrisburg, Pittsburgh, Reading, and parts of New Jersey. Pennsylvania law threatened the state's suspending banks with loss of their charters, but a special session of the legislature temporarily relieved them of that penalty.[29]

Suspension in Philadelphia was a severe blow to the banks in New York, but on September 28 thirteen of them bravely announced that they would continue specie payments. Their depositors were not convinced, and as the pressure continued each of them had to fend for itself. Early in October several of the weaker banks suspended, and on the thirteenth there was a run on all of them. By mid-afternoon eighteen had closed their doors, and that evening all but one agreed to suspend the following morning. Two days later the last of them, the Chemical, succumbed.[30]

After the action of New York's banks, general suspension was inevitable. The banks of New England followed a day later. "We have now reached the height of financial calamity," wrote an angry Boston editor, who quite unjustly held the "arrogant" New York financiers responsible for it. Their "pitiful exhibition of weakness and folly," he charged, had "drawn others into the pit with them." From New York and New England, bank suspensions spread throughout the West and South. When the last Detroit bank had suspended specie payments, the *Free Press* predicted that there would be no quick recovery from a financial disaster as severe and prostrating as the one then in progress. The only banks to avoid suspension were the branches of the state Bank of Indiana, most of those in Kentucky, and all but one in New Orleans.[31]

Although others may have been badly hurt, the country's bankers were quite relieved once the suspension of specie payments had become general. Free from the pressure of their own creditors, they now had time to increase their specie reserves, and they could deal more patiently with those who had borrowed from them. In any case, the financial panic, though severe, was soon over. In New York City the banks were able to resume specie payments by December 14, in New England before the end of the month, and in most other places early the following year. However, the accompanying economic recession was equally severe and lasted much longer. Eventually it resulted in more than 5000 business failures, as well as disastrous losses to countless investors in farmlands, town properties, railroad bonds, and other securities.[32]

Reviewing the early weeks of the recession, *Hunt's Merchants' Magazine* recalled that each day brought news of failures among business enterprises once considered strong enough to survive any crisis. "Now it was a banking house, now a railroad corporation, or a large manufacturing establishment; and again, saddest of all, some old mercantile firm that had stood through all previous storms, which went crashing down like the old forest oak." The New York papers carried their daily lists of failures or suspensions: Harper & Brothers, publishers; Wood & Grant, grocery house; Connelly & Adams, tobacco dealers; Lyman A. George & Co., straw and ribbon dealers; Hall, Dana & Co., commission house; Fenton & Lee, dry-goods house. Similar lists appeared in the papers of Boston, Philadelphia, and other cities. Retail merchants tried to save themselves by cutting prices and advertising sales of many kinds. "Almost every shop has its placards," observed George Templeton Strong, "announcing a great sacrifice, vast reduction of prices, sales at less than cost. . . . Great dry-goods houses like Bowen & McNamee's condescend to implore mankind to come in and buy at retail and notify the universe that 'this store will be kept open till 9 P.M.'"[33]

In Boston, Amos A. Lawrence feared that the "financial derangement" and recession would "spread ruin over every interest." New England manufacturers, he reported, were "for the present completely broken down and discredited," and some of them had been "beggared." Charles Francis Adams, noting the failures among many of Boston's great business houses, believed that the ultimate result would be a heavy blow to those who had "wielded so great an influence over State Street for the last thirty years." Some had suddenly fallen from opulence to poverty, and Beacon Street now awaited "a new set of occupants." "I think it bids fair to mark an epoch in the social history of Boston," Adams concluded. "Such are the vicissitudes of life."[34]

The West suffered from the drastic decline in land values and commodity prices and from a shortage of credit. For a time the Illinois Central tried to help those who were buying its lands on credit by postponing installment payments or accepting payment in produce, but eventually both farmers and railroad were caught up in the general ruin of panic and recession. Carl Schurz recalled that in rural Wisconsin money was so scarce that many of the small transactions of daily life were carried on by barter. Bankruptcy "appeared to be the natural condition of businessmen who owed any money." One Wisconsin railroad after another fell into the hands of receivers, victims not only of the economic recession but all too often of managerial incompetence, misuse of the company's funds, and other forms of corruption. Farmers who had helped finance their construction by purchasing railroad stock with mortgages on their farms now faced foreclosures as dividends stopped and the stock itself lost most of its value. Before long the railroad promoters had lost their reputation as the harbingers of a golden age.[35]

The blight of the panic and recession grievously hurt bankers, merchants, manufacturers, railroad entrepreneurs, investors in land and securities, and farmers, and it ruined a distressing number of them. Even so, none of these economic interests endured the hardships of the urban clerks, mechanics, factory employees, domestics, and day laborers, both immigrants and native-born, who were turned out on the streets as employers retrenched or shut down their businesses. Discharged salesmen, bookkeepers, and other office workers wrote pathetic letters applying for government employment, usually without success. Most of the jobless had nowhere to turn. Late in October, *Hunt's Merchants' Magazine* reported that in New York City "nearly twenty thousand persons were thrown out of employment in a single fortnight, and throughout New York and New England the distress in large manufacturing towns, for want of work, made the prospect of winter absolutely sickening." Estimates of unemployment in New York and Brooklyn eventually ranged from 30,000 to 100,000.[36]

In New England some textile mills tried to keep all their workers on the payrolls by reducing their hours, but unemployment mounted as most of them cut the work force or closed down. Among those still employed, wage cuts of 10 percent or more were common. The Charlestown Navy Yard in Boston received at least a thousand applications for work every day. Pennsylvania was hit extremely hard as textile mills, machine shops, foundries, furnaces, and coal mines discharged workers by the thousands. By November, Philadelphia's unemployed numbered nearly 40,000; and among the state's iron workers some 20,000 were without jobs.[37]

Unemployment was most severe in the industrial Northeast, but it spread to Cincinnati, Chicago, and other western cities as well. The cessation of urban building caused a loss of jobs in the Michigan and Wisconsin lumber camps, and the insolvency of western railroads resulted in the discharge of construction gangs. In November, William H. Clement, superintendent of the recently completed and much celebrated Ohio and Mississippi Railroad, was obliged to dismiss some employees and to cut the wages and postpone payment of the rest. "I am looked upon now by most of the men as a destroying angel," he wrote Samuel L. M. Barlow, president of the company, "[and] I prefer that you should address me a note on the subject, which I will use as a reason for the reductions." Southern cities had their troubles, too. "The winter is fast coming on," a Nashville editor observed, and economic conditions would have "the sad effect of throwing many honest people out of employment."[38]

One day in October the Chicago *Tribune* tried to give meaning in human terms to the endless reports of factory closings and growing unemployment. To be thrown out of work, it reminded its readers, "means thrown out of homes, thrown out of bread, thrown into the street. The failure of this or that cotton or iron mill means the failure of so many human beings in the items of food, fuel and shelter. Failure is but another word for famine and suspension is synonymous with starvation." The *Tribune*'s subsequent advice to the poor on how to survive the hard times was inadequate and naïve, but it was squarely in the mainstream of contemporary middle-class thought. The first rule, it advised, was to give up luxuries such as strong drink and tobacco, both of them threats to morals and health as well as a needless expense. The second was to abandon the prevailing fancy for fine clothes and to "wear the garments thrown aside last season." The third was to restrain the taste for "good living" and consume only the "plainest food," thus assuring health and a longer life.[39]

In the stricken centers of industry and commerce, apprehension was mounting among those with a stake in the preservation of social order that such well-meant advice might not satisfy the growing numbers of destitute families. "A nightmare broods over society," wrote a worried Philadelphian. "Scores of thousands are out of work. Bread riots are dreaded. . . . God alone foresees the history of the next six months." The *Herald* fed the anxieties of conservative New Yorkers with reminders that near the tenement houses of the hungry unemployed were "stores piled to the roof with flour, and beef and pork, and not much further off, banks with safes full of coin." The city police, it feared, could not suppress a mob of desperate men bent on plunder and food for their families. Military companies might be compelled "to deluge the streets with blood . . . in order to preserve peace and order."[40]

Humanitarian impulses fortified by fears of violence led churches, benevolent societies, and individual philanthropists to increase their charitable work among the poor. But charity alone was not enough, and a few suggested that federal and state governments reverse their traditional policies of retrenchment in times of economic adversity and provide employment on public works. An officer at the New York customhouse urged the Secretary of the Treasury to continue work on public buildings in order to ameliorate to a small degree the problem of unemployment. From a political point of view, he warned, a reduction of federal expenditures at that time "would act most injuriously to the Democratic party in this state." A Philadelphia editor advised the city and state to consider how many of the jobless could be profitably employed on public works.[41]

In October, Mayor Fernando Wood, while campaigning for re-election, asked the City Council to appropriate funds to feed the hungry through a program of public employment. The Council approved the hiring of a few thousand men to work in Central Park but rejected most of Wood's relief proposals. Philadelphia, Newark, Rochester, Providence, and several industrial cities in eastern Massachusetts also appropriated funds for useful public works. The policy of the federal government was to continue building projects then under way but to postpone new projects. Everywhere proposals for government action to assist the unemployed met strong opposition from those who thought that the problem should be left to the public almshouses and private charities. According to the hostile New York Republican press, Mayor Wood's program was an example of pure political demagoguery. To the antislavery Washington *National Era,* the arguments for public assistance had "a flavor of communism about them" and suggested "a foreign origin." It was a "European idea," wrote a Maine editor, "contrary to the theory of our government, which supposes every man capable of taking care of himself, and leaves him to do so." Honest citizens would be unjustly taxed for "extravagant and unnecessary" public works, and the "thriftless and disorderly" would be taught to look to government for support. In short, the unemployed were told that self-help was the American way.[42]

Some did try self-help in the limited ways that were open to them. Interest in trade unions increased among skilled artisans. Wage cuts in the textile mills and other industries often provoked workers, both men and women, to go out on strike. The common response of the owners was to suspend operations, and the local press usually defended their action. When a strike led to the closing of a cotton mill in Lancaster, Pennsylvania, the Harrisburg *Telegraph* denounced the "hasty and inconsiderate action" of the operatives and accused them of failing to understand the plight of their employers. In Philadelphia, speakers at mass meetings of the unemployed voiced their demands in language sufficiently threatening to elicit a sharp response from an alarmed Democratic editor. In a time of crisis such as this, he charged, "selfish demagogues . . . take advantage of the calamity under which all classes groan, for the purpose of advancing their own peculiar interests. These men do not speak for the working people of Philadelphia."[43]

The largest disturbances occurred in New York City, where the unemployed were most numerous and poverty, especially among the Irish, was most severe. Mayor Wood, in his October message to the City Council, outraged conservative New Yorkers, who accused him of deliberately attempting to incite class conflict. When the country prospered, he said, poor working men labored "for a mere subsistence, whilst other classes accumulate wealth, and in the days of general depression, they are the first to feel the change, without the means to avoid or endure reverses. Truly may it be said that in New-York those who produce everything get nothing, and those who produce nothing get everything. They labor without income whilst surrounded by thousands living in affluence and splendor who have income without labor." The New York *Times* described the message as "fiery communism." George Templeton Strong suspected Wood, "that archdemagogue," of trying "to get up some movement among the 'dangerous classes'" in order to win their votes in the approaching election.[44]

Early in November leaders of the unemployed organized a series of demonstrations in Tompkins Square. At a rally on November 6, speakers praised Mayor Wood and called on the City Council to adopt his program to aid those without jobs. After the speeches a "disorderly, fierce and noisy" procession marched to Wall Street carrying banners and placards demanding work. When they arrived one of the speakers, a blacksmith, warned that workingmen did not intend to starve while $20 million in specie was lying unused in the city banks. Three days later a large crowd gathered at City Hall for another demonstration, and Wood, growing apprehensive, called out the police to preserve order. On the following day a second mass meeting at Tompkins Square sent a delegation to confer with the mayor, who again summoned the police to clear the City Hall corridors and stairs. November 11 marked the climax of Tompkins Square demonstrations. By then Wood had ceased to be the hero of the jobless, and speakers denounced him for failing to fulfill his promises and for using the police against them. "If we cannot get work peacefully," cried one speaker, "we must get bread by violence; for it is better before God and man to steal than to lie down and die." On this occasion the mayor, now the defender of law and order, not only called out the police but asked for the militia, while federal troops guarded the customhouse.[45]

"This city is going through a somewhat threatening, and possibly a perilous, process of agitation," a New York Democrat informed President Buchanan, "but the extravagance of the demands of some of their leaders . . . will, I think, have a powerful influence in preserving the public peace." Demonstrations of the unemployed did diminish after the Tompkins Square rally on November 11, and by the end of the month they had almost ceased. Neither charity nor government assistance had been adequate to serve the needs of those without jobs; yet the kinds of organized self-help to which they had resorted met with strong public disapproval. They were often advised to consider their own shortcomings. They were told that the rich men of New York, "so much abused and hooted," had nearly all begun as "poor men and hard workers." They were urged to remember "the troubles to which the employer is subjected in stemming the current of the present financial pressure," and to do everything within their power "to lighten his labors."[46] Thus both public policy and private expectations required the unemployed to wait out the recession with patience and fortitude. Eventually they did.

The South, like the rest of the country, was shaken by the panic that followed the failure of the Ohio Life and Trust. "The pressure of the financial crisis has been severely felt here," a Charleston merchant reported in late October. By then most southern banks had suspended specie payments. Cotton and tobacco prices fell sharply. Planters, who had placed orders with merchants and factors when they anticipated better returns on their crops, now had trouble settling their accounts.

Few Southerners had doubts about the source of their distress. "It is not the bursting of bubbles among ourselves," claimed the Charleston *Mercury*, "that has produced whatever stringency we feel in the condition of our money market." Rather, the trouble had come on an ill wind blowing from the North. New York, Jefferson Davis charged, "by extravagance, by her speculation in railroad stocks and western land," had become bankrupt, and her commercial crisis had spread to the South. A Texas editor traced the cause to the tariff on foreign goods and to the concentration of bank capital in New York City. Money from the sale of southern staples was drawn off to the North, "and in its place we have Yankee goods at an enormous premium shoved upon us." Northern profits from the southern trade, he argued, provided the capital for stock gambling and land speculation, for costly private mansions and ostentatious display. In fact, the South was "the very slave of the North, notwithstanding the vain-glorious motto of 'Cotton is King.'" How sad, then, was the lot of the southern planter, who was the innocent victim of the calamity "which well nigh prostrates him."[47]

One of the results of the panic was to strengthen the South's conviction that its economic welfare was at the mercy of reckless northern bankers and speculators and rapacious northern merchants. On the other hand, since the South recovered rapidly from the financial crisis, and since prices for its staple crops improved early the following year, it escaped the severe recession that afflicted northern agriculture, industry, and commerce. This good fortune fortified the traditional southern belief that its agricultural economy was built on a more stable foundation than the commercial economy of the North. During the crisis, gloated the Richmond *Enquirer,* the maligned South had presented evidence of "solid substance." Had the North avoided speculation in banks, western lands, and fancy railroad stocks, remarked a Texas editor, and, like the South, employed its energy "in developing the true resources of the country, this financial crash . . . never would have transpired."[48]

Proslavery Southerners seized the reports of suffering and unrest among unemployed northern workers to vindicate their own social institutions. "The gloomy scenes that darken the Northern horizon," the Richmond *Enquirer* claimed, had brought the public mind to a better understanding of the relative merits of the northern and southern labor systems. In the South the public was not shocked by the cries of workers for relief from starvation. Under its "patriarchal and conservative institutions . . . [the] laboring population suffer no pangs of penury, no diminution of the comforts or necessaries of life." Professing deep sympathy for northern workingmen, the *Enquirer* wished them a "speedy delivery" from their present misery. It also reminded the South's enemies of the "gross injustice" it had suffered from them. A Tennessee editor invited northern philanthropists to apply their benevolence to their own "ragged starving poor." Unlike the North, the Mobile *Register* claimed, the South feared no conflict between labor and capital. The black slave was both labor and capital and was therefore "as tenderly guarded as the humanity and avarice of its owners can induce." Momentarily at least the northern friends of free labor found themselves on the defensive.[49]

The contemporary quest for causes of and remedies for the economic disaster of 1857 led to critical evaluations of government policies affecting the economy, to numerous reaffirmations of traditional community values, and to a great deal of individual self-criticism. The puzzling question repeatedly asked was how a country with a rapidly growing population, rich in fertile soils and natural resources, producing food in abundance, busily engaged in manufacturing and commerce, could get itself into such a predicament. "It seems indeed very strange," wrote one bewildered observer, "that in the very midst of apparent health and strength . . . the whole country . . . should suddenly come to a dead stop and be unable to move a step forward—and that we should suddenly wake up from our dreams of wealth and happiness, and find ourselves poor and bankrupt."[50]

Even those who wrote commercial columns for metropolitan newspapers and business publications, although alluding to the conditions preceding the panics of 1819 and 1837, rarely showed much understanding of the stages of modern business cycles. At best they identified disparate elements of the present crisis, such as the decline of European markets for western grain, or the contraction of domestic and foreign sources of credit, but they seldom put them together in a coherent pattern. Instead, they mixed sensible analysis with fanciful speculation. For example, one of the causes for the panic listed in *Hunt's Merchants' Magazine* was the ability of the telegraph network to disseminate bad news quickly, thus causing "a fever of excitement" and inciting runs on local banks.[51]

Inevitably the debate over causes and remedies found its way into politics and revived an ancient controversy over money and banking. Old Whigs, again sniffing a potential issue, returned to the attack on Jacksonian Democrats for destroying the second Bank of the United States. That nationally chartered institution, claimed a Tennessee Whig-American, had been "a fiscal agent competent to furnish a *national* paper currency, and to act as a safeguard and remedy against the imprudence and ignorance of the local banks." Congress, unwilling to admit its error, had abdicated its authority over the country's currency and given it to the "blundering control and regulation of the separate states." The authority once exercised by the Bank of the United States, claimed the *National Intelligencer,* was now in the hands of the irresponsible banks of New York City. As a result, "we have all the Bank's power for evil without its compensating power for good. Instead of the 'monster' with one head, we have a monster with many heads." After years of Democratic misrule, asserted the Richmond *Whig,* the country "never stood more in need of the [Whig] party than it does now."[52]

Democrats ridiculed Whigs for their pathetic attempt to revive an idea as obsolete as the chartering of another Bank of the United States. The majority of them, like the Republicans, accepted the existing system of state banking but agreed that in most states the banks needed to be more strictly regulated. Some wanted to prohibit banks from paying interest on demand deposits; some wanted to stop the issuance of bank notes in small denominations; nearly all wanted to require banks to maintain larger specie reserves than in the past. President Buchanan, in his first annual message to Congress, expressed the most popular contemporary idea of the principal cause underlying the panic: It had resulted "solely from our extravagant and vicious system of paper currency and bank credits, exciting the people to wild speculations and gambling in stocks."[53]

Buchanan agreed that banks and their paper currency, if properly regulated, "might continue with advantage to the public." If existing abuses could not be avoided, he believed that it would be better to deny them the power to issue bank notes altogether. He thus alluded to a remedy that some traditional Jacksonian Democrats advocated with undiminished conviction: the abolition of all forms of paper money and the exclusive use of "hard money"—that is, gold and silver— in all business transactions. The principal objection of most banks, charged a Tennessee Democrat, was to "get a circulation for their worthless rags" for purposes of speculation; the remedy was a return to a hard money standard. Paper money, claimed another critic, was "a British institution" used to drain off American gold and silver without the expense "of employing an army and navy to make the seizure." In Philadelphia a meeting of hard-money Democrats strongly opposed permitting Pennsylvania banks to suspend specie payments and demanded a return to a metallic currency. Paper money, the *Missouri Democrat* insisted, was "the first great cause" of the economic recession, from which every other suggested cause was in fact merely "a consequence or effect."[54]

Some Jacksonians still believed that the best remedy was to abolish not only bank notes but the banks themselves. Henry D. Cooke, Republican editor of the Sandusky *Register,* warned John Sherman that banks, because of their recent conduct, had incurred the hostility of nine-tenths of the voters. Republicans, he advised, should "keep clear of all 'entangling alliances'" with them. The Democratic Cincinnati *Enquirer* thought it outrageous that, at a time when the whole banking system had collapsed, some desired to "rebuild these rickety, false and rotten edifices of financial frauds." Every banking system that had ever been tried, it asserted, proved to be no better than its predecessors. In Nashville another Democratic editor argued that all banks were evil and "at war with the vital interests of the country." Accordingly, he deemed it "a high privilege to war upon them to the knife, and to expose their rottenness by every means within our power." Corporate banking, predicted an Indiana Democrat, was destined soon to be "numbered among the things that were."[55]

While the majority considered the banks and their note issues to be the prime villains in bringing on the panic and recession, doctrinaire protectionists, especially the iron interests in Pennsylvania, were equally certain that the root of the disaster lay in the modern heresy of free trade. The low tariff schedules adopted by Congress the previous March, they claimed, had caused the country's unfavorable trade balance, the exporting of specie, the banking and commercial crisis, the closing of factories, and the widespread unemployment and misery among American workingmen. Henry C. Carey, the Philadelphia apostle of protectionism, having failed to persuade Republicans to insert a tariff plank in their national platform the previous year, now urged the Buchanan administration to restore prosperity by asking Congress to adopt a policy favorable to American industry and labor. A protective tariff, he promised, would soon restore harmony between the sections and place the country "in the lead of the world." In December the Philadelphia *North American* began publishing a long series of Carey's letters addressed to the President and lecturing him on the advantages of protection. His efforts were endorsed by Pennsylvania's politicians and by a cascade of editorials in the state's newspapers. Give Pennsylvania's iron manufacturers adequate protection against British competition, begged the Harrisburg *Telegraph,* and "this important interest would soon rise to a magnitude superior to any industrial interest of the country."[56]

The recession increased protectionist sentiment among manufacturing interests in other parts of the North as well. "The tariff looms up again," wrote one of Seward's upstate New York correspondents. "It is going to be the great question now and will enter largely I think into the canvass of 1860." Present economic conditions, another believed, would "open the eyes of the People ... to the necessity of protection to home industry." Manufacturers had suffered enough from the folly of revenue tariffs, still another complained. Northern labor, he contended, rather than capital or commerce, now needed protection. Its unhappy condition had been caused by the "Southern Lords" who, "true to their instincts," had voted down every proposal to protect free labor. Free trade, wrote an Indiana Whig-American, was "an error that needs speedy correction." Republican politicians, who had previously ignored Carey's blandishments, soon began to take notice. As the recession developed in the fall of 1857, some party leaders saw in the tariff a potential economic issue for the next presidential campaign. Conservative voters in pivotal Pennsylvania, who had been indifferent or hostile to the party's antislavery Philadelphia platform, might find Republicanism more attractive if it promised protection to the state's vital industries.[57]

Pennsylvania Republicans hastened to make their position clear. Senator Cameron warmly endorsed a proposal to establish a protectionist trade journal devoted exclusively to the interests of his state. David Wilmot, during his campaign for governor of Pennsylvania, denied that he had ever favored free trade and demanded "adequate protection" for the country's industrial interests. In New York, Greeley's *Tribune* resumed its protectionist crusade, insisting that the revenue tariff was the single cause of the financial crisis and recession. It predicted that if American industries were protected with duties of 40 to 80 percent, confidence would soon revive and the mills, foundries, and factories would be calling for additional hands. Republicans took up the cause in the new Congress when it assembled in December. Massachusetts' Senator Henry Wilson found reason enough for the recession in "revenue laws which were not wisely adjusted to protect the productive industry and capital of the country." Seward denounced the recent "unreasonable preference for the manufactures of other countries."

Senator James Dixon of Connecticut, pointing to the closed factories and the workers searching for employment, held Virginia's Senator Hunter, chairman of the Committee on Finance, and his Democratic friends responsible for these conditions. They were the fruits, he charged, of their indifference to the interests of northern industry and labor.[58]

There were numerous Republican dissenters. In the centers of protectionism, Sumner of Massachusetts and Chase of Ohio, for example, were reputed to be advocates of free trade and therefore ideologically "unsound." Former free-soil Democrats in the party were especially prominent among the unconverted. The Chicago *Democrat,* organ of John Wentworth, the Republican mayor of Chicago, noted that some editors "with Whig proclivities" were taking advantage of the financial crisis to foist their "antiquated doctrine" of protection upon the public. William Cullen Bryant's New York *Evening Post* waged a running battle with the *Tribune* over the issue. "Greeley is trying very hard to get up a clamor for *protection,*" editor John Bigelow reported during Bryant's absence, and he promised to speak out in defense of "the free trade we now enjoy."[59] Nevertheless, in 1860 the protectionists would prevail.

The flawed banking system and free-trade policy were the alleged institutional and political causes of the panic and recession, and the remedies for them required state action to reform banking practices and federal action to give increased protection to American industry. Many, however, believed that amending the state banking laws and raising the tariff would not by themselves be sufficient to cure the general malaise, to restore the vitality of the national economy, and to enable the country to fulfill its mission to serve as a model republic. Abolitionists and other secular reformers, as well as much of the clergy, had long been urging their countrymen, first, to look inward and examine their own behavior, then to look outward and consider the values of their increasingly urban, commercial, and industrial social order. Had the American people lost their way? Had the growing city populations rejected the traditional values and simpler ways of their fathers? In fact, was not a large-scale moral regeneration the remedy above all others required to cure the nation's ills?

For a time there was much soul-searching, and there were many cries of remorse. "The truth is," wrote an upstate New York editor, "we have been too extravagant, have not lived within our means, have been too hasty to accumulate vast wealth, have produced too little, and squandered profusely." Anyone who visited New York or Philadelphia and examined the "style and habits of life" in those cities, asserted a Pennsylvanian, would have no doubt about what caused the panic. That disaster was brought on by "the CRIMINAL EXTRAVAGANCE of the times," and the remedy was "a return to plain honest dealing, [and] frugal and economical habits." Male critics deplored the "growing love of display in both sexes," but they usually accused women of being the greater sinners. They had dressed "like Babylonian courtesans," one of them charged, rather than like "the daughters of a republican commonwealth." One wholesome effect of the recession would be "the humbling of snobs and pretenders—the collapse of *parvenues* in the fashionable world."[60]

Those who stressed moral causes for the economic crisis also censured the traders on the New York Stock Exchange, for their operations looked too much like searching for wealth without labor. "We are gamblers in our ventures," wrote a critic of the speculators, "we have cut clear of ancient landmarks in . . . trade. We dare the gamble's loss to win the gamble's gain." The older forms of speculation in farm lands and town properties were bad enough, complained the Chicago *Tribune,* but Wall Street's den of plunderers had expanded the practice to new extremes of depravity. Merchants and capitalists, observed a New England editor, had not been content with the prosperity derived from a gradual and prudent development of the country's resources. Searching for greater profits, they had "overinvested in western lands, in needless railroads, in mushroom cities, and profitless factories." They had withdrawn capital from legitimate business enterprises and "sunk it in the mad vortex of speculation, whence there are no returns." This recent orgy of reckless speculation, wrote a Boston reformer, "will teach good and much needed lessons . . . and will reduce all things here to a more sober, sound, and healthy condition."[61]

The extravagance in personal expenditures, the reckless speculations in land and securities, and the headlong pursuit of wealth, charged the critics, went hand-in-hand with the corruption of both politicians and businessmen. The principal cause of the present distrust of banks and other business enterprises, wrote a Philadelphia editor, was the "*want of moral principle* and nothing else." The failure of the Ohio Life and Trust and the discovery of a huge embezzlement proved to be only the first of a long series of revelations that left in tatters the good reputations of many business leaders. Half the railroad companies, he charged, had been managed dishonestly. Men of the highest business character, known not only for sagacity but for honor and integrity, had stolen funds and used credit in a manner calculated to generate suspicion instead of confidence. Eventually "all saw, what few had believed before, that the man who had taken even his own money from his lawful and regular business to speculate . . . had been committing a moral wrong and was not to be trusted." That was the real difficulty, Charles Francis Adams believed. It was "the destruction of confidence in individual character."[62]

Abolitionists perceived the wrath of God in the economic crisis—indeed, they had been anticipating His judgment for years. The primary cause, asserted the *National Anti-Slavery Standard,* was northern partnership with the "fraud and robbery" of southern slaveholders. The nation had been hurled from the height of prosperity into bankruptcy and ruin, Garrison claimed, because it had tolerated "centuries of bloody oppression" and had shown an "atheistical contempt for the 'higher law' of God." Every nation had its peculiar source of corruption. "Ours is to be found in that Vesuvius of crime, that maelstrom of blood, that pandemonium of oppression, the slave system." The lesson of history, according to Garrison, is that despotism "curses the soil, fetters industry, paralyzes invention, destroys wealth . . . and breeds exterminating judgments. Freedom brings prosperity and abundance."[63]

Great numbers of professing Christians, feeling contrite for their misdeeds, confessed that the autumn catastrophe was punishment well deserved. "I declare to you, Sir," wrote one of the many who recognized divine justice, "I see the hand of an avenging God in our present calamity." Clergymen inveighed against a "corrupt and sinful generation running after strange gods." In their misery the guilty, while accepting the judgment of Heaven, also sought God's comfort and mercy. Such calamities, the Rev. A. L. Stone warned his Boston congregation, are "too much for human strength," and the delicate tissues of the brain frequently give way under the heavy burden. "Infinite Power alone," he advised, "can avail under such circumstances."[64]

After considering the accumulating evidence of a "want of integrity" among Boston merchants "of the best name and connection," Robert C. Winthrop hoped that the business recession would have at least one salutary effect. Perhaps it would bring both men and women "to a sense of religious obligation in regard to business and pleasure and all the affairs of this life." They were too much inclined, he thought, to reserve their religion for Sunday and church, and to think that it was never Sunday "in the backyard, or in the counting room." Winthrop's hope was realized, for a time at least, in a "Great Prayer Meeting Revival" that gathered strength in the autumn of 1857 and continued through the following year. It was the most recent of a series of antebellum Protestant revivals which began with the Great Awakening of the 1730s and 1740s, continued with a Second Awakening around 1800, and followed with at least two other revivals in the early decades of the nineteenth century.[65]

All revivals shared certain common goals. They would bring the word of God to those who had not received it, thus preparing them for the purifying experience of conversion and giving them the hope of salvation, while they also revitalized the faith of those already converted. Yet each revival had its own unique features, some spawning new evangelical sects, some developing new organizational methods, such as the camp meeting, some more active in one region of the country, some in another. The revival of 1857-58 was distinct in several ways. While its predecessors had drawn their principal support from rural regions, such as the South or upstate New York, the present one was strongest in the urban centers of the Northeast. Previous revivals had attracted a disproportionately large number of women, but on this occasion there was a substantial increase in the percentage of converts among men. Still another difference was the active involvement of the more sedate churches, such as the Episcopalians and Unitarians, which had traditionally stood aloof from the religious excitements promoted by their evangelical Baptist, Methodist, and Presbyterian brethren. Finally, this revival was unique for its popular noon-hour interdenominational prayer meetings attended by, among others, worried businessmen, who sought forgiveness and renewed prosperity based upon a firmer commitment to live by Christian precepts.[66]

Neither this nor any other revival was solely the product of economic adversity. As early as February, long before the panic, a resident of Trumbull County, Ohio, reported that the "religious mania [was] going ahead in our midst." Nor were interdenominational prayer meetings an entirely new phenomenon. In 1835, Mrs. Phoebe Palmer of New York, a well-known Methodist evangelist, had inaugurated Tuesday prayer meetings at which men and women united with the clergy to feel the presence of God and to search for ways to achieve a state of holiness. In October 1857, during the early stages of the revival in New York, Mrs. Palmer and her husband, a successful physician and philanthropist, were leading a revival in Hamilton, Canada West, after which they carried its message to Britain. Everywhere the goal was more than the mere recovery of economic prosperity. Its other objectives included the promotion of temperance, the conversion of Catholics to Protestantism, the restoration of harmony between the sections and among the Protestant churches, and the purification of both individuals and the community.[67]

Nevertheless, the term "Businessmen's Revival," although too much of a simplification, described one of its most arresting features. On September 23, Jeremiah C. Lanphier, a missionary of the Old Dutch Church on Fulton Street in New York, organized a program of interdenominational noontime prayer meetings. They were similar to those being held in other churches, but Lanphier helped to give the movement considerable momentum. The meetings soon became so popular that they attracted not only bankers, merchants, and clerks from the financial district but lawyers, physicians, tradesmen, and artisans. Before long the union prayer-meeting movement had spread to the churches of cities in upstate New York and New England. Those who attended were deeply moved, often to tears, by the prayers, hymns, inspirational talks, and occasional spontaneous confessions of misdeeds.

"It is the prevailing feeling," wrote a New England observer, "that 'the times' are peculiarly adapted to religious awakening, partly because the people have plenty of time to attend to religious matters, and partly because the ruin of earthly hopes naturally drives men to other sources of consolation." In addition to the prayer meetings, revivals were reported in Newark, Brooklyn, Rochester, Boston, Philadelphia, and Pittsburgh. The churches were unusually full, and the demand for religious services sometimes required the use of public halls and theaters as well. Gambling, drinking, and theater attendance declined. Before the revival of 1857-58 had run its course, the evangelical churches counted tens of thousands of new members, the Methodists alone claiming to have baptized close to 180,000.[68]

"If the pressure should be lifted," a cynical editor wrote in early November, "we fear Wall Street would lose its interest in the noon prayer meeting, and return to its old modes of preying."[69] The decline that he anticipated came soon enough, but in the last months of 1857 the revival was flourishing and had yet to reach its peak. Meanwhile, the current upsurge of religious enthusiasm was encouraging those who were affected by it not only to attune their private lives to a higher moral standard but to examine the behavior of men in public life with a more critical eye. As a result, in late autumn, when the problems of Kansas Territory again became the central issue in national politics, the behavior of territorial politicians, Congressmen, and the national administration came under the same close scrutiny that bankers, railroad promoters, and speculators had endured. Unfortunately, in that crucial test many fell far short of the moral standards subscribed to at the Fulton Street prayer meetings.

CHAPTER 9

Northern Politics:
The Parties in Equipoise

By mid-November, affairs in Kansas had become so critical that the highly polit-ical national press was devoting an increasing amount of attention to territorial news and less space to news of the economic recession. In contrast, before the renewal of the Kansas controversy, a series of important autumn gubernatorial and legislative campaigns in the northern states had met with considerable public apathy. George Templeton Strong, who had filled his diary with political com-mentary the previous year, ignored the New York campaign until a terse entry on November 2: "State election comes off tomorrow. Nobody cares. Twelve months and a [business] crisis have toned down people's interest in politics won-derfully." The voter turnout in off-year elections normally declines, of course, but the decline in 1857, especially among Republican voters, was unusually steep. In Massachusetts, for example, the participation of eligible voters dropped from 82 to 62 percent; in New York from 89 to 64 percent; in Wisconsin from 81 to 55 percent.[1]

Even so, these northern elections were significant indicators of the direction the party system was taking after the presidential campaign of 1856 and before the reopening of the conflict over Kansas. The results greatly encouraged north-ern Democrats, because, in spite of the Dred Scott case, they polled an increased percentage of the popular vote in every state which held an election. Especially gratifying was their victory in New York, where the Republicans had defeated them decisively in 1856. Significantly, the northern Democratic press attributed these party gains to Buchanan's and Governor Walker's commitment to honest elections in Kansas. The President had redeemed his pledge, claimed the Detroit *Free Press,* and to his "unyielding firmness and steadiness" free-state Democrats owed their brightening prospects. His policy, predicted the Philadelphia *Press,* "vigorously carried forward by Governor Walker," would forever remove from national politics the vexatious issue of Kansas.[2]

The desperate northern Whigs and Fillmore Americans saw a glimmer of hope in the falling off of the Republican vote. A New York Whig, still anticipating a Republican collapse, believed that his party, "by the same name or any other," could provide at least the nucleus for a new conservative political organization to oppose the Democrats. Many Republicans, he claimed, now saw "the great mistake they made two years ago in disbanding the Whig party."[3] His optimism was based on fantasy more than fact. True, the Republican vote did decrease both numerically and, in most states, as a percentage of the whole. Nevertheless these autumn elections demonstrated, even more clearly than the presidential election of 1856, that the Republican party was the sole serious rival of the northern Democracy. Both the Whig and American parties were far along the road to extinction. In the New England states, save for Massachusetts, and in Wisconsin and Iowa they had nearly lost their independent identities. To the extent that Whigs and nativists continued to have political influence, most of them exerted it as pressure groups within the Republican party.

In the elections for governors, legislatures, and other state officers, the Republicans easily carried Maine and Iowa, although by reduced majorities, and the Democrats had little trouble electing their ticket in California. The major battles were waged in five states: Massachusetts, New York, Pennsylvania, Ohio, and Wisconsin. Only in one of them, Massachusetts, could the Republicans find much to celebrate, and even there some party members were less than satisfied with the manner in which the victory had been won. Critics complained that the Massachusetts party was afraid to stand on its own feet and boldly repudiate the Know Nothings. In 1856, in order to win American party votes for Frémont, it had nominated no candidates for state offices, thus assuring the re-election of the nativist Governor Henry J. Gardner. Now, in what one party leader called a "practical union" of all who opposed the national Democracy, Republicans again flirted with the American party "for the purpose of gaining power." The antinativist "straight" Republicans protested in vain. "How miserably they behave in Mass.," a New England neighbor commented. The Washington *National Era* found the Republican campaign "so complicated and embarrassed by Know Nothingism" that it preferred not to comment at all.[4]

The problem confronting Massachusetts Republicans was not as simple as their critics thought. They had carried their state for Frémont by nearly a two-thirds majority, but only because the great majority of Americans had voted for him. In 1857 Massachusetts was the only northern state in which the American party, if united, probably had sufficient strength to win an election. It was by no means certain that Republicans, standing alone, could defeat the nativists if the latter were to choose a free-soil North American such as Nathaniel P. Banks as their candidate for governor. The Democrats were not likely to be a major force in the campaign, but the American party was at the very least a formidable threat. The majority of Republican leaders concluded that the threat could not be ignored.

They turned to Banks, a former Democrat and Free Soiler, a three-term Congressman and Speaker of the House in the last Congress, and an adroit politician who had joined the Know Nothings less from conviction than from a recognition of the realities of Massachusetts politics. The acknowledged leader of the state's antislavery North Americans, Banks had persuaded the Republicans in 1856 not to oppose the re-election of Gardner and then campaigned vigorously for Frémont. Although that seemed to make him a plausible Republican candidate in 1857, a complication developed before the state convention met. In June the American party held its own convention, adopted a nativist platform, and chose Banks as its candidate for governor. When Banks formally accepted the nomination, the most militant antislavery, anti-nativist Republicans, led by Francis W. Bird, mobilized to demand a better Republican candidate. On Bird's invitation, Charles Francis Adams attended a meeting of "former active free soil men," but he reluctantly concluded that Banks's nomination could not be avoided. Adams, a convention delegate, acknowledged his irritation that the Americans, "both in words and in acts," had insulted the Republicans. Yet he respected Banks and would judge him "by his own acts and nobody else's."[5]

Later in June, Bird and his rebels carried their fight to the Republican convention in Worcester, where they tried to secure the nomination of John Z. Goodrich, a member of their faction. As Adams observed, their opposition to the "double and ambiguous position" that Banks occupied "was warm but without hope." The Americans were well represented among the delegates, but their leader, Anson Burlingame, after some nativist rhetoric, assured the convention that Banks was a true Republican. After an animated debate, Banks was nominated on the first ballot, but a motion to make the nomination unanimous was defeated. The platform was thoroughly Republican, fully in harmony with the Philadelphia platform of 1856, and Banks, in his letter of acceptance, gave it his unqualified approval. Adams did not vote for Banks but announced after the vote was taken that he would support him. Privately he noted that there still remained a feeling of distrust, "which scarcely any impartial man in the body could at his heart disavow."[6]

Distrust no doubt increased when a post-convention conference between Republican and American party leaders resulted in the withdrawal of two Republican candidates for other state offices and their replacement by Americans. "You know," Senator Henry Wilson explained to the abolitionist Wendell Phillips, "Massachusetts is not half so anti-slavery as she pretends to be, and we could not do anything better." Nevertheless, the Bird faction preferred honorable defeat to victory with a candidate who attempted "to face both ways." The radical Republicans, Edward L. Pierce assured Chase, would nominate their own candidate and hoped to poll at least 10,000 votes. "I want no mongrel party," Pierce declared, "which shall talk blarney to the naturalized alien in the West and spit in his face in New England." In October a small but militant "straight Republican" convention met at Chapman Hall in Boston and nominated Dr. Caleb Swan for governor. Swan reluctantly accepted in a speech full of "good-humored indignation against slavery and know nothingism." In an address to the public the convention took a stand for pure antislavery Republicanism cleansed of nativism.[7]

Throughout the summer one dissident after another had deserted the cause and announced his support for Banks. In September the desertions increased when two conventions of anti-Banks Americans joined ranks at Faneuil Hall in Boston and nominated Governor Henry Gardner for another term. Convention resolutions denounced Sumner, promised enforcement of the Fugitive-Slave Act, and opposed state financial aid for Kansas. Amos A. Lawrence, still the friend of Kansas but not of Republicanism, spoke earnestly, as he had often before, against a politically united North confronting a politically united South. The nomination of Gardner was enough to cause most Republican critics of Banks to reconsider their position. Banks himself encouraged them with campaign speeches stressing his antislavery views rather than nativism. Late in September, even before the "straight Republican" convention had met, the bottom fell out of the anti-Banks movement when John Z. Goodrich announced that he was now satisfied that Banks was an antislavery man and would support him. "Let us try Mr. Banks fully and fairly," Adams urged his friends. "If he does his duty, as we expected of him, well and good." On the eve of the election, even Sumner wrote a letter endorsing Banks![8]

The Democratic candidate for governor, Erasmus D. Beach, was, according to the Springfield *Republican,* "a gentleman, a very respectable and well-praised lawyer, and a good citizen," but inexperienced in public life and, like his party, a tool of the Slave Power. Gardner, it charged, was the tool of the "Massachusetts Magi," the rich, powerful, proslavery aristocrats of State Street, and of the cotton manufacturers of Lowell and Lawrence. As a former Boston merchant and a conservative old Whig, he was their natural leader, for they would not have a man like Banks, who had come from a working-class family and had himself worked in a Waltham cotton textile factory, elected governor of Massachusetts. Gardner tried to focus the campaign on local issues; but the Republicans, apart from attacking his record as governor, stressed national issues—the Slave Power, Buchanan's response to the Silliman letter, and free soil. At a Banks rally in Boston, Anson Burlingame, forgetting his nativism, asserted that the chief issue of the campaign was slavery. Two national parties had formed, he said. One, upholding the dogma of Calhoun, would "establish slave labor as the national system," the other would defend the rights of free labor. Neither the business recession nor Kansas was much discussed during the campaign, and neither appeared to have a significant effect on the result.[9]

Adams, in a letter to Sumner, predicted a plurality for Banks "as the most creditable choice," but he found "little appearance of the enthusiasm which had been expected from the nomination."[10] The general apathy was evident in the sharp decline in voter turnout. Superficially, the returns appeared to give the Republicans little cause to rejoice, because their popular vote declined from 108,000 in 1856 to 60,000 in 1857, and their percentage of the total vote declined from 65 to 47. Republicans had lost a substantial part of their American party support to Gardner, who won 38,000 votes, or 29 percent. Yet, this was far from an American party victory. Comparing total votes and percentages, the Republicans, with Banks stressing antislavery rather than nativist issues, had in fact defeated Gardner quite decisively. The American party would never recover from that defeat. The Democrats' share of the vote increased only slightly, to 24 percent. As for poor Dr. Swan, the "straight Republican" candidate, a few loyal friends of Francis Bird gave him 213 votes. Before the end of 1857, the Republican party, now an amalgam of antislavery radicals such as Sumner, of moderates such as Charles Francis Adams, and of former North Americans such as Banks and Burlingame, had become the dominant party in the state.

Having elected their entire ticket for state offices and overwhelming majorities in both houses of the legislature, Massachusetts Republicans soon forgot whatever reservations they might have had about Banks and congratulated themselves on their remarkable growth in the past three years. Goodrich expressed "real satisfaction" at the result and hoped that good would come from it not only for the state but for the whole country. Adams was gratified that the defeat of Gardner had removed the "last point of concentration for [the nativists] in the Free States." It remained for the last of the conservative old Whigs to mourn their party's death. Edward Everett found all three gubernatorial candidates unacceptable and abstained from voting. "You and I must accept it, I think, as a *finality*," John C. Clifford advised Robert C. Winthrop. "We may as well sit down therefore and comfort ourselves with the reflection that as the 'gone men' of Massachusetts we have in our day . . . done something not altogether unworthy for the good name and fame of the old Commonwealth."[11]

In the New York election the decline in voter turnout was even sharper than in Massachusetts, in part because it lacked the excitement of a gubernatorial campaign. The contest was for several lesser state offices and for a new legislature. Although Republicans needed substantial support from present or former Know Nothings to win, their principal competitors were the Democrats, not the fading Americans. Republican prospects were weakened by intra-party friction, notably between Horace Greeley and his former political friend Thurlow Weed, the Albany boss, lobbyist, and editor of the *Evening Journal*. Greeley felt that Weed and Seward did not appreciate his services to the party; he also disliked the not-always-faint odor of corruption that rose from the present Republican legislature under Weed's management. Early in the year Greeley had worked against Weed to secure the election of the former Democrat Preston King to the United States Senate, and thereafter relations between them steadily worsened.[12]

When the Republican state convention met at Syracuse in September, Greeley joined David Dudley Field and other former Democrats to control proceedings. Weed sat uncomfortably on the sidelines. All factions were represented—onetime Free Soilers, Whigs, Democrats, and Americans—and all were given a place on the state ticket. The platform was a forthright antislavery document. It denied the right of one man to enslave another; repudiated the Dred Scott decision and Buchanan's reply to the Silliman letter; affirmed the right of Congress to prohibit slavery in the territories; and asserted that New York would never permit slaveholding within its borders. Another series of resolutions must have added to Weed's discomfort. They proclaimed that American institutions were threatened not only by slavery but by official corruption. They denounced special legislation for private interests, condemned both lobbyists and the practice of lobbying, and opposed the distribution of free railroad tickets to public officials. Finally, the platform threw a small bone to the nativists with a demand for legislation to end the "monstrous frauds at elections," especially in (Democratic) New York City.

In addition to the platform, David Dudley Field read an address to the voters of New York, which the convention adopted unanimously. Field stressed the same twin dangers: slavery and corruption. From the nation's birth, slavery had been "the great disturbing element" in national politics; it was ever "grasping, encroaching, arrogant, and domineering." Had Frémont been elected, the Supreme Court would not have dared put forth the Dred Scott decision, "so alien to the principles we have received from our forefathers." What next? The Court would soon hold that the Constitution authorized slaveholders to reside with their slaves temporarily in the free states. Field called on the electorate to lay aside minor differences and rescue the country "from that curse greater than slavery—that of loving, praising, and extending it." Turning to the other danger, he attacked the jobbers in political favors who hung about the federal and state capitols offering bribes for the votes of legislators. These practices must be stopped, "for they sap the foundations of our institutions."[13]

At the Democratic convention in Syracuse the "Hards" and the "Softs" waged their customary battle, but they emerged with a ticket representing both factions and with a platform praising the national administration, denouncing slavery agitation, and, like the Republicans, deploring corruption at Albany and Washington. Southern Democrats watched the New York campaign closely to determine what strength remained to the party in the North. The outcome was a matter of great consequence, Senator David L. Yulee of Florida believed. A Democratic victory there would "preserve the hope and strength" of the party elsewhere, especially in Pennsylvania and other border states. New York Democrats were optimistic. Thanks to Buchanan and Walker, they insisted that the slavery issue was settled and Kansas was certain to be admitted as a free state. The issues of the campaign, therefore, were local, and Democratic speakers focused on waste and corruption under a Republican governor and legislature in Albany. Only the Democrats could provide the "radical and sweeping reform" that was required.[14]

New York Republicans were vulnerable on the corruption issue and could only promise to live up to the pledges in their platform. Their new canal commissioner would not be a servant of the contractors; their candidates for state offices had clean records; a new Republican legislature would put an end to waste and rebuff the lobbyists. In short, Republicans hated corruption, waste, and high taxes as much as Democrats. All this amused an upstate nonpartisan editor. However the election turned out, he predicted, "one result will surely follow—the discovery that the people have placed in power the most unmitigated set of scamps that ever disgraced the State. At least this will be the discovery of two badly beaten parties."[15]

Party speakers and editors felt more comfortable discussing slavery and continued to insist that it was the central issue of the campaign. "The Republican party is the party of Freedom and Progress," David Dudley Field told a party rally in New York City. "The Democratic party has sunk into a society for the propagation of slavery." Kansas was still not free, warned the *Tribune*. The Lecompton convention might yet force slavery on its people without their consent. Moreover, "the Slave Power to-day rules our Nation as relentlessly as ever, makes and unmakes its rulers, and is plotting new exactions and encroachments." After the initial shock of each new aggression, the Democratic party always submitted meekly to its demands. Reminders of Bleeding Kansas, Brooks's attack on Sumner, and the Dred Scott decision also figured prominently in the Republican campaign.[16] However, the immediacy of the slavery issue, felt by Republican voters in 1856, was lost in the continued widespread confidence that the battle for a free Kansas had already been won. The panic and recession had turned men's thoughts to other things. Edwin D. Morgan, chairman of the Republican National Committee, found fund raising a good deal more difficult than a year earlier.

In the election on November 3 the Republicans suffered a shocking defeat; the Democrats found cause to hope for a revival of their party in the northern states; and the American party had reason to fear that the end was near. The Republican vote declined from 276,000 in 1856 to 177,000, and from 46 to 40 percent. The Democratic vote held steady at 195,000, but its percentage of the whole increased from 33 to 45. The American party's vote of 67,000 was scarcely more than half of its total the previous year, a decline from 21 to 15 percent. It had lost strength to the Republican party in counties that once had been Know-

Nothing strongholds. Thus, in spite of their defeat, New York Republicans by 1857 had established themselves securely as the only formidable opponent of the Democrats.[17]

In considering ways to avoid future defeats many New York Republicans were convinced that it was essential to cut further into the American party vote. To this end they accepted the mildest and most reasonable of its demands—the adoption of a state voter-registration law to reduce election frauds. On the other hand, Seward, who despised the Know Nothings, believed that Republican "manifestations of sympathy" for them had driven all the naturalized urban voters into the arms of the Democracy. This left the rural and small-town vote to the Republicans, and they had brought it out successfully in 1856 during the excitement over slavery in Kansas. In 1857, Seward concluded, the prevailing "calmness and quiet" on the subject of slavery, together with a spell of bad weather, had kept one-fourth to one-third of the farmers away from the polls. But he was confident that, because support for nativism was declining, northern voters would soon be confronted with a clear choice between the proslavery Democrats and the antislavery Republicans. When the free-state electorate faced that choice, Seward predicted, the Republican party would add urban support to its rural constituency. Putting it another way, the New York *Evening Post* claimed that the party had been organized around national issues and fared best when the electorate responded to them.[18]

The victorious Democrats seemed to agree. They could focus on local issues, claimed the Albany *Atlas and Argus,* because the public was satisfied that the Kansas question had been permanently resolved. The New York *Herald* foresaw a long era of Democratic rule, for the Know-Nothing party had diminished to a "mere remnant" and the large Frémont plurality of 1856 had "vanished like a dream." The Republican decline, it was confident, was permanent. "The tremendous Kansas excitement, which gave them their prodigious vote of last November, has passed away with the causes which created it, and the confidence of the people in the Kansas policy of Mr. Buchanan has diverted attention to other subjects of a more practical character." That was early November, when northern Democrats believed that not only had Republicans lost the Kansas issue but that nothing to replace it was in sight.[19]

A month later New York City had its own election for mayor and aldermen. The campaign was waged mostly as an intraparty feud among Democrats, but it took on the aspect of a reform crusade. Fernando Wood had been nominated by one faction of Tammany Hall, and Daniel F. Tiemann, a member of the Board of Aldermen, had been nominated by an anti-Wood reform faction, led by Samuel J. Tilden and Congressman Daniel E. Sickles. The Republican and American parties made no nominations, joining a coalition of anti-Wood Democrats and virtually the whole New York business community. Prominent merchants met and formed a nonpartisan committee to raise a campaign fund for Tiemann. The coalition waged its crusade against a man accused not only of corruption but of demagoguery and, most heinous to many, of inciting unrest among the poor and the unemployed. "There is a very strong desire among the best men in our party to get rid of Wood," Sickles informed Buchanan. His "outrageous message, arraying . . . the poor against the rich" had aroused widespread feeling against him. Another anti-Wood Democrat warned Buchanan that the party could not afford to lose the support of the "leading merchants and distinguished men of the city," who had raised the money to carry Pennsylvania for the Democrats in the last presidential election.[20]

Although Wood partisans arranged the naturalization and enfranchisement of several thousand pro-Wood immigrants on the eve of the election, Tiemann defeated him by a thin margin of 2300 out of some 84,000 votes cast. George Templeton Strong thought it appalling "that so notorious and certified a cheat and swindler" could poll more than 40,000 votes. Nevertheless the *Evening Post* proclaimed it "a triumph of the people . . . gloriously won." The city had rid itself of "a great public nuisance" and inaugurated "a new order of things" by electing an honest mayor. Tiemann promptly assured Buchanan that he was a sound Democrat and an administration man. Since his sole aim was "to give the blessings of good government to New York," he asked the President to order federal officeholders to cooperate with him. Few did, and two years later, with the reformers dispersed, Fernando Wood, having organized Mozart Hall to rival Tammany Hall, triumphantly returned to City Hall.[21]

Pennsylvania voters were to choose a governor, two judges of the state supreme court, a canal commissioner, and a legislature. "It must be admitted that such an event usually attracts much more attention than it does now," wrote a Philadelphia editor. "But the financial troubles . . . are of too engrossing a nature to leave room for much of public interest beside."[22] In spite of the general apathy, Democrats hoped to strengthen the Buchanan administration by another victory in his home state. Their task would not be difficult if the opposition remained divided as it had been in 1856, when the Republican party had polled 32 percent of the vote and the American party 18 percent. Republicans drew their strength from the northern and western counties, Americans from the eastern, especially from Philadelphia. Coalition was on the minds of most opposition leaders, but each group hoped to control the coalition and set the agenda.

State Republican leaders issued a call for a "Union" convention to meet at Harrisburg on March 25—a convention they clearly intended to control. "I aid the Union movement," wrote a confident Pittsburgh Republican, "because I know it will eventuate in bringing every right thinking 'American' to our side."[23] Republican and nativist members of the state legislature subsequently issued a second call for a convention, to meet at the same time and place, for the purpose of writing a platform and nominating candidates acceptable to both parties. They appealed not only to those who would exclude slavery from the territories but to those who opposed "the union of church and state," the exclusion of the Bible from the common schools, and the "corrupt influences" that threatened the purity of the ballot box. The result of the two calls was the appearance of contesting delegations from several eastern counties and an agreement to seat them all.

Nevertheless, the Republicans dominated the convention and nominated their candidate, Judge David Wilmot, for governor. Wilmot, a former free-soil Democratic Congressman, had won fame during the war with Mexico by introducing a Proviso to prohibit slavery in territory acquired by the treaty of peace. To balance the ticket the convention nominated Americans for canal commissioner and for one of the judgeships. The platform made minor concessions to the nativists but stressed the party's opposition to slavery expansion and to the aggressions of the Slave Power, as did Wilmot's letter of acceptance. He denounced the attempt to subject Kansas to the "curse of slavery" and attacked the Dred Scott decision for closing the courts "against an entire race of men." Eventually, he asserted, "the verdict of this great Commonwealth must be pronounced on the issues forced upon the country by the advocates of human bondage." But he assured conservative Pennsylvanians that the defenders of free labor did not wish to elevate the black race to a position of equality with the white; nor would they interfere with slavery in the southern states. In a brief and vague concession to the anti-Catholic nativists, Wilmot told naturalized citizens that they must acknowledge "no earthly power superior to the Constitution and the sovereignty of the American people." In short, although nominated at a Union convention and running as the candidate of the "People's Party," Wilmot began his campaign as a Republican who endorsed an essentially Republican platform.[24]

Few in the American party considered this an acceptable coalition platform or Wilmot an appropriate coalition candidate. Early in the campaign the American State Council submitted five questions to him which covered issues of special concern to nativists, and he responded at great length. He would prefer to have native-born citizens hold public office, but he would support a naturalized citizen if he were better qualified. He accepted the nativists' vague demand for the protection of "American labor, America rights, and American interests." He deplored electoral frauds but preferred state action against them rather than changes in federal naturalization laws. He welcomed "honest and industrious immigrants" but would prevent European governments from shipping "cargoes of criminals and paupers to our shores." Like many other Republicans, he enthusiastically subscribed to the nativists' anti-Catholicism, denouncing the intervention in American politics of a "priestly order . . . acknowledging as their head a foreign potentate." Injecting a favorite Republican argument, he accused "the votaries of this church" of being the allies of slavery and the Slave Power. Finally, Wilmot affirmed his opposition to the exclusion of the Bible from the public schools.

Wilmot's nativism was not sufficiently pure to satisfy the hard-core Americans, who nominated their own slate of candidates, including Isaac Hazlehurst, Philadelphia's city solicitor, for governor. Knowing that the continued division of the opposition virtually assured a Democratic victory in the October election, a few Americans continued to seek a workable coalition. In a speech at Harrisburg late in the campaign, Wilmot reiterated his earlier concessions to them. According to a local reporter, he avowed himself in favor of "rebuking the impudent assumptions of foreigners, and restricting and counteracting the political machinations of the Catholic Church." All efforts at coalition failed, primarily because Republicans would make no further concessions to a movement so obviously on the wane. Defeat, if it came, would be at the hands of the Democrats, not the Americans.[25]

The Democrats had met at Harrisburg in February and transcended their factional differences with relative ease. To head their ticket they nominated William F. Packer, an able and experienced politician, a former auditor general, canal commissioner, state senator, and speaker of the state House of Representatives. With a platform endorsing popular sovereignty and pledging support to the Buchanan administration, the party entered the campaign brimming with confidence. In the spring, after a tour of the state, Senator Bigler reported to Buchanan that the Democrats were "certain of a most triumphant victory," thus giving the new administration "a glorious endorsement." Packer flatly refused Wilmot's proposal for a series of joint debates as undignified and unprecedented. "His object undoubtedly was to get up an excitement where none exists," Packer wrote Bigler. "He now has to get up his own meetings and listen to his own thunder. He gets no Democratic help."[26]

Nothing went well for Wilmot, and before the end of the summer defeat was a near certainty. Having already lost the immigrant vote without gaining the united support of the Americans, he soon found himself at a considerable disadvantage on another major issue when the panic and recession aroused the protectionists. Pennsylvanians remembered his vote for the low Walker Tariff of 1846, and his conversion to protectionism was too recent to be convincing. Democrats ridiculed his attacks on the Tariff of 1857, calling him a notorious associate of New York free traders. They interpreted his opposition to slavery expansion as sympathy for abolitionism, his attacks on the Dred Scott decision as belief in racial equality. As a result, during an intensive speaking campaign, Wilmot found himself devoting as much time to explaining and defending his own positions on nativism, slavery, race relations, and the tariff, as to attacking those of the Democrats.[27]

Local issues, insofar as they had a bearing on the state campaign, gave the Republicans no compensating advantage. In Pittsburgh and Allegheny County, both parties took the popular side of a taxpayers' revolt against the use of city and county bonds to help finance railroad construction. The sale in 1857 of the

Main Line of the state-owned Pennsylvania canal system to the Pennsylvania Railroad on terms highly favorable to the corporation aroused considerable criticism, but both Republican and Democratic legislators had voted for it. The transaction eliminated a major source of political corruption and deprived the Democrats of a great deal of patronage, but it put the managers of the Pennsylvania Railroad in the debt of the legislature's Democratic majority. In September a Republican leader complained that the company had shipped the "biggest brawlers" and "red mouthed locofocos" among its employees to Newport to lend support to the Democratic ticket.[28]

In August and September, Republicans throughout the state reported "a feeling of apathy in our party" and complained of a lack of funds. "Have our [state] Committee any *funds?*" ran one appeal. "We have a hard district here—no enthusiasm—can get nothing done without paying for it. . . . I confess I cannot give you much to encourage." Another complained that the campaign either had no organization or it was pursuing "a most 'masterly inactivity.'" Feeling deserted by other leaders of his party, Wilmot begged Senator Cameron to assist him, "not in achieving a victory . . . but in getting through the campaign in a manner that shall bear no just responsibility upon me for defeat if it should come." Cameron responded with a contribution of $200, thereby winning another grateful friend. "I accept your generous and truly magnanimous offer of friendship," Wilmot wrote, "and trust that I shall live to prove that I am not ungrateful for it."[29]

The election in October brought no surprises. The Democrats elected their entire state ticket and won large majorities in both houses of the legislature. Packer's plurality over Wilmot was 43,000 in a total vote of 360,000. Wilmot's support came largely from the counties bordering New York and Ohio; in Philadelphia he came in a humiliating third, losing the city by a margin of more than five to one. Although the Republican party suffered an overwhelming defeat, the Pennsylvania returns nevertheless gave evidence that it had established itself decisively as the second major party in that crucial state. Its share of the total vote increased from 32 percent in 1856 to 40 percent in 1857. For the American party the Pennsylvania election was truly a disaster, its popular vote shrinking from 83,000 to 28,000 and its percentage from 18 to 8. Here, too, nativism was becoming less an independent political force than one of several competing influences within the Republican party.[30]

"I am not . . . either disheartened or discouraged," Wilmot assured Cameron after it was over. "We have the material for a triumphant party in this State whenever it can be cordially combined in one organization, and this cannot much longer be prevented." Wilmot was ready to assist in achieving that end, but, with uncommon prescience, he left that task to the "controlling influence" of Pennsylvania's ambitious Republican Senator.[31]

In the western state elections the clear Republican victory in Iowa was offset by two narrow escapes from defeat in Ohio and Wisconsin. Republican professions of satisfaction with the results were far from convincing. In Ohio, interest was focused on Governor Salmon P. Chase's difficult campaign for re-election, for he was one of the antislavery founders of the Republican party. Born in New Hampshire, Chase had settled in Cincinnati to practice law, pursue a minor literary career, and participate actively in the reform movements of the 1830s and 1840s. In spite of the unpopularity of abolitionists in southern Ohio, he supported their cause and pleaded the cases of several fugitive slaves in state and federal courts. Turning to political action, he joined the Liberty party in 1840 and the Free-Soil party in 1848. In 1849 a coalition of Democrats and Free Soilers in the Ohio legislature elected him to the United States Senate, and in 1855 a coalition of Republicans and Know-Nothings elected him governor.[32]

Chase had been a candidate for the Republican presidential nomination in 1856, and he intended to be a candidate again in 1860. He would be one thereafter every four years until his death. Life for this handsome and gifted man became one of everlasting tension between his conscience and his unquenchable political ambition—between moral imperatives, such as his commitment to the antislavery crusade, and the expedient divergences that tempted him in his presidential quest. No doubt it had been distasteful for him to run for governor in alliance with Know Nothings, for whom he had no sympathy, but since he could not have won without them, he did.

Professing no desire for a second term in 1857, he hesitated before deciding to accept the nomination. He would do what was best for the party, he said, but his decision no doubt was governed by thoughts of 1860 as well. There was one good reason for not running: the possibility of defeat. "Politically we . . . are in a rather critical position," observed a Republican legislator. "If the Fillmorites go over to the [Democrats] they will beat us next fall, and it is a serious question whether we can prevent that if Chase is our candidate for Governor." One adviser warned Chase that Republicans would not have an easy time in the campaign with him at the head of the ticket, because a remnant of the old Whig party, numbering 20,000 to 30,000, could not be persuaded to vote for an antislavery radical. Re-election, he suggested, would do little to advance his presidential prospects, whereas a defeat would do him great harm.[33]

In normal circumstances Chase might have found this advice convincing, but in June his decision was affected by the revelation of a sensational scandal that might have seriously damaged his reputation. The scandal involved the embezzlement of more than a half-million dollars of state funds by the previous Democratic state treasurer, John G. Breslin, and the concealment of the theft by his Republican successor, William H. Gibson. Chase handled the affair skillfully, forcing Gibson to resign, taking care to meet the state's financial obligations, and initiating an investigation of the records of both state treasurers. The Democratic press, anticipating a campaign against Republican corruption, portrayed Gibson as the principal culprit, until Breslin was indicted and fled to Canada to escape trial. Nevertheless, Chase concluded that he had to risk a campaign for re-election in order to avoid suspicion either of involvement with Gibson in the concealment or of retreating under fire.[34]

The Republican state convention took its chances with Chase, renominating him unanimously, and relied on the party's own strength, giving only one Know Nothing a place on its ticket. The Democrats nominated Henry B. Payne of Cleveland, and the remnants of the American party found a doughty old Whig, Col. Philadelph Van Trump, willing to carry their banner for one last campaign. Van Trump "adheres tenaciously to his old Whig notions," a friend informed Chase, "and, in his own estimation is too pure and too upright, to coalesce or identify himself with either the Republican or Democratic party. . . . He professes not to have any information or to have formed any opinion on the effect of his Ticket on the canvass."[35]

With neither party in a position to exploit the corruption issue, much of the campaign involved Republican attacks on the Dred Scott decision and proslavery expansionism, and Democratic attacks on disunionists, abolitionists, and racial "amalgamationists." In accepting the Republican nomination and in campaign speeches Chase described his party as bearers of the standard of human rights and reform. He accused the Supreme Court and the Buchanan administration of converting the territories from a home for free labor into "one great slave pen." In the name of state sovereignty he demanded the denationalization of slavery, and in the name of freedom its exclusion from the territories. Slavery, he promised, would one day be abolished, but it would be accomplished by constitutional means, not suddenly by violence.[36] Chase was not an impressive stump speaker, but he delivered his message with conviction.

The failure of the Ohio Life Insurance and Trust Company and the subsequent financial panic gave the Democrats one potent economic issue. Since the company had served as a depository for state funds, the shocking exposure of its affairs increased support for a Democratic proposal to remove public funds from private banks and place them in a state-owned sub-treasury. On the other hand, the Republican majority in the legislature, with Chase's approval, had placed a referendum on the October ballot proposing an increase in the number of banks in the state. Capitalizing on the rash of bank failures and an upsurge of anti-bank sentiment, Democratic politicians and editors exploited the referendum to link the Republicans with bankers and paper-money speculators. It was the wrong year for such a proposal, and it was overwhelmingly voted down.[37]

With Chase as the Republican candidate, Ohio Democrats believed that their best issue was that "undisguised Abolitionist," Chase himself. He was the perfect target for their now familiar demagogic attacks on "Black" Republicans as fanatical advocates of racial equality. The Cincinnati *Enquirer* delivered nearly the whole message in one late-summer editorial. The present campaign, it claimed, involved "as its main issue, the immensely important social and political question, whether the black or African race shall possess and enjoy, in this State, equal rights with the white or Caucasian race." All other issues were insignificant compared with this. Chase would grant blacks political, legal, and civil equality, seating them beside whites "in the jury-box, on the bench, [and] in public offices." He would mingle them with whites in the schools and academies. "Social equality would be an inevitable consequence . . . and the degradation of our white blood and race would be the . . . brilliant result of the Chase doctrine and policy." Were the people of Ohio prepared for such a revolution? the *Enquirer* asked. Were they prepared "to open this magnificient State to the hordes of fugitive or emancipated negroes from the South, who would, immediately upon the triumph of such a party, pour into it?"[38]

Chase *was* a political abolitionist, and his racial attitudes were relatively liberal for his time—far too liberal for the conservative voters of southern Ohio. The heavy vote against him there, the decline of the Republican majority in the Western Reserve region of northeastern Ohio, and the more than 9000 Whig-American votes cast for Col. Van Trump made the gubernatorial race very close. It took several days to determine that Chase had defeated Payne by a plurality of 1500 votes in a total of 330,000. All but one of the Republicans were elected to other state offices by slim margins, but the Democrats won control of the state legislature. Actually, compared with the previous year, the Republican share of a smaller total vote remained the same, nearly 49 percent. The Democrats increased their percentage from 44 to 48, while the Americans fell from 7 to 3. Thus, in an essentially two-party race, Republicans and Democrats were almost dead even.[39]

Republicans could plausibly claim that Chase's success without American party support, even though narrow, was more significant for the future of their party than his coalition victory in 1855. Chase was not modest about his contribution. "They required me to take a renomination," he wrote Sumner, "and I consented, truly, on many accounts, against my will. Then they left me to fight the battle almost alone, so far as the state canvass was concerned. . . . God, in his goodness, gave me health and strength for the work, and our ticket was elected."[40]

In the Wisconsin election the governorship, other state offices, and control of the legislature were at stake. The contest was strictly one between the Republican and Democratic parties. Although Know-Nothing lodges had been organized in the state and a nativist newspaper was published in Milwaukee, the American party was never significant as an independent political organization. Instead, nativists used their influence within the Republican party, pressuring the Republican legislature of 1855 to adopt two prohibition laws, both of which were vetoed by Democratic Governor William A. Barstow. That year Republicans lost control of the legislature and barely elected their candidate for governor, Coles Bashford. But in 1856 the issue of Bleeding Kansas helped them to give Frémont a 13,000-vote majority over Buchanan, to elect all three Congressmen, to regain control of the legislature by a large majority, and thereby to send Republican James R. Doolittle to the United States Senate. Republican control of Wisconsin then seemed solid and unshakable.[41]

Early in 1857 the new legislature adopted a "personal-liberty law" prohibiting state officials from assisting in the enforcement of the federal Fugitive Slave Act. It also submitted a referendum on black suffrage to the voters at the November election. In Milwaukee, on June 17, a mass meeting of confident antislavery Republicans greeted with "hearty applause" speeches by the abolitionists Gerrit Smith and John Brown. Among the resolutions approved by the audience, one denounced the "alarming encroachments of the Slave Power" and deplored the Dred Scott decision, which nationalized slavery and denied free blacks the rights of citizenship. Another reaffirmed the duty of Congress to prohibit slavery in the territories but challenged its authority to legislate for the recovery of fugitive slaves. Still another, in an assertion of state rights, noted that the Wisconsin supreme court had ruled the federal Fugitive Slave Act unconstitutional; therefore, whoever seized a fugitive in the state would be guilty of kidnapping. Finally, the meeting resolved that, "as slavery is a crime against humanity . . . it can no more be constitutionalized or legalized, than theft, murder or robbery."[42]

Conservative Republicans were worried about the presence of abolitionists at the Milwaukee meeting and about the radical tone of its antislavery resolutions. Nevertheless, when the Republican state convention met at Madison in September, it incorporated the substance of the resolutions in the party platform. Focusing entirely on national issues, the platform devoted more space to an attack on the Dred Scott decision than to any other subject. Repeating many of the arguments of the two dissenting justices, it charged that the majority decision was extrajudicial and wholly political. Having clearly established its antislavery position, the convention, in a bid for at least the Protestant German vote, made a clean break with nativism. The platform denounced the proscription of any person because of birth, creed, or color and called for equal rights for all citizens, native or foreign-born. Indirectly, and somewhat vaguely, this plank was an endorsement of the black-suffrage referendum as well.[43]

Several Republicans sought the gubernatorial nomination, but on the seventh ballot the convention chose Alexander W. Randall, a New Yorker by birth, a former Free Soiler, a supporter of black suffrage, and an effective campaigner. In 1855, as a member of the legislature, Randall had helped to expose corruption in the administration of Democratic Governor Barstow, and the following year he had become a circuit court judge. In choosing a candidate for lieutenant governor, the party distanced itself further from the nativists. After Randall's nomination, Sherman M. Booth, a radical antislavery Republican, made an eloquent and effective appeal for the nomination of Carl Schurz, a German exile who had actively supported the Revolution of 1848 and recently settled in Watertown, Wisconsin. Even though Schurz would not become a naturalized citizen until November, the convention nominated him on the first ballot. Tall and angular, clad in a frayed and ill-fitting suit, he cut a strange figure when he delivered his acceptance speech, but he was a superb orator and won the audience with his moving exposition of the antislavery cause.[44]

When the Democrats convened in Madison, Republicans charged that ex-Governor Barstow and his corrupt followers were "quietly managing affairs" and would control the party's candidates. When the convention refused to nominate Dr. Franz Huebschmann, a prominent Milwaukee German-American, for governor, Republicans accused it of catering to the Know-Nothings, some of whom had in fact joined the Democrats. The delegates chose instead James B. Cross of Milwaukee, a wealthy businessman who had twice served as mayor. To appease their disgruntled German constituency they nominated Germans for state treasurer and attorney general.[45] The party platform, besides praising the Buchanan administration, made it clear that charges of abolitionism, partiality to blacks, and hostility to immigrants would be major themes in the Democratic attack on Republicanism.

In the campaign the panic and recession were more significant as distractions from politics than as issues that either party could effectively exploit. To the limited extent that political corruption was a subject of debate, Republicans had an advantage, because the bribery scandal involving Governor Coles Bashford was still only a rumor. They exploited Cross's association with Barstow, whose administration was remembered for election frauds and for corruption in the awarding of construction contracts, in the sale of school lands, and in the use of the school fund. Wisconsin voters would elect Cross governor, asserted the *State Journal*, when a majority favored "defalcation, forgery, ballot-box stuffing, and corruption in office generally."[46]

For the most part Republican editors and stump speakers interpreted the campaign as a crusade of the opponents of slavery against the proslavery Democracy. In listing the major issues before the electorate, the Milwaukee *Sentinel* mentioned nothing else. The Republican party was pledged to resist the expansion of slavery, it claimed, while the Democratic party held that the Constitution *"protects Slavery everywhere."* Republicans believed that the Union had been formed "not to propagate and perpetuate *Slavery,* but '*to secure the blessings of liberty* to ourselves and our posterity.'" They believed in "the inalienable right of every human being to life, liberty and the pursuit of happiness." Every Republican vote was "a plumper for Freedom and a protest against Slavery." In contrast, the "Sham Democracy" was the lackey of the Slave Power and had willingly done its bidding in Kansas. The *Sentinal* admonished voters to use their ballots to repudiate "the infamous doctrine embodied in the Dred Scott decision," and to rebuke those who would inflict upon Kansas "that blasting iniquity," slavery.[47]

As in Ohio, Wisconsin Democrats responded with racial demagoguery. They accused Republicans of believing that blacks were superior to white European immigrants. They held up the Republican-sponsored black-suffrage referendum to prove that these fanatics preferred Africans to "the representatives of the German, Celtic, French, English, and Norse races among us." Even the corruption issue elicited from one Democratic editor a racist attack upon "the nigger loving, Kansas shrieking, pulpit thundering" "Black" Republicans. In spite of these appeals to race prejudice, most Republican editors supported black suffrage, but many party members backed away from it, denying that it was a test of party loyalty. Carl Schurz, whom Republicans featured and flattered throughout the campaign, was their best response to the charge of nativism—a charge, incidentally, which they repeatedly turned against the Democrats.[48]

On election day, November 3, the Republican vote was 21,000 less than it had been the previous year, and its percentage declined from 55 to 50. The Democratic vote declined by only 8000, and its percentage increased form 44 to 50. Randall was elected governor by a majority of less than 600 votes in a total of 90,000. The Republicans retained control of the legislature and elected two other candidates for state offices by margins as small as Randall's, but Carl Schurz was defeated in the race for lieutenant governor by 107 votes. Apparently the German evangelical support that Republicans may have gained from Schurz's candidacy was not sufficient to offset the refusal of some other Republicans to vote for a still unnaturalized immigrant. Schurz, who had been confident of success, was bitter about his defeat, calling it "a disgrace to the name of Wisconsin." One Republican friend assured him that the party was "under the strongest debt of gratitude" to him. Defeat had come "through the ignorant, unreasoning prejudice of here and there a vagabond native, whose prejudices were stronger than his principles."[49]

The Republicans had won the Wisconsin election, but the Democrats had nevertheless recovered from their decisive defeat in 1856 and, as in Ohio, virtually tied them in the popular vote. The black-suffrage referendum, although receiving much support in areas of Republican strength, was defeated by a 13,000-vote majority and doubtless lost votes for the party among conservatives. However, that was not a sufficient explanation for the Republican decline from 66,000 to 45,000 votes. In addition to the expected lower turnout in the wake of a presidential election, the panic and recession may have distracted more Republicans than Democrats. Probably the major cause for the large Republican decline was the changed political situation. In 1856 the assault on Sumner and the civil war in Kansas had upset most Wisconsin voters and given the Republican party's antislavery campaign the kind of immediate relevance to a specific threat that it lacked in 1857. Democrats now argued that the Kansas question was closed, and Republicans had no evidence to prove them wrong.

When all the returns were in from these northern state elections, Republican strategists could congratulate themselves on their victories in Maine and Iowa, but even more on their defeat of the American party in Massachusetts and on clear evidence of its continued decline everywhere. At the same time, northern Democrats had good reason to celebrate their impressive recovery from the losses of the previous year. The apparent balance of strength that existed between the parties in Ohio and Wisconsin after the elections of 1857 reflected a similar balance of strength in the North as a whole. In New York, New Jersey, and Ohio, Republicans controlled the governorships, and Democrats controlled the legislatures. Elsewhere Democrats controlled Pennsylvania, Indiana, Illinois, and California, while Republicans controlled New England, Michigan, Iowa, and, by a narrow margin, Wisconsin. If the present trend continued until 1860, the next Democratic presidential candidate might hope to add New York, Ohio, and Wisconsin to the five free states his party had carried in 1856. With victories in eight of them and a sweep of the South, the Democracy would inflict upon the Republicans a crushing defeat.

Such a prospect was by no means too unrealistic for Democrats to contemplate. It was premised, of course, on two assumptions: first, that their party would remain united and, second, that with the support of President Buchanan and Governor Walker, Kansas would have an honest election and the free-state majority would have its way. Taking these for granted, the Democracy's future looked bright. The Republican party had derived its vitality from the single issue of making Kansas a free state, claimed the Cincinnati *Enquirer* after the Ohio state election. Its life, therefore, would be "brief and ephemeral," for Kansas would "soon, beyond all question, be a free State, by the vote of its own citizens." When that happened, "where will be the capital of Black-Republicanism? Gone!—utterly exploded." The only valid fear of the "Kansas agitators," wrote a Democratic editor in upstate New York, was not that it would be a slave state, "but that its Democratic voters will outnumber the 'Topeka Republican' voters."[50] So it seemed until mid-November.

Autumn elections also occurred in Minnesota and Kansas territories, the first to elect a governor and legislature in preparation for statehood, the second to elect a new territorial legislature. Minnesota Democrats won the governorship and control of the legislature in an extremely close vote, after which Republicans claimed that only the illegal ballots of United States soldiers and hundreds of imported Irish laborers had defeated them.[51] The Kansas election was not a simple contest between Republicans and Democrats. Rather, the free-state party, consisting of Republicans, northern Democrats, and a few southern Democrats, opposed the proslavery party, consisting of southern Democrats and southern Whig-Americans.

Having refused to take part in the June election of delegates to the constitutional convention, soon to meet at Lecompton, the free-state party agreed to participate in the October territorial election only after a long and bitter debate. To vote, argued opponents such as Martin F. Conway and James Redpath, was to recognize the authority and laws of the present "bogus" territorial government. How could there be a fair vote, they asked, when many free-state men were not on the voting lists and when control of the election machinery would be in proslavery hands? Moreover, to vote would be to abandon the Topeka constitution and government, leaving the free-state party helpless if it should lose the territorial election. Encouragement to stand firm came from several eastern Republican journals, notably the New York Tribune and its Kansas correspondent, William A. Phillips.

G. W. Brown, editor of the Herald of Freedom, and "Governor" Robinson abandoned their private feud to join Governor Walker in urging the free-state party to participate. Walker weakened the opposition by pledging that ballot-box frauds would not be tolerated and by ruling, with Buchanan's approval, that payment of a territorial tax would not be required to qualify as a voter. "Heretofore," Brown argued, "we have been prevented from voting by test oaths, and the requirement of taxes." Now the only condition was residence in the territory for six months prior to the election, a condition that would exclude Missourians from the franchise. Conceding that the legislative apportionment was "a villainous affair," Brown contended that the free-state party, with a majority in every district, would still be able to win the election. The Herald of Freedom was for "making Kansas a Free State in the shortest way possible, not for its effect on parties in the States, but to give quiet to Kansas." Senator Wilson of Massachusetts and Congressman Schuyler Colfax of Indiana informed Robinson that taking part in the election was essential to maintain support for the free-state party in the East. Better to vote and lose, they advised, than to give the impression of obstreperous defiance of federal authority.[52]

The two factions carried their dispute to a free-state convention which met at Topeka on July 15-16, with "General" James H. Lane presiding. After an animated debate, the delegates agreed not to abandon the Topeka government and scheduled an election for a new legislature and state officers the following month. They resolved that the Topeka constitution was "the first and only choice of the Free State men of Kansas" and again petitioned Congress for immediate admission to statehood. They urged Governor Walker to submit the constitution to a popular vote. Another resolution warned that if the Lecompton convention refused to submit its constitution for ratification, it would be guilty of an act so flagrantly despotic as to justify "the extremest measures" to protect the people's rights. Still, the delegates claimed to represent a party of peaceful men eager to avoid collision with the federal government.

After conciliating the supporters of the Topeka state government, the convention took up the question of participation in the election of a new territorial legislature and a delegate to Congress. Eventually it resolved that since the election would be held under federal law, citizens could vote "without recognizing the validity of a bogus Legislature." Accordingly, it recommended that the people of Kansas assemble in a mass convention at Grasshopper Falls on the last Wednesday in August, "to take such action as may be necessary with regard to that election." Because of rumors that Missourians would again try to control the election, the convention authorized "General" Lane "to organize the people . . . to protect the ballot boxes."[53]

On August 3 the election under the Topeka free-state constitution "passed off quietly," according to the *Herald of Freedom*, with some 8000 voters casting their ballots. Some regarded this as the first step in a clever plan to force Congress and the administration to recognize the Topeka government. As Robinson explained it, the next step was to win free-state control of the territorial legislature in the October election. The new legislature would then meet, repeal all territorial laws, prohibit slavery, and adjourn *sine die*. Next, according to Robinson, the Topeka legislature would enact a code of laws and "set the state government in motion." By then, he was confident, all opposition would have ceased, Governor Walker would have departed, and Congress would be "compelled to admit us under the *'treasonable'* Topeka Constitution or suffer the reproach of the country."[54] Fortunately, the plan, which naïvely assumed the acquiescence of a hostile administration and congressonal majority, was never put to the test.

Grasshopper Falls, the site of the free-state mass convention, was a small village located in northeast Kansas. In addition to a half-dozen stores and a sawmill, it had one hotel with a single room occupying the entire second floor. On the night of August 25, the room was occupied by thirty-five convention delegates, one of whom found "the nasal concert . . . anything but musical and soul-soothing." Other delegates slept in stores, private houses, and tents. The next day, after an uncomfortable night, the well-attended convention reached a decision that profoundly affected not only the people of Kansas but, in due course, the entire nation.

Both supporters and opponents of voting in the territorial election were fully represented. The debate, although rehearsing mostly familiar arguments, was protracted and intense. Phillips of the New York *Tribune*, finding the advocates of voting in the majority, proposed the tactic of winning the election, dissolving the territorial legislature, and installing the Topeka government, but the convention rejected it. At length "General" Lane announced his willingness to try the ballot box once more. Prudent men with wives and children wished "to try their hand at this peaceful remedy," he said, "and we must concede to them the right to do so. [Cheers.] If they fail they will join us in sustaining the Topeka Constitution and Government. [Loud applause.]"

Relying on Governor Walker's pledge, the convention adopted by acclamation a resolution favoring participation in the October election. It petitioned territorial authorities to review and correct the legislative apportionment, and it instructed Lane to offer Walker the services of the men he had organized to protect the ballot boxes. The convention nevertheless affirmed its determination to adhere to the Topeka government and put it into operation "in a legitimate manner, at an early date." In addition to the resolutions, a group of more radical delegates subsequently published an address, written by Lane, explaining that the convention had acted in response to "urgent appeals" from eastern friends. Enumerating the advantages enjoyed by the proslavery party, they found little reason to expect a favorable result. In any case, this should be understood "as the only attempt which will ever be made to adjust our great difficulty under the territorial government. What may be done after that, however, it is not our province to declare."[55] In this manner, for the first time in more than two years, the free-state party prepared to participate in the affairs of the regular territorial government, holding in reserve the Topeka government if their attempt should fail.

Pleased with the free-state party's decision, Walker assured the administration that a "fair and peaceful election" would get the territory safely past its "most dangerous crisis." "Without fraud the day is ours," Robinson assured Amos A. Lawrence, "and with fraud blood may flow in the future. . . . Mr. Buchanan and Gov. Walker will have to pay some respect to the popular will in Kansas or they will find plenty of employment for their troops." Senator Wilson raised money in the East to help finance the free-state campaign. "General" Lane, commanding the Kansas Volunteers from his headquarters in Lawrence, issued General Orders which urged free-state men to form companies and elect officers and which divided the territory into military districts. "Kansas expects every man to do his duty," Lane boldly proclaimed. "The despotism which has been forced upon us must be overthrown. We must look to the ballot-box as the instrumentality of our disenthrallment." An alarmed Kansas Democrat called Lane's flamboyant pronouncements "undisguised rebellion" and declared the territory again on the verge of civil war.[56]

During the two-day election, October 5 and 6, General Harney, at the request of Governor Walker, posted troops in a number of precincts where trouble was anticipated. Fortunately, after the polls had closed, Harney was able to report to Secretary Floyd that the election had "passed off very quietly, no disturbance or tumult having occurred." Both free-state Republicans and Democrats whose names were on the voting lists turned out in full force. The mass of free-state Democrats, reported a Lecompton Democratic editor, was determined "to remain in the single position of Free-State men, until the question of slavery was decided." Proslavery partisans, reported another free-state Democrat, had made themselves so odious that they could not face the people, "even under the banner of democracy." In spite of anticipations of another "border-ruffian" invasion, voting by Missourians was relatively small. Most proslavery polling officials, under the scrutiny of Lane's free-state volunteers, seemed to have conducted themselves properly. All the early signs indicated that Kansas Territory had at last experienced a peaceful and relatively honest election.[57]

The returns came in slowly, but it soon became evident that Marcus J. Parrott, the free-state candidate for delegate to Congress and a former Democrat, would be elected by a majority of more than 4000 votes. The news, gloated a Boston editior, was "almost too good to be true," even though the unfair apportionment might give the legislature to the proslavery party. Before the polls closed a free-state delegation from Lawrence had gone to the various precincts in Johnson and Douglas counties to observe proceedings and obtain the results as soon as they were available. "No one, free state or pro-slavery," wrote a correspondent of the *Missouri Democrat*, "doubted for a moment but what this district ... had gone overwhelmingly in favor of freedom." One of the observers from Lawrence visited the Oxford precinct in Johnson County and counted 88 voters, including a coachload of Missourians. Oxford, a village of six houses located on the Missouri state line about twelve miles south of Westport, contained a handful of voters. However, when the official returns reached Lecompton, Oxford precinct reported 1628 proslavery votes, which greatly exceeded the number of eligible voters in the whole of Johnson County. The Oxford vote was sufficient to carry the district for three proslavery councilmen and eight proslavery representatives, and thereby to give the proslavery party a majority in the new legislature.[58]

This astounding result led representatives of the free-state party to search for the Johnson County judges of election to ask for an explanation, but the judges had disappeared and could not be found. Returning to Lecompton, they notified Governor Walker and asked him to investigate. Walker and territorial secretary Stanton took a carriage to Johnson County, where they found the voting lists but no trace of the judges of election. At the hotel in Lawrence they unrolled a remarkable list, more than fifty feet long, containing 1601 names, all written by the same hand. When Stanton began to read off the names, several members of the audience recognized one or another of them as former neighbors in Cincinnati. They soon discovered that some 1500 of the names had been copied in alphabetical order out of Williams's Cincinnati Directory for 1855. The fraud was so crude, so blatantly contemptuous of public opinion, that the editor of the Lecompton *Kansas National Democrat* joined the free-state party in denouncing it, expressing his suspicion that John Calhoun, the Democratic surveyor-general, was one of its perpetrators.[59]

On October 19, Governor Walker issued a proclamation detailing the facts of the Oxford fraud and declaring that the returns from that precinct must be wholly rejected. Having previously been notified by the administration that he had no authority to act as a judge in a contested election, Walker contended that he was not presuming to act in such a capacity. Rather, he based his action on the requirement that the election returns, to be valid, must be in "perfect compliance with all the essential provisions of the law." In this case it appeared that the judges of election had failed to take the required oath to discharge their duties impartially. Moreover, the paper presented from Oxford precinct was not "the genuine record of the votes taken at the election." Instead, it was a "copy of some other document . . . made up for the occasion." On his visit to Oxford, Walker found the people "astonished by the magnitude of the return; and all persons of all parties . . . treated the whole affair with derision and indignation." He absolved Missourians from responsibility for the outcome, declaring the returns, "beyond all doubt . . . simulated and fictitious." Accordingly, Walker, claiming no right to go behind the returns, held that the returns themselves were clearly "defective in form and in substance, and therefore inadmissible."

Three days later, on October 22, Walker issued a second proclamation regarding a similar case involving election returns from three precincts in McGee County. This county was located in southeastern Kansas and contained lands of the Cherokee Indians which were not open to preemption or settlement. Fewer than one hundred qualified voters lived in the entire county, and the previous June only fourteen votes had been cast for delegates to the constitutional convention. Yet three precincts now reported more than 1200 votes. No Missouri voters were involved, and the fraud was as transparent as it had been in the Oxford precinct. Walker gave the same reasons for rejecting the returns, noting in addition that the lists did not designate the office for which a candidate was supported. Again he denied going behind the returns, claiming only that no legal returns had been submitted. In his second proclamation Walker also spoke as a loyal Democrat. An election won "by frauds so monstrous," he warned, "would be more fatal to our party than any defeat, however disastrous."[60]

Walker's rejection of the fraudulent votes had the effect of ratifying a peaceful political revolution, for it gave the free-state party a majority in the new territorial legislature. On October 23, Judge Sterling G. Cato attempted to reverse the outcome by issuing a writ of mandamus ordering Walker and Stanton to grant certificates of election to the eleven proslavery candidates from the district containing Oxford precinct. The governor and secretary, denying Cato's right to issue the writ, refused to comply, and the matter was pursued no further. On November 3, Walker forwarded copies of his proclamations and reply to Judge Cato to Secretary Cass, together with an explanation and defense of his action. Had he not rejected the fraudulent returns, he claimed, "immediate revolution would have followed throughout Kansas, and the pacification of the territory have been indefinitely postponed."[61]

Apart from expressing gratification that the Kansas election had occurred without violence, Buchanan indicated neither approval nor disapproval of the manner in which Walker had dealt with the frauds. On November 11, Stanton wrote to the President concerning various reports emanating from Washington that he and Walker were to be reprimanded for their action. Having earlier tendered his resignation, effective January 1, Stanton wished it to be known that he assumed his full share of responsibility for the action taken on the Oxford and McGee returns. Still, he refused to believe that Buchanan could be so far misled as to "approve the hasty condemnation . . . pronounced against us by a few interested individuals."[62] Stanton's virtual plea for some word of approval went unanswered. Although the administration never reversed or condemned Walker's action, its stubborn silence was the first significant sign that the President was growing uneasy about the governor's handling of Kansas affairs.

In Kansas Territory, public opinion was clear enough. Walker was quite justified in his statement to Cass that his action had won the "cordial approval of an overwhelming majority of the people of all parties." The Lecompton *Kansas National Democrat,* although a friend of the Buchanan administration and critical of the free-state party, strongly supported the governor against a small local faction of proslavery partisans. This faction, it charged, consisted of Know Nothings, "notorious disunionists," and those who had participated in or expected to benefit from the election frauds. Even in Lecompton, "once the very citadel of the pro-slavery party," majority opinion was clearly favorable to the governor. The *Herald of Freedom* reminded the eastern press that the free-state victory had not been won by Republicans alone, for at least a third of the votes had come from Democrats. At the time of the election the Republican party did not exist in the territory as a separate political organization.[63]

In the northern states, praise for Governor Walker was almost universal. Democrats understood their debt to him, for his rejection of the fraudulent returns had prevented Republicans from reviving the Kansas issue in the closing days of the autumn campaigns. Praising "the strict justice and impartiality" of Walker's course, the New York *Herald* remarked that administration approval "was simply a question of life or death to the national democratic party." The Albany *Atlas and Argus* ridiculed Republican reports that Buchanan intended to remove the governor. He had promised Kansas self-government, and he had now clearly redeemed his pledge. "We honor Gov. Walker for his act of manly courage," declared an Indiana editor. The Cincinnati *Enquirer* confidently denied that a true Democrat "could have had anything to do with the frauds committed at the Oxford Precinct." The Detroit *Free Press* expected the President to give Walker's action his full approval. Considering the nature of the frauds, it was hardly the time for him "to look very closely at the mere technicalities of the law." Speaking through the Chicago *Times,* Senator Douglas celebrated the free-state victory as the result "of that good, sound Democratic policy," the Kansas-Nebraska Act, "which Walker went to Kansas to enforce." Whatever Buchanan's private feelings may have been, northern Democrats let him know theirs, showering him with compliments for standing by his plucky little Kansas governor.[64]

Most Republican editors, in response to reports of Walker's imminent dismissal, were prepared to admit him, as they had ex-Governor Geary, to their pantheon of Kansas free-state martyrs. Although the New York *Tribune's* Kansas correspondent continued to snipe at him and read private ambition into his every act, the reaction of the *Illinois State Journal* was more typical. After repeatedly branding Walker an agent of the Slave Power, it now asked indignantly whether Buchanan would reward his "honesty and fairness" with dismissal. Evidently the administration had decided to cast its lot with the southern disunionists, whom the governor was "too patriotic to follow."[65] "The latest news from Washington is that Governor Walker will be removed," ran an oft-repeated item in the Republican press. It originated partly in the current rumors and partly, perhaps, in an unconscious wish.

The governor's critics came almost entirely from the South. Even there none defended the frauds; not many denied that they had occurred. Instead they brushed aside Walker's argument that the Oxford and McGee returns were defective and accused him of usurping authority belonging to the court or to the territorial legislature, both of which happened to be in proslavery hands. He had, raged a South Carolina editor, "stepped beyond the limits of vapid speech-making and impertinent advice" and had "illegally defeated the success of pro-slavery candidates." Walker deserved the praise he was receiving from Republicans, growled a Georgian, "for never was laborer better worthy of his hire. He went to Kansas with the deliberate resolve to defeat the pro-slavery party, and ... he has pursued his purpose with ... patient duplicity and persistent treachery." His goal, charged an Alabama editor, was the presidency, and his whole policy had been guided by that aspiration. A resolution of the Alabama legislature expressed "profound regret" that Buchanan had not removed him and demanded an explanation for his "apparent continued acquiescence" in the governor's "atrocious policy." The rather lame complaint of a Memphis editor was that Walker had exposed frauds only on the proslavery side. Had Lane and his party "polled no illegal votes to challenge his scrutiny?"[66]

Although the critics were in the majority, some Southerners were not impressed with their case. The Richmond *Enquirer* was unsure whether Walker had exceeded his authority, but it had no doubt that he had defeated "an infamous effort at a stupendous fraud." Nor did it doubt that he could justify his conduct "in a moral point of view." The Louisville *Democrat* hoped that there was virtue enough in the South to disavow "with scorn and abhorrence" a fraud performed in its behalf. Southern honor would not permit it to denounce a man for exposing a fraud, for the corruption of the ballot box was "infinitely more dangerous than the slavery question ever was." A New Orleans editor could not believe that any Southerner would defend "such scandalous abuses of the elective franchise." If Kansas were lost to the South, he urged, "let us at least preserve dignity and honor to the end."[67]

By early November it was clear that Governor Walker, by his action in the Kansas territorial election, had achieved two important political results. First, he had denied the Republicans any political advantage from the frauds in the Oxford and McGee precincts. Second, he had provided the northern Democrats with one of the indispensable requirements for their survival as a strong political party—that is, an honest vote in Kansas and a legislature that represented the majority of its people. Thereby, the political balance between northern Democrats and Republicans remained undisturbed.

Most, but not all, proslavery Southerners fumed at Walker's "treachery." Yet his action had given them no sharp sense of unbearable injustice, no resplendent principle, around which to rally. Save for the chronic secessionists, none would imperil the Union for the sake of a small and rather hapless set of territorial scoundrels, whose attempts at fraud were so utterly lacking in imagination and finesse. In short, the secessionists required a clearer grievance and a better cause.

Early in October, Walker, exhausted by his trials in Kansas and concerned about his business affairs in the East, had asked the President for a leave of absence during the month of November. Buchanan granted the leave but asked him to remain in the territory until the Lecompton constitutional convention had adjourned. Reluctantly, he agreed.[68]

Politics as Farce:
The Lecompton Constitution

On the seventh of September delegates to the Kansas constitutional convention, elected by the small proslavery minority the previous June, were to meet at Lecompton, the drab little territoria. capital overlooking the Kansas River. That was just two weeks after the shocking failure of the Ohio Life and Trust, when the financial panic filled the columns of the press and was foremost in the public mind. Yet, even then a conservative Philadelphia editor believed that the panic was a more transitory event than those he feared would soon occur in Kansas. He described the ingredients of a crisis which, "unless averted in season and with decision," would bring with it "more intense and bitter strife" than that territory had yet experienced. Fearing that the convention would attempt to coerce the admission of Kansas with a constitution "framed and adopted by a packed jury," he begged the administration to honor its commitment to determine the will of the majority by an honest vote. Failing that, the convention would "stir up the embers of discord again, and raise a fire which human agency may not easily extinguish."[1]

Prior to their election, the delegates from Douglas County, among them, John Calhoun, had publicly pledged to vote for the submission of the Lecompton constitution for popular ratification. That was before the free-state party, at its Grasshopper Falls convention, had decided to take part in the election of a new territorial legislature. Its decision made it likely that free-state partisans would also turn out if they were given an opportunity to vote on the constitution. Pro-slavery support for submission consequently declined. "This constitution," the St. Louis *Missouri Democrat* boasted, "if submitted to the people ... at a fair and free election, would be voted down by an overwhelming majority. The members know it. ... They are trying, therefore, to avert this inevitable result."[2]

Their strategy was delay. Meeting only briefly in September, the convention elected Calhoun president and appointed committees to write preliminary drafts of the constitution's major sections. In an address to the delegates, as reported in the *Kansas National Democrat,* Calhoun expressed his "firm belief and trust, that by framing a proper Constitution and submitting it to the true citizens of Kansas, the slavery question would be settled, the Black Republican party ruined, [and] the peace and prosperity of Kansas secured." He thus honored his pledge both to those who had nominated him and to Senator Douglas, to whom he owed his appointment as surveyor-general. On September 11, having transacted its preliminary business, the convention adjourned until October 19, when delegates would know the result of the territorial election. A free-state victory, Calhoun informed Douglas, would make it very difficult to obtain a vote for constitutional submission.[3]

In the interim the Buchanan administration and the delegates were exposed to a great deal of pressure both for and against popular ratification. By then a pro-Walker Democratic organization, supported by the Lecompton *Kansas National Democrat,* had met and almost unanimously agreed to oppose the Lecompton constitution if it were not submitted to the voters. Sovereignty, argued the *National Democrat,* could not be delegated to any "intermediate body"; it must be exercised by the people themselves. Striving to unite proslavery and free-state Democrats, it begged convention delegates to show a spirit of "forbearance and conciliation," not the "bigotry of sectional zeal." Would the chivalry of the South, it asked, "stoop to trick, chicane or quibble, to shield them from an issue they are afraid to meet? . . . The pro-slavery party . . . cannot create a majority, if it does not exist." An angry free-state Democrat complained to the administration that the convention had begun "by setting itself in hostility to Gov. Walker in the election of Calhoun," and that proslavery Democrats had refused to support his own candidacy for the territorial legislature. *"There is no slavery party in Kansas,"* another Democrat informed Buchanan. "The attempt to establish slavery there is a fraud. . . . We are driven to support the principle of submission . . . and, in my judgment, upon our fidelity in this trying hour, depends the Union itself."[4]

Outside the territory, Republicans charged that Buchanan was involved in a "concerted plan" to bring Kansas into the Union as a slave state. "The truth is," reported the New York *Tribune,* "the Constitution is *already framed"* and would be put in operation at once if the proslavery party lost the territorial election. Responding to these reports, worried northern Democrats bravely assured the public that Buchanan would not fail to require ratification. The Oxford election fraud, asserted the New York *Herald,* betrayed "a depth of corruption" that rendered the proslavery party "unworthy of further respect or toleration." Douglas's Chicago *Times* was convinced that Kansas would be a free state. To force a proslavery constitution upon an unwilling people, it warned, "would add thousands to the vote of the Republican party in every state . . . and give to that organization, what it has never had yet—a show of justice and truth."[5]

The pressure on the administration from proslavery Southerners was equally unrelenting. Whether the Lecompton constitution was to be submitted to the voters, they insisted, was a matter within the exclusive jurisdiction of the convention. It was a simple question of expediency, wrote a Memphis editor, better settled by the delegates than by outsiders. The convention, he suggested, might decide against submission in order to avoid a threat of political chaos. Senator Hunter of Virginia, in a statement published in the Richmond *Examiner,* noted that the act providing for the convention did not require the constitution to receive a vote of popular approval. He refused to believe that Buchanan would oppose Kansas statehood "merely because its convention did not choose to submit the constitution to the people for ratification." However, southern Democrats were still not nearly as united as northern Democrats on the ratification issue. The Richmond *Enquirer,* among others, continued to argue for it. A meeting of the Democracy of Rockingham County, Virginia, resolved that if the convention failed to submit the Kansas constitution to the voters, it would violate "the spirit and letter of the act creating her Territorial Government." In that event, the constitution "ought to be returned by Congress to the residents of Kansas for endorsement."[6]

During the critical weeks of September and October, surviving records indicate that the Buchanan administration, although making no public pronouncements, refused to yield to the proslavery pressure from the South. There is no evidence to suggest that the President had abandoned his effort to secure ratification of the Lecompton constitution. In a letter to Governor Walker, dated October 22, published many years later, but appearing to be authentic, Buchanan "rejoiced to learn . . . that the convention of Kansas [would] submit the constitution to the people." He believed that everything was "gliding along smoothly" and anticipated "a happy conclusion to all the difficulties in that Territory."[7]

Meanwhile, Secretary Cobb continued to serve as Buchanan's principal defender against his southern critics. In September, Cobb assured Alexander H. Stephens that Walker was "fully sustained by our friends in Kansas," and he expressed confidence that the constitution would be submitted for ratification. Failure to secure popular approval, he feared, would "produce the most dangerous crisis we have yet had on the Kansas question." Cobb confessed that the administration had no plan of action for that contingency, because it did not expect it to occur. After reading Stephens's argument against required ratification, he replied that a case of "overwhelming power" could be made that denying a popular vote "was the result *alone* of a fear that a majority would condemn it." Cobb would have been gratified if Kansas came in as a slave state, but only if it could be brought about "upon the recognized principle of carrying out the will of the majority." Early in November he begged Stephens to "save us from the fatal blunder of committing the Democracy of Ga. against the submission of the constitution." John J. McElhone, in testimony before a congressional committee a few years later, recalled a letter that Cobb had dictated to him, addressed to "some influential man in Kansas," perhaps Hugh M. Moore, reminding him of the pledge regarding Kansas that the Democratic party had made during the presidential campaign of 1856. Cobb himself testified that he had written an "urgent and strong" letter to Moore, the vice-president of the Lecompton convention, in favor of submission.[8]

Secretary of the Interior Jacob Thompson also assisted Buchanan in defending the administration's Kansas policy, but he acted with less conviction and more reservations than Cobb. According to his account, he sought to "harmonize" the territory's free-state and proslavery Democrats and to persuade them to unite in support of a vote on the Lecompton constitution. Like Cobb, this Mississippian hoped that Kansas would enter the Union as a slave state, and, in any case, he thought that the rights of slaveholders then in the territory ought to be protected. Nevertheless, although he did not believe that submission was mandatory and would not oppose the admission of Kansas without it, he was convinced that it would be "most unwise and impolitic, under the circumstances," for the convention to refuse to seek voter approval.[9]

In October, Col. Henry L. Martin of Mississippi, a clerk in Thompson's Department of the Interior, went to Kansas for the official purpose of examining the affairs of the federal land office in Lecompton. Unofficially his mission was quietly to represent the administration when the constitutional convention reconvened. Martin conferred with both Cobb and Thompson before he departed, and he carried Cobb's letter to Moore urging the convention to provide for ratification. Apparently he did not receive instructions directly from Buchanan, but it is highly unlikely that both his mission and Cobb's letter had not received the President's approval. Neither the purpose of the mission nor the message to Moore departed in any respect from the goals of Buchanan's Kansas policy.

Subsequently rumors spread that Martin had played a sinister role in the convention's proceedings. Some charged that he was sent to spy on Governor Walker; that he carried a proposed draft of the Kansas constitution in his pocket; that he was instructed "to ply the purse, strengthen the doubtful, [and] curb the headstrong" in behalf of the proslavery cause. None of these charges were supported with evidence. Martin later testified that the "whole drift" of Thompson's advice to him was that whatever the convention decided "ought to be submitted to the people" and ought not to be "objectionable to the free State Democrats in the Territory." He confirmed that Cobb's letter to Moore was a "strong and forcible" argument favorable to submission. He admitted that he was, "a good deal of the time," in the basement of the Lecompton convention hall, where the land-office records were kept. Martin also admitted that he "conferred with the delegates freely" and that some consulted him. He testified that he had pressed for submission until it was defeated by a vote of the convention itself.[10] In short, if Buchanan or any member of the administration, whatever his private feelings may have been, abandoned the cause of full constitutional ratification before that fateful convention vote, they covered their tracks remarkably well.

On October 19, convention delegates began straggling into Lecompton, but several days passed before they had a quorum and could begin their deliberations. Numerous reporters, many of them highly opinionated, were there to interpret proceedings. The military was much in evidence, with instructions to protect the convention from any possible interference. In the basement of the two-story wooden hall, Col. Martin was ever ready to advise the delegates, but not many cared much for what he had to say. They were in a defiant mood, furious that Governor Walker had meddled in the territorial election, and determined to retaliate by stripping him of his powers. With the free-state party now holding majorities of nine to four in the territorial Council and twenty-four to eleven in the House of Representatives, the Lecompton convention was the last refuge of the proslavery minority.

Compared with the conventions that had framed constitutions for other new states, the Lecompton convention was in most respects uniquely unrepresentative of the people in whose name it pretended to act. It had been elected by a small fraction of the adult male population; fifteen counties were without delegates; and the apportionment had been heavily weighted in favor of the remaining pockets of proslavery sentiment. Of the fifty-three delegates identified by a New York *Tribune* correspondent, thirty-four were Democrats, seven were Whigs, and the other twelve were probably Democrats but called themselves "proslavery," or "states rights," or "ultra-southern." Free-state Republicans, who far outnumbered the territory's proslavery Democrats, were, by their own choice, wholly unrepresented. Only four of the delegates had been born and lived in the North before coming to Kansas; two had been born in the South but lived in the North; six had been born in the North but lived in the South; and the remaining forty-one had been born and lived in the South. Of the nineteen Missourians, only a few were identified with the "border ruffians" of previous years, among them one of the elusive election judges at Oxford precinct. The ages of the delegates were more typical of territorial conventions, thirty-five being under forty and only two over sixty. Occupationally, twenty-two were professional men, fourteen of them lawyers; twenty were farmers; eight were merchants; and three were skilled craftsmen.[11]

Among the delegates, perhaps a half-dozen owned slaves, but in sentiment they were solidly proslavery. In at least one respect they represented the majority of free-state party members well enough, namely, in their racial prejudices and in their determination to prevent free blacks from settling in the state of Kansas. Two years earlier, when free-state voters had ratified the Topeka constitution, a

large majority betrayed similar racial attitudes by approving a provision excluding free blacks. According to the *Herald of Freedom,* some had favored it in order
to reduce proslavery opposition to the Topeka state government. Unfortunately,
it confessed, much of the sentiment for exclusion grew "out of a spleen of prejudice against color." For this it offered no defense, hoping that the people would
"soon put themselves in a correct position."[12]

Sixty delegates had been elected to the convention, but several did not
appear, and only forty-seven remained until final adjournment. The New York
Tribune's correspondent sent regular reports of drunkenness and disorder among
them. A New England correspondent claimed that even New York City's notorious Five Points could not produce men "whose characteristics of depravity were
more marked than those . . . who have usurped the office of law-makers of the
people of Kansas." These biased comments aside, the convention did not in fact
bring together a body of men well suited, either by temperament or training, for
the demanding task of writing a state constitution for Kansas at that critical
time. Frontier territories seldom produced distinguished constitutional conventions, but the performance of these Lecompton delegates was well below average.
The relatively balanced report of the New York *Herald's* correspondent,
although describing the convention as a body of "ordinary respectability,"
thought it "little qualified to frame an organic law or perform a work of such
immense responsibility and requiring so much legal, political, and historical
knowledge." He found only one or two of the delegates sufficiently trained for
that task.[13]

John Calhoun, president of the convention, played a curious role. A Boston-
ian by birth, he had settled in Illinois and served in the legislature as a Douglas
Democrat. Moving to Kansas as surveyor-general in 1854, he continued his political friendship with Douglas but allied himself with the proslavery party and
became one of its ablest leaders. Free-state partisans hated him for tolerating the
"border ruffians" and for his suspected role in the Oxford precinct frauds. Yet,
Calhoun led the moderates at the convention, urging the delegates to submit their
constitution to a popular vote. Rush Elmore, another moderate leader, had been
an Alabama lawyer and came to Kansas with fourteen slaves and an appointment
as a judge of the territory's supreme court. Elmore was recognized by all parties
as a man of good character and one of the few delegates of superior ability. Hugh
M. Moore, the convention's vice-president and a third moderate leader, was a
young Georgia Democrat who had settled in Leavenworth to practice law.
Moore had hesitated for a time, but he accepted Cobb's advice and joined those
favoring constitutional submission.[14]

After the territorial election, most delegates were not easily persuaded by
the arguments of the moderates. Their anger increased when free-state orators,
addressing an antislavery meeting in Lecompton almost under their noses, called
them "the creatures of a miserable minority" and urged them to go home. Breath-

ing defiance, the radicals were determined to adopt a proslavery constitution and send it directly to Congress without a popular vote. They were uncompromising in pressing their cause. William H. Jenkins, an "ultra states rights" Democrat from South Carolina, opposed the popular election of judges, fearing that the free-state party might get the upper hand. Jenkins and Lucius L. Bolling, a Mississippian, objected to a restriction on the transportation of slaves into Kansas for sale. Although the purpose of the restriction was to prevent traders from bringing in rebellious or physically unsound slaves, opponents argued that slaves were property and trade in them should not be interfered with. The majority agreed and thus, contrary to the policies of several southern states, would have opened Kansas to the commercial interstate slave trade.[15]

Most of the Lecompton constitution's provisions relating to the structure and powers of the state government were neither novel nor likely to cause debate, and much of its wording was lifted from the constitutions of other states. Even so, some of its provisions were highly controversial, notably, the manner of selecting judges, the permanent location of the state capital, legislative apportionment, qualifications for voting and officeholding, and state policies concerning banking, land grants, and internal improvements. Collectively, these issues would seem to have been sufficient to require submission of the constitution to a popular vote.

However, Article VII alone, which legalized slavery and incorporated nearly the whole of Kentucky's and Missouri's slave codes, would have led any reasonable body of men to conclude that submission was indispensable. "The right of property, is before and higher than any constitutional sanctions," it declared, "and the right of the owner of a slave to such slave and its increase is the same and as inviolable as the right of the owner to any property whatsoever." In other clauses it granted the customary powers and protection to the master, required him to treat his slaves humanely, provided for the recovery of runaways, and attempted to guard the community against slave insurrections and other forms of violence. It denied the legislature the power to emancipate slaves without full compensation to and the consent of their owners. Finally, it granted new emigrants to Kansas the right to bring their slaves with them. Thus, the Lecompton constitution would have made Kansas the sixteenth slave state.[16]

On November 6, having approved the substance of the constitution, the convention confronted the final major question: whether to honor the commitment of the President, the governor, and some of its own members to insist that the document be submitted to the Kansas electorate. On this issue the delegates were divided between a radical proslavery majority, who denied any obligation to have their work ratified, and a moderate proslavery minority, who urged submission in one form or another. Calhoun, Elmore, Moore, and other moderates, speaking as national Democrats and administration men, urged submission, but their pleas lacked the passion of the radicals. John D. Henderson, a native of Pennsylvania who had lived in Virginia before coming to Kansas, was one of the more determined moderates. He defended the record of the northern Democracy in upholding the rights of the South, and he claimed to be a proslavery man himself. Yet, he could not accept this constitution without giving the people of Kansas a full and fair vote. The radicals, brandishing letters of support from prominent Southerners, including Virginia's Senator Hunter, asserted their sovereign right to act for the territory and denied that either Congress or the President would insist upon ratification. Moreover, Jenkins claimed, the national interest would be served best by the admission of Kansas as a slave state. Repeatedly he and other radicals charged that the free-state party would reject *any* constitution adopted by the convention, and, having refused to vote in the delegate election, they did not deserve the opportunity.[17]

At the end of the first day of debate the majority, stubbornly ignoring all appeals to reason and warnings of disaster, voted to send the constitution directly to Congress. Another angry debate followed before the radicals, long after midnight, agreed to adjourn without bringing the entire document to final passage. It was then, in the early morning hours, that a desperate band of moderates, led by Calhoun and Col. Martin, decided to offer what they considered a compromise. Its terms had been in the air for several months and were known to the New York *Tribune*'s correspondent soon after the convention reconvened. Rather than submitting the whole constitution for ratification, the compromise proposed to submit only the article on slavery, thus assuring the survival of the remainder of the constitution however the electorate might vote. Edwin G. Dill of the Washington *Union* subsequently recalled that Senator Bigler, late in summer, had expressed the opinion that, "as the slavery question was the only one upon which the people were divided," partial submission was probably the best the convention could achieve. Calhoun won support for the compromise by claiming that it had the approval of Senator Douglas. Having written to Douglas for advice, and having received no reply, he chose, quite erroneously, to interpret an editorial in the Chicago *Times* of October 14 as evidence that Douglas endorsed the compromise.[18]

On the morning of November 7, the moderates persuaded the convention, by a slim margin, to reconsider its vote on submission. They then introduced their proposal for partial submission, and the debate resumed, lasting most of the day. Eventually the compromisers won just enough support to secure its approval. Later in the day, when the constitution came up for final passage, only a few delegates voted against it, and forty-five of them put their signatures on the engrossed document. Several proslavery radicals, opposing even partial submission, refused to sign. One of them, George P. Hamilton, a physician from Georgia, explained that he had used his "utmost efforts to make Kansas a slave State." Now, to his dismay, he found that "designing politicians" had seen fit "to sacrifice the pro-slavery party at the altar of 'national democracy.'" Most of the radicals, although voting against the compromise, found it not too difficult to

accept. Later that night, after the completion of a few formalities, President Calhoun, to the relief of the restless and weary delegates, proclaimed the convention
adjourned. At that moment, reported the New York *Tribune's* correspondent, a
familiar feature of the convention exhibited itself. "One prominent member
exclaimed with a loud voice, 'Now, boys, let's come and take a drink!'" Many,
apparently, had not waited that long.[19]

The refusal of a few proslavery radicals to approve the constitution with its
provision for submitting the article on slavery was not surprising. What might
have seemed surprising was the ultimate willingness of the great majority to
accept it—that is, until the terms of the compromise were read in full. By no
means did it give the voters of Kansas a clear choice between a free state or a
slave state, and the wonder is that any of the moderates could have hoped that
opponents of slavery would have found it acceptable. In fact, the "schedule" that
was added to the constitution, spelling out precisely what the voters could decide
and how the election would be conducted, was a triumph for the territory's proslavery minority.

According to the schedule, before the vote was taken and during the interim
between the vote and admission to statehood, the powers of both Governor
Walker and the new free-state territorial legislature were to be taken from them
and given to the president of the convention, John Calhoun. He was instructed
to provide for an election on December 21. Three commissioners in each county,
appointed by him, were in turn to appoint three judges of election in each precinct. In the election the Lecompton constitution was to be submitted for ratification or rejection in the following manner: The ballots were to be endorsed,
"Constitution with slavery," or "Constitution with no slavery." After the election, President Calhoun and two or more members of the convention were to
examine the poll books. If the majority voted for the constitution with slavery,
it was to be transmitted to Congress at once. If the majority voted for the constitution with no slavery, the article providing for it was to be deleted. Then, the
schedule declared, slavery would no longer exist in Kansas, *except* that the right
of property in slaves then in the territory would "in no manner be interfered
with."

Therein lay the explanation for the convention majority's acceptance of the
compromise. Whatever the voters decided, Kansas would enter the Union with
at least a small slave population—and with Calhoun, rather than Walker, in control, the election might well turn out in favor of opening Kansas to additional
slaves. If it went the other way, the two hundred or so slaves already there would
be protected. And how, even then, could others be kept out? Missouri slaveholders with claims to land in Kansas would surely assert their right to settle with
their slaves. Moreover, no slaveholding state had yet been successful in preventing the smuggling of slaves across their borders in defiance of laws against further

importations. Those who protested that the election gave voters no real choice did not raise a false or insignificant issue.

The schedule also provided for an election, to be held the first Monday in January, to choose a governor, other state officers, a legislature, and a member of Congress. These officers were to take control from Calhoun as soon after admission to statehood as possible. The same officials were to control this election as had controlled the vote on the constitution. Again Walker and the territorial legislature were to play no role.

Finally, in case the free-state party should win the first state election, the schedule attempted to prevent any immediate revision of the Lecompton constitution. No amendment was to be permitted until after the year 1864. Then the legislature, by a two-thirds majority, could recommend to the voters at the next general election the calling of a constitutional convention to consider revisions. If a majority of the state's qualified voters (not just a majority of those voting) favored a convention, the legislature at its next session would provide for the election of delegates. The convention would meet within three months after the election. Even then the schedule prohibited any amendment which affected "the rights of property in the ownership of slaves." In short, by the terms of the Lecompton constitution, even if the majority voted for it "with no slavery," Kansas could conceivably remain a slave state forever.[20]

After trying and failing to win Governor Walker's support for the compromise, Calhoun could have had no illusions about the response it would elicit from the free-state majority in Kansas and from the North. Disputing Calhoun's assertion that it was the policy of the administration, Walker showed him Buchanan's letter of July 12 with its firm commitment to full submission. Calhoun replied that administration policy had changed, but he could offer no evidence to support his claim. Walker later testified that he had "long since ceased to have any confidence in [Calhoun's] veracity." Buchanan's subsequent denial of responsibility, he recalled, was "so solemn, so serious, so grave, that I believed him then, and have believed him ever since on that point." Although Walker suspected that some member of the Cabinet was responsible for the compromise, Colonel Martin did not carry it with him from Washington. Rather, he and moderate leaders themselves put the compromise together in Lecompton, believing that it was all they could salvage and, quite mistakenly, that it was better than nothing.[21] They would have served themselves, the administration, their party, and the Union far better by remaining loyal, even in defeat, to their commitment to full submission than by being party to a fraud.

After the Lecompton delegates had finished their work and gone home, little was heard of them or their small following of proslavery partisans. There were no public celebrations, no party rallies, and few campaigners, prior to the December 21 election, canvassing the territory for votes for the constitution with slavery. The proslavery editor of the Leavenworth *Herald,* who had served as a delegate to the convention, boldly congratulated the people of Kansas "upon the immediate prospect of a just, a manly, a noble settlement of the distracting issue which has been involved." Admitting that the constitution was proslavery in its protection of vested rights in slaves already in the territory, he asked who could object to that, "save those who want no peace in Kansas?" His was a solitary voice amid the roar of protest when news of the proceedings at Lecompton reached the public. The *Herald,* according to the Democratic Leavenworth *Journal,* was the only paper, among some twenty published in the territory, that favored the constitution's adoption.[22]

Conspicuous among the dissenters was the Lecompton *Kansas National Democrat,* a pro-administration journal and a critic of the free-state party for its refusal to participate in the delegate election. "It is vain to talk of parties in reference to such a matter as this," it warned. "The subject is far beyond the range of party action. . . . No respectable portion of the people can ever be rallied to the support of such an instrument." In addition to the fact that the people were denied the right to reject the constitution altogether, it asserted that "nothing substantial" was involved in the choices open to them. Moreover, the legislative apportionment gave Johnson County representation based on the Oxford returns, thus legalizing "that most outrageous fraud." Repeating its suspicion that Calhoun had been involved, the *Democrat* asserted that the people had good reason not to trust him. Predicting that the free-state party would again refuse to vote, it foresaw another crisis if the constitution were forced upon a hostile population. In despair it asked, "Will the troubles of this unhappy Territory never have an end?"[23]

The Lecompton delegates were probably correct in their charge that the free-state party would spurn any constitution they submitted, no matter what its provisions. Long before the convention met "Governor" Robinson had assured Amos A. Lawrence that the party would stand by the Topeka constitution and "vote down all opposing constitutions" if given a chance. In July the *Herald of Freedom* had urged voters to reject the Lecompton constitution. "It matters not what the character of that Constitution may be. Though it is the Topeka Constitution itself, or one which is wholly unexceptionable . . . it is foreign to our soil, imposed upon us by fraud, and it *must be voted down.*" The majority, of course, could claim the right to vote it down for any reason it chose, but it was denied a chance to do so for even the best of reasons. The issue now, claimed the *Herald of Freedom,* was whether power should be given to "a class of scoundrels," with John Calhoun usurping the authority of both governor and legislature. To resist them the free-state party had attracted men from every state and all parties. "Abolitionists, Free Soilers, and Moderate Pro-Slavery men are united in a common cause against Border Ruffian usurpation."[24]

In late November, mass meetings in Lawrence, Leavenworth, and many smaller towns repudiated the constitution "with loathing and scorn." They vowed to take no part in the vote on ratification and to resist any attempt to put the constitution in operation. They urged Walker or Stanton to call a special session of the new territorial legislature. On December 2, a convention of delegates representing all parts of the territory met at the Congregational church in Lawrence, with Robinson presiding and Lane in charge of a committee on resolutions. After a series of fiery speeches the convention unanimously resolved "NEVER, under any circumstances" to permit the Lecompton constitution to become the organic law of Kansas. It declared the territorial legislature elected in October to be "the only legitimate law making body" ever to meet in Kansas. It endorsed the Topeka constitution and agreed to "maintain it against all opposition." Finally, the convention called on the legislature to frame a fair election law and submit both constitutions to a vote of the people. Robinson warned Congressman John Sherman that the Lecompton constitution could not be forced upon Kansas "without the shedding of blood."[25]

News of the Lecompton convention's work reached the northern states soon after the autumn elections had revealed a decline in Republican strength and a more promising future for the Democrats. In those circumstances Republican leaders would have transcended human frailty if their words of condemnation did not sometimes betray a degree of elation at the prospect of another major crisis over slavery in Kansas. If northern confidence in the territory's early admission as a free state were shaken, their appeal would regain its relevance to a specific and immediate proslavery threat. Once again the party could gird itself to defend free labor against an aggressive Slave Power—the perceived danger, above all others, that had called it into being. The next Congress, predicted the *National Era,* would be "the theatre of a complicated and desperate struggle on the Slavery Question," one that would define the issues "to be decided by the election of 1860." The great battle between Freedom and Slavery had yet to be fought, claimed the Chicago *Tribune.* Soon it would be transferred "from Lecompton to Washington, from the Territory to the whole Republic. Thus it daily enlarges its fearful proportions."[26]

Republicans placed the Lecompton fraud in a still developing pattern of proslavery aggression. The repeal of the Missouri Compromise, the "border ruffian" legislature, the Dred Scott decision, Buchanan's reply to the Silliman letter, the Lecompton convention, charged a Chicago editor, were all parts of a single plot, having its "instigators and prime movers in the South and its [Democratic] accomplices in the North." Its ultimate goal was "to give the slave power the dominion for all time in the National Councils; to settle the slavery question at once and for ever by making it a national institution. . . . Slavery will never be satisfied with anything short of this." In the face of such aggression, asserted a Massachusetts Republican, the North had every right to fight back—"to attack

INTO slavery. . . . To win slave states to freedom. To restrict slavery's present rights." Save Kansas for freedom, urged the Chicago *Tribune,* and all the remaining territories would be saved. Missouri would then be won to the side of free labor, and the western half of Texas would become a free state. "When this is accomplished, slavery will be surrounded and left to wither, smother, and expire."[27]

In this new Kansas crisis, Republicans found themselves obliged by circumstances to take a stand in support of Douglas's doctrine of popular sovereignty, rather than acting on their belief that it was the duty of Congress to exclude slavery from the territories. Neither their platform nor the Dred Scott case had any bearing on the question of whether the people should be permitted to vote on a proposed state constitution. In principle, even the most extreme proslavery partisans did not question the right of the majority to exclude slavery from a new state at the time its constitution was framed. At most they denied that it was obligatory for the delegates elected to a constitutional convention to submit their document for ratification. There were precedents on both sides. Some early state constitutions had not been ratified, but in the last two decades all of them had been, and the recent Minnesota enabling act had explicitly required it. Many Republicans, therefore, like the New York *Tribune,* described the Kansas issue as one involving not only slavery but the right of the people to approve or reject the whole of their constitution—in short, the acceptance of popular sovereignty as previously defined by most Southerners themselves. In justification they stressed other controversial issues that were raised by the Lecompton constitution—for example, its specific provisions for certain railroad land grants and for a state banking system.[28]

The action of the Lecompton convention and its threat to revive the Kansas conflict had a chilling effect on the recently buoyant northern Democrats. Even they, remarked the Republican Milwaukee *Sentinel,* had been startled by this last act of proslavery aggression, for they were being "fairly crowded to the wall by their Southern allies." With rare exceptions, free-state Democrats saw only one way to avoid the loss of the entire North to the Republicans: The party must repudiate the Lecompton fraud quickly and without reservation; the Democratic Congress must reject the constitution or send it back to Kansas for ratification; and President Buchanan must stand by his commitment to secure submission and an honest vote. Some, like the Indianapolis *Sentinel,* spoke gently: "If the constitution is wise and just in its provisions, it would be far better to submit it to the approval of the people than to force it upon them." Some, like the Detroit *Free Press,* spoke angrily: "The Kansas convention has disgraced itself in the eyes of all decent men." Any northern politician "who shall lend his aid to . . . defeat the will of the majority . . . will be punished with political annihilation." Southern extremists should not delude themselves that northern Democrats would support them "in any juggle to fetch Kansas into the Union as a slave State against the wishes of its actual inhabitants."[29]

Northern Democrats lavished praise on Governor Walker for the courageous and honorable role he had played amid "the many personal and political perils which surrounded him from the moment he set foot on the soil of Kansas." The New York *Herald* assured the fire-eaters that, in spite of their "last desperate trick," they had lost Kansas and must agree to surrender it. Some parts of the Lecompton document, wrote Forney in the Philadelphia *Press,* "would disgrace a despotism, others [were] merely ridiculous." When it was presented to Congress, he predicted that it would be "thrown out of both branches by a unanimous vote." On one point the northern Democratic press was quite emphatic: Kansas would never enter the Union "under a democratic administration" until its whole constitution had been submitted to a popular vote. The administration, declared the Detroit *Free Press,* "has but to pursue steadily the course upon which it started. . . . That it will do so we feel the most perfect assurance." Buchanan's commitment to submission, affirmed a New York editor, had given the Democracy its recent victory in that state. Writing directly to the Attorney General, a Pennsylvania Democrat reported that Walker was "standing very strong," and he hoped that the administration would give him its "cordial support." That, he believed, was "a matter of mighty consequence to the Democracy of the North."[30]

Some southern Whig-Americans, after reading the northern Democratic press, once more assumed their role as the South's most militant defenders, protesting that it had been betrayed by the national Democracy long enough. There were many more points of agreement between northern Democrats and "Black" Republicans, claimed an Alabama Whig editor, than between northern and southern Democrats. The protection of southern rights, therefore, required "cutting loose from all party associations at the North" and yielding nothing more to its demands. That, he predicted, would occur soon enough. Indeed, before the end of the first session of the new Congress the Democratic party would be "divided into two irreconcilable and antagonistic factions." Lacking common principles and sentiments, all that held it together was "devotion to the spoils and plunder of the Government."[31]

Most southern Democrats needed no pressure from the Whigs. Having almost abandoned hope of winning Kansas, they were suddenly and unexpectedly presented with an opportunity to make it a slave state. After fretting over Buchanan's tolerance of Walker's behavior in Kansas, they demanded acceptance of the Lecompton constitution as a rebuke to the governor and as a test of the readiness of northern Democrats to protect southern interests. The Memphis *Appeal* abandoned its earlier support of submission and argued that the convention, having been legally called and legally elected, was entitled to decide the question of ratification without interference from the governor or Congress. More than one proslavery journal joined the Mobile *Register* in congratulating the convention for having devised "a most ingenious scheme to rob the [free-state] rioters of their anticipated repast." Its submission scheme, reported the Kansas correspondent of the Jackson *Mississippian,* "was the very best proposition for making Kansas a slave state. . . . Calhoun is the great man of the Territory."[32]

Pro-Lecompton Southerners, ignoring all evidence to the contrary, repeatedly asserted that the convention had expressed the will of the people. Resolutions adopted by the Alabama legislature promised to maintain, "to the last extremity, the right of the people of Kansas, acting through their legally appointed Convention . . . to adopt a constitution with or without submitting the same for subsequent ratification." In Georgia, a Democratic convention, meeting in Milledgeville with former Governor Herschel V. Johnson presiding, resolved that Congress had no authority to require constitutional ratification or to examine the manner in which a territory had prepared for statehood. "If Kansas is rejected with a pro-Slavery Constitution because of the failure to refer for ratification," Thomas R. R. Cobb had earlier warned his brother Howell, "the most doubtful battle ever fought for the Union will be ahead of us. I tremble for the result."[33]

Nevertheless, Southerners, in their reaction to the Lecompton constitution, as in their reaction to the Kansas territorial election, were not nearly as united as Northerners. Some doubted that the fate of the South depended upon the future of slavery in Kansas; others had no taste for the tactics of the Lecompton convention. Whig Congressman John A. Gilmer of North Carolina believed that slavery would have only a brief and feeble life in Kansas in any case; and Governor Thomas Bragg opposed any drastic measures if the constitution should be rejected. Governor Wise of Virginia, in a public letter to the *Enquirer,* took issue with Senator Hunter and called on Congress to demand a vote on the Lecompton constitution before admitting Kansas to statehood.[34]

The southern press also had its prominent dissenters. In support of Wise, the Richmond *Enquirer* asked whether it was "in accordance with Democratic principles that the will of a minority should control. . . . Can it be claimed that a Constitution expresses the wishes and opinion of *the people* of Kansas, when there are thousands of those people who have never voted even for the men who framed it?" In the Deep South the New Orleans *Picayune* conceded that the free-state party had a commanding majority and argued that southern interests could not be advanced by "continuing to urge a lost cause." To attempt to protect slavery "by artifice, or fraud, or denial of popular rights" would be "a grave blunder in policy, and a fatal error in principle." If Kansas were lost to the South, "let us at least preserve dignity and honor to the end." The Louisville *Democrat,* showing no sympathy for the many proslavery Kentuckians in the Lecompton convention, could think of no reason for refusing to submit the constitution other than a fear that the people would reject it. "The policy proposed is a most infallible way to make Kansas ... not only a free State, but a violent anti-slavery State—a shrieking State after the model of Massachusetts. Such a policy would fill the Black Republicans with ecstasy."[35]

In mid-November, as the Lecompton debate raged in the press, Governor Walker departed for the East to look after his personal affairs and to urge Buchanan to stand by his commitment to full submission. Before leaving Kansas and on his journey to St. Louis, he spoke bluntly of the convention's misdeeds and expressed confidence—more, perhaps, than he felt—that the President would sustain him. After a detour to Chicago for a conference with Douglas, he traveled by train to Washington. On November 26, Walker had a long interview with Buchanan in which he described public sentiment in Kansas and the likely consequences of administration acquiescence in the Lecompton fraud. His argument was sound, but it came too late.[36]

When a President is obliged to make a crucial policy decision, he may consider himself fortunate if the dictates of justice, political expediency, and his own prior commitments all unmistakably point in the same direction. That seemed to be James Buchanan's advantageous position when, soon after the adjournment of the Lecompton convention, reliable information concerning its action reached Washington. He knew the background well enough. A territorial legislature elected with the aid of thousands of illegal votes had decided, without the authority of a congressional enabling act, to call a constitutional convention. Proslavery delegates had been elected by a small fraction of the qualified voters. Those events, Buchanan thought, could not be undone without great turmoil, and he had recognized the convention as legally qualified to frame a constitution.

Yet, the evidence that the Kansas population was overwhelmingly antislavery was so convincing that he had, since his inauguration, repeatedly stressed that justice required ratification, assuring Governor Walker that he was ready to "stand or fall" on that demand. His political goal was to deprive Republicans of the Kansas issue, and speedy admission to statehood after an honest vote was the only practicable way it could be achieved. Until late October, Buchanan seemed to expect that the Lecompton convention would respect his wishes concerning ratification. Knowing that a proslavery constitution would be voted down, he hoped that the delegates would accept the inevitable, seek to reunite the territory's northern and southern Democrats, and thereby win control of the free state of Kansas. Perhaps the first inkling Buchanan had of possible trouble was the news of the frauds in the Oxford and McGee precincts during the October territorial election.

Although there is no record of the President's initial reaction to the convention's rejection of full ratification, he could have felt nothing less than bitter disappointment. Given its open defiance of his known wishes, acquiescence could hardly have been his first impulse. He must have sensed the injustice of the convention's action and remembered his pledge to Walker. With a united North at his back and less than a united South against him, why not repudiate this crude betrayal of the Democratic doctrine of popular sovereignty? He would doubtless cause some angry southern protests, and the proslavery radicals would surely fill the columns of the Charleston *Mercury,* New Orleans *Delta,* and other papers of that ilk with secession threats. But Buchanan would have a considerable advantage over them. By rejecting the Lecompton fraud he would give them no better cause for radical action than Walker's rejection of the election frauds. Considerations of political expediency might also have suggested this course. Would not his administration, as well as his party's existence as a national organization, be threatened more seriously by ignoring the northern Democrats' solid opposition to partial submission than by risking another flurry of secession agitation in the South?

If, as seems likely, these thoughts passed through Buchanan's mind, they soon gave way to others. Again, there are no records of discussions at Cabinet meetings or other sources to show precisely how his policy developed. Secretary Cobb later testified that he himself had no knowledge of a plan for partial submission until its adoption by the Lecompton convention, and there is no reason to doubt his word. Eventually, however, the administration decided to reverse the policy it had consistently pursued for the past eight months. It reached the astonishing conclusion, as Cobb explained, that since slavery, "the only question at issue," was to be submitted, "the material point had been attained." Hence it agreed to accept the action of the convention "as virtually carrying out the policy of submission."[37]

In this manner the President and his Cabinet joined Calhoun and the convention's proslavery moderates in urging Congress and the country to endorse a fraud. Somehow Buchanan managed to persuade himself that he had never in fact demanded full submission—only a vote on the future of slavery in Kansas. That was sufficient to fulfill the terms of the Kansas-Nebraska Act. Somehow the convention persuaded him that slave property then in the territory was entitled to continued protection even if the majority voted against the constitution with slavery. In any case, he concluded that it would be folly to oppose the Lecompton constitution simply because it protected the owners of a few hundred slaves! Looking back, knowing the ultimate consequences of Buchanan's policy decision, it stands as one of the most tragic miscalculations any President has ever made.

Buchanan decided to announce his Lecompton policy through an editorial in the Washington *Union,* and Attorney General Black accepted the task of writing it. During the preceding month the *Union* had been silent about Kansas affairs, making the impact all the greater when, on November 18, the administration organ finally spoke. Black opened his editorial on a bold and cheerful note: "The vexed question is settled—the problem is solved—the dead point of danger is passed—all serious trouble about Kansas affairs is over and gone. Kansas comes into the Union on the principle of the great act which organized her and Nebraska as territorial governments." The schedule attached to the constitution acknowledged the people of Kansas to be the only tribunal entitled to determine what its domestic institutions should be, and they would decide the question of slavery or no slavery when they voted on December 21. Perhaps an "ultra abolitionist here and there" might object to the protection of slave property then in the territory, but "the justice and propriety of this is as clear as noon-day."

Black congratulated the administration "on this auspicious event." He commended the Lecompton convention for "adhering to the great truths of the democratic creed in the midst of temptations which the virtues of most men would have been too weak to resist." Concluding on a malevolently partisan note, he asserted that the news, "so full of hope to every American patriot," would bring sorrow only to the "black-republican politicians [who] had all their capital staked on the chances of disorder and confusion in Kansas." Their enterprise had failed, and the Republican party would soon be reduced "to its original nothingness." After accusing Republicans of concealing or distorting the truth about the constitution, Black failed to explain why the people were denied the option of rejecting it.

Several editorials in subsequent issues of the *Union* rounded out the administration's defense. One of them argued that the clause in the Kansas-Nebraska Act authorizing the people of a territory to regulate their own domestic institutions was written "with exclusive reference to the slavery question." To object to the Lecompton constitution because of its protection of existing slave property was a "contemptible quibble," for if the majority voted for the constitution without slavery Kansas would be free "to all intents and purposes." Moreover, it claimed, the property rights of slaveholders then living in Kansas were protected by the Dred Scott decision even after statehood. Admitting that it had once strongly favored submission of the entire constitution, the *Union* claimed to have changed because of "considerations of high duty to the country." Those who would vote against the slavery clause, it explained, "would also vote against every other clause," because they denied the legality of the convention and preferred the Topeka constitution. In short, the constitution could not be submitted because the majority would vote it down![38]

How Buchanan, a shrewd and experienced politician, one of the best trained Presidents the country has ever had, could have been responsible for a political disaster of such magnitude has been variously explained by hostile contemporaries and by historians. According to his modern biographer, Buchanan was a legalist and accepted the constitution because the Lecompton convention was a legal body, and no law required it to provide for full ratification.[39] It is true that neither he nor Governor Walker had questioned the manner in which the delegates were elected or their authority to meet and write a constitution. But Buchanan had understood the convention's legality in July when he vowed that he would stand or fall on the issue of ratification. Never before had he indicated that he would be helpless if the convention refused his advice. He was, in fact, not helpless, for he could have urged Congress to reject the constitution if it were not approved by the voters. He knew that Congress had no constitutional obligation to admit a territory to statehood without examining its constitution and, if the majority chose, requiring that it be ratified. In the past, Congress had refused to admit Missouri before certain conditions were met; it had twice rejected petitions for admission from Utah Territory; and it had made popular ratification of Minnesota's constitution a requirement for statehood. A majority was available in the House of Representatives to impose the same condition on Kansas—as it ultimately did.

By far the most common explanation among political opponents and critical historians focused on the character of the man. Buchanan, they claimed, was weak, unable to resist the immense pressure of proslavery Southerners, frightened by the secessionists, and dominated by the strong men in his Cabinet, notably Cobb, Thompson, and Black. That southern pressure on him was strong and persistent was true. His friend Robert Tyler tried to poison his mind against Walker, describing the governor's Kansas policy as either a "gross blunder" or a "revolting act of treachery." Walker, he suggested, was trying to make a great man of himself, "and this *outside* the Democratic Party." John Slidell, Jefferson Davis, and other southern Senators warned of terrible consequences if Kansas were not admitted with the Lecompton constitution.[40]

Even so, Buchanan's decision to support the constitution was not a sign of inability to resist pressure, for northern Democrats were at least as insistent that he stand by his commitment to full submission. Loyal Kansas Democrats warned him that the party would be ruined in the territory if the convention were sustained. One reported that Walker had the support of nineteen-twentieths of the administration's friends. "I have consulted freely with our best and leading democrats," he wrote, "who all concur with me that [he] has done his duty well and faithfully."[41] Clearly, Buchanan was strong enough to ignore heavy pressure when he disagreed with those who applied it.

The charge that he was a puppet in the hands of a powerful proslavery Cabinet clique had its origin in the partisan Republican press of his day, but there is a good deal of evidence to refute it. None of the President's advisers, including Cobb and Thompson, would have had the temerity to usurp his authority to determine administration policy toward the Lecompton constitution. One incident made clear who was in charge. After Black had written the *Union* editorial of November 18, he gave it to Buchanan to read and approve. When it was published, Buchanan was annoyed to discover that Black had deleted a flattering reference to Walker's performance as governor of Kansas. He immediately sent a sharp note to Black: "What is the reason for this? It will give just cause for offence to Governor Walker's friends; and I confess I am much worried myself at the omission." The next day, another editorial in the *Union* tendered Walker "heartfelt congratulations" for urgently pressing the policy of submission, even though it did not come in quite the form he had demanded. Black had rectified his error.[42]

A more plausible explanation for Buchanan's Lecompton policy is that there was no significant difference between his own outlook and that of the Southerners in his Cabinet. They shared an extreme dislike of abolitionists and Republicans, and they saw no great wrong in the existence of black slavery. Ultimately they gravitated easily toward the position of the Lecompton moderates and concluded that the choice offered the Kansas voters was sufficient to redeem their pledge. Congressional approval of the Lecompton constitution was, after all, the quickest way to dispose of the divisive Kansas issue. After admission, Kansans could deal with their problems as they saw fit without creating a national crisis. The conclusion seems warranted that Buchanan's policy, while pleasing to most Southerners, was nevertheless *his* policy, not one forced upon him by others.

Buchanan seemed confident that, following the vote in Kansas on December 21, executive pressure would be sufficient to bring enough northern Democrats in line to get an admission bill through both houses of Congress. Meanwhile, if the Lecompton issue caused a political storm in the North, Senator Douglas himself had provided an instructive precedent in 1854. For a time, his Kansas-Nebraska Act had also raised one "hell of a fuss." Yet, within two years, the Democrats had pulled themselves together sufficiently to win another presidential election. This, after all, was only 1857, and three years should be time enough for another crisis to pass. Apparently these calculations induced a normally cautious President to risk the future of both his party and the Union.

In less than a month after the autumn elections Republican optimism had returned. The administration had handed them the Kansas issue, and the national Democracy was in disarray. An Ohio Republican congratulated Governor Chase "upon the present highly auspicious state of things in Kansas. They never were better because they never were worse. . . . [For] like some diseases, the only hope of betterment lies in their getting worse." The action of the Lecompton convention "is just what I would have had it. It is but the denouement of a drama cast some three years ago and was a necessary part of the original plot which would have lacked artistic harmony and unity without it." A member of the Ohio Republican Executive Committee found the Kansas question "more exciting and interesting than ever. Let our friends stand fast. . . . There is to be a 'good time coming.'" The administration, a friend wrote to Sumner, "has determined that gentlemen of your way of thinking shall not speedily find your occupation gone." The Kansas-Nebraska Act seemed to have left "a running sore from which we are destined never to recover."[43]

According to the Republican press, the Lecompton fraud was the logical consequence of the repeal of the Missouri Compromise, and Douglas therefore was as responsible for it as Buchanan. A Chicago editor claimed that Buchanan had violated no principle of Douglas's Kansas-Nebraska Act, or of the Democratic party. The Slave Power, scoffed the *National Era,* had forced the Democracy "from one position to another" until no ground was left for it but "indecent and absolute submission to its imperious will." Conservative northern Whigs and Americans shared the indignation of Republicans. Millard Fillmore considered the action of the Lecompton convention "so infamous a fraud" that it would provoke the entire North to rise up against it. The Washington *National Intelligencer* deplored the convention's "tortuous plan of indirect and partial submission" and predicted that it would simply prolong sectional agitation.[44] By his endorsement of the Lecompton "juggle," Buchanan had provided another bridge for Fillmore voters to cross into the camp of the Republicans.

After the Washington *Union* had stated Buchanan's position, most southern critics of the Lecompton convention fell into line and agreed that the slavery issue had been fairly presented to the Kansas voters. For the Richmond *Enquirer* the switch was obviously painful. Although it now praised the work of the convention, it remained "firmly convinced" that it would have been better to submit the whole constitution to the people. It agreed with those who denied that partial submission fully carried out the principle of popular sovereignty, and it credited northern Democratic critics with "honest and patriotic intentions." But it urged them to accept the President's policy in order to avoid "a renewal of civil strife in Kansas, and increasing the bitterness of the sectional contest." A few southern dissenters would not yield. The Louisville *Democrat* still questioned the legality of the Lecompton constitution and urged Congress to reject it. "The Black Republicans," it lamented, "may rest from their labors just now if their opponents will do so well for them."[45] As for those Southerners who had been indifferent to the issue of slavery in Kansas, there is no evidence that Buchanan's support of the Lecompton fraud made them any less so.

Nevertheless, many Democrats, especially in the Deep South, were prepared to risk alienating their northern political allies in pressing Congress to admit Kansas to statehood immediately after the December 21 election. A Georgia editor anticipated a crisis "more violent and more dangerous" than any in the past, but he was ready to test "severely" the reliability of northern Democrats. The Memphis *Appeal* hoped that "no good Democrat [would] be found acting with the Black Republicans in their diabolical effort to keep the [Kansas] question open." It was a simple matter of law and order, asserted the Richmond *Sentinel.* "Is Kansas to be governed by an organized social community or is it to be ruled by a mob?" To submit the entire constitution to the free-state mob "would be casting pearls before swine, simply that they might have the satisfaction of trampling them under foot." The opposition Whig-Americans in the Deep South, if anything, tried to outdo the Democratic fire-eaters in their shrill demands for congressional approval of the Lecompton constitution.[46]

The response of northern Democrats to the *Union* editorial was panic. All the optimism of recent weeks vanished as there now seemed to be no way to avoid disaster for their party and, many feared, for the Union as well. The choice they had to make between repudiating their own administration or supporting it regardless of public opinion promised to lead, one as much as the other, to an almost certain Republican victory in 1860. In the first instance, the national Democracy would be fragmented; in the second, it would face defeat in every northern state. For the past three years Kansas had indeed been a "running sore," and now it seemed to have intensified the sectional conflict to a point where no national political organization could survive.

If there were any possibility of escape from this dilemma, Buchanan would have to be persuaded to alter his course—to support Governor Walker and, without condoning the tactics of the free-state party or passing judgment on the Lecompton constitution, to ask Congress to return the document for ratification. A favorable result was not likely, for Walker, during his interview, had not moved him with warnings of renewed violence in Kansas.[47] Still, there was a chance. The President had not yet spoken officially, and he might be persuaded to reconsider his course before his first annual message was sent to Congress in early December. There would be angry protests from the South, but most northern Democrats, concerned first about their own survival, were prepared to take that risk. Accordingly, in the three weeks between the unofficial *Union* editorial and the organization of the new Congress, they made one last effort to change Buchanan's mind.

From New Hampshire he heard of the "very deep anxiety" that Kansas would again "break down the Democracy" and "sever the country." To ask for full submission of the constitution "causes delay merely and is in no event fatal, while the imposition of a Constitution against the . . . wishes of the people would be disastrous and may cause a civil war." From New York, George Bancroft wrote: "I entreat you, as one who most sincerely wishes honor and success to your administration, not to endorse the Lecompton Constitution. The democracy regard that usurpation as a stab at their principles. . . . Justice, the peace of the country, the present strength of your administration, its standing with posterity, all point to the same policy." A Pennsylvanian warned Black that most Democrats "loudly proclaim that the Constitution should be repudiated by Congress and that upon this depends the very existence of our party in the North. . . . This movement is much more serious than you imagine."[48]

From the West, James P. France, editor of the Springfield *Illinois State Reg-*

ister, appealed to the President through his old friend, Senator Bigler. His was a letter not to be taken lightly. On a table in his office he had "nearly a bushel of letters and communications" concerning Kansas affairs. After reading them he was convinced that to admit Kansas with its constitution unratified would cause the Democratic party to lose the entire Northwest, and not only to be defeated in 1860 but "ruined beyond redemption." The opposition was so overwhelming, France asserted, that "Gen. Jackson rising from the dead and advocating the Lecompton constitution would not receive one hundred votes in Illinois."[49]

Buchanan, thinking he knew better, was not impressed. Sooner or later every Democratic editor and party leader had to decide which horn of the dilemma to seize. Many considerations entered into their decisions: personal relations with the President; patronage expectations; political ambitions; how to minimize damage to the party; individual feelings about slavery and the South; and, by no means a minor factor, the morality of the Lecompton convention's action. Not surprisingly, some hesitated, and some changed their minds as the controversy developed. One observer expected to witness "odd incidents of crossing over, and 'forward and back' among the Democratic journals of the North." He was not disappointed. On November 18, before news of the *Union* editorial had arrived, Bennett's New York *Herald* denounced the Lecompton convention as "a contemptible farce" and was certain that the President would oppose the admission of Kansas under any constitution that had not been ratified. Three days later, after learning where Buchanan stood, Bennett decided that it would be best not to "chaffer upon secondary issues" but "to seize upon the first chance for a compromise, and make the most of it." The Cincinnati *Enquirer* and Albany *Atlas and Argus* went through a bewildering series of switches—first denouncing the Lecompton fraud, then giving it qualified support, then condemning both Kansas parties, then returning to qualified support—before joining a scattering of other Democratic journals on the administration's side.[50]

The Philadelphia *Pennsylvanian* was in the pro-Lecompton minority, but its influence was insignificant compared with that of Forney's Philadelphia *Press*. That "organ of the disaffected," federal District Attorney James C. Van Dyke informed Buchanan, had "thrown itself into the embraces of the abolition and disorganizing presses of the North." In spite of his bitterness, Forney made his break with Buchanan slowly and with seeming reluctance. Sometime after the *Union* editorial he called on the President and tried to persuade him to stand by his commitment to full submission. Impelled "by a thousand considerations of self-respect and political associations," the *Press* deeply deplored the necessity of differing with the administration. Yet, without saying a harsh word against Buchanan, Forney maintained his opposition to the "Kansas-Calhoun Constitution." He ridiculed the idea that the constitution should not be submitted to the voters "*because* they do not approve of it." As to the reasons for their opposition, "are we to set up the principle that *the motives which influence voters . . . are to be canvassed?*"[51]

Like Forney, most other anti-Lecompton editors directed their attacks against the Washington *Union* rather than against Buchanan. Refusing to believe that the *Union* could have spoken for him, the Detroit *Free Press* accused the editor of a "deliberate attempt to bring the great democratic doctrine of popular sovereignty into ridicule and contempt" and to "disintegrate and destroy the democratic party." The *Union* editor, asserted the *Illinois State Register,* "in the insanity of his course," had proved himself "unworthy of the confidence or support" of the Democracy. The Indianapolis *Indiana State Sentinel,* hitherto the organ of the state's proslavery Senator Bright, after declaring its confidence in Buchanan, asserted that the Lecompton convention had committed "an act of despotism, which should be reprobated by the Democratic party," as it had been "with singular unanimity" by the northern Democratic press.[52]

With each passing day it became more and more difficult for Democrats to attack the Lecompton fraud while persisting in the fiction of Buchanan's innocence. The *Union,* with the administration's blessing, grew increasingly truculent in its references to dissenting editors. It began by expressing regret that some were "warmly cooperating with the abolition organs," and it hoped that, after a sober second thought, they would renounce their present "odious association." It followed with a warning that no Democrat would be held guiltless who sought "to promote his peculiar views by association with black republicanism." To adopt even briefly the "fanatical appeals of the enemy" would be regarded "as the preliminary steps of a formal desertion." Finally, in anger, it turned on Forney and the Philadelphia *Press:* "By common consent that journal has won the distinction of leadership in the onslaught upon the late Kansas convention." Threatening Forney with serious consequences for his posture of "political bravery," the *Union* accused him of joining the "black republicans whom he so gallantly fought in former contests."[53] Buchanan's message to Congress soon followed, putting an end to the game of hide-and-seek with his northern Democratic critics.

Although Senator Douglas had made no public statement, rumors were afloat that he would oppose any attempt to admit Kansas with a constitution which had not been approved by a popular vote. "Now this is no news to us," declared the Columbus *Ohio Statesman.* "Mr. Douglas is a statesman of the first order, a democrat of unquestioned integrity, and a man of unsullied honor." To accept the "Calhoun usurpation" would be to "disgrace himself as a man, and to leave him without a political friend in the North."[54]

Brooding at his home in Chicago, Douglas had ample cause for disappointment, regret, and anger. His Kansas-Nebraska Act had failed to fulfill his hope that popular sovereignty would enable Congress to avoid divisive conflicts over slavery expansion. His "great principle" had thus far produced only corrupt territorial elections, an unrepresentative constitutional convention, and a constitution that Kansas voters would reject overwhelmingly if given a chance. Perhaps Douglas now regretted that he had not raised his voice against the first territorial legislature, or against the manner in which delegates to the constitutional convention had been chosen, and that he had failed to respond to Calhoun's request for advice. It was too late for him to question the legality of the convention, nor could he cite a constitutional provision or an act of Congress explicitly *requiring* the constitution to be submitted for ratification. At best he could argue that the popular sovereignty provision of the Kansas-Nebraska Act *implied* ratification, or he could invoke the clear right of Congress, at its discretion, to refuse Kansas statehood without it. Douglas could not accept Buchanan's policy without publicly abandoning his principle of territorial self-determination and majority rule.

His decision to oppose the administration was a crucial turning point in his career and an event of major historical significance. Yet it lacked the drama and suspense that he would have created if he had gone through a period of agonizing indecision before resolving to risk all for the sake of a great principle. Instead, Douglas knew at once the truth of a tart observation in the Springfield *Illinois State Journal* that, "without a change of front," his re-election to the Senate the following year would be "a moral impossibility." Moreover, if the repeal of the Missouri Compromise resulted in the admission of Kansas as a slave state, he would be "dead as a herring" even in his own party. In short, the cost of loyalty to the President, for whom he felt little affection, would be a humiliating end to a proud and powerful Senator's political career.[55]

Unquestionably there was a moral dimension to his decision, for he was truly appalled at the shabby attempt of a proslavery minority to force its will upon so large an antislavery majority. But the morality of the case so obviously coincided with political expediency that he never doubted the position he must take. He had merely to decide upon the appropriate time formally and publicly to make his position known. To him a break with Buchanan was less distressing than the resulting loss of political friends in the South. For that loss he blamed Buchanan's failure to honor his own commitment to ratification, which doubtless helped to explain the anger his words would soon reveal.[56]

Douglas did receive a few appeals from Kansas friends to accept the Lecompton compromise as "the best submission we could get," because so many delegates opposed submission in any form. A. J. Isaacs, a former district attorney in Kansas, denounced Walker for deserting them and "making war upon the constitution." A former Kansas surveyor informed Douglas that the constitution had been written by his friends with the aim of taking the territory out of national politics and making it a Democratic state. From an old St. Louis friend, Samuel Treat, he received an impressive defense of the convention's legality and of its exclusive right to decide for or against submission. Its decision, Treat maintained, was "prudent," because the territory was filled with Topeka "rebels" whose object was "anarchy, for partisan and, it may be, worse purposes. To submit to them the whole [constitution], would be to prolong indefinitely the Kansas trouble."[57]

This scattering of pro-Lecompton letters was insignificant compared with the deluge of indignant protests against it. Some were from politically active Democrats, such as James W. Sheahan, editor of the Chicago *Times,* who urged Douglas not to yield an inch. To admit Kansas as a slave state, he asserted, "would be destructive of everything in Illinois. We could never recover from it." John A. McClernand, a former Illinois Congressman, advised him, as chairman of the Senate Committee on Territories, to introduce a bill for a new Kansas convention before the Republicans did. But the great majority of letters came from rank-and-file Democrats who neither held nor sought public office. Many, claiming that they had never written to a politician before, apologized for intruding on his time. Most took for granted that Douglas would resist approval of an unratified constitution and simply pledged support. Typically, an Urbana correspondent wrote: "Your course in regard to the admission of Kansas under a constitution *not* submitted to her people cannot be doubted by your friends." A Chicago Democrat reported that he had assured friends in Indiana that Douglas would never agree to any action "that would violate the Kansas bill." Another constituent looked forward confidently to the day when he would make known his intention to wage "an uncompromising war against the sentiments . . . of the Administration."[58]

Letters poured in from every state in the old Northwest. From Iowa, Douglas heard that Democrats looked to him "for the safety and success of the party for the next three years," after which they hoped to elect him President. A Michigan Democrat assured him that there was "but one sentiment—that Gov. Walker must be sustained," or "we resign ourselves to a hopeless minority." An angry letter from a Democratic member of the Wisconsin legislature asserted that if Buchanan supported the Lecompton fraud, "he will have politically d———d himself and d———d he will deserve to be." An Ohio admirer reported that the Senator's friends had been "waiting anxiously" for him to speak out, for it would "act as a tonic to the party." From the East, George Bancroft begged him not to permit the Kansas-Nebraska Act "to become in the hands of timid or unprincipled men an imposture and a sham." A Pennsylvanian assured Douglas that Buchanan could not have carried his state without a Democratic pledge that the people of Kansas would be permitted to vote on their constitution.[59] Douglas's self-image at the time of the Lecompton crisis was that of a man on a dangerous mission, risking all to vindicate his "great principle"; yet he had at his command nearly the whole of the northern Democracy, and he obviously relished the role he played. Outside the South the administration held the support of a handful of editors, most of the officeholders, and a small fraction of the party rank-and-file. Buchanan, not Douglas, was the man besieged.

Douglas would make no public statement until the President had formally announced his policy in his first message to Congress. Meanwhile, the Chicago *Times* spoke for him. As soon as the proceedings of the Lecompton convention were known, it asserted that the fate of the constitution was sealed, for the people would never accept a fundamental law making slavery a perpetual institution. That document was not worth the paper it disfigured, and any officers elected under it would have no more authority than those of the Topeka government. The *Times* ridiculed the system of "submission" which denied the people the right to vote against it.

On November 26, Douglas, betraying the anger he felt, used the *Times* for an anonymous response to Black's editorial in the Washington *Union*. "The *Union* may exult," his organ retorted, "but the *Union* is not the administration and the *Union* is not the Democratic party." Claiming no authority to speak for Douglas, it ventured the prediction that he would not "stand coldly back while the South [crammed] slavery down the throats of the people of that or any other territory, without the consent of the people themselves." Moreover, "We . . . refuse to accept the new teaching; deny the authority of the oracle that proclaims it and hesitate not to stamp it as one of those impudent exhibitions of folly which are the natural result of a diseased mind." A week later the *Times,* still observing the fiction that the *Union* did not express the views of the administration, deplored its "political heresies" which were "calculated to . . . destroy the Democratic party." The issue was no longer slavery or no slavery but whether Congress should admit Kansas with a constitution which everyone knew "would be repudiated by the people."[60]

Although Douglas would speak publicly only through editor Sheahan and the Chicago *Times,* he expressed his feelings freely and bluntly in letters to friends and in private conversations with both Democrats and Republicans. Buchanan, he wrote, had made "a fatal mistake, and got us all into trouble." Douglas's course was plain: he must stand on the principle of the Kansas-Nebraska Act and "defend it against all assaults from any quarter." The battle would soon begin, he cautioned the editor of the *Illinois State Register.* "Keep the ball rolling, and the party united. It will be all right in the end." At a meeting with several Republican leaders in Chicago, Douglas made their "eyes stick out" by his belligerent speech. Boasting that he had "made Mr. James Buchanan," he reportedly vowed that he would "unmake him!" Late in November he traveled east, "leaving quite a smoke in his rear," conferring with Walker in New York before going on to the capital for the opening of Congress.[61]

Arriving in Washington on December 2, Douglas had an interview with the President the following day. Precisely what was said at that historic meeting is uncertain, for the newspaper reports came from persons who were not present, and from Douglas's recollection several years later. The traditional account is as dramatic as the occasion demanded. The interview began on a friendly note but quickly turned sour when Buchanan confirmed what Walker had reported to Douglas in New York. Without the courtesy of consulting him as chairman of the Senate Committee on Territories, Buchanan had made up his mind to ask approval of the Lecompton constitution. He had completed his message to Congress and had sent the relevant section on Kansas to Acting Governor Stanton. Insisting upon a speedy resolution of the Kansas issue, he refused Douglas's request to delay his decision until after the territorial vote on December 21. Douglas then asserted angrily that approving the Lecompton fraud would put a potent weapon in the hands of the Republicans and that he intended to oppose it. Buchanan threatened party discipline, demanding that Douglas give his support to the administration's policy. He advised Douglas to remember that two Democratic Senators who had defied President Jackson had been driven from the party. Douglas's reply was a virtual declaration of war: "Mr. President, I wish you to remember that General Jackson is dead."[62]

Republicans, who had already been forced by circumstances to defend Douglas's principle of popular sovereignty in Kansas, were of two minds about how to deal with Douglas himself. Could the author of the Kansas-Nebraska Act, the man they had damned as an agent of the Slave Power, redeem himself? Some, believing that he would be forced out of the Democratic party, were ready to accept him as an ally in the struggle to make that territory a free state. One Ohio "out and out Republican" urged him to become "*the man for the hour* and make to yourself troops of *new* friends in all the land." Two former Democrats from New York and Indiana assured him that their trust would be restored if he steadfastly demanded that the Lecompton constitution be submitted to the Kansas electorate. Douglas, the New Yorker believed, could still leave as his legacy "the fairest record of any man now living." A Massachusetts Republican editor thought that Douglas might yet prove that he was a statesman if he led the fight for a new Kansas constitutional convention. In that battle he would win "the friendship, not just the cooperation, of the Republican party."[63]

Others, especially Illinois Republicans who thought they knew Douglas better, were skeptical. One of them was convinced that his object was "to raise the standard of rebellion and detach as many republicans as possible to follow him as leader." Charles H. Ray, editor of the Chicago *Tribune,* believed that he was "playing the part of injured innocence, saying to Republicans 'I have been unjustly accused. I will show you that I will do what I promised.'"According to Ray, Douglas had even sent a man to the *Tribune* office "to say that we ought not to pitch into him so when he is doing what we all want to do." Ray and others feared that he would make "a good deal of capital" out of his proposal to introduce an enabling act for Kansas, similar to that of Minnesota, requiring constitutional ratification. They urged Senator Lyman Trumbull to introduce his own bill, "and let him follow *our* lead." Observing that many Republicans were "relenting a little" toward Douglas, one of the skeptics insisted that he did not "merit endorsement or absolution for an act which after all is but one of self-preservation."[64]

Both Douglas and Trumbull were in Washington for the opening of the first session of the Thirty-fifth Congress. In that body a final epic battle over slavery in Kansas would be waged. Facetiously, unaware of its consequences, an Illinois Republican wrote, "We are looking for fun in Congress early in the session."[65]

CHAPTER **11**

Politics as Tragedy: Buchanan's Decision

In the late autumn of 1857, news of the new crisis in Kansas filled the columns of the press, troubled state and national politicians, and seemed to arouse strong feelings among much of the electorate. Kansas deserved the public attention it received, for the manner in which Congress and the administration dealt with the Lecompton issue ultimately would affect the lives of everyone. Yet, at that time, many regarded this political controversy as less important than various concurrent events that touched their lives more immediately and directly. Historical events overlap, interrelate, and are invariably complex, and those who experienced them rarely understood their consequences. To millions of southern slaves, tens of thousands of unemployed urban workingmen, most isolated residents of California and Utah, and unnumbered rural, provincial Northerners and Southerners, Kansas was too remote to elicit more than casual concern.

Even the central figures in the Lecompton imbroglio were distracted by problems arising from other sources. Residents of Kansas Territory worried about the impact of the economic recession on commodity prices and land values as well as about the future of slavery when they achieved statehood. Governor Walker hastened east in November not only to confer with the President about Kansas affairs but to deal with his faltering private business interests. Seward, like numerous other Congressmen, was severely hurt by the commercial panic and struggled with his personal finances as he helped to shape Republican strategy for the Senate debate on Lecompton. Douglas waged his battle against the administration while deeply distressed about the illness of his wife and frantic about heavy losses from speculative investments.

As for Buchanan, although Kansas was by far the most serious problem confronting him, it was only one of many. He devoted most of his first annual message to Congress to other matters: to the proposed transcontinental railroad, for which he urged federal support; to the financial panic and the need for currency and banking reforms; to the affairs of the Mormons in Utah and his reasons for dispatching a military expedition; to foreign relations, especially to events in Nicaragua, from which the State Department had recently secured a treaty granting transit rights across its territory.

In mid-November, at the very moment that the President was making his crucial Lecompton decision, his attention was diverted by a second attempt of the filibuster William Walker and another ragtag army to overthrow the government of Nicaragua. Walker, still claiming to be that country's legitimate president, began to plan a triumphant return soon after his expulsion the previous May. With the enthusiastic support of numerous editors and politicians in the Deep South, he went about openly and confidently raising men and money When Walker's intentions became clear, Buchanan ordered federal officers to prevent his departure from any American port, and he assured the British Minister, Lord Napier, that a filibustering invasion of Nicaragua would not be tolerated.

On November 10, Walker was arrested in New Orleans, brought before a United States district judge on a charge of preparing a military expedition in violation of federal neutrality laws, and released on $2000 bail. That night some two hundred filibusters boarded Walker's ship, the *Fashion,* escaped from New Orleans, and sailed to Mobile. Walker and his staff followed them on a mail steamer. On November 14 the expedition, having managed to deceive federal customs inspectors, set sail for Nicaragua. On November 24, after eluding United States naval vessels, Walker and most of his filibusters landed at San Juan del Norte, expecting reinforcements to follow. Early in December, Commodore Hiram Paulding arrived on his flagship the *Wabash* with two other vessels and a body of marines sufficiently large to surround the filibusters' camp and force Walker to surrender. According to Paulding, "this lion-hearted devil," when taken on board, "wept like a child." Late in December, Walker was sent to Washington, where Secretary of State Cass informed him that he would not be held in custody unless some charge was brought against him in a federal court. None was, and this grim and obsessed man was therefore free to mount still another invasion of Nicaragua, one that ended in 1860 with his death before a Honduran firing squad.[1]

Although Paulding's instructions were vague, he clearly had no authority, once the filibusters had landed on Nicaraguan soil, to arrest them for violating the laws of the United States. For a time southern proslavery expansionists attacked the Commodore violently for his "most unparalleled and unpardonable outrage." Resolutions adopted at a large public meeting in Mobile praised the invasion as the "forerunner of the Americanization of Nicaragua," promising "new power to the southern States," and urged Southerners to aid the movement "in every proper form." In the Republican press, however, Paulding was the hero, and his bold action was "the most creditable thing" that had happened during the Buchanan administration.[2]

This episode gave Buchanan an opportunity, in his annual message and in a special message the following month, to refute the charge that he was the loyal servant of the Slave Power. Conceding that Paulding had "committed a grave error" by capturing the filibusters on Nicaraguan soil, he asserted that this "gallant officer" nevertheless had acted from "pure and patriotic motives" in the sincere belief that he was "vindicating the honor of his country." Buchanan announced his determination to enforce federal neutrality laws and condemned the action of Walker and other filibusters as "robbery and murder." Ever the expansionist, he affirmed that it was "the destiny of our race to spread themselves over the continent of North America," but this would occur peacefully and for the good of all if permitted to take its natural course. Unfortunately the filibusters had caused the people of Central America "to regard us with dread and suspicion," and the United States had lost much of its influence in consequence of their "lawless expeditions."

Nicaragua briefly provoked an animated debate on the floor of Congress, but it was a mere contretemps, soon lost in the furious controversy over Lecompton.

Early in December, Congressmen began to arrive in Washington, the Republicans cheerful and confident, the Democrats worried and uncertain. If Kansas could be saved for freedom, wrote a New York Republican, it would be "the first grand victory won over Slavery during the present generation." James Gordon Bennett's Democratic New York *Herald,* having first firmly denounced the Lecompton fraud and then quickly switched to the administration's position, now joined the waverers, contending that it was too early to decide one way or the other. The "alarming entanglement" of Kansas affairs, it feared, threatened not only a violent disruption of the Democratic party but a shock that would shake the Union to its foundations.[3]

Democratic leaders tried frantically to prevent a party split. Alexander H. Stephens and other moderate Southerners called on Douglas at his home and begged him to avoid a break with the administration and with his friends in the South. Secretary of the Navy Toucey urged him to reconsider, and Buchanan conferred with him a second time. Prior to the opening of Congress the House Democratic caucus agreed not to discuss the Lecompton issue or to put members on record. It nominated James L. Orr of South Carolina, a moderate Unionist, for Speaker and two friends of Douglas for the offices of House clerk and printer. The Senate Democratic caucus agreed to continue Douglas as chairman of the Committee on Territories. All appeals to party loyalty and gestures of appeasement left him unmoved. In a curt reply to another word of caution from Buchanan, he said something to the effect that, having taken a through ticket and checked all his baggage, he would not turn back. "He is against us," reported Stephens unhappily. "I fear he will do us great damage." The battle would soon begin, a determined Douglas wrote to a friend, vowing that he would "defend the right of the people to govern themselves against all assaults from all quarters."[4]

On December 7 the Thirty-fifth Congress met and organized for its first session. The Senate elected Benjamin Fitzpatrick, senior Senator from Alabama, President *pro tem,* and the House elected Orr to replace Banks as Speaker. The Democratic candidates for other congressional offices were quickly chosen, and a few days later the standing committees were appointed. Early in the session, in a pleasant ceremony, Speaker Orr led the members of the House out of their cramped and poorly ventilated old quarters into an elegant new and more spacious chamber just completed in the south wing of the Capitol. The occasion provided a rare interlude of warmth and amiability in a session otherwise full of tension.

In the Senate the Democrats held thirty-seven seats, giving them a majority of fourteen. Twenty-five of the Democrats came from the slave states and included three newly elected members destined for fame: Jefferson Davis of Mississippi, James Henry Hammond of South Carolina, and Andrew Johnson of Tennessee. Five Whig-American Senators also came from the South. Seven of the twenty Republicans were serving their first terms, among them Zachariah Chandler of Michigan, a sturdy antislavery radical and rough but effective debater who would long dominate his party's state organization. Sumner, recently returned from Europe and looking much improved, was still unsure whether he had recovered from Brook's attack sufficiently to resume his Senate duties. Threatened by violence if he appeared in Washington, urged by friends to stay away until fully recovered, he was nevertheless in his seat on December 7, welcomed by Republican colleagues and ignored by most Democrats. He remained in the capital for only two weeks, taking no part in the Kansas debate, and thereafter returned only occasionally to cast a vote.[5]

The House membership consisted of 128 Democrats, 75 of them Southerners and 53 Northerners, 14 Whig-Americans, all of them Southerners, and 92 Republicans. In the House, as in the Senate, Southern Democrats enjoyed not only a numerical advantage within their party caucus but a decided edge in seniority. As a result, they dominated the committees. In the House two-thirds of the major committee chairmanships went to Southerners. In the Senate the important Committee on Commerce, for example, contained four southern and two northern Democrats, with only one Republican representing the entire Great Lakes area, New England, and New York. Republicans protested bitterly. Senator Hannibal Hamlin of Maine described the whole committee structure as "unjust, disproportionate, and sectional." Congress, the judiciary, and the executive department, charged Senator Wilson, were all proslavery, demonstrating that the Democratic party and the proslavery party were identical. "The history of the one, during the past twenty years, must ever be the history of the other." Senator Chandler warned Southerners that the day was close at hand "when the measure you mete to us to-day shall be meted to you." Democratic Senator George Pugh of Ohio agreed that the committees had not been fairly constituted but voted with his party nonetheless.[6]

On December 8, in an atmosphere already charged with hostility, the two houses of Congress listened attentively to the reading of the President's message. Halfway through, when he took up the matter of Kansas, it was quickly evident that all the blandishments of northern Democrats had made no more impact on him than his warnings had made on Douglas. In sketching the background of the Lecompton convention, Buchanan placed the entire responsibility for the present crisis upon the free-state party. The territorial law providing for the election of convention delegates, he claimed, had been "in the main fair and just," and it was regrettable that many had refused to register and vote. Instead they had formed a "revolutionary organization" with the avowed object of overthrowing the lawful government and replacing it with one of their own under the spurious Topeka constitution.

Because the territorial legislature had not required the submission of the constitution for ratification, Buchanan granted that many Kansans had justly feared that slavery would be forced upon them against their will. In this manner he tried to narrow the controversy to the single issue of slavery or no slavery rather than the right of voters to approve or reject the entire constitution. Yet, he did not deny that his instructions to Governor Walker had favored the latter policy and that he had assumed that the Lecompton convention would provide for it. Buchanan strongly recommended that a requirement for submission, made explicit in the Minnesota enabling act, be adhered to on all future occasions.

In the case of Kansas, although he wished that the entire Lecompton constitution had been submitted to the voters, he contended that this requirement had not been written into the Kansas-Nebraska Act, and that the term "domestic institutions" used therein referred only to slavery. Accordingly, the convention's sole obligation was to submit that question to the electorate. In spite of his instructions to Governor Walker and subsequent commitment to full submission, Buchanan now insisted that all he had ever intended was that the people of Kansas should be given a chance to vote for or against slavery, which, he claimed, was the only controversial constitutional issue. The convention had agreed to this, and Kansas voters were now free to settle the matter at the approaching election "in the very mode required by the organic law." Those who refused to vote would do so as "their own voluntary act," and they would be responsible for the consequences.

The slavery question, Buchanan argued, could never be presented to Kansas voters "more clearly nor distinctly" than at present. If this opportunity were rejected, the territory might be involved "for years in domestic discord, and possibly in civil war" before another chance for a peaceful settlement arose. "Kansas has for some years occupied too much of the public attention," he complained. "It is high time this should be directed to far more important objects." Once admitted to the Union, with or without slavery, Kansas would be free to manage its own affairs without causing excitement elsewhere. If any provision of the Lecompton constitution displeased a majority of the people, "no human power [could] prevent them from changing it within a brief period." Was not the peace and quiet of the whole country, Buchanan asked, more important "than the mere temporary triumph of either of the political parties in Kansas?"

Finally, Buchanan referred to the provision in the Lecompton constitution which protected the property of slaveholders then in the territory even if the popular vote was for the constitution without slavery. To him it was a matter of no great consequence and he saw no reason why it should deter the free-state party from voting. The number of slaves in Kansas was small, he said, but even if there had been more "the provision would be equally just and reasonable." As the Supreme Court had ruled in the Dred Scott case, the Constitution of the United States protected slaveholders who had brought their chattels with them to Kansas. Therefore, to have "summarily confiscated the property in slaves already in the Territory would have been an act of gross injustice and contrary to the practice of the older States of the Union which have abolished slavery."

In the light of this argument, Buchanan's support of the Lecompton constitution meant that he advocated the admission of Kansas as a slave state no matter what the voters might decide. By defending the right of slaveholders to remain there with their property in spite of a vote against slavery, he introduced an entirely new issue into the territorial controversy. Buchanan's argument went well beyond the rights given slaveholders in the Dred Scott case, for the Court did not question the authority of a territory, when ready for statehood, not only to prohibit the future introduction of slaves but to abolish whatever slavery might then exist within its borders. In effect, his novel doctrine denied the right of *any* territory where slaveholders had chosen to settle to become entirely a free state regardless of the wishes of the majority. Perhaps Buchanan's doctrine, as incorporated in the Lecompton constitution, would be tested in another case before Taney's proslavery Court.

At the very least his doctrine was full of mischief. Moreover, it was based on bad history. The older states of the Northeast, when they abolished slavery, had in fact deprived slaveholders of their property without compensation, some gradually, as in Pennsylvania, some immediately, as in Massachusetts. His reasoning was equally faulty. By prohibiting all slavery in Kansas at the time of

statehood the convention would have been no more guilty of confiscating property than of violating the Dred Scott decision. The option would have remained
open to every slaveholder still in Kansas to remove his slaves promptly and settle
somewhere else, as some already had done.

Nevertheless, Buchanan was now publicly committed and seemed remarkably confident that ultimately he would have his way.

As soon as the President's message had been read, the eyes of colleagues and
spectators turned to Douglas as he rose for a brief response. Moving that the
message be printed, he remarked that he had listened to it with great pleasure
and concurred cordially in most of what it contained. On the subject of Kansas,
however, he dissented totally from its approval of the proceedings of the Lecompton convention. At an appropriate time he would give the reasons for his dissent
and vindicate the right of the people of Kansas "to form and regulate their
domestic institutions in their own way according to the organic act." Several
others spoke briefly in defense of or opposition to Buchanan's position, usually
by way of announcing their intention to speak at length at a later date. Seward
simply expressed his opinion that, in its statements on Kansas affairs, the message
had been "very lame and impotent," and he therefore awaited the arguments of
those who promised to support it. He and other Republicans also awaited the
replies of Democratic dissenters, cheerfully standing by as they carried on their
debate. Only bring it to a close as early as possible, he urged, for Kansas was
again threatened with civil war.[7]

On December 9, the day set for Douglas's reply, the galleries were packed,
the floor was filled with Senators, reporters, and special guests, and the capitol
halls and lobbies swarmed with those unable to gain entrance to the Senate chamber. The Illinois Senator, quick-witted, combative, and sharp-tongued, always
attracted an audience when scheduled to speak, whatever the subject, for his dramatic style of delivery, his pacing and posturing, produced a masterly performance, especially in debate. On this day his audience witnessed an event rare in
the annals of American politics: the spectacle of a major national party leader
rising in a public forum to repudiate the President he had helped to elect. It was
the climax of the Kansas crisis.

His three-hour speech was angry and uncompromising, loaded with sar-
casm, much of it relentlessly logical, some of it painfully self-righteous, all of it
suggesting an occasion no less consequential than Armageddon. Douglas opened
by pretending to believe, after reading the President's message a second time, that
he had not actually recommended the admission of Kansas under the Lecompton
constitution. Rather, he had offered an "unanswerable argument" against it by
expressing regret that the constitution had not been submitted to a popular vote
and by asserting that ratification ought to be the general rule. Douglas agreed

with the President and proposed to apply that rule to the case of Kansas. It was proper that this matter should be submitted to Congress for its consideration, not as an administration measure, but as one for it to approve or reject.

Since Congress was free to act as it saw fit, Douglas declared it essential to inquire whether the Lecompton convention had complied with the provisions of the Kansas-Nebraska Act. Buchanan apparently believed that this organic act merely required the slavery clause in the constitution to be submitted to a popular vote. However, "with profound respect for the President," Douglas claimed that on this point he had committed a "fundamental error." His error was quite understandable, for he was in London when the act was debated and passed. Douglas explained to a presumably misinformed President that its principle of self-government entitled the people of a territory to decide upon all their domestic institutions, not slavery alone. This was his error—an error "radical, fundamental, and, if persevered in, subversive of that platform upon which he was elevated to the Presidency." Therefore, "out of respect to him," Congress ought to return the Lecompton constitution to the people of Kansas to determine whether "each and every clause of it" met their approval.

Douglas then launched into a devastating attack on the behavior of the Lecompton convention. It had met without the authority of an enabling act; it had violated every pledge of the President, of Governor Walker, and of many of its own delegates; it had refused to submit the constitution for ratification because the delegates knew that it would be voted down. Buchanan had no right to tell the people of Kansas that it was a good constitution. "Whether good or bad, whether obnoxious or not, is none of my business and none of yours." As to the constitution's slavery clause, Douglas did not care whether it was "voted down or voted up," but he would not forfeit his honor "in order to enable a small minority of the people of Kansas to defraud the majority."

He loved his party and would sacrifice anything for it except principle. "But if this constitution is to be forced down our throats, in violation of the fundamental principles of free government, under a mode of submission that is a mockery and insult, I will resist it to the last." He would regret to see social and political ties severed, but he would defend the great principle of popular sovereignty even if that were the price. "I will follow that principle wherever its legal and logical consequences may take me," he concluded, "and I will endeavor to defend it against assault from any and all quarters."

When Douglas sat down the applause from the galleries was so loud and prolonged that Senator James M. Mason of Virginia angrily demanded that the galleries be cleared. Mason was persuaded to relent but let the audience know his own judgment of the speech: It was "of little moment . . . a series of monstrous fallacies." Bigler then spoke briefly in defense of the President, urging Douglas to consider what was best for the country and how renewed strife in Kansas could be avoided. He had himself heard free-state people in the territory declare that they would reject any constitution framed at Lecompton. That was what impelled the convention to say, in effect, "If you will not judge of this instrument why should it be submitted to you." Bigler reminded Douglas that in 1856 he had supported the unsuccessful Kansas enabling act, known as the Toombs bill, even though it contained no provision for constitutional ratification. Douglas retorted that it was implied in the bill and emphatically, but not altogether convincingly, denied that he knew that some supporters had preferred not to require it. His position was further compromised by the fact that he had incorporated an explicit provision for ratification in the Minnesota enabling act. Why then had he not demanded it in the Toombs bill?[8]

At length the Senate agreed to postpone further debate until December 14, giving both Douglas and the administration time to mobilize their forces and plan strategy. By the time the debate resumed it was evident that Douglas would have few allies among Democratic Senators. Charles A. Stuart of Michigan, his loyal friend, and David Broderick of California, nursing patronage grievances, were firmly committed to his support and made their positions known. George Pugh of Ohio sympathized with Douglas, knew the sentiment of his constituents, but wavered and could not bring himself to break with the administration. Of the eight remaining northern Democrats, Bigler of Pennsylvania, Jesse Bright and Graham N. Fitch of Indiana, and William M. Gwin of California were staunch administration men, and the others had political reasons of their own for ignoring public opinion in their states and supporting the President. Douglas would have the unanimous support of the Republicans, but they decided, as Seward had advised, not to participate in the December debate, thus permitting Democrats to have their quarrel undisturbed.[9] Three administration Democrats, James S. Green of Missouri, Bigler, and Fitch, spoke for the administration. Until December 23, the last day before the Senate's Christmas recess, when Stuart and Broderick spoke, Douglas waged his battle alone.

His anger mounted as the debate progressed. Green scolded Douglas for opposing a policy that promised peace to the country while favoring one that would prolong indefinitely the controversy over "this most unfortunate subject." The captious opposition to the Lecompton constitution was intended purely to keep up the excitement, and Douglas had given "that fanatical element the benefit of his powerful talents." Douglas replied that he hoped to terminate the Kansas controversy as much as anyone, but "no system of trickery by which the majority are cheated by the minority, will settle this question." He proposed to restore peace by ignoring both the Lecompton and Topeka conventions, passing an enabling act, and authorizing the people to form a constitution and state government for themselves. "Such an act," he predicted, "will restore peace to the country in ninety days. In fact, the day you pass it everything will be quiet in Kansas." Green retorted that Douglas did not know what the people of Kansas wanted. In a remarkable flight of fancy he asserted that a "large majority" of them favored the Lecompton constitution and did not want to bear the expense and risk the excitement of another election.

Bigler deplored the "tone and temper" of Douglas's dissent, especially his resort to "sarcastic ridicule when dealing with the views of the President," his readiness to incite slavery agitation, and his effort to weaken public confidence in the leaders of his own party. Contrary to Douglas, the Lecompton constitution *was* an administration measure, and he endorsed Buchanan's reasons for urging its approval. Bigler did not defend the convention's behavior altogether but claimed that it had been "sufficiently provoked by its enemies."

When he had finished, Douglas engaged the ponderous Pennsylvanian in a running debate, tormenting him unmercifully with questions about what precisely administration policy was. In fact, he said, nothing was before the President, no vote having been taken in Kansas and no application for admission having been made. Well, replied Bigler, Buchanan had approved what had happened in Kansas thus far, "and so far it is an administration measure." He spoke of "other sources" of information concerning administration policy, and Douglas demanded to know who the sources were that authorized him to read men out of the party for not supporting the President. In exasperation Bigler denied that he had read anyone out of the party and asked Douglas, "an experienced and skillful debater," not to take advantage of an "unpracticed debater" like him. Douglas then accused him of insinuating that he had deserted the party and joined the "Black" Republicans. "There are men here," he charged bitterly, "personal enemies of mine—men who would be willing to sink an Administration if they could kill off northern men, and get them out of the way in the future; such men are getting out their tools to denounce me as having abandoned the party." He had heard reports that the President and his Cabinet intended to make an issue "with their patronage, with their favors, against any man merely because he opposed the Lecompton constitution." If differences of opinion on this question were tolerated, the party could act in harmony, but Douglas would maintain his position "whether there be harmony or not."

Fitch, a first-term Senator with a rather dubious claim to his seat, began his speech with startling impudence, assuring the veteran Douglas that he did not intend to read him out of the party. Nevertheless, "a man may, by his own voluntary acts, either by promoting discord within a party, or some other equally obnoxious course, place himself beyond the pale of party organization." Such a man, who would attempt to destroy his party "in return for some past grievance, real or fancied," should consider the lessons to be learned from the ruined careers of Aaron Burr and Martin Van Buren, who similarly betrayed their party. No man could be held guiltless who abandoned the great conservative Democratic party—"the only national party"—over a question of "so little practical importance . . . perhaps, to subserve his selfish purpose." Fitch preferred the course proposed by the President, an old man "with no schemes of personal ambition to subserve," to that of the young, ambitious Douglas, "a candidate past, and perhaps future."

In an acid response, Douglas baited Fitch by claiming that he had himself disagreed with the President's interpretation of the Kansas-Nebraska Act and, with mock earnestness, defending his right to disagree. "God forbid," he said, "that I should ever surrender my right to differ from a President of the United States of my own choice! . . . I know that the President would not respect me if I should thus receive a *dictum* from any authority contrary to my own judgment." Near the close of the long debate Douglas shouted his defiance to the administration and his senatorial critics: "I ask no mercy in relation to this matter. . . . I shall not shrink from the avowal of my opinions and the vindication of my character whenever I choose to do it. . . . It may be an object to worry out my strength by these constant attacks. . . . Whenever I find it failing I will reserve myself, and then come back and take a raking fire at the whole group. [Laughter.]"[10]

By December 23, when it was Stuart's and Broderick's turn to speak, the arguments for and against the Lecompton constitution had been fully aired. Stuart's long speech, although not forcefully delivered, was a temperate, well-reasoned statement of the case for a fair vote on the constitution prior to the admission of Kansas to statehood. Given the strife in that territory, he asked, what was to be expected of an irregular convention whose delegates were chosen in a rigged election? By denying Kansans the option of voting against the constitution it clearly intended to defeat the majority by "a trick and a fraud." Stuart stressed the provision against interfering with the slaves then in the territory, as well as their increase. "Is that a fair submission of the question of slavery to the people of Kansas?" He asked each colleague whether he would, in his own state, "consent to go into an election when the prime man of [his] opponents [John Calhoun] was to appoint the inspectors, receive the returns, and count the votes." He was as eager as any man to be rid of "this eternal and interminable question of slavery," but accepting the Lecompton constitution would simply "light up the torch of civil discord throughout this Union." Alternatively, if the people of Kansas were permitted to settle the question by a majority vote, "all will be peace."

Broderick then rose to speak, "very much embarrassed in doing so," he said, because it was his first attempt to address the Senate. He quickly warmed to his task. In his brief, blunt remarks Broderick held Buchanan wholly responsible for the present state of affairs. He was the first President ever to step down from his exalted position and "attempt to coerce the people into a base submission to the will of an illegal body of men." The slavery question, Broderick claimed, had already been submitted to the people of Kansas in their October territorial election, and they had settled it conclusively by electing a free-state legislature. He was astonished at their forbearance. If they had seized the Lecompton delegates "and flogged them, or cut off their ears, and driven them out of the country, I would have applauded them for the act." On that note the Senate recessed until January.[11]

Because Douglas was the central figure, the debate in the Senate was more dramatic than that in the House of Representatives, but it was less crucial. The upper chamber, with its twenty-five southern and at least eight loyal northern Democrats, would approve the Lecompton constitution by a comfortable margin. In the House, however, among the 53 Northerners in the Democratic majority, the administration could not confidently assume the support of more than half. Their votes combined with those of the 75 southern Democrats left the pro-Lecompton group fifteen to twenty votes short of the 118 required for a majority. Since the fourteen southern Whig-Americans could hardly be trusted to come solidly to the support of a Democratic administration, the only hope for success in the House was to convert most of the anti-Lecompton Democrats. That would not be an easy task, even with the President's power to exert pressure with promises of patronage favors or threats of political punishment. Apart from much personal doubt about the administration's course, the elections of 1858 were much on the minds of northern Congressmen, and many, especially those from districts with slim Democratic majorities, feared defeat at the hands of an overwhelmingly anti-Lecompton electorate.

In spite of Buchanan's apparent confidence of success, he made few converts among party dissenters before the Christmas recess. During a debate in the House on a motion to print the President's message, Samuel S. Cox of Ohio stated the views of the anti-Lecompton Democrats in one of the ablest and most witty speeches of the session. Like most of them, he denied that he was indifferent, "let alone unfriendly," to the success of the administration. His purpose was simply to uphold established Democratic policy by demanding the submission "of the whole constitution to the whole people." The President accepted that policy, but for the sake of peace he thought it inexpedient to apply it in the present case. That was an error, and Cox claimed the right, in behalf of his constituents, to protest "against any doctrine which would seem to approve of the conduct of the constitutional convention in Kansas." Its scheme of constitutional submission was "a device so thin as to have no upper nor under side. . . . True, very true, [the constitution] would have been voted down, and therefore it is not to be submitted to a vote. This is Democracy, is it? Let us, then, rewrite our lexicons. Democracy means, does it, to withhold the right of suffrage to all who may vote against you?" If the South wished to turn the Democracy into a sectional party, "let her place the northern Democracy in the wrong, where it can be reproached and insulted, taunted and despised."

Representative James Hughes of Indiana rebuked Cox for attacking the administration when it was conceived to be in trouble. Where would he go if he left the Democratic party to carry out his personal idea of popular sovereignty?

Cox replied that Hughes could not drive him out of the party "by any little scornful indignation from Indiana."[12] Everywhere, as Congress recessed, there was talk of men leaving the party, of defectors being expelled, of party disruption in one form or another.

Douglas's proposal for a Kansas enabling act and a new constitutional convention had won no support among southern Senators or northern "doughface" Senators such as Bright, Fitch, Bigler, and Gwin. He knew, however, that the rank-and-file of the northern Democracy, all but a handful of party editors, most of the state and local politicians, and even some federal officeholders were with him in his fight against Lecompton. It was a heady time for him. Flattering editorials in the press and letters of praise in his mail, some from Republican voters, must have erased bitter memories of 1854 when he was the target of angry northern attacks for his role in repealing the Missouri Compromise. In the Milwaukee *Sentinel*, as in many other Republican papers, charges that he was the worst of the doughfaces, a truckling servant of the Slave Power, gave way to words of appreciation for his "gallant stand." "[We] are all with you now," wrote a Pennsylvania Republican. "If you manage your cards right, we will make you President." From an Ohio Republican, Douglas heard that "thousands and thousands" who had been his most severe critics, now looked to him as "the very man destined to save the country in this awful crisis." A Chicago attorney claimed to speak for many local Republicans in expressing "unfeigned pleasure and admiration" for his bold course. Douglas and Sumner, he said, were the first men on the Senate floor to resist "the giant efforts which Slavery is making for dominion in this country." Douglas and Sumner in tandem? No doubt Douglas winced![13]

Numerous Republican leaders, especially in the East, responded cordially to his leadership in the anti-Lecompton battle. Gideon Welles, the Connecticut editor, sent him warm congratulations for his speech. Thurlow Weed, in a friendly letter, told Douglas that he would have called on him in Washington, "if it had been wise for *so Black* a Republican to be seen in your company." Greeley, who vowed "to write so as not to weaken him," visited him at his home, as did Schuyler Colfax, Benjamin F. Wade, and Nathaniel P. Banks. Earlier Wade had expressed surprise at Douglas's speech, because, as he wryly claimed, he had "never expected to see a slave insurrection." Connecticut Senator James Dixon thought that Douglas might be "indulging in the luxury of a conscience" but would not scrutinize his motives too closely. "He is right now, and if he will continue so, I am willing to forget the past, and cordially act with him and his friends in the future." Preston King was convinced that Douglas, Broderick, and Stuart, although still nominally Democrats, had severed their ties with the party and were "prepared for whatever results may come."[14]

Douglas had no intention of abandoning his party, but he welcomed a working relationship with the Republicans during the conflict over Lecompton. On the night of December 14, by his invitation, Congressmen Colfax and Anson Burlingame had conferred with him for three hours at his Washington residence. According to Colfax's memorandum of the meeting, Douglas opened the discussion with a long statement of his conviction that Jefferson Davis and other Southerners were seeking an opportunity to break up the Union. The best policy, he suggested, "was to put the Disunionists in such a position that when the break was made ... they would be in the position of insurgents ... so that, they being the rebels, the Army and the power of the Nation would be against them." He confessed that he had not expected such formidable opposition to his demand for justice for the people of Kansas. Nevertheless, he was determined to maintain his position inflexibly, "making all else subservient to it, even if it drove him to private life." Douglas claimed that the administration had sent agents to Kansas to get the slavery clause in the constitution "voted out or returned out" in order to increase its chances for congressional approval. If they succeeded, he would still demand an enabling act, or any other measure "which provided for a full fair vote of the people of Kansas on the whole Constitution."

In response, Colfax admitted having had strong prejudices against Douglas politically, but he, too, made justice for Kansas the paramount issue. He feared that Douglas underestimated the power of the administration, that he "would be beaten in the end" and forced out of the party if he continued his opposition. Colfax would make no commitments "in regard to the Presidency or future affiliations," except that he was with Douglas on the Lecompton issue. That was as it should be, Douglas replied. If slavery expansion continued to be the dominant issue, "the future would decide our duties and our positions." If new issues arose, "we should all divide again." In short, political collaboration would be limited solely to Kansas.[15]

Late in December, Douglas went to New York and conferred with a group of Republicans in Banks's room at the St. Nicholas Hotel. John Bigelow of the New York *Evening Post* met him there and, after hearing him speak about his plans "without the least reserve," was convinced that he was in earnest. Banks predicted that Douglas would find no "half way house" between supporting the administration and Republicanism, and Douglas agreed that the South would never forgive him. If that were true, Bigelow believed that he would give Republican sentiment in the Northwest a more "competent exponent" than it had had in the past. In any case, he seemed disposed "to go as far as the farthest now for freedom in Kansas."[16]

Douglas's Senate speech and subsequent behavior left many Republicans puzzled and less sure how to respond. "Is it a *ruse* or an act of *bona fide* patriotic effort?" an Ohio party leader asked Senator Trumbull. "We are at a loss to know ... what construction to place upon his eccentric conduct." Charles H. Ray, editor of the Chicago *Tribune,* confessed that he was "confounded" by Douglas's anomalous position and did not know what line to take. Ray's personal inclination was to "give him the lash," but he wanted to do nothing that would impair the struggle for a free Kansas. "Please write to us," he begged Trumbull. "We are in the dark and need light." Douglas may be sincere, wrote another Illinois Republican, but he had "fellowshipped with wrong and outrage" so long as to justify misgivings. A Pennsylvanian was fearful that he would "so retrieve himself with the North as to be a very formidable candidate in 1860."[17]

Other Republicans were convinced that he was not to be trusted. His goal, they asserted, was simply to secure his re-election to the Senate. To this end he was seeking to regain the support of Democratic voters who had deserted the party over the Kansas-Nebraska Act. "What does the New-York Tribune mean by its constant eulogizing, and admiring, and magnifying [of] Douglas?" an indignant Abraham Lincoln asked Trumbull. Had Washington Republicans concluded that the cause could be "best promoted by sacrificing us here in Illinois?" Their course served but one purpose, remarked a critical New York Republican: "Douglas will be returned to the Senate again in spite of everybody."[18]

After his friendly visit with Douglas, Senator Wade soon changed his mind. "He does not occupy his present position from choice," Wade observed. "He is driven to it by the folly and misdeeds of Buchanan and his southern masters." The Chicago *Tribune,* although agreeing with Douglas in his anti-Lecompton stand, reminded Republicans that there were fundamental differences between him and them. Douglas believed that the majority in a territory "may make a man a slave"; he denied the power of Congress to prohibit slavery in the territories; and he would admit a slave state to the Union as readily as a free state. "Judge Douglas is no more a Republican, no more a friend of freedom and of human rights at the present moment than James Buchanan," another editor insisted. "Let our Republican friends read [his] speech, on the Kansas question, and find if they can a single aspiration in favor of freedom or humanity." The best course for Republicans was to stand by while Douglas and the administration waged their battle. "We are in the position of the woman whose not over-loving husband was engaged in a deadly struggle with a bear: we do not much care which whips."[19]

Whatever differences existed among Republicans concerning Douglas, all knew that his conflict with the pro-Lecompton administration was for them the most fortuitous event of the year. Their disappointment at their losses in the autumn elections was forgotten; they were convinced that the results would have been different if the elections had occurred after the President's message to Congress. Lecompton, exulted one partisan, promised "a beautiful rent in the ranks of the Democracy, which augurs well for the success of the Republican cause next fall." In Washington, Senator Dixon reported, congressional Republicans viewed the controversy as one almost certain to destroy the northern Democracy. A Massachusetts editor believed that Buchanan might have broken the Republican party and made his own party unbeatable in the North if he had honored his commitment to a fair vote on the Kansas constitution. Instead, bowing to the southern Slave Power, he had mistakenly gambled that the northern Democracy would submit even to the Lecompton fraud. None could think of another rational explanation for his "great blunder at the very outset of his administration."[20]

Meanwhile, during the last weeks of the year, Democrats watched helplessly as their party began to disintegrate as a national political organization. The administration had announced its official stand on the Kansas issue, Douglas had announced his. As one northern peacemaker regretfully observed, "I cannot see how Douglas can back down . . . without fatally compromising himself." Nor could the administration retreat. Since neither would yield or compromise, party members—editors, officeholders, state and local officials, and ordinary voters—eventually were obliged to choose between them. Most Southerners would give their support to the administration, most Northerners to Douglas. Thus, wrote a bitter Wisconsin Democrat, the harmony "of the hitherto invincible democracy is to be broken by one paragraph in the Message of President Buchanan," and the party "is now ready to fly into a million pieces." A dour editorial in the New York *Herald* foresaw the "disruption of the democracy, North and South, and the reconstruction of all parties for the succession upon sectional platforms and sectional candidates."[21]

Some still searched for a plan of reconciliation or sought to minimize the issue that divided them. An Indiana Democratic editor, professing his friendship for Senator Bright and the administration and sympathy for Douglas's stand on Lecompton, begged them not to risk "driving off another battalion of Democrats." If both sides would avoid harsh words for a few weeks, "some plan of conciliation and compromise might be agreed upon. . . . There is no vital question of principle involved in the dispute, and no cause for an internal war among Democrats." Henry B. Payne of Ohio, the defeated candidate for governor, assured Douglas that few disagreed with him, "but all deplore a breach and division in the party. On all hands I am besought to interpose and prevent a split, until it becomes evident that it can no longer be avoided." An Iowa Democrat urged Douglas to consider "an exercise of judicious diplomacy." Why not name some discreet friends of both parties to arrange a fair settlement? A Democratic meeting in Detroit, like many others, tried a straddle. It expressed confidence in "our patriotic President" and pledged him hearty support in defending the Constitution and the Union. It also asserted the right of the people of Kansas to have any constitution framed for them "fully submitted for their rejection or approval."[22]

Unfortunately, the administration demanded complete loyalty and quickly set about to mobilize its friends in the North, usually under the command of federal officeholders or office-seekers. From the Philadelphia Post Office, Bigler was assured that every employee was loyal to the President. Joseph B. Baker, Collector of the Port, informed the President that "persons connected with the

Federal Government" in that city were a unit for him. There and elsewhere in the state, friends of the administration reported, the principal voice of disaffection was Forney's Philadelphia *Press.* His paper circulated widely in Pennsylvania, they noted, and had considerable influence on other party editors, and his friends among government appointees were either openly or secretly pro-Douglas. Bigler urged Buchanan to subsidize Forney's faltering rival, the loyal Philadelphia *Pennsylvanian,* with a Post Office printing contract even though that paper badly needed a new editor. William H. Smith, editor of the Pittsburgh *Post,* also eager for a printing contract, ignored local public opinion and supported the administration "against all malcontents." Late in December, James C. Van Dyke, United States District Attorney in Philadelphia, arranged a pro-administration meeting at Jayne Hall. "The meeting will be a large one," he promised the President, "and have the complexion of not being controlled by officials but by the people outside of office." In other states the officeholders made similar efforts in the administration's behalf. In New York City, for example, Congressman Daniel E. Sickles, trying to win control of the patronage for his party faction, informed Buchanan that he was "endeavoring to get up a good meeting . . . and I have no doubt the result . . . will be gratifying to you."[23]

Before the end of the year Democratic Congressmen who sided with Douglas began to feel the administration's pressure. "[The] *thumb screw* is being applied with much force," wrote one Washington observer. Many appointments were being delayed until the vote on Lecompton had been recorded. The House clerk and printer, both friends of Douglas, had been "compelled to cave and now [could] not say a word . . . except to disavow their concurrence in his views." Douglas heard reports from various northern cities that applicants for office were kept dangling "in order to secure their active co-operation, or at least their *prudential silence.*" A Cincinnati friend warned him that the numerous candidates for unfilled local appointments would try "to harmonize the President's views with popular sovereignty."[24]

One of the crudest administration efforts to win the support of an anti-Lecompton editor involved Buchanan's old friend Forney. On December 18, David Webster, a Philadelphia lawyer and friend of both Forney and Black, complained to Black about the failure of the administration to give Forney a Post Office printing contract. Webster reminded the Attorney General of an earlier promise that "our good friend Forney should be taken care of" when the opportunity arose. In reply, Black invited Webster to come to Washington to discuss the matter. After the interview Webster returned to Philadelphia with the administration's terms: Forney was to write a small statement in the *Press* to the effect that he intended to remain a Democrat, that Lecompton was an issue that should be settled within the party, and that he would abide by the party's decision. In return Forney would receive the Post Office printing contract, worth about $80,000. According to Webster, Forney "indignantly refused to comply with

Judge Black's wishes, and was very emphatic in expressing his refusal." He thought that his many years of service to Buchanan and the party ought to be sufficient, and he would not endure the humiliation of making such a declaration in his paper.[25]

Forney was by then solidly committed to Douglas, calling him a statesman who "never failed in the right" and his Senate speech "overwhelming in its logic." Before long he was sending Douglas advice and assuring him that his support in Philadelphia was "absolutely astonishing." Every mail brought Forney "the strongest expressions of sympathy and support from our leading men throughout the state." On December 23, when Douglas stopped at the Girard House in Philadelphia, Forney appeared on the balcony with him when a crowd gathered to hear him speak. Forney also spoke briefly, pledging his loyalty to Douglas and the anti-Lecompton cause as ardently as he had once pledged it to Buchanan.[26]

With the northern Democracy now fighting for its own survival, Forney's defection was only one of many signs that the President and the federal officers loyal to him would not be able to control the party even in his own state. William F. Packer, the newly elected governor, deserted him. Douglas heard from sources other than Forney that Philadelphia Democrats were with him and "fast showing their colors . . . despite the jeers and taunts of all the office holders here." Western Pennsylvania, he was told, supported him "almost as a *unit.*" The pro-Lecompton editor of the Pittsburgh *Post* apologized to Bigler for sending bad news but confessed that he could find "but few who [were] in favor of voting Kansas into the Union with the Lecompton Constitution."[27]

Similar encouragement reached Douglas from Democrats in every northern state. Correspondents from Boston, Albany, and Buffalo urged him not to back down and assured him that he would be sustained by the northern Democracy. "We expected better things from old Buck!" wrote an Ohio Democrat. "Stand firm! . . . We *will* make you our next President!" In Detroit, according to the *Free Press,* sentiment among party members was overwhelmingly pro-Douglas, and reports from the interior indicated that the city was an index of the entire state. An Indiana state legislator asserted that Bright's and Fitch's support of the administration was "against the wishes of their constituents." Prior to an Indiana state Democratic convention, scheduled for January 8, a large majority of the county conventions demanded the submission of the whole Lecompton constitution to Kansas voters. "That is unquestionably the general feeling," reported a Democratic editor, "though the politicians dislike the idea of breaking with the administration." A prominent Wisconsin party leader informed Douglas that the administration, "with all their drill, and allowing for official subordination, [could not] poll 1000 votes against you on this issue."[28]

The Illinois state organization was securely in Douglas's hands. James W. Sheahan, editor of the Chicago *Times,* informed him that every Democratic paper had taken an anti-Lecompton stand except the Joliet *Signal,* whose editor was the town postmaster. Letters of support poured in from Illinois Democrats, along with anti-Lecompton resolutions from many local party meetings. A mass meeting called by the Chicago Democratic Association rang with praise for Douglas and demands for submission of the entire Lecompton constitution to the voters of Kansas. "Your position takes the wind clean out of the B[lack] Republican leaders," wrote a Galesburg friend. "Their only hope is that you will yet waver and back down."[29]

Northern Democrats were dismayed to find Southerners supporting the administration's Lecompton policy. "We cannot conceal our astonishment at the attitude of the South," wrote the Detroit *Free Press,* for its leaders had never before advanced the doctrine that Congress was "bound by the acts of a convention having no other authority than the Territorial Legislature." In the past, complained an Ohio Democrat, the northern wing of the party had always stood by the South, but it could not survive if it betrayed the principle of popular sovereignty in Kansas. Who would then defend Southerners against abolitionism? Did they not realize that by saving the northern Democracy they were saving themselves? A New York Democrat thought that the South, in attempting to force a government on Kansas against the will of the majority, was involved in a "dangerous and fearful" experiment and hoped its leaders would "see the folly of the thing and abandon it."[30]

Dismay often gave way to anger. The Chicago *Times* resented the "impudence" of a Virginia editor who had read Douglas out of the party. One anti-Lecompton Democrat deplored the "unholy alliance" of doughfaces and the "Slavocracy," whose goal was "to make the Democratic party stand Godfather for the dissemination of the accursed institution of slavery throughout this entire nation." Another believed that the sole concern of the South was "protecting and enhancing the value of its slave property." It felt no gratitude for the support the northern Democracy had given it in the past. "The South squeezes the lemon and throws away the peel." Still another was convinced that if Buchanan had insisted upon ratification of the Lecompton constitution, the result would have been "the usual muttering of fire eaters of the Delta school—and nothing more."[31]

Confronted with overwhelming evidence that the northern Democracy could be neither persuaded nor coerced to accept its Lecompton policy, the administration vented its own anger through increasingly reckless arguments and accusations in the Washington *Union.* There were reasons enough why the constitution should not be submitted to the electorate, it asserted. To do so would immerse it "in the dirty mire of abolition politics" and expose it "to the ruffian handling of rowdies and rebels such as Lane and Brown." In fact, the *Union* now argued, submitting whole constitutions to the voters was always bad policy. These documents were invariably long and complicated, and popular ratification of them could be "little more than a farce." The best policy was "to leave details to the representative convention . . . and to single out one or two leading provisions for direct vote." Accordingly, the Lecompton convention, had chosen to determine the will of the majority solely on the "angry question of slavery." Unfortunately, Senator Douglas, in a manner "wanton and mischievous," threatened to frustrate the hopes of his party and "all honest men." His attempt to obstruct a settlement "by a peaceful and final vote," the *Union* charged, was giving powerful support to the abolitionists in their effort to continue this fierce controversy.[32]

The administration could not even persuade all southern Democrats that support of the the Lecompton constitution would, in the long run, be to their advantage. The Richmond *Enquirer,* after strongly advocating ratification, eventually endorsed the policy without much enthusiasm, while praising Douglas for the service he had rendered the South. Governor Wise of Virginia stubbornly persisted in his opposition. "I am determined," he informed Robert Tyler, "that neither the Democratic party nor slavery shall be injured irreparably by marching over the doctrine of popular sovereignty. . . . I want to cure the egregious blunders of pro-slavery blind leaders." Douglas's "able and conclusive" speech on the Kansas issue met with the governor's "heartfelt approbation." In a public letter to the Tammany Society of New York City, dated December 30, Wise shocked the administration by denouncing the Lecompton convention for its "unveiled trickery and shameless fraud." One prominent border newspaper, the Louisville *Democrat,* viewed administration policy as a major blunder. "We are opposed to sectional issues about trifles," it protested, "when no principle is at stake." Lecompton was such an issue. "It is not pretended that the South is to gain anything by the acceptance of the Lecompton Constitution; on the contrary, she is certain to lose friends, influence, and credit by insisting on it."[33]

Among the many letters of support that Douglas received each day was a scattering from the South. A Virginia slaveholder praised his speech against the "political legerdemain" of Lecompton. A Nashville Democrat sent his "decided approbation" and assured him that he had significant support in Tennessee. "You are of course abused by the whole Southern press," wrote a correspondent from Mobile, "but there are individuals, even in the South, who can appreciate the efforts of a statesman . . . in battling for the right." An admirer in New Orleans expressed "total and entire approval" of Douglas's stand on the "Lecompton swindle." There were others, among them a letter from Dr. Samuel A. Cartwright, a prominent New Orleans racist who specialized in "Negro diseases." Upon reflection, Cartwright concluded that Douglas was trying to "preserve the integrity and moral power of the Democratic party" and to prevent it from "falling to a level with any petty Banking Corporation, by losing its soul."[34]

These words of encouragement were decidedly not typical of current southern sentiment. Public opinion in that section was better expressed by a Memphis carpenter who felt "sorely grieved" because of Douglas's stand and therefore denied that he was a *"genuine democrat"* and consigned him "to the tomb of the Capulets." For a Texas editor "the charm of the name of Douglas is broken forever. His political reputation now shrinks within the narrow compass of free-soilism." He now stood, others said, side-by-side with the Sewards, the Greeleys, and the Sumners. Alfred Huger, the Charleston postmaster, was not altogether surprised at his defection, for there always had been "a manner about him . . . at variance with an elevated feeling." The Richmond *South* believed that Douglas had once shown considerable political promise. "Association with southern gentlemen had smoothed down the rugged vulgarities of his early education," but he must now be regarded "as an enemy to the South and the Democratic Party."[35]

To southern defenders of Lecompton the evidence that a majority of Kansans opposed the constitution was legally irrelevant. The convention, they maintained, was lawfully elected by a majority of those who voted; it was given authority to frame a constitution and apply at once for admission to the Union without the formality of ratification. As John Tyler argued, the convention "was the creature of the popular will, as far as the voting class could make it so, and that is the only standard to which we can refer." If the majority refused to vote, "their acquiescence is fairly to be inferred. There is no other criterion to which we can refer but the results of the ballot-box." In the light of early precedents, the failure to submit the constitution for ratification provided no ground for congressional rejection. Indeed, a Mississippi editor contended, the convention's decision to submit the slavery question to the voters was an "extraordinary act of liberality." As for the protection given to slaveholders then living in Kansas, that was clearly required by the Court's decision in the Dred Scott case. Therefore, concluded the Memphis *Appeal,* there was no justification "for prolonging the controversy, consistent with patriotism and the peace of the Union." Opposition to the immediate admission of Kansas after the territorial vote on December 21 would be "a mere quibble, used as a disguise for deadly hostility to the institutions of the South."[36]

That the fire-eaters in the Deep South threatened disunion if Congress rejected the Lecompton constitution or returned it for popular ratification surprised no one. They had found an issue and made the most of it. The Mobile *Register* called the Kansas controversy "pregnant with consequences . . . to the harmony of the Democratic party and of the Union." The Jackson *Mississippian* told northern Democrats that they alone had the power to "decide the question fairly" and thus to save the Union. Meanwhile, the South should prepare for the worst and consider calmly "the alternatives that may soon be presented for our choice as Southern men." In Texas, Governor H. R. Runnels asserted that the rejection of Kansas as a slave state would further disrupt the sectional balance and expose the South "to the lust of an aggressive and dominant sectional majority." Since Texas would not remain in the Union at the cost of her rights and honor, Runnels urged "the thorough military organization and training, indispensable to the liberties of every Free State."[37]

Pro-secession sentiment among the radicals in the southern Democracy was at that time probably no more extensive than pro-Douglas sentiment among the conservatives, perhaps less. In between was a solid pro-Lecompton majority concerned simply with the immediate issue of Kansas. Although they were not radicals, those in the majority were heedlessly risking the survival of the Democracy as a national organization—the very organization which southern party leaders had claimed to be the South's last line of defense within the Union.

Southern Whig-Americans were, as usual, of two minds about Lecompton. The Richmond *Whig* named all the prominent northern Democrats who had, one time or another, betrayed the South. Douglas had only "acted after his kind." On the other hand, a Whig editor in Tennessee praised Douglas for the "strength and truthfulness" of his Senate speech. "And in both these respects his position is in striking contrast with the fatuous and stultifying course of the President." The Lecompton constitution, wrote a Kentucky Whig, was a "base cheat," and Buchanan would be "the most odious President" in the country's history. George D. Prentice, the Louisville Whig-American editor, took neither side but, in an intensely partisan mood, thought that a fight among Democrats would kindle "joy in the bosom of every patriot." Could not a plain Whig or American be excused "for taking especial delight in so pretty a quarrel as this? We can't help enjoying it excessively for the life of us."[38]

Before the year was out Kansas Territory would have a new governor, the fifth in little more than three years. Governor Walker was distracted by his business speculations and doubted in any case that the Senate would confirm his appointment. Returning to Washington, he sought advice from Douglas, after which he again discussed Kansas affairs with the President. On December 15 he resigned. In a long and characteristically verbose letter of resignation, Walker reminded the President that he had accepted his appointment with the clear understanding that the Kansas constitution was to be submitted to the people for approval or rejection. To this the President had explicitly agreed. By that commitment alone he had prevented violence in the territory and, in October, persuaded the whole people "to go, for the first time, into a general and peaceful election." Walker declared it "as a fact," based on his long association with the people of Kansas, that an overwhelming majority opposed the Lecompton constitution, and he explained in detail a variety of reasons in addition to slavery for their opposition. One that he felt deeply was the proposed legislative apportionment giving Johnson County representation for all the fraudulent votes counted in Oxford precinct the previous October. He claimed that much of the responsibility for that "extraordinary" document rested on Calhoun and other federal officeholders in Kansas. Because of the administration's support of the constitution, Walker could not remain as governor "without personal dishonor and the abandonment of fundamental principles."[39]

Secretary of State Cass loyally but unhappily signed a curt letter in which he accepted Walker's resignation and denied that the President had changed his Kansas policy. He had "never entertained or expressed the opinion that the convention [was] bound to submit any portion of the constitution to the people, except the question of slavery." Delegates to the convention had merely exercised "the right belonging to them" not to submit the whole constitution. It was then the President's duty, "in strict conformity with previous instructions," to take care that a fair election was held on the slavery question "and thus give peace to the Union." He had no authority to insist upon full submission merely because that was his own preference. Finally, the letter claimed that Walker had been sent to Kansas only to make sure that the people had a fair chance to vote for or against slavery. In short, contrary to his pledge of the previous July to "stand or fall" on the issue of submission, Buchanan would do neither.[40]

Meanwhile, since the departure of Walker in November, Frederick P. Stanton, the territorial secretary, had been serving as acting governor. During his brief tenure he faced a political crisis that brought Kansas dangerously close to another explosion of violence. News of the action of the Lecompton convention and of the President's endorsement of its proslavery constitution led many free-state partisans to conclude that peaceful political action had failed. From November until early January a renewal of the bloodshed of 1856 seemed a distinct possibility. Even as conservative a man as Amos A. Lawrence could urge "Governor" Robinson to use force to rid the territory "of the renegades who have disgraced it." "You cannot imagine the state of excitement . . . that has prevailed here," a Kansas friend informed Black. "We live in the midst of threats of fire and sword. . . . Suspicion, distrust and every kind of horror of impending civil war haunt us. . . . The Ultras of both sides seem itching for a fuss." Robinson learned that a bitter dispute between free-state and slave-state partisans over land claims near Fort Scott might precipitate an armed conflict. The territory, he feared, was "on the eve of a bloody page in [its] history."[41]

In late November the most serious threat to peace was a movement among militant free-state leaders to activate the Topeka government and seize political control of the territory. They urged Robinson to convene a special session of the Topeka legislature with a view toward nullifying the Lecompton constitution and the authority it had delegated to John Calhoun. Robinson refused to comply, appealing instead to Stanton for action that would avert civil strife. On November 27 a large mass convention at Leavenworth asked Stanton to call the free-state territorial legislature into special session and threatened to "put the Topeka Government in motion" if he refused. A majority of the members of the legislature and more than a hundred "leading citizens of Kansas" signed a letter to

Stanton urging him to comply with the convention's request. They promised to take no action other than to give the people an opportunity legally to vote for or against the entire Lecompton constitution.[42]

Accepting their assurance of a limited agenda, Stanton issued a proclamation calling a special legislative session to meet on December 7, thus ending the immediate threat of violence. On December 2 a free-state convention then meeting at Lawrence expressed its appreciation for his action. It denounced the December 21 vote on the constitution and the January 4 election of state officers, both under the supervision of Calhoun, as swindles and threats to the peace of the territory. It advised free-state voters to participate in neither, proposing instead a preferential vote on both the Lecompton and Topeka constitutions. Lane, leader of the militants, boasted that 18,000 warriors stood ready to defend the people's rights.[43]

On the day the legislature assembled at Lecompton, free-state partisans paraded the streets with music and banners, Lane's military companies showed their strength, and orators entertained the crowds that gathered throughout the day. The next day Stanton delivered his message. He acknowledged that a "sense of wrong and injustice" had aroused the people of the territory to a condition of "dangerous excitement," and he held the Lecompton convention responsible for the present state of alarm. That body, representing a small minority of the voters, had no right to deny a popular vote on its constitution. Although the legislature was not entitled to interfere with the convention's provision for a partial vote on December 21, Stanton had no doubt of its right to require a second vote for or against the constitution as a whole. If it were voted down, he asserted that Congress could not accept it "without a violation of all popular rights." Stanton proposed further the adoption of an election law making it a felony for any judge or clerk of election to compile false returns. These measures, he believed, would be sufficient to dispel the excitement which threatened the peace of the territory.[44]

The legislature responded with an act providing for the submission of the Lecompton constitution to another vote on January 4. This time voters were to be given three choices: they could approve of it with slavery, or they could approve of it without slavery, or they could reject it altogether. The conservatives defeated an effort to secure a vote on the Topeka constitution as well. The legislature also provided penalties for electoral corruption. Violating its commitment not to take up other matters, the majority passed two measures over Stanton's veto. It repealed the law authorizing the Lecompton convention, and it took control of the territorial militia and made Lane a major general. In addition the majority adopted a concurrent resolution, which did not require executive approval, demanding the admission of Kansas to statehood under the Topeka constitution. Since the terms of these legislators would not begin until January, all of their acts were of dubious legality.[45]

Having convened the territorial legislature to deal with an immediate crisis, Stanton had acted without waiting for administration approval. The approval never came. A letter from Cass, dated November 30, instructed him to see that the election of December 21 was conducted with the "utmost fairness and security." On December 2, Cass sent the portion of the President's annual message dealing with Kansas. A few days later he sent the whole message and instructed Stanton to conform strictly to administration policy in his official conduct. The present opportunity to end the slavery agitation in Kansas, Cass cautioned, must not be lost.

Stanton waited until December 9 before notifying the administration of his action and forwarding a copy of his message to the legislature. He had done what was necessary, he explained, to avoid bloodshed. He thought that "the peace of the territory would be cheaply maintained at the expense of a short session of the legislative assembly." He considered its provision for a popular vote on the whole Lecompton constitution to be "just and proper." Before Stanton's report arrived Buchanan had read accounts of his action in the press and on December 10 peremptorily dismissed him. Subsequently, in a letter to Walker, Stanton expressed satisfaction for having found a way to enable the electorate to vote down the Lecompton fraud. "My head will not have fallen in vain."[46]

Buchanan selected General James W. Denver, the federal commissioner of Indian affairs, to replace Stanton as territorial secretary and acting governor, and the following month the Senate confirmed his appointment as governor. Denver, a competent and conscientious administrator, was a Virginia lawyer who, in the early 1850s, had moved to the Kansas border in western Missouri. In his instructions to Denver, Cass alleged that Stanton had been removed for throwing "a new element of discord among the excited people of Kansas," thus undermining the peaceful policy of the administration. Denver was to preserve the peace and see that voters had safe access to the polls on December 21. To avoid a dangerous confrontation, he was also instructed to recognize and protect the legislature during its current meeting. Moreover, should that body authorize an election for any purpose, it "should be held without interruption, no less than those authorized by the convention." These elections could cause no harm, Cass concluded, for their results would receive only "their due weight under the constitution and the laws."[47]

Before the first Kansas election on December 21 several northern Democrats advised the administration to do everything possible to obtain a majority vote for the Lecompton constitution without slavery. Such a result, they hoped, would weaken the anti-Lecompton forces and improve its chances for approval in the House of Representatives. Bigler wrote to friends in Kansas urging them to bring out a large antislavery vote. Douglas charged that agents of the administration were prepared to resort to fraud if necessary to secure a majority for the constitution without slavery. The effort failed. "It is useless for me to attempt to persuade the people to vote on the 21st of December," wrote one Kansas Democrat, "they will not do so." Another reported that he knew of no one in his county who would vote and believed that most of the election returns would be fraudulent. With Calhoun in charge, "votes may be put in by handfuls and there is no remedy."[48]

On election day Acting Governor Denver made one last appeal to Kansans to vote in spite of their objection to the manner in which the issue had been presented to them. The outcome gave no advantage to the administration. Calhoun's election officials reported more than 6000 votes for the constitution with slavery, fewer than 600 for the constitution without slavery. Hardly a member of the free-state party had voted. "Your friends here . . . [have] done the thing you desired," Bigler was assured. "I am sorry . . . that our efforts have not prevailed."[49]

Many wondered how the small proslavery party, which had cast fewer than 2000 votes for convention delegates the previous June, had managed to poll so large a vote in December. An anti-Lecompton Democrat in Leavenworth informed Douglas that a third of the ballots had been cast by Missourians who had come over to Kansas for the day. Forney was probably closer to the truth when he charged that Calhoun, that "mighty manufacturer of votes . . . had things all his own way." A subsequent legislative investigating committee reported that more than half the proslavery votes were fraudulent. Nevertheless, Calhoun certified that the Lecompton constitution with slavery had been approved. If Buchanan were to accept these returns as valid, he would be obliged to ask Congress to admit Kansas as a slave state.[50]

As the January 4 election for a legislature and state officers approached, the free-state party was uncertain whether or not to abandon its position against participation. Again the voting would be in the hands of Calhoun's appointees, and fraud would be difficult to prevent. On the other hand, the Lawrence *Herald of Freedom* predicted that if Congress approved the Lecompton constitution and the state government was proslavery, thousands of slaveholders would come to Kansas and make it a slave state forever. Every avenue for peaceful political change would be closed, and a resort to violence would be suppressed with federal bayonets. The best hope, the *Herald of Freedom* advised, was to nominate candidates and "*compel* honesty on the part of those commissioned to count returns." With the state offices in its hands, the free-state party would have the political leverage needed to persuade Congress to reject the Lecompton constitution.[51]

On December 23 a free-state convention in Lawrence debated the matter at length and with considerable heat. Lane led the radicals who opposed any action that would give legitimacy to the proceedings of the Lecompton convention. The conservatives led by "Govenor" Robinson, Thomas Ewing, Jr., and George W. Brown of the *Herald of Freedom,* favored the expedient course of contesting the election. When the Lane radicals persuaded a majority to vote against participation, the conservatives withdrew and organized a convention of their own. They nominated candidates for state offices and called on the people in the districts to support free-state candidates for the legislature. If Congress accepted the Lecompton constitution, their candidates were pledged to adopt measures enabling the people, "through a new Constitutional Convention to obtain such a Constitution as the majority shall approve." Lane and some of the radicals finally yielded and gave the free-state ticket their support.[52]

In the January 4 election for state offices many free-state partisans still refused to vote, and many proslavery votes again turned out to be fraudulent, leaving the result uncertain and the returns in Calhoun's hands. However, the vote on Lecompton, sponsored by the territorial legislature and held the same day, probably sealed the fate of the constitution in the national House of Representatives. Denver reported less than 200 votes for the constitution either with or without slavery and more than 10,000 against it altogether. Most proslavery partisans had not participated, but when compared with their own vote total on December 21, the free-state party had won an impressive victory. Subtracting the fraudulent proslavery votes, the free-state victory was overwhelming.[53] Perhaps some small irregularities also occurred in this election—the pattern was well established in Kansas—but the free-state party had the numbers to make major frauds unnecessary. Buchanan had not questioned the authority of the legislature to hold this election, yet he continued to press his pro-Lecompton policy as if it had never occurred.

In the life of a nation, every year has its failures and disappointments, but 1857 had more than its share. The solemn reflections at year's end contrasted sharply with the pervasive optimism so evident just twelve months before. "The year is growing old," a Philadelphia editor wrote sadly in late December. "Few, comparatively, of our readers have failed to encounter storms of adversity ... that seem to leave them more than a year older in experience at least." The economic panic and recession had "scattered fair and bright hopes like autumn leaves. . . . Many a brown stone house is tenantless, and many an humbler cottage and hearth bare and desolate."[54]

Political prospects were gloomy enough for the Democracy. The New York *Herald* feared that the country now confronted "the inevitable contingency of a Northern anti-slavery coalition in 1860, which will sweep everything before it as with the force of a whirlwind." It found "something positively awful in the rise, progress and growth of this Northern anti-slavery movement." In South Carolina, Senator Hammond was apprehensive that the "*final and decisive* Crisis" was at hand, which would "settle the destiny of the Slaveholders of the South *forever*."[55]

Charles Francis Adams, noting the sudden change in the fortunes of the Democracy, reflected that in politics "events have an overruling influence, and they always defy calculation." Just when it appeared that a prosouthern administration, supported by a solid majority in Congress, was firmly in control, the President was unexpectedly weakened by an assault from Senator Douglas, followed by another from Senator Stuart, and still others from Governor Walker, from Forney, and from numerous western Democratic editors. All of the President's troubles, Adams believed, sprang from his "obstinate and preposterous policy ... favorable to the old and musty conservatives of the democratic party." The New York *Evening Post* believed that Buchanan possessed "less of the confidence of the country at the commencement of his first Congress, than Pierce possessed at the close of his."[56]

On December 30, an outburst in the Washington *Union* betrayed the administration's frustration. "The whole population of Kansas," it protested, "does not yet equal that of a suburb of one of our populous Atlantic cities." Why should the troublemakers in that territory be permitted to "usurp a prominence in our affairs beyond that of our foreign policy, our financial condition, and our widespread commerce[?]" Why should Kansas monopolize the business of Congress? Why, indeed, asked the *Union*, "should a few thousand men possess the faculty of changing great federal issues, in order to gratify individual ambition at the expense of the harmony of the Union?"

That, of course, was a considerable oversimplification. Even so, that the national Democratic party, and with it the Union, should finally begin to crumble in a wretched dispute over the Lecompton constitution, seemed to trivialize a profound and deeply felt controversy over the future of black slavery in America. But that, as it happened, was how things came to a head—how Douglas, who was quite willing to see any territory become a slave state if the majority wished, found himself on this occasion standing with Seward and other "Black" Republicans in defiance of the Slave Power. No doubt the Lecompton issue was not worthy of the cause which it now appeared to represent—and some have made much of that fact, transforming the cause itself into a shabby squabble among irresponsible politicians. Yet, in many historic crises which culminated in violent conflict, some incident, often small in itself, marked the point where discussion and negotiation gave way to accusations and inflexible demands, and where concession was equated with humiliating defeat. When that point was reached, events no longer seemed to be controllable. The crisis had gathered so much momentum that the peacemakers could find no way to stop it from running its course.

In all probability, the American sectional conflict reached that point in December 1857. After Lecompton the self-inflicted wounds of the national Democracy never healed. Three years later, demoralized and fragmented, it would surrender the presidency to the Republicans. Meanwhile, for Republicans at least the approaching new year was full of promise. "We are certainly now in good heart and cheer," wrote one party leader in late December, "and believe all that [we] have to do is stand by our guns, and victory will perch on our banner."[57]

CHAPTER 12

1858:
The Fruits of Lecompton

The Kansas crisis ran its destructive course well into the summer of 1858. Although the arguments for and against accepting the Lecompton constitution had been exhausted in December, the debate continued after Congress reconvened in January and grew increasingly acrimonious with each passing day. Except for a few wavering northern Democrats and southern Whig-Americans, members of the House had taken firm positions before the Christmas recess. The 75 southern Democrats unanimously demanded the admission of Kansas as a slave state; the 92 Republicans unanimously opposed. A small majority of the 53 northern Democrats appeared ready to defy their constituents and support the administration, but more than twenty of them, led by Thomas L. Harris of Illinois and Samuel S. Cox of Ohio, were determined anti-Lecompton rebels. A few Whig-Americans from the Upper South also appeared likely to join the opposition. Throughout the debate the division was close and the outcome in doubt.

None was more adamant in his pro-Lecompton stand than Buchanan. A budget of discouraging news during the winter merely drove him to fight more desperately, apparently heedless of the cost. A confidential letter from Governor Denver, dated January 16, advised him in the strongest terms not to press for the approval of the Lecompton constitution. The result of approval was certain to be renewed violence in Kansas. Denver urged the President to favor instead the passage of an enabling act providing for another convention to write a new constitution. Kansas moderates, he predicted, would then organize in opposition to the extremists and save the state for the Democracy. A delegation of anti-Lecompton Democratic Congressmen called on Buchanan to plead with him and to warn him that he would not have the votes to win. Impatiently he responded that he was both committed and confident and was determined, if necessary, to drive Lecompton through "naked."[1]

Every sign in the northern states indicated that pro-administration Congressmen were not speaking for the party rank-and-file. At the Indiana state Democratic convention on January 8, the Bright machine dominated the platform committee and, amid loud protests, prevented the passage of anti-Lecompton resolutions. The result was a rebellion, the calling of a second convention in February, and the adoption there of a ringing endorsement of Douglas. Federal officeholders controlled the Pennsylvania state convention in March, but it was overshadowed by a huge anti-Lecompton meeting in Philadelphia the previous month. Forney introduced Stanton, the principal speaker, and read supporting letters from Douglas, Walker, Wise, Stuart, and other anti-Lecompton notables. The Kansas vote of January 4, Douglas asserted, "conclusively and undeniably" established that the Lecompton constitution did not embody the popular will. The Rhode Island, New Jersey, and Michigan legislatures denounced Lecompton, and the Ohio legislature instructed Senator Pugh to vote against it. The spring elections in New Hampshire, Connecticut, and Rhode Island resulted in crushing Democratic defeats. Republicans swept local elections in Michigan and maintained their control of Chicago.[2]

In February, John Calhoun appeared in Washington with the January 4 Kansas state election returns in his pocket and the results still unannounced. He arrived amid reports that an investigating committee of the territorial legislature had uncovered election frauds fully as crude as the ones perpetrated in the Oxford and McGee precincts the previous October. On March 2, a member of the investigating committee brought the evidence to Washington, and an angry Douglas asked Calhoun whether he would certify results based on fraudulent returns. This was more than the administration could bear, and on March 19, under considerable pressure, Calhoun certified an anti-Lecompton majority in the prospective state legislature but left the other results undecided.[3] Proof of another corrupt Kansas election under the supervision of Calhoun's appointees damaged the administration cause at a time when it already appeared all but lost.

On January 30, Buchanan received an official copy of the Lecompton constitution, and on February 2 he transmitted it to both houses of Congress with a special message that constituted his last public appeal for approval. By then his argument was familiar. Again he accused the free-state party of rebellion under a military leader "of a most turbulent and dangerous character." Had the constitution been submitted to these dissidents, it would have been rejected, not upon its merits "but simply because they have ever resisted the authority of the government authorized by Congress from which it emanated." He repeated his assertion that he had never believed that the Lecompton convention was bound to submit any question to the voters "except the all-absorbing question of slavery."

The people of Kansas, Buchanan maintained, had framed a constitution in strict accordance with the provisions of the Kansas-Nebraska Act. They now asked for admission to statehood, and although the decision was in the hands of Congress he was decidedly in favor of admission, "thus terminating the Kansas question." If the majority of Kansans wished to get rid of slavery, there was no quicker way to accomplish it than by prompt admission. Then they could "make and unmake constitutions at pleasure" regardless of the Lecompton constitution's provision against amendments before 1864. Meanwhile, the Dred Scott decision had established that slavery existed in Kansas by virtue of the federal Constitution, and Kansas was at that moment "as much a slave State as Georgia or South Carolina."

Buchanan concluded with a solemn warning that refusal to admit Kansas would renew the agitation in a form more dangerous than in the past. Given the behavior of the free-state party, the people of the slave states would resent the rejection keenly. This Kansas controversy had "alarmed the fears of patriots for the safety of the Union." The "dark and ominous clouds" that hung over it could only be dissipated by the admission of Kansas during the present session of Congress. If it refused, he feared that the Union might not survive.

In the Senate the Lecompton constitution and Buchanan's message were referred to Douglas's Committee on Territories. Control of the committee was in the hands of pro-Lecompton Senators, and on February 18, James S. Green of Missouri submitted a majority report and a bill for the admission of Kansas as a slave state. Douglas and the Republican members submitted separate minority reports. The Senate debate raged for more than a month, contributing little of substance to the controversy but producing a surfeit of hot rhetoric. The Republicans now entered the battle and made clear that their support of popular sovereignty in Kansas was linked to their determination to check the spread of slavery. On March 3, Seward spoke at length of the inevitable conflict between the two "antagonistical systems" of slave labor and free labor. Slavery would ultimately give way and perish as additional free states, among them Kansas, entered the Union. Buchanan, Seward charged, had conspired with Chief Justice Taney, at the time of the inauguration, to bring forth the Dred Scott decision; and now he would further the proslavery cause by urging Congress to approve the Lecompton fraud.[4]

The following day Senator Hammond of South Carolina, a wealthy planter and master of several hundred slaves, rose to deliver a carefully prepared and long rehearsed defense of the proslavery South. He ridiculed Douglas's doctrine of popular sovereignty, denying that a territorial legislature could prohibit slavery and claiming that only a sovereign state could exercise that power. Seward, Hammond charged, had revealed the hostile intentions of the North toward the South. Yet, he and others had underestimated the South's economic power based on its control of the world's cotton supply. "No, you dare not make war on cotton," he asserted. "No power on earth dares make war on it. Cotton is King." After that long-remembered boast, Hammond praised the South's social system for its inherent harmony and its underlying strength. Every advanced society required a docile underclass to perform menial labor—the "mud-sills" who freed those with superior skills and intelligence to build great civilizations. This was the role played in the South by black slaves and in the North by exploited laboring men and women. The North claimed to have abolished slavery, Hammond scoffed, but it had abolished only the *name*, not the *thing*. "All the powers of the earth cannot abolish that."[5] The letters of praise Hammond received from admirers in the South should have been matched by letters of appreciation from Republicans in the North. What better proof did they need of the Slave Power's contempt for free labor and threat to its interests? Mud-sills indeed! Senator Wilson indignantly defended northern artisans and laborers and proudly described his own early years as a shoemaker.

On March 17, John J. Crittenden, Whig-American Senator from the slave state of Kentucky, spoke for two hours and dealt another blow to the administration cause. He appealed to his colleagues to end their angry accusations and recriminations and deal with the Kansas crisis as statesmen. He pleaded with them to respect the clear will of the people of Kansas and to dissociate themselves from the series of frauds that had preceded the submission of the Lecompton constitution to Congress. A few days later Crittenden offered a substitute bill providing for the admission of Kansas after the referral of the whole constitution to the voters in a strictly supervised election. If the constitution were rejected, another convention would be chosen to write a new one.

March 22 was the final day of the Senate debate. Stuart reviewed the anti-Lecompton case at great length, and Broderick attacked Buchanan savagely. Douglas spoke to a densely packed chamber at the evening session. The long battle and his private worries had exhausted him, and for several days he had been confined to his bed. But the Little Giant gathered his strength for a last vigorous three-hour assault on the "void, rejected, repudiated, Lecompton constitution." He would not be intimidated, he vowed, by charges that he had deserted his party. "If, standing firmly by my principles, I shall be driven into private life, it is a fate that has no terrors for me."[6]

Toombs of Georgia followed Douglas with a bitter reply, and the next day Green made a final plea for approval of his Lecompton bill. The Senate was then ready to vote. Crittenden's substitute was rejected, and the Lecompton constitution was approved by a vote of 33-25. Joining Douglas, Stuart, and Broderick in the minority were Democratic Senator George E. Pugh, who honored his instructions from the Ohio legislature, two southern Whig-Americans (Crittenden and John Bell of Tennessee), and all the Republicans except Sumner, who was not present.

The epic battle then shifted to the House, where maneuvering for advantage had long been under way. The anti-Lecompton coalition succeeded, by a close vote, in keeping the President's Lecompton message out of the hands of the pro-administration Committee on Territories and referring it to a select committee with power to investigate Kansas affairs. The victory was a hollow one, for Speaker Orr, after making Thomas L. Harris, the anti-Lecompton leader, chairman, appointed a pro-Lecompton majority. Even in this early skirmishing tempers flared. When Republican Galusha A. Grow of Pennsylvania and fire-eater Lawrence A. Keitt of South Carolina suddenly came to blows, a score of Congressmen briefly joined in a ludicrous exchange of punches and shoves, until Speaker Orr managed to call the House to order. There were no casualties.[7]

Alexander H. Stephens led the pro-Lecompton forces, searching for some means to avoid at least the appearance of total defeat, while the administration resorted to methods fair and foul to win the votes of party rebels. Buchanan ruthlessly dismissed every pro-Douglas officeholder who dared to show his colors. In Chicago, Douglas's friend William Price was replaced as postmaster by his mortal enemy Isaac Cook, who commanded the state's loyal administration Democrats. Anti-Lecompton Congressmen listened to tearful presidential pleas, were guests at lavish dinner parties, and had dangled before them every patronage and financial favor at the disposal of the executive department. Cobb was ever present in the House lobby, radiating charm and offering inducements to come to the President's support. One lobbyist, taking a more direct approach, tried to advance the administration cause with cash.[8]

A few of the rebels capitulated but the great majority of them would not yield. Congressman William Montgomery of Pennsylvania introduced a slight variation of the Crittenden substitute, and a committee of anti-Lecompton Democrats, Republicans, and Whig-Americans signed an agreement to give it their support. On April 1, with the galleries filled, the Crittenden-Montgomery substitute for the administration bill was put to a vote and passed, 120 to 112. Twenty-two anti-Lecompton Democrats and six Whig-Americans had joined the Republicans to require an honest vote in Kansas before admission under the Lecompton constitution would be approved. Even more repugnant to the administration was the substitute's provision for a new convention if Lecompton were voted down. Buchanan had gambled and lost.[9]

The Senate rejected the Crittenden-Montgomery substitute, and the House would accept nothing else. The deadlock lasted until April 13, when the Senate finally surrendered and asked for a conference committee to seek a way out. The administration then found itself in the humiliating position of pleading with anti-Lecompton Democrats, in effect, to take their victory without forcing the President to lose face altogether. Stephens worked diligently to that end, and William H. English of Indiana, who was both an anti-Lecompton Democrat and a friend of Senator Bright, agreed to support him. With the reluctant aid of a few rebels, the House vote on the proposed conference committee resulted in a tie, which Speaker Orr broke in the administration's favor.[10]

The committee consisted of Senators Green, Hunter, and Seward, and Representatives Stephens, English, and William A. Howard of Michigan—three administration Democrats, one anti-Lecompton Democrat, and two Republicans. Stephens and English together devised an extraordinary "compromise," designed to enable Kansans indirectly to vote on the Lecompton constitution while seeming to be voting on something else, thus easing the pain of Buchanan's defeat. The English bill, as it was called, reduced the enormous federal land grant that the Lecompton constitution had demanded for Kansas to a grant about the size recently given to other new states—approximately four million acres. Kansas voters would be permitted to decide whether or not they would accept the Lecompton constitution with this smaller grant of land, but the proposition as presented to them would emphasize the land issue rather than slavery. If the proposition were accepted, Kansas would be admitted at once; if it were rejected, Kansas would remain a territory until it had the population normally required for statehood, which at that time was about ninety thousand. In effect, Kansans would be given what the dissidents had demanded all along—an opportunity to vote on the Lecompton constitution. The consolation for the administration and proslavery Southerners was that the penalty for rejection would be the postponement of statehood for several years.

On April 23 the committee majority submitted the English bill to both houses along with a minority dissent from Seward and Howard. Republicans denounced the bill for its failure to permit a direct vote on Lecompton and for its refusal to admit Kansas immediately except as a slave state. Some charged, inaccurately, that the land grant was an attempt to bribe Kansans to accept the constitution. The anti-Lecompton Democrats in the House were exposed to immense pressure from the administration, which sanctioned the spending of large sums of money to break their ranks. Eventually half of them gave in and agreed to accept the English bill as substantially granting their principal demand for a vote on Lecompton. Walker, Stanton, and Forney favored the bill, and Douglas, after a conference with them, came close to a public announcement of his support. However, urgent advice not to yield from Illinois friends and a meeting with staunch anti-Lecompton congressional Democrats quickly changed his mind. Broderick angrily threatened to denounce him publicly if he backed down.

On April 29, during the Senate debate, Douglas spoke in opposition to the English bill. It did not conform to the principle of popular sovereignty, he said, for it did not permit a direct vote on the Lecompton constitution. Moreover, "where there are inducements on one side, and penalties on the other, there is no freedom of election." The next day the Senate passed the bill by a vote of 31-22, and the House by a vote of 112-103. It was a miserable subterfuge, but Buchanan accepted it with gratitude, even persuading himself that Douglas had met defeat.[11]

None could doubt how the Kansas electorate would respond. To accept the proposition offered by the English bill, asserted the Lawrence *Herald of Freedom*, would be to ratify the Lecompton constitution and all the frauds associated with it. It would be far better to remain a territory indefinitely. "The Territorial Government in the hands of the Free State party, and Uncle Sam to foot the bills, we can go along swimmingly for a year or so, with little or nothing to retard our progress." On August 2, under the strict supervision of Governor Denver, the election took place. On August 24, Denver notified Secretary Cass that the Election Board had determined that "the people of Kansas do not desire admission . . . with said Constitution under the conditions set forth in said proposition." The vote was 1,788 for the proposition, and 11,300 against.[12] Lecompton had at last been laid to rest!

Congress adjourned in June, and Democratic members went home to explain and defend their votes on the English bill. Those from the Deep South had to persuade disgruntled constituents that they had not really surrendered on the Lecompton issue. Northern administration Democrats fought for their political lives as the autumn congressional elections approached. Peacemakers worked feverishly to end the feud between Douglas and the administration and to reunite the national Democracy. By then the work of destruction had gone too far, and their efforts failed. Douglas faced a formidable opponent in Abraham Lincoln, and he apparently concluded that his prospects for re-election to the Senate would, if anything, be impaired by a reconciliation with Buchanan. Hence, he launched his campaign with another assault on the Lecompton fraud and a proud assertion of his crucial role in securing its defeat. The administration then carried the war to Illinois. Showing no concern about ultimate consequences, it used all its power to undermine Douglas's influence as a national party leader, to break his hold on the Illinois party organization, and to prevent his return to the Senate.

Douglas survived, for the new Illinois legislature, elected in November, had a small Democratic majority which, by a vote of 54-46, re-elected him the following January. Elsewhere in the North, the autumn elections revealed the damage the Democracy had suffered and foretold events yet to come. Republicans swept New York, even carrying New York City, and gained seven additional congressional seats. In Indiana they gained three seats and control of the legislature; in Ohio they gained three seats; and in Pennsylvania they gained eleven. One of the casualties was Buchanan's close friend, J. Glancy Jones. In the new Congress the number of free-state Democrats declined from the fifty-three seats they had held in the previous Congress to thirty-two, a dozen of whom were stubborn anti-Lecompton foes of the administration. The party had lost its House majority.[13] Looking to 1860, it could no longer hope to carry New York, or Ohio, or Wisconsin, or any other northern state that it had lost in 1856. Rather, it was more likely to lose several of the five it had won.

During the 1850s the proslavery South had won a series of striking political victories. In the Compromise of 1850 it had obtained a new and more stringent

Fugitive-Slave Act, which gave slaveholders the assistance of federal commissioners in their efforts to recover runaways. In 1854 southern Senators forced Douglas to agree to the repeal of the Missouri Compromise before giving their support to his Kansas-Nebraska Act. In 1857 the Supreme Court's Dred Scott decision affirmed the right of slaveholders to carry their property into all the territories of the United States. The year 1857, in fact, marked the high tide of the proslavery South's national political power. It had the sympathy of the Buchanan administration. It controlled the Supreme Court. It dominated the Democratic majorities in both houses of Congress. Pressing on, aggressive proslavery leaders ignored the advice of more cautious proslavery spokesmen, such as the Richmond *Enquirer,* not to force their northern allies to support policies that would destroy them—in short, not to endanger the survival of the Democratic party as a national organization. Instead, they disregarded election frauds and the clear will of the Kansas majority and, with the wholehearted support of the administration, demanded congressional approval of the Lecompton constitution.

With this demand they overreached themselves and brought on a genuine uprising of northern rank-and-file Democrats—and Douglas was their acknowledged leader. When Lecompton went down, the proslavery South suffered its first major defeat of the decade. Buchanan no longer had firm control of the Democracy in Pennsylvania; Bright soon lost control of Indiana. The Buchanan administration was discredited; southern control of the House of Representatives was lost; and the Democratic party was split. The Republican victory in the presidential election of 1860 was the logical result. "The South never made a worse move," wrote the angry editor of the Louisville *Democrat* at the end of 1857. "A blunder, it is said, is worse than a crime; but this is both a blunder and a crime. . . . It is calculated to break down the only national party in one section of the Union. A contest for President purely sectional will be the result, and we know how that will end; and then the object of the disunionists will be near its accomplishment."[14]

Could all of this have been avoided—would the course of the sectional conflict have been significantly altered—if Buchanan had remained true to his pledge and demanded the submission of the whole Lecompton constitution to the voters of Kansas? That is a question no historian can answer. It is doubtful that a firm stand by Buchanan would have resulted in southern secession, because the provocation would not have been sufficient to unite even the Deep South behind so drastic a response. Nor would it have been sufficient to produce a major split in the national Democratic party. Accordingly, without a divided and demoralized national Democracy, Republican successes in the elections of 1858 and the presidential election of 1860 would have been a good deal more problematic.

Yet, contrary to the optimists of 1857, removing the Kansas question from national politics, although eliminating a serious irritant, would not have assured a lasting settlement of the sectional conflict. The possibilities for other crises over slavery were far too numerous. Sooner or later, any one of them, like Lecompton, might have disrupted the Democratic party, perhaps, as in 1860, led to the nomination of two Democratic presidential candidates, and resulted in the election of Abraham Lincoln or some other "Black" Republican. The triumph of a Republican presidential candidate proved to be the provocation that turned the southern threats of secession, heard so often in the past, to reality.

On December 6, 1858, after the Democratic disasters in the northern autumn elections, Buchanan sent his annual message to the lame-duck session of the Thirty-fifth Congress. He began with his own explication of the Lecompton controversy, expressing satisfaction that Kansas at last appeared to be "tranquil and prosperous" and was attracting thousands of emigrants. The rebellious activities of the "revolutionary Topeka organization" had been abandoned, thus proving that "resistance to lawful authority . . . cannot fail in the end to prove disastrous to its authors." Although he continued to believe that approval of the Lecompton constitution would have "restored peace to Kansas and harmony to the Union" more rapidly, he "cordially acquiesced" in the English bill which Congress preferred. Still, it was "to be lamented that a question so insignificant when viewed in its practical effects on the people of Kansas, whether decided one way or the other, should have kindled such a flame of excitement throughout the country." In this manner, at the end of a disruptive party controversy, Buchanan made his case for posterity.

Rarely, it must be admitted, has any President, during his term in office, confessed publicly that he was guilty of an important error of judgment. He may on occasion, using the passive voice, concede the possibility that mistakes had been made, leaving responsibility for them in doubt. Buchanan would not concede even that. Referring to his message of February 2, 1858, which recommended approval of the Lecompton constitution, he now assured Congress and the public that he had no regrets. "In the course of my long public life," he defiantly asserted, "I have never performed any official act which in the retrospect has afforded me more heartfelt satisfaction." Let him be remembered, then, for that!

Manuscripts Consulted

Adams Family Papers, Massachusetts Historical Society
David Wyatt Aikin Diary, University of South Carolina
Robert F. W. Allston Papers (typescripts), University of South Carolina
John A. Andrew Papers, Massachusetts Historical Society
John S. Bagg Papers, Henry E. Huntington Library
George Bancroft Papers, Massachusetts Historical Society
Nathaniel P. Banks Papers, Library of Congress
Samuel L. M. Barlow Papers, Henry E. Huntington Library
Hiram Barney Papers, Henry E. Huntington Library
John Bell Papers, Library of Congress
John Bigelow Papers, New York Public Library
William Bigler Papers, Historical Society of Pennsylvania
John Houston Bills Diary, University of North Carolina
Francis W. Bird Papers, Harvard University
Jeremiah S. Black Papers, Library of Congress
James G. Blaine Papers, Library of Congress
Blair Family Papers, Library of Congress
Blair-Lee Papers, Princeton University
George Bliss Papers, Massachusetts Historical Society
Milledge L. Bonham Papers, University of South Carolina
Breckinridge Family Papers, Library of Congress
Preston S. Brooks Papers, University of South Carolina
John Brown Papers, Boston Public Library
William Cullen Bryant Papers, New York Public Library
Bryant-Godwin Papers, New York Public Library
James Buchanan Papers, Historical Society of Pennsylvania
James Buchanan and Harriet Lane Johnston Papers, Library of Congress
Benjamin F. Butler Papers, Library of Congress
Simon Cameron Papers, Historical Society of Dauphin County
Simon Cameron Papers, Library of Congress

Henry C. Carey Papers, Historical Society of Pennsylvania
Zachariah Chandler Papers, Library of Congress
Salmon P. Chase Papers, Historical Society of Pennsylvania
Salmon P. Chase Papers, Library of Congress
Salmon P. Chase Journal for 1857, New Hampshire Historical Society
Clement C. Clay Papers, Duke University
John H. Clifford Papers, Massachusetts Historical Society
Howell Cobb Papers, Duke University
Howell Cobb Papers, University of Georgia
Schuyler Colfax Papers, Indiana State Library
John J. Crittenden Papers, Library of Congress
John J. Crittenden Papers, Duke University
Caleb Cushing Papers, Library of Congress
Dana Family Papers, Massachusetts Historical Society
David Davis Family Papers, Illinois State Historical Library
Jefferson Davis Papers, Duke University
Stephen A. Douglas Papers, University of Chicago
William H. English Papers, Indiana Historical Society
Edward Everett Papers, Massachusetts Historical Society
Thomas Ewing Papers, Library of Congress
William P. Fessenden Papers, Library of Congress
Millard Fillmore Papers, Buffalo and Erie County Historical Society
Millard Fillmore Papers, State University of New York, Oswego
John C. Frémont Papers, University of California, Berkeley
William Lloyd Garrison Papers, Boston Public Library
Giddings-Julian Papers, Library of Congress
Goddard-Roslyn Collections, New York Public Library
Horace Greeley Papers, New York Public Library
Greeley-Colfax Papers, New York Public Library
John Berkley Grimball Diaries, University of North Carolina
William M. Gwin Papers, University of California, Berkeley
Hannibal Hamlin Papers, University of Maine
James H. Hammond Papers, University of South Carolina
James H. Hammond Papers, Library of Congress
Hampton Family Papers, University of South Carolina
Joseph Holt Papers, Library of Congress
Robert M. T. Hunter Papers, Virginia State Library
Andrew Johnson Papers, Library of Congress
Horatio King Papers, Library of Congress
Edmund Kirby-Smith Papers, University of North Carolina
Amos A. Lawrence Papers, Massachusetts Historical Society
Francis Terry Leak Diary, University of North Carolina
Lenoir Family Papers, University of North Carolina
Francis Lieber Papers, Henry E. Huntington Library
Francis Lieber Papers, University of North Carolina

Abraham Lincoln Papers, Library of Congress
John A. Logan Papers, Library of Congress
John A. McClernand Papers, Illinois State Historical Library
John McLean Papers, Library of Congress
Edward McPherson Papers, Library of Congress
James W. Mandeville Papers, Henry E. Huntington Library
Willie P. Mangum Papers, Library of Congress
Horace Mann Papers, Massachusetts Historical Society
William L. Marcy Papers, Library of Congress
Samuel J. May, Jr., Papers, Boston Public Library
William Porcher Miles Papers, University of North Carolina
John S. R. Miller Papers, University of North Carolina
Justin S. Morrill Papers, Library of Congress
Norcross Collection, Massachusetts Historical Society
Pettigrew Family Papers, University of South Carolina
Willard Phillips Papers, Massachusetts Historical Society
Francis W. Pickens Papers, Library of Congress
Franklin Pierce Papers, Library of Congress
William C. Rives Papers, Library of Congress
Charles and Sara Robinson Papers, Kansas State Historical Society
Charles Robinson Papers, University of Kansas
Samuel B. Ruggles Papers, New York Public Library
Thomas J. Rusk Papers, University of Texas, Austin
William Schouler Papers, Massachusetts Historical Society
Carl Schurz Papers, Library of Congress
William H. Seward Papers, University of Rochester
John Sherman Papers, Library of Congress
William Gilmore Simms Papers, University of South Carolina
Edwin M. Stanton Papers, Library of Congress
Alexander H. Stephens Papers, Duke University
Alexander H. Stephens Papers, Library of Congress
Thaddeus Stevens Papers, Library of Congress
Charles Sumner Papers, Harvard University
David S. Terry Papers, Henry E. Huntington Library
Samuel J. Tilden Papers, New York Public Library
Robert Toombs Papers, Duke University
Lyman Trumbull Papers, Library of Congress
Lyman Trumbull Family Papers, Illinois State Historical Library
John Tyler Papers, Library of Congress
Martin Van Buren Papers, Library of Congress
Benjamin F. Wade Papers, Library of Congress
Robert J. Walker Papers, New-York Historical Society
Emory Washburn Papers, Massachusetts Historical Society
Israel Washburn, Jr., Papers, Library of Congress
Elihu B. Washburne Papers, Library of Congress

Thurlow Weed Papers, Library of Congress
Thurlow Weed Papers, University of Rochester
Gideon Welles Papers, Library of Congress
Benjamin Davis Wilson Papers, Henry E. Huntington Library
Henry Wilson Papers, Library of Congress
Robert C. Winthrop Papers, Massachusetts Historical Society
Richard Yates Papers, Illinois State Historical Society
Brigham Young Papers, Archives of the Church of Jesus Christ of Latter-day Saints

Newspapers Consulted

Albany, N.Y., *Atlas and Argus*
Aurora, Ind., *Standard and Press*
Austin *Texas State Gazette*
Boston *Advertiser*
Boston *Evening Transcript*
Boston *Liberator*
Burlington, Vt., *Free Press*
Charleston *Mercury*
Chicago *Democrat*
Chicago *Times*
Chicago *Tribune*
Chillicothe, Ohio, *Scioto Gazette*
Cincinnati *Enquirer*
Cleveland *Plain Dealer*
Detroit *Free Press*
Edgefield, S.C., *Advertiser*
Harrisburg *Telegraph*
Indianapolis *Indiana State Sentinel*
Indianapolis *Locomotive*
Jackson *Mississippian*
Lawrence, Kan., *Herald of Freedom*
Leavenworth *Times*
Lecompton *Kansas National Democrat*
Lecompton *Union*
Louisville *Democrat*
Louisville *Journal*
Memphis *Appeal*
Madison *Wisconsin State Journal*
Milledgeville, Ga., *Federal Union*
Milwaukee *Sentinel*

Mobile *Register*
Montgomery *Mail*
Morrisville, N.Y., *Madison Observer*
Nashville *Republican Banner*
Nashville *Union and American*
New Albany, Ind., *Ledger*
New Orleans *Picayune*
New York *Evening Post*
New York *Herald*
New York *National Anti-Slavery Standard*
New York *Times*
New York *Tribune*
Philadelphia *North American*
Philadelphia *Press*
Philadelphia *Public Ledger*
Portland, Me., *Transcript and Eclectic*
Richmond, Ind., *Jeffersonian*
Richmond, Va., *Enquirer*
Richmond, Va., *Whig*
Sacramento *Union*
St. Louis *Missouri Democrat*
St. Louis *Missouri Republican*
San Francisco *Evening Bulletin*
South Bend *St. Joseph Valley Register*
Springfield *Illinois State Journal*
Springfield, Mass., *Republican*
Vincennes, Ind., *Gazette*
Washington *National Intelligencer*
Washington *National Era*
Washington *Union*
Waterville, N.Y., *Times*

Abbreviations Used in Notes

AH	Agricultural History
AHR	American Historical Review
ACLDS	Archives of the Church of Jesus Christ of Latter-day Saints
BECHS	Buffalo and Erie County Historical Society
BPL	Boston Public Library
CWH	Civil War History
DU	Duke University
GHQ	Georgia Historical Quarterly
HEH	Henry E. Huntington Library
HSDC	Historical Society of Douphin County, Pennsylvania
HSP	Historical Society of Pennsylvania
HU	Harvard University
ISHL	Illinois State Historical Library
IndHS	Indiana Historical Society
ISL	Indiana State Library
JAH	Journal of American History
JISHS	Journal of the Illinois State Historical Society
JSH	Journal of Southern History
KHQ	Kansas Historical Quarterly
KSHS	Kansas State Historical Society
LC	Library of Congress
LCHSJ	Lancaster County Historical Society Journal
MHS	Massachusetts Historical Society
MVHR	Mississippi Valley Historical Review
NEQ	New England Quarterly
NYHS	New-York Historical Society
NYPL	New York Public Library
OH	Ohio History
PH	Pennsylvania History
PHS	Pennsylvania Historical Society

PMHB	*Pennsylvania Magazine of History and Biography*
PU	Princeton University
SAQ	*South Atlantic Quarterly*
SCH	*Studies in Church History*
THM	*Tennessee Historical Magazine*
UC	University of Chicago
UCB	University of California, Berkeley
UG	University of Georgia
UK	University of Kansas
UM	University of Maine
UNC	University of North Carolina
UR	University of Rochester
USC	University of South Carolina
UTA	University of Texas, Austin
VSL	Virginia State Library
WMH	*Wisconsin Magazine of History*

Notes

Note: Unless otherwise indicated, all citations of newspapers, manuscripts, and published documents are for the year 1857. If a newspaper was published in more than one edition—daily, weekly, or semiweekly—I have indicated the edition consulted only if it was not the daily edition. I have deleted the words "daily" or "weekly" from the names of newspapers.

Chapter 1

1. Allan Nevins and Milton Halsey Thomas, eds., *The Diary of George Templeton Strong* (4 vols., New York, 1952), II, 317; Louisville *Journal*, January 1.
2. Washington *National Intelligencer*, January 3.
3. The best study of the formation and early years of the Republican party is William E. Gienapp, *The Origins of the Republican Party, 1852-1856* (New York, 1987).
4. The reference to polygamy was directed at its practice among the Mormons in Utah Territory.
5. *Congressional Globe*, 34 Cong., 3 sess., 10-11, 24-25, 51, Appendix, 162.
6. *Congressional Globe*, 34 Cong., 3 sess., 44-45, 71-74, 88-90.
7. Washington *National Intelligencer*, January 1; Philadelphia *North American*, January 1; Springfield *Illinois State Journal*, January 1.
8. *Harper's Weekly: A Journal of Civilization*, January 3.
9. Joseph Carlyle Sitterson, *The Secession Movement in North Carolina* (Chapel Hill, 1939), 135; Roy F. Nichols, *The Disruption of American Democracy* (New York, 1948), 48-49.
10. *Congressional Globe*, 34 Cong., 3 sess., Appendix 131; Philadelphia *North American*, January 1; Philadelphia *Public Ledger*, January 1.
11. In the free states Frémont's vote was 1,335,000; Buchanan's, 1,220,000; Fillmore's, 393,000.
12. Letter from "Essex," in St. Louis *Missouri Democrat*, January 22.
13. New York *Herald*, January 4; Washington *Union*, January 9; Nashville *Union and American*, January 11.
14. J. R. Meredith to Salmon P. Chase, January 8, Chase Papers, LC.
15. George Bancroft to James Buchanan, February 21, Buchanan Papers, HSP.

16. Cincinnati *Enquirer,* March 6; weekly Chicago *Times,* January 8; Lillian A. Kibler, *Benjamin F. Perry: South Carolina Unionist* (Durham, 1946), 286-87; J. P. Farnsley to William H. English, January 12, English Papers, IndHS.

17. Isaac G. Wilson to Lyman Trumbull, February 14, Trumbull Papers, LC.

18. *Congressional Globe,* 34 Cong., 3 sess., Appendix 125; Memphis *Eagle and Enquirer,* quoted in Montgomery *Mail,* March 26.

19. The Republicans also lost California, but its electoral vote was then very small.

20. Andrew J. McCallen to Trumbull, January 20; T. A. Marshall to Trumbull, March 2, Trumbull Papers. See also William E. Gienapp, "Nativism and the Creation of a Republican Majority before the Civil War," *JAH,* LXXII (1985), 529-59.

21. George S. Hillard to Francis Lieber, May 28, Lieber Papers, HEH; Edward Everett to Horace Maynard, October 3, Everett Papers, MHS; Nevins and Halsey, eds., *Diary of George Templeton Strong,* II, 273-74; William E. Gienapp, "The Crime Against Sumner: The Caning of Charles Sumner and the Rise of the Republican Party," *CWH,* XXV (1979), 218-45.

22. S. W. Parker to Benjamin F. Wade, January 16, Wade Papers, LC; W. S. Bailey to Chase, January 11, Chase Papers, LC.

23. Robert F. Lucid, ed., *The Journal of Richard Henry Dana, Jr.* (3 vols., Cambridge, Mass., 1968), II, 821; Nevins and Halsey, eds., *Diary of George Templeton Strong,* II, 310; John Niven, *Gideon Welles: Lincoln's Secretary of the Navy* (New York, 1973), 275; Henry D. Cooke to John Sherman, December 8, 1856, Sherman Papers, LC; Frederic Bancroft, ed., *Speeches, Correspondence and Political Papers of Carl Schurz* (6 vols., New York, 1913), I, 28-31; S. W. Parker to Wade, January 16, Wade Papers.

24. *Congressional Globe,* 34 Cong., 3 sess., 97-98; Chicago *Tribune,* January 31.

25. William K. Scarborough, ed., *The Diary of Edmund Ruffin: Volume I, Toward Independence, October 1856-April, 1861* (Baton Rouge, 1972), 37; Betty L. Mitchell, *Edmund Ruffin: A Biography* (Bloomington, 1981), 98-99; Charleston *Mercury,* January 12; Natchez *Mississippi Free Trader,* February 6, quoted in Percy L. Rainwater, *Mississippi: Storm Center of Secession, 1856-1861* (Baton Rouge, 1938), 43.

26. *Congressional Globe,* 34 Cong., 3 sess., Appendix, 140-45.

27. Scarborough, ed., *Diary of Edmund Ruffin,* I, 66; Laura A. White, *Robert Barnwell Rhett: Father of Secession* (New York, 1931), 138-39; H. J. Harris to Jefferson Davis, December 3, 1856, in Dunbar Roland., ed., *Jefferson Davis, Constitutionalist: His Letters, Papers, and Speeches* (10 vols., Jackson, Miss., 1923), III, 99; *De Bow's Review,* July 1857, 102.

Chapter 2

1. Washington *National Era,* January 1.

2. *Congressional Globe,* 34 Cong., 3 sess., Appendix, 140-45.

3. Lydia Maria Child, one of Sumner's adoring followers, wrote him on January 3 that, on meeting him, she had wanted to ask for a lock of his hair, "but that noble head, which had suffered martyrdom for Freedom, seemed too sacred for me to touch." Sumner Papers, HU. An Iowa Congregational clergyman informed him that he was "honored and beloved . . . by the freedom loving ministers of this State. . . . Their prayers and expectations will follow you . . . as you return to do something for the Savior they serve." George Magoun to Sumner, January 13, Sumner Papers.

4. D. W. Alvord to Sumner, January 29, Sumner Papers. Mary Thacher Higginson, ed., *Letters and Journals of Thomas Wentworth Higginson, 1846-1906* (Boston, 1921), 78; W. S. Bailey to Salmon P. Chase, January 11, Chase Papers, LC; Charles Sumner to William H. Seward, January 25, Seward Papers, UR; Charles Francis Adams ms. diary, entry for February 21, Adams Family Papers, MHS; David Donald, *Charles Sumner and the Coming of the Civil War* (New York, 1960), 326-28.

5. Allan Nevins, *Ordeal of the Union* (2 vols., New York, 1947), II, 446-47.

6. R. C. Griffin to Milledge L. Bonham, January 31, Bonham Papers, USC. For a full, first-hand account of Brooks's death, see John McQueen to his son, January 31, Preston S. Brooks Papers, USC.

7. *Congressional Globe*, 34 Cong., 3 sess., 499-501; William Y. Thompson, *Robert Toombs of Georgia* (Baton Rouge, 1966), 116; S. G. Haven to Millard Fillmore, January 29, Fillmore Papers, BECHS; Edgefield, S.C., *Advertiser,* quoted in Charleston *Mercury,* February 21.

8. *Southern Quarterly Review,* February 348-70.

9. Adams ms. diary, entries for January 28, 29, Adams Family Papers; Henry Wilson to Sumner, January 27; S. P. Hanscom to Sumner, January 29, Sumner Papers; *National Anti-Slavery Standard,* February 7.

10. *Hunt's Merchants' Magazine,* XXXVII (March), 327; Moses H. Grinnell to William H. Seward, February 17, Seward Papers.

11. New York *Evening Post,* March 25; Cincinnati *Enquirer,* January 21.

12. Richmond *Enquirer,* January 6; *Congressional Globe,* 34 Cong., 3 sess., Appendix, 189; Edgefield, S.C., *Advertiser,* February 25; Charleston *Mercury,* January 1, 8, 10.

13. Washington *National Intelligencer,* March 30; *Congressional Globe,* 34 Cong., 3 sess., 643, 786, Appendix, 225–28.

14. New York *Evening Post,* January 5; A. R. Corbin to Henry Douglas Bacon, January 1, Samuel L. M. Barlow Papers, HEH; Edward Corning to William H. Seward, February 17, Seward Papers; *Congressional Globe,* 34 Cong., 3 sess., 642-43; Chillicothe, Ohio, *Scioto Gazette,* January 8; Horace Greeley to Schuyler Colfax, January 3, Greeley-Colfax Papers, NYPL.

15. Thomas Andrews & Co. to William H. Seward, February 23; Jeremiah Milbank to Seward, February 25; Ziegler & Williams to Seward, February 25, Seward Papers.

16. James Fitton to William H. Seward, January 3, Seward Papers; *Congressional Globe,* 34 Cong., 3 sess., 788; J. W. Wolcott to Nathaniel P. Banks, February 5, Banks Papers, LC; Richard Hofstadter, "The Tariff Issue on the Eve of the Civil War," *AHR,* XLIV (1938), 50-55.

17. *Congressional Globe,* 34 Cong., 3 sess., 185-87, 249, 589, 642, 786, 791-92.

18. Edward Stanwood, *American Tariff Controversies in the Nineteenth Century* (2 vols., Boston, 1903), 97-109.

19. Sam Lawrence to Robert M. T. Hunter, March 6, Hunter Papers, VSL; Boston *Advertiser,* March 17; New York *Tribune,* March 4; New York *Evening Post,* March 4; Charleston Mercury, March 9.

20. *Congressional Globe,* 34 Cong., 3 sess., 969-71, 1060-62; Philadelphia *North American,* January 3; March 9.

21. W. S. Bailey to Salmon P. Chase, January 11, Chase Papers, LC; *Congressional Globe,* 34 Cong., 3 sess., 649.

22. Nevins, *Ordeal of the Union,* II, 201-2; Robert R. Russel, *Improvement of Communication with the Pacific Coast as an Issue in American Politics, 1783-1864* (Cedar Rapids, Iowa, 1948), 220-21; New York *Herald,* January 12; New York *Tribune,* January 1,3; Richmond *Enquirer,* January 13; Horace Greeley to Schuyler Colfax, January 3, Greeley-Colfax Papers.

23. Russel, *Improvement of Communication with the Pacific Coast,* 221-24; San Francisco *Evening Bulletin,* April 7; July 2.

24. *Congressional Globe,* 34 Cong., 3 sess., 587, 731, 741, 753-59, 882. The subsidy was to be reduced to $50,000 when the enterprise became profitable and was to be terminated after 25 years.

25. *Congressional Globe,* 34 Cong., 3 sess., 218-22, 378-80; Charleston *Mercury,* January 7; February 14; E. W Beatty to Clement C. Clay, Jr., January 21; Edmund Ruffin to Clay, February 2, Clay Papers, DU.

26. *Congressional Globe,* 34 Cong., 3 sess., 381-85, 399-403, 465-74, Appendix, 270-75.

27. *Congressional Globe,* 34 Cong., 3 sess., 998.

28. Susan Sutton Smith and Harrison Hayford, eds., *The Journals and Miscellaneous Notebooks of Ralph Waldo Emerson* (16 vols., Cambridge, Mass., 1978), XIV, 170; *Harper's Weekly,* March 21; Cincinnati *Enquirer,* January 15; New York *Herald,* January 13, 24. The best account of political corruption in the 1850s is Mark W. Summers, *The Plundering Generation: Corruption and the Crisis of the Union* (New York, 1988).

29. Nichols, *Disruption of American Democracy,* 189-90; Summers, *Plundering Generation,* 102-3; Glyndon G. Van Deusen, *Thurlow Weed: Wizard of the Lobby* (Boston, 1947), 222-23.

30. *Congressional Globe,* 34 Cong., 3 sess., 274-77, 760-73, 882-907, 925-53, Appendix 266-70; Washington *National Intelligencer,* February 21; March 5; New York *Tribune,* January 12, 14, 16; March 3; Nichols, *Disruption of American Democracy,* 68-69. Matteson was re-elected and regained his seat in the Thirty-fifth Congress.

31. Edward Everett ms. diary, entries for February 21,24, Everett Papers; Glyndon G. Van Deusen, *Horace Greeley: Nineteenth Century Crusader* (Philadelphia, 1953), 215, 232n.

32. Scarborough, ed., *Diary of Edmund Ruffin,* I, 24; Charleston *Mercury,* February 25; Nashville *Union and Banner,* February 15; Washington *National Era,* February 5, 26; New York, *Herald,* February 20.

33. Alexander Rives to William C. Rives, May 29, W. C. Rives Papers, LC; William E. Gienapp, "'Politics Seem to Enter into Everything': Political Culture in the North, 1840-1860," in Stephen E. Maizlish and John J. Kushma, eds., *Essays on American Antebellum Politics, 1840-1860* (College Station, Texas, 1982), 25-27.

34. Van Deusen, *Thurlow Weed,* 212-30; New York *Times,* April 13.

35. New York *Tribune,* March 23; Eugene H. Roseboom, *The Civil War Era, 1850-1873,* Vol. IV of Carl Wittke, ed., *The History of the State of Ohio* (6 vols., Columbus, 1944), 324; W. T. Bascom to Benjamin F. Wade, February 16, Wade Papers; Gayle Thornbrough, Dorothy L. Riker, and Paula Corpuz, *The Diary of Calvin Fletcher: Volume VI, 1857-1860* (Indianapolis, 1978), 74 and passim; Madison *Wisconsin State Journal,* June 5; September 22; Summers, *Plundering Generation,* 109-12; Richard N. Current, *The History of Wisconsin, Volume II: The Civil War Era, 1848-1873,* 244-47.

36. Roseboom, *Civil War Era,* 325-26.

37. Ed Davis to Willie P. Mangum, February 15, Mangum Papers, LC; Sacramento *Union,* January 22; San Francisco *Evening Bulletin,* February 8, 12; March 13; New York *Tribune,* March 30; C. H. Hempstead to James Buchanan, September 19, Buchanan Papers.

38. New York *Times,* June 1; New York *Tribune,* July 8; September 29; *Harper's Weekly,* January 17; Nichols, *Disruption of American Democracy,* 84, 207-8.

39. Boston *Advertiser,* March 13; April 3; New York *Tribune,* January 10; March 14, 24; New York *Evening Post,* April 13; Moses Pierce to Gideon Welles, March 13; Welles to Chauncey F. Cleveland, April [?]; Lancelot Phelps to Welles, April 23, Welles Papers, LC; Niven, *Welles,* 280.

40. Cincinnati *Enquirer,* April 8; Louisville *Democrat,* April 5; Don E. Fehrenbacher, *Chicago Giant: A Biography of "Long John" Wentworth* (Madison, 1957), 140-41; Robert W. Johannsen, *The Letters of Stephen A. Douglas* (Urbana, 1961), 374.

41. Waterville, N.Y., *Times* October 3, 24.

42. Cincinnati *Enquirer,* January 10; Detroit *Free Press,* January 13.

43. For the pervasiveness of politics in American culture, see Gienapp, "'Politics Seem to Enter into Everything,'" 14-69.

44. Cushing Papers for 1857, LC; William N. Chambers, *Old Bullion Benton, Senator from the New West: Thomas Hart Benton, 1782-1858* (Boston, 1956), 428-31; Cincinnati *Enquirer,* May 8.

45. Nevins and Halsey, eds., *Diary of George Templeton Strong*, II, 316-79; Pettigrew Family Papers and Lenoir Family Papers for 1857, UNC.

46. New York *Evening Post*, January 20; Philadelphia *Public Ledger*, January 27; New Orleans *Picayune*, February 21; Chicago *Tribune*, May 5.

47. William C. Rives to William C. Rives, Jr., January 22, Rives Papers; William Bingham to Aunt Sade, January 26, Lenoir Family Papers.

48. Detroit *Free Press*, January 2.

49. Waterville, N.Y., *Times*, March 3; New York *Evening Post*, June 25.

50. San Francisco *Evening Bulletin*, January 2; Milwaukee *Sentinel*, February 15; New York *Evening Post*, April 25; Waterville, N.Y., *Times*, February 28; Lucid, ed., *Journal of Richard Henry Dana, Jr.*, II, 832.

51. Herbert Aptheker, *American Negro Slave Revolts* (New York, 1943), is best as an account of the white South's fear of slave conspiracies. See also Kenneth M. Stampp, *The Peculiar Institution: Slavery in the Ante-Bellum South* (New York, 1956), 86-191.

52. William C. Rives, Jr., to his overseer, January 7, Rives Papers; Richmond *Enquirer*, January 9.

53. New Orleans *Picayune*, December 24, 1856; January 2; Austin *Texas State Gazette*, January 3; Athens, Ga., *Southern Watchman*, quoted in Ulrich B. Phillips (ed.), *Plantation and Frontier* (2 vols., Cleveland, 1910), II, 116-17; New York *National Anti-Slavery Standard*, January 31.

54. New Orleans *Picayune*, January 2; Nashville *Union and American*, January 8; Phillips (ed.), *Plantation and Frontier*, II, 116-17; Austin *Texas State Gazette*, January 3.

55. *Harper's Weekly*, June 20. On nativism and anti-Catholicism in the politics of the 1850s see especially Ray A. Billington, *The Protestant Crusade* (New York, 1938), *passim*; Michael F. Holt, "The Politics of Impatience: The Origins of Know Nothingism," *JAH*, LX (1973), 309-31; Eric Foner, *Free Soil, Free Labor, Free Men: The Ideology of the Republican Party before the Civil War* (New York, 1970), 225-60; William E. Gienapp, "Nativism and the Creation of a Republican Majority before the Civil War," *JAH*, LXXII (1985), 529-59; Gienapp, *Origins of the Republican Party, passim.*

56. Brainard Williamson to Millard Fillmore, July 18, Fillmore Papers; Amos A. Lawrence political letter, dated July 8, in Amos A. Lawrence Papers, MHS; Boston *Advertiser*, January 10; *Congressional Globe*, 34 Cong., 3 sess., Appendix, 124-25; 247; Louisville *Democrat*, April 4, 5; Louisville *Journal*, April 11; June 23; July 18; Howell Cobb to his son, June 2, Cobb Papers, UG.

57. Milwaukee *Sentinel*, September 15; Waterville, N.Y., *Times*, June 13; Sacramento *Union*, January 29; San Francisco *Evening Bulletin*, April 24; Chicago *Tribune*, April 24.

58. Nashville *Republican Banner*, August 12; Chicago *Democrat*, May 30; San Francisco *Evening Bulletin*, December 25.

59. James B. Smith to Jeremiah S. Black, June 6, Black Papers, LC; Louisville *Democrat*, May 15; Adele Cutts Douglas to her mother, June 24, in Johanssen, *Letters of Stephen A. Douglas*, 384-85; Chicago *Tribune*, July 28; San Francisco *Evening Bulletin*, December 25.

60. New York *Evening Post*, February 4; New York *Independent*, quoted in Waterville, N.Y., *Times*, February 21; Nevins and Halsey, eds., *Diary of George Templeton Strong*, II, 320; Charles Kuhn to Charles Francis Adams, February 11, Adams Family Papers.

61. For a summary of the case see *Harper's Weekly*, May 9; Nevins and Halsey, eds., *Diary of George Templeton Strong*, II, 316-17, 320-24; New York *Herald*, February 3, 12; New York *Tribune*, February 12.

62. New York *Herald*, February 4, 12.

63. New York *Herald*, May 10, 11; New York *Evening Post*, May 11.

64. San Francisco *Evening Bulletin*, December 25; Washington *National Era*, February 26; Philadelphia *Public Ledger*, February 12; *United States Democratic Review*, September, 207; New York *Herald*, February 3.

65. New York *Evening Post,* May 18; Washington *National Era,* February 26; Chicago *Democrat,* May 30; Chicago *Tribune,* June 20.

66. Current, *History of Wisconsin,* II, 191, 195; Madison *Wisconsin State Journal,* March 5; Milwaukee *Sentinel,* January 31; February 4, 14, 19.

67. Richmond *Enquirer,* February 20.

68. New York *Evening Post,* February 24.

69. Lori D. Ginzberg, "'Moral Suasion Is Moral Balderdash': Women, Politics, and Social Activism in the 1850s," *JAH,* LXXIII (1986), 601-22; Elizabeth E. Hutter to James Buchanan, December 9, Buchanan Papers.

70. *Harper's Weekly,* June 6; Milwaukee *Sentinel,* March 4; Michael J. McManus, "Wisconsin Republicans and Negro Suffrage: Attitudes and Behavior, 1857," *CWH,* XXV (1979), 39-40.

71. Philadelphia *North American,* April 7. For a discussion of women's education, written in a similar spirit and reaching similar conclusions, see *Harper's New Monthly Magazine* for November, 776-83.

72. Waterville, N.Y., *Times,* September 12; October 10; Richmond *Enquirer,* February 23; *Harper's Weekly,* January 3.

73. Mrs. Cyrus Pierce to Horace Mann, March 5, Mann Papers; Philadelphia *Public Ledger,* February 4.

74. San Francisco *Evening Bulletin,* May 5.

75. Waterville, N.Y., *Times,* April 11.

Chapter 3

1. Henry S. Foote, *Casket of Reminiscences* (Washington, D.C., 1874), 110-13.

2. Buchanan to John Y. Mason, December 29, 1856, Buchanan Papers. The best full-length biography of Buchanan is Philip Shriver Klein, *President James Buchanan: A Biography* (University Park, Pa., 1962). Elbert B. Smith, *The Presidency of James Buchanan* (Lawrence, Kansas, 1975), and Nichols, *Disruption of American Democracy,* are perceptive on the presidential years. Allan Nevins, *The Emergence of Lincoln* (2 vols., New York, 1950), portrays Buchanan as weaker than he really was.

3. Memphis *Appeal,* January 6; Milledgeville *Federal Union,* February 6; Z. L. Nabors to Clement C. Clay, January 23, Clay Papers.

4. John Appleton to Buchanan, January 11, 15; Jefferson Davis to Buchanan, February 2, Buchanan Papers.

5. John Appleton to Buchanan, February 7; George Bancroft to Buchanan, February 21, Buchanan Papers; Bancroft to H. D. Gilpin, February 6, Bancroft Papers, MHS.

6. Buchanan to James Gordon Bennett, December 29, 1856; Henry Wikoff to Buchanan, January 14; Bennett to Buchanan, February 6, Buchanan Papers; New York *Herald,* January 4.

7. Cincinnati *Enquirer,* February 15, 18.

8. Gienapp, "'Politics Seem to Enter into Everything,'" 48-49.

9. Mark L. Berger, *The Revolution in the New York Party System* (Port Washington, N.Y., 1973), 104-8.

10. Craig M. Simpson, *A Good Southerner: The Life of Henry A. Wise of Virginia* (Chapel Hill, 1985), 158-60.

11. Joseph A. Wright to Buchanan, January 15; Buchanan to Wright, January 22, Ashbel P. Willard to Buchanan, January 30, Buchanan Papers; W. F. Sherrod to William H. English, January 30, English Papers; New York *Tribune,* March 19, 23; Emma Lou Thornbrough, *Indiana in the Civil War Era, 1850-1880* (Indianapolis, 1965), 78-79.

12. Balie Peyton to John Bell, February 4, Bell Papers, LC; Sacramento *Union,* January 15; San Francisco *Evening Bulletin,* January 19; David A. Williams, *David C. Broderick: A*

Political Portrait (San Marino, Calif., 1969), 148-55; William H. Ellison, *A Self-Governing Dominion: California, 1849-1860* (Berkeley, 1950), 269-93.

13. Alexander K. McClure, *Old Time Notes of Pennsylvania* (2 vols., Philadelphia, 1905), I, 254-56; John F. Coleman, *The Disruption of the Pennsylvania Democracy, 1848-1860* (Harrisburg, 1975), 19-25, 49-54, 88-101; Nichols, *Disruption of American Democracy*, 45-47.

14. McClure, *Old Times Notes*, I, 255-58, 261-62; Coleman, *Disruption of the Pennsylvania Democracy*, 103; Nichols, *Disruption of American Democracy*, 58-59.

15. William N. Brigance, *Jeremiah Sullivan Black* (Philadelphia, 1934),41-42.

16. Buchanan to Forney, December 13, 1856; Buchanan to Henry Mott, January 7; Forney to Buchanan, January 3, 9, Buchanan Papers; Klein, *Buchanan*, 265-66.

17. Robert Tyler to Buchanan, January 5, Buchanan Papers; G. R. Barrett to William Bigler, January 5, Bigler Papers, HSP; Philip G. Auchampaugh, *Robert Tyler: Southern Rights Champion, 1847-1866* (Duluth, Minn., 1934), 158-59, 163, 171-72.

18. Forney to Buchanan, January 10, 11, 13; George Plitt to Buchanan, January 11, Buchanan Papers; Coleman, *Disruption of the Pennsylvania Democracy*, 104.

19. Thaddeus Stevens to [?], December 4, 1856, Edward McPherson Papers, LC; Philadelphia *Pennsylvanian*, January 8, quoted in Lee F. Crippen, *Simon Cameron: Ante-Bellum Years* (Oxford, Ohio, 1942), 160-61.

20. Harrisburg *Telegraph*, January 13, 14; Forney to Howell Cobb, January 30, and one undated letter, Cobb Papers, UG; McClure, *Old Time Notes*, 266-73; Klein, *Buchanan*, 265-66; Crippen, *Cameron*, 158-70; Erwin S. Bradley, *Simon Cameron: Lincoln's Secretary of War* (Philadelphia, 1966), 114-21.

21. Edward J. Fox to Cameron, January 26; Stephen Miller to Cameron, January 13, Cameron Papers, HSDC; O. Collier to Cameron, January 15; Charles B. Forney to Cameron, January 24, Cameron Papers, LC; New York *Evening Post*, January 14.

22. Philadelphia *Pennsylvanian*, quoted in Harrisburg *Telegraph*, January 16; Richmond *Enquirer*, January 20; Milledgeville, Ga., *Federal Union*, January 27.

23. Washington *Union*, January 15; Richardson L. Wright, J. Lawrence Getz, and N. B. Brown to Bigler, March 12, Bigler Papers; *Congressional Globe*, 34 Cong., 3 sess., Appendix, 387-89.

24. Jos. Veech to Cameron, January 12, Cameron Papers, HSDC; Charles W. Corrigan to Cameron, July 13, 19; J. M. Andrews to Cameron, August 5, Cameron Papers, LC; Bradley, *Cameron*, 114-21; Crippen, *Cameron*, 158-70.

25. New York *Herald*, January 9.

26. Klein, *Buchanan*, 262-65; Nevins, *Emergence of Lincoln*, I, 67-68; Bright to William H. English, April 16, English Papers; Edward Everett to Buchanan, January 19, Buchanan Papers; J. H. Garrard to John C. Breckinridge, January 26, Breckinridge Family Papers, LC; William C. Davis, *Breckinridge: Statesman, Soldier, Symbol* (Baton Rouge, 1974), 166.

27. T.R.R. Cobb to Howell Cobb, January 17; A Birdsall to Cobb, January 27, Cobb Papers, UG; R. P. Brooks, ed., "Howell Cobb Papers," *GHQ*, V (1921), 172-73; Auchampaugh, *Robert Tyler*, 170-71; James P. Shenton, *Robert John Walker: A Politician from Jackson to Lincoln* (New York, 1961), 143-45; John E. Simpson, *Howell Cobb: The Politics of Ambition* (Chicago, 1973), 93-113; William B. McCash, *Thomas R. R. Cobb (1823-1862): The Making of a Southern Nationalist* (Macon, 1983), 145-47; Nevins, *Emergence of Lincoln*, I, 69-71.

28. Royal Phelps to William M. Marcy, February 15, Marcy Papers, LC; New York *Tribune*, January 1.

29. John Appleton to Buchanan, January 15; Wise to Buchanan, January 5; Slidell to Buchanan, February 14, Buchanan Papers; John B. Lamar to Cobb, January 21, 24; W. F. Boone to Cobb, January 31; Mary Ann Cobb to Cobb, January 29, Cobb Papers, UG; Auchampaugh, *Robert Tyler*, 144-45; Nevins *Emergence of Lincoln*, I, 74; Roger P. Leemhuis, *James L. Orr and the Sectional Conflict* (Washington, D.C., 1979), 53-54.

30. Slidell to Buchanan, January 5; Bigler to Buchanan, February 5, Buchanan Papers; William L. Marcy to Martin Van Buren, January 26, Van Buren Papers, LC; Washington *Union,* January 28; February 5; Cobb to John B. Lamar, January 31, Cobb Papers, UG; Robert M. McLane to Cobb, February 14, in Ulrich B. Phillips, ed., *The Correspondence of Robert Toombs, Alexander H. Stephens, and Howell Cobb,* American Historical Association, *Annual Report* (1911), II, 395-96.

31. Newburyport, Mass., *Herald,* quoted in Morrisville, N.Y., *Madison Observer,* October 1. The best biography of Douglas is Robert W. Johannsen, *Stephen A. Douglas* (New York, 1973).

32. Cincinnati *Enquirer,* February 1, 10; Johannsen, *Douglas,* 540-43.

33. Douglas to Samuel Treat, February 5, in Johannsen, *Letters of Douglas,* 372; Slidell to Buchanan, February 14, Buchanan Papers.

34. Philadelphia *Public Ledger,* March 16, 20; Klein, *Buchanan,* 268-69; Nichols, *Disruption of American Democracy,* 63; Richard H. Sewell, *John P. Hale and the Politics of Abolition* (Cambridge, Mass., 1965), 173.

35. Bigler to Buchanan, February 12; Slidell to Buchanan, February 14; Jones to Buchanan, February 14, Buchanan Papers.

36. Slidell to Buchanan, February 19, Buchanan Papers; Frank B. Woodford, *Lewis Cass: The Last Jeffersonian* (New Brunswick, N.J., 1950), 315-16; Klein, *Buchanan,* 266-67; New York *Tribune,* March 2.

37. Cobb to Mary Ann Cobb, January 28; February 10; Martin J. Crawford to Cobb, February 15; John B. Lamar to Cobb, January 2, Cobb Papers, UG; Buchanan to Cobb, February 21, in Phillips, ed., *Correspondence of Toombs, Stephens and Cobb,* 397; Simpson, *Cobb,* 113-14; Nichols, *Disruption of American Democracy,* 66.

38. Buchanan to Jones, February 17; Jones to Buchanan, February 20; John Appleton to Buchanan, February 20; Buchanan to Jones, February 28, Buchanan Papers; Charles Henry Jones, *The Life and Public Services of J. Glancy Jones* (2 vols., Philadelphia, 1910), I, 348-72.

39. Klein, *Buchanan,* 267-68; Nichols, *Disruption of American Democracy,* 78-81; Nevins, *Emergence of Lincoln,* I, 71-72.

40. Buchanan to Jones, February 28; Buchanan to Black, March 6; Black to Buchanan, March 7, Buchanan Papers.

41. John Appleton to Buchanan, February 2, Buchanan Papers.

42. Klein, *Buchanan,* 270; Nichols, *Disruption of American Democracy,* 69-70.

43. Benjamin Perley Poore, *Perley's Reminiscences of Sixty Years in the National Metropolis* (2 vols., Philadelphia, 1886), I, 511-16; Klein, *Buchanan,* 270-71; Nichols, *Disruption of American Democracy,* 71.

44. Poore, *Perley's Reminiscences,* I, 515-16; Klein, *Buchanan,* 271-72; Nevins, *Emergence of Lincoln,* I, 88.

45. Nashville *Union and American,* March 5; Cincinnati *Enquirer,* March 4.

46. Detroit *Free Press,* March 5; New York *Herald,* March 4; Washington *Union,* March 7; W. B. Slaughter to Amos A. Lawrence, March 4, Lawrence Papers; Washington *National Intelligencer,* April 2.

47. Cobb to Black, April 26, Black Papers; Austin *Texas State Gazette,* March 21; John O. Knox to William C. Rives, March 23, Rives Papers.

48. Chicago *Tribune,* March 5; Milwaukee *Sentinel,* March 9; New York *Evening Post,* March 5; Adams ms. diary, entry for March 4, in Adams Family Papers.

Chapter 4

1. Klein, *Buchanan,* 273-74.

2. Mrs. Clement C. Clay, Jr., *A Belle of the Fifties: Memoirs of Mrs. Clay of Alabama* (New York, 1904), 114-16; Nevins, *Emergence of Lincoln,* I, 120-27.

3. Cobb to Mary Ann Cobb, March 8; June 6; Black to Cobb, April 30, Cobb Papers, UG.

4. Black to Cobb, April 30, Cobb Papers, U.G.; C.W.C. Dunnington to Robert M. T. Hunter, October 6, in Charles H. Ambler, ed., *Correspondence of Robert M. T. Hunter, 1826-1876,* American Historical Association, *Annual Report* (Washington, D.C., 1916), II, 235-36; Floyd to Buchanan, July 31, Buchanan Papers; Klein, *Buchanan,* 285. The argument that a Cabinet "Directory" dominated the Buchanan administration is presented most fully in Nevins, *Emergence of Lincoln,* I, passim. For a different perspective see Richard R. Stenberg, "An Unnoticed Factor in the Buchanan-Douglas Feud," *JISHS,* XXV (1933), 271-85; Klein, *Buchanan,* passim; and David E. Meerse, "Presidential Leadership, Suffrage Qualifications, and Kansas in 1857," *CWH,* XXIV (1978), 293-313.

5. Klein, *Buchanan,* 275-78, 285, 333; Simpson, *Cobb,* 114-15; Nichols, *Disruption of American Democracy,* 78-81; Nevins, *Emergence of Lincoln,* I, 75-78.

6. John B. Floyd to John C. Breakinridge, March 25; J. C. Van Dyke to Breckinridge, April 9, Breckinridge Family Papers; Davis, *Breckinridge,* 168-71.

7. New York *Herald,* January 20; Mobile *Register,* May 19; Bright to William H. English, April 13, English Papers.

8. Bigler to Black, April 13, Black Papers; John A. Bryan to Horatio King, November 10, King Papers, LC; Summers, *Plundering Generation,* 23-28.

9. John Coyle to Bigler, October 21, Bigler Papers; J. W. Foster to Nathaniel P. Banks, December 8, Banks Papers.

10. *United States Democratic Review,* August, 105-6.

11. Edward Stiles to Bigler, December 16, Bigler Papers; New York *Tribune,* December 4; Joseph A. Wright to Stephen A. Douglas, November 14, Douglas Papers, UC.

12. These and similar letters were culled from the papers of various politicians.

13. Louisville *Journal,* March 20.

14. Buchanan to John Y. Mason, December 29, 1856, Buchanan Papers.

15. William Porcher Miles to Buchanan, February 20, Miles Papers UNC; Black to Edwin M. Stanton, undated, 1857, Stanton Papers, LC; Cobb to Black, May 4, Black Papers; Edward Everett ms. diary, entry for May 25, Everett Papers; New York *Herald,* March 23; Washington *National Intelligencer,* May 18; Klein, *Buchanan,* 278-80.

16. Summers, *Plundering Generation,* 39-41; Simpson, *Cobb,* 116-17. The papers of Horatio King contain a voluminous political correspondence with the postmasters.

17. *Congressional Globe,* 35 Cong., 1 sess., 10; Nichols, *Disruption of American Democracy,* 58-59, 187-88; Summers, *Plundering Generation,* 44-45.

18. New York *Herald,* January 11; February 14; Cincinnati *Enquirer,* February 1; March 5; weekly Chicago *Times,* April 9.

19. John Appleton to Buchanan, January 11, Buchanan Papers; Washington *Union,* April 15; Nichols, *Disruption of American Democracy,* 92.

20. David L. Yulee to Robert J. Walker, April 4, Walker Papers, NYHS; Fernanao Wood to Buchanan, January 8; Albert C. Ramsey to Buchanan, April 6, Buchanan Papers; Klein, *Buchanan,* 280-81; Nichols, *Disruption of American Democracy,* 82-85; Nevins, *Emergence of Lincoln,* I, 130.

21. Cincinnati *Enquirer,* March 7; July 15.

22. Joseph A. Wright to Buchanan, January 15, Buchanan Papers; Bright to Black, April 9, Black Papers; Indianapolis *Indiana State Sentinel,* May 13, 16, 20, 21, 27; July 23; Nichols, *Disruption of American Democracy,* 88-89.

23. R. B. Carpenter to Robert J. Breckinridge, April 13, Breckinridge Family Papers; Douglas to Horatio King, October 9, King Papers; Nichols, *Disruption of American Democracy,* 89.

24. Isaac N. Morris to Horatio King, May 18; King Papers; Johanssen, *Letters of Douglas,* 397-98; Johanssen, *Douglas,* 550-58; Damon Wells, *Stephen A. Douglas, The Last Years, 1857-1861* (Austin, 1871), 26-27; David E. Meerse, "Origins of the Buchanan-Douglas Feud Reconsidered," *JISHS,* LXVII (1970), 154-74; Nichols, *Disruption of American Democracy,* 89-90.

25. Gwin to James W. Mandeville, April 3, 5, Mandeville Papers, HEH; Cornelius Cole to Seward, June 4, Seward Papers; San Francisco *Evening Bulletin,* June 9; Williams, *Broderick,* 156-58; Ellison, *Self-Governing Dominion,* 293-95.

26. New York *Tribune,* June 14; C. S. Weller to Horatio King, May 5; July 18, King Papers.

27. George Sanderson to Bigler, March 24, Bigler Papers; James Campbell to Buchanan, August 20, Buchanan Papers; Michael F. Holt, *Forging a Majority: The Formation of the Republican Party in Pittsburgh, 1848-1860* (New Haven, 1969), 226-27; Klein, *Buchanan,* 281-83; Nichols, *Disruption of American Democracy,* 86-87.

28. John W. Forney, *Annecdotes of Public Men* (2 vols., New York, 1873, 1881), II, 239-40; Klein, *Buchanan,* 218-19.

29. Forney to Buchanan, January 14; Mrs. Forney to Buchanan, undated, probably February, Buchanan Papers; Forney to Cobb, January 30, Cobb Papers, UG. In another letter to Cobb, written in January but undated, Forney claimed to have spent $4000 in the campaign.

30. John Appleton to Buchanan, February 5, 7; Buchanan to Forney, February 28; Forney to Buchanan, March 6, Buchanan Papers.

31. Forney to Black, March 27; April 25; May 6, 7, 19; June 28, Black Papers; Forney to Buchanan, June 6, 13, Buchanan Papers.

32. New York *Herald,* July 7; Philadephia *Press,* August 1; Forney to Buchanan, July 12, 20; Buchanan to Forney, July 18, Buchanan Papers; George E. Martin to John C. Breckinridge, July 28, Breckinridge Family Papers.

33. Forney to Black, July 30, Black Papers; Forney to Buchanan, August 18, Buchanan Papers; Forney to John C. Breckinridge, August 12, Breckinridge Family Papers.

34. Robert Tyler to Buchanan, July 16; Richard Vaux to Buchanan, August 8, Buchanan Papers; John Hastings to Bigler, August 8; William Rice to Bigler, September 1, Bigler Papers.

35. Buchanan to Joseph B. Baker, July 1; September 9; Baker to Buchanan, September 14, Buchanan Papers.

36. Forney to Black, October 3, Black Papers.

37. In the vast legal and historical literature on the Dred Scott case, three recent general studies are available. Vincent C. Hopkins, *Dred Scott's Case* (New York, 1971), is good on the background. Walter Ehrlich, *They Have No Rights: Dred Scott's Struggle for Freedom* (Westport, Conn., 1979), stresses the human dimension of the case. Don E. Fehrenbacher, *The Dred Scott Case: Its Significance in American Law and Politics* (New York, 1978), the most comprehensive study, is superb on both the legal and political background, on the litigation in state and federal courts, and on its legal and political consequences. I have used it extensively in my brief summary. Frederick S. Allis, "The Dred Scott Labyrinth," in H. Stuart Hughes, ed., *Teachers of History: Essays in Honor of Laurence Bradford Packard* (Ithaca, 1954), 341-68, is a useful historiographical essay.

38. John A. Bryan, "The Blow Family and Their Slave Dred Scott," *Missouri Historical Society Bulletin,* IV (1948), 223-25; Hopkins, *Dred Scott's Case,* 9-25; Ehrlich, *They Have No Rights,* 9-88; Fehrenbacher, *Dred Scott Case,* 239-65. Quotation on p. 265.

39. Fehrenbacher, *Dred Scott Case,* 267-83; William E. Smith, *The Francis Preston Blair Family in Politics* (2 vols., New York, 1933), I, 385-97; Stanley Harrold, *Gamaliel Bailey and Antislavery Union* (Kent, Ohio, 1986), 197; Gamaliel Bailey to Seward, May 8, Seward Papers.

40. Fehrenbacher, *Dred Scott Case,* 226-34; Nevins, *Emergence of Lincoln,* I, 100-5; John P. Frank, *Justice Daniel Dissenting: A Biography of Peter V. Daniel, 1784-1860* (Cambridge, Mass., 1964), 243-46. For brief biographical sketches of each of the justices see Leon Friedman and Fred L. Israel, eds., *The Justices of the United States Supreme Court, 1789-1969* (4 vols., New York, 1969), I, 535-46, 601-11, 635-54, 737-49, 759-84; II, 817-29, 873-83, 895-908, 927-39.

41. *Congressional Globe,* 34 Cong., 3 sess., 33, 77-78, 92, 145-47; Johanssen, *Douglas,* 546.

42. Benjamin R. Curtis, ed., *A Memoir of Benjamin Robbins Curtis* (2 vols., Boston, 1879), I, 180; Fehrenbacher, *Dred Scott Case,* 286-90.

43. *Argument of Montgomery Blair, Dred Scott vs. John F. A. Sanford, Supreme Court of the United States, December Term, 1856,* in Blair Family Papers, LC; Fehrenbacher, *Dred Scott Case,* 293-302.

44. Blair to Martin Van Buren, February 5, Van Buren Papers.

45. Fehrenbacher, *Dred Scott Case,* 302-4, summarizes the Court's options in a slightly different way.

46. Thomas E. Schott, *Alexander H. Stephens of Georgia: A Biography* (Baton Rouge, 1988), 228; Rudolph Von Abele, *Alexander H. Stephens: A Biography* (New York, 1946), 159; Robert J. Walker to Douglas, January 9, Douglas Papers.

47. Frank, *Justice Daniel Dissenting,* 257-58.

48. Fehrenbacher, *Dred Scott Case,* 305-11, and end notes which cite the proponents of the traditional explanation of the majority decision.

49. Catron to Buchanan, February 6, 10, 19, 23; Grier to Buchanan February 23, Buchanan Papers.

50. Jones to Buchanan, February 14, Buchanan Papers; Fehrenbacher, *Dred Scott Case,* 313-14.

51. Curtis, ed., *Memoir,* I, 193; Fehrenbacher, *Dred Scott Case,* 1-3, 5-7, 314-15.

52. *Dred Scott v. John F. A. Sandford,* 60 U.S. (19 Howard), 393, 399-454, for Taney's opinion. For a full discussion and perceptive critique see Fehrenbacher, *Dred Scott Case,* 335-88.

53. *Dred Scott v. John F. A. Sandford,* 60 U.S. (19 Howard), 393, 454-529, for the concurring opinions.

54. *Dred Scott v. John F. A. Sandford,* 60 U.S. (19 Howard), 393, 529-633, for Curtis's and McLean's dissenting opinions. Fehrenbacher, *Dred Scott Case,* 403-14, for comment.

55. Fehrenbacher, *Dred Scott Case,* 414; McLean to Montgomery Blair, March 30, Blair Family Papers.

56. Curtis, ed., *Memoir,* I, 212-30; Fehrenbacher, *Dred Scott Case,* 315-21; Richard H. Leach, "Justice Curtis and the Dred Scott Case," *Essex Institute Historical Collections,* XCIV (1958), 37-56.

57. Curtis *Memoir,* I, 245-63; Robert C. Winthrop to John A. Clifford, September 21, Robert C. Winthrop Papers, MHS; Charles Francis Adams to Charles Sumner, April 7, Adams Family Papers.

58. James M. Mason to George Bancroft, July 28, Bancroft Papers; Richmond *Enquirer,* March 10.

59. Nashville *Union and American,* March 15; semi-weekly Richmond *Whig,* March 13; Charleston *Mercury,* March 17; April 22; New Orleans *Picayune,* March 20; Milledgeville, Ga., *Federal Union,* March 31.

60. *Congressional Globe,* 34 Cong., 3 sess., 67, 103-4; Louisville *Democrat,* May 20; Charleston *Mercury,* April 21, 22.

61. Bancroft to James M. Mason, July 21, Bancroft Papers.

62. New York *Herald,* March 8; Washington *Union,* March 11; Taney to Cushing, November 9, Cushing Papers. A printed copy of Cushing's Newburyport speech is in the Cushing Papers.

63. Indianapolis *Indiana State Sentinal,* June 3; October 2; Detroit *Free Press,* March 14, 20; April 2; Johannsen, *Douglas,* 570-72.

64. Cincinnati *Enquirer,* March 8; Sacramento *Union,* April 15; weekly Chicago *Times,* April 2; Washington *Union,* March 18.

65. Detroit *Free Press,* April 1; weekly Chicago *Times,* April 2; October 15; Indianapolis *Indiana State Sentinel,* March 17.

66. Milwaukee *News,* quoted in Milwaukee *Sentinel,* September 25; New York *Times,* June 23; Johanssen, *Douglas,* 568-72.

67. Madison *Wisconsin State Journal,* June 27; New York *Tribune,* March 7; Sarah

Forbes Hughes, ed., *Letters of John Murray Forbes (Supplementary)* (3 vols., Boston, 1905), I, 189-90; Chicago *Tribune*, April 10.

68. *North American Review*, October, 392-415; Thomas Hart Benton, *Historical and Legal Examination of . . . the Dred Scott Case . . .* (New York, 1858); New York *Herald*, April 9; Fehrenbacher, *Dred Scott Case*, 422-27.

69. Edward Everett ms. diary, entry for August 11, Everett Papers; New York *Times*, April 10, 11; June 26; New York *Herald*, April 12; Roseboom, *History of Ohio*, IV, 326-27; Current, *History of Wisconsin*, II, 261-62; Fehrenbacher, *Dred Scott Case*, 431-35.

70. New York *Evening Post*, March 9; Milwaukee *Sentinel*, October 7.

71. Madison *Wisconsin State Journal*, June 4; October 20; Chicago *Democrat*, November 14; Milwaukee *Sentinel*, March 12; December 2; Chicago *Tribune*, March 16.

72. Chicago *Tribune*, March 11; Boston *Advertiser*, March 13; May 26; *Congressional Globe*, 35 Cong., 1 sess., 941; New York *Evening Post*, March 7; Milwaukee *Sentinel*, December 2.

73. New York *Times*, April 11.

74. Roy P. Basler, ed., *The Collected Works of Abraham Lincoln* (8 vols., New Brunswick, N.J., 1953), II, 400-7; Chicago *Tribune*, April 10; Portland, Maine, *Transcript and Eclectic*, May 23.

75. New York *Evening Post*, March 11; New York *Herald*, April 12; Hughes, ed., *Letters of John Murray Forbes (Supplementary)*, I, 189-90; New York *Tribune*, March 16; September 18; Boston *Liberator*, March 13; Springfield *Illinois State Journal*, July 23; Chicago *Tribune*, September 18.

76. *North American Review*, October, 392-415; Philadelphia *North American*, March 18; Washington *National Era*, March 12. See also New York *Times* April 11; Boston *Advertiser*, May 8, 26; July 20; Chicago *Democrat*, September 18.

77. Springfield *Illinois State Journal*, June 27; Johanssen, *Douglas*, 572-73.

78. New York *Anti-Slavery Standard*, March 14; Philip S. Foner, ed., *The Life and Writings of Frederick Douglass* (5 vols., New York, 1950-75), II, 411-12; Boston *Advertiser*, October 28.

79. J. A. Ware to William P. Fessenden, March 12, Fessenden Papers, LC; Chicago *Tribune*, March 19; Washington *National Era*, March 12; Philadelphia *North American*, March 27; Milwaukee *Sentinel*, March 12.

Chapter 5

1. Richmond *Enquirer*, October 9; *Congressional Globe*, 34 Cong., 3 sess., Appendix, 134. Republicans, on occasion, could speak with equal eloquence in defense of *northern* honor and constitutional rights—for example, in resisting the federal Fugitive Slave Act.

2. Chicago *Tribune*, February 11; Chicago *Democrat*, June 16; E. B. Crocker to Seward, January 3; James A. Fox to Seward, January 1, Seward Papers.

3. Mobile *Register*, June 16; *De Bow's Review*, September, 231; *Congressional Globe*, 34 Cong., 3 sess., Appendix, 229.

4. Richmond *Enquirer*, March 17; May 1; June 12, 16.

5. Edward Everett to Sir Henry Holland, July 25, Everett Papers; *Congressional Globe*, 34 Cong., 3 sess., Appendix, 149. Some twentieth-century historians have shown sympathy for this point of view. For a critique of these so-called revisionists see Kenneth M. Stampp, *The Imperiled Union: Essays on the Background of the Civil War* (New York, 1980), 199-220.

6. Richmond *Enquirer*, March 6; William C. Gaston to Robert J. Breckinridge, April 20, Breckinridge Family Papers.

7. Richmond *Enquirer,* January 23; April 24; Louisville *Journal,* January 30; James M. Mason to John B. Clifford, July 30, Clifford Papers, MHS.

8. New York *Herald,* September 2; Richmond *Enquirer,* June 12; Jackson *Mississippian* July 1; semi-weekly Richmond *Whig,* September 18.

9. New Orleans *Picayune,* August 27; *Congressional Globe,* 34 Cong., 3 sess., Appendix, 236; Louisville *Democrat,* January 8.

10. New Orleans *Picayune,* August 27; Louisville *Democrat,* April 8; Richmond *Enquirer,* May 19.

11. *De Bow's Review,* March, 225-48; August, 194-202; September, 228-82; October, 377-85; *Southern Literary Messenger,* August, 81-94.

12. *De Bow's Review,* October, 336-49; William Stanton, *The Leopard's Spots: Scientific Attitudes Toward Race in America, 1815-59* (Chicago, 1960), 161-83; George M. Fredrickson *The Black Image in the White Mind* (New York, 1971), 58-82.

13. *De Bow's Review,* November, 449-62; Austin *Texas State Gazette,* January 10; Scarborough, ed., *Diary of Edmond Ruffin,* I, 67-68.

14. W. J. Carnathan, "The Proposal to Reopen the African Slave Trade in the South, 1854-1860," *SAQ,* XXV (1926), 410-29; Ronald T. Takaki, *A Pro-Slavery Crusade: The Agitation to Reopen the African Slave Trade* (New York, 1971), 148-50.

15. *Congressional Globe,* 34 Cong., 3 sess., 125-26; Nashville *Republican Banner,* January 27.

16. New Orleans *Picayune,* July 3; September 12; Richmond *Enquirer,* February 20; Mobile *Register,* October 13; Clement C. Clay to John G. Shorter, C. J. Pope, and E. C. Bullock, March 30, Clay Papers.

17. Roland, ed., *Jefferson Davis Letters, Papers, and Speeches,* III, 103-5, 107-8; Winston Banks to Seward, July 8, Seward Papers; William S. Pettigrew to editor of the *Missionary Herald,* January 22, Pettigrew Family Papers.

18. Nashville *Republican Banner,* August 21; Frederick L. Roberts to Seward, December 11, Seward Papers.

19. Louisville *Democrat,* January 10. For the tactics and policies of the national Democracy during the 1850s, see Joel H. Silbey, *The Partisan Imperative: The Dynamics of American Politics Before the Civil War* (New York, 1985), 97-126.

20. Philadelphia *Press,* August 28; Washington *Union,* April 2; Cincinnati *Enquirer,* January 13.

21. Washington *Union,* April 16; *United States Democratic Review,* August, 103-4.

22. Cincinnati *Enquirer,* January 1; New York *Herald,* November 15; Mattoon Ill., *Gazette,* quoted in Springfield *Illinois State Journal,* August 27; Francis Terry Leak ms. diary, entry for March 28, UNC; Fredrickson, *Black Image in the White Mind,* 91-96.

23. Charleston *Mercury,* May 28; Cincinnati *Enquirer,* November 13.

24. Detroit *Free Press,* March 26; weekly Chicago *Times,* April 9; New York *Herald,* March 8; May 3; Cincinnati *Enquirer,* January 14.

25. Natchez *Mississippi Free Trader,* August 14, quoted in Rainwater, *Mississippi,* 48; Charleston *Mercury,* January 29; June 3; July 20; New Orleans *Delta,* quoted in Montgomery *Mail,* February 19; Harold S. Schulz, *Nationalism and Sectionalism in South Carolina, 1852-1860* (Durham, 1950), 145-46.

26. Montgomery *Mail,* March 16; Nashville *Republican Banner,* March 4; Humphrey Marshall to Millard Fillmore, November 16, Fillmore Papers; W. Darrell Overdyke, *The Know-Nothing Party in the South* (Baton Rouge, 1950), 170-210; William J. Cooper, *Liberty and Slavery: Southern Politics to 1860* (New York, 1983), 244-47.

27. *Congressional Globe,* 34 Cong., 3 sess., Appendix, 122; Alexander H. H. Stuart to William C. Rives, June 28, Rives Papers; semi-weekly Richmond *Whig,* February 6; June 26; Silbey, *Partisan Imperative,* 43-44.

28. Montgomery *Mail,* June 15, 20, 22; July 20; August 7, 8, 18; October 1; semi-weekly Richmond *Whig,* January 1, 23; July 20; August 4; Nashville *Republican Banner,* January 7; August 25; Louisville *Journal,* January 6, 12; August 7, 28.

29. Semi-weekly Richmond *Whig,* April 28; *Congressional Globe,* 34 Cong., 3 sess., Appendix, 364-70; Montgomery *Mail,* September 22; Nashville *Republican Banner,* May 12; R. S. Daniel to William C. Rives, April 11, Rives Papers.

30. Nashville *Union and American,* May 29.

31. *Southern Literary Messenger,* August, 88-89; Richmond *Enquirer,* January 6; *Congressional Globe,* 34 Cong., 3 sess., Appendix, 184; New York *Herald,* January 10.

32. New York *Herald,* January 10; Cincinnati *Enquirer,* January 17; *Congressional Globe,* 34 Cong., 3 sess., 852; Nashville *Republican Banner,* January 18; Louisville *Democrat,* January 22.

33. Richmond *Enquirer,* March 27; July 17, 21; August 7; September 4, 22; Milledgeville, Ga., *Federal Union,* May 5; November 5; Edgefield, S. C., *Advertiser,* June 24; July 8, 15.

34. Richmond *Enquirer,* January 2, 26; April 24; July 24; August 4, 11; September 1; Mobile *Register,* April 29; May 17; Edgefield, S. C., *Advertiser,* January 14. See also Milledgeville, Ga., *Federal Union,* April 7; Memphis *Appeal,* August 25; James P. Metcalf to John C. Breckinridge, June 4, Breckinridge Family Papers.

35. Milledgeville, Ga., *Federal Union,* January 27; Richmond *Enquirer,* July 17; Woodville, Miss., *Republican,* August 4, quoted in Rainwater, *Mississippi,* 47-49; Edgefield, S. C., *Advertiser,* August 5; O. C. Hartley to Black, June 2, Black Papers.

36. Louisville *Democrat,* August 9.

37. Boston *Liberator,* July 10.

38. New York *National Anti-Slavery Standard,* May 2.

39. New York *National Anti-Slavery Standard,* April 25; William Goodell to George W. Julian, June 18, Giddings-Julian Papers, LC.

40. New York *National Anti-Slavery Standard,* May 2, 9, 16; Samuel May, Jr., to "Dear Friend Webb," February 8, Samuel J. May Papers, BPL.

41. The literature on the antislavery movement is vast, but three good brief modern studies are Gerald Sorin, *Abolitionism: A New Perspective* (New York, 1972); Merton L. Dillon, *The Abolitionists: The Growth of a Dissenting Minority* (DeKalb, Ill., 1974); and James Brewer Stewart, *Holy Warriors: The Abolitionists and American Slavery* (New York, 1976).

42. Boston *Liberator,* September 4; Gerrit Smith to S. J. May, September 5; May to William Lloyd Garrison, September 12, Garrison Papers, BPL; Samuel May, Jr., to "Dear Friend Webb," February 8, Samuel J. May Papers; Foner, ed., *Life and Writings of Frederick Douglass,* II, 436-37; G. W. Chapman to Samuel J. May, March 15, May Papers.

43. New York *National Anti-Slavery Standard,* January 31; February 7; New York *Tribune,* January 17, 19, 21, 28; John L. Thomas, *The Liberator: William Lloyd Garrison, A Biography* (Boston, 1963), 391-93.

44. Boston *Advertiser,* August 28, 29; New York *Tribune,* August 31; Washington *National Intelligencer,* September 5; New York *National Anti-Slavery Standard,* September 12.

45. Boston *Advertiser,* July 6. For the feelings of an untutored rank-and-file abolitionist, see S. P. Leland to Garrison, September 7, Garrison Papers.

46. Boston *Liberator,* June 12; New York *Tribune,* January 21.

47. Foner, ed., *Life and Writings of Frederick Douglass,* II, 413; Boston *Liberator,* July 17; New York *National Anti-Slavery Standard,* January 31; February 28.

48. J. W. Bryce to John C. Breckinridge, April 19, Breckinridge Family Papers; Horace Emery to Amos A, Lawrence, July 3, Lawrence Papers, MHS; Everett to John J. Crittenden, January 31; Everett to Buchanan, January 19, Everett Papers; S. G. Haven to Fillmore, January 3; Leonard W. Kennedy to Fillmore, April 9; Fillmore to John P. Kennedy, January 29, Fillmore Papers.

49. Philadelphia *Public Ledger,* March 19; Jeter A. Isley, *Horace Greeley and the Republican Party, 1853-1861* (Princeton, 1947), 202-3; John Costigan to Seward, March 7,

Seward Papers; Edward L. Pierce published letter "To the Editor of the Republican," dated January 26, in Abraham Lincoln Papers, LC.

50. Gienapp, "Nativism and the Creation of a Republican Majority," 547-50; Ian R. Tyrrell, *Sobering Up: From Temperance to Prohibition in Antebellum America, 1800-1860* (Westport, Conn., 1979), 290-309.

51. Gienapp, "Nativism and the Creation of a Republican Majority," 552; Harrisburg *Telegraph,* January 19; Springfield *Illinois State Journal,* April 15; Chicago *Tribune,* March 2; Nevins and Halsey, eds., *Diary of George Templeton Strong,* II, 348.

52. Chicago *Democrat,* November 13; Chicago *Tribune,* July 25, 30; August 1, 13.

53. Springfield *Illinois State Journal,* February 25; Michael J. McManus, "Wisconsin Republicans and Negro Suffrage: Attitudes and Behavior, 1857," *CWH,* XXV (1979), 49.

54. Basler, ed., *Collected Works of Abraham Lincoln,* II, 405-9; Springfield *Illinois State Journal,* July 2. Lincoln's colonization idea had considerable support among Republicans. See Springfield *Illinois State Journal,* April 24; Francis P. Blair to Frank Blair, January 26; February 5, Blair Family Papers; Frank Blair to Francis P. Blair, March 25, Blair-Lee Papers, PU.

55. A. L. Robinson to Salmon P. Chase, November 30, Chase Papers, LC; Basler, ed., *Collected Works of Abraham Lincoln,* II, 391.

56. Springfield *Illinois State Journal,* May 18; September 3; Basler, ed., *Collected Works of Abraham Lincoln,* II, 405.

57. Joshua R. Giddings to William Schouler, April 11, Schouler Papers, MHS; Portland, Maine, *Eclectic and Transcript,* May 23; William H. Beecher to Francis P. Blair, January 12, Blair-Lee Papers; Washington *National Era,* May 14; Eric Foner, *Free Soil, Free Labor, Free Men,* 261-300; Stampp, *The Imperiled Union,* 105-35.

58. Washington *National Era,* September 17; New York *Tribune,* March 25; September 26; October 13; Phyllis F. Field, "Republicans and Black Suffrage in New York State: The Grass Roots Response," *CWH,* XXI (1975), 140; Morton M. Rosenberg, *Iowa on the Eve of the Civil War: A Decade of Frontier Politics* (Norman, Okla., 1972), 146-54.

59. Milwaukee *Sentinel,* August 3, 20; September 19; October 1; November 3; Leslie H. Fishel, Jr., "Wisconsin and Negro Suffrage," *WMH,* XLVI (1963), 186-89; McManus, "Wisconsin Republicans and Negro Suffrage," 36-54; Current, *History of Wisconsin,* II, 262-67.

60. W. Patterson to John Sherman, January [n.d.], Sherman Papers; Springfield *Illinois State Journal,* May 12; August 2; Rodney B. Field to Justin S. Morrill, December 31, Morrill Papers, LC; John Wilson to Seward, January 19, Seward Papers; Van Deusen, *Thurlow Weed,* 213, 219-30.

61. Mark Howard to Gideon Welles, February 21, Welles Papers; Charles Coxe to Salmon P. Chase, October 23, Chase Papers, LC; Sumner to Francis W. Bird, September 11, Bird Papers, HU; *Congressional Globe,* 34 Cong., 3 sess., Appendix, 135-40.

62. George W. Julian to Thomas Wentworth Higginson, October 24, Giddings-Julian Papers.

63. For a variety of interpretations of Republican ideology see Eugene H. Berwanger, *The Frontier Against Slavery* (Urbana, 1967); Foner, *Free Soil, Free Labor, Free Men,* 301-17; C. Vann Woodward, *American Counterpoint* (Boston, 1971), 147-48; Richard H. Sewell, *Ballots for Freedom: Antislavery Politics in the United States, 1837-1860* (New York, 1976), 321-36; Gienapp, *Origins of the Republican Party,* 347-73; Michael F. Holt, *The Political Crisis of the 1850s* (New York, 1978), 189-90; Stampp, *Imperiled Union,* 117-35.

64. Chicago, *Tribune,* September 29.

65. Stampp, *Imperiled Union,* 122; Milwaukee *Sentinel,* June 19; Joint Resolution of the Michigan legislature, dated February 4, copy in Zachariah Chandler Papers, LC; Theseus A. Cheney to Seward, November 12, Seward Papers; Salmon P. Chase to "My dear friend," February 16, Chase Papers, LC.

66. Milwaukee *Sentinel,* June 19; Chicago *Tribune,* September 29.

67. New York *Evening Post,* June 1; Charles Francis Adams ms. diary, entry for April 16, Adams Family Papers; Boston *Liberator,* July 17; Milwaukee *Sentinel,* February 9, 21.

68. Patrick W. Riddleberger, *George Washington Julian: Radical Republican* (Indianapolis, 1966), 118-19; Cincinnati *Enquirer,* June 14; Chicago *Democrat,* May 2; June 4; Roseboom, *History of Ohio,* IV, 327, 345; Madison *Wisconsin State Journal,* January 19, 22; Current, *History of Wisconsin,* II, 219-21, 235; Milwaukee *Sentinel,* June 19.

69. Hugh C. Bailey, *Hinton Rowan Helper, Abolitionist-Racist* (University, Ala., 1965), 21-42.

70. Washington *National Era,* June 23; Charlton T. Lewis to Horace Greeley, July 13, Greeley Papers, NYPL; William C. Chace to Lyman Trumbull, October 19, Trumbull Papers; Chase to Gideon Welles, November 3, Welles Papers.

71. Elbert B. Smith, *Francis Preston Blair* (New York, 1980), 235; St. Louis *Missouri Democrat,* January 9, 16, 28; March 24; April 8, 15.

72. Mobile *Register,* April 17; Springfield *Illinois State Journal,* April 9; Washington *National Era,* April 16; Foner, ed., *Life and Writings of Frederick Douglass,* II, 414.

73. George Winston Smith, "Ante-Bellum Attempts of Northern Business Interests to 'Redeem' the Upper South," *JSH,* XI (1945), 177-213; Simpson, *Life of Henry A. Wise,* 146-48; New York *Times,* April 7; Boston *Advertiser,* July 31; New York *Evening Post,* April 15; Chicago *Tribune,* April 15; Richmond *Enquirer,* March 17; Charleston *Mercury,* March 13; *Southern Planter,* May, 303-306.

74. Charles Francis Adams to Thomas Wentworth Higginson, January 10; Adams to Sumner, May 5, Adams letter book, in Adams Family Papers.

Chapter 6

1. Richmond *Enquirer,* June 26; Phillips, ed., *Correspondence of Toombs, Stephens, and Cobb,* 392; Charleston *Mercury,* April 1; S. E. Cooke to John Sherman, December 25, 1856, Sherman Papers; Hiram H. Heath to Seward, February 20, Seward Papers.

2. Horace Andrews, Jr., "Kansas Crusade: Eli Thayer and the New England Emigrant Aid Company," *NEQ,* XXXV (1962), 497-500; James A. Rawley, *Race and Politics: "Bleeding Kansas" and the Coming of the Civil War* (Philadelphia, 1969), 84; Nevins, *Ordeal of the Union,* II, 307-8.

3. Nevins, *Ordeal of the Union,* II, 308-13, 284-86; Rawley, *Race and Politics,* 79-83; Ambler, ed., *Correspondence of R.M.T.Hunter,* 160-61; Lawrence, Kansas, *Herald of Freedom,* February 28.

4. Nevins, *Ordeal of the Union,* II, 390-93, 408-11, 428-37, 472-86.

5. F. G. Adams, comp., *Transactions of the Kansas State Historical Society,* IV (Topeka, 1890), 684-85; Lawrence, Kansas, *Herald of Freedom,* February 7; June 20.

6. Johannsen, *Douglas,* 524-27; Thompson, *Toombs,* 112-14; Nevins, *Ordeal of the Union,* II, 471-72; Gienapp, *Origins of the Republican Party,* 349-50.

7. *Congressional Globe,* 34 Cong., 3 sess., 3-6, 18, 40, 68-69; New York *Tribune,* August 26; Lawrence, Kansas, *Herald of Freedom,* August 1.

8. St. Louis *Missouri Democrat,* February 18; William E. Parish, *David Rice Atchison of Missouri: Border Politician* (Columbia, Mo., 1961), 207-12; Leavenworth *Times,* March 14; Boston *Advertiser,* May 26; New York *Times,* May 28; James C. Malin, *John Brown and the Legend of Fifty-six* (Philadelphia, 1942), 166-67; Wendell H. Stephenson, *The Political Career of General James H. Lane* (Topeka, 1930), 84-85.

9. Schulz, *Nationalism and Sectionalism in South Carolina,* 138-39; Richmond *Enquirer,* June 26.

10. Richmond *Enquirer,* January 20; Charleston *Mercury,* March 31; April 1, 6, 9; Edgefield, S. C., *Advertiser,* April 15; Leavenworth *Journal,* quoted in Lecompton *Union,* June 19.

11. Lawrence, Kansas, *Herald of Freedom,* January 3; Chicago *Tribune,* February 11, 19; March 2, 27.

12. Charles Robinson to Sara Robinson, January 4, 11, 15; Robinson to William Barnes, January 30, Charles and Sara Robinson Papers, KSHS; Boston *Advertiser,* May 30; Kansas State Committee of Massachusetts appeal "To the Public," copy in Adams Family Papers; Thomas H. O'Connor, *Lords of the Loom: The Cotton Whigs and the Coming of the Civil War* (New York, 1968), 109-10.

13. New York *Tribune,* January 12; Smith and Hayford, eds., *Journals and Miscellaneous Notebooks of Ralph Waldo Emerson,* XIV, 125; Henry Steele Commager, *Theodore Parker* (Boston, 1936), 250; Charles Francis Adams ms. diary, entry for April 8, Adams Family Papers; Stephen B. Oates, *To Purge This Land with Blood: A Biography of John Brown* (New York, 1970), 181-205.

14. John Carter Brown to Amos A. Lawrence, April 2; F. B. Sanborn to Lawrence, February 19; John Brown to Lawrence, February 21, Lawrence Papers; Amos A. Lawrence to Charles Robinson, March 31, Robinson Papers, UK.

15. Ephraim Newt to Amos A. Lawrence, January 25; George S. Boutwell to Lawrence, February 23, Lawrence Papers.

16. Boston *Advertiser,* May 28; Daniel P. Livermore to Seward, February 24, Seward Papers; Samuel A. Johnson, *The Battle Cry of Freedom: The New England Emigrant Aid Company in the Kansas Crusade* (Lawrence, Kansas, 1954), 239-44.

17. St. Louis *Missouri Democrat,* March 16, 17; Leavenworth *Times,* March 14.

18. Paul W. Gates, *Fifty Million Acres: Conflicts over Kansas Land Policy, 1854-1890* (New York, 1966), 19-22, 48-55, 58-61, 65-73, 106-8; Malin, *John Brown and the Legend of Fifty-six,* 143-47, 161-62; J. W. Whitfield to William H. English, May 9, English Papers.

19. Lawrence, Kansas, *Herald of Freedom,* January 10; Charles Robinson to his wife, Sara, September 13, Robinson Papers, KSHS; Robinson to Amos A. Lawrence, June 27; July 7, Lawrence Papers.

20. Johnson, *Battle Cry of Freedom,* 237-39, 248-53; Amos A. Lawrence to Joseph I. Steele, January 12, copy in Lawrence Papers.

21. Malin, *John Brown and the Legend of Fifty-six,* 691-92; Lecompton *Union,* May 2.

22. Nevins, *Ordeal of the Union,* II, 484-85; Adams, comp., *Transactions of the Kansas State Historical Society,* IV, 693-94.

23. Geary to Buchanan, January 16, Buchanan Papers.

24. Lecompton *Union,* January 27; February 13; Lawrence, Kansas, *Herald of Freedom,* January 24; New York *Tribune,* January 24, 28, 29; Adams, comp., *Transactions of the Kansas State Historical Society,* IV, 689.

25. Edward Clark to Amos A. Lawrence, January 29, Lawrence Papers; New York *Times,* April 1; Lawrence, Kansas, *Herald of Freedom,* February 7; Malin, *John Brown and the Legend of Fifty-six,* 684-85, 688.

26. Adams, comp., *Transactions of the Kansas State Historical Society,* IV, 688-89, 699-700; Lawrence, Kansas, *Herald of Freedom,* January 17; John H. Gihon, *Geary and Kansas: Governor Geary's Administration in Kansas* (Philadelphia, 1857), 214-16; Malin, *John Brown and the Legend of Fifty-six,* 190-91.

27. Adams, comp., *Transactions of the Kansas State Historical Society,* IV, 676-87.

28. *Congressional Globe,* 34 Cong., 3 sess., 519-20, 731-33, 752-53; New York *Tribune,* March 3; New York *Times,* April 10; Leavenworth *Times,* March 7.

29. Adams, comp., *Transactions of the Kansas State Historical Society,* V, 287-88; Lecompton *Union,* January 8; February 13; Phillips, ed., *Correspondence of Toombs, Stephens, and Cobb,* 384.

30. Adams, comp., *Transactions of the Kansas State Historical Society,* IV, 695-96; V, 276-87; Lecompton *Union,* February 21; Leavenworth *Times,* March 7; Gihon, *Geary and Kansas,* 227-44.

31. Lecompton *Union,* January 8, 22.

32. Lecompton *Union,* February 21; Lawrence, Kansas, *Herald of Freedom,* February 7; St. Louis *Missouri Democrat,* March 13; Leavenworth *Times,* March 7.

33. Adams, comp., *Transactions of the Kansas State Historical Society,* IV, 717-20; Lawrence, Kansas, *Herald of Freedom,* March 14; Gihon, *Geary and Kansas,* 260-68.

34. Geary to Amos A. Lawrence, February 25, Lawrence Papers; St. Louis *Missouri Democrat,* March 17; New York *Tribune,* March 18, 21; Gihon, *Geary and Kansas,* 287-99; Nevins, *Emergence of Lincoln,* I, 136-40.

35. New York *Tribune,* March 24; A. G. Ege to Jeremiah S. Black, March 12; William A. Stokes to Black, April 12, Black Papers; New York *Herald,* March 19; New York *Evening Post,* March 21.

36. John Richter Jones to Jeremiah S. Black, March 26, Black Papers; Robert McClelland to William L. Marcy, April 11, Marcy Papers; Philadelphia *North American,* March 21.

37. Shenton, *Walker,* 2-3; Nichols, *Disruption of American Democracy,* 96-97; Nevins, *Emergence of Lincoln,* I, 144-45.

38. Buchanan to Walker, October 6, 1856, Walker Papers; Shenton, *Walker,* 141-42.

39. *Report of the Select Committee on Alleged Corruptions,* in *House Reports,* 36 Cong., 1 sess., No. 648 (Serial 1071), 105-6; David L. Yulee to Walker, April 4, Walker Papers; Philadelphia *North American,* March 28.

40. Washington *Union,* March 31; Adams, comp., *Transactions of the Kansas State Historical Society,* V, 290, 322-23; Shenton, *Walker,* 146-47.

41. New York *Herald,* March 27; Detroit *Free Press,* March 28; Charleston *Mercury,* March 18; April 16; Scarborough, ed., *Diary of Edmund Ruffin,* I, 80; Richmond *Enquirer,* March 31; Lecompton *Union,* March 27.

42. New York *Evening Post,* May 14; St. Louis *Missouri Democrat,* June 11; New York *Tribune,* March 28; Milwaukee *Sentinel,* March 26; Chicago *Tribune,* April 4; G. W. Brown to Salmon P. Chase, April 4, Chase Papers, LC.

43. New York *Herald,* March 27.

44. Adams, comp., *Transactions of the Kansas State Historical Society,* V, 324-26.

45. Lawrence, Kansas, *Herald of Freedom,* May 2; Lecompton *Union,* May 2.

46. Leavenworth *Times,* March 14; Lawrence, Kansas, *Herald of Freedom,* March 14; St. Louis *Missouri Democrat,* March 23; Malin, *John Brown and the Legend of Fifty-six,* 194-96.

47. Washington *National Era,* April 9; New York *Times,* April 1, 10; *Harper's Weekly,* April 18; Cincinnati *Enquirer,* March 25; Detroit *Free Press,* April 10.

48. Chicago *Tribune,* June 16; New York *Evening Post,* April 7; May 4; Amos A. Lawrence to Charles Robinson, March 31, Robinson Papers, UK; Seward to Greeley, May 16, Greeley Papers; Charles Francis Adams to Sumner, May 5, Adams letter book in Adams Family Papers.

49. Charles Robinson to Amos A. Lawrence, April 19, Lawrence Papers; S. W. Wood to Salmon P. Chase, April 9, Chase Papers, LC; Schuyler Colfax to Charles Robinson, April 8, Robinson Papers, KSHS.

50. Adams, comp., *Transactions of the Kansas State Historical Society,* V, 433-36; Charles Robinson, *The Kansas Conflict* (New York, 1892), 350-51; New York *Herald,* May 9.

51. *House Reports,* 36 Cong., 1 sess., No. 648 (Serial 1071), 106-7; Shenton, *Walker,* 151-54.

52. Lawrence, Kansas, *Herald of Freedom,* May 30; Robinson, *Kansas Conflict,* 351.

53. Adams, comp., *Transactions of the Kansas State Historical Society,* V, 328-41.

54. *House Reports,* 36 Cong., 1 sess., No. 648 (Serial 1071), 107-9; Lecompton *Union,* June 12; Shenton, *Walker,* 155-57.

55. Lawrence, Kansas, *Herald of Freedom,* May 30; June 6; Henry J. Adams to Salmon P. Chase, May 30, Chase Papers, LC; Adams, comp., *Transactions of the Kansas State Historical Society,* V, 326-27.

56. Adams, comp., *Transactions of the Kansas State Historical Society*, V, 291-97; Lecompton, Kansas, *Herald of Freedom,* June 20.

57. Adams, comp., *Transactions of the Kansas State Historical Society*, V, 341-43; Robinson, *Kansas Conflict, 352-55.*

58. Johannsen, *Douglas,* 567; Lawrence, Kansas, *Herald of Freedom,* June 13; New York *Times,* June 1; July 1; Chicago *Tribune,* June 24; Robert W. Johannsen, "The Lecompton Constitutional Convention: An Analysis of Its Membership," *KHQ,* XXIII (1957), 227-28; George A. Crawford to Horatio King, July 13, King Papers.

59. Washington *Union,* June 24; August 6; Cincinnati *Enquirer,* July 5; Henry J. Adams to Salmon P. Chase, May 30, Chase Papers, LC.

60. Walker to Buchanan, June 28, Buchanan Papers.

61. New York *Herald,* August 2.

62. Charleston *Mercury,* June 9, 27; Jackson *Mississippian,* July 1; Philadelphia *Press,* August 19; Lawrence M. Keitt to William Porcher Miles, June 15, Miles Papers; Phillips, ed., *Correspondence of Toombs, Stephens, and Cobb,* 401-2.

63. Horace Montgomery, *Cracker Parties* (Baton Rouge, 1950), 190-94; Rainwater, *Mississippi,* 47-48; New York *Times,* July 7.

64. A. L. Diket, *Senator John Slidell and the Community He Represented in Washington, 1853-1861* (Washington, D.C., 1982), 120; Phillips, ed., *Correspondence of Toombs, Stephens, and Cobb,* 403-6, 416-18.

65. Nashville *Republican Banner,* July 8, 12; semi-weekly Richmond *Whig,* June 12; July 10, 17, 21; Louisville *Journal,* July 16; Montgomery, *Cracker Parties,* 188-90.

66. New York *Herald,* July 3; Philadelphia *Press,* August 3; Cincinnati *Enquirer,* July 22; Albany *Atlas and Argus,* July 15.

67. John C. Knott to Black, July 31; Richard Vaux to Black, September 2, Black Papers; J. Glancy Jones to Buchanan July 14, Buchanan Papers; Douglas to Walker, July 21, Walker Papers.

68. New York *Herald,* July 8; New York *Times,* July 8; Washington *Union,* July 11; Detroit *Free Press,* July 14.

69. Charleston *Mercury,* August 19; Slidell to Buchanan, August 12; Francis W. Pickens to Buchanan, August 5, Buchanan Papers.

70. Richmond *Enquirer,* June 26; July 14, 24.

71. Memphis *Appeal,* July 17, 19; September 4; Milledgeville *Federal Union,* June 23; July 21; New Orleans *Picayune,* June 23; July 18; Montgomery, *Cracker Parties,* 196-97; Schulz, *Nationalism and Sectionalism in Sourth Carolina,* 141-42.

72. W. R. de Graffenried to Cobb, July 14; S. W. Burney to Cobb, July 15, Cobb Papers, UG; Leemhuis, *Orr,* 54-55.

73. Ambler, ed., *Correspondence of Robert M. T. Hunter,* 210-12, 214-15; Henry T. Shanks, *The Secession Movement in Virginia, 1847-1861* (Richmond, 1934), 55; A. D. Banks to Hunter, August 18; John Blair to Hunter, September 18, Hunter Papers; Richmond *Enquirer,* July 24.

74. Adams, comp., *Transactions of the Kansas State Historical Society,* V, 341-48.

75. George N. Sanders to Buchanan, June 23; Simeon M. Johnson, to Buchanan, June 20, Buchanan Papers.

76. Bigler to Buchanan, July 9, in Black Papers.

77. The contents of this letter were not made public until three years later when Walker testified before a committee of the House of Representatives, chaired by John Covode of Pennsylvania, investigating political corruption. *House Reports,* 36 Cong., 1 sess., No. 648 (Serial 1071), 112-13.

78. Washington *Union,* June 10, 26; July 7, 9, 15, 18; August 21.

79. Phillips, ed., *Correspondence of Toombs, Stephens, and Cobb,* 401-3, 407-8, 421, 423; T. Lomax to Cobb, July 21, Cobb Papers, UG; Brooks, ed., "Howell Cobb Papers," 235-36; McCash, *Cobb,* 149-50; Simpson, *Cobb,* 118, 120-22.

80. Cobb to L.Q.C. Lamar, July 27, copy in Walker Papers.

81. New York *Evening Post,* June 9.
82. Thompson to Black, July 4, Black Papers; Foote, *Casket of Reminiscences,* 114-15; Aaron V. Brown to Walker, July 8, Walker Papers; Shenton, *Walker,* 253-54; Meerse, "Presidential Leadership," 300-305.
83. Adams, comp., *Transactions of the Kansas State Historical Society,* V, 347-48, 350-58.
84. Lawrence, Kansas, *Herald of Freedom,* July 25; Lawrence, Kansas, *Republican,* quoted in Boston *Advertiser,* July 31; Adams, comp., *Transactions of the Kansas State Historical Society,* V, 358-64; Cass to Buchanan, July 31; Floyd to Buchanan, July 31, Buchanan Papers; Meerse, "Presidential Leadership," 298; Shenton, *Walker,* 159.
85. Adams, comp., *Transactions of the Kansas State Historical Society,* V, 372-74; Milwaukee *Sentinel,* July 24; Springfield *Illinois State Journal,* July 21.
86. The original of the undated Silliman letter is in the Buchanan Papers.
87. Washington *Union,* September 3.
88. Phillips, ed., *Correspondence of Toombs, Stephens, and Cobb,* 421; Thomas R. R. Cobb to Howell Cobb, October 1, Cobb Papers, UG; E.G.W. Butler to Buchanan, September 22, Buchanan Papers.
89. Washington *National Era,* September 10; St. Louis *Missouri Democrat,* September 9; Springfield, Mass., *Republican,* September 26.
90. New York *Tribune,* August 28; Boston *Advertiser,* August 29.

Chapter 7

1. Austin *Texas State Gazette,* July 4; Richmond *Enquirer,* July 4; New York *Times,* July 4. For a less optimistic view see Chicago *Tribune,* July 4.
2. Louisville *Journal,* July 20.
3. Semi-weekly Richmond *Whig,* August 7; Nashville *Union and American,* May 30; Milledgeville, Ga., *Federal Union,* July 14.
4. *Congressional Globe,* 34 Cong., 3 sess., 738-40; Louisville *Journal,* July 13; semi-weekly Richmond *Whig,* March 13; May 26; Nashville *Republican Banner,* February 5, 20; March 10; April 22; May 6, 22.
5. S. H. Lester to Robert M. T. Hunter, April 3, Hunter Papers; Nashville *Union and American,* March 1; May 29; July 28.
6. Overdyke, *Know-Nothing Party in the South,* 265-66, 268-70; Cincinnati *Enquirer,* July 14; P. H. Cooney to John C. Breckinridge, May 19; James D. Leach to Breckinridge, July 14, Breckinridge Family Papers; New York *Times,* June 2, 3; Washington *National Era,* June 4; Gerald S. Henig, *Henry Winter Davis* (New York, 1973), 94-97.
7. New York *Herald,* April 28; June 26; semi-weekly Richmond *Whig,* February 13, 17; Beverley Tucker to Buchanan, May 14, Buchanan Papers.
8. Marc W. Kruman, *Parties and Politics in North Carolina, 1836-1865* (Baton Rouge, 1983), 178-79; Overdyke, *Know-Nothing Party in the South,* 261-63, 266-68, 178-79; Joseph H. Parks, *John Bell of Tennessee* (Baton Rouge, 1950), 315-18; J. Mills Thornton, III, *Politics and Power in a Slave Society; Alabama, 1800-1860* (Baton Rouge, 1978), 359-61.
9. Sam Houston to Thomas J. Rusk, May 12, Rusk Papers, UTA.
10. Austin *Texas State Gazette,* May 10, 30; August 15; J. F. Warren and thirteen other Democrats to Rusk, June 10; John Marshall to Rusk, May 13; June 17, 18; Rusk to Marshall, June 28, Rusk Papers; Overdyke, *Know-Nothing Party in the South,* 271-73.
11. St. Louis *Missouri Democrat* for July and August; Boston *Advertiser,* August 12, 18; September 4; Overdyke, *Know-Nothing Party in the South,* 270-71.
12. Overdyke, *Know-Nothing Party in the South,* 277-78; James B. Ranck, *Albert Gallatin Brown, Radical Southern Nationalist* (New York, 1937), 152-53; Lillian A. Pereyra, *James Lusk Alcorn* (Baton Rouge, 1966), 33-36.

13. James Jackson to Cobb, August 27; Mrs. Cobb to Cobb, July 5; John H. Lumpkin to Cobb, July 14, Cobb Papers, UG; Montgomery, *Cracker Parties,* 190-94; Schott, *Stephens,* 231-32; Simpson, *Cobb,* 117-19.

14. Milledgeville *Federal Union,* July 21; Montgomery, *Cracker Parties,* 186-90; Overdyke, *Know-Nothing Party in the South,* 263-65; Von Abele, *Stephens,* 157-59, 161-62; Schott, *Stephens,* 235-38.

15. Richmond *Enquirer,* June 16; Charleston *Mercury,* January 14.

16. *De Bow's Review,* August, 192-94; September, 225-38, 290-320; Washington *National Intelligencer,* August 18, 22; John G. Van Deusen, *The Ante-Bellum Southern Commercial Conventions* (Durham 1926), 58-61.

17. Philadelphia *Public Ledger,* August 24; Letter of Willoughby Newton in Washington *National Intelligencer,* August 8.

18. Mitchell, *Ruffin,* 98-99.

19. New York *Times,* June 15; Charles H. Brown, *Agents of Manifest Destiny: The Lives and Times of the Filibusters* (Chapel Hill, 1980), 409n.

20. New York *Times,* May 29; Brown, *Agents of Manifest Destiny,* 174-243, 267-358. Walker tells his own story in *The War in Nicaragua* (Mobile, 1860). His defense of his proposed introduction of slavery is on p. 256.

21. New York *Times,* May 28, 30; June 15; New Orleans *Picayune,* May 28; Austin *Texas State Gazette,* August 29; Richmond *Enquirer,* May 29; Brown, *Agents of Manifest Destiny,* 405-8.

22. Cincinnati *Enquirer,* May 28, 30; *United States Democratic Review,* July, 9-29.

23. Washington *National Intelligencer,* May 30; Chicago *Democrat,* May 29.

24. New York *Times,* June 18; Brown, *Agents of Manifest Destiny,* 409-12.

25. Walker, *The War in Nicaragua,* 262; Louisville *Journal,* February 25; Nashville *Union and American,* January 9; Scarborough, ed., *Diary of Edmund Ruffin,* I, 39; New Orleans *Picayune,* April 19. For the background of mid-nineteenth-century expansionism see Albert K. Weinberg, *Manifest Destiny: A Study of Nationalist Expansionism in American History,* (Baltimore, 1935), esp. 160-89; Reginald Horsman, *Race and Manifest Destiny: The Origins of Racial Anglo-Saxonism* (Cambridge, Mass., 1981), esp. 272-97; and Robert E. May, *The Southern Dream of a Caribbean Empire, 1854-1861* (Baton Rouge, 1973).

26. *Congressional Globe,* 34 Cong., 3 sess., 856; O. C. Hartley to Black, June 2, Black Papers; Austin *Texas State Gazette,* November 21; Memphis *Appeal,* November 17; Richmond *Enquirer,* June 23.

27. Horatio J. Perry to Buchanan, January 7; Buchanan to Christopher Fallon, December 14, Buchanan Papers; Phillips, ed., *Correspondence of Toombs, Stephens, and Cobb,* 399.

28. Detroit *Free Press,* September 4; Fuess, *Cushing,* II, 194-95.

29. *United States Democratic Review,* July 7-8; San Francisco *Evening Bulletin,* January 21; *Harper's Weekly,* January 10.

30. Cincinnati *Enquirer,* April 21; New York *Herald,* November 7.

31. Nashville *Republican Banner,* September 1; Washington *National Intelligencer,* April 22, 27; May 28; June 4; Alexander H. H. Stuart to William C. Rives, November 11, Rives Papers.

32. Baltimore *Republican,* quoted in Washington *National Intelligencer,* June 3; George N. Sanders to Buchanan, January 4, Buchanan Papers.

33. Klein, *Buchanan,* 318-19. Buchanan related the details of the negotiations in his first annual message to Congress.

34. New York *Times,* June 1.

35. For the origins and early history of the Mormons see Fawn M. Brodie, *No Man Knows My History: The Life of Joseph Smith, the Mormon Prophet* (New York, 1945); Leonard J. Arrington and Davis Bitton, *The Mormon Experience: A History of the Latter-day Saints* (New York, 1979); Jan Shipps, *Mormonism: The Story of a New Religious Tra-*

dition (Urbana and Chicago, 1985); Leonard J. Arrington, *Brigham Young: American Moses* (New York, 1985); and Eugene E. Campbell, *Establishing Zion: The Mormon Church in the American West, 1847-1869* (Salt Lake City, 1988).

36. Arrington and Bitton, *Mormon Experience,* 206-13.

37. Arrington, *Young,* xvi-xvii, 226-49; Stephen Taggart, *Mormonism's Negro Policy: Social and Historical Origins* (Salt Lake City, 1970), 71-73.

38. Arrington and Bitton, *Mormon Experience,* 212-13; Juanita Brooks, *The Mountain Meadows Massacre* (Stanford, 1950), 7-8; Thomas Cartwright to Brigham Young, February 2; A. Calkin to Young, July 28, Young Papers, ACLDS.

39. Richard S. Van Wagoner, *Mormon Polygamy: A History* (Salt Lake City, 1986), 89-92; Arrington and Bitton, *Mormon Experience,* 194-205; Campbell, *Establishing Zion,* 163-68.

40. Van Wagoner, Mormon Polygamy, 92-104; Arrington and Bitton, *Mormon Experience,* 185-205; Alfred Bell to Young, February 25; Lewis Brunson to Young, February 16, Young Papers.

41. Susan Grant to Young, September 9; Mary Ann Barton to Young, August 18, Young Papers.

42. Philadelphia *Public Ledger,* August 19; New York *Times,* July 2; Philadelphia *North American,* April 10.

43. C. Coolidge to Justin S. Morrill, April 27, Morrill Papers; New York *Times,* June 23; Johannsen, *Douglas,* 568; weekly Chicago *Times,* June 11; Springfield *Illinois State Journal,* June 25; Chicago *Tribune,* April 24; Basler, ed., *Collected Works of Lincoln,* II, 398-99.

44. Richmond *Enquirer,* March 27. The *Enquirer's* justification of federal intervention in Utah against the Mormons was identical to the Republicans' and abolitionists' justification of federal intervention in the territories against slavery. For defenses of the Mormons' right to self-government see weekly Chicago *Times,* January 15; New York *Herald,* May 3; Charleston *Mercury,* May 26; New Orleans *Picayune,* September 4; and Sacramento *Union,* November 14, 25.

45. San Francisco *Evening Bulletin,* June 15, 18; New York *Times,* April 21; June 9; Chicago *Tribune,* May 23; A. S. Bayley to Black, April 3, Black Papers; Bigler to Buchanan, May 25; Robert Tyler to Buchanan, April 27, Buchanan Papers.

46. Norman F. Furniss, *The Mormon Conflict, 1850-1859* (New Haven, 1960), 45-59, 75-88, 91-94; Edward L. Lyman, *Political Deliverance: The Morman Quest for Utah Statehood* (Urbana, 1986), 8-9; Arrington and Bitton, *Mormon Experience,* 161-66; Arrington *Young,* 226-47; Brooks, *Mountain Meadows Massacre,* 7-8.

47. Furniss, *Mormon Conflict,* 63, 88-89; Nevins, *Emergence of Lincoln,* I, 317.

48. Furniss, *Mormon Conflict,* 95-104.

49. William S. Harney to Young, July 28, Young Papers.

50. Furniss, *Mormon Conflict,* 60-61; Arrington, *Young,* 250-51; Brooks, *Mountain Meadows Massacre,* 10-12.

51. Brooks, *Mountain Meadows Massacre,* 12, 14-15, 19-20n.

52. Brooks, *Mountain Meadows Massacre,* 13-19; Furniss, *Mormon Conflict,* 123-24.

53. Arrington, *Young,* 254-56; Furniss, *Mormon Conflict,* 104-18; Campbell, *Establishing Zion,* 233-52.

54. Isaac Bullock to Young, August 8, Young Papers; Brooks, *Mountain Meadows Massacre,* 21-23.

55. Although a little generous in stressing the extenuating circumstances, Juanita Brooks, *The Mountain Meadows Massacre,* is by far the best study of this episode in Mormon history. I have relied on it heavily in my brief account. See also her biography, *John Doyle Lee: Zealot, Pioneer, Builder, Scapegoat* (Glendale, 1961). William Wise, *Massacre at Mountain Meadows: An American Legend and a Monumental Crime* (New York, 1976), presents the circumstantial evidence for a case against Brigham Young as an accessory before and after the fact. Leonard J. Arrington, a distinguished Mormon historian, illustrates the pain that this event has caused those who have written about the Mormon

War. In his *Great Basin Kingdom* (Cambridge, Mass., 1958), he devotes fourteen pages to the conflict without mentioning the massacre. His and Davis Bitton's account in *The Mormon Experience* is brief and vague. In his biography of Brigham Young he praises Brook's study as "complete and dependable," but he places most of the responsibility for the massacre on the Indians and the emigrants.

56. N. B. Baldwin to Young, November 15, Young Papers; San Francisco *Evening Bulletin*, October 27.

57. Mascord Hedley to Young, November 18, Young Papers; Arrington, *Young*, 260-75; Furniss, *Mormon Conflict*, 168-203; Andrew L. Neff, *History of Utah* (Salt Lake City, 1940), 456-84.

58. *Harper's Weekly*, January 31; New York *Times*, April 2, 3, 8-10, 13, 15.

59. *Harper's Weekly*, March 28; New York *Times*, April 16; New York *Herald*, April 23, 27; July 15; Nevins and Halsey, eds., *Diary of George Templeton Strong*, II, 342-45.

60. *United States Democratic Review*, July, 64-79; New York *Times*, April 14; May 30; June 15, 18, 25; *Harper's Weekly*, May 30.

61. New York *Times*, July 3, 4; New York *Tribune*, July 4, 15; Samuel A. Pleasants, *Fernando Wood of New York* (New York, 1948), 77-83.

62. New York *Times*, July 6-8; New York *Tribune*, July 8; Nevins and Halsey, eds., *Diary of George Templeton Strong*, II, 346-47; Lucid, ed., *Journal of Richard Henry Dana, Jr.*, II, 823-24.

63. New York *Times*, July 9, 13-15; New York *Tribune*, July 14; Nevins and Halsey, eds., *Diary of George Templeton Strong*, II, 349.

64. New York *Herald*, July 15; New York *Times*, July 7, 8.

65. New York *Herald*, August 6; New York *Times*, August 5, 10; New York *Evening Post*, August 6; *Harper's Weekly*, August 15; Philadelphia *Public Ledger*, August 10.

66. Washington *National Intelligencer*, January 27; New York *Herald*, August 21; New York *Evening Post*, February 3; Nashville *Republican Banner*, August 19, 28.

67. Harrisburg *Telegraph*, September 7; New York *Evening Post*, September 21; New Orleans *Picayune*, September 22, 25; Waterville, N.Y., *Times*, September 26.

Chapter 8

1. Robert C. Winthrop to John H. Clifford, September 21, Winthrop Papers.

2. Cincinnati *Enquirer*, June 3.

3. Cincinnati *Enquirer*, April 4; June 3; Springfield *Illinois State Journal*, June 8-9; Chicago *Democrat*, June 20; John F. Stover, *Iron Road to the West: American Railroads in the 1850s* (New York, 1958), 135-39.

4. Milwaukee *Sentinel*, April 14-16.

5. Milwaukee *Sentinel*, January 16; Boston *Evening Transcript*, January 2; Detroit *Free Press*, January 7; Harrisburg *Telegraph*, February 7; New Orleans *Picayune*, September 23; Stover, *Iron Road to the West*, 59-93.

6. Stover, *Iron Road to the West*, 94-105, 152-53; John L. Larson, *Bonds of Enterprise: John Murray Forbes and Western Development in America's Railway Age* (Cambridge, Mass., 1984), 64-68.

7. Stover, *Iron Road to the West*, 105-11; Russel, *Improvement of Communication with the Pacific Coast*, 226-27; Robert Toombs to Howell Cobb, April 17, Cobb Papers, UG; George S. Yerger to Thomas J. Rusk, April 9, Rusk Papers; New Orleans *Picayune*, March 3; April 14; June 6.

8. William S. Wade to Trumbull, January 13, Trumbull Papers.

9. Letter of "J.S.P." in New York *Tribune*, January 13; Louisville *Democrat*, January 17; Nashville *Union and American*, April 7-9, 11.

10. Seneca W. Ely to Chase, April 14, Chase Papers, LC.

11. Cincinnati *Enquirer*, January 7.

12. Springfield *Illinois State Journal,* July 4; Chicago *Tribune,* January 29; semi-weekly Richmond *Whig,* June 26; William B. Smith and Arthur H. Cole, *Fluctuations in American Business, 1790-1860* (Cambridge, Mass., 1935), 89-94, 108-15; George Rogers Taylor, *The Transportation Revolution* (New York, 1951), 346-48; Paul W. Gates, *The Farmer's Age: Agriculture, 1815-1860* (New York, 1960), 402.

13. Bray Hammond, *Banks and Politics in America from the Revolution to the Civil War* (Princeton, 1957), 551-56, 698-710; Taylor, *Transportation Revolution,* 301-23, 347-48.

14. New York *Tribune,* July 4; Chicago *Democrat,* May 20; Gates, *Farmer's Age,* 90.

15. Springfield *Illinois State Journal,* June 6; William Hill to Thomas J. Rusk, April 17, Rusk Papers.

16. Washington *Union,* June 13; Madison *Wisconsin State Journal,* May 13; George A. Nourse to Chase, April 20, Chase Papers, LC; New York *Tribune,* July 1; *Vermont Journal,* quoted in Boston *Advertiser,* August 18; Shenton, *Walker,* 159-60.

17. Washington *Union,* June 13.

18. Philadelphia *North American,* June 20; Philadelphia *Public Ledger,* April 14; Madison *Wisconsin State Journal,* May 13; Chicago *Democrat,* May 22; Amos A. Lawrence to Charles Robinson, May 16, Robinson Papers, UK.

19. Chicago *Tribune,* April 21; Richard Yates to L. L. Linton and J. H. Kedzie, August 5; Yates to J. C. Conklin, August 6, Yates Papers, ISHL; New York *Herald,* May 5; New York *Times,* June 24; Boston *Advertiser,* August 14.

20. *Hunt's Merchants' Magazine,* XXXVII (July), 70; (August), 197; (September), 325.

21. New York *Independent,* quoted in Boston *Advertiser,* August 12; Chicago *Democrat,* August 13; letter from "JWS," dated August 26, in Waterville, N.Y., *Times,* September 5.

22. George W. Van Vleck, *The Panic of 1857* (New York, 1943), 38-59, 105, stresses the international background of the panic. Albert Fishlow, *American Railroads and the Transformation of the Ante-Bellum Economy* (Cambridge, Mass., 1965), 114-16, stresses the domestic background. James L. Huston, *The Panic of 1857 and the Coming of the Civil War* (Baton Rouge, 1987), the most recent study, is brief on the background but good on its political ramifications. Hammond, *Banks and Politics,* 707-10, and Peter Temin,"The Panic of 1857," *Intermountain Economic Review,* VI (1975), 1-12, are good on the banking background. See also Taylor, *Transportation Revolution,* 348-49; and Nevins, *Emergence of Lincoln,* I, 178-90.

23. New York *Herald,* August 25-26; Hammond, *Banks and Politics,* 710.

24. New York *Herald,* August 25; New York *Evening Post,* September 1; Philadelphia *North American,* September 3; *Hunt's Merchants' Magazine,* XXXVII (October), 452-53; Cincinnati *Enquirer,* August 28; Van Vleck, *Panic of 1857,* 64-66.

25. Van Vleck, *Panic of 1857,* 66-73; Hammond, *Banks and Politics,* 710-11; Huston, *Panic of 1857,* 14-17; Nevins and Halsey, eds., Diary of George Templeton Strong, II, 355.

26. Boston *Advertiser,* September 8; Springfield, Mass., *Republican,* September 26; New York *Tribune,* October 5-6; Chicago *Tribune,* August 29; September 17; Nashville *Republican Banner,* September 8.

27. Chicago *Tribune,* September 29; Nashville *Republican Banner,* October 4, 15, 18; Nevins and Halsey, eds., Diary of George Templeton Strong, II, 257-58.

28. Boston *Advertiser,* August 27; New York *Tribune,* October 5-6, 9; Boston *Evening Transcript,* October 7; *Hunt's Merchants' Magazine,* XXXVII (November), 582; Phillips, ed., *Toombs, Stephens, and Cobb Correspondence,* 424; Van Vleck, *Panic of 1857,* 96-100.

29. New York *Tribune,* September 28-29; Harrisburg *Telegraph,* September 26; James Beck to Simon Cameron, October 6, Cameron Papers, LC.

30. New York *Tribune,* October 9, 12-14; *Hunt's Merchants' Magazine,* XXXVII (November), 587; Huston, *Panic of 1857,* 19-22; Van Vleck, *Panic of 1857,* 71-73.

31. Boston *Advertiser,* October 15; Springfield, Mass., *Republican,* October 15; Detroit *Free Press,* October 15; Hammond, *Banks and Politics,* 711-12.

32. Springfield, Mass., *Republican,* October 15; Hammond, *Banks and Politics,* 713; Taylor, *Transportation Revolution,* 350-51.

33. *Hunt's Merchants' Magazine,* XXXVII (November), 582; John Bigelow to William Cullen Bryant, October 12, Bigelow Papers; New York *Tribune,* October 9-13; Nevins and Halsey, eds., *Diary of George Templeton Strong,* II, 367; Gunther P. Barth, *City People: The Rise of Modern City Culture in Nineteenth Century America* (New York, 1980), 123.

34. Amos A. Lawrence to Charles Robinson, October 19, Robinson Papers, UK; Sarah Forbes Hughes, ed., *Letters and Recollections of John Murray Forbes* (2 vols., Boston, 1899), I, 167-68; Charles Francis Adams ms. diary, entries for October 1, 10, 14; November 27; December 14; Adams to Sumner, October 5, Adams Family Papers.

35. Rosenberg, *Iowa on the Eve of the Civil War,* 163; Gates, *Farmer's Age,* 90; Carl Schurz, *The Reminiscences of Carl Schurz* (3 vols., New York, 1907-8), II, 75-76; Current, *History of Wisconsin,* II, 243-50; Frederick Merk, *Economic History of Wisconsin during the Civil War Decade* (Madison, Wis., 1916), 244-70.

36. Ethan A. Allen to Seward, December 14; William J. Nagel to Seward, December 22, Seward Papers; *Hunt's Merchants' Magazine,* XXXVII (November), 582; Huston, *Panic of 1857,* 25-26.

37. Boston *Evening Transcript,* October 6; Springfield, Mass., *Rupublican,* October 7, 13; November 4, 9; December 2, 5; Harrisburg *Telegraph,* October 16; Malcom R. Eiseln, *The Rise of Pennsylvania Protectionism* (Philadelphia, 1932), 244-45; Coleman, *Disruption of the Pennsylvania Democracy,* 110-11.

38. Springfield, Mass., *Republican,* November 4; William H. Clement to Samuel L. M. Barlow, November 3, 16, 20, 25, 29; December 23, Barlow Papers; Nashville *Republican Banner,* November 1.

39. Chicago *Tribune,* October 8; November 5.

40. Huston, *Panic of 1857,* 25; New York *Herald,* October 22.

41. E. B. Hart to Cobb, October 23, Cobb Papers, UG; Philadelphia *Public Ledger,* November 6; Philadelphia *North American,* October 26.

42. Samuel A. Pleasants, *Fernando Wood of New York* (New York, 1948), 85-86; Benjamin J. Klebaner, "Poor Relief and Public Works during the Depression of 1857," *The Historian,* XXII (1960), 264-79; New York *Tribune,* November 6; New York *Times,* October 23, 27; Washington *National Era,* November 12; Portland, Maine, *Transcript and Eclectic,* November 14.

43. Huston, *Panic of 1857,* 27-28; Harrisburg *Telegraph,* September 3; Philadelphia *Press,* November 12.

44. New York *Times,* October 23, 27; Nevins and Halsey, eds., *Diary of George Templeton Strong,* II, 369; Leonard Chalmers, "Tammany Hall, Fernando Wood, and the Struggle to Control New York City, 1857-1859," *New-York Historical Society Quarterly,* LIII (1969), 13-14.

45. New York *Tribune,* November 6-7, 10-12; Huston, *Panic of 1857,* 26-27; Nevins and Halsey, eds., *Diary of George Templeton Strong,* II, 370.

46. John A. Dix to Buchanan, November 10, Buchanan Papers; *United States Democratic Review,* September, 206; Binghamton, N.Y., *Republican,* quoted in Waterville, N.Y., *Times,* December 5.

47. Williams and Butler to William S. Pettigrew, October 24, Pettigrew Family Papers; Charleston *Mercury,* October 8; *Congressional Globe,* 35 Cong., 1 sess., 90; Austin *Texas State Gazette,* November 21; Huston, *Panic of 1857,* 60-63.

48. Douglass C. North, *The Economic Growth of the United States, 1790-1860* (Englewood Cliffs, N.J., 1961), 214; Richmond *Enquirer,* November 20; Austin *Texas State Gazette,* October 10.

49. Richmond *Enquirer,* November 20; Mobile *Register,* November 18; Huston, *Panic of 1857,* 80-81.

50. Nashville *Republican Banner,* October 18.

51. James L. Huston, "Western Grains and the Panic of 1857," *AH,* LVII (1983), 15-17; *Hunt's Merchants' Magazine,* XXXVII (December), 660.

52. Nashville *Republican Banner,* October 20; December 6; Washington *National Intelligencer,* October 15; semi-weekly Richmond *Whig,* October 9.

53. *United States Democratic Review,* November, 386-87; Chicago *Democrat,* October 3; Chicago *Tribune,* October 26; Boston *Advertiser,* August 28; Sidney Homer to Caleb Cushing, October 9, Cushing Papers; Huston, *Panic of 1857,* 37-40.

54. Memphis *Appeal,* November 6; Letter of "Franklin" in New York *Tribune,* October 21; New York *Tribune,* October 6; St. Louis *Missouri Democrat,* October 19.

55 Henry D. Cooke to John Sherman, November 17, Sherman Papers; Cincinnati *Enquirer,* September 26; Nashville *Republican Banner,* October 16; Indianapolis *Indiana State Sentinel,* September 26.

56 Henry C. Carey to Buchanan, October 1, Buchanan Papers; Philadelphia *North American,* October 1, 20; Harrisburg *Telegraph,* December 30; George W. Smith, *Henry C. Carey and American Sectional Conflict* (Albuquerque, 1951), 51-53; Eiselen, *Rise of Pennsylvania Protectionism,* 245-46.

57. Samuel Wilkinson to Seward, October 25; Myron H. Clark to Seward, October 15; H. D. Sharpe to Seward, November 28, Seward Papers; Vincennes *Gazette,* October 12, 16; James L. Huston, "A Political Response to Industrialism: The Republican Embrace of Protectionist Labor Doctrines," *JAH,* LXX (1983), 49-51.

58. Simon Cameron to William P. Seymour, November 16, Cameron Papers, LC; Harrisburg *Telegraph,* September 29; New York Tribune, September 28; October 2, 6, 14, 26; *Congressional Globe,* 35 Cong., 1 sess., 85-86, 89-90, 94.

59. Chicago *Democrat,* October 7; John Bigelow to William Cullen Bryant, October 12, Bigelow Papers.

60. Waterville, N.Y., *Times,* October 17, 31; Harrisburg *Telegraph,* September 26; Boston *Evening Transcript,* October 5; H. S. Randall to Robert F. W. Allston, October 26, Allston Papers, unpublished typescripts, USC; W. Hunt to Samuel B. Ruggles, November 7, Ruggles Papers, NYPL.

61. H. S. Randall to Robert F. W. Allston, October 26, Allston Papers; Chicago *Tribune,* September 4; October 20; Portland, Maine, *Transcript and Eclectic,* November 14; Samuel J. May, Jr., to "Dear Friend Webb," October 21, May Papers.

62. Philadelphia *Public Ledger,* October 11; Charles Francis Adams ms. diary, entry for November 21, Adams Family Papers.

63. New York *Anti-Slavery Standard,* October 20; Boston *Liberator,* October 20; Louis Ruchames, ed., *The Letters of William Lloyd Garrison,* Vol. IV, *From Disunion to the Brink of War, 1850-1860* (Cambridge, Mass., 1975), 492-93.

64. H. S. Randall to Robert F. W. Allston, October 26, Allston Papers; Waterville, N.Y., *Times,* October 31; Boston *Evening Transcript,* October 5; Richard Carwardine, *Transatlantic Revivalism: Popular Evangelicalism in Britain and America, 1790-1865* (Westport, Conn., 1978), 163.

65. Robert C. Winthrop to his son, November 19, Winthrop Papers. For brief accounts of earlier nineteenth-century revivals see William G. McLoughlin, *Revivals, Awakenings, and Reform* (Chicago, 1978), and Carwardine, *Transatlantic Revivalism.*

66. Carwardine, *Transatlantic Revivalism,* 159-64; Sandra Sizer, "Politics and Apolitical Religion: the Great Urban Revivals of the Late Nineteenth Century," *Church History,* XLVIII (1979), 86-87.

67. H. R. Harmon to Benjamin F. Wade, February 2, Wade Papers; Carwardine, *Transatlantic Revivalism,* 164-69; Sizer, "Politics and Apolitical Religion," 88-91.

68. Springfield, Mass., *Republican,* December 5; Timothy L. Smith, *Revivalism and*

Social Reform in Mid-Nineteenth-Century America (New York, 1957), 63-67; McLoughlin, *Revivals, Awakenings, and Reform,* 141-42; Carwardine, *Transatlantic Revivalism,* 159-62; Nichols, *Disruption of American Democracy,* 135-36.
69. Springfield, Mass., *Republican,* November 7.

Chapter 9

1. Nevins and Halsey, eds, *Diary of George Templeton Strong,* II, 368; Gienapp, "'Politics Seem to Enter into Everything,'" 19.
2. Detroit *Free Press,* October 25; November 15; Philadelphia *Press,* October 16, 30.
3. W. Hunt to Samuel B. Ruggles, November 7, Ruggles Papers.
4. Springfield, Mass., *Republican,* October 9; Israel Washburn, Jr., to Seward, September 21, Seward Papers; Washington *National Era,* September 24; Dale Baum, *The Civil War Party System: The Case of Massachusetts, 1848-1876* (Chapel Hill, 1984), 37-38.
5. Elihu C. Becker to Banks, June 4, Banks Papers; Charles Francis Adams ms. diary, entries for June 11, 18, Adams Family Papers; Fred H. Harrington, *Fighting Politician: Major General N. P. Banks* (Philadelphia, 1948), 1-26, 41-44.
6. Boston *Advertiser,* July 2; Boston *Evening Transcript,* June 30; Charles Francis Adams ms. diary, entries for June 23-24; Adams to Sumner, June 26, Adams letter book, Adams Family Papers; Martin B. Duberman, *Charles Francis Adams, 1807-1886* (Boston, 1961), 210-11.
7. Boston *Advertiser,* September 18; October 16; Springfield, Mass., *Republican,* October 18; Boston *Liberator,* August 14; Edward L. Pierce to Chase, August 8, Chase Papers, LC; Pierce to Frank Blair, October 2, Blair-Lee Papers.
8. Boston *Advertiser,* September 11; October 31; Springfield, Mass., *Republican,* September 26; Charles Francis Adams to E. Hopkins, August 20, Adams letter book, Adams Family Papers; Harrington, *Banks,* 43-44.
9. Springfield, Mass., *Republican,* October 7, 20-21, 23, 28; Boston *Advertiser,* October 8, 28; November 2; Baum, *Civil War Party System,* 40-41.
10. Charles Francis Adams to Sumner, October 5, Adams letter book, Adams Family Papers.
11. John Z. Goodrich to Henry Wilson, November 25, Banks Papers; Charles Francis Adams ms. diary, entry for November 4, Adams Family Papers; Edward Everett ms. diary, entry for November 3, Everett Papers; John C. Clifford to John C. Winthrop, November 15, Winthrop Papers.
12. Van Deusen, *Greeley,* 222-23; Van Deusen, *Weed,* 240.
13. New York *Tribune,* September 23-25.
14. William H. Ludlow to Horatio King, September 16, King Papers; David L. Yulee to Robert J. Walker, April 4, Walker Papers; Albany *Atlas and Argus,* September 29-30; October 9, 17, 31.
15. New York *Tribune,* September 28; Waterville, N.Y., *Times,* October 3.
16. New York *Tribune,* October 28-31; James A. Rawley, *Edwin D. Morgan, 1811-1883: Merchant in Politics* (New York, 1955), 73.
17. Silbey, *Partisan Imperative,* 134-35, 156-57. Silbey, in my opinion, somewhat overstates the remaining power of the New York Know Nothings as an independent political organization in 1857.
18. Silbey, *Partisan Imperative,* 142-43; Seward to Francis Preston Blair, Sr., November 5, Blair-Lee Papers; New York *Evening Post,* November 4.
19. Albany *Atlas and Argus,* November 6; New York *Herald,* November 5.
20. New York *Tribune,* November 6, 12, 16, 18, 21, 25; Daniel E. Sickles to Buchanan, November 20, 28; Reid Sanders to Buchanan, November 28, Buchanan Papers; Pleasants, *Wood,* 87-89.

21. New York *Tribune,* December 14; Nevins and Halsey, eds., *Diary of George Templeton Strong,* II, 374-75; New York *Evening Post,* December 2; Daniel F. Tiemann to Buchanan, December 8, Buchanan Papers; Pleasants, *Wood,* 92-101.

22. Philadelphia *North American,* October 9.

23. Harrisburg *Telegraph,* February 21, 27; March 17, 26; April 16; Russell Errett to Chase, March 14, Chase Papers, LC.

24. Harrisburg *Telegraph,* March 26; Coleman, *Disruption of the Pennsylvania Democracy,* 106-7; Charles B. Going, *David Wilmot, Free-Soiler* (New York, 1924), 495-503.

25. Going, *Wilmot,* 732-36; McClure, *Old Time Notes of Pennsylvania,* I, 298-306; W. P. Seymour to Cameron, June 19, Cameron Papers, LC; D. C. Gillespie to Lemuel Todd, April 21; Frank Jordan to Todd, July 13; Wilmot to Todd, August 8, 11, McPherson Papers; Harrisburg *Telegraph,* September 29.

26. Coleman, *Disruption of the Pennsylvania Democracy,* 107; Bigler to Buchanan, May 25, Buchanan Papers; William F. Packer to Bigler, August 7, Bigler Papers; Going *Wilmot,* 505-6.

27. Charles Cook to Lemuel Todd, October 5, McPherson Papers; Harrisburg *Telegraph,* September 29; Eisclen, *Rise of Pennsylvania Protectionism,* 239-41; Going, *Wilmot,* 507-13; Coleman, *Disruption of the Pennsylvania Democracy,* 107-10.

28. New York *Tribune,* August 31; Holt, *Forging a Majority,* 220-39; Coleman, *Disruption of the Pennsylvania Democracy,* 112-13; McClure, *Old Time Notes of Pennsylvania,* I, 223-27; Lemuel Todd to Jacob Gossler, July 9, McPherson Papers; A. B. Anderson to Simon Cameron, September 29, Cameron Papers, LC.

29. John P. Jones to Edward McPherson, September 19; D. L. Eaton to McPherson, September 21; John Laporte to Lemuel Todd, August 14; Todd to McPherson, September 1, McPherson Papers; J. M. Kirkpatrick to Cameron, August 24; Wilmot to Cameron, August 8; September 6, Cameron Papers, LC.

30. New York *Tribune,* October 28; Coleman, *Disruption of the Pennsylvania Democracy,* 109-10.

31. Wilmot to Cameron, October 24, Cameron Papers, LC.

32. Frederick J. Blue, *Salmon P. Chase: A Life in Politics* (Kent, Ohio, 1987), is the best and most recent biography.

33. William Slade, Jr., to Chase, July 2, Chase Papers, LC; W. T. Bascom to Benjamin F. Wade, February 16, Wade Papers; Blue, *Chase,* 115.

34. Caleb B. Smith to William Schouler, June 14; R. M. Corwine to Schouler, June 20, Schouler Papers; Roseboom, *History of Ohio,* IV, 325-26; Blue, *Chase,* 115-16.

35. John Brasee to Chase, August 28, Chase Papers, LC.

36. Boston *Advertiser,* August 27.

37. Roseboom, *History of Ohio,* IV, 327-28; Blue, *Chase,* 116.

38. Cincinnati *Enquirer,* August 9.

39. Roseboom, *History of Ohio,* IV, 328-29; Huston, *Panic of 1857,* 51.

40. William H. Bissell to Chase, October 20, Chase Papers, LC; Chase to Sumner, November 23, Sumner Papers.

41. Current, *History of Wisconsin,* II, 224-36.

42. Milwaukee *Sentinel,* June 29; Current, *History of Wisconsin,* II, 260-62.

43. Madison *Wisconsin State Journal,* September 4; Milwaukee *Sentinel,* September 8.

44. Madison *Wisconsin State Journal,* September 4; Schurz, *Reminiscences,* II, 80-82; Hans L. Trefousse, *Carl Schurz: A Biography* (Knoxville, 1982), 65-68; Current, *History of Wisconsin,* II, 262-63.

45. Madison *Wisconsin State Journal,* August 27-28, 31; Current, *History of Wisconsin,* II, 264.

46. Madison *Wisconsin State Journal,* September 19; October 6; Current, *History of Wisconsin,* II, 225.

47. Milwaukee *Sentinel,* September 8, 22; October 5, 19, 23; Madison *Wisconsin State Journal,* October 19, 29, 31.

48. Current, *History of Wisconsin,* II, 264-65; Madison *Argus and Democrat,* quoted in Madison *Wisconsin State Journal,* September 23; *Milwaukee Sentinel,* October 1, 3, 6, 8.

49. Joseph Schafer, ed., *Intimate Letters of Carl Schurz* (Madison, 1928), 179; Frederic Bancroft, ed., *Speeches, Correspondence and Political Papers of Carl Schurz* (6 vols., New York, 1913), I, 31-32; L. P. Harvey to Schurz, December 20, Schurz Papers, LC; Current, *History of Wisconsin,* II, 266-67.

50. Cincinnati *Enquirer,* October 13; Morrisville, N.Y., *Madison Observer,* September 3, 10.

51. George A. Nourse to Lyman Trumbull, November 5, Trumbull Papers; Madison *Wisconsin State Journal,* October 28-29; Springfield, Mass., *Republican,* November 4; Boston *Advertiser,* December 24.

52. Adams, comp., *Transactions of the Kansas State Historical Society,* V, 375-78, 382-84, 388-400; Lawrence, Kansas, *Herald of Freedom,* August 15, 22; St. Louis *Missouri Democrat,* August 24; Schuyler Colfax to Robinson, April 8; Henry Wilson to Robinson, June 15, Robinson Papers, KSHS; G. W. Brown to Chase, October 18, Chase Papers, LC.

53. Lawrence, Kansas, *Herald of Freedom,* July 25.

54. Lawrence, Kansas, *Herald of Freedom,* August 8; Robinson to Amos A. Lawrence, June 28, Lawrence Papers; Dwight Thatcher to Seward, June 28, Seward Papers; Boston *Advertiser,* August 3.

55. St. Louis *Missouri Democrat,* September 5, 10; Lawrence, Kansas, *Herald of Freedom,* September 5; Stephenson, *Lane,* 88-89.

56. Adams, comp., *Transaction of the Kansas State Historical Society,* V, 364-67, 374, 385; Robinson to Amos A. Lawrence, October 5, Lawrence Papers; Henry Wilson to Robinson, June 15, Robinson Papers, KSHS; Lecompton *Kansas National Democrat,* August 5; Stephenson, *Lane,* 87-88.

57. Adams, comp., *Transactions of the Kansas State Historical Society,* V, 302-6; Lecompton *Kansas National Democrat,* October 8; November 12; G. A. Crawford to William Bigler, October 3, Bigler Papers; New York *Tribune,* October 10; Springfield, Mass., *Republican,* October 16.

58. Boston *Advertiser,* October 13; Lawrence, Kansas, *Herald of Freedom,* October 10; St. Louis *Missouri Democrat,* October 20.

59. Springfield, Mass., *Republican,* November 5; Washington *National Intelligencer,* November 5; Robinson, *Kansas Conflict,* 362-65; Lecompton *Kansas National Democrat,* November 12.

60. Adams, comp., *Transactions of the Kansas State Historical Society,* V, 383, 403-8.

61. Adams, comp., *Transactions of the Kansas State Historical Society,* V, 402-10; Lawrence, Kansas, *Herald of Freedom,* October 24.

62. Adams, comp., *Transactions of the Kansas State Historical Society,* V, 401, 411.

63. Lecompton *Kansas National Democrat,* October 22; November 5.

64. New York *Herald,* October 26; November 1; Albany *Atlas and Argus,* October 31; November 3, 13; New Albany, Ind., *Ledger,* November 11; Cincinnati *Enquirer,* October 30; November 5; Detroit *Free Press,* November 6; Chicago *Times,* October 28.

65. New York *Tribune,* November 9; Springfield *Illinois State Journal,* November 3.

66. Edgefield, S. C., *Advertiser,* November 11; Macon *State Press,* quoted in Jackson *Mississippian,* November 25; Mobile *Register,* November 6; Montgomery *Advertiser,* quoted in Jackson *Mississippian,* December 9; Memphis *Appeal,* November 8.

67. Richmond *Enquirer,* November 6; Louisville *Journal,* November 7; New Orleans *Picayune,* November 11.

68. Adams, comp., *Transactions of the Kansas State Historical Society,* V, 401, 403.

Chapter 10

1. Philadelphia *North American,* September 8.

2. St. Louis *Missouri Democrat,* August 15.

3. Lecompton *Kansas National Democrat,* September 10; New York *Tribune,* September 17, 19; Johannsen, *Douglas,* 576-77.

4. Lecompton *Kansas National Democrat,* July 30; September 3; October 1; George A. Crawford to Horatio King, October 12, King Papers.

5. Milwaukee *Sentinel,* October 1; New York *Tribune,* September 22; New York *Herald,* October 30; weekly Chicago *Times,* October 22.

6. Memphis *Appeal,* September 16; Ambler, ed., *Correspondence of Robert M. T. Hunter,* 237-41; undated clipping in Hunter Papers.

7. The letter was published in full in John G. Nicolay and John Hay, *Abraham Lincoln, a History* (10 vols., New York, 1890), II, 110-12. According to the authors, the letter was then in the hands of Gen. Duncan S. Walker, of Washington, D.C. In a possible reference to reports of frauds in the territorial election, Buchanan told Walker that he hoped to see him "before you publish anything." Copies of Walkers's proclamations had not yet reached the President.

8. Phillips, ed., *Correspondence of Toombs, Stephens, and Cobb,* 422, 423-24; Cobb to Stephens, November 2, Stephens Papers, DU; *House Reports,* 36 Cong., 1 sess., No. 448 (Serial 1071), 103, 318-19.

9. *House Reports,* 36 Cong., 1 sess., No. 448 (Serial 1071), 314-17.

10. St. Louis *Missouri Democrat,* December 16; *House Reports,* 36 Cong., 1 sess., No. 448 (Serial 1071), 157-74.

11. St. Louis *Missouri Democrat,* August 15; September 3; November 30; New York *Tribune,* November 19; Robert W. Johannsen, "The Lecompton Constitutional Convention: An Analysis of Its Membership," *KHQ,* XXIII (1957), 233-35.

12. Lawrence, Kansas, *Herald of Freedom,* June 20.

13. New York *Herald,* September 22; Johannsen, "Lecompton Constitutional Convention," 230-33, 242.

14. Johannsen, "Lecompton Constitutional Convention," 237-38.

15. New York *Tribune,* November 9; Johannsen, "Lecompton Constitutional Convention," 235-36.

16. For the full text of the Lecompton constitution, see Washington *Union,* December 5; Washington *National Intelligencer,* December 7.

17. New York *Tribune,* November 19; Madison, *Wisconsin State Journal,* November 16.

18. New York *Tribune,* November 9; *House Reports,* 36 Cong., 1 sess., No. 448 (Serial 1071), 213-14; William Weer to Douglas, December 21, Douglas Papers; Johannsen, *Douglas,* 579-80.

19. *House Reports,* 36 Cong., 1 sess., No. 448 (Serial 1071), 163-74; Washington *Union,* November 22; New York *Tribune,* November 19; Nichols, *Disruption of American Democracy,* 121-24.

20. Washington *National Intelligencer,* December 7; St. Louis *Missouri Democrat,* November 23; Chicago *Democrat,* November 28. Jonathan W. Randolph, a proslavery delegate from Atchison who opposed submission in any form, bluntly accused the moderates of perpetrating a fraud. Amid laughter, he described the choice they offered the voters as one between "a Slave State Constitution and a Slave State Constitution," and he was certain that the free-state party would not be fools enough to accept it. He preferred full submission to such a "swindle." Boston *Advertiser,* November 20.

21. *House Reports,* 36 Cong., 1 sess., No. 448 (Serial 1071), 110-11, 114.

22. Leavenworth *Herald,* November 21; Leavenworth *Journal,* November 27, both quoted in Washington *National Intelligencer,* December 8.

23. Lecompton *Kansas National Democrat,* November 12, 19, 26; December 3.

24. Robinson to Amos A. Lawrence, June 28, Lawrence Papers; Lawrence, Kansas, *Herald of Freedom,* July 4; November 14, 21.

25. New York *Tribune,* December 2, 4, 7; Lawrence, Kansas, *Herald of Freedom,* December 5; Robinson to John Sherman, November 24, Sherman Papers.

26. Washington *National Era,* November 5; Chicago *Tribune,* November 11.

27. Chicago *Democrat,* November 26; Springfield, Mass., *Republican,* November 30; Chicago *Tribune,* December 1; Edward Harte to Nathaniel P. Banks, November 16, Banks Papers.

28. New York *Tribune,* November 16; December 3; George Ashmun to Robert J. Walker, December 1, Walker Papers; Madison *Wisconsin State Journal,* November 13; Boston *Advertiser,* November 19.

29. Milwaukee *Sentinel,* November 30; Indianapolis *Indiana State Sentinel,* November 23; Detroit *Free Press,* November 18-19.

30. Cincinnati *Enquirer,* November 25; New York *Herald,* November 2; Philadelphia *Press,* November 18; Springfield *Illinois State Register,* November 19, quoted in Chicago *Tribune,* November 23; Detroit *Free Press,* November 13; Albany *Atlas and Argus,* November 14; James Thompson to Black, November 14, Black Papers.

31. Montgomery *Mail,* November 14.

32. Memphis *Appeal,* December 8; Mobile *Register,* November 24; Jackson *Mississippian,* December 2.

33. Mobile *Register,* November 28; Montgomery, *Cracker Parties,* 202-3; Thomas R. R. Cobb to Howell Cobb, October 8, Cobb Papers.

34. Sitterson, *Secession Movement in North Carolina,* 142-43; Richmond *Enquirer,* November 17; Simpson, *Wise,* 162-66.

35. Richmond *Enquirer,* November 13; New Orleans *Picayune,* November 5, 11; Louisville *Democrat,* November 12, 24; December 1.

36. Lawrence, Kansas, *Herald of Freedom,* November 21; New York *Tribune,* November 28; Johannsen, *Douglas,* 580-81.

37. *House Reports,* 36 Cong., 1 sess., No. 448 (Serial 1071), 318-19.

38. Washington *Union,* November 18, 24, 29.

39. Klein, *Buchanan,* 307-8.

40. Robert Tyler to Buchanan, November 5, 16, Buchanan Papers. For the argument that Buchanan was dominated by a Cabinet "Directory," see Nevins, *Emergence of Lincoln,* I, 239-46.

41. Findley Patterson to Buchanan, November 10; John F. Shroder to Buchanan, November 22, Buchanan Papers.

42. Buchanan to Black, November 18, Black Papers; Washington *Union,* November 19; Klein *Buchanan,* 308; Stenberg, "An Unnoted Factor in the Buchanan-Douglas Feud," 276; Meerse, "Presidential Leadership, Suffrage Qualifications, and Kansas in 1857," 299n.

43. L. Case to Chase, November 30, Chase Papers, LC; W. T. Bascom to John Sherman, November 25, Sherman Papers; James C. Welling to Sumner, November 21, Sumner Papers.

44. Chicago *Democrat,* December 7; Fillmore to John Pendleton Kennedy, November 25, copy in Fillmore Papers; Washington *National Intelligencer,* November 21; December 1.

45. Richmond *Enquirer,* November 20; December 1, 4, 8; Louisville *Democrat,* November 21, 24; December 5.

46. *Georgia Constitutionalist,* November 26; Richmond *Sentinel,* November 28, both quoted in Washington *National Intelligencer,* December 1; Memphis *Appeal,* December 8; Thornton, *Politics and Power in a Slave Society: Alabama, 1800-1860,* 361.

47. New York *Tribune,* November 28; New York *Times,* November 27; New York *Herald,* November 27.

48. Nathaniel G. Upham to Buchanan, November 29; George Bancroft to Buchanan, December 5, Buchanan Papers; R. J. Haldeman to Black, November 26, Black Papers.

49. James P. France to Bigler, December 9, 14, Bigler Papers.

50. Sidney Webster to Caleb Cushing, November 27, Cushing Papers; New York *Herald*, November 18, 21; December 2; Cincinnati *Enquirer*, November 27; December 1, 11; Albany *Atlas and Argus*, November 20, 23, 25; December 4, 8, 11.

51. James C. Van Dyke to Buchanan, November 21, Buchanan Papers; Philadelphia *Press*, November 23, 30; December 3; Coleman, *Disruption of the Pennsylvania Democracy*, 113-14; Nevins, *Emergence of Lincoln*, I, 246-47.

52. Detroit *Free Press*, November 22, 29; Springfield *Illinois State Register*, quoted in Springfield *Illinois State Journal*, November 25; Indianapolis *Indiana State Sentinel*, November 26; December 3.

53. Washington *Union*, November 24; December 1, 3.

54. Columbus *Ohio Statesman*, quoted in Detroit *Free Press*, December 6.

55. Springfield *Illinois State Journal*, November 18, 28; Wells, *Douglas*, 32-33. Johannsen, *Douglas*, 582-83, argues that opposing the Lecompton Constitution was more of a political risk than supporting the administration, but he does not explain how Douglas could have retained his Senate seat after the state legislative election of 1858.

56. For a warning to Douglas from the South, see S. T. Bailey to Douglas, December 5, Douglas Papers.

57. A. J. Isaacs to Douglas, November 16, 21; W. D. Latshaw to Douglas, November 23; Samuel Treat to Douglas, December 2, Douglas Papers; Johannsen, *Douglas*, 580.

58. J. W. Sheahan to Douglas, December 9, 12; John A. McClernand to Douglas, December 2; W. N. Coles to Douglas, November 28; A. May to Douglas, December 1; A. M. Johnson to Douglas, November 25, Douglas Papers.

59. James D. Eads to Douglas, November 11; A. Logan Chipman to Douglas, December 8; William Hull to Douglas, December 5; A. M. Johnson to Douglas, November 23; Frederick Bancroft to Douglas, December 2; S. Ohl to Douglas, December (n.d.), Douglas Papers.

60. Weekly Chicago *Times*, November 12, 26; December 3, 10; daily Chicago *Times*, November 17, 18, 20; December 5.

61. Johannsen, *Douglas*, 581, 585; Douglas to John A. McClernand, November 25, Johannsen, ed., *Letters of Douglas*, 405; N. B. Judd to Lyman Trumbull, December 1, Trumbull Papers.

62. New York *Tribune*, December 4; New York *Times*, December 4; Chicago *Times*, December 5; Johannsen, *Douglas*, 586; Wells, *Douglas*, 33-34; Nichols, *Disruption of American Democracy*, 130; Nevins *Emergence of Lincoln*, I, 253.

63. James A. Briggs to Douglas, November 28; Daniel Mace to Douglas, November 28; R. H. Stevens to Douglas, December 5, Douglas Papers; Springfield, Mass., *Republican*, December 5.

64. C. H. Ray to Lyman Trumbull, November 24; Charles L. Wilson to Trumbull, November 26; N. B. Judd to Trumbull, December 1, Trumbull Papers.

65. N. B. Judd to Lyman Trumbull, November 23; O. M. Hatch to Trumbull, November 23, Trumbull Papers.

Chapter 11

1. Brown, *Agents of Manifest Destiny*, 409-57; Russel, *Improvement of Communication with the Pacific Coast*, 246-52.

2. New York *Evening Post*, December 14; Boston *Advertiser*, December 29, 31; Mobile *Register*, December 17, 29. A copy of the resolutions of the Mobile public meeting, December 15, is in the Douglas Papers.

3. John Jay to Sumner, November 25, Sumner Papers; New York *Herald*, November 28.

4. New York *Tribune,* December 3, 7, 8; Johannsen, *Douglas,* 588-89; Schott, *Stephens,* 241-42.

5. Charles Francis Adams ms diary, entry for November 20, Adams Family Papers; Sumner to John A. Andrew, December 12, Andrew Papers, MHS; "A South Carolina Plug Uglie" to Sumner, November 23; Henry Muzzey to Sumner, December 19, Sumner Papers; Edward L. Pierce, ed., *Memoir and Letters of Charles Sumner* (4 vols., Boston, 1877-93), III, 558-59; Donald, *Sumner and the Coming of the Civil War,* 328-31.

6. Springfield, Mass., *Republican,* December 5; New York *Tribune,* December 15-16; *Congressional Globe,* 35 Cong., 1 sess., 38-39, 41.

7. *Congressional Globe,* 35 Cong., 1 sess., 5-8.

8. *Congressional Globe,* 35 Cong., 1 sess., 14-22; Johannsen, *Douglas,* 588-92. The verbatim report of Douglas's speech published in the Washington *National Intelligencer,* December 12, differs in a few places from the version published in the *Congressional Globe,* perhaps because of some subsequent editing. In the *National Intelligencer* version, for example, Douglas spoke more forcefully of his readiness to "break all associations" with his party if necessary.

9. Van Deusen, *Seward,* 184; Nevins, *Emergence of Lincoln,* I, 258-59.

10. *Congressional Globe,* 35 Cong., 1 sess., 42-51, 113-22, 137-42; Johannsen, *Douglas,* 596-97.

11. *Congressional Globe,* 35 Cong., 1 sess., 158-64.

12. *Congressional Globe,* 35 Cong., 1 sess., 53-58.

13. Milwaukee *Sentinel,* December 15; Greeley to Schuyler Colfax [December ?], Greeley-Colfax Papers; Joseph Fell to Douglas, December 21; Charles Adams to Douglas, December 12; Charles B. Waite to Douglas, December 29, Douglas Papers.

14. Gideon Welles to Douglas, December 12; Thurlow Weed to Douglas, December 10, Douglas Papers; Greeley to Colfax, December 20, Greeley-Colfax Papers; New York *Evening Post,* December 10; Benjamin F. Wade to "Cal," December 20, 25, Wade Papers; James Dixon to Gideon Welles, December 15; Preston King to Welles, December 18, Welles Papers.

15. The memorandum of this interview, dated December 14, is in the Schuyler Colfax Papers, ISL. See also O. J. Hollister, *Life of Schuyler Colfax* (New York, 1886), 119-20.

16. John Bigelow to William Cullen Bryant, December 28, Bigelow Papers; Johannsen, *Douglas,* 597-98.

17. Samuel Galloway to Trumbull, December 12; C. H. Ray to Trumbull, December 18; Charles L. Wilson to Trumbull, December 14, Trumbull Papers; E. Peshine Smith to Henry C. Carey, December 6, Carey Papers, HSP; Johannsen, *Douglas,* 593-94.

18. William H. Bissell to Trumbull, December 12, Trumbull Papers; M. Day to John Sherman, December 18, Sherman Papers; Basler, ed., *Collected Works of Lincoln,* II, 430; E. A. Stansbury to William Cullen Bryant, December 27, Bryant-Godwin Collection, NYPL.

19. Benjamin F. Wade to Chase, December 25, Chase Papers, HSP; Chicago *Tribune,* December 15, 17; Chicago *Democrat,* December 23.

20. Richard M. Benbow to Trumbull, December 11, Trumbull Papers; James Dixon to Gideon Welles, December 15, Welles Papers; Springfield, Mass., *Republican,* December 10; Philadelphia *North American,* December 29.

21. George W. Houk to Samuel S. Cox, December 10, in Douglas Papers; William C. Allen to Douglas, December 15, Douglas Papers; New York *Herald,* December 18.

22. J. R. Norman to William H. English, December 21, English Papers; Henry B. Payne to Douglas, December 25; James May to Douglas, December 23, Douglas Papers; Detroit *Free Press,* December 23.

23. G. G. Westcote to Bigler, December 24; S. R. Jones to Bigler, December 30; David Lynch to Bigler, December 26, Bigler Papers; Joseph B. Baker to Buchanan, December 2; Bigler to Buchanan, December 22, 28; James C. Van Dyke to Buchanan, December 21; Daniel E. Sickles to Buchanan, December 21, Buchanan Papers; William H. Smith to Black, December 24, Black Papers; Holt, *Forging a Majority,* 240-41.

24. Anthony Ten Eyck to John S. Bagg, December 21, Bagg Papers, HEH; Benjamin Mace to Douglas, December 18; J. M. Hatch to Douglas, December 19; W. C. McDowell to Douglas, December 24, Douglas Papers.

25. David Webster to Black, December 18, 24, Black Papers; *House Reports,* 36 Cong., 1 sess., No. 648 (Serial 1071), 218-23.

26. Philadelphia *Press,* December 12, 24; Forney to Douglas, December 12, 13, Douglas Papers.

27. R. B. Deintzelman to Douglas, December 10; I. J. Cummings to Douglas, December 26, Douglas Papers; William H. Smith to Bigler, December 21, Bigler Papers.

28. "Douglas Democrat" to Douglas, December 14; Nicholas Hill to Douglas, December 31; William A. Seaver to Douglas, December 17; Dr. William Egry to Douglas, December 16; Thomas N. Stilwell to Douglas, December 17; Mat. H. Carpenter to Douglas, December 16, Douglas Papers; J. R. Norman to William H. English, December 30, English Papers.

29. James W. Sheahan to Douglas, December 31; G. C. Lanphere to Douglas, December 24, Douglas Papers; weekly Chicago *Times,* December 24; Arthur C. Cole, *The Era of the Civil War, 1848-1870,* Vol. III of *The Centennial History of Illinois* (Chicago, 1922), 158-59; Johannsen, *Douglas,* 601-2.

30. Detroit *Free Press,* December 27; Jas. Haddock Smith to Douglas, December 9, 12; D. A. Ogden to Douglas, December 15, Douglas Papers.

31. Weekly Chicago *Times,* December 24; James Anderson to Douglas, December 24; Charles E. Clark to Douglas, December 15; W. W. Wick to Douglas, December 15, Douglas Papers.

32. Washington *Union,* December 20, 23.

33. Richmond *Enquirer,* December 15; Lyon G. Tyler, *The Letters and Times of the Tylers* (2 vols., Richmond, 1885), II, 542-43; O. Jennings Wise to Thomas Fitnam, December 31, in Douglas Papers; Simpson, *Wise,* 164-70; Louisville *Democrat,* December 12, 15, 17, 30.

34. R. R. Collier to Douglas, December 13, 25; "A Douglas Democrat" to Douglas, December 28; K. B. Sewall to Douglas, December 31; Logan McKnight to Douglas, December 25; Samuel A. Cartwright to Douglas, December 21, Douglas Papers.

35. G. W. Armstrong to Douglas, December 30, Douglas Papers; Austin *Texas State Gazette,* January 2, 1858; Mobile *Register,* December 15; Alfred Huger to William Porcher Miles, December 19, Miles Papers; Richmond *South,* quoted in Milwaukee *Sentinel,* December 19.

36. This paragraph is a summary of arguments advanced in the following: John Tyler to Robert Tyler, December 24, in Auchampaugh, *Robert Tyler,* 216-17; Edgefield, S. C., *Advertiser,* December 23; Memphis *Appeal,* December 16, 29; Jackson *Mississippian,* December 23.

37. Mobile *Register,* December 1; Jackson *Mississippian,* December 9, 16; Austin *Texas State Gazette,* December 21.

38. Semi-weekly Richmond *Whig,* December 18; Nashville *Republican Banner,* December 18; R. P. Letcher to John J. Crittenden, December 26, Crittenden Papers, LC; Louisville *Journal,* December 3.

39. Washington *National Intelligencer,* December 19; Adams, comp., *Transactions of the Kansas State Historical Society,* V, 421-30.

40 Washington *National Intelligencer,* December 25; Adams, comp., *Transactions of the Kansas State Historical Society,* V, 431. For Cass's unhappy role, see Willard C. Klunder, "Lewis Cass and Slavery Expansion: 'The Father of Popular Sovereignty' and Ideological Infanticide," *CWH,* XXXII (1986), 314-16.

41. Amos A. Lawrence to Robinson, January 2, 1858, Robinson Papers, UK; George Crawford to Black (n.d.), Black Papers; Robinson to Chase, December 19, Chase Papers, LC.

42. Lawrence, Kansas, *Herald of Freedom,* December 5.

43. New York *Tribune,* December 14.

44. Lecompton *Kansas National Democrat,* December 10; Washington *National Intelligencer,* December 18; Adams, comp., *Transactions of the Kansas State Historical Society,* V, 414-19.

45. New York *Tribune,* December 27; Washington *National Intelligencer,* December 31; Stephenson, *Lane,* 93; Washington *Union,* December 17.

46. Adams, comp., *Transactions of the Kansas State Historical Society,* V, 411-13; Stanton to Walker, January 5, 1858, Walker Papers.

47. Adams, comp., *Transactions of the Kansas State Historical Society,* V, 419-20.

48. James C. Van Dyke to Buchanan, December 1; Bigler to Buchanan, November 28, Buchanan Papers; William Brindle to Bigler, December 18; M. M. Caslin to Bigler, December 18, 19, Bigler Papers.

49. Adams, comp., *Transactions of the Kansas State Historical Society,* V, 465-68; George A. Crawford to Bigler, December 28; M. M. Caslin to Bigler, December 26, Bigler Papers.

50. Josiah Perham to Douglas, December 21, Douglas Papers; Philadelphia *Press,* December 29; Leverett W. Spring, *Kansas the Prelude to the War for the Union* (Boston, 1888), 229-30; Nichols, *Disruption of American Democracy,* 55; Nevins, *Emergence of Lincoln,* I, 268.

51. Lawrence, Kansas, *Herald of Freedom,* December 5; Henry Wilson to Charles Robinson, November 26, Robinson Papers, CSHS.

52. Lawrence, Kansas, *Herald of Freedom,* December 26; Stephenson, *Lane,* 91-92.

53. Lawrence, Kansas, *Herald of Freedom,* January 9, 1858; Rawley, *Race and Politics,* 232-34; Nichols, *Disruption of American Democracy,* 155.

54. Philadelphia *Public Ledger,* December 25.

55. New York *Herald,* December 11; James H. Hammond to Benjamin F. Perry, December 31, quoted in Lillian A. Kibler, *Benjamin F. Perry: South Carolina Unionist* (Durham, 1946), 287-88.

56. Charles Francis Adams ms. diary, entry for December 9, Adams Family Papers; New York *Evening Post,* December 29.

57. Jesse K. Dubose to Trumbull, December 21, Trumbull Papers.

Chapter 12

1. Nichols, *Disruption of American Democracy,* 157-58.

2. Nevins, *Emergence of Lincoln,* I, 272-75, 295; Johannsen, *Letters of Douglas,* 408-10.

3. Lawrence, Kansas, *Herald of Freedom,* February 6, 1858; Lecompton *Kansas National Democrat,* February 11, 1858; Nichols, *Disruption of American Democracy,* 163-64; Nevins, *Emergence of Lincoln,* I, 293-94.

4. Van Deusen, *Seward,* 188-90. For the congressional debates see *Congressional Globe,* 35 Cong., 1 sess., for the months of February through April 1858. The controversy is treated fully in Nichols, *Disruption of American Democracy,* 158-75; Nevins, *Emergence of Lincoln,* I, 275-79, 287-301; and Johannsen, *Douglas,* 603-13. For an excellent briefer treatment see David M. Potter, *The Impending Crisis, 1846-1861,* completed and edited by Don E. Fehrenbacher (New York, 1976), 318-27.

5. Drew Gilpin Faust, *James Henry Hammond and the Old South: A Design for Mastery* (Baton Rouge, 1982), 345-47.

6. Johannsen, *Douglas,* 607-8.

7. Nichols, *Disruption of American Democracy,* 159-60; Nevins, *Emergence of Lincoln,* I, 288.

8. Buchanan to Robert Tyler, February 15, 1858, in Lyon G. Tyler, *The Letters and Times of the Tylers* (2 vols., New York, 1885), II, 543-44; Nichols, *Disruption of American Democracy,* 164-66; Nevins, *Emergence of Lincoln,* I, 293.

9. Nichols, *Disruption of American Democracy*, 167-68; Nevins, *Emergence of Lincoln*, I, 295-96.

10. Nichols, *Disruption of American Democracy*, 169-70.

11. Nichols, *Disruption of American Democracy*, 172-75; Nevins, *Emergence of Lincoln*, I, 296-301; Johanssen, *Douglas*, 611-13.

12. Lawrence, Kansas, *Herald of Freedom*, May 15; June 5, 12, 19, 1858; Lecompton *Kansas National Democrat*, August 19, 1858; Adams, ed., *Transactions of the Kansas State Historical Society*, V, 540.

13. Nichols, *Disruption of American Democracy*, 200-221; Johannsen, *Douglas*, 645-52.

14. Louisville *Democrat*, December 30.

Index